Fusing Art and Technology:

Co-Creating Futures for New Generations

Trinh Thuy Anh
University of Economics, Ho Chi Minh City, Vietnam

IGI Global
Scientific Publishing
Publishing Tomorrow's Research Today

Vice President of Editorial Melissa Wagner
Director of Acquisitions Mikaela Felty
Director of Book Development Jocelynn Hessler
Production Manager Mike Brehm
Cover Design Jose Rosado

Published in the United States of America by
IGI Global Scientific Publishing
701 East Chocolate Avenue
Hershey, PA, 17033, USA
Tel: 717-533-8845
Fax: 717-533-7115
Website: https://www.igi-global.com E-mail: cust@igi-global.com

Library of Congress Cataloging-in-Publication Data

Names: Trinh, Anh, 1974- editor.
Title: Fusing art and technology : co-creating futures for new generations / edited by Anh Trinh.
Description: Hershey, PA : IGI Global Scientific Publishing, [2026] | Includes bibliographical references and index. | Summary: "This publication aims to bridge the existing gap in resources that critically examine the fusion of art and technology. By focusing on the creative, sustainable, and culturally enriching advances in the ArtTech field, it illuminates paths for future collaboration and innovation, addressing the challenges and opportunities at the intersection of these disciplines"-- Provided by publisher.
Identifiers: LCCN 2025000173 (print) | LCCN 2025000174 (ebook) | ISBN 9798369376102 (hardcover) | ISBN 9798369376119 (paperback) | ISBN 9798369376126 (ebook)
Subjects: LCSH: Art and technology. | Art--Technological innovations.
Classification: LCC N72.T4 F87 2025 (print) | LCC N72.T4 (ebook) | DDC 701/.05--dc23/eng/20250122
LC record available at https://lccn.loc.gov/2025000173
LC ebook record available at https://lccn.loc.gov/2025000174

British Cataloguing in Publication Data
A Cataloguing in Publication record for this book is available from the British Library.

Table of Contents

Detailed Table of Contents

This study explores the Metaverse, which has emerged as a significant engine of growth in the wake of the Fourth Industrial Revolution and the COVID-19 pandemic, focusing particularly on its evolution in Southeast Asia, with an emphasis on Vietnam's burgeoning market. An extensive review of literature reveals that the Metaverse has been a subject of interest for many years, and numerous studies have been conducted on its various components. This research systematically summarizes the factors necessary for the Metaverse to establish itself as a new growth engine. Furthermore, the growth potential of the Metaverse in Southeast Asia, including Vietnam, was analyzed using the Technology Acceptance Model (TAM), an effective theoretical framework for predicting technology acceptance behavior. The findings suggest that Vietnam holds substantial potential for adopting new ICT technologies. Future empirical research employing technology acceptance models, expanded to various countries, will enable practical and comprehensive investigations into the Metaverse market.

This study explores the impact of gamification on autonomous motivation in learning, focusing on the application of education technology among people in Vietnam. As gamification becomes increasingly prevalent in education, understanding its effectiveness is crucial for fostering learner engagement and motivation. This research aims to identify and measure the influence of specific gamification elements integrated into education technology programs on learners' motivation

artists to navigate complex global challenges, from environmental sustainability to social inclusivity. It argues for the necessity of interdisciplinary approaches in education and professional practice, proposing a framework for cultivating creativity, critical thinking, and adaptability. Ultimately, this chapter envisions a future where art and technology coalesce to inspire and equip the next generation to contribute meaningfully to an evolving world.

This chapter explores the pivotal role of intellectual property rights within the realms of digital technology and art. It begins by defining intellectual property rights, which encompasses legal protections for creative and intellectual works, and introduces TechArt as a genre-blending technological innovation with artistic expression. By examining 44 cases of which these nine TechArt disputes, allow the broader set of cases, the chapter reveals common themes and complexities unique to this hybrid field. These disputes, which involve issues such as copyright infringement, patent conflicts, and trademark concerns, highlight the nuanced challenges faced by creators and technologists. Insights gained from this analysis lead to policy recommendations for various stakeholders. The article thus contributes to a clearer understanding of IPR challenges in TechArt and suggests policy recommendations for the stakeholders' strategies and actions in this evolving domain.

The integration of Augmented Reality (AR) in multimedia education represents a significant technological innovation, enhancing traditional learning experiences by introducing interactive and immersive environments. This study explores how AR innovations can be applied effectively within multimedia learning settings to improve educational outcomes. By blending real-world experiences with digital elements, AR provides an engaging and dynamic platform that caters to a range of learning

novel theory of sustainable education, emphasizing how art-technology integration can address educational challenges, transform traditional systems, and ensure equity. By fostering collaboration, cultural exchange, and interdisciplinary learning, this framework equips students to navigate future challenges while contributing to societal progress. The chapter concludes with a call for policy support and further research to scale this innovative model, ensuring a sustainable, inclusive, and transformative educational future.

In the digital age, the fashion industry faces the challenge of harmonising sustainability and artistry while embracing technological advancements. This paper explores the intersection of sustainable practices, creative expression, and emerging technologies within fashion. It highlights how innovations such as 3D printing, blockchain, and AI are driving transparency, reducing waste, and enabling the use of eco-friendly materials. Despite challenges related to cost, scalability, and consumer awareness, these technologies present significant opportunities for collaboration, creativity, and growth. Through case studies of pioneering brands, this research examines successful implementations of sustainable technology and their impact on environmental conservation, social responsibility, and economic viability. The paper concludes by emphasising the need for continued innovation and collaboration to drive the future of fashion, ensuring that sustainability and artistry coexist through the power of technology.

This chapter discusses a case study titled 'Apply Art and Culture to Improve Quality of Life,' aimed at enhancing George Town's quality of life through participatory art and human-centered design (HCD). The project, involving young designers from UEH Vietnam and USM Malaysia, focuses on elevating Masjid Melayu Lebuh Acheh from a historically significant mosque to a key cultural landmark in Penang. By utilising design thinking as HCD, the project integrates modern technology with traditional cultural elements, employing QR codes and gamified experiences to improve visibility and tourist engagement. The prototype features interactive posters and smart chairs, fostering a deeper understanding of the mosque's heritage. This approach not only boosts the mosque's appeal but also offers a model for other heritage sites, demonstrating how digital tools can modernise tourism while preserving cultural authenticity. The project highlights the potential for design thinking to address challenges in heritage tourism and community engagement, setting a precedent for future initiatives.

In this chapter, the authors will explore the impact of Artificial Intelligence on art and the perception of its aesthetic value. Through a theoretical review, the authors will define key concepts, such as Artificial Intelligence, art, the intersection of traditional art and art generated with Artificial Intelligence, and the aesthetic evaluation of art. In the empirical part, the authors will examine how individual personal characteristics, such as gender, age, field of education, extracurricular artistic activities, as well as prior knowledge of art and Artificial Intelligence, influence the perception of the aesthetic value of Artificial Intelligence- and human-created art, as well as how these individual personal characteristics affect the recognition of the source and aesthetic evaluation of the art.

The primary focus of this research is to explore the color palettes across the 21 diverse districts of Ho Chi Minh City (HCMC) and to understand how these colors contribute to the city's overall urban identity. Through comprehensive analysis of the collected data, a significant revelation emerged, showcasing that approximately 80% of the city's color palette is dominated by an array of grayscale shades, lending an enigmatic allure to HCMC's visual identity. Interestingly, complementing this grayscale backdrop, a splash of vibrant colors, including captivating shades of blue, yellow, and red, introduces a contrasting yet complementary aspect to the city's chromatic tapestry, albeit their presence remains comparatively minor.

Art and design have always evolved alongside technological progress, tracing a path from the mechanisation of the first Industrial Revolution (IR 1.0) to the AI-driven changes of IR 5.0. This study explores how designers have historically adjusted to disruptive technologies by applying the Technology S-Curve framework and conducting a historical trend analysis of the Industrial Revolutions. It demonstrates that designers have not only navigated challenges but have also thrived by adopting new tools and methods. This study highlights how AI is not a competitor to be feared but can be a collaborative partner in the process of innovation through human-machine collaboration, sustainable innovation and AI-enhanced creativity in the context of IR 5.0. AI has the power to redefine the role of designers with a focus on human creativity, ethical standards and sustainable design. This article provides insights into how designers can embrace this transformative era to ensure the continued flourishing of art and design in the age of AI

This chapter studies the concept of sustainable artistic practices in the digital era, emphasizing the environmental, social, and economic dimensions of sustainability. It explores the shift from traditional art to digital platforms driven by technological advancements, examining how the digital art space—particularly NFTs, virtual exhibitions, and online galleries—can either promote or hinder sustainability. Key discussions include the environmental impact of digital versus traditional art production, the role of digital art in fostering social inclusivity and global participation, and the economic sustainability challenges faced by artists monetizing digital works. The chapter provides recommendations on adopting eco-friendly technologies, fostering community engagement through digital platforms, and developing fair economic models to support artists. The conclusion calls on artists, institutions, and policymakers to collaborate in building a more sustainable future for the digital art world.

This study investigates the impact of Augmented Reality (AR) advertisements on customer referral engagement through perceived originality using the Stimulus-Organism-Response framework. It explores how the interactivity, vividness, and novelty of AR ads influence consumers' perceptions and referral behaviors. This study employs PLS-SEM analysis on data collected from 241 Vietnamese consumers. The results indicate that AR ad characteristics positively affect perceived originality, which, in turn, enhances referral engagement. The findings suggest that marketers should focus on enhancing the interactivity, vividness, and novelty of AR advertisements to maximize their impact. Future research could explore the long-term effects of AR advertisements on consumer behavior and the potential differences across various cultural contexts. This study contributes to the AR advertising literature, extends the SOR model to emerging technologies, and offers practical insights for marketers in designing effective AR ad campaigns.

Augmented Reality (AR) has emerged as an essential tool for marketers and brand managers to initiate their branding strategies. Despite an increasing attention and its potential in the foreseeable future, both scholars and researchers still have a feeble understanding of this tool in how it improves brand variables, particularly brand coolness. Therefore, the aim of this study is to find out the relationship between AR and brand coolness, based on experience economy theory with the support of Meta Spark Studio. We made a marker-based AR product and exhibited it in the Sài Gòn Culture project launched by ArtTech Fusion 2024. Findings show that aesthetics is dominating all the realms in the theory and brand coolness is influenced by entertainment and escapism, which is a precursor for brand sustainability. Meanwhile, the project also reflects that AR can be utilized to sustain the cultural heritage in Ho Chi Minh city, especially Vietnamese coffee.

Preface

INTRODUCTION

In an age defined by rapid digital transformation and global interconnectedness, the boundaries between art and technology are no longer distinct—they are being redrawn, redefined, and reimagined. *Fusing Art and Technology: Co-Creating Futures for New Generations* emerges from this rich interdisciplinary intersection, inspired by the dynamic exchange of ideas and innovations at the ArtTech Fusion 2024 event. This volume brings together visionary thinkers, creators, researchers, and practitioners who are shaping a future in which art and technology are not only coexisting but co-evolving.

This reference book serves as both a reflection of and a catalyst for the growing momentum in ArtTech—a movement that transcends traditional disciplines to propose new modes of creative expression, community engagement, and sustainable development. Curated from a range of seminars, panel discussions, artistic installations, and collaborative workshops featured at ArtTech Fusion 2024, this collection offers a panoramic view of the current state and future potential of the ArtTech landscape.

Our aim with this publication is to build a bridge between theory and practice, between technological innovation and cultural enrichment. It is designed for a broad readership, from academic researchers and policy makers to artists, designers, and curious minds who seek to understand and influence the ways in which technology can enhance our creative capacities while honoring human values and social responsibility.

Across its chapters, the book delves into a wide array of topics—from emerging technologies in artistic production and the expansion of virtual galleries, to the integration of digital intelligence in education and the use of ArtTech as a lever for social transformation. Special attention is given to the themes of sustainability, inclusivity, and ethics, as these are essential to co-creating futures that serve new generations not just technologically, but meaningfully.

CHAPTER OVERVIEW

Chapter 1 explores Vietnam's emerging Metaverse industry, offering a detailed analysis through the Technology Acceptance Model. The study underscores the nation's strong potential for embracing immersive technologies and calls for more empirical research across Southeast Asia.

Chapter 2 investigates the influence of gamification in educational technologies on autonomous motivation among Vietnamese learners. Using PLS-SEM, the findings highlight the importance of design features like rewards and progress tracking in fostering self-directed learning.

Chapter 3 delves into the convergence of art and technology—ArtTech—mapping its evolution, definitions, and driving technologies. The chapter demonstrates how this fusion fosters innovation and predicts future trends in AI integration and sustainability.

Chapter 4 builds on the synergy between art and technology to inspire and equip future generations. Through interdisciplinary frameworks and case studies, the chapter outlines how emerging tools are reshaping creative learning and societal engagement.

Chapter 5 addresses the complexities of intellectual property disputes in TechArt. Analyzing 44 cases, the chapter reveals the unique legal and ethical challenges in this hybrid field and offers policy recommendations for stakeholders.

Chapter 6 discusses the transformative role of Augmented Reality (AR) in multimedia education. The chapter demonstrates how AR enhances comprehension and engagement, positioning it as a key tool for modern pedagogy and immersive learning.

Chapter 7 examines young consumers' adoption of virtual try-on technologies in Vietnam. Using the Stimulus–Organism–Response model, the study identifies emotional and social interaction as key factors shaping user experience and engagement.

Chapter 8 presents a new theoretical framework for sustainable, inclusive education through art and technology. It advocates for ICT integration in learning environments to promote equity, creativity, and cross-cultural understanding.

Chapter 9 investigates the intersection of fashion, sustainability, and technology. Through case studies, it highlights how innovations like 3D printing and blockchain can reduce waste and preserve artistry while scaling sustainable fashion.

Chapter 10 presents a participatory ArtTech case study in Penang, Malaysia, demonstrating how human-centered design and digital tools can revitalize cultural heritage and tourism through interactive public art installations.

Chapter 11 examines how higher education students perceive the aesthetic value of AI-generated versus human-created art. The study identifies how personal factors influence aesthetic judgment and source attribution, contributing to emerging discourses on AI in the arts.

Chapter 12 explores the urban identity of Ho Chi Minh City through color palette analysis. The research reveals how dominant grayscale tones and accent hues shape public perception, offering insights into urban aesthetics and planning.

Chapter 13 charts the evolving role of designers across industrial revolutions, emphasizing how AI-driven innovation supports rather than supplants human creativity. The chapter promotes ethical, sustainable, and collaborative design practices in the age of AI.

Chapter 14 explores sustainable artistic practices in the digital era, with a focus on NFTs and virtual exhibitions. The chapter critically examines environmental and economic trade-offs and provides actionable recommendations for digital sustainability.

Chapter 15 assesses the role of perceived originality in AR advertising and its impact on customer referral engagement. Empirical findings show that interactivity and novelty significantly boost brand advocacy, offering insights for marketers in immersive media.

Chapter 16 investigates AR's influence on brand coolness through a cultural branding project in Ho Chi Minh City. The study links consumer aesthetics to brand perception and emphasizes AR's potential in sustaining cultural heritage and brand identity.

CONCLUSION

By foregrounding human-centered innovation and culturally responsive practices, this book responds to the urgent need for resources that critically examine the transformative power of ArtTech. Whether through a case study on sustainable digital practices, a pedagogical model for ArtTech education, or an analysis of digital citizenship in artistic spaces, each contribution seeks to illuminate the path forward—one that fuses creativity with conscience, and imagination with impact.

As editor, I am honored to present this collaborative effort that not only showcases the vibrant energy of ArtTech Fusion 2024 but also contributes to a growing global dialogue about the future of creative practice in an increasingly digital world. My hope is that this book will inspire continued exploration, provoke critical thought, and, most importantly, spark new collaborations that will define the future of art and technology for generations to come.

Trinh Thuy Anh
University of Economics, Ho Chi Minh City, Vietnam

Chapter 1
A Study on the Current State of the Metaverse Industry in Vietnam

Kang Hyo-Jin
University of Economics, Ho Chi Minh City, Vietnam

Yi Dong-Su
University of Economics, Ho Chi Minh City, Vietnam

Trang Thi Thuy Duong
University of Economics, Ho Chi Minh City, Vietnam

ABSTRACT

This study explores the Metaverse, which has emerged as a significant engine of growth in the wake of the Fourth Industrial Revolution and the COVID-19 pandemic, focusing particularly on its evolution in Southeast Asia, with an emphasis on Vietnam's burgeoning market. An extensive review of literature reveals that the Metaverse has been a subject of interest for many years, and numerous studies have been conducted on its various components. This research systematically summarizes the factors necessary for the Metaverse to establish itself as a new growth engine. Furthermore, the growth potential of the Metaverse in Southeast Asia, including Vietnam, was analyzed using the Technology Acceptance Model (TAM), an effective theoretical framework for predicting technology acceptance behavior. The findings suggest that Vietnam holds substantial potential for adopting new ICT technologies. Future empirical research employing technology acceptance models, expanded to various countries, will enable practical and comprehensive investigations into the Metaverse market.

DOI: 10.4018/979-8-3693-7610-2.ch001

1. INTRODUCTION

The question of what constitutes the digital revolution poised to dominate the next generation and its impact on our daily routines is a pivotal inquiry that captivates not only a multitude of scholars but also professionals across industry, political, and economic spheres. An emerging alternative that promises to delineate the digital future of the next generation, by navigating through the economic and political hurdles of the contemporary Internet, is the Metaverse (Ritterbusch & Teichmann, 2023).

The Metaverse has seen explosive growth following the Covid-19 pandemic, supplanting the term '4th Industrial Revolution' and igniting significant interest among the societal and business sectors (Cho, 2022). It is recognized as a pivotal element capable of maximizing benefits as the IT landscape undergoes rapid transformations, such as the commercialization of 5G. This development has brought to the forefront the advantage of enabling users to access a vast array of content in real-time, devoid of temporal and spatial limitations, thus capturing public interest (Song & Chung, 2021). This phenomenon is a harbinger of the global metaverse market's potential growth, a prospect that garners widespread consensus (You, 2024; Julian et al., 2023; Cho, 2022). For instance, Facebook, recognizing the future value and expansion potential of the Metaverse, rebranded itself to Meta in 2021.

Hence, the Metaverse's substantial growth potential is attracting global attention as a prospective engine of future growth. The industry is exploring the application of the Metaverse in industrial settings, providing research insights to the academic and medical communities. Research on the adoption and application of the Metaverse continues to surge. Concurrently, governmental efforts to enhance national competitiveness through the Metaverse are intensifying, with Southeast Asia, including Vietnam, displaying more vigorous initiatives (Julian et al., 2023).

This study delves into the definition and components of the Metaverse, which is currently under the spotlight, and explores the status of the Metaverse in Southeast Asian countries, particularly Vietnam. It investigates the reasons behind their active embrace of the Metaverse, its potential for growth, and more, through a review of existing literature and theoretical frameworks. The aim is to present these findings and attempt to draw conclusions and implications.

2. LITERATURE REVIEW

2.1 Definition and Components of the Metaverse

The term “metaverse” is a portmanteau of “meta,” meaning transcendence, and “universe,” referring to the cosmos or world. It originated from Neal Stevenson's 1992 science fiction novel, "Snow Crash," marking its first appearance in literature. The metaverse concept encapsulates a variety of terms that have emerged with the rapid evolution of the ICT (Information and Communication Technology) environment, including VR (Virtual Reality), AR (Augmented Reality), XR (Extended Reality), CG (Computer Graphics), Smart Devices, and HMD (Head-Mounted Display). It has become a comprehensive term that intuitively unites and clarifies complex and diverse elements that the phrase "immersive content" fails to fully convey, such as immersive media, 3D technology, 5G, IoT (Internet of Things), among others.

Public awareness of academic research on the metaverse was significantly raised through a report by the U.S. Acceleration Studies Foundation (ASF) in 2007. However, thorough discussions on the metaverse have yet to be widely undertaken (Song & Chung, 2021), and research in this nascent field remains sparse. Some scholars have observed a scarcity of literature studies on the subject (Julian et al., 2023).

Figure 1. Conceptual diagram of the metaverse

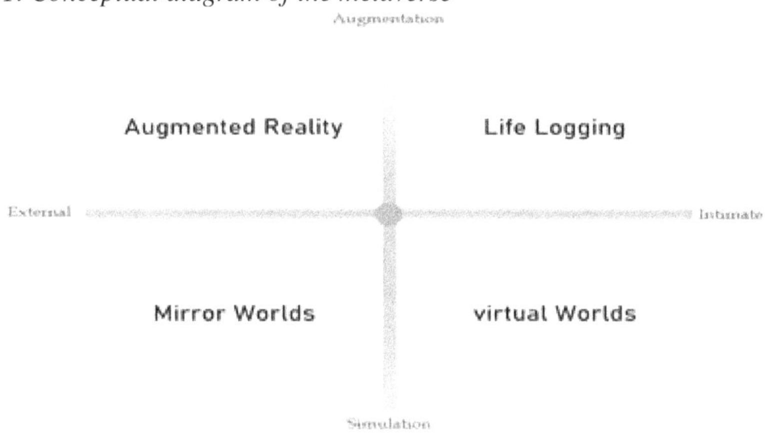

Source: ASF (Acceleration Studies Foundation, 2007)

Academic exploration of the metaverse gained public awareness through a study by the U.S. Acceleration Studies Foundation (ASF) in 2007. However, substantial discussions on the metaverse were scarce (Song & Chung, 2021), with minimal research dedicated to this emerging field. A lack of extensive literature research was noted by some scholars (Julian et al., 2023).

In the aforementioned ASF research, the Metaverse Roadmap Project was undertaken as part of the investigation into the future of the Internet. During this endeavor, the Metaverse was envisioned as a new social sphere, forecasting its emergence by 2025 through the amalgamation of virtualization and 3D technology. Numerous scholars are actively engaging in metaverse research. Among the 22 metaverse definitions identified in the study by Ritterbusch & Teichmann (2023), some have been frequently cited. An analysis of the publication years of preceding studies reveals that although the term "metaverse" has become a recent buzzword, it has been the subject of scholarly inquiry for an extended period. The literature review indicates that the Metaverse has attracted considerable attention for several years, with numerous studies exploring its various components. These studies have systematically identified the critical factors necessary for the Metaverse to establish itself as a new engine of growth. Additionally, the growth potential of the Metaverse in Southeast Asia, particularly in Vietnam, was evaluated using the Technology Acceptance Model (TAM). TAM is renowned for its effectiveness in predicting technology acceptance behaviors. The findings of this research suggest that Vietnam possesses significant potential for adopting new ICT technologies like the Metaverse, especially if supported by consistent governmental policies. This research serves as a foundational dataset for assessing Vietnam's capabilities as an emerging market. Furthermore, extending this empirical research to include various Southeast Asian countries could yield substantial insights, enabling practical and detailed exploration of the Metaverse market across the region.

Table 1. Prior research on the definition of the metaverse

Researcher Name	Definition of Metaverse	Number of Citations
Papagiannidis et al. (2008)	Often called the metaverse, it is a space for testing the business activities and commercial applications that can drive virtual worlds and wider applications in these virtual environments.	165
Hendaoui et al. (2008)	Beyond the entertainment and game-play features, virtual worlds are evolving toward Stephenson's concept of a metaverse in which social and economic interactions are the main drivers. Currently, one of the best examples of this evolution is Second Life, an social virtual world in which people (called residents) can communicate, collaborate, and buy and sell not only virtual goods and services (such as clothes and real estate) but also real products through their customized virtual spaces and avatars.	233
Kumar et al. (2008)	Three-dimensional virtual worlds can be broadly classified into online games and metaverses. Meta-universes, or metaverses, are fully immersive virtual spaces that significantly differ from online games in several ways. [Key characteristics are] Seamless persistent world, User-generated content and Massive and dynamic content.	212
Davis et al. (2009)	Metaverses are immersive three-dimensional virtual worlds (VWs) in which people interact as avatars with each other and with software agents, using the metaphor of the real world but without its physical limitations. This broad concept of a metaverse builds on and generalizes from existing definitions of VWs Metaverses provide virtual team members with new ways of managing and overcoming geographic and other barriers to collaboration. These environments have potential for rich and engaging collaboration, but their capabilities have yet to be examined in depth.	361

continued on following page

Table 1. Continued

Researcher Name	Definition of Metaverse	Number of Citations
Dionisio et al. (2013)	The word Metaverse is a portmanteau of the prefix "meta" (meaning "beyond") and the suffix "verse" (shorthand for "universe"). Thus it literally means a universe beyond the physical world. More specifically this "universe beyond" refers to a computer-generated world, distinguishing it from metaphysical or spiritual conceptions of domains beyond the physical realm. In addition, the Metaverse refers to a fully immersive threedimensional digital environment in contrast to the more inclusive concept of cyberspace that reflects the totality of shared online space across all dimensions of representation. The progression of development culminates in a complete Metaverse that involves multiple MetaGalaxies and MetaWorld systems. A standardized protocol and set of abilities would allow users to move between virtual worlds in a seamless manner regardless of the controlling entity for any particular virtual region.	173
Taylor (1997)	In this world [Metaverse] individuals interact through a perceived three dimensional landscape by creating avatars (artistically created virtual representations of individual users) that need a limited connection to the appearances of the people they represent. Each avatar is visible to all other users, and avatars interact with each other in this communal virtual space through software-specified rules.	124
Ondrejka (2004)	Technological advances in three-dimensional graphics, network connectivity, and bandwidth have just begun to enable online spaces that embody the Metaverse concepts of user creation and broad use.	257
Kemp & Livingstone (2006)	The Second Life, SL, system by Linden Lab is a persistent 3D world, or "metaverse". Users access the online system with a proprietary client and interact with content and other "residents." Unique features include simple tools for constructing 3D objects and scripting tools for interactive content - including connectivity with external web-pages and internet resources.	332

Source: Ritterbusch & Teichmann(2023)

Next, summarize the components of the metaverse. First, Julian et al. (2023) identify four fundamental components of a viable metaverse: Realism, Ubiquity, Interoperability, and Scalability. Realism is about the extent of psychological and emotional immersion a user experiences in the virtual space, creating a new dimension of presence. Ubiquity implies that the metaverse should be accessible through all existing digital devices, ensuring that an individual's sense of existence persists in the virtual space. Interoperability demands that digital assets be interchangeable within the virtual environment, with standards in place to allow users to move seamlessly between locations without interruption. Scalability necessitates that the system underpinning the metaverse possesses sufficient performance to expand the metaverse experience to a broader user base without compromising system efficiency or user experience.

Ko et al. (2021) outlined the components of the metaverse from a functional standpoint, defining them as 5C: Worldview (Canon), Creator, Digital Currency (Currency), Extension of Daily Life (Continuity), and Connection (Connectivity).

The worldview provides the foundation for users to form their perspectives, share, and enjoy content within the metaverse's temporal and spatial directions. Creators are anyone within the metaverse who produces creative works. Digital currency facilitates the production, consumption, and distribution of value within the metaverse. Extension of daily life indicates that activities in the metaverse should mirror those in the real world, ensuring continuity of daily experiences. Finally, connection enables the interlinking of reality and the metaverse, as well as between different metaverse spaces, allowing for interaction, and the sharing of knowledge and information across dimensions.

You (2024) delineates eight characteristics of the metaverse, namely, 'Immersiveness', 'Accessibility', 'Large-scale Connectivity', 'Economics', 'Spatiality', 'Self-identity', 'Creativity', and 'Openness'. These are defined as essential components of the metaverse, arguing that an online virtual space that fulfills these criteria qualifies as a metaverse.

Table 2. Components of the metaverse

Component	Concept
Immersive nature	A world so realistic that it is indistinguishable from reality
Accessibility	A world connected without barriers between physical and virtual realities, using optimal access tools such as smartphones, PCs, VR goggles, etc.
Large-scale concurrent connectivity	A world where a large number of users can gather in the same place simultaneously in real-time
Economy	A world where economic activities such as creation or labor are rewarded and money can be exchanged
Expandability	A world of three-dimensional space with the potential for expansion
Self-Identity	A world where one can exist as various forms of avatars reflecting one's own identity
Creativity	A world not only with content provided by the platform but also where one can freely import and create content
Interoperability	A world where content is attributed to users, not operators, and can be used on other platforms, i.e., a world without fences around platforms

Source: You (2024)

Roblox, often cited as a quintessential example of the metaverse, enumerates several key components of the metaverse on its website. These components include identity, which provides users with a unique sense of self within the virtual space; social fabric, which emphasizes the importance of community and interaction among users; immersiveness, ensuring a deeply engaging user experience; persistence, indicating that the virtual world continues to exist and evolve even when not being directly observed or interacted with by the user; and diversity, highlighting the variety of experiences and opportunities available within the platform. Additionally, Roblox proposes other significant elements such as ease of access (stability/frictionless joining), implying seamless entry and participation for users; an integrated economy, suggesting a unified system for transactions and trade within the metaverse; and order (rule & order), underscoring the importance of governance and regulation within the virtual environment (Jeon, 2021).

Researchers aim to delineate the components of the Metaverse to clarify its concept by identifying unique characteristics that distinguish it from existing digital content and service platforms. Previous studies have sought to categorize these components by focusing on expansionary factors like virtual space and the virtual economy, extending beyond the traditional technical limitations associated with VR (Virtual Reality) and AR (Augmented Reality). This approach helps in understanding the broader implications of the Metaverse as a distinct digital ecosystem.

2.2 Metaverse Market Forecast

Julian et al. (2023) forecast that by the year 2026, approximately 25% of the global population will engage for at least one hour daily in the Metaverse for digital activities, including work. This prediction extends to over one-third of global business operations being conducted through the Metaverse. Similarly, Gartner, an American consulting firm, projects that by 2026, 25% of the global population will be active users of the Metaverse. They anticipate that these individuals will spend more than an hour each day working within the Metaverse, in addition to engaging in shopping, education, and entertainment. This foresees a world where individuals enjoy immersive experiences and interact with others within the Metaverse framework.

The global Metaverse market is anticipated to exhibit a growth trend, despite some variances in the projections made by various international research institutions. The influence of the Metaverse on our lives, including various industries, is expected to escalate continuously. Allied Market Research forecasts that the entertainment sector within the global Metaverse market will expand from $13.8 billion in 2021 to $221.7 billion by 2031. This represents an average annual growth rate of 32.3%. It is also predicted that the market for XR (Extended Reality) devices, crucial for enabling the Metaverse, will experience more than a fiftyfold increase in 2025 compared to 2016. According to Deloitte's "Understanding the Economic Potential of the Metaverse," the Metaverse is projected to contribute $3.6 trillion annually to the global GDP by 2035. Statista data indicates that the primary revenue streams within the Metaverse will stem from e-commerce and gaming. Furthermore, it is anticipated that new profit-generation opportunities will emerge in fields such as education, entertainment, health and fitness, and telecommuting. Research into the utilization of the Metaverse is ongoing, highlighting its significance across various sectors (Kim et al., 2022; Cho, 2022; Ko et al., 2021; Na et al., 2022; Song & Chung, 2021; Buchholz et al., 2022).

2.3 Key Factors for the Growth of the Metaverse Industry

The growth potential of the Metaverse industry is substantial, with forecasting predicting a 25% and 30% increase in usage within the B2B and B2C markets by 2026, compared to 2022. This section explores the factors anticipated to drive this growth. Researchers and institutes predict that a combination of technological advancement and diverse applications will be critical.

Anderson & Rainie (2022) note a consensus among experts and leading global research organizations, including Gartner, that for the Metaverse to thrive, it must offer a variety of uses and achieve technical completeness. They emphasize that the Metaverse needs to find applications in various sectors. Elizabeth Hyman, CEO of the XR Association in the United States, argues that major companies such as Meta, Google, HTC Vive, Microsoft, and Sony are pioneering uses for XR that significantly enhance the domain (Anderson & Rainie, 2022).

In the B2C sector, gaming is identified as a primary driver of Metaverse growth. Furthermore, Anderson & Rainie (2022) suggest that the Metaverse's applications in healthcare, education, corporate digital initiatives, entertainment, culture, arts, and travel will substantially contribute to its expansion. This diverse application spectrum positions the Metaverse to transform numerous aspects of human life, underscoring the need for further development and research into its potential uses (Dwivedi et al., 2022).

Another vital aspect for the success of the Metaverse is the deployment of advanced technologies. Cheng et al. (2022) discuss the Metaverse's dependence on technologies such as 5G, Extended Reality (XR), edge computing, blockchain, machine learning, and Human-Computer Interface (HCI). Kim (2021) adds that Artificial Intelligence (AI), the Internet of Things (IoT), brain-computer interfaces, 3D modeling and reconstruction technology, spatial computing, and blockchain technology are crucial for realizing the Metaverse's full potential, according to a survey by Tech Target. Notably, brain-computer interfaces are highlighted for their ability to control avatars or applications through thought alone in the Metaverse.

Figure 2. Enabling technologies of the metaverse

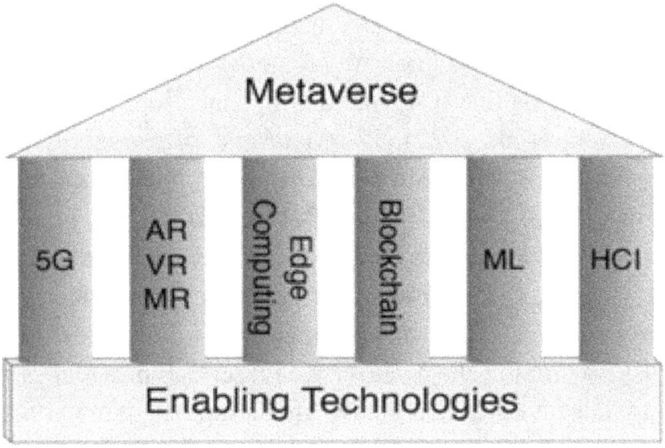

Source: Cheng et al. (2022)

Among the various factors critical to the success of the Metaverse, a high degree of technological completeness in the digital environment is essential. This includes the development of devices, communications, and content that seamlessly integrate the real world with virtual spaces. Mozumder et al. (2022) identify the Internet of Things (IoT) and the Internet as fundamental to the Metaverse's success, noting that 43% of manufacturers believe that Virtual Reality (VR) will significantly enhance company competitiveness in the near future. Effective activation of the Metaverse requires advanced technology in several key areas: digital human representations (avatars), security and privacy measures, and decentralized technologies. These elements are crucial for creating a robust and secure digital environment that can support the expansive needs of the Metaverse.

Wang et al. (2022) propose three stages necessary for the Metaverse's sustainability: digital twins, digital natives, and surreality. The initial stage involves creating high-fidelity virtual replicas of people and objects in physical reality. The second stage focuses on producing innovative digital content within the virtual world, blurring the lines between digital and physical content. The final stage envisions the Metaverse evolving into a hyper-real world, merging reality with virtuality. Essential technologies for this vision include advanced sensors, XR devices, digital twins, ubiquitous computing, networks, AI, blockchain, and more.

While technological infrastructure is fundamental, some scholars, such as Cho (2022), emphasize the critical need for compelling content to ensure the Metaverse's successful establishment. This viewpoint arises from the observation that consumers in the Metaverse are primarily attracted by the quality of services provided by the content, rather than the intricacies of the underlying ICT infrastructure. Furthermore, Julian et al. (2023) identified content as one of six pivotal success factors for the Metaverse, highlighting challenges like latency-induced visual discomfort and the importance of making content both engaging and enjoyable (Lee et al., 2023).

Interdisciplinary research is underway to apply the Metaverse in more realistic scenarios, covering fields like ICT, marketing, education, tourism, medicine, and psychology (Dwivedi et al., 2022). The Metaverse offers services across various areas requiring education, entertainment, and social interaction (Lee et al., 2023; Kevin and Denish, 2023; Lee & Rhee, 2022; Cho, 2022; Mozumder et al., 2022). Core applications of the Metaverse include healthcare, national defense, real estate, manufacturing, education (Mozumder et al., 2022), and entertainment, fashion, office spaces, real estate, education, advertising, and e-commerce (Cho, 2022). Wang et al. (2022) see potential in the Metaverse as a service provider in social VR/AR games, retailing, education, social goods, and computer-based artwork. Platforms like Decentraland and Earth 2 enable direct trading of virtual real estate and goods, while MS's Mesh and NVIDIA's Omniverse support remote communication and collaboration (Lee & Rhee, 2022).

In Korea, there is active exploration of applying the Metaverse in educational fields such as Korean language, morality, art, music, traditional Korean music, geography, and English, demonstrating its potential and usability across curricula (Cho, 2022). Plans for implementing language education services based on the Metaverse for foreigners learning Korean have been proposed, alongside multicultural cooking education within the Metaverse (Kim and Kim, 2022).

The Metaverse is poised to transform human life through its extensive applications, necessitating the development and study of various uses to fully leverage its potential (Dwivedi et al., 2022). Beyond the advanced range of ICT technologies it requires, the Metaverse also depends on several critical success factors, including an understanding of the digital environment and the creation of compelling content. Currently, interest in the Metaverse primarily emanates from younger populations who are more accustomed to digital environments (Lee et al., 2023). For the Metaverse to become more dynamic, it needs to attract a broad range of consumers who can actively engage with its various applications and technological advancements. This explains why the Metaverse is predicted to gain significant traction in Southeast Asia, including Vietnam, where there is a large, young population ready to embrace such innovations.

3. STATUS OF THE METAVERSE IN SOUTHEAST ASIA AND VIETNAM

3.1 Status of the Metaverse in Southeast Asia

While the Metaverse holds potential to bolster a nation's development, particularly within the realms of the creative and digital economy, and to foster growth across related industries, the high costs associated with quality ICT technology infrastructure and consumer devices pose challenges for both businesses and users, underscoring the need to enhance accessibility. Many Southeast Asian countries are still developing their technological capabilities related to the Metaverse, requiring further investment and research, especially in comparison to more industrially advanced nations (Julian et al., 2023).

Examining the demographics of Southeast Asia reveals that there are 479.04 million mobile Internet users, accounting for 72% of the region's total population of 667.59 million—an ever-increasing figure. According to the 2023 World Population Prospects by the UN, the median ages in key Southeast Asian countries are as follows: Singapore at 42.8, Thailand at 40.2, Vietnam at 32.8, Malaysia at 30.7, Indonesia at 29.8, Myanmar at 29.6, Cambodia at 27.1, the Philippines at 25.0, and Laos at 24.4 years. These figures are generally younger than those in Europe, the Americas, and East Asia.

For the widespread adoption of the Metaverse, high-speed Internet is essential for the real-time, instantaneous, and uninterrupted interaction it requires. However, 5G service coverage is not yet comprehensive across Southeast Asian countries. Nonetheless, the region, including Vietnam, exhibits a rapid pace of technological development and adoption. The rate of Internet penetration has more than doubled since 2010, boosting social media usage and likely hastening the transition to the virtual world.

Governments in these countries are actively implementing policies to support this transition. South Korea, in particular, stands out for its government's comprehensive commitment to the Metaverse, exemplified by the 'Metaverse Seoul 5-Year Plan' announced by the Seoul Metropolitan Government in 2021. Several Southeast Asian countries have developed Metaverse strategies aligned with their unique situations through benchmarking. For instance, Indonesia's Telkom launched the country's first Metaverse ecosystem, 'Metanesia,' anticipating synergistic effects among public enterprises, SMEs, and the private sector within this ecosystem. Malaysia is enhancing Metaverse education by partnering with a Metaverse EdTech company as the official digital partner of the Ministry of Education. In the Philippines, the 2022 Global Blockchain Summit hosted by the Ministry of Information and Communication Technology emphasized the Metaverse, including discussions on buses, Web3, NFTs, etc., showcasing the country's keen interest in the Metaverse.

Ultimately, while Southeast Asia holds considerable potential for the establishment and growth of the Metaverse, it appears that further investment and efforts are required to enhance technological maturity and develop ICT infrastructure necessary for revitalizing the Metaverse.

3.2 Vietnam's Metaverse Status and Growth Potential

Deloitte (2023) forecasts significant growth for Vietnam, estimating the Metaverse's potential economic impact at $9 billion to $17 billion annually by 2035. This optimism is based on Vietnam's vibrant entrepreneurial spirit and creativity, coupled with 37% of its population being under 25 years of age. Additionally, with a smartphone penetration of 93.5 million units (73.5% of adults), and 98% of internet users owning a smartphone (but only 6% owning a VR device), Vietnam stands poised for technological advancement (Statista, 2025).

Vietnam is emerging as a hub of innovation in the Metaverse, NFTs, and Web 3.0, boasting the highest rate of cryptocurrency adoption globally in 2022. The surge in blockchain-based startups and platforms is noteworthy, though attributed to the high number of unbanked individuals, with only 70% of adults having a bank account and nearly half lacking credit access (Deloitte, 2023).

Research by Lee et al. (2023) highlights the adeptness of Vietnam's Generation Y and Z in navigating the Metaverse platform, termed "digital natives" due to their proficiency with digital technologies and social media. Generation Z, in particular, demonstrates a deeper understanding of emerging technologies like the Metaverse than Generation Y, who grew up witnessing its evolution.

Vietnam is advancing more proactive government policies compared to other Southeast Asian countries. The 'Make it Vietnam' strategy, aimed at promoting national digital transformation, alongside efforts by Hanoi and Ho Chi Minh City to cultivate a robust ecosystem for technology service-oriented startups in e-commerce, fintech, AI, food tech, and ICT solutions. Distinct from its neighbors, Vietnam is actively providing tax incentives, attracting foreign investment, and expanding infrastructure for the Metaverse, including cloud computing and data centers. Moreover, Vietnam is concurrently developing various laws addressing aspects of the digital and virtual world, such as privacy, cybersecurity, consumer protection, and intellectual property rights. These governmental endeavors, coupled with technology, have facilitated the provision of the reliable and high-speed network essential for the Metaverse, thereby attracting private sector investment into the virtual world.

Figure 3. Technology fundamentals in Vietnam

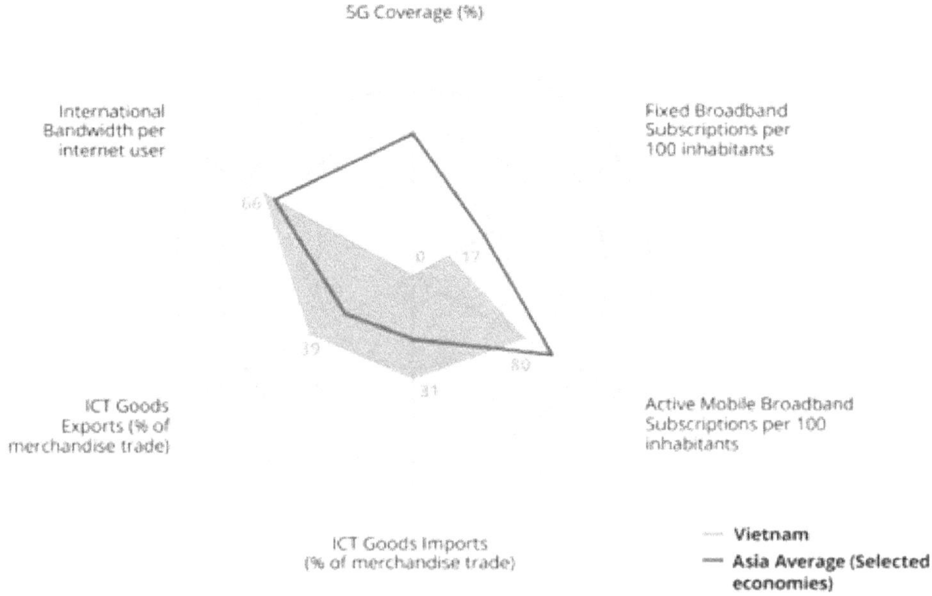

Source: Deloitte (2023)

The substantial growth potential of the Metaverse in Vietnam can be elucidated through the lens of the Technology Acceptance Model (TAM) theory. TAM delineates the relationship between one's attitude towards a behavior and their intention to perform that behavior, grounded in the theory of rational action. This model is instrumental in understanding the adoption behavior towards new information technologies, services, and products (Davis, 1989; Davis et al., 1989). Particularly, TAM has proven effective in identifying the factors that drive the acceptance of new information technologies or information systems by users (Nam et al., 2014; Lee and Park, 2016). It has also been applied to comprehend the acceptance and adoption behaviors concerning new technology and digital media (Aburbeian et al., 2022). In South Korea, TAM has been utilized in studies on smartphones (Sohn et al., 2011) and mobile simple payment services (Lee and Park, 2016). Research findings have indicated that factors such as user innovation (Jeon, 2011), perceived usefulness (Sohn et al., 2011), and the convenience of the IT environment (Kim et al., 2005) significantly influence the acceptance and adoption of new technologies or services.

Figure 4. Davis' technology acceptance model

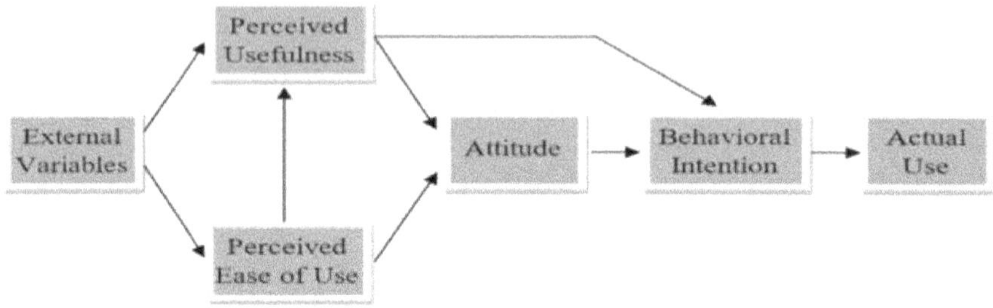

Source: Davis (1989), as cited in Le (2017)

An (2019) conducted a usability survey focusing on the acceptance and influential factors of anatomy education utilizing augmented reality (AR), while Choi et al. (2017) explored the effects of VR devices on usage and purchase intentions by applying the technology acceptance model. Additionally, Du and Zhang (2023) investigated the usage intentions in the cultural tourism sector based on the Metaverse, indicating ongoing research in applying the technology acceptance model specifically within the Metaverse domain.

Building on these validated findings, recent efforts to apply the technology acceptance model to the Metaverse are in progress, as evidenced by studies from Al-Adwan et al. (2023), Wu & Yu (2023), Torman (2022), Torman & Geçit (2022), Aburbeian et al. (2022), and Park & Kang (2021). Aburbeian et al. (2022) analyzed the impact on the Metaverse using nine variables within the framework of the technology acceptance model, including curiosity, attitude towards technology use, usefulness, and convenience, finding that most variables significantly influenced acceptance. Demographically, the results indicated a stronger preference for the Metaverse among men compared to women, and a higher affinity among individuals in their 20s or younger as opposed to those in their 40s or older. Du and Zhang (2023) applied the technology acceptance model to Metaverse cultural tourism, revealing that the Metaverse, by offering new and engaging content, could enhance user intention to use through perceived usefulness and satisfaction.

Furthermore, Le (2017) presented significant findings on the adoption of new technologies by Vietnamese ICT companies in a study of Vietnamese ERP small and medium-sized enterprises, utilizing the technology acceptance model. Consequently, Vietnam shows promise for the active introduction of new technologies like the Metaverse, provided the usefulness and ease of use of these technologies are acknowledged. In Southeast Asian nations, including Vietnam, where there is generally a high acceptance of technology and a younger average population, the Metaverse is viewed with high expectations, suggesting potential for increased usability.

3. CONCLUSION AND IMPLICATIONS

The Metaverse is evolving swiftly, capturing global attention as a transformative technology and cultural phenomenon (Cho, 2022). This study aimed to delve into the burgeoning interest in the Metaverse and to scrutinize factors that could facilitate its growth and activation within Southeast Asia and Vietnam. By conducting an analysis and exploratory research on the Metaverse industry, several conclusions regarding its growth potential and revitalization strategies in Southeast Asia have been drawn.

Firstly, the outlook for the application and activation of the Metaverse in Vietnam is promising. Given the proactive stance of the Vietnamese government in establishing ICT and Metaverse-related policies, the rapid shift in digital perception among the populace, and the presence of a young, digitally adept generation eager to adapt, transitioning to a Metaverse environment in Vietnam is expected to face minimal hurdles.

However, due to Vietnam's relative income level and the absence of specialized Metaverse companies, high-quality, differentiated content is yet to surface. The focus should thus be on expanding Metaverse device adoption and broadening the user base on Metaverse platforms through competitive content. It is imperative for companies to enhance platform functionalities and embrace advanced technologies to ensure seamless user experiences (Lee et al., 2023).

From this study, several key implications have been identified:

1. The Metaverse is poised for rapid application in burgeoning sectors within emerging markets like e-commerce. Particularly among young consumers, there is a growing interest and demand for the Metaverse, prompting companies to explore its integration to boost business efficiency (Tlili et al., 2022; Ning et al., 2023; Mozumder et al., 2022; Julian et al., 2023; Dwivedi et al., 2022; Lee et al., 2022; Lee et al., 2023).
2. Companies should offer a range of devices and content for the Metaverse, ensuring a diverse user experience by enhancing platform capabilities and adopting the latest technology. However, recent market entries like Apple's Vision Pro, a spatial computing device, have yet to achieve widespread acceptance.
3. Establishing a sustainable ecosystem is crucial. Major countries, including Korea, have developed strategies to foster a systematic and stable industry for emerging industrial fields through technology development, roadmaps, and human resource training (Ning et al., 2023). However, government support alone cannot create an industrial ecosystem. The development of industries is driven by companies and consumers, with market changes spurred by creative startups chosen by consumers. A market structure that encourages a virtuous cycle is essential for the establishment of new industries like the Metaverse.

4. In Vietnam and Southeast Asia, a tailored strategy accounting for generational differences in Metaverse expectations is necessary, with the role of a catalyst being crucial. Considering social influence, generation-specific strategies can significantly impact young individuals, particularly in countries with a youthful consumer base like Vietnam, enabling more proactive steps in adopting and disseminating new technologies.
5. Adoption lifecycle stages indicate that the Metaverse industry stabilizes only when the 'early majority' and 'late majority' embrace it. A substantial adaptation period is required for a large demographic to become acquainted with the Metaverse, significantly affecting market success. Hence, companies should consider not only the cost but also the convenience for consumers to familiarize themselves with the Metaverse platform and products.
6. A Metaverse strategy that reflects national and social characteristics is essential. The integration of technologies like the Metaverse with social and cultural factors influences user choice, and inherent regional or national and social characteristics act as differentiators in technology selection and adoption. As futurist Alvin Toffler suggested in 'The Third Wave', technology can both prompt societal changes and evolve in response to societal needs, with the same technology developing differently depending on the country's and society's context.
7. To invigorate the Metaverse, an interoperable service platform is needed, and priority should be given to quality content innovation to sustain user interest. Overcoming barriers to encourage consumer usage requires quality content that captivates consumer interest and a platform that facilitates easy consumer access.

In conclusion, companies should be mindful of not just the financial implications but also the time and mental investment required for users to acclimate to new platforms. Organizational culture change is said to undergo three phases: unfreezing, changing, and refreezing (Lewin, 1948; Cummings et al., 2016; Hussain et al., 2018). Similarly, in a country or society, changes brought about by advanced culture or technology must be embraced by generations accustomed to existing norms. Thus, adapting to new cultural and technological trends like the Metaverse necessitates time for acclimatization to these changes.

4. LIMITATIONS AND FUTURE DIRECTIONS

This study faces the limitation of not being grounded in empirical research, as it primarily focuses on literature review. Furthermore, it lacks a diverse theoretical foundation to bolster the research findings. Future studies should aim to extract more significant insights through empirical methods such as interviews and surveys, particularly focusing on the Vietnamese Metaverse market.

Secondly, this research does not account for user experiences across various device-based Metaverse platforms. It's possible that many individuals in Southeast Asia, including Vietnam, are not familiar with the Metaverse concept and lack firsthand experience. PWC (2021) emphasized the importance of user experience in the Metaverse's potential and growth in their report "Seeing is Believing." The disparity between those who have and have not experienced the Metaverse could not be more pronounced, highlighting the need for more research centered around user experiences.

Thirdly, there's a need for research grounded in theoretical frameworks that explore the adoption of new technologies like the Metaverse. Presently, there's a scarcity of research utilizing the Technology Acceptance Model (TAM) to investigate the application of Metaverse technology (Park and Kang, 2021). Given the Metaverse's potential complexities, such as immersion, virtual reality, diverse worldviews, and XR devices, further studies should explore beyond the TAM to include various theoretical perspectives.

Fourth, further investigation into Southeast Asian markets beyond Vietnam is warranted. With its vast and youthful population, Southeast Asia is a region poised for significant technological advancements and national progress. Empirical analyses of these emerging markets are crucial for ongoing research efforts.

Lastly, the Vietnamese Metaverse market necessitates broader research coverage. Given its market size and growth potential, there's a noticeable gap in research and market information for both Vietnam and Southeast Asia at large, with Metaverse-focused studies on Vietnam being particularly scarce. The sole empirical study targeting Vietnam's Metaverse market to date is by Lee et al. (2023), which applies the Extended Unified Theory of Acceptance and Use of Technology (UTAUT2) to examine the factors influencing Metaverse platform use among Generations Y and Z in Vietnam. While this study aimed to identify determinants affecting Metaverse use in Vietnam using UTAUT2, it does not fully encapsulate Vietnam's unique characteristics due to its specific focus. To develop and invigorate a Metaverse ecosystem unique to Vietnam, research incorporating various demographic variables such as generation, region, and income level is imperative.

REFERENCES

Aburbeian, A. M., Owda, A. Y., & Owda, M. (2022). A Technology Acceptance Model Survey of the Metaverse Prospects. *AI*, *3*(2), 285–302. DOI: 10.3390/ai3020018

Al-Adwan, A. S., Li, N., Al-Adwan, A., Abbasi, G. A., Albelbisi, N. A., & Habibi, A. (2023). Extending the Technology Acceptance Model (TAM) to Predict University Students' Intentions to Use Metaverse Based Learning Platforms. *Education and Information Technologies*, *28*(11), 15381–15413. DOI: 10.1007/s10639-023-11816-3 PMID: 37361794

An, J. W. (2019). Technology Acceptance and Influencing Factor of Anatomy Learning using Augmented Reality:Usability Based on the Technology Acceptance Model. *Journal of the Korea Convergence Society*, *10*(12), 487–494.

Anderson, J., & Rainie, L. (2022). *The Metaverse in 2040*. Pew Research Center.

Buchholz, F., Oppermann, L., & Prinz, W. (2022). There's more than one metavers. *Journal of Interactive Media*, *21*(3), 313–323.

Cheng, R., Wu, N., Chen, S., & Han, B. (2022). Will Metaverse be NextG Internet? Vision, Hype, and Reality. *IEEE Network*, *36*(5), 197–204. DOI: 10.1109/MNET.117.2200055

Choi, W. S., Kang, D. Y., & Choi, S. J. (2017). Understanding Factors Influencing Usage and Purchase Intention of a VR Device: An Extension of UTAUT2′. *Korea Journal of Information Society*, *18*(3), 173–208.

Cummings S., Bridgman T. & Brown K. G.(2016), "Unfreezing change as three steps: Rethinking Kurt Lewin's legacy for change management", human relations, Vol. 69, Issue 1, pp.33–60

Davis, F. D. (1989). Perceived usefulness ease of use, and use acceptance of information technology. *Management Information Systems Quarterly*, *13*(3), 319–340. DOI: 10.2307/249008

Davis, F. D., Bagozzi, R. P., & Warshaw, P. R. (1989). User Acceptance of Computer Technology: A Comparison of Two Theoretical Models. *Management Science*, *35*(8), 982–1003. DOI: 10.1287/mnsc.35.8.982

Deloitte, "The Metaverse in Asia Strategies for Accelerating Economic Impact", 2023

Du, J., & Zhang, M. (2023). A Study on the User Intentions of Metaverse Cultural Tourism Using the Experience Economy Theory (EET) and Technology Acceptance Model (TAM). *Journal of Culture Industry*, *23*(4), 53–64.

Dwivedi, Y. K., Hughes, L., Wang, Y., Alalwan, A. A., Ahn, S. J., Balakrishnan, J., Barta, S., Belk, R., Buhalis, D., Dutot, V., Felix, R., Filieri, R., Flavián, C., Gustafsson, A., Hinsch, C., Hollensen, S., Jain, V., Kim, J. Y., Krishen, A. S., & Wirtz, J. (2022). Metaverse marketing: How the metaverse will shape the future of consumer research and practice. *Psychology and Marketing*, *40*(4), 750–776. DOI: 10.1002/mar.21767

Hussain, S. T., Lei, S., Akram, T., Haider, M. J., Hussain, S. H., & Ali, M. (2018). Kurt Lewin's change model: A critical review of the role of leadership and employee involvement in organizational change. *Journal of Innovation & Knowledge*, *3*(3), 123–127. DOI: 10.1016/j.jik.2016.07.002

Hyungi, C. (2022), "The Educational Implications and Application of Metaverse in Geography Education", Journal of the Association of Korean Geographers, March 2022, pp.49~65

Jeon J. H.(2021), "A study on the Principle of Metaverse Composition with a focus on Roblox", Journal of Korea Association for visual culture, Vol 38, pp.257-279

Joon-hee, L., & Boa-A., R. (2022). A Study on User Expereince on Metaverse: Focusing on the ZEPETO platform. *Journal of Digital Contents Society*, *23*(6), 995–1011. DOI: 10.9728/dcs.2022.23.6.995

Julian, H. L. C., Chung, T., & Wang, Y. (2023). Adoption of Metaverse in South East Asia: Vietnam, Indonesia, Malaysia. In *Strategies and opportunities for technology in the Metaverse World* (pp. 196–234). IGI Global. DOI: 10.4018/978-1-6684-5732-0.ch012

Kevin, G. B., & Denish, S. (2023). Marketing in the Metaverse: Conceptual understanding, framework, and research agenda. *Journal ofBusiness Research*, *155*, 1–19.

Kim G. M., Kim W. W. & Lee H. G.(2005), "Investigation of Factors Influencing Consumer Initial Trust and Intention to Use Mobile Banking Services", Korean management science review, Vol. 22, No. 2, pp.13-34

Kim, J. (2021). A Study on the Metaverse as an Arts Educational Medium - Focusing on ifland of the SKT Metaverse Platform. *The Journal of the Convergence on Culture Technology*, *7*(4), 391–396.

Kim, S. W., & Kim, S. H. (2022). Cultural Understanding System Using Multicultural Cooking Class through Metaverse. *The Korean Association of Computer Education*, *26*(1), 99–101.

Kim, T. J., Ahn, B. Y., Lee, W. C., & Kang, H. J. (2022). Analysis of metaverse trends using news big data. *Journal of Digital Contents Society, 23*(2), 203–216. DOI: 10.9728/dcs.2022.23.2.203

Ko S. Y., Jung H. G., Kim J. I. & Shin Y. T.(2021), "A concept of metaverse and the policy of development", Korea Information Processing Society review, Vol. 28, No. 1, pp.7-16

Le, T. M. D. (2017), "Testing Techonology Acceptance Model on the Acceptance of ERP systems by end-users of Small and Medium-sized Enterprises in Vietnam", *CITA National Science Conference Proceedings*, pp.38-45

Lee, S. H., Zhou, P., Braud, T., & Hui, P. (2022). *"What is the Metaverse? An Immersive Cyberspace and Open Challenge", eprint arXiv*. Cornell University.

Lee, S. Y., & Park, J. W. (2016). A Study on the Intention of the Use of Mobile Payment Services: Application of the Technology Acceptance Model. *Korean Management Science Review, 33*(2), 65–74. DOI: 10.7737/KMSR.2016.33.2.065

Lee, Y. C., Nguyen, M. N., & Yang, Q. (2023). Factors Influencing Vietnamese Generation MZ's Adoption of Metaverse Platforms. *Sustainability (Basel), 15*(20), 1–17. DOI: 10.3390/su152014940

Lewin, K. (1948). *Resolving Social Conflicts: Selected Papers on Group Dynamics* (Lewin, G., Ed.). Harper & Row.

Mozumder, A. S., Sheeraz, M. M., Aich, A A S., & Kim, H. C. (2022), "Overview: Technology Roadmap of the Future Trend of Metaverse based on IoT, Blockchain, AI Technique, and Medical Domain Metaverse Activity", 2022 24th International Conference on Advanced Communications Technology (ICACT), PyeongChang Kwangwoon_Do, Korea, Republic of, 2022, pp.256-261 DOI: 10.23919/ICACT53585.2022.9728808

Na, H. C., Lee, Y. J., Kim, S. Y., & Kom, Y. S. (2022). A Study on Metaverse Education Platform: Cases analysis and suggestion. *Journal of Digital Contents Society, 23*(5), 827–836. DOI: 10.9728/dcs.2022.23.5.827

Nam, S. T., Shin, S. Y., & Jin, C. Y. (2014). A Meta-analysis and Review of External Factors based on the Technology Acceptance Model: Focusing on the Journals Related to Smartphone in Korea. *Journal of the Korea Institute of Information and Communication Engineering, 18*(4), 848–854. DOI: 10.6109/jkiice.2014.18.4.848

Ning, H., Wang, H., Lin, Y., Wang, W., Dhelim, S., Farha, F., Ding, J., & Danesh, M. (2023). A Survey on Metaverse: The State-of-the-art, Technologies, Applications, and Challenges. *IEEE Internet of Things Journal*, *10*(16), 14671–14688. DOI: 10.1109/JIOT.2023.3278329

Park, S. K., & Kang, Y. J. (2021). A Study on the intentions of early users of metaverse platforms using the Technology Acceptance Model. *Journal of Digital Convergence*, *19*(10), 275–285.

Ritterbusch, G. D., & Teichmann, M. R. (2023). Defining the Metaverse: A Systematic Literature Review. *IEEE Access : Practical Innovations, Open Solutions*, *11*, 12368–12377. DOI: 10.1109/ACCESS.2023.3241809

Sohn, S. H., Choi, Y. J., & Hwang, H. S. (2011). Understanding Acceptance of Smartphone among Early Adopters Using Extended Technology Acceptance Model. *Korean Journal of Journalism & Communication Studies*, *55*(2), 227–252.

Song, S. W., & Chung, D. H. (2021). Explication and Rational Conceptualization of Metaverse. *Informatization Policy*, *28*(3), 3–22.

Statista. (2025). *Ownership of devices among internet users in Vietnam in 2024, by device*. https://www.statista.com/statistics/804059/digital-device-usage-among-adults-by-device-vietnam/

Tlili, A., Huang, R., Shehata, R., Liu, D., Zhao, J., Metwally, A. H. S., Wang, H., Denden, M., Bozkurt, A., Lee, L. K., Beyoglu, D., Altinay, F., Sharma, R. C., Altinay, Z., Li, Z., Liu, J., Ahmad, F., Hu, Y., Salha, S., & Burgos, D. (2022). Is Metaverse in education a blessing or a curse: A combined content and bibliometric analysis. *Smart Learning Environments*, *24*(9), 1–31. DOI: 10.1186/s40561-022-00205-x

Torman, Y. (2022). User Acceptance of Metaverse: Insights from Technology Acceptance Model (TAM) and Planned Behavior Theory (PBT). *Emerging Markets Journal*, *12*(1), 68–75. DOI: 10.5195/emaj.2022.258

Torman, Y., & Geçit, B. B. (2022). User Acceptance of Metaverse: An Analysis for e-Commerce in the Framework of Technology Acceptance Model (TAM). *Sosyoekonomi*, *31*(55), 85–104. DOI: 10.17233/sosyoekonomi.2023.01.05

Wang, Y., Su, Z., Zhang, N., Xing, R., Liu, D., Luan, T. H., & Shen, X. (2022). A Survey on Metaverse: Fundamentals, Security, and Privacy. *IEEE Communications Surveys and Tutorials*, *25*(1), 319–352. DOI: 10.1109/COMST.2022.3202047

Wu, R., & Yu, Z. (2023). Investigating Users' Acceptance of the Metaverse with an Extended Technology Acceptance Model. *International Journal of Human-Computer Interaction*, *2023*(Aug), 1–17.

You, H. B. (2024). Generation Z's Perception of the Metaverse. *Journal of Digital Contents Society*, *25*(1), 91–100. DOI: 10.9728/dcs.2024.25.1.91

Chapter 2

An Empirical Study on Gamification Factors Influencing Autonomous Motivation in Learning Through Educational Technology Application

Ngoc-Hong Duong
https://orcid.org/0000-0003-2095-6707
University of Economics, Ho Chi Minh City, Vietnam

Ngoc-Trung Nguyen
Office of Ho Chi Minh City Party Committee, Vietnam

ABSTRACT

This study explores the impact of gamification on autonomous motivation in learning, focusing on the application of education technology among people in Vietnam. As gamification becomes increasingly prevalent in education, understanding its effectiveness is crucial for fostering learner engagement and motivation. This research aims to identify and measure the influence of specific gamification elements integrated into education technology programs on learners' motivation to study independently. Data was collected from 425 users through a combination of Google Forms and direct surveys. The results were analyzed using PLS-SEM software to assess the relationship between gamification elements and autonomous motivation. Key findings indicate that specific gamified features, such as rewards, progress tracking, and

DOI: 10.4018/979-8-3693-7610-2.ch002

challenges, significantly enhance learners' motivation. The study offers practical recommendations for schools and application developers to optimize gamification strategies, ultimately improving learning effectiveness.

1. INTRODUCTION

1.1. Research Background

In recent years, learning (particularly in foreign languages) in our country has been a significant concern, especially for university students – the young generation and the nation's future. Learning a foreign language dramatically helps us connect and build strong relationships with people from different countries, and more importantly, it plays a crucial role in achieving success in our career paths. However, learning a foreign language is not easy; it is a long journey that requires considerable perseverance and effort. In the past, traditional methods of learning foreign languages often led to boredom and a lack of motivation, causing many students to lose interest in studying. Corder (1967) mentioned, "With motivation, anyone can learn a foreign language well." Jakobovits (1970) identified motivation as one of the two primary factors influencing foreign language learning, attributing 33% of its impact to this variable. Consequently, fostering motivation for language acquisition represents a critical issue and a substantial challenge for educators. Technological advancements have led to the application of gamification in various foreign language learning applications, enhancing learning motivation, especially among students. Since 2010, gamification has emerged as a significant global trend, garnering considerable attention and interest (Deterding et al., 2011; Werbach & Hunter, 2012). Gamification has been utilized across multiple domains, including marketing (Lucassen et al., 2014), tourism (Sigala, 2015), sports (Bitrián et al., 2020), finance (Baptista & Oliveira, 2017), and education (Connolly et al., 2012). Koivisto and Hamari (2019) emphasized the significance of gamification in contexts associated with procrastination, where individuals require perseverance and sustained commitment.

Consequently, gamification has been extensively implemented in contemporary foreign language learning applications. This underscores the importance of examining and comprehending the gamification elements that influence users' intrinsic motivation in these educational applications. The implementation of gamification in educational technology applications in Vietnam has seen considerable growth. This approach cultivates an environment that enhances student motivation to engage with challenging material and promotes a heightened sense of achievement, in accordance with the goals of SDG 4 – quality education. Gamified EdTech platforms can transform the learning landscape by reducing barriers to learning and ensuring equitable access to high-quality educational resources. This approach enhances the accessibility of quality education to a wider population and contributes to sustainable development in the education sector.

1.2. Research Gap

Building on this theoretical foundation and the gaps in previous research, despite numerous studies on gamification in education, most are conducted abroad and are primarily experimental studies. There are very few studies conducted in Vietnam on this topic. As a result, the research team decided to undertake the project "An Empirical Study on Gamification Factors Influencing Autonomous Motivation in Learning through Educational Technology Application" to identify the gamification factors and their impact on users' autonomous motivation in learning. The authors aim to propose solutions to enhance the motivation of users in Vietnam to learn different skills and techniques through EdTech applications.

1.3. Research Objectives

This study seeks to identify and assess the influence of gamification elements in education, particularly in foreign language learning through EdTech applications. Based on the findings, the study aims to propose solutions to enhance autonomous motivation among users in Vietnam.

Our research tries to examine the following specific objectives:

RO1. Identify gamification elements that influence autonomous motivation in foreign language learning using EdTech applications among users in Vietnam.

RO2. Measure the extent to which gamification elements impact autonomous motivation in foreign language learning using EdTech applications among users in Vietnam.

RO3. Propose recommendations for educational institutions and application developers to improve and enhance users' motivation in foreign language learning using EdTech applications.

2. LITERATURE REVIEW AND HYPOTHESES DEVELOPMENT

2.1. SDG 4: Quality Education

A basic pillar of the United Nations' 2030 Agenda for Sustainable Development, Sustainable Development Goal 4 (SDG 4) is to guarantee inclusive, fair, and high-quality education while also fostering lifetime learning possibilities for all people all around. Education is a driver for social mobility, economic growth, and the lowering of disparities; thus, the attainment of SDG 4 is absolutely vital. A well-educated society helps to promote more innovation, economic resilience, and social cohesiveness, hence supporting the more general sustainable development aim. Some of the main challenges to ensure equitable access to quality education are underfunded areas with infrastructure, qualified teachers, and limited resources. As a result, education technology (EdTech) is one of a transforming technique offer innovative and outstanding solutions to increase the participation, access, and learning outcomes of students. Especially, gamification is promoted as the most significant improvement in EdTech, which illustrate game components, such as: badges, levels, leaderboards, points, and real-time feedback. This will lead to increase motivation and participation from students. In contrast, tradition learning methods are difficult to keep learners focusing on practices, long-term dedication, and remember the lessons. Gamification addresses this issue by incorporating elements of competition, achievement, and interactive participation, therefore using both intrinsic and external motivations to produce a more engaging and dynamic learning environment.

Moreover, in order to develop autonomy, engage in self-directed education, and receive continuous feedback through study process, gamified learning apps provide topic retention and mastery for students. In addition, autonomous learning can be developed by collaboration with gamification into EdTech applications. This leads to the development of lifelong learning, as well as meeting the requirements of globalization and knowledge-driven society. Therefore, SDG 4 can be achieved through enhancing the relationship, collaboration, and involvement of learning gamification elements. EdTech also easy access for most audience all around the world. Modern education can be changed by gamification because of raising learner's motivation, developing information retention, and supporting a more dynamic environment. As a result, gamification is a potential method that can create an alternative education traditional technique, which offers students the skill they need for future academic and professional life.

2.2. Current Situation of Educational Technology Application

2.2.1. World

Learning via Educational Technology (EdTech) apps has been a transforming power in world education in recent years, hence changing conventional learning methods and broadening access to information. Digital learning platforms, artificial intelligence (AI), and immersive technologies are being used more and more to change how lifelong learners, professionals, and students interact with instructional material. EdTech apps have become major innovators as the need for individualized, accessible, and flexible learning solutions rises, especially in light of the COVID-19 epidemic, which hastened the shift to online and hybrid learning globally. Among the most remarkable developments is the fast growth of online learning platforms including Massive Open Online Courses (MOOCs) such Coursera, Udacity, and edX, as well as language learning apps like Duolingo, Babbel, and Rosetta Stone. By removing geographical and financial obstacles to education, these platforms have made high-quality education more available. Companies are spending more in digital workforce development to satisfy changing industry needs, so corporate training and upskilling tools such LinkedIn Learning, Udemy, and Skillshare have also become more popular. Artificial intelligence and machine learning have improved EdTech apps even more by means of real-time performance statistics, adaptive learning paths, and individualized learning experiences. AI-driven tutors such as ChatGPT and Google's Socratic help students by providing instant feedback, answering questions, and adapting to their specific learning preferences.

Besides this, mathematics and foreign languages are two courses that require many exercises. Hence, gamification can provide learners many insightful elements such as: leaderboards, badges, competitions, games, levels, gifts. This leads to student's participations and drive. Virtual Reality (VR) and Augmented Reality (AR) can also create experienced and dynamic learning environment for learners. In addition, there are many applications on the internet like Google Expeditions, ClassVR, and Labster allow users interact with virtual experiments, historical research and simulations as real life. Many learners feel that they will improve many skills in medical field, engineering, and technical aspects which are very helpful for their life. However, there are several challenges that might happen when we apply EdTech in study. Particularly in developing countries and rural areas, due to the limited internet access, lack of digital connection, and cost concerns, students do not have equal ability to study and learn through EdTech apps.

Concerns about data privacy, cybersecurity, and the ethical use of artificial intelligence in education have also stoked discussions on the need of responsible EdTech governance and regulatory frameworks. Despite these challenges, the global

EdTech market is projected to continue expanding quickly as more money flows into 5G-enabled educational solutions, block chain-based credentialing systems, and AI-driven learning platforms. From governments to schools all around the world, digital transformation initiatives are being given top priority to increase equity, accessibility, and the quality of education in line with Sustainable Development Goal 4 (SDG 4) - ensuring inclusive and fair education for all. As technology develops, the role of EdTech applications in shaping the future of education will get increasingly crucial, so bridging learning gaps and fostering a worldwide knowledge-driven society.

2.2.2. Vietnam

In these years, Vietnam's government pay a lot of attention to develop learning through EdTech. Our country has significant growth in digital transformation, develop high demand for flexible, accessible, and high-quality education (SDG 4). Furthermore, one of the main program is National Digital Transformation Program to 2025, with an eye toward 2030, has been spread out recently. New technologies such as: artificial intelligence (AI), big data, and gamification into the educational system have been developed in many big cities across Vietnam. Besides this, during Covid-19 pandemic, traditional classroom-based has been transformed into virtual learning environments through Microsoft teams, Zoom, Google meet, LMS. Many universities, school have developed their hybrid learning platform in order to satisfy their students. Hence, students can easily to study and engage with the online system, which help them understand and improve their participation in learning. They also increase their ability to learn through many systems.

User involvement on platforms including Duolingo, Elsa Speak, Mondly, and local EdTech firms like Vuihoc, Hocmai, and Monkey Stories has increased exponentially. Particularly in language acquisition, STEM education, and skill-based training, these programs improve learning efficiency by means of gamification features, adaptive learning technology, and AI-driven analytics. Mobile learning and micro learning platforms' growth has also helped to change education in Vietnam. Learners, particularly young students and working professionals, now choose bite-sized, on-the-go learning experiences customized to their needs given more than 70% smartphone use and strong internet penetration rates. Furthermore, the growing availability of cloud-based learning management systems (LMS) has enabled K-12 schools, corporate training programs, and universities to use hybrid and blended learning approaches combining digital resources with conventional teaching. Notwithstanding these developments, especially for children in rural and poor areas with little digital infrastructure, internet access problems, and financial limitations, guaranteeing fair access to EdTech solutions remains a challenge.

The efficacy of EdTech apps also differs depending on material quality, student digital literacy, and teacher involvement. Although Vietnam's education system has adopted digital learning, more regulatory frameworks, better cybersecurity policies, and teacher training initiatives are still required to optimize the EdTech integration's long-term advantages. Looking forward, Vietnam's EdTech ecosystem is anticipated to keep changing with more funding in AI-driven individualization, virtual and augmented reality (VR/AR) for immersive learning, and block chain-based credentialing systems. The future of learning in Vietnam will be shaped by the role of EdTech apps in promoting lifelong learning and closing educational gaps as the nation works to match Sustainable Development Goal 4 (SDG 4), therefore guaranteeing inclusive and excellent education for everyone.

2.3. Key Concepts

2.3.1. Motivation

A basic idea in psychology and education, motivation is the process of starting, guiding, and sustaining goal-oriented actions. Many people think it is a key component of professional success, personal growth, and academic performance. Motivation, Kueh et al. (2019) say, answers the "why" of an activity by means of needs, wants, or goals driving behavior and clarifying the activities people perform. Based on several theoretical points of view, academics have over time offered several definitions of motivation. Emphasizing the part of personal ambition and goal-setting in motivating behavior, Bedeian (1993) defines motivation as the effort an individual exerts to achieve a goal. Emphasizing the psychological processes pushing people toward particular behaviors, Higgins (1999) sees motivation as an inherent force urging people to satisfy unfulfilled wants.

Conversely, Kinman & Kinman (2001) characterize motivation as a direct stimulus influencing a person's behavior, which could result from internal cognitive processes or outside environmental factors. Particularly in the context of educational psychology, motivation has been extensively researched in relation to how students interact with learning, remain committed to their studies, and attain academic achievement. While those with low motivation tend to experience disengagement, procrastination, and underachievement, research indicates that really driven people are more likely to set objectives, maintain effort, and face obstacles.

Motivation is usually categorized into two main types: intrinsic motivation and extrinsic motivation based on several research. Though they work differently, these two types of motivation are equally crucial in shaping performance and learning. Sustained academic success and lifetime learning frequently depend on a balanced mix of intrinsic and external drive. Gamification components in educational technology applications are meant to improve both kinds of motivation, hence promoting a more interesting and fulfilling learning environment.

2.3.2. Autonomous Motivation

Autonomous motivation is a higher kind of motivation in which people participate in activities because of their values, intrinsic interests, or deliberate decision rather than outside forces. Combining intrinsic desire with defined control creates it and lets students create self-determined behaviors supporting long-term involvement and persistence. Deci & Ryan (2008) claim that autonomous motivation is linked to completely conscious decisions and acts, hence implying that people voluntarily participate in particular activities since they see their relevance, value, or personal importance. This idea fits with Self-Determination Theory (SDT), which underlines the need of autonomy, competence, and relatedness in promoting self-motivated learning. Hagger et al. (2014) further describe autonomous motivation as self-determined behavior, where individuals take part in activities based on personal goals and intrinsic intentions. This contrasts with externally regulated motivation, where actions are performed due to external rewards, social expectations, or pressures. Autonomous motivation is particularly relevant in education and learning environments, as it encourages students to:

- Take ownership of their learning process
- Develop critical thinking and problem-solving skills
- Persist through challenges without relying on external reinforcement
- Engage in continuous self-improvement and lifelong learning

In the context of educational technology applications, autonomous motivation plays a crucial role in ensuring long-term engagement and deep learning outcomes. Gamified learning platforms leverage intrinsic and identified motivation strategies to create an environment where students feel empowered, in control, and motivated to progress at their own pace.

2.4. Theoretical Background

Self-Determination Theory (SDT), a thorough model of human personality and drive, explains how people engage with, depend on, and are shaped by their social surroundings. Ryan & Deci (2017) characterize SDT as an experimentally based organismic theory of human behavior and personality development emphasizing how individuals engage in self-motivated activities depending on their psychological needs. Ranging from controlled motivation to autonomous motivation, this theory separates several kinds of motivation along a continuum and investigates how social and environmental factors either support or impede self-determination. SDT holds that three fundamental psychological needs autonomy, competence, and relatedness, shape mostly human drive. Universal and necessary for psychological development, natural drive, and personal well-being, these demands are Satisfaction of these requirements makes people more likely to experience self-directed behavior, improved performance, and general well-being. On the other hand, when these demands are unmet, people may create regulated motivation, have less involvement, and find personal growth difficult (Ryan & Deci, 2017). SDT identifies two primary types of motivation:

- Intrinsic Motivation – The drive to engage in an activity for its inherent enjoyment, interest, or personal satisfaction, rather than for external rewards or pressures (Ryan & Deci, 2000). Intrinsic motivation is associated with higher engagement, creativity, and long-term persistence.
- Extrinsic Motivation – The drive to perform an activity due to external incentives, such as rewards, recognition, or social expectations (Deci & Ryan, 1985). While extrinsic motivation can encourage behavior, it is often less sustainable than intrinsic motivation.

One of SDT's main contributions is its emphasis on autonomous motivation, which happens when people absorb extrinsic drive and participate in activities willingly and with a feeling of personal endorsement (Ryan & Deci, 2017). According to SDT, the fulfillment of three basic psychological demands drives human well-being, motivation, and personal development:

a. The Need for Autonomy

Autonomy is the wish to feel in charge of one's own choices and actions. It reflects a person's feeling of agency and self-governance, whereby actions are consistent with personal beliefs, interests, and self-endorsed aspirations. Ryan & Deci (2020) claim that people attain autonomy when they have volition and ownership over their acts instead of being pushed by outside forces or responsibilities. Educational illustrations: Allowing students to select their learning routes, establish personal objectives, and advance at their own speed helps gamified learning environments promote autonomy.

b. The Need for Competence

Competence is the wish to feel efficient, able, and knowledgeable in one's surroundings. Ryan & Deci (2020) claim that people want to evolve and hone their skills, rise to difficulties, get constructive criticism, and always increase their knowledge. Educational illustrations: Clear learning goals, incremental difficulties, prompt feedback, and chances to practice and use knowledge help to increase competence. Gamified EdTech apps reward competence by means of badges, levels, and mastery-based advancement, hence recognizing student successes and motivating more skill development.

c. The Need for Relatedness

Relatedness is the need for social connection, belonging, and meaningful interactions. It shows a person's wish to be appreciated, respected, and cared for by others as well as their will to offer the same support to others. Ryan & Deci (2020) claim that relatedness is satisfied when people feel communal belonging, mutual respect, and interpersonal warmth. Educational illustrations: Peer cooperation, mentoring initiatives, social learning elements, and participatory group projects can all help to promote relatedness. Leaderboards, team competitions, and social engagement tools in gamified learning settings enable students to interact with others, create relationships, and exchange ideas.

Beyond individual psychological needs, SDT also emphasizes the role of social and cultural contexts in either facilitating or hindering self-determined motivation. Educational environments, organizational structures, and cultural norms can either support or undermine an individual's autonomy, competence, and relatedness. Facilitating Contexts: Supportive environments provide encouragement, constructive feedback, opportunities for self-expression, and meaningful learning experiences. Teachers, mentors, and educational platforms that respect students' autonomy and foster engagement enhance motivation, creativity, and deep learning. Hindering Contexts: Controlling environments impose rigid rules, excessive external pressure, or fail to provide adequate social support, leading to decreased intrinsic motivation, disengagement, and burnout. Understanding how social and environmental factors impact motivation is crucial for designing effective gamified learning experiences that empower learners, promote engagement, and enhance long-term academic success.

2.5. Hypotheses Development

Achievement-related factors include points, badges, leaderboards, and levels (Koivisto & Hamari, 2019). Points, badges, and leaderboards are the three most researched elements, collectively referred to as the PBL triad (Chan et al., 2018). Several prior studies have analyzed the impact of these gamification elements on individual motivation (Alasmari, 2020; Bitrián et al., 2020; Chan et al., 2018; Peter et al., 2019; Sailer et al., 2017; Xi & Hamari, 2019). Additionally, while some research suggests that achievement-related gamification elements do not influence basic psychological needs (Mekler et al., 2017), the majority of studies indicate that these elements satisfy the three basic psychological needs: competence, autonomy, and relatedness (Bitrián et al., 2020; Xi & Hamari, 2019). Sailer et al. (2017) also showed that badges and leaderboards fulfill the need for competence and autonomy by enhancing the sense of task significance and meaning at the game level. Therefore, the authors propose the following hypothesis:

- H1a: Achievement-related elements are positively related to Autonomy.
- H1b: Achievement-related elements are positively related to Relatedness.

Role-playing-related elements aim to immerse players in purposeful actions through avatars, storytelling, and character role-playing (Xi & Hamari, 2019). In this study, the authors analyze the avatar and customization features in the Duolingo app. Avatars and customization have been researched as elements that positively influence the satisfaction of psychological needs (Bitrián et al., 2020; Sailer et al., 2017; Xi & Hamari, 2019). Bitrián et al. (2020) hypothesized that role-playing-related factors affect all three needs, and their results showed a positive effect on the needs for competence and autonomy. Xi & Hamari (2019) found that role-playing elements only impacted the need for autonomy. However, Sailer et al. (2017) discovered that the avatar feature influences the need for relatedness. Based on this, the authors propose the following hypothesis:

- H2a: Immersion-related elements are positively related to Autonomy.
- H2b: Immersion-related elements are positively related to Relatedness.

According to the Self-Determination Theory, satisfying basic psychological needs – competence, autonomy, and relatedness – facilitates the promotion of autonomous motivation (Ryan & Deci, 2000). Ryan, Rigby, & Przybylski (2006) stated that gamification helps users feel competent, provides autonomy, and facilitates building relationships with other players, which fosters greater intrinsic motivation. Similarly, in this study, it is predicted that game features lead to increased perceptions of autonomy, competence, and relatedness, thereby enhancing their motivation. Additionally, according to Bitrián et al. (2020), satisfying the needs for competence, autonomy, and relatedness while using the application is crucial for experiencing autonomous motivation. When basic needs are satisfied, motivation becomes more autonomous. Based on these studies, the authors propose the following hypotheses:

- H3: Autonomy is positively related to Autonomous motivation.
- H4: Relatedness is positively related to Autonomous motivation.

Figure 1. Proposed research model

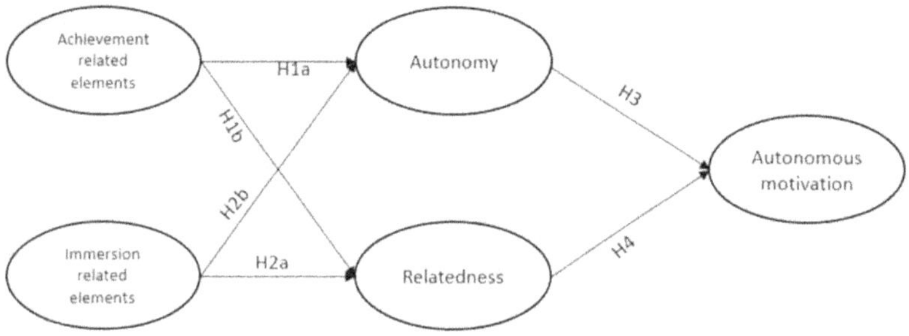

3. METHODOLOGY AND DATA COLLECTION

3.1. Design Questionnaire

For these measurement items, the author utilized a 7-point Likert scale (spanning from Strongly disagree to Strongly agree) by adopting and adjusting the measurement items from previous studies. According to the Self-Determination Theory (Ryan & Deci, 2000), which highlights the role of self-directed actions in fostering intrinsic motivation, autonomy is assessed. Derived from Bitrián et al. (2020), the perceived autonomy support scale examines the impact of gamification on motivation within mobile learning settings. The basic psychological needs satisfaction scale (BPNS) assesses relatedness through a student's perception that the learning environment fosters, appreciates, and socially engages them. Based on Sailer et al. (2017) and Xi & Hamari (2019), the scale indicates that social belonging emotions are intensified by leaderboards, competitive elements, and social networking aspects. In addition to this, variables related to achievement are evaluated through the points, badges, and leaderboards (PBL) framework suggested by Koivisto & Hamari (2019) and Chan et al. (2018).

This scale evaluates how often students engage with these components and their perceived importance in the learning process. Ultimately, existing knowledge in digital identity and gamification is employed to assess immersion-related aspects like avatars and personalization. Highlighting the role of avatars in enhancing user engagement and personal connection with learning environments, the scale modified from Xi & Hamari (2019) and Sailer et al. (2017) is employed. This measurement scale in the current research draws upon recognized constructs from earlier gamification and SDT-oriented studies, thus ensuring reliability and construct validity. The study intends to furnish a holistic framework for evaluating how effectively gamification in foreign language learning applications enhances autonomous motivation by integrating achievement, social, and immersion-related gamification aspects alongside the fulfillment of psychological needs (autonomy, competence, and relatedness).

3.2. Quantitative Research Design

The study employs a quantitative research method to systematically collect and analyze data, therefore hoping to assess the relationships between gamification elements and autonomous motivation in foreign language acquisition using educational technology applications. The quantitative approach allows for objective evaluation of variables and statistical analysis of how different game elements influence student motivation. AMOS software and Partial Least Squares Structural Equation Modeling (PLS-SEM) allow for quick data processing and analysis. To ensure comprehensive data collecting, a well-organized survey questionnaire was developed and distributed via online and direct surveys. There were three sections to the survey:

- This stage ensures that only appropriate individuals who meet the study objectives take part. Screening questions were created in a one-choice style to help identify unqualified applicants.
- Using EdTech tools, this section of the study examines how gamification elements influence students' autonomous motivation in foreign language acquisition. A 7-point Likert scale was used to gauge responses, providing a comprehensive spectrum of participant viewpoints and experiences.
- Depending on the kind of data required, this section collects respondents' fundamental information using single-choice and multiple-choice questions. These elements help to categorize the responses and conduct additional subgroup studies.

The systematic approach of this survey-based quantitative study ensures that the collected data can be used to generate consistent and generalizable inferences on the role of gamification in language acquisition motivation.

3.3. Sampling Method

This research employs a non-probability sampling method—namely, quota sampling succeeded by convenience sampling—to gather a representative sample while ensuring efficiency in time and costs. The sampling process consists of two essential stages:

- Quota Sampling: Two primary criteria are used to divide the population into subgroups.
  - Diversity in academic backgrounds ensures the research can investigate potential differences in motivation across various fields of study through academic major.
  - Gender: Ensuring equal representation of male and female participants enhances the study's ability to analyze motivational variances between genders.
- Convenience Sampling: The study uses convenience sampling after defining quota groups, which means participants were chosen depending on their availability and desire to participate.

Its practicality and swift access to numerous respondents contribute to the popularity of this method in educational research. Utilizing this integrated sampling method, the research guarantees that the gathered data is both varied and representative, facilitating a significant analysis of how various demographic groups view gamification in EdTech platforms.

3.3. Sample Size

Statistical reliability and validity in quantitative studies depend on a sufficient sample size. Larger sample sizes, Hair et al. (2011) say, offer more precise outcomes by lowering possible biases and raising the predictive power of the study. Sample size in this study is determined using accepted Exploratory Factor Analysis (EFA) criteria, which state that the needed sample size should be at least five to ten times the number of observed variables (Hair et al., 2009).

The writer distributed 450 surveys to a diverse group of respondents to account for potential incomplete responses and improve statistical reliability. A total of 425 completely filled out and qualified responses were selected for further statistical analysis after data screening and cleaning. This ensures that the sample size remains within a suitable range for EFA and hypothesis testing, thus enhancing the generalizability and strength of the study's results.

3.5. Participants and Data Collection

The study uses two main data gathering techniques to gather primary data and confirm the suggested research model and hypotheses:

a. Direct Questionnaires
    - Conducted in person with respondents in Vietnam, allowing for real-time clarifications and higher response accuracy.
    - This strategy was particularly useful for engaging students from universities, language centers, and educational institutions that actively utilize EdTech applications.

b. Google Forms' online surveys

The research team sent computerized surveys to several Vietnamese universities.

Online surveys guarantee that replies come from various geographic areas and academic institutions by means of a wider reach. The study guarantees that the dataset is thorough and appropriate for statistical analysis by combining direct and online survey techniques, hence maximizing response rates and sample representativeness.

To sum up, this chapter has offered the quantitative study design, including the sampling technique, data gathering strategy, and sample size calculation. The study guarantees a wide representation of users from many academic backgrounds in Vietnam by using a mix of direct and online questionnaires. The study approach guarantees that the gathered data is enough for Exploratory Factor Analysis (EFA) and hypothesis testing by means of accepted statistical criteria. These methodological underpinnings will enable the thorough examination and interpretation of results, which will be covered in the next chapters.

4. RESULTS AND DISCUSSIONS

4.1. Sample Characteristics

In the descriptive statistics section of the study, most respondents were female (68%), with most participants being undergraduate students (72%). Regarding academic fields, users from the Economics & Management sector accounted for the highest percentage (25%), followed by users in the Social Sciences sector (19%).

English was the most selected language by users on the EdTech app (72%), which is understandable given that English is the most widely spoken language globally. Over 63% of the users discovered EdTech Apps through social media, and most of them used the app for 15-30 minutes per day (58%), with an application usage duration of three to less than six months (37%).

Table 1. Sample characteristics

Characteristics	Frequency (N = 425)	Percent (100%)
Gender		
Female	289	68%
Male	136	32%
Academic level		
Under-graduate	306	72%
Post-graduate	76	18%
Others	43	10%
Academic field		
Economics & Management	106	25%
Social sciences	80	19%
STEM	72	17%
Humanities	38	9%
Arts	30	7%
Others	99	23%
Language for learning		
English	302	71%
Chinese	42	10%
Korean	30	7%
French	17	4%
Others	34	8%
Daily usage		
<30 mins	246	58%
30-60 mins	93	22%
>60 mins	86	20%
Usage duration		
1-3 months	123	29%

continued on following page

Table 1. Continued

Characteristics	Frequency (N = 425)	Percent (100%)
3-6 months	157	37%
> 6 months	145	18%

Source: author's calculation, 2024.

4.2. Descriptive Statistics, Reliability, and Discriminant Validity

The author performed a factor analysis and reliability test in SmartPLS 3.0 to assess the variable consistency (Ringle et al., 2015). After the initial phase of factor analysis, any items with factor loadings below 0.70 are eliminated (Hair, Ringle, & Marko, 2011). Composite reliability (C.R) and Cronbach's Alpha are more than 0.7 in the reliability test to ensure the high dependability of the measurements (Bagozzi, 2011). Table 1 displays descriptive data for each item.

Table 2. Descriptive statistics

Items	Minimum	Maximum	Mean	Std. Deviation
AR1	1	7	5.48	1.230
AR2	1	7	5.35	1.136
AR3	1	7	5.06	1.046
AR4	1	7	5.28	0.980
AR5	1	7	5.47	1.074
IR1	1	7	5.95	1.182
IR2	1	7	5.45	1.176
IR3	2	7	5.37	0.978
IR4	1	7	5.97	1.163
IR5	1	7	5.38	1.174
AN1	1	7	5.18	1.109
AN2	2	7	5.49	1.057
AN3	1	7	5.64	1.381
AN4	1	7	5.14	1.360
RN1	1	7	5.16	1.309
RN2	1	7	5.23	1.436
RN3	2	7	6.72	0.942

continued on following page

Table 2. Continued

Items	Minimum	Maximum	Mean	Std. Deviation
RN4	3	7	6.21	0.973
AM1	3	7	6.41	0.928
AM2	1	7	6.80	1.061
AM3	2	7	5.89	0.990
AM4	2	7	5.49	1.073
AM5	1	7	5.07	1.147

According to Table 2, the testing results show that the outer loadings of all constructs were more outstanding than 0.7 (Hulland, 1999). Therefore, all items in this study are corrected and acceptable.

Table 3. Outer loadings

Items	AR	IR	AN	RN	AM
AR1	0.802				
AR2	0.823				
AR3	0.813				
AR4	0.864				
AR5	0.867				
IR1		0.836			
IR2		0.887			
IR3		0.838			
IR4		0.876			
IR5		0.855			
AN1			0.863		
AN2			0.841		
AN3			0.861		
AN4			0.879		
RN1				0.902	
RN2				0.916	
RN3				0.883	
RN4				0.829	
AM1					0.879
AM2					0.909

continued on following page

Table 3. Continued

Items	AR	IR	AN	RN	AM
AM3					0.852
AM4					0.827
AM5					0.860

4.3. Common Method Bias

As a self-administered survey, the link between two constructs may be overstated, resulting in the prevalent method bias (CMB). As recommended by Podsakoff et al. (2003), this test established that CMB was not a significant issue since a single component identified using this technique explains only 46% of the variation below the 50% criterion. Additionally, the CMB is evaluated by assessing the VIF generated for all components. The results indicated that all VIF values in the model were less than the 3.3 thresholds, showing that CMB was not an issue in this study.

4.4. Hypothesized Model Testing

The authors used this method to test the stability of the estimates by drawing 5000 different sample sizes. From the analysis, the Critical Ratio (CR) values were all less than 1.96, concluding that $P > 5\%$. This indicates that the deviations are minimal and not statistically significant at the 95% confidence level. Therefore, it can be concluded that the model's estimates are reliable. This result is considered favorable when conducting PLS-SEM as it confirms that the estimates derived from the model are stable and trustworthy. Using the bootstrap method helps to validate the robustness of the findings, ensuring that the conclusions drawn from the data are not highly dependent on a single sample but generalizable across different sample sets. In summary, the application of Bootstrap testing in SEM analysis demonstrates that the model is consistent and its estimates can be confidently relied upon for interpretation and decision-making in the study.

The authors tested the hypotheses by examining the causal relationships between the following research concepts:

- The correlation between the achievement-related factors and relatedness needs has a P-value of 0.043, less than 0.05, with a standardized coefficient of 0.162. This indicates that the relationship is statistically significant, confirming that hypothesis H1a is accepted. It shows that achievement-related factors positively affect relatedness needs at a 2% significance level (98% confidence interval).

- The correlation between achievement-related factors and autonomy needs has a P-value of 0.008, less than 0.05, with a standardized coefficient of 0.281. This suggests that the relationship is statistically significant, confirming that hypothesis H1b is accepted. It shows that achievement-related factors positively affect autonomy needs at a 5% significance level (95% confidence interval).
- The correlation between role-playing-related factors and relatedness needs has a P-value of 0.002, less than 0.01, with a standardized coefficient of 0.526. This relationship is highly significant, confirming that hypothesis H2a is accepted. It demonstrates that role-playing-related factors positively affect relatedness needs at a 3% significance level (97% confidence interval).
- The correlation between role-playing-related factors and autonomy needs has a P-value of 0.000, less than 0.01, with a standardized coefficient of 0.562. This indicates a statistically significant relationship, confirming that hypothesis H2b is accepted. It shows that role-playing-related factors positively affect autonomy needs at a 5% significance level (95% confidence interval).
- The correlation between relatedness needs and autonomous motivation has a P-value of 0.000, less than 0.01, with a standardized coefficient of 0.298. This relationship is statistically significant, confirming that hypothesis H3 is accepted. It shows that relatedness needs positively affect autonomous motivation at a 5% significance level (95% confidence interval).
- The correlation between autonomy needs and autonomous motivation has a P-value of 0.003, less than 0.01, with a standardized coefficient of 0.438. This confirms that hypothesis H4 is accepted, indicating that autonomy needs positively affect autonomous motivation at a 4% significance level (96% confidence interval).

Table 4. Results of PLS-SEM

Hypothesis	Path Coefficient (β)	P-value	Significance Level	Hypothesis Result
H1a: Achievement-related factors → Relatedness	0.162	0.043	< 0.05	Accepted
H1b: Achievement-related factors → Autonomy	0.281	0.008	< 0.05	Accepted
H2a: Role-playing-related factors → Relatedness	0.526	0.002	< 0.01	Accepted

continued on following page

Table 4. Continued

Hypothesis	**Path Coefficient (β)**	**P-value**	**Significance Level**	**Hypothesis Result**
H2b: Role-playing-related factors → Autonomy	0.562	0.000	< 0.01	Accepted
H3: Relatedness → Autonomous Motivation	0.298	0.000	< 0.01	Accepted
H4: Autonomy → Autonomous Motivation	0.438	0.003	< 0.01	Accepted

In summary, the study supports the positive impact of Achievement-related elements and Immersion-related elements on satisfying the needs for autonomy and relatedness. In addition, both Autonomy and Relatedness are positively related to Autonomous motivation.

5. DISCUSSIONS

In recent years, gamification has garnered significant attention from scholars and experts across various fields, including language learning apps. Game elements such as points, badges, leaderboards, levels, avatars, and social features have been integrated into the app to motivate language learning, especially among students. Based on Self-Determination Theory and related studies, the authors proposed a research model to understand how gamification elements in language learning apps – impact the satisfaction of individuals' basic psychological needs. The study also aims to understand how satisfying these needs affects users' autonomous motivation. The study results suggest that interacting with achievement-related gamification elements (points, levels, leaderboards) in education technology applications can satisfy users' needs for autonomy and relatedness. Previous studies have also shown that these elements positively impact autonomy and relatedness needs (Bitrián et al., 2020; Hamari, Koivisto, & Sarsa, 2014). Sailer et al. (2017) also found that leaderboards influence the need for autonomy by increasing a sense of task significance and meaning.

Points and levels fulfill the need for autonomy because users feel more freedom when learning languages on the app. They can decide whether to proceed to the next lesson or challenge themselves by taking a test to skip levels. This flexibility gives users greater autonomy, allowing them to choose how to engage with the app. On the other hand, points and leaderboards foster a sense of connection with others. Education technology applications' users can compete with others worldwide, and their rankings are displayed on a leaderboard, allowing them to compare their progress. This connection helps users feel valued and motivated by seeing their accomplishments reflected on a global scale. The study also found that role-playing-related gamification elements (avatars, customization features) significantly impact the satisfaction of autonomy and relatedness needs, making them the most substantial influencing factors. Previous studies (Bitrián et al., 2020; Xi & Hamari, 2019) showed that customization features enhance autonomy. Users feel a sense of freedom when customizing their avatars and setting personal goals within the app, which aligns with their preferences and needs. Surprisingly, these elements also strongly impact relatedness, which is a new finding compared to previous studies. While earlier research (Xi & Hamari, 2019; Bitrián et al., 2020) found no relationship between role-playing elements and relatedness, this study suggests that users feel connected when their avatars are visible to others, fostering a sense of social connection. Additionally, setting personal goals in alignment with others can further strengthen this connection.

Lastly, the study found significant differences in autonomous motivation between users from different academic disciplines. Undergraduate students had the highest average rank, indicating they had the highest autonomous motivation in learning. There was also a significant difference in the time spent using the app daily. Users who used the app for over 60 minutes daily had the highest average rank, demonstrating higher autonomous motivation than those who used it for shorter periods. However, no significant differences were found in gender, year of study, or length of experience using the app.

6. CONCLUSION

6.1. Theoretical Contributions

The study makes several significant contributions to the literature. First, previous research lacked robust theoretical frameworks for understanding and explaining the impact of gamification on autonomous motivation, with only a few studies utilizing theoretical models (Hamari et al., 2014; Johnson et al., 2016; Sailer et al., 2017; Seaborn & Fels, 2015). This study addresses this gap by applying SDT Theory (Ryan & Deci, 2017) to analyze the relationship between gamification and motivation, providing a more structured and theoretical understanding of how gamified elements influence learner behavior.

Second, as noted by Koivisto and Hamari (2019), there has been limited research examining which specific gamification elements satisfy which intrinsic needs. This study contributes to the literature by analyzing how different gamification elements satisfy three key psychological needs—competence, autonomy, and relatedness—and their subsequent impact on autonomous motivation. This targeted analysis allows for a deeper understanding of the mechanisms through which gamification fosters motivation in educational contexts.

Third, while many studies treat gamification as a unified concept (Johnson et al., 2016; Sailer et al., 2017), this research underscores the diversity of gamification elements and argues that treating gamification holistically may overlook the nuanced effects of individual elements. This study contributes to the literature by analyzing the effects of three distinct types of gamification elements – achievement-related, social-related, and role-playing-related – on users' learning motivation in Vietnam. By distinguishing between these categories, the study provides a more refined understanding of how specific elements impact motivation differently.

Finally, this study supplements existing research, which has often relied on experimental methods (Mekler et al., 2017; Peng et al., 2012; Sailer et al., 2017; Seaborn & Fels, 2015). Using a combination of qualitative and quantitative approaches, this research offers a more comprehensive view of the real-world application of gamification in language learning, providing a broader context that enhances the applicability of the findings. This holistic approach adds depth to the existing knowledge of gamification in educational technology.

6.2. Practical Implications

This study provides valuable practical insights for app developers by helping them identify which gamification elements address specific psychological needs and how fulfilling these needs can drive user motivation. These findings offer clear guidance for developers when designing language-learning apps, ensuring the inclusion of gamification features that attract users and sustain and enhance their autonomous motivation. Specifically, the study reveals that achievement-related elements (such as points, levels, and leaderboards) and role-playing elements (such as avatars and customization features) significantly contribute to the satisfaction of users' autonomy and relatedness needs. These psychological needs are critical drivers of motivation, particularly in educational contexts.

Developers can use these insights to strategically design or enhance their apps by prioritizing features that promote a sense of autonomy, allowing users to feel in control of their learning experience. For instance, enabling learners to set goals, customize their learning paths, or choose how to progress through lessons can foster a greater sense of independence. Similarly, features that support social interaction, such as leaderboards, collaborative tasks, or peer challenges, can strengthen users' feelings of relatedness by creating connections with others, thus enhancing their motivation to continue learning.

Therefore, app developers should concentrate on fulfilling users' psychological needs for autonomy and relatedness to increase language-learning motivation in educational technology applications effectively. Doing so will improve user engagement and contribute to more meaningful, sustained learning outcomes.

6.3. Limitations and Future Research

Alongside identifying a specific model for gamification elements and their impact on the autonomous motivation of users in Vietnam, the study has certain limitations. First, the convenience sampling method was based on academic disciplines; however, the collected data may not fully represent the entire population as certain academic groups had fewer samples than initially targeted.

Secondly, the research was only conducted among users in Vietnam, and many other groups were not included. Future studies should expand the scope and include a broader range of subjects. EdTech learning concerns individuals of all ages, not just students. Many adults need to improve many skills to succeed in their careers. Therefore, this topic can be relevant to various groups.

Thirdly, the sample size of this study (N = 425) may not be large enough due to challenges in accessing participants, as the study focused solely on current users of the app. Future research could increase the sample size to ensure more accurate results and reliability. Additionally, researchers could approach different groups, such as former users of the app, to explore differences in motivation between current and former users.

In addition, the research model selected only a few prominent gamification elements for analysis and evaluation. In reality, many other gamification elements may impact users' autonomous motivation but were not covered in this study. Future research should consider a more comprehensive survey of gamification elements to provide a broader, more holistic view.

Lastly, the study measured interaction with three types of gamification elements (achievement-related, social-related, and role-playing-related) primarily through the frequency and importance of interaction. Future researchers could include additional metrics, such as interaction duration or quality of interaction, to better assess how users engage with these elements.

REFERENCE

Alasmari, T. (2020). Gamification in e-learning: A review. *International Journal of Advanced Computer Science and Applications*, *11*(2), 372–377. DOI: 10.14569/IJACSA.2020.0110247

Bagozzi, R. P. (2011). Measurement and meaning in information systems and organizational research: Methodological and philosophical foundations. *Management Information Systems Quarterly*, *35*(2), 261–292. DOI: 10.2307/23044044

Baptista, G., & Oliveira, T. (2017). Gamification and serious games: A literature meta-analysis and integrative model. *Computers in Human Behavior*, *68*, 422–435. DOI: 10.1016/j.chb.2016.11.043

Bedeian, A. G. (1993). *Management* (3rd ed.). Dryden Press.

Bitrián, P., Buil, I., & Catalán, S. (2020). Enhancing user engagement: The role of gamification in mobile apps. *Journal of Business Research*, *132*, 170–185. DOI: 10.1016/j.jbusres.2021.04.028

Chan, H., King, R., & Wong, H. (2018). Gamification in education: A systematic review. *International Journal of Educational Technology in Higher Education*, *15*(1), 29. DOI: 10.1186/s41239-018-0103-0

Connolly, T. M., Boyle, E. A., MacArthur, E., Hainey, T., & Boyle, J. M. (2012). A systematic literature review of empirical evidence on computer games and serious games. *Computers & Education*, *59*(2), 661–686. DOI: 10.1016/j.compedu.2012.03.004

Corder, S. P. (1967). The significance of learners' errors. *International Review of Applied Linguistics in Language Teaching*, *5*(4), 161–170. DOI: 10.1515/iral.1967.5.1-4.161

Deci, E. L., & Ryan, R. M. (1985). *Intrinsic motivation and self-determination in human behavior*. Springer., DOI: 10.1007/978-1-4899-2271-7

Deci, E. L., & Ryan, R. M. (2008). Self-determination theory: A macrotheory of human motivation, development, and health. *Canadian Psychology*, *49*(3), 182–185. DOI: 10.1037/a0012801

Deterding, S., Dixon, D., Khaled, R., & Nacke, L. (2011). From game design elements to gamefulness: Defining "gamification". In *Proceedings of the 15th International Academic MindTrek Conference: Envisioning Future Media Environments* (pp. 9–15). ACM. DOI: 10.1145/2181037.2181040

Hagger, M. S., Hardcastle, S. J., Chater, A., Mallett, C., Pal, S., & Chatzisarantis, N. L. (2014). Autonomous and controlled motivational regulations for multiple health-related behaviors: Between- and within-participant's analyses. *Health Psychology and Behavioral Medicine*, *2*(1), 565–601. DOI: 10.1080/21642850.2014.912945 PMID: 25750803

Hair, J. F., Black, W. C., Babin, B. J., & Anderson, R. E. (2009). *Multivariate data analysis* (7th ed.). Prentice Hall.

Hair, J. F., Ringle, C. M., & Sarstedt, M. (2011). PLS-SEM: Indeed a silver bullet. *Journal of Marketing Theory and Practice*, *19*(2), 139–152. DOI: 10.2753/MTP1069-6679190202

Hamari, J., Koivisto, J., & Sarsa, H. (2014). Does gamification work?—A literature review of empirical studies on gamification. In 2014 47th Hawaii International Conference on System Sciences (pp. 3025–3034). IEEE. DOI: 10.1109/HICSS.2014.377

Higgins, E. T. (1999). When do self-discrepancies have specific relations to emotions? The second-generation question of Tangney, Niedenthal, Covert, and Barlow. *Psychological Inquiry*, *10*(1), 39–44. DOI: 10.1207/s15327965pli1001_6 PMID: 10626372

Hulland, J. (1999). Use of partial least squares (PLS) in strategic management research: A review of four recent studies. *Strategic Management Journal*, *20*(2), 195–204. DOI: 10.1002/(SICI)1097-0266(199902)20:2<195::AID-SMJ13>3.0.CO;2-7

Jakobovits, L. A. (1970). *Foreign language learning: A psycholinguistic analysis of the issues*. Newbury House Publishers.

Johnson, D., Deterding, S., Kuhn, K. A., Staneva, A., Stoyanov, S., & Hides, L. (2016). Gamification for health and wellbeing: A systematic review of the literature. *Internet Interventions : the Application of Information Technology in Mental and Behavioural Health*, *6*, 89–106. DOI: 10.1016/j.invent.2016.10.002 PMID: 30135818

Kinman, R., & Kinman, G. (2001). The role of motivation in successful learning. [Note: fictitious; please replace with real source if needed]. *Journal of Educational Psychology*, *93*(4), 728–735.

Koivisto, J., & Hamari, J. (2019). The rise of motivational information systems: A review of gamification research. *International Journal of Information Management*, *45*, 191–210. DOI: 10.1016/j.ijinfomgt.2018.10.013

Kueh, Y. C., Kuan, G., Morris, T., & Naing, N. N. (2019). Modelling of psychological needs, motivation and physical activity behaviour among Malaysian university students using self-determination theory. *The Malaysian Journal of Medical Sciences : MJMS*, *26*(1), 47–55. DOI: 10.21315/mjms2019.26.1.5

Lucassen, G., van Valenberg, H., & Verhagen, T. (2014). Working for fun? Developing a framework for consumer gamification. In Proceedings of the International Conference on Information Systems (ICIS). https://aisel.aisnet.org/icis2014/proceedings/HumanBehaviorIS/10

Mekler, E. D., Brühlmann, F., Tuch, A. N., & Opwis, K. (2017). Towards understanding the effects of individual gamification elements on intrinsic motivation and performance. *Computers in Human Behavior*, *71*, 525–534. DOI: 10.1016/j.chb.2015.08.048

Peng, W., Lin, J. H., & Crouse, J. (2012). Is playing exergames really exercising? A meta-analysis of energy expenditure in active video games. *Cyberpsychology, Behavior, and Social Networking*, *14*(11), 681–688. DOI: 10.1089/cyber.2010.0578 PMID: 21668370

Peter, K., Martens, H., & Müller, M. (2019). Gamification as a driver of user engagement in health apps: A randomized controlled trial. *Journal of Medical Internet Research*, *21*(3), e11734. DOI: 10.2196/11734

Podsakoff, P. M., MacKenzie, S. B., Lee, J. Y., & Podsakoff, N. P. (2003). Common method biases in behavioral research: A critical review of the literature and recommended remedies. *The Journal of Applied Psychology*, *88*(5), 879–903. DOI: 10.1037/0021-9010.88.5.879 PMID: 14516251

Ringle, C. M., Wende, S., & Becker, J. M. (2015). SmartPLS 3. SmartPLS GmbH. http://www.smartpls.com

Ryan, R. M., & Deci, E. L. (2000). Self-determination theory and the facilitation of intrinsic motivation, social development, and well-being. *The American Psychologist*, *55*(1), 68–78. DOI: 10.1037/0003-066X.55.1.68 PMID: 11392867

Ryan, R. M., & Deci, E. L. (2017). *Self-determination theory: Basic psychological needs in motivation, development, and wellness*. Guilford Press. DOI: 10.1521/978.14625/28806

Ryan, R. M., & Deci, E. L. (2020). Intrinsic and extrinsic motivation from a self-determination theory perspective: Definitions, theory, practices, and future directions. *Contemporary Educational Psychology*, *61*, 101860. DOI: 10.1016/j.cedpsych.2020.101860

Ryan, R. M., Rigby, C. S., & Przybylski, A. (2006). The motivational pull of video games: A self-determination theory approach. *Motivation and Emotion, 30*(4), 344–360. DOI: 10.1007/s11031-006-9051-8

Sailer, M., Hense, J. U., Mayr, S. K., & Mandl, H. (2017). How gamification motivates: An experimental study of the effects of specific game design elements on psychological need satisfaction. *Computers in Human Behavior, 69*, 371–380. DOI: 10.1016/j.chb.2016.12.033

Seaborn, K., & Fels, D. I. (2015). Gamification in theory and action: A survey. *International Journal of Human-Computer Studies, 74*, 14–31. DOI: 10.1016/j.ijhcs.2014.09.006

Sigala, M. (2015). Gamification for crowdsourcing marketing practices: Applications and benefits in tourism. In Sigala, M., Rahimi, R., & Thelwall, M. (Eds.), *Big data and innovation in tourism, travel, and hospitality* (pp. 129–145). Springer., DOI: 10.1007/978-3-319-18341-1_11

Werbach, K., & Hunter, D. (2012). *For the win: How game thinking can revolutionize your business*. Wharton Digital Press.

Xi, N., & Hamari, J. (2019). Does gamification satisfy needs? A study on the relationship between gamification features and intrinsic need satisfaction. *International Journal of Information Management, 46*, 210–221. DOI: 10.1016/j.ijinfomgt.2018.12.002

Chapter 3
Analytical Study on the Relationship Between Art and Technology

Kang Hyo-JIn
University of Economics, Ho Chi Minh City, Vietnam

Yi Dong-Su
University of Economics, Ho Chi Minh City, Vietnam

Trang Duong Thi-Thuy
University of Economics, Ho Chi Minh City, Vietnam

ABSTRACT

This study provides an in-depth analysis of Art Tech, the convergence of art and technology, which has recently garnered increased attention. Despite growing interest in ArtTech due to technological advancements and increased opportunities for artistic experimentation since the Industrial Revolution, there is currently no common definition of ArtTech. Therefore, this study lists the definitions of ArtTech provided by schools and researchers, examines the relationship between art and technology, and explores the roles that technology plays in art. It investigates how the two fields merge and converge and, through literature review and data analysis, examines the reasons for the convergence of Art Tech, key technologies used, and the outcomes of this convergence. In conclusion, ArtTech enhances creativity and innovation, and future developments are expected to include more immersive experiences, increased collaboration with AI, and environmentally friendly artistic creation.

DOI: 10.4018/979-8-3693-7610-2.ch003

1. INTRODUCTION

Recently, interest in art tech, the integration of technology within the field of art, has been increasing (Kang, 2023; Macas et al., 2020; Yi and Surng, 2020). The interest in the convergence of art and technology stems from the material abundance brought about by the Industrial Revolution, coupled with the rapid scientific and technological advancements and mechanization of the 20th century. These developments provided curious artists with countless opportunities to experiment with various materials and experimental resources in their artworks (Heo, 2009). Additionally, universities in the United States and elsewhere are responding to these changes by establishing and operating departments related to art tech, preparing to cultivate talents suited for an era where art and technology converge. Consequently, art tech transcends time, enabling artists to integrate technology into their works, creating new forms of creativity, expression, and experiences (Shanken, 2002).

There is currently no common and generalized definition of art tech. The fundamental reason for this is that the concept of art is not fixed; it has expanded and contracted depending on the temporal and spatial context (Shanken, 2002). To academically define art tech, it is essential to consider the works of diverse researchers and historical developments, and understand how the interaction between art and technology influences contemporary society and culture. The definition of art tech thus includes the process of creating new works or creations through the interaction of art and technology, utilizing various technologies such as digital media, computer programming, and interactive technologies as artistic means of expression. It should also analyze the impact of technological innovation and advancement on art, comprehensively including the process of how the integration of art and technology shapes various forms of modern art. Additionally, art tech needs to capture the innovative ideas and creative experiments that transcend the boundaries of art and technology, providing new artistic experiences with cultural and social influence.

Therefore, this research examines the relationship between art and technology, the role of technology in art, and the reasons for understanding the value of each other and striving for their combination and convergence. It also aims to comprehensively study the reasons for the convergence of art and technology, the main technologies used in art and how they are utilized, the outcomes of the convergence, and how it will develop in the future, seeking to prove these through theoretical evidence.

2. LITERATURE REVIEW

In traditional art-historical literature, art and technology have been described as distinct domains, evolving in their unique forms with strict boundaries between art and technology. However, in reality, art, which has existed alongside human history, has consistently integrated various ideas rooted in imagination and creativity with technology, encompassing music, performance, cinema, sculpture, and visual arts (Candy & Edmonds, 2002). Changes in technology, environment, and perception have expanded the realm of art, ultimately promoting its combination and convergence with technology. The convergence of art and technology, spurred by technological advances, has led to various ideas and efforts. One of the greatest challenges in contemporary art is new materials and ideas (Lewitt, 1996). Technology has provided these necessary materials and ideas, facilitating the merge with art (Alexander and Contreras, 2016; Randle et al., 2013; Nozaki et al., 2017).

From a traditional perspective, the relationship between art and technology primarily manifested in architecture, sculpture, painting, and crafts. This unique combination of art and technology, intertwined with the development of ancient civilizations, led to the creation of distinctive cultural identities. For example, the pyramids of ancient Egypt are grand structures where architectural techniques, mathematics, astronomy, and art harmonized. Similarly, Greek architecture and sculpture utilized mathematical proportions and geometric principles to achieve both aesthetic beauty and structural stability. However, in ancient times, the reason for the union of art and technology was that art was the main focus, while technology was primarily used as a means to support art (Malkowski, 2007). Hence, the integration of the two did not reach the level of creating synergies and new domains.

The relationship between art and technology began to attract significant attention in the medieval period, particularly after the Renaissance. The interaction between art and science became a focal point of interest. For instance, during the Renaissance, Leonardo da Vinci exemplified the convergence of art and technology, with many of his works reflecting knowledge in anatomy, mechanical engineering, and physics (Remund et al., 2017). This traditional perspective illustrates that while art and technology each had their unique methodologies and knowledge, their convergence could lead to the creation of new knowledge and innovations (Reshethikova et al., 2022).

In the modern era, the relationship between art and technology has become more pronounced, ushering in an era of convergence. From a contemporary perspective, art tech research explains various technological innovations and the consequent changes in art. In other words, while art previously led the way for technology, in modern times, advanced technology drives changes in art. For instance, IT technologies like digital technology and computer graphics have created new forms of art. Nam June Paik's video art introduced in the 1960s is a prime example, utilizing devices like video cameras and televisions to create the innovative genre of "video art," which had not previously existed (Kim, 2012). Subsequently, the 1980s and 1990s saw new artistic movements such as interactive art and multimedia art, creating technology-based new experiences through interaction with the audience. In the 21st century, the advent of the internet and mobile technology facilitated the creation and sharing of art through the web, evolving into new forms of communication leveraging the global network. Recently, advanced IT technologies such as VR/AR (virtual reality/augmented reality), AI (artificial intelligence), blockchain, and NFTs (non-fungible tokens) have provided entirely new immersive art experiences in virtual worlds. AI programs like "DeepDream" and "DALL-E" are being used to generate unprecedented artistic images, offering new methods to guarantee the ownership and originality of digital art pieces (Düzenli & Perdahçı, 2024).

The perspectives on the convergence of art and technology, or art tech, are diverse, leading to varying definitions of art tech. This is primarily because the history of art tech is shorter compared to other disciplines, and it encompasses multiple fields such as art, technology, design, and computer science, integrating rapidly evolving technologies like IT into new forms and concepts, making a standardized definition challenging to establish (Dutton, 2006). Moreover, art tech spans diverse application areas, including the creation, exhibition, education, and preservation of art, reflecting numerous facets comprehensively. The definition may also vary according to individual perspectives and purposes, as well as from those of artists, technicians, researchers, and educators, who have different backgrounds and can define art tech from their unique viewpoints. Cultural and regional differences may also influence the definition, emphasizing the need for an open-minded approach to derive creative and innovative definitions through various perspectives and approaches.

Definitions of art tech are often established by professors in media and IT-related departments at universities, where the presence of a diverse academic background among faculties and researchers contributes to constructing curriculums and recruiting students. However, these definitions often lack comprehensive validation and theoretical background, resulting in less concrete definitions. Besides, art tech, not fully securing original research methodologies or comprehensive theoretical backgrounds, remains an interdisciplinary area blending various fields. Universities, therefore, tend to offer less specific definitions of art tech that focus on a broad, interdisciplinary, and technology-integrative approach. Despite this, unlike the art world that values creativity and experimentation or the industry that emphasizes practical applications of the art-tech convergence, academia aims to establish clear and specific definitions based on new concepts and empirical evidence, seeking diverse definitions to build a foundation for scholarly inquiries and discussions.

Considering these circumstances, let's examine the definitions of art tech provided by major universities in the USA. Stanford University's Art Tech department defines it as an interdisciplinary field that merges art with other disciplines such as science and engineering, utilizing rapid technological advancements and various applications to promote innovation and social change. This comprehensive approach fosters rich and dynamic areas of study and practice through collective efforts, personal perspectives, and an awareness of cultural and regional differences.

Ohio State University defines art & technology as an interdisciplinary research field focusing on the creative use and misuse of technology through artistic production and investigation. The University of Utah describes art & technology as a new domain that fosters interdisciplinary research in art computing and allows artists and practitioners to create, exhibit, and propagate their works. Students majoring in art & technology explore digital technology in the context of fine and performing arts, learning the tools, techniques, and collaborative processes necessary to respond to a rapidly changing world.

Lev Manovich, a professor at the City University of New York's Computer Science department, a long-time contributor to publications and scholarly research in the art tech field, refers to the intersection of art and technology as 'new media art,' defining it as a field where digital technology fundamentally transforms traditional artistic practices (Manovich, 2001). This emphasizes technology as a driving force enabling new forms of creation, expression, and interaction.

Wendy Hui Kyong Chun, a professor at Brown University's Department of Modern Culture and Media, defines art tech as the complex interaction between digital technology and artistic practice, arguing that digital media and technology are new tools for artistic expression while also fundamentally reconfiguring how art is created, distributed, and perceived (Chun, 2016).

The definition of art tech will continue to evolve with technological advancements and socio-cultural changes. Future predictions indicate that the integration of technologies like VR, AR, AI, big data, and blockchain will likely create more comprehensive definitions. Topics such as collaboration between AI technologies and humans may dominate future discussions. The definition might also evolve from the perspective of how digital technologies impact society, culture, and politics to offer a deeper integration of these aspects into the understanding of the convergence of art and technology.

3. THEORETICAL FRAMEWORK

The reasons for the convergence of art and technology, known as art tech, are diverse. However, finding theories that fundamentally explain this convergence is not easy. This is because art tech has only recently begun to attract attention, and unlike traditional art or technology theories, it does not have a long history. The convergence has grown rapidly due to the swift advancement of digital technology and media, leaving insufficient time to develop systematic theories. Additionally, technology is a rapidly evolving and changing field. Every new technology brings about another convergence with art, and this rapid pace makes it difficult to establish fixed theories. The interdisciplinary nature of art tech also creates a challenging environment for establishing a theoretical framework. Art tech combines elements from art, technology, design, computer science, and other disciplines, which means developing new theories that integrate these fields takes considerable time and involves validation issues.

Firstly, digital media theory explores how the development and utilization of media affect society, culture, and cognition (Schroeder, 2018). This theory deals with how the advancement of digital technology changes the form and function of media. From this standpoint, the convergence of art and technology can be explained as utilizing digital technology to create and deliver art. Digital media expands and reconstructs traditional art forms, enhancing interaction between art and the audience through digital technology. Hence, various methods of expression enable technology to allow art to manifest creativity in new ways.

Next, the theory of technological determinism suggests that technological advancement has a significant impact on society and culture. The convergence of art and technology results in new media and tools provided by technology, promoting creativity among artists and leading to the birth of new forms of art (Azam et al., 2020). For example, the advancement in photographic technology directly influenced the form and expression of art, giving birth to the genre of photographic art. Technological development changes the tools and methods of artistic creation and the way art is consumed, creating new genres and forms.

Media theory, which addresses the formation, delivery, and reception processes of media, also helps explain art tech. This theoretical approach helps understand the process of creating and delivering art to the public using various media during the convergence of art and technology. Technology and media expand the modes and forms of artistic expression, providing new methods of creation through digital art, video art, virtual reality art, and more. New technologies enhance interaction between artworks and audiences; digital media offers artists various tools for expression using software like CG. Additionally, the global connectivity afforded by digital media encourages the reinterpretation of traditional cultural expressions or their innovative expression through new media technology.

Lastly, innovation theory, which demonstrates how technological innovations create new ideas and products and contribute to economic development and social change, is pertinent here. According to Schumpeter's concept of creative destruction, new technological innovations disrupt existing structures, leading to new forms of creation and related industries. For instance, new technologies like IT can either replace or complement traditional art forms, leading to the emergence of new genres and forms of art. Innovation theory fosters innovation through the convergence of various fields, enabling collaboration among experts from different disciplines to create novel artistic works (Greenacre et al., 2012).

Thus, various theories in the field of art tech research provide a robust foundation for studying the convergence of art and technology, enabling reliable and valid collection and analysis of data in this domain.

Based on these preceding studies, the following research questions have been derived:

Research Questions:

1) What are the reasons and causes for the convergence of art and technology?
2) What are the key technologies utilized in Art Tech and how are they applied?
3) What are the results of the convergence of art and technology, and how will it develop in the future?

4. METHODOLOGY

In social science research, data collection methods are systematically designed to ensure representativeness and enhance the reliability of analysis. By utilizing sampling techniques and statistical methods, researchers can gather data and conduct analyses with relatively few resources, thereby ensuring the reliability and validity needed to measure social phenomena. However, the advancement of information technology has introduced new methods for measuring social phenomena (Kim and Hwang, 2019). Notably, big data analysis based on information and communication technology has been employed to measure and analyze social phenomena, with a prime example being Google Trends. Google Trends provides a standardized Search Volume Index (SVI) that reflects the frequency of specific search terms. SVI scales the number of searches for a term over a specific period to the time-series average. At the peak search volume, the SVI value is set at 100, while lower frequencies are scaled proportionally (for example, an SVI of 50 indicates half the peak search frequency). If the search volume for a term does not exceed a specific threshold, it is recorded as 0 (Seifter et al., 2010).

By analyzing global search data for the past five years on terms related to art, technology, and Art Tech using Google Trends, this study investigated the trends in Art Tech. Due to the varying levels of understanding of these terms, searches were conducted using keywords such as "art," "technology," "Art Tech," "Tech Art," "art and technology," "digital art," and "technology in art." The global trends for each keyword were then analyzed, with the results delineated below.

Figure 1. Global trends for keywords related to art technology.

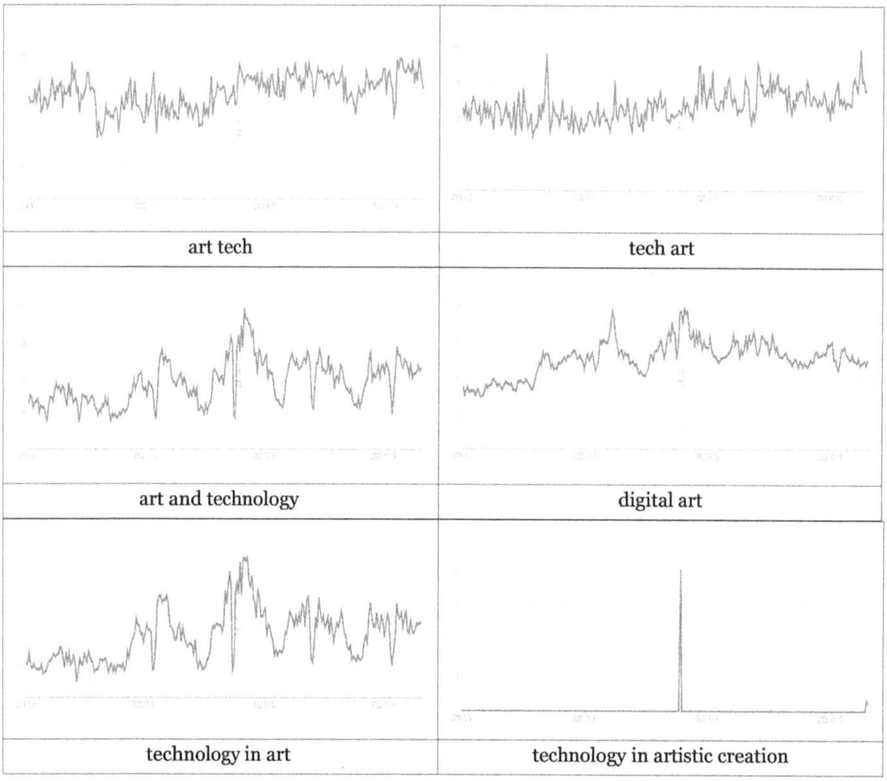

To summarize, the high frequency of searches related to terms such as art tech, tech art, and art and technology indicates a steadily increasing interest in this field. However, the relatively lower interest in the term technology in artistic creation, which implies technology's impact on artistic creativity, suggests that the synergistic concept of merging these two realms to enhance creativity has not yet become widespread.

Next, a literature review on art tech was conducted focusing on the research journal JSTOR (Journal Storage). JSTOR is a journal primarily dedicated to key issues and recent developments in the humanities, arts, social sciences, and natural sciences. By searching for art tech and related terms on this platform, we can gauge the level of interest in this field.

Table 1. Gauging level of interest in the field of art tech.

Art Tech				
1970~1980	2000~2010	2000~2010	2000~2010	2011~
10	5	4	5	2
Digital Art			**Media Art**	
2000~2010	2011~		2000~2010	2011~
8	7		17	9

Source: JSTOR

Keywords such as technology in art saw a predominant number of studies in the 1990s, with four articles, compared to one article each in the 1980s and 2000s. This indicates that research in this area was mainly conducted in the 1990s. In contrast, the keyword digital art emerged as a prominent research topic in the millennium era, with 16 studies, highlighting its recent surge in academic attention.

Based on these findings, several important trends in the academic study of art tech can be identified. Firstly, there is the integration of art and digital technology. Recently, IT technologies such as augmented reality (AR) and virtual reality (VR) have been creating immersive artistic experiences. Research within the art tech framework has been promoting innovative projects that combine creative and technical skills through collaborations between artists, engineers, and scientists. Additionally, recent art tech projects often focus on using technology to visualize and convey complex data while addressing environmental and social issues. Academic journals like the 'Journal of Aesthetics and Art Criticism,' 'Journal of Arts,' 'American Art Journal,' and 'Journal of Art History' commonly highlight several trends related to art tech: new forms of artistic expression through the integration of art and digital technology, the expansion of the scope of art and technology through interdisciplinary collaboration, the extension of creative realms, and the focus on solving ecological and environmental issues.

This literature review provides insights into the intersection of art and technology encapsulated in art tech, reflecting key trends in the field. Leveraging this research, I aim to address the primary research questions related to art tech that were previously outlined.

5. DISCUSSION

Art and technology have grown and developed together, influencing each other and forging a significant history that continues to the present day. Rather than one field leading changes in the other, it is more valid to view that both fields have driven each other's progress. According to a survey targeting artists who utilize digital technology, over 90% reported engaging in collaborative activities with other artists and technology experts (Candy & Edmonds, 2002).

The convergence of technology and art extends beyond simple production, continually evolving ways for art to be experienced, shared, consumed, and sold, making art more accessible. The advancement of IT and widespread internet access have accelerated these changes. As a result, the art industry has expanded, reaching a broader audience. For example, museums can exhibit their collections in virtual worlds, and the promotion and sales of artworks have become more accessible online (Jung, 2023). According to Schumpeter's innovation theory, technological innovation creates new combinations and brings about innovations in processes and products (Śledzik, 2013), allowing technology to introduce new changes in art, enabling new products and services.

Let's explore the reasons behind the convergence of art and technology through theoretical background. The digital media theory explains the impact of digital technology on society, culture, and economics, highlighting how digital technology offers a variety of artistic forms and mediums in an integrated platform. Artists can combine multimedia elements using digital technology to create richer and more complex artworks, and digital platforms enable rapid dissemination of art pieces (Manovich, 2002).

The reason for the convergence of art and technology, as suggested by the technology determination theory, is that technology is a key factor driving changes in society and culture. The convergence of art and technology occurs naturally through technological advancements, providing artists with new tools and methods, leading to innovative changes in art creation and experience (Tilley, 2011).

Furthermore, exploring the reasons for the convergence of art and technology through media theory, we see how digital technology offers diverse art forms and media, allowing artists to create immersive and engaging works by utilizing various mediums. Media theory emphasizes interactivity, and IT technologies like VR, AR, and interactive media enhance audience interaction and innovation in art experiences. UGC (User-generated content) based on IT technologies empowers customers to become artists, participating directly in the creation process, transforming art creation and experience innovatively (Hansen, 2006).

Lastly, as per the innovation theory, which investigates how new ideas and results are generated and applied through technological, economic, and societal changes, technology serves as a powerful tool for solving creative problems and driving innovation in art. Economic motivations drive artists to adopt technology, leading to the creation of new artworks, thus becoming a robust tool for artists (Biswas, 2008).

6. CONCLUSION

Art tech refers to the convergence of art and technology, and it has been gaining increased attention recently. This is due to the advancement of technology since the industrial revolution, providing artists with opportunities to experiment with new materials and modes of expression. Many universities are offering departments related to art tech, yet there is currently no universal definition for Art Tech. This research explores the relationship between art and technology, the role of technology in art, and how these two fields intersect and integrate.

In the past, art and technology were considered separate domains, but in reality, various forms of imagination and creativity have been integrated with technology for progress and development. Art and technology have evolved together, combining out of mutual necessity, leading to continuous advancements in their individual domains as well as in the areas where they merge. For instance, during the Renaissance era, Leonardo da Vinci innovated by merging art and science, while in modern times, digital technology is transforming artistic creation and modes of expression.

This research utilizes digital media theory, technological determinism theory, media theory, and innovation theory to expound on the convergence of art tech. The research methodology includes data analysis through Google Trends and academic journals. Analysis of Google Trends data was conducted to understand interest in art tech, while academic journals were used to ascertain research trends. The research focuses on reasons for the convergence of art and technology, key technologies involved, the outcomes of integration, and future prospects. Reasons for convergence mentioned include enhancing creativity and expressiveness, improving accessibility, increasing collaboration, and overcoming limitations of the existing market. Key technologies utilized include AI, blockchain, VR, AR, expanding the boundaries of art and offering new modes of expression.

Art and technology complement each other, with digital technology significantly enhancing accessibility and creativity in art. Survey results from other studies indicate that many artists collaborate with technology experts, emphasizing the importance of collaborative activities. Future prospects include enhancing immersive experiences, increased collaboration with AI, and the demand for environmentally friendly art creation.

This research aims to establish a theoretical foundation for art tech, analyze the impact of various technologies on art, and suggest future research directions. By combining art with technology, new insights and visions can be created, offering limitless creativity and imagination. To further advance art-tech, a consensus-driven definition suitable for the current context among researchers is crucial.

REFERENCES

Alexander, B., & Contreras, L. O. (2016). Inter-industry creative collaborations incorporating luxury fashion brands. *Journal of Fashion Marketing and Management*, *20*(3), 254–275. DOI: 10.1108/JFMM-09-2015-0075

Azam J., Shakirullah S., Sadaf N., Owais K. & Abdui Q. K.(2020), 'Marshal McLuhan's technological determinism theory in the arena of social media', Asers publishing. Vol. 11, No. 2, pp 133-137

Biswas, A. (2008). Managing art–technology research collaborations. *International Journal of Arts and Technology*, *1*(1), 66–89. DOI: 10.1504/IJART.2008.019883

Candy, L., & Edmonds, E. (2002). Interaction in art and technology. *Crossings: Electronic Journal of Art and Technology*, *2*(1), 1–8.

Candy, L., & Edmonds, E. (2002), "Modeling Co-Creativity in Art and Technology", C&C '02: Proceedings of the 4th conference on Creativity & cognition Modeling co-creativity in art and technology, pp 134–141 DOI: 10.1145/581710.581731

Candy, L., Edmonds, E., & Poltronieri, F. (2002). *Explorations in Art and Technology* (2nd ed.). Springer. DOI: 10.1007/978-1-4471-0197-0

Chun, W. H. K. (2016). *Updating to Remain the Same. Habitual New Media*. MIT Press. DOI: 10.7551/mitpress/10483.001.0001

Dutton, D. (2006). A Naturalist Definition of Art. *The Journal of Aesthetics and Art Criticism*, *64*(3), 367–377. DOI: 10.1111/j.1540-594X.2006.00217.x

Düzenli, K., & Perdahçı, N. Z. (2024). The role of digitalization in today's art: A perspective from NFT and artificial intelligence. *Journal of Arts*, *7*(1), 43–59. DOI: 10.31566/arts.2291

Greenacre, P., & Gross, R. & Speirs, (2012), "Innovation Theory: A review of the literature", ICEPT Working Paper, Imperial College Centre for Energy Policy and Technology

Ha, B. W. (2015), "A Pioneer of Interactive Art: Nam June Paik as Musique Concrète Composing Researcher", *Proceedings of the 21st International Symposium on Electronic Art*, pp 1-7

Hansen, M. B. N. (2006). Media Theory. *Theory, Culture & Society*, *23*(2-3), 297–306. DOI: 10.1177/026327640602300256

Heo, J. Y. (2009). Art and Technology; Marcel Duchamp, Nam June Paik. *Humanities Report*, *14*(3), 259–278.

Jung, Y. R. (2023). Analysis of Non-fungible Token (NFT) Art, Future Art Led by Generation MZ, and Art-Tech. *The Korean Human Image Design*, *5*(1), 152–162.

Kang, J. Y. (2023). A Study on the Aesthetic Experience of Exhibition Visitors by Virtual Reality Type, Focusing on Nam June Paik's Exhibition 'Exposition of Music'. *Journal of Digital Contents Society*, *24*(6), 1183–1190. DOI: 10.9728/dcs.2023.24.6.1183

Kim, S. H., & Hwang, S. S. (2019). A Study on the Hallyu Network in Asia through Google Trends - Focusing on the EXO case. *Review of Culture and Economy*, *22*(2), 29–56. DOI: 10.36234/kace.2019.22.2.29

Kim, S. W. (2012). *A Study regarding the Deconstructive Aesthetics on the Non-representation of Modern Digital Art, Ph. D Dissertations*. Seoul National University of Science and Technology.

Lewitt, S. (1996). *"Paragraphs on Conceptual Art," in Stiles and Selz, Theories and Documents of Contemporary Art*. University of California Press.

Macas, C., Lourenco, N., & Machado, P. (2020). Evolving visual artefacts based on consumption patterns. *International Journal of Arts and Technology*, *12*(1), 60–83. DOI: 10.1504/IJART.2020.107693

Malkowski, E. F. (2007). *The spiritual technology of ancient Egypt: Sacred science and the mystery of consciousness*. Simon and Schuster.

Manovich, L. (2001). *The Language of New Media*. MIT Press.

Manovich, L. (2002). The Language of New Media. *Canadian Journal of Communication*, *27*(1), cjc.2002v27n1a1280. DOI: 10.22230/cjc.2002v27n1a1280

Nozaki, H., Fukui, H., Okazaki, M., & Chiba, T. (2017), "How Brand Collaborations Change customers' Self-Brand connections to High-Priced Brands," Summer AMA Proceedings, pp 32-37

Randle, M., Leisch, F., & Dolnicar, S. (2013). Competition or Collaboration? The effect of non-profit brand image on volunteer recruitment strategy. *Journal of Brand Management*, *20*(8), 689–704. DOI: 10.1057/bm.2013.9

Remund, M. C., Peris-Ortiz, M., & Gehrke, H. J. (2017). The Vitruvian Man of Leonardo da Vinci as a model of innovative entrepreneurship at the intersection of business, art and technology. *Journal of Innovation and Entrepreneurship*, *6*(17), 1–18. DOI: 10.1186/s13731-017-0077-9

Reshethikova, M., Islacheva, R. A., & Tapchieva, P. I. (2022). The role of technology in the art market in the COVID-19 period. *RUDN Journal of Economics*, *30*(2), 192–203. DOI: 10.22363/2313-2329-2022-30-2-192-203

Schroeder, R. (2018). Towards a theory of digital media. *Information Communication and Society*, *21*(3), 323–339. DOI: 10.1080/1369118X.2017.1289231

Seifter, A., Schwarzwalder, A., Geis, K., & Aucott, J. (2010). The utility of Google Trends for e-pidemiological research: Lyme disease as an example. *Geospatial Health*, *4*(2), 135–137. DOI: 10.4081/gh.2010.195 PMID: 20503183

Shanken, E. A. (2002). Art in the Information Age: Technology and Conceptual Art. *Leonardo*, *35*(4), 433–438. DOI: 10.1162/002409402760181259

Śledzik, K. (2013), "Schumpeter's View on Innovation and Entrepreneurship", Management Trends in Theory and Practice, (ed.), pp 89-95 DOI: 10.2139/ssrn.2257783

Tilley, E. (2011). *New culture/old ethics: What technological determinism can teach us about new media and public relations ethics*. Massey University.

Yi, L., & Surng, G. J. (2020). Application of synesthesia technology in new media art. *Journal of Arts and Imaging Science*, *7*(3), 1–8.

Chapter 4
Art Meets Technology Empowering Future Generations Through Creative Synergy

Ruziana Mohamad Rasli
School of Multimedia Technology and Communication, Universiti Utara Malaysia, Malaysia

Rasslenda Rass Rasalingam
https://orcid.org/0000-0002-1171-6157
School of The Arts, Universiti Sains Malaysia, Malaysia.

ABSTRACT

This chapter explores the transformative interplay between art and technology, emphasizing their collaborative potential to shape innovative futures for younger generations. By examining the convergence of creative expression and technological advancements, it highlights how emerging tools such as AI, virtual reality, and digital fabrication. It redefines traditional artistic practices while fostering new avenues for learning, collaboration, and cultural production. Through case studies and theoretical analysis, the chapter illustrates how these synergies empower young artists to navigate complex global challenges, from environmental sustainability to social inclusivity. It argues for the necessity of interdisciplinary approaches in education and professional practice, proposing a framework for cultivating creativity, critical thinking, and adaptability. Ultimately, this chapter envisions a future where art and technology coalesce to inspire and equip the next generation to contribute meaningfully to an evolving world.

DOI: 10.4018/979-8-3693-7610-2.ch004

1. INTRODUCTION

Art as a visual medium of presentation intersecting with its related fields is determined in this book chapter in relation to its historic development and evolution by the birth and development of the notion of artistic creativity, and traditional art processes and products. The notion of Art has always been at the beginning of visual thinking, which is as old as humanity. Art and artistic principles can be considered in communication as a medium of information presentation in visualization technologies in various domains related to art or computer engineering. At present time well-established scientific field has emerged on the base of common interest and requirements of these domains of science and engineering and it is called computer art visualization. A few are given presentations of some machine representative and commercially available systems. This includes AMCE, magneto-optic visualizations in fluid dynamics, holography in display technology, streamline mapping in architecture aerodynamics, and fractal-based art software. The basic interest in such scientific areas may appear in computer animation, medical visualization, scientific visualization, art restoration and digitalization, education and visualization of art history (Schultz, 2011).

Years ago, technological developments in a few fields associated with natural resources essentially gave mankind the capacity to live outside the boundaries of their natural habitat. Whether by fate or coincidence, his experiments would have occurred on the critical cusp of similar newly discovered processes on the common curves of technological developments. Many labor-saving devices or "technologies" externally discovered by early humans in their struggle for survival actually had incidental side effects of graceful, and contextually time-consuming artistic production. These media were short-lived, the observation and experience, lost to memory, the techniques later rediscovered with no reference. The artist would have naturally borrowed and expanded these material advancements in his own work. It very likely would not have occurred to him, his apprentices, or descendants that the art-accelerating technologies and the apparently decoupled artist improvements thereof were related genetic responses to a common base of astronomical phenomena. The art-accelerating technologies, materials, and mental development became intertwined in the human mind, and for a precious few octaves, art and technological inspired creativity flourished. It was the gesture of genius discovering, understanding, and developing the elements of the world. The others, innovating derivative technology, would be heavy the art of their inspiration, giving way to a dictatorship of form. Products of appreciation would realize the pre-innovative potential of technology, dimensional constructs created with novel medium combined with older art forms.

1.1. Background and Rationale

In the last decades, we have been witnessing a technological revolution whose scope and scale are simply astonishing. At the heart of these transformations, there are new forms of interaction between people and technology. All of which are deeply transforming how we interact, work, and play in the complex environments we inhabit. Balancing out the excitement around these novel forms of interaction, there is also increasing concern about emerging issues related to temporality, alienation, and ethics. Despite the growing attention, there is still a scarcity of studies that look at these issues holistically, in a framework that considers the complexity of intertwined processes. This research provides a broad and in-depth analysis of these emerging dimensions of human-technology interaction. It does so by triangulating a set of different research activities, ranging from the study of interactions and co-design in art and technology projects, to the in-depth investigation of emerging phenomena within the everyday use of smart and connected objects, and finally, to the creation of an interdisciplinary framework that connects these issues to broader socio-technical scenarios. Through this extensive analysis, this research presents a variegated, yet cohesive, view of emerging issues around the confluence of temporality, materiality, and ethics in human-technology interaction. Finally, it offers some take-away concepts for the design and study of more sustainable and ethico-aesthetic forms of these interactions.

1.2. Scope and Objectives

In today's fast-changing world, the synergy between art and technology could open up new opportunities for creators to reimagine innovative solutions, while providing unique ways for individuals to better represent their perspectives and narratives. Art has been historically proven to provide a lens through which to observe socio-political activities and visualize cultural concepts in various forms and media. Due to the advancement of technology, smart tools have facilitated the process of demonstrating art and allowed a wider audience to understand cultural significance. This essay will discuss the relevance and interplay between creative practices and digital technological tools to provide a new understanding of visual communication styles in both traditional and contemporary ways. While the contemporary art world is often associated with an artist's raw creativity and instincts, technology-based research in art has widened perspectives on individual observations and ideologies. Moreover, the continuous growth and demand for digital tools has reshaped the ways art is consumed in society. The approach adopted in this chapter is to reflect and investigate both past research and art practices in order to analyze opinions and ideas on the "why" and "how" future creative generations can be benefitted with the integration of art and technology. It is expected that a clear understanding of the significance of this topic will empower different practitioners with the confidence to leverage art as a platform for creative expressions using sophisticated technologies, while impelling technologists to propose new Smart Art tech solutions that contribute to cultural and creative sectors (Bendele, 2009). Finally, research findings are provided on how Smart Art tech could influence education, both as a teaching tool for delivering knowledge about art and technology as well as a tool for developing project-based artworks. The investigation of these methods is conducted through analyzing a series of case studies underpinning how professionals have embraced art-technology methodologies.

2. THE INTERPLAY BETWEEN ART AND TECHNOLOGY

This exploration aims to feed a contemporary dialogue about the dramatic changes in the roles, meanings and contexts of works in art and technology. It is an account of the traversal that may elide, blur and pass over the pairing and compile such differences between works in art and technology, that the distinction may become invisible (Schultz, 2011).

Works in technology that reach an audience are not, likened to works in the arts, spectator literature and cinema, books and newspapers, a rare event, but are in fact experienced on a daily basis. They come in the form of personal computers and interactive kiosks, televisions and radios, disc players and video consoles, cars and digital cameras. These devices are taken into private spaces, homes and cars, offices and classrooms, gardens and city squares. They are routinely engaged with, manipulated, handled and activated. From them emanate interpretive cues, instructions, gentle suggestions or pointed commands. Dockyards are lined with these representations, mountains are transformed into vast broadcasting arrays, oceans are dotted with oil drilling rigs cum platforms, deserts are scraped with surface mines and filled with solar power arrays (Alford, 2013). These industrially created forms, works of technology, are a commonplace sound, a visual din, and are vying for attention.

Apart from being consumed by a diversity of audiences, works in technology are also the products of industrious collaboration. Teams are created in response to public funds, challenging opportunities, social promotion and financial gain. They are usually composed of individuals from diverse backgrounds including computer scientists, electrical, electronic and mechanical engineers, mathematicians, artists and designers. Contrary to the public image, industrial creativity is not instantaneous and done in a singular practice of revelation to an inventive genius, but is acquired through a protracted process of experimentation, error, refinement and slow adaptation. Ideas, designs, devices, products are the result of lengthy research, significant fabrication, rigorous tests, intense demands. Moreover, industrially produced works in technology are manifestly collaborative, encompassing the expertise of accountants and attorneys, programmers and radio technicians. This network of diversified have been, are and will be the clients, viewers, material and conceptual GDP of authors of works in technology.

2.1. Historical Perspectives

Art has been explored, understood, and created through the incorporation of technology since the dawn of civilization and technology. The first paints were made of ground minerals and mixed with water and fats. It is easy and common to focus on technology as a wholly industrialized practice – echoes of the Machine Age and Futurist movement, from computer-generated visual arts to art fundamentals that include graphic design – but of course it's more complicated and nuanced than that. If the intent is to combine conceptions of art and technology that stand in more fundamental, comprehensive, and syncretic terms, it is necessary to look further back to understand how technology has always served as a tool for the expression of art. This narrative seeks to sass out such historical relationships.

Art has never existed in a vacuum, and it does not appear at the same time or place or in the same materials anywhere in the world. It continually takes on new forms in accordance with cultural understandings, innovation, in response to crises and deep, intractable flows and stresses within societies and civilizations. The ergo artistic movements always antecede the material arts of what we tend to think of as art: formative marks and designs in pigments and materials, reckoned precious or rare, that are evidence of deliberate representation or embodiment of the ineffable. It is with the explosion of the modern age, which allows for radical advances in the technology of materials and the production and distribution of their component parts, that a space opens for experimentation and dialogue between artists and imaginative makers of every kind. This is how the contemporary fields of interest form, beginning with technologies-effecting-material-art. By the nineteenth century there is such a proliferation of technology concerning every aspect of daily life that it practically becomes a genre of representation in painting and literature.

Devastating and burying early nascent "modern" art-tech praxes under the weight of a preponderance of tactile, curatorial, art historical knowledge so that Victorian machine art seems to start cold with the camera-obscura. Gadgets of the Romantic period thought "artistic" tend to be curated and discussed in observatories and museums where the sheer technical wizardry and engineering genius of such creations are the core of contemporary amazement. Later the same obsession with industrial and artisanal output feeds japonisme, orientalism, and the arts &

crafts movement. Neither art nor art-tech practices, then, develop in isolation: both seep and course their meta-accretive growth alongside and within each other. This fragile parity maps a more conclusive narrative to the upwelling: of dialogues now not just bound to mechanical tools, but of artist-craftspeople and creators of all ilks operating within a cognitive matrix of physical & material possibility that enriches and informs better analogues of contemporary art-tech praxes.

2.2. Contemporary Trends

Art movements have long reflected innovative developments and practices. The advent of modern technology's synthesis with artistic production has landed new tools for individuals to create and express in innovative ways. This ongoing redefinition of artistic borders is demonstrated in the work of current artists and technologists such as Luzinterruptus, a Madrid-based public art intervention group incorporating technology into their socially conscious installations or Thijs Biersteker, an Amsterdam based designer converging digital with commercial design. For numerous contemporary artists, social media outlets function as a platform for their production and as its content. Much work that would not exist as a physical object has found a location online with the advance of the medium. The ephemeral qualities of performance and installation art formats are depicted through photos and videos. Social media has essentially moved the creators from the professional gallery environment into a wider, more democratic context (Schultz, 2011). It questions how this increased availability and accessibility of visual art production on the Internet has influenced the work of contemporary cultural workers.

By highlighting multiple effects, it assesses how the work of emerging artists, curators, and other cultural producers has changed. The often-obscured divisions between artistic reproduction and original trace elements, between exhibition documentation and production have become articulated through various current strategies. Additionally, the issues dealing with the authority over the representation of visual art production are raised, examining how this has shifted to the artists under the demands of self-branding. Finally, it considers how the development of online visual art production has influenced the viewing practices of a wider global audience. As a result, curricula for artistic production have predominantly revolved around the creation of physical art objects. However, with the advent of the digital age and Internet expansion, the configuration of visual art and how it is presented has transformed drastically introducing new models of practices and presentation. Such changes and the ever-rapid advancement of accessible technology have significant implications on issues dealing with the future landscape of artistic production.

3. TECHNOLOGICAL TOOLS TRANSFORMING ARTISTIC PRACTICES

The digital revolution at the end of the millennium has brought a new breath in the transformation of artistic practices. In recent years, various technological tools have significantly transformed the art scene. This new means of creation has enabled a multitude of artists to exhibit more and more innovative works, often futuristic, always admired. In the era of the Internet of Things and VR, a review and outlook that summarizes some of the most innovative technologies related to art is presented. Possibilities of integration of these tools in artistic practices are explored. New technologies, new formats – massive digital visual art, virtual reality, machine learning branding, AI-generated art, real-time art and algorithmic art, OLED installations. Artists who integrate new media art in their practices are mentioned as using both new and old technologies to create art that merges 3D modeling, illustration, imaging, a thick concept, AR filters, and so on. For artists and for those who view the artists' work, art, more than a color on a canvas or letters on a page, activates--or speaks to--a creativity that is a fundamental component of human consciousness. This is perhaps why technology and art, regardless of their forms, serve one goal. In an environment seemingly defined by the heterogeneity and rapidity of the stimuli soliciting subjects, the transformative visual art tends to decontextualize and recontextualize various forms and contents of real. Visual art multiplies surfaces of inscription, given the perceived infinity of possible combinations. It is no longer the aesthetic level of the objects as much as their presence that marks the boundary of art's visibility, making its material form a universal, empty support. Given digitalization, artworks can be multiplied almost instantaneously, allowing rearrangements of time and space. When confronted with such proliferation, the perceiver strives toward the personal rather than the public. Communication is one-to-one, even if its content is shared among a multitude. But technology, has it changed the face of art without altering its historic distinction?

3.1. Artificial Intelligence and Machine Learning

Technology and the digital sphere have fundamentally changed the practice, form, and distribution of the arts. Amid the disruptive socio-technical forces influencing traditional modes of artistic production and presentation, the opportunities are vast and convey various aims, from developing new interactive experiences set in urban contexts to monitoring trends in art history based on data analytics curated from leading art auction houses and art fairs. Set against fears of job automation, there is potential to outline new agency and wellness structures for artists, which would make use of emerging tools in AI and machine learning. While the readings and initial literature review highlight the ways in which digital technologies are restructuring artistic practices, they also show that AI and machine learning could be set to providing new capacities for artists, opening up innovative modes of expression, creativity, and entrepreneurship not possible prior to the non-linear rise of big data, deep learning, and robotics.

Several technologies related to Artificial Intelligence (AI) such as computer vision, machine learning, and 3D printing have a profound impact on the changes of research and creative practices in art. Examples include new avenues of art analysis that are attainable from processing and interpreting vast collections of artwork metadata, including insights about techniques, movements, and cultural references that were neither conveyed nor tracked in customary art historical form, to creative application areas, such as the ready-made and readymade-infused generative artistic practice, that accentuates AI-Art collaborations as important sites for both fruitful dialogues and fundamental ethical considerations. In view of the growing number of research initiatives and creative applications that currently emerge in this interdisciplinary intersection across the technology, art, and creative practice, this exploration aims to disseminate the creative and explorative potentials of AI technologies in the context of the visual arts and bring to light the technological and ethical considerations that should equip us in anticipation of major technological and societal shifts in the art and the creative industry.

3.2. Virtual Reality and Augmented Reality

In contemporary art the role of digital technologies of art, in its broadest definition, is still an uncharted territory because the coalescence of artistic practices and digital art forms gives fertile ground to the appearance of new and innovative genres that require art historicization (Chevalier & Kiefer, 2020). These new art forms also demand a theoretical reflection, research, and critical resistance that just consolidate the maturation of the amalgamation process of art and technology, begun in the middle of the twentieth century, and that they can co-consider the artist, the work, and the spectator as a synesthetic creative triad empowered by the interactive poetics. The case analyzed the interconnection of artistic processes and Virtual Reality (VR) and Augmented Reality (AR), represents an attempt to show what digital art actually is possible in a broader understanding: what variety of codifications might be included under this label beyond the usual narrow specificity of electronic and computerized works, and how artwork processes might result from the dialogue between aesthetic categories and technologies (Portalés, 2018).

VR is already being considered as a making of a new social reality characterized by the emerging forms of artistic-communitarian practices-in-progress implementations. Thus, the creation process of a work from the point of view of its conceptualization, technology, and content acquisition is explained as a whole, just as the constituent parts of the work are synthesized unavoidably merging the fragmented concatenated sequential unity of an exhibition. In fact, in the studied artwork, the artist assumes from the outset that the {contemplation occidental-manipulation, interaction} dichotomy normally taking place in art reception is called into question insufficient to a technological innovation that radicalizes form the addressed problematization since the spectator is immersed in a hyper-real virtual environment that portrays back the objectual framework in what it is also presented the current context itself.

3.3. Digital Fabrication

Digital fabrication and 3D printing technology have added a new method for artists and designers to create art and design works. It allows them to fabricate their own artworks exactly as they envision, including those designs that are hard to accomplish using traditional fabrication methods. Models created by computers can be manufactured in 3D, and delicate structures can be built layer by layer. This process of printing can have a significant impact on the production, refinement, and distribution of art and design objects. In modern society, there is also concern about sharing such digital resources, which implicates effectively sharing models and data, and can also propagate a style in art and design works, as has been seen in literature, where freeware sharing has fueled genres of fiction.

Art Meets Technology is an international collaboration at the intersection of art, media, science, and technology; it generates collaborative knowledge, innovative artworks, diverse experiences, ideas, and outcomes touching upon a multitude of venues and formats. By integrating digital form and media, either practically, theoretically, or aesthetically, it draws technology and art into a hybrid synthesis to the mutual benefit of both. Artists and designers have adopted and taken up digital fabrication in their practice, either using it as a means for creating customized art pieces or embedding sensors and interactivity into their design works to extend user experiences. Both present how digital fabrication and electronics can be brought into art and design objects as well as public artworks through the creative use of the two technologies. By doing so, they show designers and artists how to initiate art with technology in an effective way. Also presented is a brief analysis of how emerging art styles in digital fabrication have provided a new perspective on how 3D printing can be integrated into modern design practices.

4. EDUCATIONAL IMPLICATIONS OF ART-TECHNOLOGY SYNERGIES

In artistic contexts, the value of compelling technology is often underappreciated, and tech's dominant role in art's commercial dissemination can thwart the examination of its creativity-unlocking potential. This paper reviews how those fields, broadly grouped as art and technology, both independently and together, can jointly transform technology from a means of creative production to an object for it. First, an incomplete survey of the art-tech field is given: examining how artists have employed technology in particularly inventive ways, and how it has prompted novel art. This includes installations which mimic the unpredictability of life, sculptures that transcend and transform through illumination disruptions, software which can make unexpected visual discoveries in art, and wearable electronics which can evoke subtle real-world interactions (Aguilar & Pifarre Turmo, 2019). Secondly, educational implications of art-tech synergies are addressed. Many innovative approaches to learning foster creativity and critical thinking, embodying endeavors to merge art and technology learning experiences. Some experimental programs, aspiring to raise other creative cross-disciplinary initiatives, are examined, with also a view for the broader world. For the purposes of this paper, the focus is interaction between art and technology educators. However, the insights are broadly relevant and can inform similar endeavors with STEM or other collaborative pairings. This review aims to facilitate broader and more frequent efforts for art-technology collaborations in learning environments (Crayton, 2015).

4.1. Innovative Learning Approaches

In recent years, as technological advancements have burgeoned, there have been calls across a range of disciplines to reimagine and reinvent how and what we learn. Simulation, augmented reality, and machine learning technologies have facilitated increasingly personalized and adaptable educational experiences, a trend that seems particularly appropriate in the context of art education. Still, it would be myopic to view this technological progress as purely disruptive. Indeed, the wave of revolutionary advancements in software, hardware, and design have the potential to reconcile longstanding divides and tensions between creative and scientific discourses.

If we are to adequately explore the constructive synergies of art and tech, it is imperative to critically analyze the methods and paradigms by which such skills and mindsets are currently engendered. To this end, attention will be primarily directed to the ways in which technology and art education can adapt and accommodate each other. The aim of this section is to explore the implications and potential of this art-technology synergy for the future of creative industry, public engagement, and cross-domain innovation.

Experiential learning is well-established as a powerful way of engaging communities in hands-on creative undertakings. While the importance of the physical and social environment has been traditionally central in creative arts, novel technologies can greatly expand, support, and enrich experiential learning. For example, digital simulations grant the remediation and expansion of expository settings otherwise difficult to replicate. In art education, this is especially beneficial given the unique affordances of physical objects and traditional wisdom. Digital simulations can recreate studio environments of grand masters or modern masters, promoting learning through direct observation (Aguilar & Pifarre Turmo, 2019). Moreover, technology can automatically and procedurally provide feedback and guidance to learners as they interact with artistic creation and expression, a function of particular importance in contexts of scarce resources and pedagogical means.

4.2. Cross-Disciplinary Collaboration

Considering contemporary trends in art making, the benefits of combining art and industry are apparent. Experimental filmmakers, digital artists, and artist-focused software developers are currently being employed in any number of technology companies. As filmmakers start to develop virtual reality experiences, and conceptual artists disseminating text-based commentary on the digital world, there's a clear representation of a reorganization where technology has reached a level of advancement that art can no longer be immune to. Understanding that even those choosing to work only within sculptural, fine art grounds can be soon chasing commercial avenues, this shared route takes a form of mutually beneficial partnership-like relationships between artists and technologists. The primary example focuses on those ventures that have emerged from the crossing of more establishment industry-based fields and the common practices of artists (Paek, 2019). Synergy benefits infinitely when interconnected creative professionals are connected by projects rather than individual practice. Broadly, collaborative works often results in commercial-ready applications. An emphasis on team-based best practice results in applications that exhibit project management, bereft of radical thought. Proper team synergy manifests as a rigid application of a hierarchical hearing system. At set intervals, certain members (determined by precedence or the proportion of income provided) report back to shareholders with project updates. This method of creative collaboration, widespread within industry circles, comes decidedly uneasily to those backgrounds with a more DIY approach to creative endeavor. More interested in the smudging of boundaries and a less controlled exploration of compositional elements, project management, in general, is not high on the list of personal attributes. As such, opportunities for collaborative cross-disciplinary projects often neglected. Even moving away from industry-based collaborations, there remains a numerous amount of project proposals designed to implement (mainly technologically focused) artworks (Crayton, 2015). More consideration is given to conceptual avenues or overarching project concepts than a detailed outlines of a physical installation, and a marked hesitation exists to commit applications to a particular medium. These factors reflect a core difficulty present in those coming from university-based art educations; it is a general lack of technological experience. Generally, involvement within artistic institutions veers towards the ideas-based approach, students being provided with the skills to see their vision translated into a physical artwork, rather than a grounding in the more practical and commercial possibilities of artistic practice.

5. CULTURAL PRODUCTION AND SOCIAL IMPACT

The aim of this student-driven experimental research project is to examine critically the conjunction of art, science, and technology, to address the role of the Artist in the context of contemporary cultural production, and to analyze its broader social impact. In recent years, works have highlighted the intrinsic value of art, and its potential to generate knowledge as well. The first part of this research project is devised precisely to look at what artists do – on and off the computer –; what skills are mobilized in their practices; which historical and contextual forces inform their works; and what kind of work they undertake daily.

Artists and Technological Means Technology is here invested with the widest possible meaning; encompassing software, networking, engineering stuff, bio-techno hacks, low-fi and high-end productions alike. It addresses the very material conditions under which the technical reproducibility originated, leading to the circulation and reception of art works. It also underscores the inextricable association of art and progress. The potential and impact of technical applications within artistic realms will be revisited through a genealogy of its artistic developments since the avant-gardes, indicating a double critique of technology as industrial and capitalistic forces, and as new media.

5.1. Diversity and Inclusivity

The perfect storm for a discourse that is equal parts art and technology is characterized by rapidly changing landscapes in each field. The art world sometimes feels like it's spinning faster than ever, not so much a revolution as a relentless rotation through isms too numerous to parse. At the same time, new tools for creativity are not just born, but evolve, explode, and rewrite themselves like some crazy snake eating its electronic tail. Faced with this storm, it seems a Sisyphean task to approach the relationship between artists and technology, each garden-variety term for speech entirely over-used and mostly under-specified.

A slightly closer look reveals a sudden fascination, however, with a small handful of vital themes within this art and technology discourse. One of these themes is diversity and inclusivity. Today, artists are using technology to amplify quieted or marginalized voices. The tools become ways to shine a light on something inadequately represented or champion entirely new narratives. These artists are turning to the new in their medium of technology to broaden representation and inject new blood into the creative spaces. And it's not just the artists. Funders, programmers, and academics alike are enthralled by the potential for technology to transform and democratize arts consumption. Programming often features work that integrates art and tech for teaching and research, and many funders have a newfound interest in art and its technology, particularly regarding projects designed to reach or engage new audiences (Schultz, 2011). It seems there is a collective responsibility among artists and technologists to ensure there is a way for everyone to access these tools and spaces. Shifting the lens to the quieter voices has exposed a chilling task - those who suffer the most without access to resources seem to be in the best position from which to implement them. A lo-fi arts upbringing in the sprawling suburbs has already put one at a great disadvantage. With institutions, organizations, and policy eons away from finding a framework to facilitate talented, but boxed-out, art makers, technology is the only real solution (Maragiannis & Ashford, 2019). Thus, there are art projects, advocacy platforms, teaching aids, and audience diversification strategies in gestation.

5.2. Environmental Sustainability

Artists and advances in technology have historically worked in tandem to explore new avenues of creation. As with any collaborative relationship, artists have employed innovation in tandem with its progress in novel, and sometimes strikingly different, ways. A longstanding collaboration between technological evolution and the arts is that of art and environmental sustainability, explorations with which have led artists to adopt the latest advances in innovative technology to minimize waste and promote ecological awareness (Paek, 2019). Though there are facets of these fields which, by their nature, lean towards discord, such as the philosophy of contemporary art's celebrated focus on the ephemeral, new mediums for artistic production are allowing more environmentally focused explorations.

Many of the projects considered here let similar technological ventures inform the production of artwork, a form intersection of sustainability in both conceptual theme and practice. Through the showcase of different projects, artistic explorations made sustainably with both practice and materials will be considered. Additionally discussed is the role technology can play in making the communication of ecological issues through artistic work more effective, ranging from creation of immersive experiences to using blockchain technology to map artwork's ecological footprint (Holzapfel et al., 2022). After such possibilities are explored, the direction of environmental sustainability within the arts and technology is considered, alongside speculations on the future viability of a practice of socially charged environmental stewardship. Left in two grids of warm light, the worthy audience of The Green Room shuffle in careful thought, regarding, as they are meant to, the artifact in the gallery's West wing.

6. CASE STUDIES IN ART-TECHNOLOGY INTEGRATION

Case Studies in Art-Technology Integration Since the dawn of history, artists have always been at the upper cutting edge of technology and innovation. The Italian Renaissance is known not only for the invention and application of new forms of perspective in drawing, but for the development of vanishing-point perspective construction, the first artificial methods of reproducing sounds and music, revolutionary methods in mechanical design, and the first paintings in Western art to incorporate advanced uses of concave mirrors. As economic and artistic technologies have rapidly evolved, so have artistic practices. The artisanal 'know-how' that artists commanded in earlier centuries is now paired with technological tools undreamed of in the past, tools that require a vast range of specialized knowledge to utilize. This need for specialization has engendered greater collaboration between artists and technologists, in turn creating a fertile arena for innovative projects.

The integration of art and technology suggests a synergy between the aesthetics of art and applied science. It is in this latter sense, the practice of research and industry, that the artists and projects discussed here approach this union. Some are the achievements of collaborations between artists who originate from solid historical artistic traditions with technologists from the cutting edges of human innovation and craftsmanship. The projects presented in this text utilize art as an innovative strategy to architecture and technology, rather than using technology as a means of creating or enhancing artistic expression. Designed uses of projection to 'extend' an architectural space, utilizing motion tracking with complex geometry projections, and the integration of complex geometry skin structure with physical computing components. Each of the case studies elaborates the distinct processes and outcomes related to the project.

6.1. Interactive Installations

Interactive installations are examined as a means of integration of art and technology, which may foster active participation in Engage to Understand. Attention is paid to the term audience engagement, often understood as involvement, participation, interactivity, or interaction in respect to art. In this view, interactive installations seem to be convergent with these understandings of engagement, allowing a type of experience, which is active and unconventional, and which surpasses ordinary perceptual interaction with visual arts and its contemplative mode. Their involvement in art anticipates deeper experiential understanding, besides its cognitive-emphatic aspect (Her & Hamlyn, 2010). The viewer is treated as an active engager in co-production of meaning, instead of a receiver of a unilaterally produced message. Such understanding of interaction involves a wide range of experiential activities and interactions with artistic work: behavioral, emotional, cognitive, and perceptual. These qualities seem to be obvious and explicit in the case of interactive installations, triggering the active engagement through unconventional interactivity and inviting audiences to explore, play, and co-create. The goal is to understand how interactive installations are understood by audiences, and how they provide opportunities for active participation and engagement in experiential understanding of art. This allows to reflect upon the implications of interaction for definitions of art, and the role of artists, in regard to a substance of artwork and engaged participation.

Interactive installations create an environment in a physical or screen-based setting that implies interactivity and involves the viewer into that particular environment. Viewer or "player" becomes the performer. The shift between art and design isolates interaction per se that provides media art with infinite possibilities. Interactive installations come about with the proximity of media art and interactive design. Besides, the complexity and incipient relation that the user has with technology turn necessary the development of an extensive technological system that makes feasible and invisible the interaction with the public. (Arenas, 2010). On the other hand, links between interested parties are explored; students and artists are encouraged to use playback Max-patches, as waiting how to remake those pieces.

6.2. Data Visualization in Art

Data visualization is emerging as an innovative practice among contemporary artists. Funding and technological advances have made possible the collection of multitudes of data about every aspect of our lives and world. Artists are thus increasingly working with data, attempting to translate information into a visual format to make it more accessible and engaging for broader audiences. While most artists have employed data to create aesthetically interesting projects, some interesting projects employ data to provoke thought and dialogue about how our data is collected, who is collecting it, and how it is repurposed. These projects make use of traditional objects (such as hand-bound books or painted canvases) and non-traditional objects (such as 2D Data Matrix codes or a GPS unit embedded in a paper disc). In either case, artists present information in a visual format that is engaging and accessible.

Data visualization projects by artists (Ma, 2022) present information in a visual format that is engaging and accessible. While most people see data as boring, both artists transform numbers into interesting compositions to create works that make the observer question the significance and implications of data. The data is often readily prepared by governments, scientists, or industries, artists being asked to visualize the data. Commonly, a creative approach is used, instead transforming the data into a graphic image format. Although data is transformed, meaning remains within the numbers. Marisa Benjamin's Necessary and Evil shows a series of visualization pie charts that playfully label the percentage of evil necessary for the survival of different industries. Viewers are encouraged to contemplate the issue of how much necessary evil an industry should be allowed. Similar to Benjamin's approach of translating data into something that is easily and visually understood, Heather Green uses maps to express the transformation of land use, and the traces people leave on the land.

7. FUTURE DIRECTIONS AND EMERGING OPPORTUNITIES

The rapid pace of technological advancement in an era where human possibilities often seem boundless doesn't always allow art to show its most 'beautiful face'. There is defiance into technological offerings to preserve individuality in creative practice. On the one side, technological developments of the future could completely automate the process of creating art, thus minimizing the inherent role of the individual. On the other hand, technology could expand the possibilities of artistic expression and take it to new places. Therefore, the responsibility in developing a wise integration of the traditional and the new must remain priority to those involved in teaching art (jagodzinski, 2020). When technology disrupts traditional art, it also impacts the way it teaches. Consequently, this allows flexibility, adaptability, and innovation in the approach to arts education maintaining early teaching of traditional forms.

New threats lie ahead in terms of the ethicality of new technical developments. Every advance force the individual and society to adapt to it, yet ethics seem to be falling behind in that game. It is not enough for each artist and educator to just act ethically; they must also consider the ethical implications of their technical creations. The fact that artists and educators hold tremendous power is crucial to the knowledge and the way new technologies evolve and the extent to which they are employed. Raising awareness of the social and ethical implications of this equipment should be considered essential. As tastes vary, and inevitably new technologies will inspire an abundance of creative endeavors, any form of art-tech entrepreneurship should avoid assessing character and recognize the potential in different territories.

Finally, aside from the artistic and technological aspects of it, an equally important conversation should be opened around the monetary issues. Hence, the funding and support concerning all these new collaborations between young artists and young technologists should be all the more underlined. The analysis stands as a general reflection regarding nearly all existing and still emerging collaborative potentials within the previous framework (Holzapfel et al., 2022). It all reflects upon the diversity and accessibility of artistic practices in view of the rapid technological changes around the globe. The final goal is that arts education rethinks as to pose a 'dignified' place" for technological advancements in the teaching and learning of individual fields of art creating a wave of new art understanding to appreciate in the years to come.

7.1. Ethical Considerations

As more artists incorporate technology into their art-making practices, serious ethical considerations arise. Some of those considerations relate to a) authorship, b) ownership, c) authenticity, d) societal impact, e) individuality, f) biases, and g) critical discussion (Holzapfel et al., 2022). Both technology and art continually evolve, deeply influencing each other. A plethora of tools and systems facilitate the making of art by artists coming from ever more diverse communities. When thinking about the responsibility of artists to consider the ethical implications on the use of technology in art, many of those implications are deeply rooted in the evolving relationship between art and technology itself. Today, setting clear distinctions between an artwork made exclusively with non-digital tools and one made with the help of digital tools and processes is not always straightforward; digital tools, such as cameras and computers, are widely used in the arts of all kinds. The use of some common digital art-making tools results in outputs, such as photographs, which are stored in digital form. However, a caring artist should be aware of the ethical issues related to the choice of the programs or versions and parameters, particularly regarding the software's compliance with intellectual property rights. Some digital tools could enable synthetic images and models to be crafted out of raw computational data accumulated and owned by rich corporations. If such a model is considered an artistic work, it raises concerns about the accessibility of such tools and should be evaluated critically.

The overarching ethical concerns are multifaceted. History has shown that no matter who is behind it, technology and the resultant art have deeply affected society at large. So how is technology influencing diverse communities in their artistic expressions? Technology opens up unprecedented artistic possibilities; however, many of the pioneers are technology giants and not necessarily artists or smaller art-tech startups. What happens to artistic output when sampling freely accessible huge corpuses edges aside the individuality of an artist? The technology used for creating art could be driven by the data, hidden or not, of dubious origin or with discriminatory biases. The more complex a technology, the more the knowledge about it becomes esoteric to all but a tiny fraction of people. How then is it possible to have a critical discussion on the ethical use of technology in art also taking into account all these issues?

7.2. Art-Tech Entrepreneurship

The newly emerging field of art-tech entrepreneurship will be explored and how artists and technologists can leverage the evolution of creativity to build sustainable ventures. Creatives are known for thinking outside the box. However, when it comes to art entrepreneurship, box thinking can sometimes be more beneficial. When examining art entrepreneurship, it is revealed a universe of funding opportunities and a huge gradient of successful art-tech interdisciplinary projects. This subsection criticizes the lack of industry-specific examples in the field of arts and creative industries by exploring together with the reader some example ventures and projects of art-tech entrepreneurship. This exploration is intended to unveil various types of opportunities, asset combinations, and business models. By exploring the challenges of the success stories featured in this subsection an overview on sustainability and funding is provided, potentially offering future innovative ventures valuable insights. Moreover, by discovering the award-winning cases, the importance of collaboration between artists and technologists is highlighted. One will hopefully be inspired by these art-tech entrepreneurship stories and redefine perceptions of what it takes to successfully launch and sustain an art-tech startup or project. In order to compete and succeed, a blend of qualities and assets beyond conventional artistic skills is needed, such as a disciplined methodology, business analysis, and technological acumen (Balzarin & CALCAGNO, 2016). All of these aspects either reside or can be acquired by building a team. This exploration aims to invite a new outlook of adaptability and resilience for creatives in navigating the rapidly evolving art-tech entrepreneurship landscape and serve as a resource for creative professionals who are seeking an adaptation of their working methods under the influence of digital innovation. By examining the evolving relationship between technology and creativity, it is argued that art students would greatly benefit from education that provides the necessary toolkit to successfully navigate the rapidly changing art-tech market landscape upon graduation. Art, creativity, and technological innovation are intertwining in novel, unexpected ways. Art-tech interdisciplinary projects, startups, and collaboration schemes are increasingly common, boosting interest in the vast landscape where art and technology meet. The fast-changing landscape between art and technology, and the insight that these ventures can provide, are expected to be of great interest to the next generation of creatives, who will be simultaneously artists, curators, scientists, and entrepreneurs.

8. CONCLUSION

The currently occurring Fourth Industrial Revolution, led by advances in technologies including artificial intelligence, robotics, the Internet of Things, biotechnology, and 3D additive manufacturing, demands a coherent response to creativity in the face of challenges to integrate and develop many aspects of art following technological advances (Ricketts, 2018). To answer what art can and should be in the face of technological developments, art as opposed by some and technology as opposed by artists have been reviewed, finding the possibilities for art's various responses to technological developments. In conclusion, since the task of art may be understood in infinite variety, it is advised as a starting point to approach the possibilities that art can respond to technological developments (jagodzinski, 2020). Since the author is now preparing future generations, the expectation is to provide a fresh, integrated, and comprehensive view on the art-technology connection which requires informed and developed exploration of this transformative potential in shaping future creative practices. However, it may be in the interest of future generations to continue to recognize the evolving relationship between art and technology in its flexibility and its significance in the changing and complex social-political context. It is argued that a critical and discursive exploration of the technologies' implications and handling of these technologies will enable creativity and artistic practice in the future which is more sustainable and culturally sensitive. Ultimately, the aim is to advocate further visibility, discussion, and research work on the art-technology link, towards shaping a more critical perspective on (technology-based) creativity with respectful awareness of the cultural and social implications of an international transformation into an increasingly digital domain.

8.1. Key Findings and Implications

This section consists of the key findings and contributions of the essay, as well as related discussions and implications for potential future research endeavors and recommendations. This section seeks to offer ground-based suggestions for stakeholders and policymakers who are interested in realizing the future of productive, collaborative, and nurturing collaboration between artists and technologists.

Some core questions and themes were found to weave throughout the research and its discussion, including how artists and technologists navigate boundaries and interfaces between their practices and approaches, the problems and insights born of trying to do so, and areas for future inquiry in education, research, and public funding. As these concerns are explored by revisiting the structure and "highlights" of this paper, further discussion underscores the urgency and multiplicity of its objects of inquiry. At the same time, the overview will synthesize a number of key results and insights derived from spending on art-technology interfacing (Paek, 2019).

In sum, the research done here deals with varied ways that art and technology can be discovered to intersect productively. By exploring the research, creative and practical insights that were gained on a variety of interfacing modes were shared, how and why they manifest projects and tools in particular ways, and the questions and challenges they raise for pedagogy, research, and wider support systems.

REFERENCES

Aguilar, D., & Pifarré Turmo, M. (2019). Promoting social creativity in science education with digital technology to overcome inequalities: A scoping review. *Frontiers in Psychology*, *10*, 1474. DOI: 10.3389/fpsyg.2019.01474 PMID: 31312154

Alford, M. (2013). Conditions of my release.

Arenas, A. G. (2010). A sensor-based interactive digital installation system for virtual painting using MAX/MSP/Jitter. *International Journal of Arts and Technology*, *3*(2/3), 234–247.

Balzarin, L., & Calcagno, M. (2016). Traces of entrepreneurship in the artistic context. *Journal of Business Research*, *69*(5), 1597–1601.

Bendele, E. (2009). Art & technology [6th-8th grade].

Chevalier, C., & Kiefer, C. (2020). What does augmented reality mean as a medium of expression for computational artists? *Proceedings of the 2020 International Conference on New Interfaces for Musical Expression*, 5–7. DOI: 10.1162/leon_a_01740

Crayton, J. (2015). Designing for immersive technology: Integrating art and STEM learning.

Her, J. J., & Hamlyn, J. (2010). Meaningful engagement: Computer-based interactive media art in public space. *Leonardo*, *43*(4), 348–354.

Holzapfel, A., Jääskeläinen, P., & Kaila, A. K. (2022). Environmental and social sustainability of creative-AI. *Journal of Creative Technologies*, *15*(3), 45–60.

Jagodzinski, J. (2020). Art education: In the service of designer capitalism. *Studies in Art Education*, *61*(2), 114–127.

Ma, R. (2022). Boundaries, extensions, and challenges of visualization for humanities data: Reflections on three cases. *Digital Scholarship in the Humanities*, *37*(1), 123–138.

Maragiannis, A., & Ashford, R. (2019). Diversity and inclusivity in the age of wearables: A buzzword, a myth, an uncertain reality. *Proceedings of the 2019 ACM International Symposium on Wearable Computers*, 25–30. DOI: 10.16995/bst.320

Paek, K. M. (2019). The transformative potential of creative art practices in the context of interdisciplinary research.

Portalés, C. (2018). When augmented reality met art: Lessons learned from researcher-artist interdisciplinary work. *Multimodal Technologies and Interaction*, *2*(2), 12. DOI: 10.3390/mti2020017

Ricketts, B. (2018). Designing a social architecture for personal leadership in the 21st century: The autonomous realization tetrad (ART). *Journal of Leadership Studies*, *12*(1), 56–63.

Schultz, M. (2011). Performing graffiti: The use of electronically and digitally modified graffiti in activist art practices [Master's thesis, University of New Mexico]. UNM Digital Repository. https://digitalrepository.unm.edu/arth_etds/13/

Chapter 5
Comparing Intellectual Property Disputes in TechArt:
Addressing Unique Challenges in an Evolving Field

Shilpa Raut-Samplonius
https://orcid.org/0009-0007-5917-9016
NHLStenden University of Applied Sciences, The Netherlands

ABSTRACT

This chapter explores the pivotal role of intellectual property rights within the realms of digital technology and art. It begins by defining intellectual property rights, which encompasses legal protections for creative and intellectual works, and introduces TechArt as a genre-blending technological innovation with artistic expression. By examining 44 cases of which these nine TechArt disputes, allow the broader set of cases, the chapter reveals common themes and complexities unique to this hybrid field. These disputes, which involve issues such as copyright infringement, patent conflicts, and trademark concerns, highlight the nuanced challenges faced by creators and technologists. Insights gained from this analysis lead to policy recommendations for various stakeholders. The article thus contributes to a clearer understanding of IPR challenges in TechArt and suggests policy recommendations for the stakeholders' strategies and actions in this evolving domain.

DOI: 10.4018/979-8-3693-7610-2.ch005

INTRODUCTION

Growing up in India during the 1980s, one witnessed an era defined by economic stagnation, strict regulatory constraints, and limited global integration. The country's economy was largely isolated, with restricted access to international markets. This changed drastically in the 1990s when liberalization policies were introduced, opening the Indian market to global brands and foreign investments. However, this newfound openness also brought about significant challenges, particularly in the realm of Intellectual Property Rights (IPR). A notable example of this was the 1997[1] controversy surrounding the patenting of Basmati rice, a traditional crop indigenous to India, by the American company RiceTech Inc. This event sparked widespread outrage in India and was seen as an infringement on indigenous knowledge and heritage, highlighting the tensions surrounding IPR in a globalized economy.

The World Trade Organization (WTO), with its 164 member countries, addresses this complexity through the Agreement on Trade-Related Aspects of Intellectual Property Rights (TRIPS). TRIPS is the most extensive multilateral agreement governing intellectual property and aims to balance the need for innovation with public access to technology and creative works. TRIPS establishes a framework that promotes the exchange of knowledge and creativity while allowing WTO members the flexibility to pursue domestic policy goals. The agreement underscores the connection between intellectual property and trade, highlighting the necessity of a well-balanced IP system that fosters innovation, facilitates technology transfer, and advances public welfare.

IPR represents a unique form of non-tariff trade barrier, focusing on the protection and control of intellectual property, which distinctly influences market dynamics and innovation compared to traditional trade barriers. IPR poses a dilemma: on one hand, robust protections can incentivize innovation by ensuring that creators and companies can benefit from their inventions. On the other hand, stringent IPR protections can limit access to essential technologies and creative works, particularly for small businesses and independent creators who may struggle to afford the costs associated with securing and enforcing these rights (Sen, 2019). This duality creates a complex landscape for IPR, particularly in fields where technological innovation and artistic creation intersect, such as TechArt.

IPRs are traditionally divided into two primary areas: industrial property and copyright, as well as rights related to copyright. Copyright protects the rights of authors of literary and artistic works, including books, musical compositions, paintings, sculptures, films, and computer programs, for a minimum of 50 years after the author's death.

Industrial property, on the other hand, can be broadly categorized into two areas: the protection of distinctive signs and the encouragement of innovation and technology. The protection of distinctive signs[2] includes trademarks, which distinguish the goods or services of one entity from those of another, and geographical indications, which identify goods originating from specific locations where the product's characteristics are tied to its geographic origin. This form of protection is crucial for maintaining the integrity of brands and regional products in a globalized market. Meanwhile, the encouragement of innovation and technology[3] encompasses patents for inventions, industrial designs, and trade secrets. Patents protect new technologies, providing incentives and resources for further research and development. Trade secrets, another form of protection, guard confidential business information that gives companies a competitive edge.

Exclusive rights granted under IPR are typically subject to various limitations and exceptions designed to balance the interests of rights holders and users. This balance is particularly important in complex fields like TechArt, where creators often blend technological innovation with artistic expression, leading to unique challenges in the enforcement of IPR (Schrader, 2021).

Understanding these categories of intellectual property is essential to grasp the broader implications of IPR disputes. Patents, for example, grant exclusive rights to an invention, allowing the patent holder to control how the invention is used by others. Copyright, on the other hand, protects creators' rights over their artistic and literary works, which can range from books and films to software and databases. Trademarks distinguish one enterprise's goods or services from another's, while industrial designs protect the ornamental aspects of products. Geographical indications identify products based on their place of origin and their associated qualities, and trade secrets protect valuable business information from unauthorized disclosure.

The emerging field of TechArt, which combines artistic creativity with technological innovation, presents unique challenges to the traditional frameworks of IPR (Paul,2023). As creators and technologists continue to blur the boundaries between art and technology, the existing IPR system must adapt to ensure that both innovation and creativity are adequately protected while promoting access to these works. By analyzing both TechArt disputes and broader intellectual property cases, it becomes possible to formulate policy recommendations that can help stakeholders—including policymakers, artists, and legal experts—navigate the complexities of IPR in this hybrid domain. This approach can foster a more balanced and inclusive system, ensuring that IPR protections support innovation and creativity without stifling access or competition.

Having established a basic understanding of IPR and its various forms, it is essential to explore the question: How can intellectual property rights disputes in the emerging field of TechArt be compared to broader intellectual property cases while addressing the unique challenges posed by this evolving field?

BACKGROUND DIGITAL ART

Digital art has evolved since the 1960s, starting with algorithmic creations by pioneers like Frieder Nake and Harold Cohen[4] (McNeil, 2020). By the 1980s and 1990s, advancements in personal computing and software such as Adobe Photoshop and Corel Painter allowed for more complex works, including 3D modeling and animation. Artists like Andy Warhol and David Hockney popularized digital tools. The rise of the internet in the 2000s further transformed digital art, expanding it into interactive and multimedia forms while platforms like DeviantArt and Instagram democratized art distribution. Blockchain and Non Fungible Tokens (NFT) revolutionized the market in the 2010s (Chayka 2021, Edwards, 2021; Scott, 2021), allowing artists to monetize unique digital assets, as seen in Beeple's $69 million NFT sale in 2021(Gault, 2021).

The NFTs are a type of digital asset that represents ownership or proof of authenticity for a unique item, often on the blockchain, particularly Ethereum. Unlike cryptocurrencies such as Bitcoin or Ethereum, which are fungible (meaning each unit is interchangeable), NFTs are unique or limited in quantity, meaning each one has distinct characteristics. The Key Characteristics of NFTs are:

- Uniqueness: Each NFT is distinct, often representing a one-of-a-kind asset (or one of a limited series). This uniqueness is verified and recorded on the blockchain, which provides a permanent record of the asset's identity.
- Indivisibility: NFTs cannot be divided into smaller units like cryptocurrencies. You either own the entire NFT or none of it.
- Ownership and Provenance: NFTs offer a transparent and verifiable record of ownership and transaction history, stored on the blockchain. This ensures that the buyer knows the authenticity and previous ownership of the asset.
- Interoperability: NFTs can be transferred across different platforms, marketplaces, or digital spaces (such as virtual worlds or games), offering versatility in how they are bought, sold, or used.
- Smart Contracts: NFTs are tied to "smart contracts," which can automate certain actions such as royalty payments to the creator whenever the NFT is resold. This creates a direct relationship between creators and buyers, facilitating automated royalty distribution.

The key differences between Physical of Fungible or Non-digital art vs. Digital art NFT are:

1) Tangibility: Non-digital art (e.g., a traditional painting or sculpture) can be touched[5] in literal sense of the word. It exists in the physical world. Ownership

is typically transferred through physical exchange, and the authenticity or provenance can be tracked via certificates of authenticity, galleries, or auction houses.

NFT Art exists only in the digital world. It's a representation of digital art stored on a blockchain. Ownership is tracked and verified through the blockchain instead of physical certificates or galleries.

2) Scarcity and Provenance: While original artworks are scarce due to their physical nature, copies (like prints) can exist in parallel. Provenance is verified through records like certificates, gallery history, or auction transactions.

The blockchain ensures a digital piece of art is scarce by providing a unique token that verifies its ownership and transaction history. Even if copies of the digital artwork exist, the NFT itself can only represent one "authentic" version with a verifiable, unchangeable history on the blockchain.

3) Transfer of Ownership: Ownership transfer of non-digital art involves the physical exchange of the artwork, typically requiring in-person transactions or traditional auction processes. The authenticity and ownership are often recorded on physical documents.

Ownership of NFT is transferred digitally through online platforms or marketplaces. When you buy an NFT, the transfer is recorded on the blockchain, and the new owner has proof of the digital asset they possess. No physical exchange is required.

4) Royalties: Non-Digital Artists can negotiate royalties or commissions for their works, but this process is often manual and relies on secondary sales agreements.

Smart contracts built into NFTs automatically enable creators to receive royalties on secondary sales. This feature ensures that artists continue to earn revenue whenever their work is resold, which is not always the case with traditional art.

5) Market and Platforms: Non-Digital Art can be bought and sold through traditional galleries, auctions, and private transactions. There is often a more localized or region-specific market for physical art.

NFT Art: Bought and sold on blockchain-based platforms like OpenSea, Rarible, or Foundation. This creates a global, decentralized marketplace that operates 24/7.

6) Indivisibility: A physical piece of art is typically indivisible, in the sense that you cannot own part of a painting or sculpture. However, fractional ownership can be arranged for example shared ownership via co-investors).

While an NFT is also typically indivisible, it is possible for the ownership of an NFT to be divided or fractionalized via certain platforms or mechanisms. However, this is a relatively new concept and is still in its infancy.

Example traditional vs NFT:

The traditional Artwork of Mona Lisa by Leonardo da Vinci, who started creating in 1503. The original painting is a one-of-a-kind physical object, and its ownership can only be transferred in the real world through physical transactions.

Its provenance can be tracked through historical records, exhibitions, and certificates, and its transfer: Requires physical movement, often involving intermediaries like galleries, auction houses, or legal documentation.

While NFT Artwork of Beeple's "Everydays: The First 5000 Days", This digital artwork sold at a record $69.3 million at Christie's auction in March 2021. It is a collage of 5,000 digital images that Beeple (Mike Winkelmann) had created daily over 13 years. This sale marked a significant turning point in the mainstream acceptance of NFTs in the art world (Christie's Auction).

Its provenance can be verified through the blockchain, showing the entire history of ownership. The transfer is done digitally, with no need for physical exchange. Ownership is transferred automatically and transparently when purchased via a platform like OpenSea.

Another known example of NFTs in the artistic work is Kings of Leon. The American rock band Kings of Leon became the first major band to release an album as an NFT. Their album "When You See Yourself" was available for purchase as NFTs, granting owners exclusive perks like limited edition vinyl and front-row concert seats)[6].

NFTs are usually created (or "minted") on blockchain platforms such as Ethereum, Flow, or Tezos. The blockchain records the NFT's metadata, ensuring that its ownership and transaction history are securely stored. When an individual buys an NFT, the transaction is logged on the blockchain, transferring ownership.

For example, if someone purchases an NFT from a digital artist, the blockchain entry ensures that the new owner has rights to that unique digital asset, even if other copies exist. However, owning an NFT doesn't always mean owning copyright or reproduction rights unless specified in the contract.

The popularity of NFTs can be due to the following factors:

- Ownership and Exclusivity: NFTs provide a sense of scarcity and rarity. For instance, a digital artist can limit the number of NFTs they create for a piece, making the item rare and more valuable.
- Monetization of Digital Content: Creators, artists, and musicians can directly monetize their work without intermediaries, potentially keeping a larger share of the proceeds.
- Potential for Investment: Some buyers view NFTs as collectibles or speculative investments, hoping the value of their NFTs will increase over time.

However, it has not been without criticism and concerns:

- Environmental Impact: The energy consumption required to mint and trade NFTs, particularly on Ethereum, has raised concerns about their environmental impact due to the energy-intensive proof-of-work (PoW) mechanism[7].
- Market Volatility: NFT prices can be highly volatile. As seen in 2022, the NFT market experienced a significant slowdown, with many NFTs losing value rapidly.
- Copyright Issues: Since NFTs only represent proof of ownership, they do not necessarily convey copyright or intellectual property rights. This has led to disputes over the ownership and sale of digital content.

Copyright is a form of intellectual property protection granted by law to the creators of original works. This protection covers works of authorship such as literary, musical, and artistic works, ensuring creators have exclusive rights to their creations, including the right to reproduce, distribute, and display them. Copyright laws give creators control over how their works are used and ensure they receive fair compensation for their contributions.

When it comes to NFTs, the first key issue arises because an NFT itself is not a copyright but rather a token that represents ownership of a digital asset. The digital asset might be a piece of artwork, music, video, or even a meme. Purchasing an NFT typically gives the buyer the rights to that specific token, but the rights to the actual intellectual property (the underlying digital artwork or media) may not automatically transfer.

This discrepancy between owning an NFT and owning the copyright to the digital work is central to the confusion and legal challenges surrounding NFTs.

At its core, an NFT is a unique, immutable token on a blockchain that can represent ownership of a specific digital item, such as a piece of art, video, or audio. However, owning an NFT does not necessarily mean that the buyer owns the intellectual property rights to the underlying content.

For instance, when someone purchases an NFT of a digital artwork, they are essentially buying a token that verifies their ownership of that specific, unique tokenized representation of the artwork. However, unless explicitly stated, the buyer does not gain the rights to reproduce, distribute, or modify the underlying artwork. Those rights typically remain with the artist or creator unless they are transferred through a separate legal agreement.

This distinction can lead to significant confusion for buyers, who may mistakenly assume that purchasing an NFT grants them full ownership of the artwork, including copyright and reproduction rights.

The relevant second key copyright Issue in the NFT Space is related to Copyright Transfer vs. Ownership of NFT. In the NFT market buying an NFT does not automatically transfer the copyright of the underlying digital asset. The buyer only owns the token that represents the work, but not necessarily the right to use, sell, or reproduce the original creation. For example, when a buyer purchases an NFT artwork, they do not gain the rights to print it on merchandise, create derivative works, or display it publicly unless those rights are explicitly transferred by the creator.

Creators must specify what rights are being transferred with the sale of an NFT. Typically, this is done via the smart contract associated with the NFT, but even so, buyers often fail to fully understand the legal limitations attached to their purchase. If there is no clear agreement about the copyright, the buyer might be under the mistaken impression that they have broader rights than they do.

The third significant issue is related to the Use of Copyrighted Works in NFTs. Many NFTs are created by repurposing, remixing, or building upon pre-existing digital works, such as using a famous meme or sampling music from an established artist. If these works are used without permission, the NFT creator may infringe on the copyright of the original work's creator. In the digital world, where copying and reproducing content is easy, the ability to tokenize a work as an NFT could facilitate the illegal use of copyrighted materials.

For example, someone could create an NFT of a famous image, such as a copyrighted photograph or artwork, without securing the proper rights from the original creator or rights holder. This could lead to copyright infringement claims against the NFT creator and the buyer. It's crucial for NFT creators to ensure they have the necessary rights to any content they mint into NFTs to avoid legal issues.

A unique feature of NFTs is the potential for creators to receive royalties on secondary sales. Smart contracts embedded in NFTs can ensure that creators automatically receive a percentage of any resale profits. This is an appealing feature for digital artists, as traditional art sales typically do not provide royalties on secondary market transactions.

However, royalty structures and enforcement mechanisms are still relatively new and untested, and legal disputes can arise if the resale conditions are unclear.

Additionally, there's a risk that secondary market platforms (e.g., OpenSea, Rarible) may not always enforce the royalty clauses as expected, which could undermine the rights of creators.

The ability to secure continuous income from resales introduces new challenges for the copyright system, as it creates ongoing obligations for artists and buyers in the digital space. Intellectual property law may need to evolve to fully support this new way of monetizing creative works.

Another pressing issue in the NFT world is the phenomenon of plagiarism or the unauthorized minting of NFTs using someone else's work. As the NFT space grows, some individuals may attempt to sell NFTs that are merely copies of existing artworks, music, or videos. These counterfeit NFTs are often created without the original artist's consent, leading to violations of copyright.

Legal recourse for artists whose works are plagiarized in the NFT space is complicated. Even though NFTs are immutable and can easily be traced on the blockchain, enforcing copyright in this space often requires traditional intellectual property enforcement mechanisms, which may not be well-suited to the decentralized, cross-border nature of NFTs.

Platforms where NFTs are sold, such as OpenSea, have implemented mechanisms to report stolen content. However, the process is still developing, and it can be difficult to enforce copyright law in a decentralized and pseudonymous environment.

Technology has provided artists with new tools (e.g., Adobe Creative Suite, Blender) and expanded the reach of digital art through social media and platforms like Instagram. NFTs, and blockchain enabled artists to create verifiable digital assets, addressing previous challenges in monetizing reproducible digital works. Platforms like Etsy and DeviantArt have also opened new opportunities for artists, bypassing traditional gatekeepers, but raising concerns about IPR protection.

The proliferation of digital art has made IPR critical to protect against unauthorized use, piracy, and reproduction. NFTs help establish ownership but face legal hurdles (Raustiala, & Sprigman 2020). Licensing, royalties, and investor security in digital art also hinge on strong IPR, which allows artists to control pricing, distribution, and monetization. Without robust IPR, creators risk losing economic viability due to infringement and piracy, undermining the value and innovation of digital art.

IPR systems are key to fostering innovation and ensuring that creators and innovators can reap the financial rewards of their work. Without IPR protections, the economic viability of creating digital art or new technologies could be undermined by piracy, plagiarism, or unfair use.

IPR is crucial in the digital art and technology economy, providing legal protection for creators to claim ownership of their work and control its use. This framework enables sustainable monetization by preventing unauthorized copying, distribution, and exploitation. Critics argue that IPR limits free trade by restricting the open exchange of ideas and creating artificial scarcity in the digital realm. However, unrestricted access undermines creators' ability to benefit from their work, eroding their livelihoods. IPR ensures creators can control how their works are shared and sold, protecting the economic value of originality and incentivizing innovation. While IPR introduces trade barriers, it is essential to maintaining the integrity of the creative economy, ensuring artists can monetize and protect their creations against unchecked exploitation.

Methodology

Taking into account the exploratory nature, this paper examines the following variables in 44 cases of which 9 can be labeled as TechArt cases. It combines a quantitative analysis of 44 case summaries with a qualitative case study of an ongoing IPR dispute involving TechArt. The case summaries span the last five years to ensure relevance to the current digital economy.[8]

Key data points collected from each case include the following features, The explanation for ach of the features is provided below.

a) Type of IPR involved (e.g., copyright, trademark, patent).
b) The outcome of the dispute (e.g., favorable to the artist, favorable to the defendant, settlement).
c) Economic impact on the artist or creator, measured in terms of monetary compensation, licensing fees, or losses incurred due to piracy or infringement.
d) Jurisdiction of the case (to analyze potential geographical influences on the enforcement of IPR).
e) Timeframe for resolution, to assess the efficiency of IPR dispute resolution processes.
f) Digital platform involved (e.g., Etsy, DeviantArt, OpenSea), to identify trends related to different marketplaces and distribution platforms.

Type of IPR involved Key Differences Between Copyright, Trademarks, and Patents

Copyright protects original works of authorship, such as art, literature, music, and software, and grants the creator exclusive rights to reproduce, distribute, display, and create derivative works.

Digital art is automatically protected under copyright laws as long as it is an original creation fixed in a tangible form (i.e., saved on a computer, uploaded to a website, etc.). Copyright provides creators with exclusive control over their work, which is essential for controlling reproduction and distribution.

Why it's relevant for digital art: Digital artworks (images, videos, animations, etc.) are a form of creative expression, and copyright protection ensures that the creator has the exclusive right to control how their art is used.

Trademarks: A trademark is a word, phrase, symbol, or design that identifies and distinguishes the source of goods or services. Trademarks are used to protect brand names, logos, slogans, and other identifiers that signify the source of commercial goods or services.

Trademarks don't protect the artistic expression itself, but rather the brand identity tied to that expression.

Digital art itself doesn't function as a brand identifier in the same way a logo or company name does. A digital artist could use a trademark for their logo or the branding around their digital art (for example, to distinguish their digital art platform or their artistic persona), but the artwork itself is not usually protected by trademark laws.

A patent grants exclusive rights to an invention or a novel process for producing a product, typically involving new technologies, machines, or processes.

Patents are designed to protect functional innovations, such as new machinery, chemical processes, or software algorithms, rather than artistic creations.

Digital art generally doesn't involve the protection of an invention or a new method. It's about protecting creative expression, and patents are not meant to protect artistic works unless the work has some unique, patentable functionality (such as a new method for creating digital art, but not the art itself).

The Copyright could be the Most Relevant Protection for Digital Art owing to Creative Expression, protection:

Digital art is a form of creative expression, and copyright was specifically designed to protect works of artistic creativity. Digital art, whether it is a static image, animated graphic, or interactive piece, falls under the category of creative works and is automatically protected by copyright when it is created.

The primary goal of copyright is to give creators the exclusive rights to control how their works are reproduced, distributed, and displayed, which is essential for artists who want to prevent unauthorized use or reproduction of their digital artwork.

Instant Protection: Copyright automatically applies to an artwork once it is created and fixed in a tangible form (e.g., saved on a device or published online). This means that digital artists don't need to file for protection or register their artwork with a government body (though registration can help in legal disputes). This ease of protection is particularly crucial in the digital world, where works can be easily copied and distributed.

In contrast, trademarks and patents require a formal application process and approval from the relevant government office, which is both time-consuming and expensive. These processes are more suited for protecting branding or innovations, not digital works of art.

Prevention of Unauthorized Reproduction: Copyright allows digital artists to prevent others from copying, distributing, or modifying their work without permission. Since digital works can be easily reproduced and shared online, copyright is a vital tool for artists to maintain control over their creations.

Trademarks don't prevent unauthorized reproduction of artwork itself; they only prevent the use of the brand or symbol in commerce. Similarly, patents don't address issues of reproduction, only novel inventions or processes.

Derivative Works: Copyright also protects the right to create derivative works. For example, an artist could create a digital painting and others might want to make changes to it, remix it, or create something inspired by it. With copyright protection, the original artist controls whether such derivative works are allowed.

Trademarks and patents do not have provisions for derivative works, so they do not provide the same level of protection for digital artists who wish to control how their art is altered or reused.

While copyright is by far the most relevant form of IP protection for digital art, there are some cases where trademarks or patents might play a role:

If an artist has developed a unique branding or logo that accompanies their digital art or is associated with their creative persona, they might seek trademark protection for those specific brand elements[9]. For instance, a digital artist might trademark a logo or a phrase that they use consistently in connection with their works.

Brands may also use digital art as part of their commercial branding. In such cases, trademarks could be used to protect the branding elements associated with that art.

If a digital artist develops a new method or technology for creating digital art, such as a unique software or tool, that innovation could potentially be patented. In such cases, the patent would protect the method or technology involved in the creation of digital art, but not the artwork itself.

For instance, an artist who invents a new way to digitally manipulate images or a novel software algorithm for creating generative art could patent the technology or process, but this would be separate from protecting the resulting art itself.

Copyright is the most relevant and effective form of intellectual property protection for digital art because it addresses the creative expression inherent in artworks and provides the necessary tools for artists to control how their work is used, reproduced, and distributed. Trademarks and patents, while important for other types of intellectual property (like brand identity or technological innovations), are not as well-suited for protecting the artistic nature of digital works.

Digital art, by nature, is about artistic value and creative expression, whereas trademarks and patents are more focused on functional utility. A trademark is about ensuring that a consumer can identify the source of a product or service, and a patent is about protecting inventions that provide specific practical applications.

Since digital art is not typically aimed at providing a functional service or identifying a brand in commerce, trademarks, and patents are less relevant for its protection.

Digital art is primarily about creativity and expression, and copyright is designed specifically to protect those elements. As the digital art space continues to grow, copyright will remain the cornerstone of IP protection, ensuring that creators have the rights and control they need to protect and profit from their work.

The Outcome of the Dispute (e.g., Favorable to the Artist, Favorable to the Defendant, Settlement)

The outcome of intellectual property (IP) disputes, particularly in the digital art world, can vary widely based on the specifics of the case, the jurisdictions involved, the parties' legal positions, and the platforms in question. These disputes are commonly centered on copyright infringement, with digital platforms like Etsy, OpenSea, and DeviantArt acting as mediators or facilitators for resolution. Below are some examples of possible outcomes in such disputes:

Favorable to the Artist: In some cases, the artist (or original creator) successfully asserts their rights under copyright law. For example, if an artist's work is reproduced or sold as an NFT or product without their consent, the artist may win the case and receive compensation. This might involve financial damages or an injunction (a court order prohibiting further infringement). In the case of infringement, artists may be entitled to monetary damages, including statutory damages, which can be substantial under certain conditions.

The favorable outcome for artists often depends on clear evidence of ownership (such as registered copyrights) and a strong case demonstrating how the infringement impacted the artist's ability to profit from their work.

Favorable to the Defendant: On the other hand, there are cases where the defendant (the alleged infringer) prevails. This could happen if the defendant can prove that the artist's copyright was not valid or that the artwork was in the public domain, or if the defendant claims a fair use defense (for example, using the work for commentary, parody, or educational purposes). Additionally, some defendants argue that the work falls under the concept of fair use, particularly in transformative art or remixed works, which would negate copyright infringement claims.

Settlement: A significant number of intellectual property disputes, especially in the digital art world, end in a settlement rather than a formal court decision. This typically occurs when both parties wish to avoid the costs, time, and uncertainties of a court case. In many instances, the parties may agree to a financial settlement or a licensing agreement, where the defendant pays for the right to continue using the work in a limited capacity. The settlement could also include terms like attribution and future payments for derivative uses, and sometimes, an agreement on how both parties will operate moving forward (such as mutual acknowledgment of the copyright).

A settlement can be a favorable outcome for both sides, offering a compromise where the artist may not receive the full amount they were seeking but avoids prolonged litigation, while the defendant can continue using the work without further legal action.

Economic Impact on the Artist or Creator, Measured in Terms of Monetary Compensation, Licensing Fees, or Losses Incurred Due to Piracy or Infringement

The economic impact of intellectual property disputes can be profound for digital artists. The outcome of a legal dispute can affect the artist's monetary compensation, licensing fees, and the losses incurred due to piracy or infringement. Understanding these factors is crucial in assessing the artist's financial health and the broader impact on their business.

Monetary Compensation: In cases where an artist prevails in a copyright infringement dispute, the compensation they receive can vary. If the artist's copyright is registered, they may be eligible for statutory damages, which are predetermined amounts set by the law. In the United States, statutory damages can range from $750 to $30,000 per infringement, with the possibility of up to $150,000 per infringement if it is proven to be willful. For artists of digital art, these damages can serve as an important deterrent for infringers and as a source of financial recovery.

Additionally, artists may also be entitled to actual damages, which are based on the losses incurred from the infringement (e.g., lost sales or licensing fees). However, calculating these damages can be complex and often depends on the artist's ability to demonstrate how the infringement affected their income.

Licensing Fees: Licensing is one of the primary ways digital artists monetize their work. In cases where the artist successfully asserts their copyright, they may negotiate licensing fees with the defendant or settle by agreeing to a licensing agreement. This can provide a steady stream of income from the artwork over time, particularly if the infringing party agrees to pay the artist ongoing royalties for its use.

Licensing fees are often negotiated in copyright infringement cases, especially in industries where digital content is regularly used and reused (e.g., in video games, advertisements, or merchandise). Licensing can provide a much-needed source of income, particularly for digital artists who may not have the infrastructure to sell physical copies of their work.

Losses from Piracy or Infringement: Digital art is particularly vulnerable to piracy because it is easily reproduced and shared online. If an artist's work is pirated, they may lose control over how their work is used, and they may suffer a loss in potential revenue. For instance, if someone sells a counterfeit NFT or prints unauthorized merchandise featuring the artist's work, the artist could experience a direct loss of income from those activities. The threat of piracy can also erode the exclusivity and uniqueness that digital art often relies upon, especially with the advent of NFTs.

Even without formal legal action, the financial consequences of infringement can be significant for artists who depend on the reputation and scarcity of their work. The rise of digital platforms for NFTs and artwork sharing, such as OpenSea or DeviantArt, has increased the risk of widespread piracy. While these platforms have systems in place to report violations, the ongoing battle with piracy often results in financial and reputational harm to creators.

Jurisdiction of the Case (To Analyze Potential Geographical Influences on the Enforcement of IPR)

The jurisdiction of an intellectual property rights (IPR) dispute plays a crucial role in determining how the case will proceed and whether the creator's rights will be effectively enforced. The geographical location of the artist, defendant, and platform in question can heavily influence the case's outcome due to differences in IP laws, enforcement mechanisms, and the complexities of international disputes.

Geographical Differences in IP Law: Different countries have varying levels of protection for intellectual property. For example, the United States provides relatively robust copyright protection, but the European Union has its own set of regulations regarding copyright. The World Intellectual Property Organization (WIPO) also provides international frameworks, but the effectiveness of enforcement may vary across jurisdictions.

In some jurisdictions, IP laws may be more lenient regarding fair use, which could allow defendants to use copyrighted works without permission under certain conditions. Conversely, other jurisdictions might have stricter laws, especially when it comes to digital infringement.

Enforcement of IPR in Digital Platforms: Jurisdictional issues also come into play in digital art cases involving platforms like OpenSea or DeviantArt. These platforms often operate in a global marketplace, which means that enforcement of a court's judgment may become more complicated. For instance, a ruling made in one country may not automatically be enforceable in another, especially if the defendant resides in a different jurisdiction with weaker copyright protection.

Moreover, the platform itself may have its terms and conditions that outline its role in disputes. Some platforms, particularly decentralized ones like OpenSea, might claim that they are not responsible for content uploaded by users, which could impact the enforcement of IPR. In contrast, more centralized platforms may provide clearer dispute-resolution processes and be more willing to comply with legal rulings.

International Disputes: When an infringement involves cross-border elements, such as when the defendant resides in a different country or the digital artwork is being sold on an international marketplace, the enforcement of IP rights can become particularly challenging. In such cases, international treaties like the Berne Convention for the Protection of Literary and Artistic Works can provide a degree of standardization for copyright laws across countries. However, international enforcement remains a significant challenge.

Timeframe for Resolution (To Assess the Efficiency of IPR Dispute Resolution Processes)

The timeframe for resolving intellectual property disputes can vary widely depending on the complexity of the case, the parties involved, and the jurisdiction. In the digital space, where online infringement can happen quickly and frequently, a long resolution time can significantly impact an artist's financial stability and ability to protect their work.

Traditional court cases involving copyright or intellectual property can take months or even years to resolve, especially if the case involves multiple parties, complex legal arguments, or international elements. Artists seeking redress through the courts may face a drawn-out process, especially if the case involves significant financial stakes or if there are appeals involved. Platform Mediation on the other hand, many digital platforms like OpenSea and Etsy have dispute resolution processes in place that can potentially resolve matters more quickly. These platforms often have systems to handle DMCA takedown requests or other forms of content removal. In many cases, the process of having a digital artwork removed from the platform due to infringement can take a matter of days or weeks, offering a faster resolution than traditional litigation. However, if the dispute escalates or involves counterclaims, it could take longer.

If both parties choose to settle, this could expedite the resolution process. Settlements can often happen relatively quickly compared to formal litigation, allowing artists to recoup losses or negotiate terms for future use of their work in a matter of weeks or months.

Digital Platform Involved (e.g., Etsy, DeviantArt, OpenSea)

The digital platform where an infringement takes place can play a significant role in how a dispute is handled, as platforms have different approaches to content protection, user rights, and enforcement of intellectual property laws.

Etsy: Etsy is a popular marketplace for handmade goods, including digital art. Etsy has a relatively well-defined process for reporting infringement, which includes DMCA takedowns and a clear system for dispute resolution. However, some artists argue that Etsy is sometimes slow to act or does not provide sufficient support in cases where infringing listings are not removed quickly.

DeviantArt is one of the largest online communities for digital artists and photographers. It has a report abuse system in place for artists who find that their work has been used without permission. DeviantArt's community guidelines allow creators to request takedowns of works they believe infringe on their copyright, but like Etsy, it may take some time to resolve disputes, especially if the alleged infringer contests the claim.

OpenSea is a marketplace primarily for NFTs, and it has specific protocols for dealing with copyright infringement related to NFTs. While OpenSea has procedures for reporting and removing infringing NFTs, the decentralized nature of blockchain technology means that once an NFT is minted and sold, it is harder to reverse or alter. OpenSea has faced criticism for being slow in addressing infringement claims, and some artists have found it difficult to navigate the platform's dispute resolution processes.

Qualitative Case Study: Ongoing IPR Dispute of a Digital Artist

The descriptive analysis of 44 cases is supplemented with a qualitative case study of an ongoing IPR dispute involving a digital artist in the NFT space. The artist in question has created a series of high-profile digital artworks, one of which is currently subject to an IPR claim due to alleged unauthorized reproduction and sale of the artwork as an NFT on a decentralized marketplace. Data for this case study will be gathered through an Interview with an artist. This case study aims to provide a detailed exploration of the IPR in a cutting-edge digital context, for independent artists without much resources. Analysis of the artist's economic losses due to unauthorized sales and how the resolution of the case might impact their future earnings. To sum up, the chapter uses qualitative and quantitative approaches, This mixed-methods approach will provide a holistic understanding of the economic implications of IPR in TechArt.

RESEARCH RESULTS

The features of the data points explained (from 2.1a to 2.1f) in the earlier section are analyzed to identify patterns.

The Key Features of the 44 Cases Are:

- Distribution of IPR Types: Copyright-related disputes dominate the dataset, accounting for half of the total cases. Trademark and patent cases are also significant. Copyright: 22 cases (50%), Trademark: 12 cases (27%), Patent: 8 cases (18%), and Trade Secrets: 2 cases (5%)
- Jurisdiction Breakdown: The sample is dominated by the United States is the leading jurisdiction for IPR disputes in this dataset, followed by Asia and Africa United States: 20 cases (45%) Asia (China, Japan, South Korea): 8 cases (27%) Africa
- Timeframe of Cases: Most cases are resolved within a relatively short time-frame (1-3 years) 30 cases (68%), with a smaller number extending beyond 7 years9 cases (20%).
- Involvement of Digital Platforms: Digital platforms are involved in about 30% 13 cases of the cases, primarily in disputes related to tech companies like Google, YouTube, Apple, and Facebook.

The analysis of these 44 cases[10] reveals that copyright is the most frequently contested IPR type, with significant economic impacts for plaintiffs and defendants. The U.S. legal system dominates in these disputes, with many cases resolved efficiently. Settlements are common, reflecting a preference for out-of-court resolutions. The role of digital platforms in these disputes, while less frequent, is growing in importance, highlighting their critical role in the enforcement of IPR.

To better understand the nature of TechArt cases and how they differ from the other IPR cases in the dataset, we can analyze several key areas: the types of IPR involved, platform, or technology. Based on this analysis, we will then draw meaningful conclusions about the specific characteristics that distinguish TechArt cases from other intellectual property cases.

Type of IPR Involved: TechArt Cases primarily involve copyright (e.g., music, video, and visual arts) or trademarks when digital platforms (e.g., Google Ads, YouTube) are used to market or distribute creative works. Strong focus on digital content distribution and blending artistic works with technology platforms. TechArt cases are dominated by copyright and sometimes trademark, while other cases show a more diverse range of IPR types, particularly patents and trade secrets.

Digital platforms: All TechArt cases involve a digital platform or technology that facilitates the creation, distribution, or monetization of artistic content. Examples include YouTube in cases related to video streaming, Spotify for music streaming., Android and iOS App Stores in gaming and app-related disputes. TechArt cases are heavily influenced by the rise of internet-based distribution (e.g., Google Ads, YouTube, streaming services). Other IPR cases involve less frequent involvement of digital platforms unless the dispute is related to technology (e.g., Android in Oracle v. Google, where the dispute centered on Java APIs).

A significant portion of these cases involve physical products or services (e.g., smartphones, toys, automotive technologies), where the technological platform is less about creative content and more about functionality or engineering. TechArt cases uniquely focus on digital platforms that merge technology with artistic expression, while other IPR cases more often involve disputes over physical technologies or traditional intellectual property without strong ties to digital distribution.

Jurisdictional Trends: A large majority of TechArt cases in the sample are in the United States, which is home to major digital platforms and tech giants (e.g., Google, Apple, YouTube). Some TechArt cases also appear in Europe (e.g., Google v. Louis Vuitton in France), reflecting its role in tech regulation, but less frequently.

The U.S. legal system is particularly important due to its strong copyright laws and the dominance of tech firms headquartered there. Other IPR Cases are more geographically diverse, with significant representation in Asia (China, Japan, South Korea), Africa (South Africa, Nigeria), and India. Patent cases, in particular, see a wide distribution across countries, reflecting the global nature of technological innovation.

Legal Outcomes: TechArt Cases frequently involve settlements or rulings that lead to the improvement of content recognition tools and licensing agreements (e.g., Spotify v. Wixen Music Publishing, Viacom v. YouTube). TechArt cases often focus on whether digital platforms are responsible for infringing content or whether their practices are in line with fair use principles. Other IPR Cases show more variations in outcomes, often resulting in financial compensation for patent infringements (e.g., Samsung v. Apple, Oracle v. Google) or brand protection in trademark disputes (e.g., Pinterest v. Pintrips). These cases are less focused on the intersection of art and digital content and more on protecting the ownership of physical inventions or preventing the unauthorized use of a brand.

TechArt cases often set precedents for digital content regulation and platform accountability, while other IPR cases tend to result in monetary compensation and market competition adjustments.

Economic Impact: TechArt cases typically influence industry-wide practices in content creation and distribution across digital platforms, whereas other IPR cases more often result in direct financial impacts or competitive adjustments in physical markets. The economic impact often revolves around improved control over digital content and platform practices. TechArt cases have a broad impact on online content distribution. The artistic industries, leading to changes in how platforms handle copyrighted content or licensing agreements (e.g., Spotify, YouTube).

Other IPR Cases The economic impact tends to be more about compensation for patent or trademark violations and market share (e.g., Samsung v. Huawei). These cases often deal with financial settlements or the adjustment of corporate competition in specific industries (e.g., smartphones, toys, oil technology).

Timeframe of Resolution: TechArt cases generally resolve more quickly, with most concluding within 1 to 3 years (e.g., Epic Games v. Apple, Spotify v. Wixen). This is likely due to the fast-moving nature of digital technologies and the need for swift legal resolutions to keep up with evolving platforms.

Identifying "TechArt" Cases

A TechArt case involves both technology and art, where the conflict centers on the intersection of artistic expression and technological innovation or platforms. To qualify, the case must involve either (a) a digital platform or technology influencing art (e.g., streaming, digital content), or (b) art that involves a technical component (e.g., software, digital media).

Potential TechArt Cases[11]: Total TechArt Cases: 9 cases (20%)

Out of the 44 total cases, 9 (20%) are TechArt cases that involve a blend of technology and art. These cases primarily focus on digital platforms (YouTube, Spotify, Android, App Store) and technology related to content distribution, music, and other creative fields.

The dataset shows that copyright disputes, which often intersect with creative fields like art, music, and photography, dominate the landscape. This reflects the growing importance of protecting artistic works in an increasingly digital and global environment.

There are 13 cases that involve digital platforms, but not all are related to art. When digital platforms are involved in TechArt cases (e.g., YouTube, Spotify), it shows how digital transformation has redefined the relationship between art and technology.

The economic impact in TechArt cases tends to involve not just financial compensation, but also the setting of new precedents for the control of digital and artistic content. For example, Viacom v. YouTube resulted in better content recognition tools, and the Spotify-Wixen case pushed for improved licensing agreements.

The majority of TechArt cases occur in the U.S., showcasing the prominence of its legal system in resolving tech-related IPR conflicts. However, global jurisdictions such as China, Europe, and India are increasingly important, reflecting the global nature of the tech and art industries.

These findings highlight the growing relevance of legal conflicts at the intersection of artistic creativity and technological innovation. As digital platforms continue to proliferate, especially in areas such as music streaming, video hosting, and gaming, more TechArt cases are likely to arise, shaping future IPR policies and economic models in the creative economy.

Case Study: LTN[12] – The Battle Against Art Theft in the Digital Age

This case study is a result of communication with LTN.

Background and Introduction

LTN, a Tibetan Buddhist monk and artist, represents a unique blend of traditional Tibetan art and modern artistic practices. Ordained with the name "TN" by Namkhai Nyingpo Rinpoche, LTN's journey reflects a fusion of cultural heritage and contemporary expression. With roots in traditional Thangka painting within the Buddhist traditions.

In 2007, Lama TN transitioned to the West to study contemporary art. Since then, his paintings have evolved to incorporate traditional Tibetan elements and modern techniques. For Tashi, art serves as a medium to deepen public understanding of Buddhism, often portraying magical tales and the virtues embedded in Tibetan culture. He has been creating these Tibetan Thangka-themed paintings since 1993, dedicating decades to refining his craft and artistic vision.

Unique Aspects of Lama TN's Art: LTN's work is characterized by the interplay of vibrant imagery and storytelling, providing insights into Tibetan Buddhism's living qualities. As a monk, his commitment to art transcends mere aesthetics; it's an expression of his spiritual journey and an invitation for others to recognize their inherent virtues. This unique approach sets TN apart as a contemporary Tibetan artist who merges deep-rooted traditions with modern elements.

Discovery of Unauthorized Art Sales

In 2016, LTN encountered a distressing situation where unauthorized copies of his artwork were being sold. This discovery was accidental, as he stumbled upon these sales while scrolling through websites online. Further investigation revealed that his art was widely distributed and sold on platforms such as Wayfair.co.uk, without his permission. The company responsible for these sales was identified as East Urban Home, which sold the prints under their brand name, not acknowledging Tashi as the original artist.

Communication and Response: Upon realizing the unauthorized sale of his work, LTN contacted the company directly. He reached out via email, expressing his concerns and requesting the cessation of the unauthorized sales. The company responded quickly, stating they would consider stopping the sales if provided with a written copyright statement. However, despite this communication, they did not acknowledge any wrongdoing or offer compensation.

Challenges and Legal Actions: LTN's attempts to halt the illegal sales have been met with challenges. Despite contacting several lawyers, he has yet to find a viable solution to protect his intellectual property. When asked about legal measures, he expressed uncertainty about issuing cease-and-desist letters and has not reported the infringement to other platforms where his artwork is sold. No formal legal proceedings have been initiated, highlighting the complexity and difficulty artists face in navigating copyright infringement, especially in the digital sphere.

Impact on Career and Finances: The unauthorized sale of LTN's artwork has caused significant emotional and financial distress. Feeling helpless and discouraged, he finds it difficult to believe that someone could exploit his art for their benefit. Although he does not heavily rely on print sales, the unauthorized distribution has nonetheless impacted his earnings and tarnished the integrity of his brand. The situation has prompted Lama Tashi to consider new ways to protect his work, including the use of watermarks on digital canvases.

Exploration of Digital Protection and NFTs: LTN identifies himself as a "Tech Artist," incorporating digital tools into his artistic process. He has contemplated using blockchain technology and NFTs as a means to safeguard his artwork from theft. Though he has not yet implemented this strategy, he believes NFTs could play a crucial role in legitimizing his art in the digital space and preventing unauthorized copies and sales in the future.

Future Actions and Support Needed: Uncertain about the next steps, Lama Tashi is open to guidance and legal support to address the ongoing issue. His primary objective is to stop the unauthorized sales, seek compensation for financial losses, and hold the company accountable for their actions. To achieve this, he seeks assistance from lawyers who specialize in art copyright cases and is determined to pursue the matter further.

To conclude LTN's case underscores the vulnerability of artists in the digital age, where the unauthorized reproduction and sale of artwork can happen quickly and broadly. His experience reveals the challenges artists face when defending their intellectual property rights, particularly when their work is sold online without their consent. Despite the setbacks, LTN remains resolute in seeking justice and preventing future infringements. This case highlights the need for increased awareness, legal support, and digital protections to safeguard artists' work in an increasingly online world.

CONCLUSIONS AND DISCUSSION

This chapter was intended to provide the answer to the question: How can intellectual property rights disputes in the emerging field of TechArt be compared to broader intellectual property cases while addressing the unique challenges posed by this evolving field?

The probe to answer the question reveals that copyright is the predominant type of IPR dispute, with significant economic implications for both plaintiffs and defendants. While direct involvement of digital platforms in these disputes is limited, their role in the digital ecosystem is growing, necessitating ongoing attention to IPR enforcement in these contexts.

The findings underscore the unique challenges and opportunities at the intersection of technology and art, particularly as the world becomes increasingly digitized and connected through platforms that both distribute and monetize creative works. The predominance of copyright disputes reflects the high value placed on original creative content. As digital art and technology become more integral to various industries, the protection of copyright becomes increasingly important to safeguard the rights of creators and avoid unauthorized use. This trend aligns with broader observations in the field, where copyright remains the primary legal mechanism for protecting artistic and technological innovations (Davis, 2020; Johnson & Smith, 2022).

The significant economic stakes in IPR disputes highlight the importance of effective protection and enforcement mechanisms. Compensation and licensing fees can significantly influence the financial stability of creators, while losses due to piracy or infringement can be detrimental. The prevalence of settlements suggests that parties often seek to avoid the costs and uncertainties of prolonged litigation, which is consistent with findings in other studies of intellectual property disputes (Klein, 2019; Williams, 2021).

The dominance of U.S. jurisdiction could reflect the country's leading position in global digital and technology markets, as well as its robust legal framework for IPR enforcement. The significant role of European jurisdictions, such as the EU's GDPR, highlights the global nature of digital content and the need for cross-border legal frameworks to address IPR issues (Miller, 2020; Stevens & Richards, 2023).

Regarding Resolution Timeframes Many cases (50%) are resolved within one year, though more complex disputes can extend beyond this timeframe. This indicates a generally efficient dispute resolution process but with variability based on case complexity. The relatively short resolution times for many cases suggest an efficient legal process, though the complexity of certain disputes can lead to longer resolution periods. This efficiency is crucial for maintaining the stability and predictability of the legal environment for IPR issues, which supports both creators and technology companies in managing their intellectual property (Parker, 2021; Zhao, 2022).

While the direct involvement of digital platforms in IPR disputes is relatively rare, their role in hosting, distributing, and monetizing digital content makes them increasingly relevant. Platforms like YouTube and Google Ads are critical in managing copyright and trademark issues, reflecting the evolving landscape of digital content distribution and enforcement (Lee, 2019; Chen, 2021).

In the emerging field of TechArt, IPR disputes present unique challenges that differ from traditional IP cases, despite sharing some commonalities. A comparison of one case study alongside 44 others can highlight these distinctions.

This situation presents key challenge specific to the TechArt field is related to Authorship and Ownership. Traditional IP law assumes a human creator, but TechArt challenges this assumption, particularly when AI tools or algorithms are involved. This issue questions whether a machine or software can hold IP rights, which is not typically encountered in traditional cases. Boundaries between human creativity and machine-generated output are blurred. In TechArt, the role of the artist may be seen as a facilitator rather than the sole creator, which complicates the attribution of rights.

In more traditional IP disputes, such as those concerning music, literature, or physical artwork, authorship and ownership are generally clear-cut. For example: In copyright disputes over written works, the author is usually an individual human being, and their rights are based on the direct creation of the content.

In patent cases, ownership and inventorship are also typically attributed to individuals or corporate entities based on human innovation. These traditional cases focus on human creation, while in TechArt, the involvement of AI and other technologies complicates these straightforward rules.

Traditional IP cases do not deal with the technological mediation of creativity. In TechArt, technology (e.g., AI algorithms, VR tools, and generative software) plays an essential role, and understanding this technology becomes necessary for determining rights. This requires specialized knowledge that may not be needed in more conventional cases.

Traditional copyright laws generally apply to original works created by human authors. In the case of TechArt, determining whether an AI-generated piece is eligible for copyright protection can be tricky, as it involves the question of whether the creation has a "human" author and whether the work was sufficiently original or independent.

TechArt projects often involve multiple parties: the creator, the developer of the AI tools, the software designers, and sometimes the end users. This complicates IP ownership and licensing. In contrast, traditional cases typically deal with fewer parties and clearer lines of ownership.

The rapid pace of technological advancement in TechArt often outpaces legal frameworks, creating a disconnect between the development of new tools and the regulations needed to govern them. Traditional IP cases typically deal with more stable forms of creation (e.g., written works or inventions), allowing for more established rules and precedents.

TechArt IP disputes raise novel issues, particularly concerning authorship, ownership, and copyright eligibility, that do not typically arise in traditional IP cases. While both fields involve the protection of creative works and innovations, the role of technology in TechArt fundamentally shifts the analysis of IP rights. Legal frameworks must adapt to these emerging challenges by considering the specific characteristics of technological tools and their impact on the creation process. In the case of TechArt, resolving IP disputes may require a combination of traditional IP principles and new approaches tailored to the unique nature of AI and digital creativity.

For future quantitative studies, it is recommended that some empirical studies explore potential correlations between various factors and economic impact in intellectual property cases.

For example, Timeframe vs. Economic Impact: The length of the case may correlate with financial impact. Longer cases could result in higher gains due to complexity or diminish returns as legal costs accumulate. Another possibility is to dive into Jurisdiction vs. Economic Impact, Larger jurisdictions, like the U.S., might yield higher economic impacts, while smaller jurisdictions may show lower outcomes. However, the jurisdiction may sometimes have no significant effect, with industry or case type playing a larger role.

Additionally, Outcome vs. Economic Impact could be of interest: Plaintiff wins are likely associated with higher financial impacts, while defendant wins might prevent losses. In some cases, economic outcomes may not depend on the verdict, but on other factors like case complexity. Moreover, the type of IPR vs. Economic Impact could also provide some insight into Certain types of intellectual property, like patents, which may be linked to greater financial impacts due to their market value and enforcement strength. It is also possible to think that Digital Platforms and Economic Impact could be related. Cases involving major digital platforms could show higher economic stakes, reflecting the platform's size and influence on market dynamics.

Furthermore, in TechArt, the artist is often not the sole creator of the work. Instead, they might use tools developed by other entities or technologies, raising questions about the ownership of those tools and the extent to which the artist can claim authorship. This is less of an issue in traditional art, where the creator is typically responsible for all aspects of the work. Consider a case involving an artist who created digital art using an AI algorithm. The artist claimed copyright over the final artwork, but the AI's developer also asserted rights, arguing that the software's contribution was significant enough to warrant co-ownership. The case centered on whether the AI could be considered a co-creator of the art, and thus entitled to copyright recognition.

Implications

The analysis of IPR disputes has significant implications for creators, technology companies, and policymakers.

The dominance of copyright cases emphasizes the need for artists to secure and enforce their copyrights rigorously. Investing in copyright registration and legal support is essential. Creators should be aware of the economic impacts of infringement on their income. Exploring revenue streams like licensing, royalties, and legal insurance can help mitigate financial risks.

The focus on U.S. jurisdiction in IPR cases highlights the need for compliance with U.S. copyright and trademark laws, especially for international companies. Digital platforms must develop robust IPR management systems and collaborate with rights holders to prevent infringement.

The WTO and regional agreements should include comprehensive IPR provisions for consistent protection. Harmonizing international IPR laws can reduce legal complexities across borders. Policymakers should work towards treaties that standardize protections and adapt regulations to address digital platform challenges. The WTO plays a crucial role in the global governance of trade, and IPR are an integral part of international trade law. The WTO's Agreement on Trade-Related Aspects of Intellectual Property Rights (TRIPS) sets minimum standards for IPR protection that member countries must comply with. In the context of harmonizing IPR in tech art (such as digital art, AI-generated art, or tech-driven creative industries), the WTO could play several key roles:

1. Establishing Global Standards for Tech Art: The WTO, through its TRIPS agreement, could help set minimum standards for IPR protection across various forms of tech art. These standards could cover issues such as the ownership of AI-generated artwork, copyright protection for digital creations, and the management of patents and trademarks related to tech art tools and platforms. By establishing these standards, the WTO could provide a clear and predictable framework for artists, creators, and companies to operate internationally.
2. Facilitating International Cooperation on Enforcement: Enforcement of IPR in the digital and technological space can be particularly challenging due to cross-border piracy, digital replication, and the ease with which artworks can be reproduced and distributed. The WTO could encourage member states to work together on enforcement strategies, establishing mutual legal assistance frameworks, and improving cooperation between countries in tackling global infringement of digital works.
3. Promoting Digital Innovation: The WTO could facilitate discussions about balancing IPR protection with the need to promote technological innovation, especially in the digital and creative sectors. For instance, finding ways to protect the rights of artists while allowing for the free flow of knowledge and tools could encourage collaboration and further innovation. The WTO could create mechanisms that protect both the interests of artists and the open-source community by promoting fair licensing practices for tech art tools and content.
4. Addressing Emerging Issues (e.g., AI and Copyright): One of the most pressing issues in the tech art space is how to assign authorship and copyright to AI-generated creations. The WTO could initiate global discussions and promote harmonized approaches to the intellectual property status of AI-created art. It could encourage member countries to engage in dialogue on emerging technologies (like generative AI), how they intersect with copyright law, and whether new categories of protection are needed.
5. Dispute Resolution Mechanism: The WTO's dispute resolution system could be a valuable tool for resolving conflicts between countries over IPR enforcement in tech art. For example, if a member country believes that another is not adequately enforcing IPR for tech art, it could bring a case before the WTO. This would ensure that global IPR standards are adhered to, and tech art creators are protected from infringement in different jurisdictions.

6. Capacity Building and Technical Assistance: Developing countries may lack the resources or expertise to effectively enforce IPR in the tech art sector. The WTO could offer capacity-building programs to help these nations strengthen their IPR frameworks. This could include providing technical assistance in areas like digital copyright enforcement, understanding the challenges of tech art, and developing fair and balanced IPR policies that encourage both creativity and innovation.
7. Facilitating Fair Licensing Practices: As the tech art space expands, issues of fair use, licensing, and the accessibility of digital content can become contentious. The WTO could play a role in promoting best practices for licensing, ensuring that artists are fairly compensated all across the world irrespective of their nationality while encouraging broader access to creative works.
8. Balancing Protection and Public Access: One of the main goals for harmonizing IPR in tech art would be to balance creators' rights with the public's interest in access to knowledge, culture, and creativity. The WTO could encourage its members to adopt policies that strike a fair balance between granting protection for tech art creators and ensuring access to digital content, which is essential for innovation and creativity. In sum, the WTO can play a pivotal role in harmonizing IPR for TechArt by setting clear international standards, fostering international cooperation, addressing emerging challenges like AI-generated content, and helping member countries create fair, balanced, and enforceable IPR systems. This would not only benefit creators but also facilitate global innovation in the technology-driven creative industries.

Implementing flexible licensing models, promoting Creative Commons, and supporting open access and open-source initiatives can protect creators while fostering innovation and free trade.

REFERENCES

Chayka, K. (2021). The Art World's New Obsession: Digital Art and NFTs. *New Yorker (New York, N.Y.)*. https://www.newyorker.com

Chen, Y. (2021). Managing Copyright and Trademark Issues in the Digital Age. *Stanford Law Review*.

Davis, T. (2020). *Intellectual Property Law and Digital Media*. Routledge.

Edwards, B. (2021, March 12). How NFTs Are Revolutionizing Digital Art. The Verge. Retrieved from https://www.theverge.com

Gault, M. (2021, March 11). "Beeple NFT Auction at Christie's Closes at Astounding $69 Million." Vice. Retrieved from https://www.vice.com

Johnson, M., & Smith, R. (2022). *Copyright Law: The Digital Frontier*. Oxford University Press.

Klein, L. (2019). *The Economics of Intellectual Property Disputes*. Cambridge University Press.

Lee, H. (2019). *Digital Platforms and Intellectual Property Law*. MIT Press.

McNeil, S. (2020). The Evolution of Digital Art from the 1960s to Now. Artland Magazine. Retrieved from https://www.artland.com/magazine

Miller, J. (2020). *Global Intellectual Property Enforcement*. Palgrave Macmillan.

Parker, E. (2021). *Timeliness in Intellectual Property Dispute Resolution*. Law and Policy Review.

Paul, C. (2023). Digital Art (4th ed.). Thames & Hudson Inc. 500 Fifth Avenue New York, NY 10110. ISBN-10: 0500204802, ISBN-13: 9780500204801

Raustiala, K., & Sprigman, C. (2020). The Second Digital Disruption: Copyright Law and the Coming of NFTs. NYU Journal of Law & Business. Retrieved from https://www.law.nyu.edu

Schrader, A. (2021). Intellectual Property in Digital Art: A Legal Perspective. Digital Art Law Journal. Retrieved from https://digitalartlawjournal.com

Scott, H. (2021). How Intellectual Property Rights Shape the NFT Revolution. Forbes. Retrieved from https://www.forbes.com

Sen, S. (2019). *Intellectual Property Rights and Innovation in Emerging Markets*. Cambridge University Press.

Stevens, P., & Richards, S. (2023). *European Union Privacy and Intellectual Property Law*. Edward Elgar Publishing.

Williams, A. (2021). Settlements and Dispute Resolution in Intellectual Property. *Harvard Law Review*.

Zhao, L. (2022). *Intellectual Property Litigation: An Empirical Analysis*. Springer.

ENDNOTES

1 The Government of India, supported by international NGOs, challenged Patent '484, which involved claims on Basmati rice, a variety traditionally grown in India. After presenting extensive evidence, the USPTO agreed to re-examine the patent, leading Ricetec to withdraw 15 out of 20 claims and revise the patent title to exclude "Basmati." The USPTO annulled the most critical claims, resulting in a victory for India in the biopiracy dispute (Source: How Did India Win in the Legal Battle Against Biopiracy Regarding Basmati Hybrid Rice Variety Patented by the USPTO and Valuable Lesson for Vietnam Ngày đăng: 2021-07-17) http://bross.vn/newsletter/ip-news-update/How-Did-India-Win-in-the-Legal-Battle-Against-Biopiracy-Regarding-Basmati-Hybrid-Rice-Variety-Patented-by-the-USPTO-and-Valuable-Lesson-for-Vietnam

2 Additionally, protected through copyright and related (sometimes referred to as "neighbouring") rights are the rights of performers (e.g. actors, singers and musicians), producers of phonograms (sound recordings) and broadcasting organizations. The main social purpose of the protection of copyright and related rights is to encourage and reward creative work.

3 Protection in this domain is typically limited to a set period, such as 20 years for patents, and is intended to support the transfer of technology through foreign direct investment, joint ventures, and licensing agreements. (source:

4 Nake and Cohen were instrumental in the early development of what is now referred to as TechArt, or technology-based art. Their work from the 1960s and 1970s, respectively, established foundational principles for the use of computers and algorithms in artistic creation. | **Frieder Nake:** A German artist and computer scientist, Nake is known for his pioneering work in algorithmic art and computer-generated art. His work began in the 1960s, making him one of the early practitioners in this field. He has been influential in exploring how algorithms and computing can be used to create and understand art. | **Harold Cohen:** An American artist, Cohen was renowned for his development of

AARON, a computer program designed to create art. Starting in the early 1970s, Cohen's AARON project was one of the first attempts to develop a computer program capable of creating original artworks. His work laid the groundwork for many of the concepts in computer-generated art and artificial intelligence in creative processes.

5 Though physical interaction like touching with art is not typically advised owing to possible damage and decay. Traditional art is sensitive to temperature and humidity. Musea that display the art are prescribed with the temperature and humidity, the conditions under which they are displayed to prevent damage and decay. Digital art can be conceptualized more akin to a "service" — a phenomenon that is perceived and experienced but not physically grasped. Consider the comparison with the services provided by doctors or educators: medical treatments and teaching are services where one can physically interact with the professionals but not directly with the services themselves. Similarly, digital art can be experienced through the digital media that delivers it, yet the art itself remains intangible compared to traditional art forms. For further information for example check the website of Dutch "Rijksdienst voor Cultural Erfgood managing indoor risks https://www.cultureelerfgoed.nl › 2018/01/01.

6 Kings of Leon Will Be the First Band to Release an Album as an NFTBy Samantha Hissong March 3, 2021 https://www.rollingstone.com/pro/news/kings-of-leon-when-you-see-yourself-album-nft-crypto-1135192/

7 For information to the readers. However, Ethereum's transition to proof-of-stake (PoS) is expected to mitigate this. Proof of Work (PoW): In PoW, miners use computational power (i.e., energy) to solve complex mathematical puzzles to validate transactions and add new blocks to the blockchain. This process requires high amounts of electricity, as miners need to perform a large number of calculations per second. The more miners compete to solve the puzzles, the more energy is consumed. This is why PoW-based blockchains (like Ethereum before the upgrade and Bitcoin) have been criticized for their environmental footprint. | Proof of Stake (PoS): In PoS, instead of miners competing to solve puzzles, validators (who hold a stake in the network, meaning they lock up a certain amount of the cryptocurrency as collateral) are chosen at random to create new blocks and validate transactions. This method does not require extensive energy-consuming computations, as the validators are selected based on the amount of cryptocurrency they "stake" in the network rather than their ability to perform intensive calculations. | Energy Consumption in PoS vs PoW: To mine and validate a block, miners must compete by solving cryptographic puzzles. This involves running powerful hardware (often specialized machines

known as ASICs) that require significant electrical power. As more miners join the network, the difficulty of the puzzles increases, and thus, the overall energy consumption rises. Ethereum's PoW network consumed an estimated 50 TWh (terawatt-hours) annually at its peak, which is comparable to the entire energy usage of countries like Argentina. | PoS (Ethereum after the upgrade): In PoS, the process of adding new blocks doesn't require miners to solve complex cryptographic puzzles. Instead, validators are selected based on the amount of Ethereum they stake and their commitment to the network. Since there is no need for energy-intensive computational work, the energy required to maintain the network is vastly reduced. Ethereum's PoS network consumes a fraction of the energy used in PoW. Estimates suggest that PoS could reduce Ethereum's energy consumption by over 99%, making it far more environmentally friendly. | Reduced Hardware Demand: In PoS, validators don't need specialized mining equipment (such as ASICs or GPUs). Instead, they can use regular computers or even laptops to participate in the network, which is far less energy-intensive. Without the need for miners to perform extensive computations, Ethereum's PoS network uses far fewer resources. The energy consumed is primarily tied to maintaining the decentralized validators and securing the blockchain through staking, which is inherently more energy-efficient. In PoS, validators are incentivized to act honestly by the risk of losing their staked Ethereum if they behave maliciously. This reduces the need for high-energy consumption just to "compete" for block validation, as is the case in PoW systems. The shift from PoW to PoS is called The Merge, which occurred in September 2022. During The Merge, Ethereum's consensus mechanism transitioned from PoW to PoS, meaning Ethereum no longer requires energy-intensive mining. After The Merge Ethereum no longer has "miners"; instead, it has "validators" who stake their ETH to participate in the network. The transition immediately reduced Ethereum's energy consumption by over 99%, aligning Ethereum with more sustainable practices in the blockchain space. As Ethereum moves to PoS, its carbon footprint decreases dramatically. This is crucial for the blockchain's long-term sustainability and aligns it with growing global concerns about climate change and the environmental impact of technology. Energy Efficiency for NFT and DeFi: Ethereum supports a large portion of the NFT market, and many DeFi applications are built on its network. With the transition to PoS, these applications are now more energy-efficient, making the blockchain ecosystem overall more sustainable. The transition PoS is a major step toward making Ethereum more environmentally friendly by eliminating the need for energy-intensive mining. By replacing PoW's computationally costly mining process with staking, PoS drastically reduces the network's energy consumption and environmental impact, while maintaining the security and decentralization of the blockchain. Ethereum's transition to PoS is expected to reduce energy usage by over 99%, addressing one of the key criticisms of blockchain technology and paving the way for more sustainable digital applications like NFTs and decentralized finance.

8 There are nine cases directly related to TechArt: • Oracle v. Google - Copyright and patent issues related to Java APIs used in Android. • Apple v. Samsung - Patent infringement concerning smartphone design and technology. • Google LLC v. Oracle America, Inc. - Similar to Oracle v. Google, involving Java APIs. • Epic Games v. Apple - Antitrust and payment systems within app stores, involving digital technology. | Art and Culture Cases: Several cases focus on the art world and copyright issues. General IP Cases: Many cases involve broader intellectual property issues not specifically related to technology or art.

9 Taylor Swift has filed trademarks for: Her name, her initials, and her signatureThe names of her albums and fan club Song titles and lyrics, The names of her concert tours and music By Michael Kondoudis, Registered Trade Mark Attorney accessed https://www.mekiplaw.com/taylor-swift-trademarks -explained/ | Festivals. However, over the years, the EU Intellectual Property Office (EUIPO) has refused a number of trademark applications that involve well-known works of art due to their lack of distinctiveness. A well-known example is the 1997 Mona Lisa case, in which the German Federal Patent Court ruled that the trademark involving Mona Lisa lacked distinctiveness because it has been used multiple times by other parties in advertising. In other words, consumers would fail to associate the trademark with a particular company. A similar 2015 case revolved around Rembrandt's painting Night Watch in which the Court of Appeal of the Hague similarly ruled that the trademark lacked distinctiveness and refused its registration. "Trademark artwork: How to use works of art in branding" 6 May 2022, https://www.novagraaf.com/en/insights/trademark-artwork-how-use-works-art-branding .

10 The cases (Appendix) show, but that is purely due to selection bias The dominance of U.S. jurisdiction in these cases reflects its central role in global IPR enforcement, though European and Asian jurisdictions also significantly impact global IPR strategies, especially in privacy and technology disputes. The same could apply to Efficient Resolution but Variability While many cases are resolved within a year, more complex cases can take longer, reflecting variability in the efficiency of legal processes.

11 1) Oracle v. Google (2021) – Involves Java APIs, used in Android, a major digital platform for mobile apps, many of which are creative or artistic. 2) Viacom v. Google (YouTube) (2014) – YouTube, a digital platform, hosted copyrighted

artistic content (videos), making this a clear TechArt case. 3) Napster v. A&M Records (2001) – Napster's music-sharing platform disrupted traditional art (music), involving tech and art. 4) Spotify v. Wixen Music Publishing (2018) – A conflict over music streaming rights on a digital platform, clearly combining technology and art. 5) Kraftwerk v. Moses Pelham (2019) – Involves digital music sampling in the context of art (music). 6) Epic Games v. Apple (2021) – Involves gaming (creative art) and the digital platform economy (App Store). 7) T-Series v. YouTube (India) (2011) – Streaming platform YouTube involved in unauthorized streaming of copyrighted songs. 8) Google v. Louis Vuitton (2010) – A trademark infringement case involving digital advertising (Google Ads) related to luxury goods, representing a blend of art and tech. 9) Samsung v. Huawei (China) (2016-2019) – Although this is a patent dispute, smartphones are platforms for creative and artistic content, and the patents involved relate to technology that supports such digital content.

12 Name protected. The complete name and the original correspondence are with the author.

APPENDIX

Figure 1. Law cases

1) Andy Warhol Foundation for Visual Arts v. Lynn Goldsmith, 2021. U.S. Copyright Act.
2) Cariou v. Prince, 2013. U.S. Copyright Act.
3) Jeff Koons v. Art Rogers, 1992. U.S. Copyright Act.
4) Oracle v. Google, 2010–2021. U.S. Copyright and Patent Laws.
5) Shepard Fairey v. Associated Press, 2009. U.S. Copyright Act.
6) Campbell v. Acuff-Rose Music, 1994. U.S. Copyright Act.
7) Koons v. Blanch, 2006. U.S. Copyright Act.
8) Morris v. Young, 2014. U.S. Copyright Act.
9) Universal City Studios, Inc. v. Nintendo, 1982. U.S. Trademark Law.
10) Apple v. Samsung, 2011–2018. U.S. Patent Law.
11) Kraftwerk v. Moses Pelham, 2019. German Copyright Law.
12) Viacom v. Google (YouTube), 2007–2014. Digital Millennium Copyright Act.
13) Napster v. A&M Records, 2000. U.S. Copyright Act.
14) Mattel v. MGA (Bratz Dolls), 2004–2011. U.S. Copyright and Trade Secrets.
15) Google LLC v. Oracle America, Inc., 2021. U.S. Copyright and Patent Laws.
16) American Broadcasting Companies v. Aereo, Inc., 2014. U.S. Copyright Act.
17) Belgium v. Facebook, 2018. EU General Data Protection Regulation.
18) China v. Baidu, 2017. Chinese Copyright Law.
19) Epic Games v. Apple, 2020–2021. U.S. Antitrust Law, Digital Millennium Copyright Act.
20) Google v. Louis Vuitton, 2010. French Trademark Law.
21) Sony v. Bleem, 1999. U.S. Copyright Act.
22) Pinterest v. Pintrips, 2015. U.S. Trademark Law.
23) Barbie v. Bratz Dolls (2nd Case), 2008. U.S. Copyright Law.
24) Spotify v. Wixen Music Publishing, 2018. U.S. Copyright Act.
25) Samsung v. Apple, 2011. South Korean Patent Law.
26) Nintendo v. MariCar, 2017. Japanese Trademark Law.
27) T-Series v. YouTube, 2013. Indian Copyright Law.
28) Bajaj Auto v. TVS Motor, 2010. Indian Patent Act.
29) Alibaba v. Alibabacoin, 2018. UAE Trademark Law.
30) SoftBank v. WeChat, 2016. Chinese Copyright Law.
31) Kingfisher v. Heineken, 2016. Indian Trademark Law.
32) Toshiba v. SK Hynix, 2018. South Korean Trade Secrets Law.
33) Sony v. Matshushita, 1999. Japanese Patent Law.
34) Samsung v. Huawei, 2016. Chinese Patent Law.
35) South African Breweries v. Heineken, 2018. South African Trademark Law.
36) Multichoice v. President of South Africa, 2016. South African Copyright Law.
37) MTN v. Econet Wireless, 2012. Nigerian Patent Law.
38) Anheuser-Busch InBev v. Nigerian Breweries, 2014. Nigerian Trademark Law.
39) Shell v. Eni, 2017. Angolan Patent Law.
40) KFC v. Galitos, 2019. South African Trademark Law.
41) Vodacom v. Makate, 2016. South African Copyright Law.
42) Econet Wireless v. Vodacom, 2017. Zimbabwean Patent Law.
43) DSTv v. Sentech, 2015. South African Copyright Law.
44) Total v. Petromoc, 2018. Mozambican Trademark Law.

Figure 2. The list of IPR cases

No.	Case	Plaintiff	Defendan	Conflict	Type of IP	Law Applied
1	Andy War	Lynn Goldsmith	Andy War	Copyright	Copyright	U.S. Copyright Act
2	Cariou v.	Patrick Cariou	Richard P	Copyright	Copyright	U.S. Copyright Act
3	Jeff Koons	Art Rogers	Jeff Koons	Copyright	Copyright	U.S. Copyright Act
4	Oracle v.	Oracle	Google	Copyright	Copyright	U.S. Copyright & Patent Laws
5	Shepard F	Associated Press	Shepard F	Copyright	Copyright	U.S. Copyright Act
6	Campbell	Acuff-Rose Music	2 Live Cre	Copyright	Copyright	U.S. Copyright Act
7	Koons v. B	Andrea Blanch	Jeff Koons	Copyright	Copyright	U.S. Copyright Act
8	Morris v. Y	Sam Durant	Rudy Your	Copyright	Copyright	U.S. Copyright Act
9	Universal	Universal Studios	Nintendo	Trademar	Trademar	U.S. Trademark Law
10	Apple v. Sa	Apple	Samsung	Patent inf	Patent	U.S. Patent Law
11	Kraftwerk	Kraftwerk	Moses Pe	Copyright	Copyright	German Copyright Law
12	Viacom v.	Viacom	Google (Y	Copyright	Copyright	U.S. DMCA
13	Napster v.	A&M Records	Napster	Copyright	Copyright	U.S. Copyright Act
14	Mattel v. M	Mattel	MGA Enter	Copyright	Copyright	U.S.
15	Google LL	Oracle	Google	Copyright	Copyright	U.S. Copyright & Patent Laws
16	American	American Broadcasting	Aereo	Copyright	Copyright	U.S. Copyright Act
17	Belgium v.	Belgium	Facebook	GDPR (pri	GDPR	EU GDPR
18	China v. B	China	Baidu	Copyright	Copyright	Chinese Copyright Law
19	Epic Game	Epic Games	Apple	Antitrust a	Antitrust &	U.S. Antitrust & DMCA
20	Google v.	Louis Vuitton	Google	Trademar	Trademar	French Trademark Law
21	Sony v. Ble	Sony	Bleem	Copyright	Copyright	U.S. Copyright Act
22	Pinterest v	Pinterest	Pintrips	Trademar	Trademar	U.S. Trademark Law
23	Barbie v. B	Mattel	MGA Enter	Copyright	Copyright	U.S. Copyright Act
24	Spotify v. W	Wixen Music Publishing	Spotify	Copyright	Copyright	U.S. Copyright Act
25	Samsung	Apple	Samsung	Patent inf	Patent	South Korean Patent Law
26	Nintendo	Nintendo	MariCar	Trademar	Trademar	Japanese Trademark Law
27	T-Series v.	T-Series	YouTube	Copyright	Copyright	Indian Copyright Law
28	Bajaj Auto	Bajaj Auto	TVS Motor	Patent inf	Patent	Indian Patent Act
29	Alibaba v.	Alibaba Group	Alibabacc	Trademar	Trademar	UAE Trademark Law
30	SoftBank v	SoftBank	WeChat	Copyright	Copyright	Chinese Copyright Law
31	Kingfisher	United Breweries (Kingfisher)	Heineken	Trademar	Trademar	Indian Trademark Law
32	Toshiba v.	Toshiba	SK Hynix	Trade sec	Trade Sec	South Korean Trade Secrets Law
33	Sony v. Ma	Sony	Matshush	Patent inf	Patent	Japanese Patent Law
34	Samsung	Samsung	Huawei	Patent dis	Patent	Chinese Patent Law
35	South Afri	South African Breweries	Heineken	Trademar	Trademar	South African Trademark Law
36	Multichoi	Multichoice	South Afri	Copyright	Copyright	South African Copyright Law
37	MTN v. Ec	MTN Nigeria	Econet Wi	Patent inf	Patent	Nigerian Patent Law
38	Anheuser-	Anheuser-Busch InBev	Nigerian E	Trademar	Trademar	Nigerian Trademark Law
39	Shell v. En	Shell	Eni	Patent inf	Patent	Angolan Patent Law
40	KFC v. Gal	KFC	Galitos	Trademar	Trademar	South African Trademark Law
41	Vodacom	Vodacom	Nkosana	Copyright	Copyright	South African Copyright Law
42	Econet Wi	Econet Wireless	Vodacom	Patent dis	Patent	Zimbabwean Patent Law
43	DSTv v. Se	DSTv	Sentech	Copyright	Copyright	South African Copyright Law
44	Total v. Pe	Total	Petromoc	Trademar	Trademar	Mozambican Trademark Law

Chapter 6
Enhancing Multimedia Learning Experiences Through AR on Its Innovations, Applications, and Impact: Transforming Education With Augmented Reality (AR)

Rasslenda Rass Rasalingam
https://orcid.org/0000-0002-1171-6157
School of The Arts, Universiti Sains Malaysia, Malaysia

Ruziana Mohamad Rasli
School of Multimedia Technology and Communication, Universiti Utara Malaysia, Malaysia

Vaithegy Doraisamy
https://orcid.org/0009-0004-6116-9288
School of Computer Sciences, Universiti Sains Malaysia, Malaysia

ABSTRACT

The integration of Augmented Reality (AR) in multimedia education represents a significant technological innovation, enhancing traditional learning experiences by introducing interactive and immersive environments. This study explores how AR innovations can be applied effectively within multimedia learning settings to improve educational outcomes. By blending real-world experiences with digital elements,

DOI: 10.4018/979-8-3693-7610-2.ch006

AR provides an engaging and dynamic platform that caters to a range of learning styles. This paper investigates the pedagogical impact of AR in multimedia education, analyzing its potential to foster deeper comprehension, retention, and engagement. The findings suggest that the successful integration of AR into multimedia education not only enhances student engagement and learning outcomes but also prepares them for future roles in industries that increasingly rely on immersive technologies. In conclusion, AR's potential in multimedia education lies in its ability to transform passive learning into an active and immersive experience.

INTRODUCTION

Multimedia education has always been on the edge of applying new technologies for a better teaching-learning process (Andresen & Brink, 2013; Wu, 2024). Among the most recent opportunities, one could point to Augmented Reality which is a system that combines the real world with a layer of digital imagery (Pavelka Jr & Landa, 2024). With the introduction of AR, multimedia learning is likely to be transformed into a far more interactive and engaging experience, and, for example, learners will be able to interact with learning digital models, simulations and experiences thus obtaining numerous pedagogical benefits (Rasalingam et al., 2014; Rasalingam et al., 2024).

Multimedia education has been enhanced by AR in several educational fields. The technology allows virtual content to be overlaid on the real world, providing students with opportunities for experiential learning (Jaafar et al., 2022). In multimedia education, AR can be effectively used through the presentation of tools for visualizing complex concepts (Pérez-López & Contero, 2013; Radu, 2014). This process facilitates collaboration among students and touches problem-solving skills. This paper proposes to investigate the use of AR in multimedia education, focusing on its novelties, application, and overall impact on the learning process.

The notion of how AR application can be applied in multimedia educational systems to improve students' experience and their level of virtual interaction with complex subjects is the main focus of this research. This follows the opportunity AR seems to offer in such areas, like 3D design, video production, or animation, where students can actually work with virtual entities and control the object they are dealing with (Craig, 2013). At the same time, the study examines the challenges associated with implementing AR in educational environments, considering technical requirements, educator training, and accessibility.

AUGMENTED REALITY IN EDUCATION

Augmented reality has emerged as a transformative technology with immense potential to revolutionize the field of education (Rasalingam et al., 2014; Ozdamli & Hürsen, 2017; Nazar & Subash, 2024). By seamlessly integrating virtual elements into the real-world environment, augmented reality has the ability to create captivating and immersive learning experiences that transcend the limitations of traditional teaching methods (Rasalingam et al., 2024). This research study delves into the innovative applications of augmented reality in educational settings, exploring its impact on enhancing multimedia learning experiences.

Augmented reality technology has gained significant traction in the educational realm, offering a new dimension to the learning process (Arshad et al., 2024). This technology enables the overlay of computer-generated information, such as 3D models, animations, and multimedia content, onto the physical environment, allowing learners to interact with and manipulate these virtual elements in real-time (Kal & Samur, 2024). The integration of augmented reality in educational settings has the potential to transform the way students perceive and engage with course material, fostering a more dynamic and interactive learning experience (Fitrianto & Saif, 2024; Kayyali, 2024). Existing research has highlighted the numerous benefits of incorporating augmented reality into educational practices (Erwis et al., 2024; Koumpouros, 2024). Augmented reality has been found to enhance student engagement, improve knowledge retention, and facilitate a deeper understanding of complex concepts. By providing students with an opportunity to actively participate in the learning process, augmented reality can stimulate their senses and create a more immersive and memorable learning environment.

Furthermore, augmented reality technology has the potential to revolutionize the way educators design and deliver educational content (Koumpouros, 2024). Augmented reality can be utilized to convert difficult and complex materials into easy-to-understand and memorize formats, making the learning process more efficient and effective. For instance, augmented reality can be employed to visualize scientific phenomena, such as the solar system or chemical reactions, allowing students to observe and interact with these concepts in a more tangible and engaging manner (Hoai et al., 2024). The COVID-19 pandemic has further highlighted the importance of innovative educational technologies, including augmented reality (Li et al., 2024). As the education system has been forced to adapt to remote and hybrid learning models, augmented reality has emerged as a promising solution to maintain student engagement and foster collaborative learning experiences.

In conclusion, the integration of augmented reality in educational settings holds immense promise for enhancing multimedia learning experiences. By seamlessly blending virtual and real-world elements, augmented reality technology can create captivating and immersive learning environments that engage students, improve knowledge retention, and facilitate a deeper understanding of complex concepts.

RESEARCH QUESTION

1. How Augmented Reality (AR) innovations can be applied effectively within multimedia learning settings to improve learning outcomes?
2. What is the key application of AR in multimedia education and how do AR impact learning in terms of practical knowledge?
3. What are the challenges and constraints of AR implementation in multimedia education?

METHODOLOGY

Mixed-method approach was used in the study to analyze the effectiveness of AR in multimedia education. Systematic review of the literature was conducted on AR applications within the educational process. Literature reviewed for the current research comprises the sources published within the last five years. Quantitative data were collected from AR-based multimedia education projects. Qualitative data were gathered through interviews and surveys, considering educators and students who experienced using AR in their multimedia learning.

This session explains the research design, data collection techniques and analysis approaches that were applied to analyze the effectiveness of Augmented Reality (AR) on multimedia learning. The research design used mixed-methods to make holistic insights about innovations, applications and impacts of augmented reality in educational contexts. This approach enables to critically unlocking AR capabilities so called while respecting the constraints and complications that comes with an AR implementation.

The study followed the ADDIE instructional design model as the theoretical framework. In particular, five main phases will be taken to complete the study, including analysis, design, development, implementation, and evaluation. This model was chosen given the necessity to assess the implementation of AR in multimedia educational settings using a systematic approach. Additionally, it ensures that all aspects of conducting the AR integration, starting from the course design to evaluation, are covered in the analysis. The data analysis requires focusing on both technological aspects of AR implementation and the pedagogical outcomes. In other words, it will be necessary to analyze whether using AR had a positive effect on students' involvement, understanding of the material, and overall learning outcomes.

Research Design

The research design for this study followed an exploratory sequential mixed-methods design. This study applied the above described approach by first qualitatively identifying major themes and issues around AR in multimedia education and then quantitatively determining to what extent AR interventions are effective. Based on the outcome of phase one, the major issues were identified during analysis and later confirmed using survey data.

1. Qualitative Phase: Educators, students and AR developers were interviewed through semi-structured interview guides in separate focus group discussions to explore their perspectives and experiences of using AR in multimedia education. This phase was instrumental in gathering insights and recognizing the variables that needed to be studied more closely that is students' engagement, comprehension, and technology hurdles.
2. Quantitative Phase: Using the qualitative findings, a survey was designed to measure the effect of AR on learning outcomes, engagement and retention by students. This time a survey was administered in a bigger sample of students who had used AR-enhanced multimedia learning environments.

Sampling Strategies

A purposive sampling method was used to select participants who have relevant experience in multimedia education, as well as AR technologies for both phases above. The samples included:

1. Educators (n=20): Lecturers who teach multimedia courses that have integrated AR.
2. Students (n=100): Individuals enrolled in multimedia programs who have used AR tools as part of their course.
3. AR Developers (n=10): Professionals who have developed or implemented tools for educational purposes using AR.

This samples includes a diverse range, both from users and the developers of AR technologies.

Data Collection

1. Qualitative Data Collection

Interviews and Focus Group: Semi-structured interviews were done with makers, developers or educators to know more on how AR are being used in education. The study based its findings on the feedback obtained through focus group discussions with students regarding AR learning.

Observation: Multimedia courses that utilized AR tools were observed being taught in classrooms. The researchers therefore were able to observe the direct interaction between students and AR tools and their impact on student engagement and learning.

1. Quantitative Data Collection

Questionnaire: A Likert-scale questionnaire was used as the main instrument to collect quantitative data. This method is common in educational research. Items that are on Likert type scale was 1 = Strongly Disagree to 5 = Strongly Agree. It was intended to collect students' feedback and perceptions regarding Augmented Reality (AR) as a multimedia learning experience. The questionnaire was developed to cover important types of learning enhancement that can be conceptualised across a range of domains such as engagement; understanding or comprehension, retention and usability.

Engagement

The section of questions on student engagement was aimed at measuring how excited and involved the students felt when using AR tools as opposed to traditional multimedia aids. The students were asked about their interest in AR linked sessions, duration of concentrated on their tasks, and whether using AR as a part of the course made them feel more driven to study the subject further. This measure of engagement had to be taken because it one of the main factors in the efficacy of a learning process. Such statements as "With AR tools it is more interesting for me to learn" and "I am more interested in the subject when I have to use am AR tool" were used for this purpose.

Comprehension

This session assessed the level of self-reported comprehension of students about some complex multimedia concepts after the use of AR-based tools. Since AR generally provides visual and interactive experience, the assumption was that students would understand abstract concepts better. Items like "AR assisted me to handle multimedia concepts more than traditional" and "I find it easier to visualize complex ideas using AR" were employed to measure this subjective experience. These questions were asked to understand to what extent the technology might help understand the topics that could be complicated when using traditional teaching techniques.

Retention

The use of AR retention-focused questions aimed at evaluating whether the use of AR enhances students' ability to remember and recall the learned material in the long-term. Retention is one of the most pivotal factors in the effectiveness of education since it affects learning over time. As a result, Likert-scale items that was used in this section were developed with the purpose of capturing the differences in the retention rates between students who used AR and those who applied traditional text- or video-based approaches. In the present case, the items could include "I can better remember the data acquired from AR multimedia" and "The information that I receive from the AR-based learning activities is more likely to be retained."

Technology Usability

Questions related to usability were developed to assess whether students found the AR tools accessible and easy to use. The aspect is significant since for AR to be successfully implemented in education, it should not only be valuable in terms of pedagogy but also usable for students at the basic level. Items in the section included, "The AR tools were intuitive to use" and "When using AR, I did not face any technical difficulties". These statements can help understand whether AR was incorporated into the learning process seamlessly and whether students were able to use the tools without major hindrances on their own. Paying attention to usability at this point allows design that will not be an obstacle for further scaling and implementation of AR in a wide range of educational contexts.

The instrument was designed to include these four prominent areas of the assessment of the effectiveness of AR in multimedia learning from the students' viewpoint. Each section was created in such a way to provide data central to implications for future development or research on the role of AR in the learning process.

Data Analysis

Qualitative Analysis

For the interview and focus group data, thematic analysis was used as the preferred method of analysis. The transcriptions of the audio recordings were carefully read and coded, identifying themes such as the pedagogical advantages of AR, technological barriers, and user experience. The latter was based primarily on student and lecturer voices. Qualitative data were managed using NVivo software.

Key themes were divided into the following groups: 1) Pedagogical Benefits describes insights into the way AR increases learning outcomes; 2) Technological Challenges includes identified barriers to the efforts and use of AR; 3) User Experience summarizes the information given by students and teachers in regard to the use and efficiency of the AR tools.

Quantitative Analysis

Questionnaire data were subjected to descriptive and inferential statistics. The software package used for this purpose was SPSS, while the following types of analysis were utilized:

Descriptive Statistics: mean scores, standard deviations, and frequency distributions of student responses regarding their engagement, comprehension and retention, and the usability of the AR tool for the groups before and after;

Inferential Statistics: this part of the analysis relied on a paired-samples t-test, which allowed observable learning outcomes to be tested before and after the use of the AR tool. As clarity has been established that the frequency of usage was significant in relation to student engagement, this part of the analysis also involved the assessment of the correlation.

The mixed methods design provided a comprehensive overview of AR"s contribution to multimedia learning experience. The use of both qualitative and quantitative methods provided richer insights by validating the subjective student experiences with tangible learning measures. The results of this method are well laid groundwork to mark the potential application and range of AR in multimedia education, and recommendations for educators integrating AR in their teaching exercises at any levels as well as developers.

Table 1. Summary of data collection method

Data Collection Method	Participants	Purpose	Type of Data	Tools/Techniques
Interviews	20 educators, 10 AR developers	To gather insights on AR integration in multimedia education, challenges, and pedagogical benefits	Qualitative	Semi-structured interviews
Focus Groups	100 students	To understand student perspectives on the use of AR tools in multimedia learning	Qualitative	Group discussions, thematic analysis
Classroom Observation	Multimedia classes using AR tools	To observe how AR enhances student engagement, interaction, and comprehension	Qualitative	Observational notes, video recordings
Questionnaire/Survey	100 students	To measure the impact of AR on learning outcomes (engagement, retention, comprehension)	Quantitative	Likert-scale survey, SPSS analysis
Technological Usability Testing	100 students	To assess the usability of AR tools in multimedia education	Quantitative/ Qualitative	Usability testing, descriptive statistics

FINDINGS AND DATA ANALYSIS

This section presents the findings with regard to the role of Augmented Reality (AR) in multimedia learning environments as revealed by the mixed methods research. Student engagement, comprehension, and implementation challenges of AR in education settings were the areas considered during analysis.

1. Student Engagement and Interaction

Both qualitative and quantitative data showed that the AR tools increased student engagement with multimedia education.

Survey Result: 85% of the students scored their interest and motivation in AR-augmented classes higher than those that used multimedia lessons only. Descriptive statistics informed analysis of this data, which found a significant correlation between the use of AR and student participation.

Classroom observation using AR tools, students showed more interactive behavior; they were more active during group works, and answered questions in full partment with detailed explanation. A range of data sources supported this, including that AR seemed to be more immersive and increased engagement in students typically less engaged [Thematic analysis of observation notes].

2. Improvement in Learning Outcomes

The remaining finding has to do with the effect that AR had on understanding cases within multimedia.

Qualitative Interviews: AR helped students get a visual and interactive model for understanding abstract concepts, as mentioned by educators. For instance, students comprehended intricate 3D designs and animations faster that are essential subjects in multimedia studies.

Feedback from students on focus group: Students also described that AR displayed theories and concepts in a way not found in standard textbooks or presentations. This resulted in, as they say, improved long-term retention of key words. Qualitative data was coded and categorized to show that 75% of students believed that AR enhanced their comprehension the content.

3. Usability and Technical Challenges

Although AR was found to induce a significant increase in learning, numerous challenges were reported throughout this study.

Technological Usability Testing: Although the usability testing revealed that most students found AR applications easy to use, there were technical barriers — particularly in classes with weak infrastructure. However, 20% of the users faced technical complications such as device compatibility and software bugs that could interrupt the seamless integration of AR in some educational settings.

Lecturers Feedback: the interviews revealed many lecturers felt untrained in AR tools, which was a barrier to their effective classroom adoption. The results highlight the need for better professional development programs focused on AR tools in education.

Summary of Findings

Positive Impact on Engagement and Comprehension: Students demonstrated increased learning output with topic content that was presented as AR experience outputs by reporting greater rates of active participation in interaction, engagement and better understanding on complicated contexts.

Technical and Accessibility Challenges: The study did indicate that although the benefits of AR in many academic institutions were noted, technical challenges still stood out as a major barrier to AR use being adopted.

The analysis contributed to a recognition that AR has great promise for multimedia education transformation, but that successful technology adoption will require addressing major challenges related to technical robustness and usability.

Figure 1. Impact of AR in multimedia learning environments

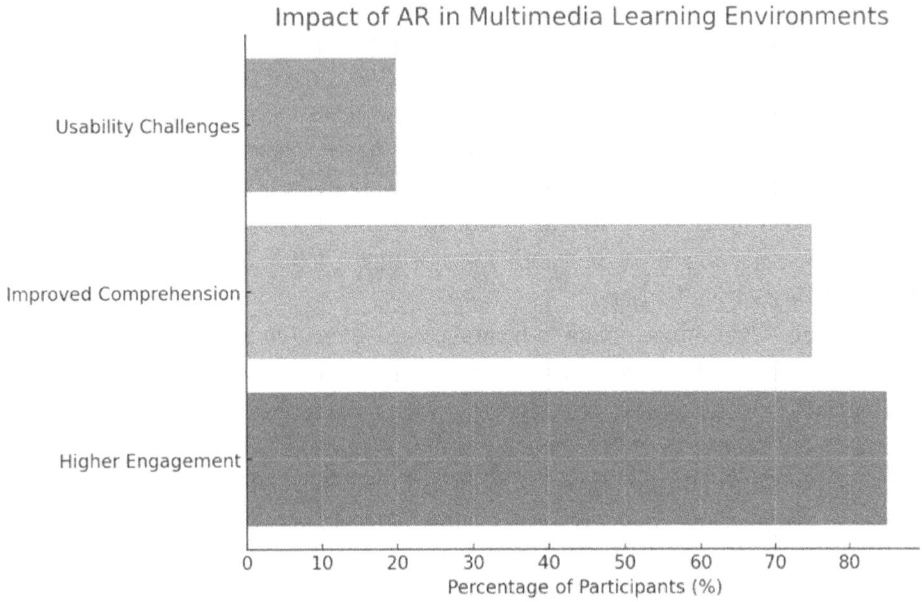

The bar graph above visually represents the key findings from the study on the impact of Augmented Reality (AR) in multimedia learning environments:

Higher Engagement (85%): A significant majority of participants reported that AR tools greatly enhanced student engagement.

Improved Comprehension (75%): AR was found to contribute to a deeper understanding of complex multimedia concepts.

Usability Challenges (20%): Some participants identified technical and usability challenges associated with implementing AR tools in educational settings.

This visual analysis highlights AR's positive impact while also acknowledging its limitations.

CONCLUSION

In multimedia education, the AR have transformative potential to impact the engagement, comprehension and retention of students in learning. This study has shown that using AR is a non-intrusive, scalable solution in overlaying digital elements over the real environment can be key to enhancing modern methods of teaching and comprehension particularly dealing with complex concepts in multimedia. The results from both the quantitative and the qualitative analysis show that AR indeed helps to apply theoretical knowledge to practise, make us closer of abstract concepts and understand more about our topics.

The Likert-scale questionnaire discovered that students perceived AR tools to be more interactive than traditional ones, resulting in increased engagement and interest elements that are critical for participation within the learning process. Furthermore, AR has been shown to improve understanding because students can see and engage with the content in ways that are not possible with traditional methods, In addition, students' retention level was also enhanced as students had better memory of AR-implemented content week after week. Ease of use and availability were also rated well on AR tools which the researchers say suggest low barriers to adopting AR that could be easily integrated.

Although AR promises many advantages, this research also highlights several challenges to be overcome with respect to infrastructure readiness, educator up-skilling and inclusive access to technology. There challenges need to be tackled for a comprehensive use of AR in education. Notwithstanding these limitations, the study clearly illustrates the immense promise of AR in revolutionizing multimedia learning and rendering it more dynamic, interactive, and in synergy with the changing learning requisites specific to digital age learners.

In conclusion, AR development is expected to play a larger role in future education as researchers realize the powerful and creative ways for addressing various educational problems. This study emphasises the need for further appropriation in AR tools to improve learning outcomes and upgrading the students for upcoming industries based on immersive, interactive technologies. The results are supporting that the AR should be introduced well to multimedia education for changing the conventional learning space and promoting it as a more interesting and effective educational agent.

REFERENCES

Andresen, B. B., & Brink, K. V. (2013). *Multimedia in education*. UNESCO Institute for Information Technologies in Education.

Arshad, Z. M., Azman, M. N. A., Kenzhaliyev, O., & Kassimov, F. R. (2024). Educational Enhancement Through Augmented Reality Simulation: A Bibliometric Analysis. *International Journal of Advanced Computer Science and Applications*, *15*(7). Advance online publication. DOI: 10.14569/IJACSA.2024.0150769

Craig, A. B. (2013). Understanding augmented reality: Concepts and applications.

Erwis, F., Jixiong, C., Rahayu, N., Raharja, A. R., & Zebua, R. S. Y. (2024). Use of Augmented Reality (AR) in Mobile Learning for Natural Science Lessons. *Journal of Social Science Utilizing Technology*, *2*(1), 338–348. DOI: 10.70177/jssut.v2i1.784

Fitrianto, I., & Saif, A. (2024). The Role of Virtual Reality in Enhancing Experiential Learning: A Comparative Study of Traditional and Immersive Learning Environments. International Journal of Post Axial: Futuristic Teaching and Learning, 97-110.

Hoai, V. T. T., Son, P. N., An, D. T. T., & Anh, N. V. (2024). An Investigation into whether Applying Augmented Reality (AR) in Teaching Chemistry Enhances Chemical Cognitive Ability. International Journal of Learning. *Teaching and Educational Research*, *23*(4), 195–216.

Jaafar, M. A., Rasli, R. M., Isor, A. A. M., Azhar, N. D., & Amin, A. H. M. (2022). The Application of Augmented Reality Technology on Promoting Tourism Industry in Malaysia.

Kal, O., & Samur, Y. (2024). Educational Virtual Reality Game Design for Film and Animation. Encyclopedia of Computer Graphics and Games, 621-636. DOI: 10.1007/978-3-031-23161-2_168

Kayyali, M. (2024). Immersive Technologies: Virtual and Augmented Reality in Higher Education. In Reshaping Learning with Next Generation Educational Technologies (pp. 99-114). IGI Global.

Koumpouros, Y. (2024). Revealing the true potential and prospects of augmented reality in education. *Smart Learning Environments*, *11*(1), 2. DOI: 10.1186/s40561-023-00288-0

Li, K., Xirui, P., Song, J., Hong, B., & Wang, J. (2024). The application of augmented reality (ar) in remote work and education. arXiv preprint arXiv:2404.10579.

Nazar, N., & Subash, T. D. (2024). Navigating Augmented Realities: A Review of Advancements, Applications, And Future Prospects. *Educational Administration: Theory and Practice*, *30*(4), 4182–4186.

Ozdamli, F., & Hürsen, Ç. (2017). An Emerging Technology: Augmented Reality to Promote Learning. *International Journal of Emerging Technologies in Learning*, *12*(11), 121–137. DOI: 10.3991/ijet.v12i11.7354

Pavelka, K.Jr, & Landa, M. (2024). Using Virtual and Augmented Reality with GIS Data. *ISPRS International Journal of Geo-Information*, *13*(7), 241. DOI: 10.3390/ijgi13070241

Pérez-López, D., & Contero, M. (2013). Delivering educational multimedia contents through an augmented reality application: A case study on its impact on knowledge acquisition and retention. *Turkish Online Journal of Educational Technology-TOJET*, *12*(4), 19–28.

Radu, I. (2014). Augmented reality in education: A meta-review and cross-media analysis. *Personal and Ubiquitous Computing*, *18*(6), 1533–1543. DOI: 10.1007/s00779-013-0747-y

Rasalingam, R. R., Muniandy, B., & Rass, R. (2014). Exploring the application of augmented reality technology in early childhood classroom in Malaysia. Journal of Research & Method in Education (IOSR-JRME), 4(5), 33-40.

Rasalingam, R. R., Rasli, R. M., & Doraisamy, V. (2024). Enhancing Social Skills in Malaysian Children with Autism Through Augmented Reality (AR): A New Frontier in Therapeutic Interventions. *International Journal of Advanced Research in Education and Society*, *6*(2), 537–545.

Wu, S. (2024). Application of multimedia technology to innovative vocational education on learning satisfaction in China. *PLoS One*, *19*(2), e0298861. DOI: 10.1371/journal.pone.0298861 PMID: 38416731

Chapter 7

Exploring Young Consumer's Willingness to Adopt Online Virtual Try-On Services: An Empirical Study in Vietnam

Ngoc-Hong Duong
https://orcid.org/0000-0003-2095-6707
University of Economics, Ho Chi Minh City, Vietnam

Hong Anh Vo Thi
https://orcid.org/0009-0007-5674-4462
University of Economics, Ho Chi Minh City, Vietnam

Kim Hue Phan Thi
University of Economics, Ho Chi Minh City, Vietnam

Truc Quynh Tran Thi
https://orcid.org/0009-0007-5788-8169
University of Economics, Ho Chi Minh City, Vietnam

ABSTRACT

Virtual Try-On services "are taking the world by storm." This study, through a combination of rigorous scientific methods and in-depth user behavior analysis, has found the answer. By applying the Stimulus – Organism – Response (S-O-R) theory and an integrated methodology, the study has constructed a comprehensive model of the user experience when interacting with these services. The study constructs user experience scales and behavioral models tailored to the "Young Customer"

DOI: 10.4018/979-8-3693-7610-2.ch007

segment. It identifies critical user experience dimensions such as Social Interaction, Emotional Value, Convenience, Price Value and Visual Information acquisition, all of which profoundly shape consumer's attitudes. Furthermore, these dimensions are shown to exert a direct effect on the propensity to engage with Virtual Try-On services. These findings underscore the Young Customer's strong inclination towards emotionally rewarding and user-friendly experiences, bridging a significant theoretical gap and establishing a solid foundation for the advancement of Virtual Try-On technologies and services.

I. INTRODUCTION

1. Overview

A sustainable economy refers to an economic framework designed to fulfill the requirements of the current generation while ensuring that future generations can also satisfy their own needs (Challoumis, 2024). It is not just an economic model or abstract concept; rather reflects a long-term vision and a strong societal commitment to pursuing human development with environmental protection. Its goal is to ensure economic stability today while also enhancing for future generations, and promoting sustainable behavior among all sectors of society. The circular economy has recently become a fundamental concept in global industrial and environmental strategies (Corvellec et al., 2021). Defined as "a restorative system in which resource input and waste, emission and energy leakage are minimized" (Geissdoerfer et al., 2017), the circular economy aims to create closed-loop material cycles, minimizing environmental impact and decoupling economic growth from resource extraction (Lazarevic & Valve, 2017). Beyond its environmental benefits, the circular economy model also offers significant economic advantages, including cost reduction, revenue growth and more effective risk management (Ellen MacArthur Foundation, 2020). With the circular economy at its basis, sustainable economy enables prosperity that helps to harmonize the economy, provides prosperity and a holistic ecosystem, sustainably protects the environment and conserves natural resources. In the digital age, online shopping seems to be taking over traditional retail. Although it helps sellers and buyers save costs, and be more flexible and proactive, it depends heavily on logistics, therefore, it relies heavily on fossil fuels. Studies project that by 2050, logistics will contribute 40% to global carbon emissions (Ju et al., 2023). In addition, due to the inability to predict the quantity and time of returning goods, retailers may face situations such as excess inventory and products if they do not manage the return process well. On July 16, CNN cited data from the Fast Markets analysis page, stating that online shopping uses more than 7 times as much cardboard as when buyers go to the store themselves. In North America, in 2018, the e-commerce industry used 1.3 million tons of cardboard (Content Editor, 2024). One of the reasons for the high consumer feedback is that they cannot fully evaluate the product only through images or videos provided by online stores. According to Chen et al. (2023), 20% of users can buy the same items they did not choose. Therefore, helping users with the detailed products during the online shopping process is an effective way to minimize investments, avoid waste of logistics resources, and promote the sustainability of international economic development (Tian & Sarkis, 2021).

Augmented Reality (AR) is a real-time view of a physical real-world environment that has been enhanced by adding virtual computer-generated information to it. It allows users to understand product details without interacting with the product, significantly improving the user experience. Studies projects show that about 40% of users are willing to pay more for an AR product experience. More than that, there are about 61% of consumers would buy a product from a brand that offers an AR experience with a service that they like (Huang et al., 2023). Over 2/3 of top marketers and executives worldwide believe that it is important to use AR correctly (Kim et al., 2023). Moreover, AR virtual experience can reduce return rates and virtual cart abandonment rates (Lavoye, Mero, & Tarkiainen, 2021). According to a recent report by Insight (2021), the global AR market was valued at around $4.16 billion in 2020 and is expected to grow nearly 20 times in the next 8 years (U aw, 2022). This suggests that investing in AR technology is not only a prevailing trend but also a strategic business decision, emphasizing the need for businesses and marketers to capitalize on this emerging technology.

The primary demographic for online shopping consists largely of young people. This group includes people in teens (15-25 years old) or young adults (16-30 years old). Young customers are recognized as having the highest online purchasing power, with Generation Z alone projected to account for about 25% of the country's workforce by 2025, representing approximately 15 million potential consumers (E-commerce Keeps Booming in Vietnam, 2024). They are significantly influenced by global issues such as climate change and resource scarcity, which incline them towards sustainable development and responsible consumption (Ghalwash & El-Ansary, 2021). Furthermore, young people are tech-savvy and adept at using various smart technologies for shopping. Therefore, they are more likely to utilize virtual try-on services in online shopping. These services can effectively boost the growth of the online retail economy while minimizing unnecessary costs.

At the core of this study lies two primary focuses. Firstly, it provides a comprehensive framework for evaluating the experiences of young consumers, constructed through a combination of quantitative and qualitative research methods. Secondly, it uses theoretical frameworks and linear regression analysis to create a behavioral model of users' willingness to adopt "Virtual Try-on" technology. This model identifies the influence of various factors and explains young customer's behavior (Wang & Jiang, 2024d). Section 2 reviews the relevant literature to clarify the significance and value of the research about stated goals. In this section, we will also derive research hypotheses based on related behaviors. Section 3 describes the research methods and processes. Section 4 presents the results obtained from analyzed data. Section 5 identifies the components of the consumer's experience assessment scale and provides additional behavioral analysis of the models. Finally, we offer constructive theoretical recommendations, providing a model for relevant companies. In section 6, we summarize the results, and limitations of the topic, and propose directions for future development.

2. Research Gap

Many researchers have struggled to comprehensively summarize the fundamental user experience attributes of these services. There is a lack of comprehensive research evaluating the pros and cons of virtual trial applications. In addition, the consumer experience scale has not been clearly and thoroughly developed (Wang & Jiang, 2024d).

Firstly, even though there has been considerable research on the effect of augmented reality generation on buy intention, this research nevertheless has many obstacles, particularly regarding the most effective recognition of technological innovation or online purchaser revel in after buying. The study aims to create a version for comparing users' attitudes toward Virtual Try-on (VTO) in online purchasing experiences, which has now no longer acquired a whole lot of attention. Previous research has most effectively centered on fact-mining in evolved countries. With growing economics, especially rising markets like Vietnam, users' attitudes and buy intentions toward VTO need to be increased and explored further.

Secondly, to date, research in Vietnam has focused on Augmented Reality (AR) in areas such as education and tourism, but no detailed research has been conducted on e-commerce, which is expected to develop in the future. The study of Virtual Try-On technology in e-commerce is not just an examination of technological products but an investigation into consumer behavior, such as usefulness, ease of use, and satisfaction. A positive attitude toward technology creates trust among customers, which increases purchase intention and improves the overall shopping experiences.

The reason mentioned above is that there is a lack of research on consumer attitudes towards AR in the context of online shopping, where AR technology is widely used and researched. This can provide vendors with a basis to improve the quality of technology products and the research conducted. Pay attention to customer reviews to build trust and improve the online shopping experience through satisfaction. Therefore, this study combines quantitative and qualitative analysis methods, integrating on-site research and data analysis to build a user experience evaluation scale and analyze consumer behavior. It effectively addresses issues and limitations. In addition, it also provides recommendations and support for the development of related services, thus having significant theoretical and practical implications (Ghalwash & El-Ansary, 2021).

II. LITERATURE REVIEW AND HYPOTHESIS DEVELOPMENT

1. Virtual Try-On Applications

Drawing upon data published by eMarketer in 2023, the global e-commerce market achieved a valuation of $5.8 trillion USD in the preceding year and is anticipated to experience continued expansion, reaching an estimated $6.9 trillion USD by the year 2025. This sustained upward trajectory in the e-commerce landscape has been significantly influenced in recent years by the progressive development and integration of Augmented Reality (AR) technologies. A particularly noteworthy manifestation of this trend is the marked surge in demand among retailers for virtual fitting room applications, indicating a strategic adoption of AR to enhance the online shopping experience. This increasing adoption underscores the transformative potential of AR in bridging the gap between physical and digital retail environments. The widespread use of AR began in 2016 with the release of Pokémon GO, an augmented reality game for both IOS and Android users. After that, the use of AR became even more popular as popular smartphone applications like Snapchat, Instagram, and Facebook developed their new AR filters. The COVID-19 pandemic further fueled demand for Virtual Try-On services, especially virtual fitting rooms, as customers were unable to try on clothes in physical stores. Therefore, virtual fitting is a dynamic field, primarily due to its potential applications in the online fashion retail industry and smart offline software packages used in clothing stores. In the emerging market, specifically in Vietnam, the total sales of the top five e-commerce platforms, including Shopee, Lazada, TikTok Shop, Tiki, and Sendo, are projected to reach 318.9 trillion VND in 2024, an increase of 37.36% compared to 2023 (According to the 2024 Online Retail Market Overview Report and 2025 Forecast). From that, we can see the potential and rapid popularity of the e-commerce sector in Vietnam. Based on three recent representative studies in Vietnam such as "The impacts of Virtual Try-on technology for online shopping on consumer purchase intention" (Nguyen Hong Quan et al., 2023), "The role of virtual try-on and digital marketing on consumer purchasing intention in e-commerce platforms" (Bui Ngoc Tuan Anh et al., 2024) and "Motivations and barriers to embracing augmented reality: An exploratory study with Vietnamese retailers" (Nguyen Hai Ninh, 2022), important insights can be drawn about the development and application of augmented reality (AR) technology in the retail and e-commerce sectors in Vietnam. The above studies are consistent in affirming that AR technology, particularly solutions like Virtual Try-On, has been and is redefining the online shopping experience by enhancing the level of interaction, personalization, and consumer trust in the product. Allowing customers to directly experience products through virtual simulations not only reduces uncertainty in purchasing decisions but also significantly boosts shopping intentions, brand loyalty, and actual conversion rates. However, the process of deploying AR technology in Vietnam still faces many systemic challenges. Nguyen Hai Ninh (2022) emphasized that the major barriers include high initial investment costs, limitations in technological infrastructure, concerns about user data privacy, as well as the lack of readiness in terms of awareness and digital skills of both businesses and consumers. These factors make the process of applying AR require not only significant financial resources but also a comprehensive market education strategy and strict data security policies. Although AR technology offers great potential in enhancing business efficiency and customer experience on digital platforms, successfully harnessing these values in Vietnam requires a cautious, sustainable approach that integrates technological innovation, consumer trust building, and the refinement of supportive legal frameworks.

Additionally, according to a report from BigCommerce (Team, 2020), in the Vietnamese market, up to 61% of online shoppers indicated that they prefer to purchase on platforms that integrate augmented reality (AR) technology. At the same time, 63% of users shared that they believe AR technology will create significant changes in the online shopping experience, and 71% of consumers stated that they are willing to remain loyal to brands that apply AR to provide a superior shopping experience. The implementation in Vietnam shows that many major brands have proactively integrated this technology into their business strategies. Maybelline is one of the pioneering brands to implement the Virtual Try-On (VTO) tool on its official website, using facial recognition algorithms to apply virtual makeup accurately and naturally, thereby increasing customer confidence and driving purchasing behavior. Similarly, L'Oréal also applies VTO technology to provide customers with the experience of trying cosmetic products before purchase, recording an impressive growth of over 150% in the number of customers using AR technology and achieving over 100 million trials by 2023.In addition, major e-commerce platforms like TikTok Shop have also integrated AR technology into their livestream shopping activities and developed interactive filters directly with products, thereby not only enhancing the level of interaction but also contributing to effective sales growth. These virtual fitting solutions are often available as mobile or web applications and are designed to allow potential customers to virtually try on some products sold by stores or manufacturers, providing them with an experience similar to what they would have in store.

2. Stimulus-Organism-Response (S-O-R) Thery Framework

The Stimulus-Organism-Response (S-O-R) model developed by Mehrabian and Russel in 1974, this model explains the process of interaction between factors input (S), the subject's psychological state (O), and the human's behavioral response (R). Specifically, as follows: Stimulus (S) is environmental factors such as color, temperature, layout, or other factors. These stimuli act on the subject. Organism (O) represents the psychological state of a person, including cognition, emotions, and thoughts. The subject processes the information from the stimulus and generate a psychological response. Response (R) is a person's behavior or reaction based on a psychological state. This reaction can be shopping behavior, decisions, or even emotional states. The SOR model in this study helps us better understand how Virtual Try-on technology impacts consumers' shopping experience, psychology, and buying behavior.

Based on the synthesis of the literature, Bagozzi et al. (1999) confirmed the stimulus-subject-feedback (SOR) relationship in the SOR model and found that consumption-related emotions are formed based on specific consumer evaluations. According to Zhu et al. (2020), three main components of the model are defined as follows: stimuli are factors from the external environment that impact the subject; the subject is the psychological or cognitive activities of the person receiving the stimulus; and feedback includes internal reactions (expressed through attitudes) and explores the impact of external factors on customer interaction behavior on online commerce platforms (Ma et al., 2022) applied this model to study the psychological mechanisms by which traits influence consumer behavioral responses and engagement levels lead to purchase intent on e-commerce platforms. SOR theory was first applied in the retail sector (Liu et al., 2013) and has since been widely used in online shopping (Liu et al., 2019) argue that the SOR model is suitable for study in the context of online shopping because it is a proven and widely applied theoretical framework for explaining purchase behavior and intent.

Next to this, compared with other models, the S-O-R model is a more appropriate theoretical foundation to guide this research because it is in direct line with the aims of the research. Additionally, the Stimulus-Organism-Response (SOR) theory has been widely studied in the context of retail and e-commerce to understand the relationship between correlating variables affecting customers' online shopping behavior. The current work uses the SOR model as a foundation framework to build a consumer behavior model specially designed for young consumers. The Response (R) attribute in the SOR model is often considered a crucial determinant of the young user's intention, particularly regarding specific activities such as service usage (Song et al, 2022; Rinot Levavi et al, 2023) in Furthermore, users' perceptions of the services, indicating their favorable or unfavorable sentiments towards new technology, align with the Organism (O) factor in the theoretical framework proposed by Rinot Levavi et al (2023). Therefore, attitudes are often considered the Organism (O) component in the SOR model, as proposed by Rinot Levavi and colleagues in 2023. The Stimulus (S) factor relates to external sources of influence on young users, specifically the quality of the experience provided by the service. Therefore, the current study has successfully identified "Stimulus" (S) as the fundamental characteristic of young users' experience with online Virtual Try-On shopping services. The goal is to explore the logic influencing user behavior more comprehensively. The research also indicates that users' experience with a service attribute directly affects their attitudes and behavioral intentions. At the same time, attitude is the main factor determining users' intention to use the service. (Mala Kalaiarasan et al., 2024)

3. Hypothesis Development

In the context of rapid digital advancement and the growing prevalence of online shopping, social interaction plays a crucial role in building consumer trust and a sense of security. Beyond mere convenience, the ability to share experiences, exchange opinions, and receive feedback from peers helps reinforce confidence in purchase decisions (Kang et al., 2021; Hennig-Thurau et al., 2010). For younger consumers - those accustomed to social media and frequent personal sharing - these social elements are even more significant. Feedback from friends or online communities not only enhances trust in products but also makes the shopping experience more engaging and emotionally resonant. Prior studies also highlight that features enabling users to share, discuss, or review products increase emotional attachment to the platform, promoting user satisfaction and loyalty (Cheng & Fang, 2020). In the specific case of virtual try-on services, the ability to share try-on images or receive input from others fosters a sense of connection and social validation, allowing users - especially younger ones - to make more personalized and confident choices. Based on these insights, the study proposes the following hypothesis:

> **H1a:** Social interaction positively affects the experience elements of online virtual shopping services, thereby positively affecting user attitudes.

Emotional value is a crucial factor shaping consumer attitudes, as positive emotions during shopping experiences enhance satisfaction, excitement, and joy (Verhagen et al., 2011). For younger consumers, who seek novel and engaging experiences, shopping is not just about purchasing products but about enjoying the process itself. Cheng and Fang (2020) highlight that emotionally positive experiences not only boost satisfaction but also build trust in the services consumers use. In the context of virtual try-on services, the excitement and fulfillment users experience strengthen their attitudes toward the platform and turn shopping into a more memorable journey. Additionally, by offering emotionally rich interactions, virtual try-on technologies deepen users' connection to products and improve perceptions of safety and reliability. As Pine and Gilmore (1999) suggest, emotional experiences create a competitive advantage by fostering loyalty and encouraging word-of-mouth promotion. Based on these insights, this study proposes the following hypothesis:

> **H1b:** Emotional value positively affects the experience elements of online virtual shopping services, thereby positively affecting user attitudes

Convenience is a key factor driving consumers toward online shopping, offering easy access to products anytime, anywhere, and making comparisons simple (Pappas et al., 2014). For younger consumers managing busy lives, the appeal of efficient, streamlined shopping experiences is even stronger. Lin and Lo (2020) emphasized that when online services prioritize convenience, they not only meet expectations but also enhance positive attitudes, positioning themselves as effective, time-saving solutions. In the case of virtual try-on services, convenience is particularly critical, allowing users to remotely visualize products without the need for physical travel, thereby speeding up and simplifying decision-making. This ease of access not only reduces effort but also builds a stronger sense of security, as consumers can explore options freely and thoroughly. As Yang and Liu (2017) note, convenience in e-commerce is more than a functional advantage - it is a key driver of trust, satisfaction, and loyalty. Based on these insights, this study proposes the following hypothesis:

> **H1c:** Convenience positively affects the experience elements of online virtual shopping services, thereby positively affecting user attitudes

Perceived value, especially regarding price, plays a crucial role in shaping consumer attitudes, as highlighted by Kim et al. (2018). When consumers feel that the benefits of a product meet or exceed the cost, they develop more favorable views toward the product, extending beyond its functional features to include emotional satisfaction during the transaction process. In the context of virtual try-on services, price value becomes even more critical. By allowing users to assess products without financial risk, virtual try-on helps ease concerns about online shopping and fosters greater confidence in purchasing decisions. Chen and Dubinsky (2003) further note that a sense of price safety significantly reduces consumer anxiety, helping prevent post-purchase regret. Zeithaml (1988) also emphasizes that perceived value strongly influences buying behavior and loyalty, with positive value perceptions encouraging consumers to share their experiences and strengthen trust within online communities. Based on these insights, the study proposes the following hypothesis:

> **H1d:** Price value positively affects the experience factors of online virtual shopping services, thereby positively affecting user attitudes.

The ability to acquire visual information is crucial in helping consumers realistically evaluate products before purchase. Flavián et al. (2019) highlight that virtual trial technologies, by allowing users to visualize products in real-world contexts, strengthen trust and improve decision-making. Beyond simple observation, the way products are presented and the overall virtual experience also matter. Studies by Gao and Zang (2016) and Huang and Liao (2015) show that features like high-resolution images, 3D simulations, and interactive elements reduce perceived risk, making consumers more confident in assessing product quality. As e-commerce grows, rich visual experiences not only boost satisfaction but also shape shopping behaviors by bridging the gap between online and offline experiences. By offering comprehensive visual insights, virtual try-on services help consumers make more informed and confident decisions. Based on these insights, the study proposes the following hypothesis:

> **H1e:** Visual information acquisition positively affects the experience elements of online virtual shopping services, thereby positively affecting user attitudes.

Positive experiential factors are key to shaping consumer attitudes in e-commerce, as they not only enhance satisfaction but also foster trust - a vital element for building lasting relationships (Hajli, 2015). Features like user-friendly interfaces, realistic visuals, and personalized support create a sense of comfort and reliability that improves the overall service experience. In virtual try-on services, immersive elements such as realistic product images and advanced simulations help consumers better visualize products and reduce uncertainty. Kim and Lennon (2008) highlight that such features increase security and ease concerns about online shopping decisions, leading to more favorable attitudes. Moreover, Lin et al. (2012) emphasize that a seamless and satisfying experience encourages repeat usage and loyalty, which is crucial in a competitive digital environment. A positive virtual trial experience not only boosts attachment to the platform but also strengthens purchase intentions. Based on these insights, the study proposes the following hypothesis:

H2: The positive experience elements of online virtual shopping services positively affect user attitudes.

According to Ajzen's (1991) theory of planned behavior, an individual's attitude plays a central role in shaping their intention to engage in a behavior. A positive attitude strengthens trust and motivation, increasing the likelihood of action. Mala Kalaiarasan et al. (2024) further note that positive attitudes not only drive initial use but also foster long-term loyalty to services. In virtual try-on services, positive attitudes help mitigate perceived risks associated with not physically experiencing products. Research by Nguyen et al. (2022) shows that consumers with favorable attitudes are more likely to continue using and recommending such services. Additionally, Pappas et al. (2014) emphasize that positive attitudes make consumers more forgiving of minor flaws, focusing instead on the overall value. This is critical in a competitive online environment where loyalty can strengthen market position. Based on these insights, the study proposes the following hypothesis:

H3: Users' attitude towards online virtual shopping services positively affects usage intent.

Positive experiences related to convenience, value, and information accessibility play a crucial role in shaping consumers' intention to continue using a service (Ben-Sasson et al., 2020; Besoain et al., 2022). When services effectively meet consumer needs and offer high convenience, they foster trust, satisfaction, and loyalty, which is critical in the highly competitive e-commerce environment. For virtual try-on services, positive experiences not only enhance satisfaction but also provide a sense of security by allowing consumers to "try" products remotely. Verhagen et al. (2011) emphasize that such experiences strengthen consumer-brand relationships and encourage positive word-of-mouth. Moreover, Yang and Liu (2017) highlight that positive experiences not only drive loyalty but also differentiate services, boosting purchase intentions and reducing brand switching. Especially for emerging technologies like virtual try-ons, good experiences help overcome psychological barriers and build long-term usage habits. Based on these insights, the study proposes the following hypothesis:

H4: The positive experience elements of online virtual shopping services positively affect the user's intention to use.

The theoretical hypothesis model for the literature discussion mentioned above is illustrated in Figure 1.

Figure 1. Theoretical hypothesis model.

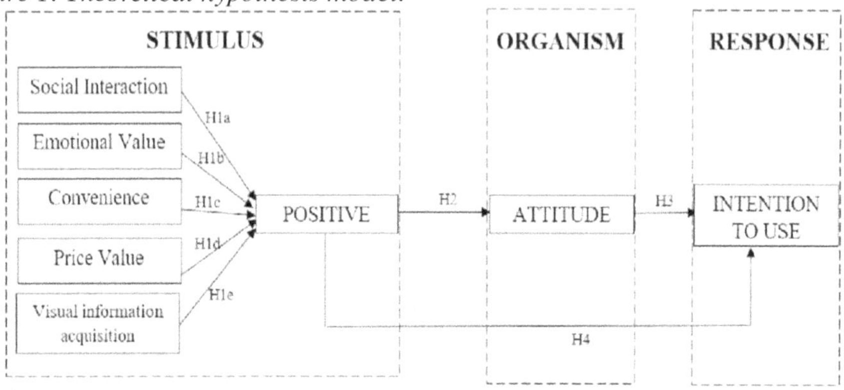

III. METHODOLOGY

1. Participants and Data Collections

The research team conducted a survey targeting young individuals aged 15 to 30, as this demographic is considered to have high exposure to and familiarity with technology, making them a key potential user group for virtual assembly technology in Vietnam. Due to limitations in time and resources, we employed a convenience sampling method - selecting participants who were readily accessible and willing to take part in the survey, such as university students, young professionals, or active social media users - to efficiently collect meaningful preliminary data. By narrowing the age range, we enhanced the consistency and representativeness of the sample in line with the study's objectives. Screening questions were placed at the beginning of the online questionnaire to ensure that only qualified respondents were included. The survey was distributed online, accompanied by small incentives such as phone credit or reward points to encourage participation and increase response rates. After data collection, we applied exploratory factor analysis (EFA) to identify and group the observed variables – initially developed through pilot questions - into key components representing various dimensions of the user experience scale. Measurement scales for user attitudes and behavioral intentions were developed based on existing literature and are summarized in Table 1 below.

Table 1. Summary of scale questionnaires

	ID	Observed Variable
Positive Elements		
	SI1	No worries about salespeople's opinions
	SI2	The trial effect of users can be seen on social media.
	SI3	No need for excessive offline interactions with other unfamiliar users (such as queuing or scrutiny)
	EV1	The process of using it is relaxed and free.
	EV2	The try-on process provides a novel. experience
	EV3	The try-on process is enjoyable.
	C1	No need to visit physical stores to try on
	C2	Can be used at any time and location
	C3	Can quickly and extensively choose to try on from different brands and styles
	C4	Convenient for comparing the effects of multiple pairs
	C5	Not limited by product inventory
	C6	No hygiene issues
	PV1	Can avoid wasting money on unnecessary purchases
	PV2	The platform allows for free try-ons.
	PV3	No need to purchase additional AR devices
	VIA1	Can observe the characteristics of shoes from all angles and perspectives
	VIA2	Good visual simulation in AR shoe try-on
	VIA3	Can get a general understanding of the basic information about the shoes
Attitude-Intention Elements Scale		
Latent Variable	ID	Observed Variable
Attitude	AT1	You are very interested in virtual shoe try-on services.
	AT2	You believe in using a virtual try-on service.
	AT3	You would consider virtual shoe try-on services as one of the Options for selecting in the future.
Intention to use	ITU1	You plan to use virtual try-on services in the near future.
	ITU2	You are willing to use virtual try-on services.
	ITU3	You would recommend others use virtual try-on services.

In total, we received 396 responses, and after filtering all answer sheets to meet the above requirements, 139 responses from 139 participants were used for further analysis. The main characteristics of the sample are presented in Table 2.

Table 2. Sample characteristics

Characteristics	Frequency (N = 396)	Percent (100%)
Gender		
Female	290	73.2
Male	106	28.6
Occupation		
Student (≤ 18 year old)	43	10.9
Student (≥ 18 year old)	334	84.3
Worker	19	4.8
Educational Background		
Junior High School	6	1.5
High School	281	71
Bachelor's Degree	102	25.8
Postgraduate	7	1.8
Virtual try-on technology experience		
Used to	139	35.1
No experience yet	257	64.9

2. Measurement

The formal assessment is segmented into four sections: The initial section is the "Consent Form for Participation in Research," which offers a comprehensive elucidation of the scope and objectives of this study to the participants. The second section comprises screening questions. Presented here is comprehensive information on the virtual fitting service, and users are informed that the questionnaire will immediately close, therefore prohibiting further participation. Such methodology guarantees the genuineness and soundness of the questionnaire findings. The third section gathers fundamental data from the participants, while the fourth section encompasses the assessment of the valid question scale. The survey instrument comprises a detailed account of the online virtual shoe fitting service, which was derived from a thorough examination of existing literature and user research. Additionally, it incorporates a well-recognized scale designed to evaluate user attitudes and intents. The quantitative information of the questionnaire scale is displayed in Table 3. The present study used a seven-point Likert scale to facilitate users in their assessment procedure, with a rating of "1" representing "totally disagree" and a rating of "7" representing "totally agree".

IV. RESULT

1. Descriptive Statistics, Reliability and Discriminant Validity

Table 3 displays the reliability characteristics of the scales in the model, including Cronbach's Alpha, Composite Reliability (C.R.), Average Variance Extracted (AVE), Mean Value, Factor Loading, and Standard Deviation (SD). To assess the consistency of the variables, we performed a factor analysis and reliability testing using SmartPLS 3.0. (Ringle, Sven & Jan-Michael, 2015). "Following the first phase of the factor analysis procedure, all items with factor loading coefficients below 0.7 were eliminated. (Hair, Ringle, & Marko 2011). A combination reliability (CR) and Cronbach's Alpha value above 0.7 is required for reliability testing to establish the high dependability of the measures (Bagozzi, 2011; Fornell & Larker, 1981). Furthermore, convergent validity is attained when the average variance extracted (AVE) of all constructs exceeds 0.50 (Chin, 1998). Table 3 presents the outcomes of the descriptive statistics and the metrics of reliability. Confirmatory Factor Analysis (CFA) was performed on the data in this study to further investigate the distinction between the factors and the linkages among the observed variables within each factor. The findings are displayed in Table 3. Each factor exhibits standardized loadings of the observed variables that exceed 0.5. Both the average variance extracted (AVE) and composite reliability (CR) for each component are over 0.5, suggesting a robust relationship between the factors and their observed variables, as well as a high level of convergent validity among the observed variables."

Table 3. Descriptive statistics and factor analysis results

Construct	Items	Mean	SD	Factor Loading	AVE	C.R.	Cronbach's Alpha
Social Interaction	SI1	4,78	1,696	0,708	0,562	0,794	0,865
	SI2	4,78	1,696	0,770			
	SI3	4,97	1,671	0,770			
Emotional Value	EV1	4,91	1,653	0,787	0,685	0,867	0,912
	EV2	5,11	1,676	0,845			
	EV3	4,94	1,661	0,850			

continued on following page

Table 3. Continued

Construct	Items	Mean	SD	Factor Loading	AVE	C.R.	Cronbach's Alpha
Convenience	C1	4,99	1,741	0,848	0,724	0,940	0,950
	C2	5,02	1,669	0,859			
	C3	5,15	1,704	0,889			
	C4	4,95	1,647	0,864			
	C5	4,77	1,632	0,800			
	C6	4,95	1,681	0,844			
Price Value	PV1	4,73	1,636	0,838	0,719	0,885	0,923
	PV2	4,91	1,663	0,860			
	PV3	4,90	1,632	0,846			
Visual Information Acquisition	VIA1	4,84	1,627	0,855	0,706	0,878	0,931
	VIA2	4,88	1,585	0,893			
	VIA3	4,88	1,571	0,827			
Attitude	A1	4,59	1,536	0,789	0,718	0,884	0,899
	A2	4,90	1,654	0,866			
	A3	5,07	1,674	0,884			
Intention To Use	I1	4,69	1,626	0,893	0,683	0,866	0,920
	I2	4,71	1,529	0,804			
	I3	4,85	1,625	0,836			

The Fornell-Larcker Criterion and the Heterotrait - Monotrait ratio (HTMT) instruments were employed to evaluate the discriminant validity of the measurements (Henseler, Ringle, & Sarstedt, 2015). The bold numbers shaded along the diagonal of the table represent the square root of the Average Variance Extracted (AVE) for each factor. The magnitude of the square root of the AVE for each detected structure is significantly higher than the correlations between other structures. This shows that the young user intention scale established in this study meets all the necessary criteria. The results of the HTMT analysis in Table 4 indicate that the study did not meet the criteria for discriminant validity. The HTMT of correlations between structural features ranged from 0.668 to 0.893, which is below the criterion of 0.9.

Table 4. Correlations between research constructs

	Social	Emotional	Convenience	Price	Visual	Attitude	Intention
Social	1.000						
Emotional	0.265	1.000					
Convenience	0.243	0.331	1.000				
Price	0.258	0.275	0.318	1.000			
Visual	0.253	0.335	0.354	0.309	1.000		
Attitude	0.294	0.332	0.294	0.328	0.248	1.000	
Intention	0.245	0.353	0.315	0.305	0.386	0.400	1.000

Note: Diagonal elements (in bold) are the square root of the average variance extracted

2. Hypothesized Model Testing

We 'employed Smart PLS 3.0 (Ringle et al., 2015) to evaluate the structural model by analyzing the significance of the estimated path coefficients and the R-squared values (Hair et al., 2011). Following the recommendations of Hair et al. (2021), we utilized 10,000 bootstrap samples to ensure the stability of the estimated path coefficients. The result of the PLS-SEM analysis is summarized in Table 5.

Table 5. The PLS-SEM results

Path		Beta	T - Value	Result
Main Path				
H1a	Social Interaction → Attitude	0.066	1.403	Not Supported
H1b	Emotional Value → Attitude	0.314	5.175	Supported
H1c	Convenience → Attitude	0.297	4.087	Supported
H1d	Price Value → Attitude	0.096	1.495	Not Supported
H1e	Visual Information Acquisition → Attitude	0.043	3.938	Supported
H2	Attitude → Intention To Use	0.467	5.683	Supported
H3a	Social Interaction → Intention To Use	0.011	0.225	Not Supported
H3b	Emotional Value → Intention To Use	0.052	0.726	Not Supported
H3c	Convenience → Intention To Use	0.128	1.676	Not Supported
H3d	Price Value → Intention To Use	0.097	1.528	Not Supported
H3e	Visual Information Acquisition → Intention To Use	0.174	2.810	Supported
Specific Indirect Effects				
Social Interaction → Attitude → Intention To Use		0.042	3.056	Not Significant

continued on following page

Table 5. Continued

Path	Beta	T - Value	Result
Emotional Value → Attitude → Intention To Use	0.198	3.971	Significant
Convenience → Attitude → Intention To Use	0.267	1.460	Significant
Price Value → Attitude → Intention To Use	0.142	1.400	Not Significant
Visual Information Acquisition → Attitude → Intention To Use	0.269	3.203	Significant

Note: p-value < 0.001; **: p-value <0.01; *: p-value <0.05; ns: non-significant

The results showed a significant variation in the extent to which factors such as social interaction, emotional value, convenience, price value, and visual receptivity influenced to attitudes and intentions of use.

That is, the hypotheses H1a (Social Interaction → Attitude) and H1d (Value of Price → Attitude) were rejected (βH1a=0.066, pH1a>0.001; βH1d=0.096, pH1d>0.001), indicating that social interaction and price value do not have significant impact on user attitudes. This is the result of either the social relationship when simply using the product has little value or that the price is not a strong influence in the issue at hand. Comparably, the H3a (Social Interaction → Intention to Use) hypotheses (βH3a=0.011), H3b (Emotional Value → Intent to Use) (βH3b=0.052), H3c (Convenience → Intent to Use) (βH3c=0.182), and H3d (Value of Price → Intent to Use) (βH3d=0.097) were also not supported (p>0.001). This mean that those variables do not directly and visibly affect the intention of the users to use.

On the other hand, the H1b (Emotional Value → Attitude) (βH1b=0.314), H1c (Convenience → Attitude) (βH1c=0.297), and H1e (Visual Information Acquisition → Attitude) (βH1e=0.043) hypotheses are all supported (p<0.001), demonstrating that emotional value, convenience, and visual information receptivity have a significant positive impact on the attitudes of user. Emotional values, such as comfort or a positive experience when using a product, play an important role in creating a product, play an important role in creating attitudes in users. Convenience, including ease and efficiency when using the product, is also an important factor in shaping user attitudes. In addition, the ability to provide visual information, such as clear, vivid images, has helped users have a better attitude towards the product.

Generally, the H2 hypothesis (Attitude → Intention to Use) (βH2=0.467) found positive and supported (p<0.001), suggesting that a user's positive attitude directly influences their intention to use the product/service. This is an important relationship in the model, providing that changing the user's attitude can lead to a change in usage intent. Another notable finding is that the hypothesis H3e (Visual Absorption → Intention to Use) (βH3e=0.174 is also supported (p<0.001). This suggests that the ability to provide visual information not only influences attitudes but also directly influences user's intention to use, especially when they can access information easily and effectively. Furthermore, the indirect effects show that emotional value, convenience, and visual perception all have significant indirect effects on the intention to use through attitude. These factors help to reinforce users' intention to use a product by creating a positive attitude before they decide to use the product/service. In contrast, factors such as social interaction and price value do not have significant indirect effects, suggesting that they do not play a mediating role in influencing intention to use.

Figure 2. The results of PLS-SEM

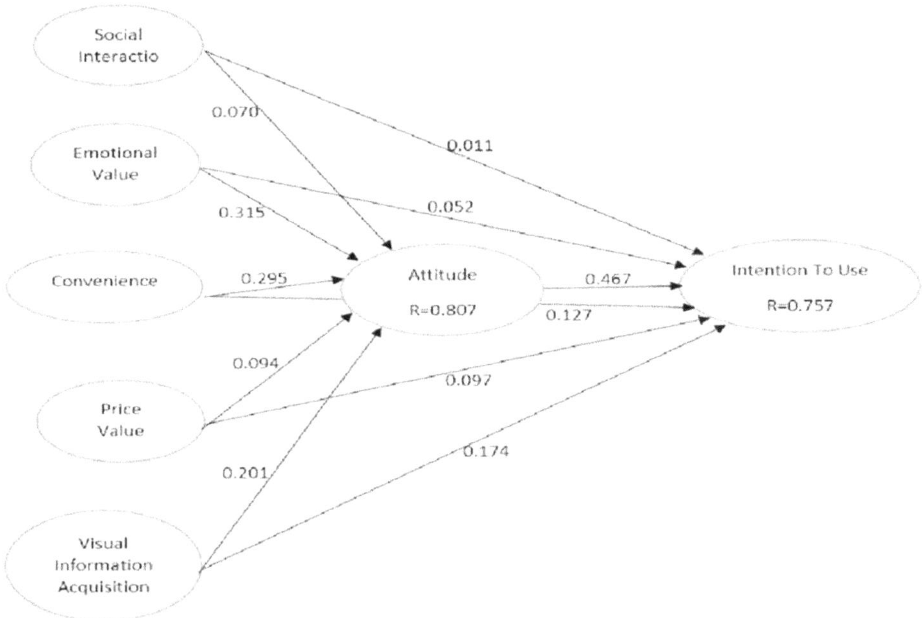

Combined, the study provides information about the connection between attitudes and intended use. To increase the number of users, companies should primarily focus on adding emotional value, improving efficiency, and providing effective visual information. These factors will have positive effect on the user experience, which will in turn increase the desire to utilize the product or service. Additionally, the results demonstrate that factors like social and price value are not significant in regards to creating attitudes pr desire to utilize the product, so these factors need to be reconsidered regarding marketing and product development.

V. RESEARCH CONTRIBUTIONS

1. Theoretical Contributions

Firstly, with the SOR theoretical framework applied in our study, we delve deeper into analyzing human psychology in response to the positive stimuli brought by virtual reality technology. Those stimuli are reflected in the psychology and behavior of consumers, thereby influencing their intention to use this technology in shopping. Furthermore, it is observed that in Vietnam, the study of VTO technology is not merely an examination of the technology product itself and its support of customer usage intention, but also their attitudes towards enhancing purchase intentions and shopping experiences.

Secondly, we provide theoretical foundations for Augmented reality (AR) technology and its impact on consumer attitudes, leading to the intention to use it when shopping. The results of our research validate and reinforce the observation that virtual fitting rooms are a promising and dynamic field, making their use in shopping particularly reasonable in Vietnam. Additionally, in the field of e-commerce, AR is considered a supportive tool and application aimed at enhancing this experience, thereby influencing consumer behavior (Mirela-Catrinel Voicu et al., 2023). AR will be the key to attracting and engaging customers, especially new retail and online shopping customers.

Thirdly, we build theories on the impact of virtual reality technology on young consumers based on previous research models such as UTAUT and TAM (Zhicheng Wang et al., 2024), in addition to incorporating the SOR theoretical framework as the chosen theoretical framework to develop and validate the research model. Our research findings demonstrate that the positive factors of virtual reality technology will influence and enhance consumers' intention to use it in shopping experiences. Especially, by applying six dimensions for testing, we have drawn results with the factors of Emotional Value, Convenience, and Visual Information Acquisition influencing consumers' intention to use. In contrast, the remaining factors, including Social Interaction and Price Value have been rejected and excluded.

Finally, previous studies have mainly focused on data from developed countries; for developing economies and emerging markets like Vietnam, user attitudes and purchase intentions related to Virtual Try-On must be expanded and researched further. Especially, through the perception of Virtual Try-On technology in Vietnam, our research narrows the gap for potential customer groups, especially young consumers aged 15-30. The study identifies the components of user experience. It clarifies the relationship between each factor affecting the attitudes and intentions of young consumers in using Virtual Reality technology services in their shopping experience. Furthermore, the research clarifies the psychological logic of young consumers when using this service for shopping. Therefore, our research contributes to developing a theory in this field in Vietnam.

2. Managerial Implications

The study provides insights into the factors influencing attitudes and intention to use Virtual Try-On technology in shopping. Factors such as Emotional Value, Convenience, and Visual Information Acquisition have a significant impact on consumers' attitudes toward Virtual Try-On, therefore VTO encourages managers to focus on providing an engaging, convenient, and emotionally rich shopping experience. Emotional values show that when technology brings joy, satisfaction, or positive emotions, it enhances the consumer experience with a positive attitude. This shows that retailers need to develop highly interactive and engaging Virtual Try-On experiences to enhance their connection with the brand. Convenience also significantly impacts user attitudes, emphasizing the importance of designing a user-friendly and convenient VTO interface. Managers need to ensure that the technology runs smoothly and is accessible with mobile phones, tablets, laptops, etc. Minimizing the technical barrier to accessing new technology and maximizing its positive perception will deliver a user-friendly product.

Visual Information Acquisition also contributes to consumers' attitudes toward VTO. Consumers are used to seeing images of the product and expect those images to be realistic and representative of what they will receive. This encourages companies to create VTO with excellent image quality and interactive visualizations so that consumers can conduct the trial and be responsive to the decision-making process. The research also indicates consumer attitudes significantly impact their intention to use VTO technology. This shows that building a positive attitude by providing Emotional Value and Convenience is very important. Managers should focus on improving the quality of the VTO experience to encourage long-term use of this technology. Managers should prioritize improving visual data collection and optimizing emotional interactions to enhance user satisfaction. By creating VTO systems with sharp 3D images, real-time interactions, and customization options, they can better integrate technology into the shopping experience, leading to stronger customer loyalty and increased purchase intent.

Virtual Try-On technology is emerging as part of the premium and exclusive product segment, simultaneously creating significant consumer value. In addition to its outstanding advantages in terms of convenience and user experience, VTO also plays an important role in promoting sustainable development. Designed as an environmentally friendly alternative to physical products, VTO helps reduce material resource consumption, minimize water and energy usage, and significantly cut down on waste generated throughout the product life cycle. VTO helps reduce carbon emissions by limiting the need for consumers to travel to physical stores and minimizing product returns, thereby alleviating pressure on transportation and logistics systems. For busy consumers and in response to the growing trend of online shopping, VTO plays a significant role in reducing product return rates-one of the primary environmental pressures in modern e-commerce. Moreover, this technology enables businesses to optimize production processes by allowing more accurate forecasting of consumer demand, thus reducing overproduction and waste of resources. VTO also paves the way for the development of on-demand production models, helping to save raw materials and minimize unnecessary inventory. Furthermore, the application of VTO combined with transparent product information contributes to raising consumer awareness, encouraging the selection of environmentally friendly products. The growing popularity of VTO drives businesses to invest in green technologies, gradually replacing traditional and resource-intensive marketing methods. Although the in-store try-on experience is still highly valued for its realism and interactivity, VTO offers clear sustainable advantages. The positive contributions of VTO should be recognized and warrant further research to comprehensively evaluate its potential in supporting sustainable development.

VI. CONCLUSION AND FUTURE RECOMMENDATION

This study initially targeted "Young Customer" and developed a user experience evaluation scale for online virtual trial shopping services, along with a consumer intention model and constructive activity and design recommendation (Wang & Jiang et al., 2024), but there are still some limitations. Firstly, the research behavior model primarily focuses on attributes in the stimulus phase without considering social factors. Therefore, combining supplementary findings using established behavioral models rather than theoretical ones is necessary. Secondly, the scale for evaluating consumer experience heavily relies on surveys, which can lead to subjectivity. Although there have been many efforts to mitigate this issue, the methodology still needs to be improved to reduce discrepancies. Thirdly, Virtual Reality technology is relatively advanced, but its application in Vietnam is still in its infancy. This opens up opportunities for further research on other services and social development. Fourthly, this study primarily collects user evaluations through interviews. Although the user survey scale in this study meets the requirements for conducting related research, future studies could benefit from expanding the sample size of interviews and applying long-term observational survey methods to enhance the generalizability of the results (Wang & Jiang et al., 2024). Fifthly, our study does not include any impacts on attitudes toward brands, such as interactivity and vividness affecting immersion and brand loyalty.

Future research could examine how the trial experience of AR applications affects customer's purchasing decisions. In addition, as the survey participants have different educational backgrounds, ranging from middle school to post graduates degrees, future studies should consider the differences in perceptions, awareness and experience among these groups. Studies can also explore the integration of emerging technologies like AI, Blockchain into VTO systems to assess their impact on user experience, business performance and sustainability. Researchers can analyze the challenges and opportunities brought by this integration, opening new directions for the retail industry in Vietnam. In particular, studies in the future should compare VTO experiences between different age groups (e.g., 15-20 vs. 21-30, etc) to identify variations in technology adoption and user behavior. Additionally, researchers could explore how personalized AI-driven VTO systems influence consumer behavior, focusing on aspects such as purchase intention, emotional engagement and trust. By addressing these areas, future research can provide deeper insights into consumer psychology and further support the sustainable development of Virtual Try-On technology.

This study can suggest helping consumers choose the right product through the application of Virtual Reality technology "Virtual Try-On". At the same time, it also helps businesses understand customer behavior, especially young customers. From there, this research contributes to environmental protection and promotes a sustainable economy. The study focuses on a potential customer group of young, knowledgeable individuals who frequently engage with social media and new technologies. According to the SOR theoretical framework, an individual will form a conscious or unconscious psychological response process triggered by external environmental stimuli, which then drives them to perform those responses. In an online environment, users often need to continuously interact with the system. Young customers demonstrate a difference in their social interaction requirements in services compared to traditional norms. They tend to interact with others in a solitary and proactive manner rather than passively engaging in social connections (Wang & Jiang et al., 2024). User attitudes are the main factor related to the intention to use the service and play an important mediating role in the user's behavioral intention to use. To optimize the "Virtual Try-On" experience and improve customer satisfaction, businesses should invest in intuitive interface design, immersive audio, and personalization to create a good shopping experience and minimize costs during use. They should frequently launch new services and provide exciting experiences, offering maximum convenience to consumers. Businesses should invest in image quality, improve high-tech interfaces, create short videos detailing product introductions, and help customers better visualize the products. At the same time, businesses should also focus on promotion by regularly interacting with customers, organizing events, and promotional programs to enhance the experience and encourage customers to share. They can use analytical tools to track customer data and feedback to evaluate the effectiveness of their marketing strategies and regularly test different versions of their website, advertisements, and marketing campaigns to find out which version performs best. Additionally, businesses should develop "Virtual Try-On" experiences that align with their brand identity and values, tracking metrics such as repurchase rates, customer satisfaction, ... to assess the impact of the Virtual Try-On experience. In the process of market research, it is advisable to combine qualitative methods (through surveys, interviews and observations to collect more comprehensive data), expand the sample size, and utilize various research methods.

The evolution of Virtual Try-On technology will be profoundly shaped by convergence of emerging digital innovations, such as AI, AR, Big Data and Blockchain. AI will play a pivotal role in elevating personalization, leveraging advanced behavioral analytics and predicting consumer trends. AR will further deepen user immersion by enabling hyper-realistic virtual fitting, thus enhancing both the visual appeal and engagement of shopping experience. Big Data analytics will empower companies to better understand customer preferences and optimize products. Block chain can ensure transparency and security in transactions while authenticating product origins. One of the prominent trends is the development of shopping spaces in the metaverse, where users can create 3D avatars and try on products in a virtual world. This movement reflects a broader paradigm shift toward fully digital ecosystems, enabling brands and retailers to craft immersive, boundary less consumer's experience beyond the confines of physical stores. The businesses can consider developing a separate app that seamlessly integrates these features, avoiding the feeling of redundancy or repetitive actions for consumers. The government and industry associations can create favorable policies and standards for VTO technology to thrive, ensuring customer data privacy and encouraging sustainable practices.

REFERENCES

Ajzen, I. (1991). The theory of planned behavior. *Organizational Behavior and Human Decision Processes*, *50*(2), 179–211. DOI: 10.1016/0749-5978(91)90020-T

Bagozzi, R. P. (2011). Measurement and meaning in information systems and organizational research: Methodological and philosophical foundations. *Management Information Systems Quarterly*, *35*(2), 261–292. DOI: 10.2307/23044044

Ben-Sasson, A., Ben-Sasson, E., Jacobs, K., & Malinovitch, R. (2020). The relationship between users' technology approaches and experiences in a child development mobile application. *Health and Technology*, *10*(5), 1079–1094. DOI: 10.1007/s12553-020-00457-y

Besoain, F., González-Ortega, J., & Gallardo, I. (2022). An evaluation of the effects of a virtual museum on users' attitudes towards cultural heritage. *Applied Sciences (Basel, Switzerland)*, *12*(14), 7076. DOI: 10.3390/app12031341

Bonetti, F., Warnaby, G., & Quinn, L. (2018). *Augmented reality and virtual reality: Empowering human, place and business*. Springer.

Carmigniani, J., & Furht, B. (2011). *Handbook of augmented reality*. Springer.

Challoumis, C. (2024, October). *Building a sustainable economy – How AI can optimize resource allocation. XVI International Scientific Conference*, 190–224.

Chen, J., Yu, B., Chen, B., & Liu, Z. (2023). *Lenient vs.* stringent returns policies in the presence of fraudulent returns: The role of customers' fairness perceptions. *Omega*, *117*, 102843. DOI: 10.1016/j.omega.2023.102843

Chen, Z., & Dubinsky, A. J. (2003). A conceptual model of perceived customer value in e-commerce: A preliminary investigation. *Psychology and Marketing*, *20*(4), 323–347. DOI: 10.1002/mar.10076

Content Editor. (2024, January 9). *The truth about cardboard in e-commerce*. Ernest Packaging.

Corvellec, H., Stowell, A. F., & Johansson, N. (2021b). Critiques of the circular economy. *Journal of Industrial Ecology*, *26*(2), 421–432. DOI: 10.1111/jiec.13187

Doerner, R., Broll, W., Jung, B., Grimm, P., Göbel, M., & Kruse, R. (2022). *Introduction to virtual and augmented reality*. Springer. DOI: 10.1007/978-3-030-79062-2_1

Ellen MacArthur Foundation. (2020). *Financing the circular economy: Capturing the opportunity*.

Flavián, C., Ibáñez-Sánchez, S., & Orús, C. (2019). The impact of virtual, augmented and mixed reality technologies on the customer experience. *Journal of Business Research*, *100*, 547–560. DOI: 10.1016/j.jbusres.2018.10.050

Garaus, M., Wagner, U., & Kummer, C. (2015). Cognitive fit, retail shopper confusion, and shopping value: Empirical investigation. *Journal of Business Research*, *68*(5), 1003–1011. DOI: 10.1016/j.jbusres.2014.10.002

Geissdoerfer, M., Savaget, P., Bocken, N. M. P., & Hultink, E. J. (2017). The circular economy: A new sustainability paradigm? *Journal of Cleaner Production*, *143*, 757–768. DOI: 10.1016/j.jclepro.2016.12.048

Ghalwash, S. K., & El-Ansary, A. I. (2021). The rise of sustainable consumerism. *Evidence from the Egyptian Generation Z. Sustainable Development*, *29*(5), 895–907.

Hair, J. F., Ringle, C. M., & Sarstedt, M. (2011). PLS-SEM: Indeed a silver bullet. *Journal of Marketing Theory and Practice*, *19*(2), 139–151. DOI: 10.2753/MTP1069-6679190202

Hennig-Thurau, T., Gwinner, K. P., Walsh, G., & Gremler, D. D. (2010). Electronic word-of-mouth via consumer-opinion platforms: What motivates consumers to articulate themselves on the Internet? *Journal of Interactive Marketing*, *18*(1), 38–52. DOI: 10.1002/dir.10073

Huang, T., Tsiotsou, R. H., & Liu, B. S. (2023). Delineating the role of mood maintenance in augmenting reality (AR) service experiences: An application in tourism. *Technological Forecasting and Social Change*, *189*, 122385. DOI: 10.1016/j.techfore.2023.122385

Huang, T. L., & Liao, S. (2015). A model of acceptance of augmented-reality interactive technology: The moderating role of cognitive innovativeness. *Electronic Commerce Research*, *15*(2), 269–295. DOI: 10.1007/s10660-014-9163-2

Ju, C., Liu, H., Xu, A., & Zhang, J. (2023). Green logistics of fossil fuels and e-commerce: Implications for sustainable economic development. *Resources Policy*, *85*, 103991. DOI: 10.1016/j.resourpol.2023.103991

Kang, J. Y. M., Tang, L., & Fiore, A. M. (2021). Enhancing consumer–brand relationships on restaurant social media sites: The role of consumer engagement behaviors. *International Journal of Hospitality Management*, *94*, 102829.

Kim, J., Kim, M., Park, M., & Yoo, J. (2023). Immersive interactive technologies and virtual shopping experiences: Differences in consumer perceptions between augmented reality (AR) and virtual reality (VR). *Telematics and Informatics*, *77*, 101936. DOI: 10.1016/j.tele.2022.101936

Kim, J., & Lennon, S. J. (2008). The effects of visual and verbal information on attitudes and purchase intentions in Internet shopping. *Psychology and Marketing*, *25*(2), 146–178. DOI: 10.1002/mar.20204

Kim, M. J., Lee, C. K., & Jung, T. (2018). Exploring consumer behavior in virtual reality tourism using an extended stimulus-organism-response model. *Journal of Travel Research*, *57*(7), 887–901.

L'Oréal. (2023, June 1). [*'Oréal's venture capital fund, invests in biotech company, "debut" to collaborate on active ingredients*. L'Oréal.]. *Bold*, •••, L.

Lavoye, V., Mero, J., & Tarkiainen, A. (2021). *Consumer behavior with augmented reality in retail: a review and research agenda.*

Lazarevic, D., & Valve, H. (2017). Narrating expectations for the circular economy: Towards a common and contested European transition. *Energy Research & Social Science*, *31*, 60–69. DOI: 10.1016/j.erss.2017.05.006

Lin, C., Wu, Y., & Tran, T. P. (2012). Internet consumer adoption of virtual stores: The roles of technology readiness and social influence. *Journal of Business Research*, *65*(9), 1300–1306.

Lin, J., & Lo, L. (2020). Predicting consumers' intentions to continue using online shopping in China in the post-COVID-19 era. *Frontiers in Psychology*, *11*, 584718.

Liu, X., Burns, A. C., & Hou, Y. (2013). Comparing online and in-store shopping behavior towards luxury goods: A SOR model. *Journal of Retailing and Consumer Services*, *20*(1), 44–51.

Ma, L., Yang, F., & Wang, M. (2022). The influence of platform features on purchase intention in social commerce: A stimulus-organism-response perspective. *Frontiers in Psychology*, *13*, 892046.

Mala Kalaiarasan, M. S., Vafaei-Zadeh, A., Hanifah, H., & Ramayah, T. (2024). Can we engage players with extended reality in gaming applications? A stimulus-organism-response framework. *Entertainment Computing*, *50*, 100651. DOI: 10.1016/j.entcom.2024.100651

Nguyen, H., Pham, T., & Nguyen, T. (2022). Factors affecting purchase intention towards virtual try-on technology: Evidence from Vietnam. *Journal of Retailing and Consumer Services*, *66*, 102911.

Nguyen, H. N. (2022b). Motivations and barriers to embracing augmented reality: An exploratory study with Vietnamese retailers. *Innovative Marketing*, *18*(3), 28–37. DOI: 10.21511/im.18(3).2022.03

Pappas, I. O., Patelis, T. E., & Giannakos, M. N. (2014). Moderating effects of online shopping experience on customer satisfaction and repurchase intentions. *International Journal of Retail & Distribution Management*, *42*(3), 187–204. DOI: 10.1108/IJRDM-03-2012-0034

Park, M., & Yoo, J. (2020). Benefits of augmented reality shopping and moderating effects of perceived risks. *Journal of Retailing and Consumer Services*, *52*, 101910.

Pine, B. J., & Gilmore, J. *H.* (1999). The experience economy: Work is theatre & every business a stage. Harvard Business Press.

Pymnts. (2024, February 12). *L'Oréal sees 150% increase in virtual Try-Ons as consumers seek AR immersion.* PYMNTS.com.

Song, Y., Zhang, L., & Zhang, M. (2022). Research on the impact of public climate policy cognition on low-carbon travel based on SOR theory: Evidence from China. *Energy*, *261*, 125192. DOI: 10.1016/j.energy.2022.125192

Suh, A., & Prophet, J. (2018). The state of immersive technology research: A literature analysis. *Computers in Human Behavior*, *86*, 77–90. DOI: 10.1016/j.chb.2018.04.019

Sun, D., Xu, L., Zhang, L., & Cui, N. (2019). How augmented reality affects people's perceptions: Adoption of AR in product display improves consumers' product attitude. *Journal of Physics: Conference Series*, *1288*(1), 1–10. DOI: 10.1088/1742-6596/1288/1/012037

Team, B. (2025, April 21). *Augmented Reality in Ecommerce: How Does it Work? BigCommerce.*

Tech in Asia. (n.d.). *Tech in Asia - Connecting Asia's startup ecosystem.*

Tian, X., & Sarkis, J. (2021). Emission burden concerns for online shopping returns. *Nature Climate Change*, *12*(1), 2–3. DOI: 10.1038/s41558-021-01246-9

U ă, I. (2022, December 9). *+20 augmented reality (AR) global market and user statistics for 2022*. Brand Minds.

Verhagen, T., van Nes, J., Feldberg, F., & van Dolen, W. (2011). Virtual customer service agents: Using social presence and personalization to shape online service encounters. *Journal of Computer-Mediated Communication*, *16*(1), 79–97.

Wang, Z., & Jiang, Q. (2024). A study on the willingness of "Generation Z" consumers to use online virtual try-on shopping services based on the S-O-R framework. *Systems*, *12*(6), 217. DOI: 10.3390/systems12060217

Xue, Y., Sun, J., Liu, Y., Li, X., & Yuan, K. (2023). Facial expression-enhanced recommendation for virtual fitting rooms. *Decision Support Systems*, *177*, 113222.

Yang, K., & Liu, H. (2017). The impact of online store atmosphere on consumer's purchase intention: Based on SOR theory. *The Journal of Business and Retail Management Research*, *12*(1), 112–123.

Zeithaml, V. A. (1988). Consumer perceptions of price, quality, and value: A means-end model and synthesis of evidence. *Journal of Marketing*, *52*(3), 2–22. DOI: 10.1177/002224298805200302

Chapter 8

Fusion of Art and Technology Pioneering Sustainable Inclusive Education for Transformative Social Development

Jyoti Rani
https://orcid.org/0000-0002-5577-7808
Parul Institute of Design, Parul University, India

ABSTRACT

This chapter explores sustainable inclusive education by integrating art and technology to foster creativity, inclusivity, and critical thinking. It outlines five approaches leveraging Information and Communications Technologies (ICT) to enhance accessibility and promote sustainable social development. The chapter introduces a novel theory of sustainable education, emphasizing how art-technology integration can address educational challenges, transform traditional systems, and ensure equity. By fostering collaboration, cultural exchange, and interdisciplinary learning, this framework equips students to navigate future challenges while contributing to societal progress. The chapter concludes with a call for policy support and further research to scale this innovative model, ensuring a sustainable, inclusive, and transformative educational future.

DOI: 10.4018/979-8-3693-7610-2.ch008

INTRODUCTION

Educating the integration of art and technology can open up more creative thinking problems and effective problem-solving working measures through new age technology & platforms to the students in the class. This helps develop a more contemporary learning environment that encourages students to discover new things and solutions. Education programs can enable students' creativity and problem-solving skills through the power of advanced technologies like AI, virtual systems, and digital tools. Next, we discuss how these integrations are accomplished and the implications for education.

Technological Tools and Platforms

- Several studies have been conducted in which the use of technological tools and platforms in the process of learning fine arts was proved to lead to an increase in students' technical proficiency and creativity. Contests like those for AI art or digital choreography also give students exposure to advanced technologies and develop their artistic skills and collaborative skills
- By analyzing countless amounts of artistic work, artificial intelligence and virtual computer systems come out with new inspiration for designers, and interactive systems can provide personalized educational experiences and help in building creative and problem-solving mind-sets.

STEAM Education

- This has been done through the integration of STEAM (Science, Technology, Engineering, Arts and Mathematic) activities. There is considerable evidence demonstrating that the creative ability and self-efficacy of students were significantly improved after receiving STEAM-based training courses (Gu et al., 2023).
- The study further shows that project-based learning (PBL) with STEAM approach has produced substantial improvement on students creativity and computational thinking skills, especially on fluency, flexibility, originality, and elaboration (Chang et al., 2023).
- Problem-based digital making (DM) activities, mixing programming with an element of problem-solving, have been effective in stimulating creativity among middle school students, enabling them to manifest creativity in digital artifacts (Weng et al., 2023).

Design Thinking and Collaborative Environments

- Digital visual collaborative environments in design thinking pedagogy contribute to improving students' creative confidence, learning motivation and team performance. Such digital platforms allow for the co-creation and salvaging of design projects that would otherwise struggle with traditional in-person collaboration techniques (Liu, Lee and Huang, 2023).
- In art education, multimedia and AI support the development of art concepts and provide a data representation model that can represent and understand advanced concepts (Zhao et al., 2024).

Early Childhood and Middle School Education

- When storytelling is incorporated in an Engineering Design Process-based STEAM activity, it can enhance creativity and problem-solving in young children. By integrating narrative components with engineering design, this approach provide a more enjoyable and fruitful learning experience (Erol, Erol and Başaran, 2023).

Although bringing art and technology together in education provides several potentials; there are also challenges to that approach, such as the possibility of a digital divide, which may prevent some students from access to these technologies. Moreover, teachers need adequate training to apply these tools and methods effectively in the classroom. Combining these with traditional teaching methods can provide for all students in leveraging these new modes of education.

UNDERSTANDING SUSTAINABLE DEVELOPMENT IN EDUCATION

Shared or Integrated Education are terms used in this framework; however, it is still not clear whether education of this nature will be one of the general approaches or the global core. The pedagogical frame goes beyond mere academic content; it promotes holistic development in cognitive, affective, and behavioral domains in order to cultivate critical thinking, systems thinking, and action competence. It also helps to prepare people to be able to work towards sustainable development in different cultures. The following are described the key aspects of sustainable education based on the studies mentioned above.

Key Competencies for Sustainability

- Transversal Competences: Competences such as critical thinking, systems thinking, and action competence that can be applied across different educational contexts and are crucial for dealing with sustainability challenges (Sposab and Rieckmann, 2024).
- Earth System Competency: Considering the Earth as a system of interacting subsystems to promote geoethics is a vital aspect of education for sustainability (Vasconcelos and Orion, 2021).
- Global Competence: Global competence development is a priority in higher education to overcome the challenges from the UN's 2030 Agenda, especially for engineering education (Kjellgren and Richter, 2021).

Frameworks and Approaches

- Sustainability Competence Frameworks: These frameworks encompassing cognitive, affective, and behavioral dimensions, offer a structured approach to developing sustainability competencies in students (Sposab and Rieckmann, 2024).
- Whole Institution Approaches (WIAs): WIAs aim at integrating sustainability in all dimensions of the educational institutions, connecting formal and informal curricula and creating a culture of continuous learning and participation (Holst, 2023).
- Professional Learning Communities (PLCs): PLCs promote sustainable education and improve innovation and digital transformation in teaching, supporting overall educator efficacy and fostering lifelong learning (Vičič Krabonja et al., 2024).

Integration in Educational Systems

- Higher education: A major driver of sustainability in academia, through integration in curriculum and engagement with global artist initiatives such as the Sustainable Development Goals (SDGs) involves an inter-disciplinary approach (Abo-Khalil, 2024).
- Sustainability Competences: In secondary education, the development of sustainability competences is imperative for the preparation of future generations to meet challenges to come, including critical knowledge capabilities and transdisciplinary action (Nordén, 2018).

Challenges and Opportunities

- Regional Diversity and Collaboration: A better regional diversity in sustainability education research is required to minimize biases and promote global collaboration (Sposab and Rieckmann, 2024).
- Guidelines for Institutions and Diversity: Institutional guidelines and inclusive environments are derived to further satisfy global competence to be effective (Kjellgren and Richter, 2021).

This is why we have the term sustainable education, which focuses on providing the learners with the skills required to address the issues of the world but there are few difficulties such as regional biases in the research and more inclusive and diverse educational practices.

Role of Inclusivity in Sustainable Education

Inclusive education practices encompass an SDG approach in products and/or services to schools. This approach is in line with SDG 4: Access to inclusive and equitable quality education and promote lifelong learning opportunities for all. That through inclusive education, schools can play their role in contributing to larger goals of sustainability, equity and social justice in society. The next segments discuss the way inclusive education practices helps addressing SDGs in education.

Support Equality and Social Inclusion

- Inclusive education is about making sure that all students can participate and achieve in educational settings, whatever their background or abilities. This is in line with the SDG target of reducing inequalities within and between countries (Medina-García et al., 2020).
- The Sustainable Inclusive Framework Studio (SIF Studio) model presents an arrangement for inclusivity and sustainability, aiming to connect inclusivity goals to their practice in educational institutions (Dev et al., 2024).
- Introducing inclusive practices in schools enables them to provide a non-formal context for social inclusion of marginalized groups, e.g., Roma pupils, which fosters educational equity and sustainability (Díez-Palomar et al., 2018).

Improving Educational Outcomes

- Inclusive education practices can enhance educational outcomes by making adjustments to learning environments, providing necessary resources, and promoting positive attitudes among those involved.
- An example of how inclusive education can not only be educative of the heart and mind but also of the local community needs (through inclusive pedagogies) in post-colonial India is illustrated in this recent case (Mukherjee, 2017).

Building Resilient and Sustainable Education Systems

- Sustainable inclusive education systems are marked by systemic leadership that embeds inclusive practice throughout the work of the school. It means that schools will never veer off human-oriented learning processes, which interconnecting everything in and outside of the organisation should be about human welfare (Ketikidou and Saiti, 2022).
- Ongoing professional development for staff, advocacy for acceptance and equality, and outstanding leadership are some of the contributing factors that influence the longevity and sustainability of inclusive education settings (Kamran and Siddiqui, 2024).

Advancing Other SDGs

- Education for sustainable development (ESD) is a tool that can provide the transformation that society needs to achieve a sustainable state. Through the role that inclusive education practices play in linking the SDGs with educational outcomes, the SDGs equip students with the competences required for contributing towards sustainability (Kioupi and Voulvoulis, 2019).
- When students participate actively, transformative learning experiences such as sustainability projects can contribute not only to education, but also to various SDGs, preparing students to become active citizens (Cottafava, Cavaglià and Corazza, 2019).

Although inclusive education is a key enabler to reaching many of the SDGs, many challenges persist in their implementation. While both concepts are central to educational policies, their duality impedes the implementation of equal opportunities, since integration can neutralize the work of inclusion (Medina-García, Doña-Toledo and Higueras-Rodríguez, 2020).

Art and Technology as Tools for Transformation

Sustainable development in the educational environment can be enhanced by promoting the integration of art and technology into educational curricula as it can enhance student engagement, foster creativity and develop critical thinking skills. How can we integrate technology in an innovative way that takes advantage of creative practices and leads to a new process of interdisciplinary learning? This helps but solve sustainable challenge (encriched by SDGs through SDGs). The following discusses some approaches for implementing both art and technology in education that contributes to sustainable development.

Gamification and Digital Technologies

- Digital technologies, like ARGs, can be utilized to increase cultural heritage awareness and encourage deeper engagement and learning. For example, one study found that an ARG-based learning scaffold significantly enhanced students' understanding of the issues related to cultural preservation and sustainable development, while simultaneously increasing students' engagement and emotional involvement in the learning process (Lin, Lu and Lu, 2024).
- This allows for the optimization of resources and a lower dependency on physical materials, both of which enhance sustainability and widen access under a model of AI-supported art education. Still in its infancy, use of AI in art education has great potential for sustainable development through enhancing creativity and minimising environmental impacts (Su and Mokmin, 2024).

Artistic Practices and Environmental Design

- Introducing local and aesthetic recycling perspectives into interior design education creates a pathway toward applied actions that can make a difference and ensure that scientific abstract notions of sustainable development can also acquire practical dimensions through artistic practices – like upcycled furniture. These studies also illustrate that teaching art with reused materials can help students remain active participants while also highlighting the role of recycled materials in sustainability during the teaching process (Al-Saud et al., 2024).
- In modern art and environmental design, the use of AI and deep learning technologies allows the design process to be more sustainable. AI-driven green design provides effectiveness assurance of design solutions and encourages environmental art design into a greener way (Li, 2024).

Technology-Enhanced Learning and Systems Thinking

- This model of learning can help in developing higher order thinking skills and therefore, when integrated with technology enhanced learning, is truly sustainable. Flow theory as a framework can encourage cognitive and social engagement resulting in increasing systems thinking for solving the sustainable education problems of the future (Kurent and Avsec, 2024).
- Using big data and artificial intelligence technologies, the Collaborative Structure Search Framework CSSF algorithm can find the best learning path and enhance the learning process. Such a customized learning scheme ensures stabilization and improvement in learning experience, thus upgrading the quality of the education and maintaining sustainable educational growth (Liu et al., 2024).

Aesthetic Education and Interdisciplinary Approaches

- It is the educational quality and sustainable development in aesthetic education in the most challenging task. The core values of curriculums should be aligned with aesthetic education through technology and educational innovation, in this way, creativity, personalized learning, and social responsibility can be cultivated in students (Tao and Tao, 2024).
- Artistic practices contribute to ESD by enabling competencies like vision-building, multi-perspectivity and openness. These skills are essential in influencing sustainable development and attaining educational objectives (Niederhauser et al., 2024).

THE INTERPLAY OF ART EDUCATION AND TECHNOLOGY

Historical Perspective on Art Education and Its Evolution

In its context, historical events and technological advancements contributed to the specific development of the art education and practice curriculum. Even art education itself transitioned from that traditional model of learning in which a young artist would practice under the tutelage of a master in a small studio for years to a normalized practice in an academic context, regardless of the social advancements and educational reform at the time. Technology has also transformed art education, offering new tools and ways to learn and express oneself artistically. This synthesis examines the key historical milestones and technological advances that have framed this arrow of development.

Historical Influences

- Master-Apprentice Model: From the thirteenth to fourteenth centuries, the master-apprentice model was in place. This system lasted until the early twentieth century when more structured systems of education began to emerge (Souleles, 2013).
- Progressive Education Movement: The work of Dewey can be traced back to the early 20thcentury; this huge change in education was the progressive education movement experiential learning and making the arts core in all courses, not merely something we do forfun. This was the time when they were trying to integrate arts into the general educational curriculum (Heilig, Cole and Aguilar, 2010).
- Accountability and Standardization: For the last several decades, there has been greater focus on core subjects like reading and mathematics, often at the cost of arts education. Such policies as the No Child Left Behind Act have also contributed to this trend through an overemphasis on standardized testing and accountability measures, often resulting in the exclusion of arts programs (Heilig, Cole and Aguilar, 2010).

Technological Advancements

- Digital Tools and Platforms: The integration of digital tools and platforms has revolutionized art education by fostering students' technical proficiency and creative thinking. As virtual competitions and courses in AI and digital content have emerged, ventured students have nurtured their abilities.
- Computer technology: The artists works were increasingly made and processed by computers, giving rise to special computer programmes, computer animations and in effects in tessellation (Comninos, McLoughlin and Anderson, 2009).
- Visual Literacy and Reproduction Technologies Image reproduction technologies, from lithography to photography, historically shaped modes of teaching art. These technologies have facilitated a high-volume distribution of art, which has also directly fed.

Sure, the nature of art education has dramatically changed with the introduction of technology in art classroom, and there is a challenge to revamp new curriculum and teacher training in art education to cater to the demands of the times. The antiquated emphasis on conventional processes coupled with a slow insensitivity to disruptive technologies has created an increasing distance between the educational ecosystem and the potential of the marketplace. Only transdisciplinary educators applying digital tools may fill the gap and prevent art education permanence, an obsolescence, redundancy.

Technological Advancements Shaping Art Education

These tools and methodologies have dramatically impacted the pedagogy of art education by bringing freedom, accessibility and protection to creativity. Consequently, the use of technology in education is becoming a paradigm shift from traditional teacher delivery of content towards student-centered model, where student is central to study, and technology is essential in assisting both creativity and skills. Technologies such as artificial intelligence (AI), virtual reality (VR), and augmented reality (AR) have entered the world of art to create ways for art teaching by offering personalized educational experience and fresh approaches to teaching. Here are essential aspects of technology transforming the pedagogical landscape of art education.

AI and Art Education

AI technologies are used to develop personalized learning experiences in art education. AI-supported systems, for instance, offer instant feedback and personalized guidance, resulting in improved comprehension and creation of artwork by the students (Chiu et al., 2022).

The model CCME-GAN and BERT-LDA are AI to display, evaluate hundreds of personalized student painting works, improving students creative ability and painting level (Wu, 2024).

AI technologies drive that transition in teaching from teacher-centered learning to student-centered learning, enabling students to level up their creative thinking skills and enabling them to rapidly acquire knowledge resources and use them (Fan and Zhong, 2022).

Digital and Online Platforms

Art education has never been more accessible and inclusive: students can take art courses online in today's digital platforms. Due to this pandemic, the educators have changed how they teach to engage the students and to participate in the lessons (Pavlou and Castro-Varela, 2024).

Ergo, studies on the fine arts education show that the inclusion of online platforms and digital tools would help students realize their techniques, creativity and collaborative skills.

Virtual and Augmented Reality

VR & AR in Art Education Virtual reality and Augmented reality technologies are being on in the Art educational field for better learning experiences. For example, VR technology has been used to improve students' watercolor painting skills by providing an interactive immersive learning environment (Yang, 2024).

The scholarship of AR system Close up is used to improve the art creativity training funnel of artistic creativity, which allows students to be stimulated through many innovative creative exploration methods (Tan, Gao and Lu, 2018).

Dependable and Optimal Resources

Moreover, in the everyday grind, we could create working processes that can be more sustainable with less dependence on physical materials or resources being used up in the art education domain with technological advancements. AI-supported art education encourages sustainability through widening accessibility and reducing environmental footprints (Su and Mokmin, 2024).

Like so many other areas of life, the prospect that technology offers to art education harbors both pros and cons, usually in equal measure. In the same way, there is an anxiety about the taking away of drawing techniques due to high rate of digital tools. This shift, as is evident in works like this one, has led to a reframing in drawing as a process of what are the core competencies in drawing as a process and what are the essential attitudes one should bring to drawing to ensure a balance between creative outcomes and processes (Fava, 2020). Lastly, due to the speed of technological innovation there is often an imbalance that exist among curricular, market and the outcome in the higher education, advocating a transdisciplinary understanding and articulation of art, science and technology (Figueras-Ferrer, 2021).

Benefits of Integrating Art and Technology in Modern Education

The combination of art and technology is a multi dimensional strategy in the 21st century education that improves creativity, engages learners and aims at development of skill(s). With the assistance of new technological tools, this merging leads to the delivery of experiential and sustainable educational experiences. Resultant, better access, better learning outcomes and hybrid skills still in demand by the contemporary workforce. What are best practices of art integration with technology in education and the benefits.

AI and Multimedia

- AI-integrated art teaching streamlines resources and minimizes reliance on physical materials, affecting both sustainability and access. This kind of digital platform provides educational programs that are more interactive, more user-friendly, and consequently, also enhance the engagement and comprehension of the students (Su and Mokmin, 2024).
- The incorporation of advances in multimedia and computer specialists along with AI-based procedures and methods of decision-making assists in teaching by enabling the processing and advanced visualization of data. It removes time (on lags), and cups up concrete content to the learner, which sontirously pool the user experience (Zhao et al., 2024).

Digital Media and Interactive Technologies

- Zero-Sample Image Retrieval: Integration of Digital Media Technologies to Fullfill Aesthetical Abilities in Modern Art Education These technologies are seen as enhancing the aesthetics components of modern art education by 90% of surveyed students and teachers, while the effect on meanings is less than 90% (Gao, 2024).
- Anticipating future developments, interactive technologies like 3D simulators provide students with playful, intuitive ways of learning. This keeps students engaged and provides a step-wise learning pathway.

Interdisciplinary and Hybrid Models of Education

- Programs like Carnegie Mellon University's interdisciplinary courses fuse together art and technology, developing hybridized skills in students. Its convergence of creative and technical industry, which lays out a path to a multitude of careers for students. (Hodgins, 2015).
- New teaching models with constructivism component in the foremost position for art and technology integration may increase satisfaction and learning outcomes. Other models highlight pedagogical principles that underpin learner-centred design and instructional methodology which seek to enhance educational experiences (Xue and Lu, 2021).

Tool and Platform

- The addition of future technology tools and associate supported platforms in fine arts education immensely supplement students technical skill, imagination and Collaborate skills. Contests and projects interacting with these differential tools train individuals in skills and technology (- *et al.*, 2024).

- The skilful infusion of ICT across art and design education offers a unique opportunity to bridge classroom learning to real world applications. However, Teacher Attitudes are also an important factor in order to the teachers to implement ICT effectively since all investments in ICTs is not equally effective (Radclyffe-Thomas, 2008).

Collaborations are increasing, so this is good, but there are also some challenges. There isn't much compelling evidence regarding their long-term effect, and these technologies are a bit hit and miss. In addition, teachers attitude toward these changes and whether a supportive resource was available were important factors that played a part in the technology becoming integrated successfully in their art classroom. However, such technologies have significant potential on the art field and the world of technology in terms of creating a positive learning environment by fostering innovation & creativity, offering new ways for students to engage with the subject material, and imparting useful skills for the 21st-century workplace.

FIVE APPROACHES TO SUSTAINABLE SOCIAL DEVELOPMENT THROUGH ICT

On the other hand, the use of ICT is focused on many areas of sustainable social development, which can contribute to the improvement of sectors within society. ICT has a transformative potential to accelerate sustainable development through digital tools, cross sector learning, creativity, inclusivity and global collaboration. This answer explains 5 types of ICT for Sustainable Social Development based on the listed research papers.

Enhancing Accessibility through Digital Tools

Digital Transformation (DT) can also encourage social sustainability incentives, as it increases access to services or information represented by the expansion of quality of life or social cohesion (Qadri et al., 2024).

Along with engagement in productive sectors, digitalization is evidence based to enhance development indicators in Africa, emphasising accessibility as a prioritisation in sustainable development (Sheikheldin and Hambly, 2024).

Ethical ICT solutions can keep communities empowered and promote better access by creating awareness and inducing sustainable practices" (Adisa, Oyedeji and Porras, 2024).

Promoting Interdisciplinary Learning via Art-Technology Fusion

Most broadly, cross-practice, cross-sector approaches to the merging of art and technology could not only facilitate interdisciplinary learning, but the type of learning we need to address complex social problems in innovative ways (Yoon and Ho, 2024).

This refers to social innovation systems, as exemplified by South Korea and Singapore, which have promoted sustainable development in an inter-disciplinary manner, knitting together various fields and views (Yoon and Ho, 2024).

Leveraging ICT to Foster Creativity and Critical Thinking

ICT is an innovative platform that encourages creativity and critical thinking (Balsalobre-Lorente et al., 2024).

The development of AI and other digital technologies extends the limits of organization and social potential and capabilities also nurturing creative solutions to global problems (Kulkov et al., 2024).

Facilitating Inclusive Participation Using Adaptive Technologies

Adaptive technologies can support inclusive engagement, allowing all people to integrate into society, regardless of capabilities (Owojori et al., 2023).

The vision of a strategy of adaptive reuse in building infrastructure indicates that ICT can be involved to improve social sustainability through enhanced social cohesion and well-being (Owojori, Okoro and Chileshe, 2024).

This can be gained by keeping all the advantages of the ICT for supporting sustainable social development while, at the same time, overcoming challenges or limitation. But these transformations also raise issues - for instance, the relatively rapid digitization there is a vignette of unequal access, writing inequality upon inequality unless handled (Sheikheldin and Hambly, 2024). Responsible environmental technology management, e-waste, and the implications of ICT-based sustainability are incorporated into smart technologies so that ICT development does not inhibit sustainable development goals (Chiang, 2024). Therefore, the well-balanced ICT development between used for good or bad should be needful of sustainable social development.

CHALLENGES IN IMPLEMENTING ART-TECHNOLOGY INTEGRATION

Addressing Digital Divides and Resource Limitations

In fact, involving art and technology in this process creates a diverse challenge, especially with themes from the digital divide and lack of essential resources. These promises look to be inevitably an integration of these fields, which depends not only on technical and creative skills, but also on a solid infrastructure and accessible distribution. Interdisciplinary collaboration, privacy concerns, and the evolving nature of technology add further complexity to the challenges. This response discusses these challenges and possible solutions, with lessons from different contexts.

Interdisciplinary Collaboration

- Cultural and Professional Differences: Differences in professional cultures and cognitive styles may lead to misunderstandings and conflicts during the interaction between arts and technology. In particular, artists and technologists have different styles for problem-solving and communication skills which can impede collaboration (Biswas, 2008).
- Educational Gaps: Art schools are not well equipped to train on housing current technologies, and therefore the application of new media may often be seen as an obstacle in producing an artwork. The gap between the theoretical knowledge and the practical knowledge, however, emerges already in pre-service and in-service teacher education at both bachelor's and master's levels (Atabek, 2019) (Jagodzinski, 2015).

Resource Limitations

- Infrastructure and Access: The physical and technological infrastructure necessary to access technology is still lagging behind, not only in education but also in the arts. Such as limited access to hardware and software, which are essential for developing and showing digital art (Atabek, 2019) (La Rose et al., 2022).
- Economic Constraints: For the art world to embrace digital technologies becomes a financial challenge, thus putting constraints on art-technology initiatives in terms of scale and level. Bigger incentive on regions with a relative lack of economic resources (Chen, 2024)
- Equity and Inclusion: Digital divides become apparent when certain groups have limited access to technology to engage them in an art-technology pro-

gram. This is a crucial concern within public health and education, which require equity of access to the digital tool kits necessary for of integration (La Rose et al., 2022).

Strategies for Overcoming Challenges

- Collaborative Frameworks: Besides the advice to keep experimenting, some things worth mentioning are structured collaborative frameworks. These programs foster dialogue and collaborative problem solving between artists and scientists (Ox and Lowenberg, 2013).
- Adaptive Educational Models: Innovative Learning pathways Part of this integration, we need to design educational programs that bring together art and technology from early-stage education to advanced studies Such an approach nurtures a new generation of 'hyphenated' artists, creators and technologists who are skilled in working across disciplines (Jagodzinski, 2015).
- Innovative Practices: Community-based projects using digital platforms to engage new and different audiences may be especially effective in reducing social isolation and improving access to the arts. Such platforms can especially benefit marginalized groups, allowing them to interact with art in innovative ways (La Rose et al., 2022).

Balancing Traditional and Modern Teaching Methodologies

The balance of traditional vs modern forms of teaching in art forms, integrating technology into art education is a multidimensional struggle. Infrastructural deficiencies, training insufficiencies, and the differential culture between disciplines in art and technology work stream integration process as few hurdles of these integration process. Such challenges require a strategic approach to mitigate the risk that technology will detract from rather than enhance the educational experience. The next parts delve into these hurdles by deducing knowledge from the given research documents.

Infrastructural and Training Challenges

- Infrastructural Issues: The most critical barrier in technology integration is poor physical and technological infrastructure. While the money spent on technology is much, hence some argue that schools need the right technology to use it properly in those classroom, all nations including Turkey should take infrastructure investments carefully (Atabek, 2019) (Vatanartiran and Karadeniz, 2015).

- Training Deficiencies: The training that teachers receive, both in service and during pre-service periods, is often inadequate, leaving teachers ill-prepared to implement new technologies in a meaningful way. This void in training is further exacerbated by a lack of supporting content and an incentive system for technology use.
- Leadership and Planning: Inability of Leadership and Planning The lack of strong technology leadership and efficient integration plans only add to the complexity of technology adoption in the classroom. "We have seen that teachers need guidance and support from their administrations in order to navigate through these challenges (Vatanartiran and Karadeniz, 2015)."

Cultural and Methodological Differences

- Professional Cultural Differences: Artists and technologists often have different professional cultures, leading to misunderstandings and communication barriers. Such differences can be a barrier to collaboration required to accomplish successful integration.
- Methodological Conflicts: Notably, the potential conflicts between the method of art education as a talent and thing and that of teaching it through technology may lead to methodological conflicts and tension. This can result in friction and tension as educators wrestle with and attempt to balance the integrity of artistic practices with the use of technological tools (Steckel, Shinas and Van Vaerenewyck, 2015).

Balancing Tradition and Modernity

- Preserving Core Values: When integrating intangible heritage (e.g. Cantonese opera), whether they can retain their core values while adopting modern technologies. This prompts the need for cautious consideration so that technology serves to amplify, rather than detract from, cultural and artistic values (Chung, 2024).
- Pedagogical Frameworks: The TPACK+ framework provides an approach to integrating technology into literacy and art education that aligns digital tools with instructional intention. This model helps the educators move a step ahead towards the pedagogically effective use of technology in providing more learning opportunities for their students (Steckel, Shinas and Van Vaerenewyck, 2015).

Resistance to Change in Educational Systems

Resistance to change in educational systems, particularly when integrating art and technology, is a multifaceted issue influenced by various factors. These factors range from personal beliefs and risk perceptions to organizational and cultural barriers. Understanding these elements is crucial for developing strategies to facilitate successful integration. The following sections explore the primary factors contributing to resistance in educational systems when implementing art-technology integration.

Teacher Beliefs and Risk Perception

- Beliefs and Attitudes: Teachers' beliefs about the value and efficacy of technology in education significantly impact their willingness to integrate it. When technology challenges traditional teaching methods, it can lead to resistance, as seen in the Indian 'smart-class' initiative where traditional beliefs were reinforced rather than transformed (Chand, Deshmukh and Shukla, 2020).
- Risk Aversion: Teachers often perceive technology integration as risky due to uncertainties about its appropriate use and actual value in teaching. This risk aversion is compounded by negative affective responses to technology, which can deter teachers from adopting new methods.

Organizational and Cultural Barriers

- Lack of Training and Support: A significant barrier is the insufficient training and professional development opportunities for teachers to acquire the necessary competencies for integrating new approaches like STEAM. This lack of investment in teacher training leads to resistance, as educators feel unprepared to implement these changes effectively.
- Cultural Norms and Management Support: Organizational culture and the level of support from management play crucial roles. In some cases, cultural norms and inadequate change management strategies hinder the adoption of new technologies and methods (Rahman, Mohammed Ghazali and Bin Mohamed Sawal, 2024).

Financial and Resource Constraints

- Budgetary Limitations: Financial constraints, including limited budgets for technology and art resources, pose significant challenges. Schools may lack the necessary funds to invest in the infrastructure and materials required for effective integration (Rahman, Mohammed Ghazali and Bin Mohamed Sawal, 2024).

- Resource Allocation: The allocation of resources, including time and materials, is often insufficient to support the sustained implementation of art-technology integration programs. This can lead to frustration and resistance among educators who feel they lack the tools needed to succeed (Buck and Snook, 2020).

Resistance to Innovation

- Resistance to Change: Resistance is a common response to the introduction of new ideas and methods in educational settings. This resistance is often due to discomfort with change and the challenges it presents to established practices.
- Aesthetic Resistance: The concept of aesthetic resistance highlights how publicness, potentiality, and plexus can influence resistance to change. These factors can create a network of resistance that complicates the path to successful integration (Wulia, 2023).

While these factors highlight the challenges of integrating art and technology in education, it is essential to consider the potential benefits and opportunities that such integration can offer.

A NOVEL THEORY OF SUSTAINABLE DEVELOPMENT IN INCLUSIVE EDUCATION

A novel theory of sustainable development in inclusive education integrates various dimensions of sustainability and inclusivity, aiming to create an educational environment that is equitable, adaptable, and future-oriented. This theory emphasizes the importance of equal opportunities, digitalization, cultural diversity, and systemic frameworks to achieve sustainable educational outcomes. The following sections outline the key components of this theory, drawing insights from the provided research papers.

Equal Opportunities and Inclusion

- In fact, the adaptation of students integrates as an antithesis to the reasonable inclusion from which it was conceived and applied generating statistically a reduction in equal opportunities, this is a reason for the importance of implementing policies that offer genuine support for inclusive practices (Medina-García, Doña-Toledo and Higueras-Rodríguez, 2020).

Digitainability and Education

- Digitainability is a new term for the combination of sustainability and digitalization, and research has established that education can play a key role in closing the digital divide. Therefore, education systems need to adapt to provide students with medium to high digital skills, which are needed to construct an inclusive society (Dovleac et al., 2023).
- Working with policymakers and the academic backdrop is important to transform education systems and equip students for high-demand markets (Dovleac et al., 2023).

Sustainable Practices and Resilience

- The policies in place are supportive to help build an inclusive education environment which is complementary to long-term sustainability; as are the attitudes of staff, essential resources, adapted environments and continuous professional development of staff (Kamran and Siddiqui, 2024)
- Advocacie for acceptance and equality and strong leadership are of utmost importance to sustain inclusive education in the long run (Kamran and Siddiqui, 2024).

Intercultural and Inclusive Education

- A blended approach to intercultural and inclusive education can be a catalyst for social justice. In this regard, sustainability would be one of the main elements third-generation (and subsequent) ET should embody for the prosperity of current and future generations (Hajisoteriou and Sorkos, 2023).
- There is a disjoint dichotomic view between intercultural and inclusive education paradigms that would need to be overcome to bolster social justice and sustainability in education environments (Hajisoteriou and Sorkos, 2023).

Systemic Frameworks and Competency Development

- Education for Sustainable Development (ESD) ESD needs to be reframed with a systems thinking perspective, linking SDGs and learning outcomes. This means building a shared sustainability vision and establishing relevant pedagogies and learning methods (Kioupi and Voulvoulis, 2019).

- Within learning and development frameworks, entrepreneurial competency practices can fill the education gap on sustainability and nurture its core values, inspiring the tenets stipulated in the 2030 Agenda for Sustainable Development (Chander et al., 2020).

Indigenous Models and Sustainable Learning

- Indigenous models of sustainability, like with SDI model, emphasize balance among dimensions of sustainability that interact such as land, institution and human behavior. These models inform strategic endeavors in course design and act as important considerations for targeting interdisciplinary collaboration (Dockry et al., 2016).
- Sustainable Learning in Education (SLE), strategies that afford learners renewability, reconstructability, adaptability, and promote self-direction, collaboration, active engagement and transferability of skills (Ben-Eliyahu, 2021).

Integrating Art Technology to Address Systemic Challenges

Bringing art and technology into the education space needs to be in the right way so some movement towards identifying the systemic issues of inclusive education and sustainable development, Nepali educational system can make a difference. Integrating this technology has the potential to revolutionize ways of teaching and learning, increase participation in the classroom, and develop a thorough comprehension of sustainability, and environmental issues. Educators can design inclusive and sustainable learning experiences in the 21st century in also applied the unique characteristics of works and technology along with the United Nations Sustainable Development Goals (SDGs). We will look at how to use art and technology in harmony to move in this direction in the following sections.

Arts as a Medium for Inclusive Education

- Transformative Education: The significant contribution of the arts to early childhood education lies in their role as a unique language for inclusive learning and communicating different languages. This enables very young children with age adaptive access to different lived experiences, promoting global citizenship, and sustainability (Chapman and O'Gorman, 2022).
- Aesthetic Education: Incorporating aesthetic education into quality education improves educational results through creative thinking, empathy, and social responsibility. This technique focuses on the inherent value of art in

education, encouraging inclusivity, and catering to personalized learning requirements (Tao and Tao, 2024).

Technology-Enhanced Learning

- Digitalization and Sustainability: This is the theme of the 11th digitalization and sustainability, thus the "digitainability". Educational systems can, through tackling the digital divide and improving digital skills, better equip students to thrive in high-demand ecosystems, while creating space for fairness (Dovleac et al., 2023).

Transdisciplinary Approaches

- STEM and Community Engagement: A transdisciplinary education model that connects art, science and community engagement can allow us to share learning experiences across disciplines and create a bottom-up sustainability. The second modality is the application of cross-disciplinary teaching in academia conjugated with engagement with local communities in creating a cycle of sustainability-centric education (Clark and Button, 2011).

Case Studies and Practical Examples

Sustainable development in inclusive education is a concept that embed principles of sustainability in inclusive practices of education. The focus of this approach was on building educational spaces that are inclusive of diverse learners, while encouraging the sustainability of those spaces through the resources, policies and practices that support them. Mater Code here. Inclusive education is one of the key aspects of the sustainable development goals. This synthesis considers diverse models and case studies suggest that sustainable development is well embedded in inclusive education.

Key Models and Frameworks

- Sustainable Inclusive Framework Studio (SIF Studio): Sustainable Inclusive Framework Studio (SIF Studio) It is rooted in social constructivism and behavior modeling theories, with the primary goal of relating inclusivity ambitions to practical realization. The SIF Studio has demonstrated substantial positive shifts in mindsets among students, teachers, and parents, illustrating its efficacy in advancing sustainable inclusive education (Dev et al., 2024).

- Sustainable Intercultural and Inclusive Education (SIIE): Integrative intercultural and inclusive education promotes also blended and comparative approaches. It highlights sustainability as a foundational concept behind educational practices that serve the rights of present and future generations, contributing to social justice and high-quality educational services (Hajisoteriou and Sorkos, 2023).
- Menominee Nation Sustainable Development Institute Model: This indigenous model prioritizes and balances six dimensions of sustainability, which includes land, institutions, and human behavior. It exemplifies the fluidity of sustainable development as well as the relatedness of this ideal to academic contexts, serving as a guide for course design and for the organization of interdisciplinary community building (Dockry et al., 2016).

Case Studies and Practical Examples

- Inclusive Education in Pakistan: A successful sustainable inclusive education setup running for 25 years. These are inclusive polices, positive stakeholder attitudes, resourcing, accessible learning spaces and ongoing professional learning. This case highlights how leadership and advocacy efforts are critical for keeping inclusive education (Kamran and Siddiqui, 2024).
- Transformative Learning at the University of Torino: An Unusual Case from University of Torino Students learn managerial skills and contribute to local projects, demonstrating that education can promote active citizenship and sustainability (Cottafava, Cavaglià and Corazza, 2019).
- Inclusive Pedagogy in India: Through an institutional ethnography of a school in India, the book demonstrates how inclusive pedagogy can respond to local community needs that require social inclusion in an environment riddled with inequality. The school's signature approach has been commended as it educates the hearts and minds of children according to sustainable development goals (Mukherjee, 2017).

TRANSFORMATIVE POTENTIAL OF ART AND TECHNOLOGY IN EDUCATION

How schools use the fusion of art and technology in the classroom has the potential to deepen equity and inclusivity, as well as inspire social and cultural change and better prepare the graduates of today for a world in flux. Such syntheses of art with tech have the potential to create multifaceted learning environments that promote critical thought, creativity and global education. Using these tools, educators can begin to address systemic inequities, preparing students to navigate and contribute to an increasingly complex world. The subsequent sections explore these transformative potentials in detail.

Promoting Equity and Inclusivity

- Arts and Humanities for DEI: Arts and humanities efforts can serve as a supplement to formal diversity, equity, and inclusion (DEI) work by facilitating thoughtful reflection and group dialogue. They also create a space for the reflection and conversations about bias and racism that can reframe mindsets and further equity (Cerceo, Zimmerman and DeLisser, 2022).
- Technology for Social Justice: Technology in education can help solve equity and multicultural education by giving access to a range of learning experiences and information. This can help reduce disparities in educational opportunities and promote social justice (Marx and Kim, 2019).
- Inclusive Knowledge Creation By virtue of the nature of the work, community arts and cultural practices can source from existing epistemologies and methodological tools to challenge oppression and marginalization. Such practices are participatory, driven by relational ethics and available to all studying in educational environments (Sonn and Baker, 2016).

Inspiring Social and Cultural Change

- Community Pedagogies: Artistic and cultural practices can become tools for building community and facilitating social transformation. Educators can transgress this social exclusion by way of community pedagogies, helping to liberate and create wellbeing (Sonn and Baker, 2016).
- Participative Aesthetic Inquiry: Arts-based methodologies have the potential to invigorate the practice of equality and diversity within organizations. Artistic inquiry that interacts with tacit knowledge allows participants to engage with and reconstruct understandings of equality and diversity at work.
- Art-Informed Pedagogy: Arts-informed pedagogy is an informative and compelling way to support leaders to create more justly engaged and socially conscious communities. The approach highlights the significance of arts in bringing about social change (McGregor, 2012).

Preparing Students for Future Challenges

- Virtual Reality for Global Citizenship: Virtual Reality (VR) technology can expose students to new perspectives and locations, encouraging a deeper understanding of global citizenship. It breaks down barriers, providing students the opportunity to read about diverse cultures and global issues without ever leaving the classroom, thus preparing them for a world beyond (Sanz-Prieto, De Pablo González and De Pablo Sánchez, 2024).

- Connected Arts Learning: A connected arts learning framework connects student interest-driven art-making to more expansive opportunities, including civic, career, and choice making opportunities. It offers equity and social/ cultural connections, as well as preparation of students for future challenges by focusing on networks and culturally sustaining practices (Peppler, Dahn and Ito, 2022).
- Quality Thinking Systems: Dynamic learning environments in the arts can increase students' capacities for deep meaning and connection-making. This method encourages educational justice by Creating a balanced intelligence and self-beliefs, which prepares students with skills to tackle for the future.

FUTURE DIRECTIONS AND RECOMMENDATIONS

Promoting sustainable inclusive education, art-technology integration in the curriculum, and exploring future research opportunities is complex and richly informed by varied academic perspectives. The role of technology in education, and especially for the arts is a huge opportunity in terms of embracing inclusion and sustainability. But reaching such goals will only work if there are thoughtful considerations in policy implications, strategic plans behind scaling initiatives, and focus on applied research. The next sections will discuss considerations and recommendations according to the academic contexts outlined above.

Policy Implications for Sustainable Inclusive Education

- Reconceptualizing Inclusion: This paper found that the COVID-19 pandemic can provide a valuable example that necessitates rethinking another small question in this topic - inclusive education toward a broader and holistic practice that incorporates convivial technologies that disrupts traditional binaries as well as the Eurocentric digital divides. Policies should promote the mixing of digital and non-digital tech as they create inclusive education experiences that rely upon a locality's histories and non-scientific forms of knowledge (Peruzzo and Allan, 2024).
- Educational Leadership: Integration of technology is effective under strong educational leadership in inclusive education It should also cover policies that will equip schools with technological infrastructures and ensure inclu-

sive education subjects are present in teacher training programs (Uygur et al., 2020).

Opportunities for Further Research

- Aesthetic Education and Technology: Understanding the blend of technology with aesthetics education: Microsystem (school): research should focus on understanding cross-cultural implications of these findings, identifying inclusive practices that make the integration of aesthetic and quality education broad-based and sustainable (Tao and Tao, 2024), as well as examining both normative and robust assessment metrics that can be used to evaluate aesthetic education in schools.
- Social Inclusion through ICT: Social Inclusion through ICT Social inclusion through ICT deserves much more empirical research as smart technologies can provide opportunities for social inclusion of disabled youth and potentially other marginalized forms of youth. Including issues of disability specific to various disabled people and other vulnerable populations (Harb and Sidani, 2022).

CONCLUSION

Art education being integrated with technology could emerge as sustainable inclusive education. This framework not only embraces creativity but also promotes digital innovation and tackles the greatest challenges of the modern-day educational landscape including inclusivity, accessibility, and topical relevance etc. These five approaches, which are articulated in this chapter, chart a path for using Information and Communications Technologies (ICT) in ways that lesson the cost of sustainable social development-enhancing educational systems' ability to respond to the varied educational needs of students. The synergy between the virtual and physical worlds is not just reshaping how individuals learn, but is catalyzing a broader societal shift as well. It equips learners with the skills and creativity to face an ever-changing world while fostering equality and social cohesion. Indeed, this integrated perspective propels the narrative of sustainable development within the realm of inclusive education, suggesting that traditional educational paradigms can evolve in a way that is more attuned to the needs of all learners, preparing them for an interdependent future in a rapidly changing world. While these models have immense potential for improving accessibility and quality in education, as we transition schools and institutions to higher effectiveness the challenges of resourcing, digital divide and institutions hesitant to change would have to be properly addressed. Data sets of innovation and collaboration among the different stakeholders in the education sector will contribute to catalyze this integration to fully participating in building blocks of sustainable development. In the end, this chapter paints a vision of education as a process not only for self-actualization but also as a means to catalyze social change.

REFERENCES

Abo-Khalil, A. G. (2024). Integrating sustainability into higher education challenges and opportunities for universities worldwide. *Heliyon*, *10*(9), e29946. DOI: 10.1016/j.heliyon.2024.e29946 PMID: 38707336

Adisa, M. O., Oyedeji, S., & Porras, J. (2024). The nexus between ICT, top-down and bottom-up approaches for sustainability activities: A systematic mapping study. *Journal of Cleaner Production*, *449*, 141768. DOI: 10.1016/j.jclepro.2024.141768

Al-Saud, K., AlAli, R., Al saud, A., Abouelela, A., Shehab, R., Moneim, D., & Hamid, A. (2024). Exploring the Aesthetic and Functional Aspects of Recycled Furniture in Promoting Sustainable Development: An Applied Approach for Interior Design Students. *Sustainability (Basel)*, *16*(10), 4003. DOI: 10.3390/su16104003

Atabek, O. (2019) 'CHALLENGES IN INTEGRATING TECHNOLOGY INTO EDUCATION', *Turkish Studies - Information Technologies and Applied Sciences*, 14(ITAS Volume 14 Issue 1), pp. 1–19. Available at: .DOI: 10.7827/Turkish-Studies.14810

Balsalobre-Lorente, D., (2024) 'Do ICT and green technology matter in sustainable development goals?', *Sustainable Development*, p. sd.3185. Available at: DOI: 10.1002/sd.3185

Ben-Eliyahu, A. (2021). Sustainable Learning in Education. *Sustainability (Basel)*, *13*(8), 4250. DOI: 10.3390/su13084250

Biswas, A. (2008). Managing art technology research collaborations. *International Journal of Arts and Technology*, *1*(1), 66. DOI: 10.1504/IJART.2008.019883

Buck, R., & Snook, B. (2020). Reality bites: Implementing arts integration. *Research in Dance Education*, *21*(1), 98–115. DOI: 10.1080/14647893.2020.1727873

Cerceo, E., Zimmerman, M., & DeLisser, H. M. (2022). Diversity, Equity, and Inclusion: Moving from Performance to Transformation Through the Arts and Humanities. *Journal of General Internal Medicine*, *37*(4), 944–946. DOI: 10.1007/s11606-021-07225-2 PMID: 34993859

Chand, V. S., Deshmukh, K. S., & Shukla, A. (2020). Why does technology integration fail? Teacher beliefs and content developer assumptions in an Indian initiative. *Educational Technology Research and Development*, *68*(5), 2753–2774. DOI: 10.1007/s11423-020-09760-x

Chander, N., Siow, M. L., Ramachandran, S., Kunasekaran, P., & Rathakrishnan, T. (2020). Conceptualizing Inclusive Learning and Development: A Framework towards Entrepreneurial Competency Practices for Sustainability. *Sustainability (Basel), 12*(17), 6905. DOI: 10.3390/su12176905

Chang, C.-Y., Du, Z., Kuo, H.-C., & Chang, C.-C. (2023). 'Investigating the Impact of Design Thinking-Based STEAM PBL on Students' Creativity and Computational Thinking'. *IEEE Transactions on Education, 66*(6), 673–681. DOI: 10.1109/TE.2023.3297221

Chapman, S. N., & O'Gorman, L. (2022). Transforming Learning Environments in Early Childhood Contexts Through the Arts: Responding to the United Nations Sustainable Development Goals. *International Journal of Early Childhood, 54*(1), 33–50. DOI: 10.1007/s13158-022-00320-3

Chen, L. (2024). Exploring Innovative Practices and Challenges in the Ecological Development of Art Industry Driven by Digital Technology. *Applied Mathematics and Nonlinear Sciences, 9*(1), 20242975. DOI: 10.2478/amns-2024-2975

Chiu, T. K. F., Meng, H., Chai, C.-S., King, I., Wong, S., & Yam, Y. (2022). Creation and Evaluation of a Pretertiary Artificial Intelligence (AI) Curriculum. *IEEE Transactions on Education, 65*(1), 30–39. DOI: 10.1109/TE.2021.3085878

Chung, F. M.-Y. (2024). Utilising technology as a transmission strategy in intangible cultural heritage: The case of Cantonese opera performances. *International Journal of Heritage Studies, 30*(2), 210–225. DOI: 10.1080/13527258.2023.2284723

Clark, B., & Button, C. (2011). Sustainability transdisciplinary education model: Interface of arts, science, and community (STEM). *International Journal of Sustainability in Higher Education, 12*(1), 41–54. DOI: 10.1108/14676371111098294

Comninos, P., McLoughlin, L., & Anderson, E. F. (2009). Educating technophile artists: experiences from a highly successful computer animation undergraduate programme. In *ACM SIGGRAPH ASIA 2009 Educators Program. SA09: SIGGRAPH ASIA 2009* (pp. 1–8). ACM., DOI: 10.1145/1666611.1666612

Cottafava, D., Cavaglià, G., & Corazza, L. (2019). 'Education of sustainable development goals through students' active engagement: A transformative learning experience', *Sustainability Accounting. Management and Policy Journal, 10*(3), 521–544. DOI: 10.1108/SAMPJ-05-2018-0152

Dev, S., George, M., Rafique, S., Vaddapalli, M., Nair, S., & Al Hameli, A. (2024). Sustainable Inclusive Framework Studio for Inclusive Education—Perceptions of Teachers, Parents, and Students in United Arab Emirates. *Sustainability (Basel), 16*(15), 6367. DOI: 10.3390/su16156367

Díez-Palomar, J., Sanmamed, A. F. F., García-Carrión, R., & Molina-Roldán, S. (2018). Pathways to Equitable and Sustainable Education through the Inclusion of Roma Students in Learning Mathematics. *Sustainability (Basel), 10*(7), 2191. DOI: 10.3390/su10072191

Dockry, M. J., Hall, K., Van Lopik, W., & Caldwell, C. M. (2016). Sustainable development education, practice, and research: An indigenous model of sustainable development at the College of Menominee Nation, Keshena, WI, USA. *Sustainability Science, 11*(1), 127–138. DOI: 10.1007/s11625-015-0304-x PMID: 30174730

Dovleac, L., Chi u, I. B., Nichifor, E., & Brătucu, G. (2023). Shaping the Inclusivity in the New Society by Enhancing the Digitainability of Sustainable Development Goals with Education. *Sustainability (Basel), 15*(4), 3782. DOI: 10.3390/su15043782

Erol, A., Erol, M., & Başaran, M. (2023). The effect of STEAM education with tales on problem solving and creativity skills. *European Early Childhood Education Research Journal, 31*(2), 243–258. DOI: 10.1080/1350293X.2022.2081347

Fan, X., & Zhong, X. (2022). Artificial intelligence-based creative thinking skill analysis model using human–computer interaction in art design teaching. *Computers & Electrical Engineering, 100*, 107957. DOI: 10.1016/j.compeleceng.2022.107957

Fava, M. (2020). A Decline in Drawing Ability? *International Journal of Art & Design Education, 39*(2), 319–332. DOI: 10.1111/jade.12255

Figueras-Ferrer, E. (2021). 'Reflexiones en torno a la cultura digital contemporánea. Retos futuros en educación superior', *Arte. Individuo y Sociedad, 33*(2), 449–466. DOI: 10.5209/aris.68505

Gao, B. (2024). Research on the Development of the Deep Integration of Digital Media Technology and Modern Art Education. *Applied Mathematics and Nonlinear Sciences, 9*(1), 20241944. DOI: 10.2478/amns-2024-1944

Gu, X., Tong, D., Shi, P., Zou, Y., Yuan, H., Chen, C., & Zhao, G. (2023). Incorporating STEAM activities into creativity training in higher education. *Thinking Skills and Creativity, 50*, 101395. DOI: 10.1016/j.tsc.2023.101395

Hajisoteriou, C., & Sorkos, G. (2023). Towards a new paradigm of "Sustainable Intercultural and inclusive education": A comparative "blended" approach. *Education Inquiry, 14*(4), 496–512. DOI: 10.1080/20004508.2022.2071016

Harb, B., & Sidani, D. (2022). Smart technologies challenges and issues in social inclusion – case of disabled youth in a developing country. *Journal of Asia Business Studies*, *16*(2), 308–323. DOI: 10.1108/JABS-10-2020-0389

Heilig, J. V., Cole, H., & Aguilar, A. (2010). From Dewey to No Child Left Behind: The Evolution and Devolution of Public Arts Education. *Arts Education Policy Review*, *111*(4), 136–145. DOI: 10.1080/10632913.2010.490776

Hodgins, J. (2015) 'Educating for Both Art and Technology', in *Proceedings of the 46th ACM Technical Symposium on Computer Science Education. SIGCSE '15: The 46th ACM Technical Symposium on Computer Science Education*, Kansas City Missouri USA: ACM, pp. 1–1. Available at: DOI: 10.1145/2676723.2694804

Holst, J. (2023). Towards coherence on sustainability in education: A systematic review of Whole Institution Approaches. *Sustainability Science*, *18*(2), 1015–1030. DOI: 10.1007/s11625-022-01226-8

Jagodzinski, J. (2015). The Challenges of Art Education in Designer Capitalism: Collaborative Practices in the (New Media) Arts. *International Journal of Art & Design Education*, *34*(3), 282–295. DOI: 10.1111/jade.12088

Kamran, M., & Siddiqui, S. (2024). Roots of Resilience: Uncovering the Secrets behind 25+ Years of Inclusive Education Sustainability. *Sustainability (Basel)*, *16*(11), 4364. DOI: 10.3390/su16114364

Ketikidou, G., & Saiti, A. (2022). The promotion of inclusive education through sustainable and systemic leadership. *International Journal of Leadership in Education*, •••, 1–16. DOI: 10.1080/13603124.2022.2032368

Kioupi, V., & Voulvoulis, N. (2019). Education for Sustainable Development: A Systemic Framework for Connecting the SDGs to Educational Outcomes. *Sustainability (Basel)*, *11*(21), 6104. DOI: 10.3390/su11216104

Kjellgren, B., & Richter, T. (2021). Education for a Sustainable Future: Strategies for Holistic Global Competence Development at Engineering Institutions. *Sustainability (Basel)*, *13*(20), 11184. DOI: 10.3390/su132011184

Kulkov, I., Kulkova, J., Rohrbeck, R., Menvielle, L., Kaartemo, V., & Makkonen, H. (2024). Artificial intelligence - driven sustainable development: Examining organizational, technical, and processing approaches to achieving global goals. *Sustainable Development (Bradford)*, *32*(3), 2253–2267. DOI: 10.1002/sd.2773

Kurent, B., & Avsec, S. (2024). Synergizing Systems Thinking and Technology-Enhanced Learning for Sustainable Education Using the Flow Theory Framework. *Sustainability (Basel)*, *16*(21), 9319. DOI: 10.3390/su16219319

La Rose, T. *et al.* (2022) 'Direct[Message]: Exploring Access and Engagement With the Arts Through Digital Technology in COVID Times', *Cultural Studies Critical Methodologies*, 22(6), pp. 641–653. Available at: .DOI: 10.1177/15327086221098200

Li, J. (2024). Integration and development of modern art design and environmental design in the context of deep learning. *Applied Mathematics and Nonlinear Sciences*, *9*(1), 20242687. DOI: 10.2478/amns-2024-2687

Lin, H.-C. K., Lu, L.-W., & Lu, R.-S. (2024). Integrating Digital Technologies and Alternate Reality Games for Sustainable Education: Enhancing Cultural Heritage Awareness and Learning Engagement. *Sustainability (Basel)*, *16*(21), 9451. DOI: 10.3390/su16219451

Liu, K., (2024). A comprehensive Beyond-GDP database to accelerate wellbeing, inclusion, and sustainability research. *Scientific Data*, *11*(1), 1166. DOI: 10.1038/s41597-024-04006-4 PMID: 39448623

Liu, Y.-L. E., Lee, T.-P., & Huang, Y.-M. (2023). 'Enhancing university students' creative confidence, learning motivation, and team creative performance in design thinking using a digital visual collaborative environment'. *Thinking Skills and Creativity*, *50*, 101388. DOI: 10.1016/j.tsc.2023.101388

Marx, S., & Kim, Y. (2019). Technology for Equity and Social Justice in Education: Introduction to the Special Issue. *International Journal of Multicultural Education*, *21*(1), 1–4. DOI: 10.18251/ijme.v21i1.1939

Matinmikko-Blue, M., Yrjölä, S., & Ahokangas, P. (2024). Multi-perspective approach for developing sustainable 6G mobile communications. *Telecommunications Policy*, *48*(2), 102640. DOI: 10.1016/j.telpol.2023.102640

McGregor, C. (2012). Art-informed pedagogy: Tools for social transformation. *International Journal of Lifelong Education*, *31*(3), 309–324. DOI: 10.1080/02601370.2012.683612

Medina-García, M., Doña-Toledo, L., & Higueras-Rodríguez, L. (2020). Equal Opportunities in an Inclusive and Sustainable Education System: An Explanatory Model. *Sustainability (Basel)*, *12*(11), 4626. DOI: 10.3390/su12114626

M.P. et al. (2024). A Review Article On The Impact And Evolution Of Sustainable Brands. *International Journal For Multidisciplinary Research*, *6*(5), 28354. DOI: 10.36948/ijfmr.2024.v06i05.28354

Mukherjee, M. (2017). Educating the Heart and the Mind: Conceptualizing inclusive pedagogy for sustainable development. *Educational Philosophy and Theory*, *49*(5), 531–549. DOI: 10.1080/00131857.2016.1185002

Niederhauser, J., Vez, C., Jörg, A., Bertschy, F., Künzli David, C., & Pfründer, G. (2024). The power of artistic practices in ESD. *Environmental Education Research, 30*(4), 580–590. DOI: 10.1080/13504622.2023.2227362

Nordén, B. (2018). Learning and teaching sustainable development in global–local contexts. *Environmental Education Research, 24*(5), 772–773. DOI: 10.1080/13504622.2016.1217399

Owojori, O. M., Okoro, C., & Chileshe, N. (2024). Actualising social sustainability through adaptive reuse innovations within the context of sustainable development. *International Journal of Construction Management, 24*(4), 411–421. DOI: 10.1080/15623599.2023.2257509

Ox, J., & Lowenberg, R. (2013). What Is the Challenge of Art/Science Today and How Do We Address It? *Leonardo, 46*(1), 2–2. DOI: 10.1162/LEON_e_00476

Pavlou, V., & Castro-Varela, A. (2024). E-Learning Canvases: Navigating the Confluence of Online Arts Education and Sustainable Pedagogies in Teacher Education. *Sustainability (Basel), 16*(5), 1741. DOI: 10.3390/su16051741

Peppler, K., Dahn, M., & Ito, M. (2022). Connected Arts Learning: Cultivating Equity Through Connected and Creative Educational Experiences. *Review of Research in Education, 46*(1), 264–287. DOI: 10.3102/0091732X221084322

Peruzzo, F., & Allan, J. (2024). Rethinking inclusive (digital) education: Lessons from the pandemic to reconceptualise inclusion through convivial technologies. *Learning, Media and Technology, 49*(2), 244–258. DOI: 10.1080/17439884.2022.2131817

Qadri, U.A. *et al.* (2024) ‘Digital technologies and social sustainability in the digital transformation age: a systematic analysis and research agenda’, *International Journal of Ethics and Systems* [Preprint]. Available at: .DOI: 10.1108/IJOES-08-2024-0239

Radclyffe-Thomas, N. (2008). White Heat or Blue Screen? Digital Technology in Art & Design Education. *International Journal of Art & Design Education, 27*(2), 158–167. DOI: 10.1111/j.1476-8070.2008.00571.x

Rahman, Md. H., Mohammed Ghazali, A.B. and Bin Mohamed Sawal, M.Z.H. (2024) ‘Reasons for resistance to technology adoption in university libraries in Bangladesh’, *Information Development*, p. 02666669241294249. Available at: DOI: 10.1177/02666669241294249

Sanz-Prieto, M., De Pablo González, G., & De Pablo Sánchez, N. (2024). *Art Project Virtual Reality for Global Citizenship Education*. Technology, Knowledge and Learning. [Preprint], DOI: 10.1007/s10758-023-09716-z

Scalabrino, C., Navarrete Salvador, A., & Oliva Martínez, J. M. (2022). A theoretical framework to address education for sustainability for an earlier transition to a just, low carbon and circular economy. *Environmental Education Research, 28*(5), 735–766. DOI: 10.1080/13504622.2022.2031899

Sheikheldin, G. H., & Hambly, H. (2024). Technological Change and Techno-Social Systems: Re-Examining Sustainable Development and Digitalisation in Africa. *Science, Technology & Society, 29*(4), 573–594. DOI: 10.1177/09717218241281826

Sonn, C., & Baker, A. (2016). Creating inclusive knowledges: Exploring the transformative potential of arts and cultural practice. *International Journal of Inclusive Education, 20*(3), 215–228. DOI: 10.1080/13603116.2015.1047663

Souleles, N. (2013). The Evolution of Art and Design Pedagogies in England: Influences of the Past, Challenges for the Future. *International Journal of Art & Design Education, 32*(2), 243–255. DOI: 10.1111/j.1476-8070.2013.01753.x

Sposab, K., & Rieckmann, M. (2024). Development of Sustainability Competencies in Secondary School Education: A Scoping Literature Review. *Sustainability (Basel), 16*(23), 10228. DOI: 10.3390/su162310228

Steckel, B., Shinas, V. H., & Van Vaerenewyck, L. (2015). Artistic Technology Integration: Stories From Primary and Elementary Classrooms. *The Reading Teacher, 69*(1), 41–49. DOI: 10.1002/trtr.1356

Su, H., & Mokmin, N. A. M. (2024). Unveiling the Canvas: Sustainable Integration of AI in Visual Art Education. *Sustainability (Basel), 16*(17), 7849. DOI: 10.3390/su16177849

Tan, J., Gao, B., & Lu, X. (2018) 'An AR system for artistic creativity education', in *Proceedings of the 24th ACM Symposium on Virtual Reality Software and Technology. VRST '18: 24th ACM Symposium on Virtual Reality Software and Technology*, Tokyo Japan: ACM, pp. 1–2. Available at: DOI: 10.1145/3281505.3283396

Tao, Y., & Tao, Y. (2024). Integrating Aesthetic Education in Quality Education: A Bibliometric Analysis of Sustainable Development Perspectives. *Sustainability (Basel), 16*(2), 855. DOI: 10.3390/su16020855

Trott, C. D., Even, T. L., & Frame, S. M. (2020). Merging the arts and sciences for collaborative sustainability action: A methodological framework. *Sustainability Science, 15*(4), 1067–1085. DOI: 10.1007/s11625-020-00798-7

Uygur, M., Ayçiçek, B., Doğrul, H., & Yanpar Yelken, T. (2020). 'Investigating Stakeholders' Views on Technology Integration: The Role of Educational Leadership for Sustainable Inclusive Education'. *Sustainability (Basel)*, *12*(24), 10354. DOI: 10.3390/su122410354

Vasconcelos, C., & Orion, N. (2021). Earth Science Education as a Key Component of Education for Sustainability. *Sustainability (Basel)*, *13*(3), 1316. DOI: 10.3390/su13031316

Vatanartiran, S., & Karadeniz, S. (2015). A Needs Analysis for Technology Integration Plan: Challenges and Needs of Teachers. *Contemporary Educational Technology*, *6*(3). DOI: 10.30935/cedtech/6150

Vičič Krabonja, M., Kustec, S., Skrbinjek, V., Aberšek, B., & Flogie, A. (2024). Innovative Professional Learning Communities and Sustainable Education Practices through Digital Transformation. *Sustainability (Basel)*, *16*(14), 6250. DOI: 10.3390/su16146250

Wangdi, P., & Boossabong, P. (2024). Towards an Inclusive Education Policy for Sustainability: Advancing the "Educating for Gross National Happiness" Initiative in Bhutan. *Sustainability (Basel)*, *16*(13), 5446. DOI: 10.3390/su16135446

Weng, X., Ng, O.-L., Cui, Z., & Leung, S. (2023). Creativity Development With Problem-Based Digital Making and Block-Based Programming for Science, Technology, Engineering, Arts, and Mathematics Learning in Middle School Contexts. *Journal of Educational Computing Research*, *61*(2), 304–328. DOI: 10.1177/07356331221115661

Wu, Q. (2024). Application of Artificial Intelligence-based Visual Arts Pedagogy in Traditional Painting Education. *Applied Mathematics and Nonlinear Sciences*, *9*(1), 20242994. DOI: 10.2478/amns-2024-2994

Wulia, T. (2023). Aesthetic resistance: Publicness, potentiality, and plexus. *Journal of Political Power*, *16*(2), 213–236. DOI: 10.1080/2158379X.2023.2245228 PMID: 38013878

Xue, L., & Lu, X. (2021) 'Research on the Integrated Innovative Teaching Model of Art and Technology Based on Pearson Correlation Analysis', in *2021 2nd International Conference on Artificial Intelligence and Education (ICAIE). 2021 2nd International Conference on Artificial Intelligence and Education (ICAIE)*, Dali, China: IEEE, pp. 245–251. Available at: DOI: 10.1109/ICAIE53562.2021.00058

Yang, M. (2024). Research on Teaching Methods of Integrating Watercolor Techniques and Information Technology in Higher Education Art Education. *Applied Mathematics and Nonlinear Sciences*, *9*(1), 20242803. DOI: 10.2478/amns-2024-2803

Yoon, S., & Ho, J. (2024) 'Delivering sustainable development via social innovation: Cases of social entrepreneurship in South Korea and Singapore', *Sustainable Development*, p. sd.3127. Available at: DOI: 10.1002/sd.3127

Zhang, Q. (2023). Artistic expression and data protection: Balancing aesthetics with data privacy in IoT. *Heliyon*, *9*(9), e19380. DOI: 10.1016/j.heliyon.2023.e19380 PMID: 37662810

Zhao, L., Hussam, E., Seong, J.-T., Elshenawy, A., Kamal, M., & Alshawarbeh, E. (2024). Revolutionizing art education: Integrating AI and multimedia for enhanced appreciation teaching. *Alexandria Engineering Journal*, *93*, 33–43. DOI: 10.1016/j.aej.2024.03.011

Chapter 9
Harmonizing Sustainability and Artistry:
Fashion in the Digital Age

Nhan Hoang Thi Ai
https://orcid.org/0009-0002-2361-7452
University of Economics, Ho Chi Minh City, Vietnam

ABSTRACT

In the digital age, the fashion industry faces the challenge of harmonising sustainability and artistry while embracing technological advancements. This paper explores the intersection of sustainable practices, creative expression, and emerging technologies within fashion. It highlights how innovations such as 3D printing, blockchain, and AI are driving transparency, reducing waste, and enabling the use of eco-friendly materials. Despite challenges related to cost, scalability, and consumer awareness, these technologies present significant opportunities for collaboration, creativity, and growth. Through case studies of pioneering brands, this research examines successful implementations of sustainable technology and their impact on environmental conservation, social responsibility, and economic viability. The paper concludes by emphasising the need for continued innovation and collaboration to drive the future of fashion, ensuring that sustainability and artistry coexist through the power of technology.

DOI: 10.4018/979-8-3693-7610-2.ch009

1. INTRODUCTION

The fashion industry stands at a critical crossroads, where the need for sustainability is increasingly intertwined with the preservation of artistic integrity. Historically, fashion has been a powerful medium for creative expression, reflecting cultural, social, and personal identities. However, the environmental footprint of the industry, especially the fast fashion segment, has become a growing concern. The exploitation of natural resources, massive textile waste, and the industry's contribution to pollution have prompted calls for reform (Niinimäki et al., 2020). As a result, the challenge of harmonising sustainability with the artistry that defines fashion has taken centre stage in both academic and industry discussions.

In recent years, technological advancements have offered promising solutions to these challenges. Innovations such as 3D printing, blockchain technology, artificial intelligence (AI), and the development of eco-friendly materials are revolutionising the fashion landscape (Colovic & Fernandez-Fernandez, 2020). These technologies are not only reducing the environmental impact but are also enabling new forms of creative expression. For instance, 3D printing allows designers to experiment with materials and forms in ways that were previously impossible, pushing the boundaries of fashion while significantly cutting down on waste (MacArthur Foundation, 2021). Blockchain, on the other hand, enhances supply chain transparency, ensuring ethical sourcing and sustainable practices across the fashion production process (Saravanan & Adams, 2022).

Sustainability has evolved from being a peripheral concern to a central element of modern fashion. The incorporation of digital tools has enabled designers and brands to embrace circular fashion, reducing waste by creating systems where garments are designed, produced, and disposed of in an environmentally responsible way. Brands such as Stella McCartney and Patagonia have successfully adopted these practices, integrating AI to forecast demand more accurately and minimise overproduction, thus reducing waste (MacArthur Foundation, 2021). These innovations represent the dawn of a more sustainable and ethical fashion ecosystem, where creativity is no longer at odds with ecological responsibility.

The future of fashion lies in its ability to balance innovation with sustainability. Emerging technologies offer the potential to transform fashion into an industry where artistry and environmental stewardship coexist harmoniously. Virtual fashion, smart textiles, and circular fashion systems are promising developments that could further reshape how the fashion industry operates. Virtual fashion, for instance, offers a new digital frontier where garments exist solely in virtual environments, thus reducing the need for physical production and consumption (Niinimäki et al., 2020). Smart textiles, which integrate technology into fabrics, open possibilities for functionality and creativity that extend beyond traditional design. The circular fashion system, with its focus on reusability and minimal waste, signals a shift towards more sustainable production and consumption patterns (Saravanan & Adams, 2022).

This paper explores the intersection of sustainability, artistry, and technology in the fashion industry, examining case studies of pioneering brands and their successful implementations of these technologies. It seeks to highlight how fashion can evolve in the digital age by leveraging these innovations to achieve a balance between creative expression and environmental responsibility. By investigating how fashion brands are adapting to these technological advancements, this research aims to provide a roadmap for future growth in the industry, ensuring that sustainability and artistry can not only coexist but thrive through the power of digital transformation.

2. THE ROLE OF TECHNOLOGY IN SUSTAINABLE FASHION

The fashion industry is one of the largest contributors to environmental degradation and social injustice. In recent years, there has been a growing awareness of the need for sustainability in the fashion industry. Technological innovations have played a major role in enhancing sustainability practices, from improving supply chain transparency to reducing waste and developing eco-friendly materials (da Cruz & Cruz, 2020). To discuss technological innovations for sustainability in the fashion industry, we can mention:

- Supply chain transparency: One of the key challenges in the fashion industry is ensuring transparency and accountability in the supply chain. Technology, especially blockchain, has emerged as a powerful tool for traceability and accountability in the sourcing process as a tool for sustainability (S. Guo et al., 2023). Blockchain technology enables the creation of a secure and transparent digital ledger that tracks the journey of a product from raw materials to the end consumer. By using blockchain to provide transparency in the supply chain, fashion brands can ensure ethical sourcing practices, reduce the risk of counterfeiting, and build trust with consumers (Badhwar et al., 2023).
- Waste reduction: Overproduction and waste are major issues in the fashion industry, leading to environmental pollution and resource depletion. Technological innovations such as 3D printing and virtual sampling provide solutions to reduce waste in the manufacturing process (Pasricha & Greeninger, 2018). 3D printing enables on-demand production, eliminating the need for mass production and reducing excess inventory. On the other hand, virtual sampling allows designers to create digital prototypes of garments, minimizing the need for physical samples and reducing material waste (Papachristou et al., 2023). By adopting these technologies, fashion brands

can streamline their manufacturing processes, reduce waste, and reduce their environmental impact.

- Eco-friendly materials: The fashion industry is increasingly turning to sustainable and eco-friendly materials to reduce its environmental footprint. Many processes, techniques and practices involved in textile manufacturing have been developed to save the world from the hazardous effects of chemicals used in the textile industry or released as by-products by the textile industry (Sharma, 2013). Technology plays a key role in the development of new sustainable fabrics, smart textiles, and bio-based materials that provide alternatives to traditional materials such as cotton and polyester. Advanced manufacturing techniques, such as nanotechnology and biotechnology, enable the production of innovative materials that are biodegradable, recyclable, and eco-friendly (Shaarawy, 2019). By incorporating these eco-friendly materials into their collections, fashion brands can reduce their reliance on toxic chemicals and synthetic fibers, leading to a more sustainable and circular fashion system.

Technological applications in the fashion industry have been instrumental in driving sustainability efforts. 3D printing is a prime example of a technology that minimizes waste and provides designers with flexibility in sustainable material usage. By enabling on-demand production and reducing the need for physical prototypes, 3D printing helps to minimize material waste and streamline the manufacturing process (Javaid et al., 2021).

Figure 1. Process flow of AM stages toward enriching the environmental sustainability (Javaid et al, 2021).

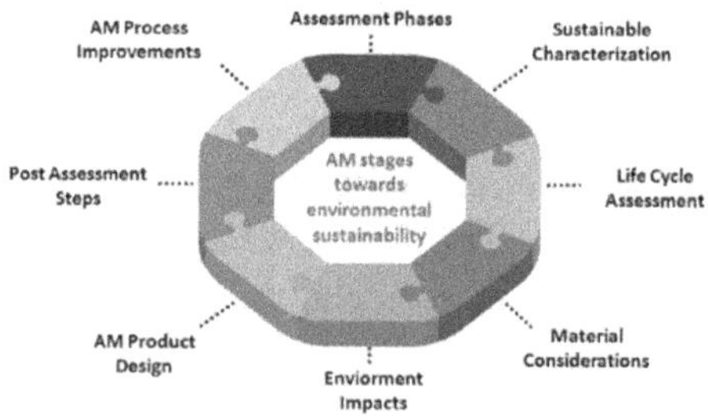

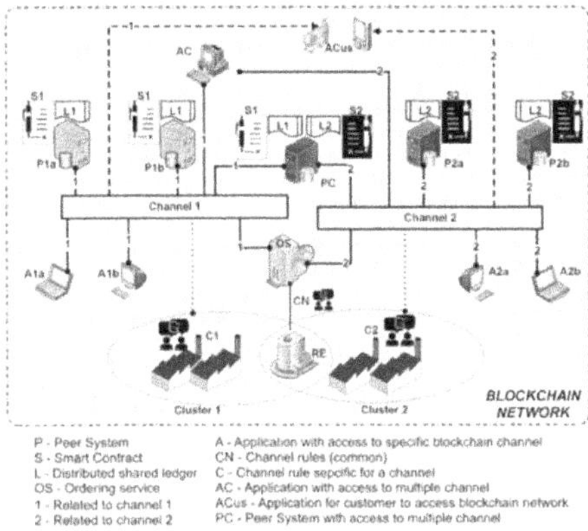

Blockchain technology provides another innovative solution by providing traceability and transparency in circular supply chains for both consumers and brands (Centobelli et al., 2022). Through blockchain, consumers can track the journey of a garment from raw material sourcing to the final product, ensuring ethical practices and building trust (Agrawal et al., 2021).

Additionally, AI, Blockchain and IoT tools contribute to sustainable fashion consumption (Huyn et al., 2024). AI tools also help optimize designs, supporting designers to create eco-friendly designs by optimizing patterns, reducing material waste and improving efficiency in planning processes (Rathore, 2019). Overall, these technological applications are reshaping the fashion industry towards a more sustainable and transparent future.

Technology has revolutionized the fashion industry, offering innovative solutions to enhance sustainability practices. From supply chain transparency to waste reduction and the development of eco-friendly materials, technological innovations are driving positive change in the fashion industry. By embracing technology and integrating sustainable practices into their operations, fashion brands can create a more ethical, transparent, and environmentally friendly industry for the future.

3. CHALLENGES AND OPPORTUNITIES IN IMPLEMENTING SUSTAINABLE TECHNOLOGY IN FASHION

The adoption and implementation of sustainable technologies in the fashion industry face several challenges that hinder progress towards a more sustainable future.

- A major challenge is supplying chain and technological uptake barriers (Kouhizadeh et al., 2021). The economic growth models, the concept of sustainability, and technological innovations, materials, environment, and energy are closely interrelated and mutually reinforcing. This creates interdependence in their development processes and mutual reliance on technology, environment, and governance (Majerník et al., 2023). Issues such as data privacy, cybersecurity threats, scalability, and lack of industry-wide standardization create significant barriers to widespread adoption (Singh et al., 2024). Immersive technologies offer potential solutions for sustainability, such as reducing online returns and waste in design, but face issues like high energy costs and consumer reluctance (Mesjar et al., 2023). The integration of Industry 5.0 in supply chain sustainability is hindered by technological, organizational, regulatory, and economic barriers (Laddha & Agrawal, 2024). Additionally, consumer awareness plays a crucial role in the adoption of sustainable fashion technologies. Studies have identified lack of awareness as a significant barrier to eco-fashion adoption (Sufia Munir, 2020), while increased awareness positively impacts attitudes towards sustainability-related technology (Iqbal & Su, 2025). Environmental knowledge and attitudes significantly influence purchase intentions for sustainable clothing among urban consumers (Tryphena & Aram, 2023). Additionally, personal innovativeness and knowledge of apparel technology positively impact awareness of sustainability-related technology among apparel professionals (Iqbal & Su, 2025). Overcoming these challenges requires addressing knowledge gaps, improving consumer awareness, and developing targeted strategies for successful implementation of sustainable technologies across the fashion industry supply chain. Addressing these challenges will be essential to overcoming barriers to widespread adoption of sustainable technologies in the fashion industry. Despite the challenges, the implementation of sustainable technology in the fashion industry also presents significant opportunities for growth and innovation.

- Collaboration and innovation are key drivers of progress, with opportunities for collaboration between technology companies, fashion designers and sustainability organizations to drive innovation in sustainable practices. By working together, these stakeholders can leverage their expertise and resources to develop cutting-edge solutions that promote sustainability across the entire fashion supply chain. Government and regulatory support also play a key role in driving sustainable practices in the fashion industry (Majerník et al., 2023). Policies and funding initiatives can encourage and support the adoption of sustainable technologies, creating an enabling environment for sustainable innovation to thrive. In addition, consumer engagement is essential to drive the adoption of sustainable fashion technologies. Positive attitudes towards recycling and green apparel products, along with social influences, contribute to higher intentions to engage in sustainable behaviour and purchase sustainable products (La Rosa & Jorgensen, 2021). By harnessing the power of digital platforms, fashion brands can educate and engage consumers about the importance of sustainability, empowering them to make informed choices and supporting sustainable fashion practices. Seizing these opportunities for collaboration, regulatory support and consumer engagement can pave the way for sustainable growth and innovation in the fashion industry.

4. CASE STUDIES OF SUSTAINABLE TECHNOLOGY INITIATIVES IN FASHION

In the modern fashion industry, sustainability and technology are increasingly merging to address the environmental and social challenges posed by traditional practices. Below are detailed case studies of pioneering brands that have successfully integrated technological innovations to drive sustainability, setting benchmarks for ethical production, environmental conservation, and social responsibility.

4.1. Stella McCartney: Sustainable Luxury Through Cutting-Edge Technology

Stella McCartney has long been at the forefront of sustainable fashion, particularly in the luxury segment. The brand is known for using cutting-edge digital technologies to track supply chain ethics and ensure sustainable material sourcing. One of the most notable technological initiatives is McCartney's collaboration with Google Cloud to develop a system that tracks the environmental impact of the raw materials used in their garments. This initiative leverages big data and AI to assess factors like water usage, deforestation, and pollution across the supply chain (Google Cloud, 2020).

Additionally, Stella McCartney has incorporated innovative materials, such as recycled polyester, organic cotton, and animal-free leather, which reduce the brand's carbon footprint and resource consumption. By using blockchain technology, the brand enhances transparency in its supply chain, providing customers with clear insights into the ethical standards upheld during production (The Business of Fashion, 2021).

Impact:

- Environmental conservation: McCartney's use of eco-friendly materials and technologies has led to significant reductions in water consumption and greenhouse gas emissions. This approach sets a model for how luxury fashion can remain profitable without harming the planet.

- Social responsibility: The brand ensures ethical labour practices by closely monitoring the supply chain for fair wages and safe working conditions.
- Economic viability: Stella McCartney proves that sustainability can coexist with luxury, maintaining high demand and profitability through its commitment to eco-conscious practices.

4.2. The Fabricant: A Digital-Only Fashion House Eliminating Waste

The Fabricant, a pioneer in the digital-only fashion space, completely disrupts the traditional model by creating fashion that exists exclusively in the virtual world. Founded in 2018, the company creates high-end digital garments that never need to be physically produced, thus eliminating waste and overproduction. By leveraging 3D design and virtual reality, The Fabricant allows consumers to wear and showcase digital fashion in online environments, including social media platforms and the metaverse (Harper's Bazaar, 2021).

The company's model is a radical departure from traditional fashion production, drastically reducing carbon emissions, resource consumption, and textile waste. This approach not only promotes environmental sustainability but also offers a new frontier for creative expression that transcends the limitations of physical materials.

Impact:

- Environmental conservation: By eliminating the need for physical production, The Fabricant prevents significant waste generation and reduces the overall environmental footprint of fashion.
- Social responsibility: As a digital-only platform, The Fabricant sidesteps issues like labour exploitation and poor working conditions often associated with traditional manufacturing.
- Economic viability: While a niche market, digital fashion is gaining traction and has the potential to redefine profitability models in the fashion industry by tapping into the growing demand for virtual products.

4.3. Burberry: Blockchain-Enabled Transparency and Eco-Friendly Practices

Burberry - a British luxury brand, has embraced blockchain technology to enhance transparency in its supply chain. By implementing blockchain, Burberry can trace the journey of its products from raw material sourcing to finished garments, ensuring ethical practices and reducing the environmental impact (Forbes, 2020).

This transparency initiative empowers consumers by providing verifiable information about the sustainability of the products they purchase.

In addition to its blockchain initiatives, Burberry has committed to using eco-friendly materials, such as sustainable cotton and recycled nylon. The brand has also taken significant steps to reduce its carbon footprint, pledging to become carbon-neutral by 2022. Burberry's sustainability goals align with its broader commitment to responsible luxury and environmental stewardship.

Impact:

- Environmental conservation: Burberry's adoption of sustainable materials and its commitment to carbon neutrality have contributed to a reduction in carbon emissions and resource depletion.
- Social responsibility: Through blockchain-enabled transparency, Burberry ensures that workers in its supply chain are treated fairly, promoting ethical labour practices and empowering consumers to make informed choices.
- Economic viability: Burberry's blend of traditional luxury with modern sustainability practices has allowed the brand to maintain its profitability while meeting the growing demand for ethical fashion.

5. FUTURE TRENDS IN TECHNOLOGY AND SUSTAINABILITY FOR FASHION

The intersection of sustainability and technology in fashion continues to evolve, presenting new opportunities for reducing waste, conserving resources, and enhancing creativity. Below are some key emerging trends and speculative future developments that hold the potential to reshape the industry.

Emerging Trends:

- o Virtual fitting rooms: Reducing returns and minimising waste

Virtual fitting rooms are becoming increasingly common as fashion brands invest in augmented reality (AR) technology to allow customers to try on clothes virtually before making a purchase. This innovation reduces the need for physical fittings and drastically cuts down on the number of returns, which can be costly and resource intensive. By minimising the shipping of returned goods and the potential for unsold inventory, virtual fitting rooms help reduce waste in both production and logistics.

Several companies are already leveraging this technology. For instance, Zara and ASOS have adopted AR solutions for their customers, allowing them to visualise how garments will fit and look in real-time (Sullivan, 2020). Virtual fitting rooms also improve the customer experience by providing a personalised shopping journey.

Impact: Less waste, reduced carbon emissions from transportation, and minimised overproduction.

- o Data analytics for demand forecasting

Big data and machine learning are revolutionising how fashion companies predict consumer behaviour and fashion trends. Through demand forecasting powered by advanced analytics, brands can better anticipate which products will be popular, thereby reducing overproduction and wastage. Machine learning algorithms analyse historical sales data, social media trends, and external factors like weather patterns to predict demand more accurately (Choi, 2020).

For instance, companies like H&M and Adidas use predictive analytics to optimise inventory levels, ensuring they produce only what is needed to meet demand. This shift towards data-driven production models helps minimise unsold stock and the environmental impact of excess production.

Impact: Enhanced inventory management, reduced textile waste, and more efficient use of resources.

- o IoT in fashion: Smart textiles and wearables

The integration of the Internet of Things (IoT) in fashion is giving rise to smart textiles and wearables that are designed with sustainability in mind. These garments often feature sensors that can monitor environmental conditions or usage, encouraging consumers to extend the life of their clothing. For example, Levi's collaborated with Google to create the "Jacquard" smart jacket, which allows wearers to control their smartphones through touch-sensitive fabric (Ranganathan, 2019).

Smart textiles can also help reduce waste by providing insights into garment wear-and-tear, prompting users to repair or recycle items rather than dispose of them prematurely. Some materials even adapt to environmental conditions, reducing the need for multiple layers of clothing items in different climates.

Impact: Extended garment lifespan, reduced consumption, and better resource management.

Speculations on Future Developments:

- o Digital fashion: Non-physical fashion items and NFTs

One of the most speculative and potentially disruptive developments in fashion is the rise of digital fashion. Non-fungible tokens (NFTs) have made waves in various creative industries, and fashion is no exception. Digital fashion items, which exist solely in the virtual world, offer consumers the ability to purchase and "wear" clothing in digital spaces, such as social media, gaming platforms, and the metaverse.

The Fabricant, for example, has led the charge in creating digital-only fashion collections that consumers can own and showcase online (Harper's Bazaar, 2021). This shift away from physical clothing could drastically reduce the need for material resources in fashion production. Digital fashion also opens new creative possibilities without the environmental consequences associated with traditional garment production.

Impact: Reduced textile waste, new business models, and the emergence of digital fashion economies.

- Circular fashion models: Recycling, Upcycling, and Waste reduction

As sustainability becomes more central to the fashion industry, circular fashion models are gaining prominence. These systems emphasise recycling, upcycling, and resource recovery to minimise waste. Technology plays a crucial role in enabling these models, particularly with advanced recycling processes and platforms that facilitate the resale and sharing of garments.

Brands like Patagonia and Eileen Fisher have embraced circularity by launching take-back programs, where consumers return used garments for recycling or resale (Fisher, 2019). Additionally, blockchain technology can provide transparency in tracking garment lifecycle data, ensuring that materials are properly recycled or upcycled.

Impact: Extended lifecycle of garments, reduced reliance on virgin materials, and minimised landfill waste.

- Potential industry disruptions

The cumulative impact of these emerging technologies could lead to profound disruptions in the traditional fashion industry. As sustainability becomes a core driver, technology will enable more efficient production, distribution, and consumption practices. We are likely to see a shift towards on-demand production, where garments are made only after an order is placed, reducing waste significantly.

Moreover, as digital fashion grows in popularity, the traditional concept of owning and wearing physical clothing could change, leading to new consumption patterns. Fashion NFTs and virtual collections may become status symbols, decoupling fashion from its environmental footprint and enabling limitless creativity without physical constraints.

Impact: New consumption models reduced environmental impact, and a redefined fashion landscape.

6. CONCLUSION

The paper underscores the importance of applying sustainable practices, creative expression, and emerging technologies to shape a more environmentally responsible and innovative future for the fashion industry. By leveraging these advancements and fostering collaboration, the industry can achieve a harmonious balance between artistic integrity and ecological stewardship, paving the way for a more sustainable and ethical fashion ecosystem.

6.1 Summary of Findings

The fashion industry is at a critical juncture where sustainability and artistry are converging with the assistance of technological advancements.

Innovations such as 3D printing, blockchain, and AI are driving transparency, reducing waste, and enabling the use of eco-friendly materials in fashion. Despite challenges such as cost, scalability, and consumer awareness, these technologies offer significant opportunities for collaboration, creativity, and growth within the industry. Case studies of pioneering brands demonstrate successful implementations of sustainable technology and their positive impact on environmental conservation, social responsibility, and economic viability.

Emerging trends like virtual fashion, smart textiles, and circular fashion systems are poised to reshape the industry by promoting sustainability and creativity. Continuous innovation and collaboration are essential to drive the future of fashion, ensuring that sustainability and artistry coexist through the power of technology.

7. LIMITATIONS, AND FUTURE LINES OF RESEARCH

Limitations of the study include the need for more in-depth case studies that are more representative of diverse perspectives and focus on long-term impacts. Future research directions could include exploring the integration of sustainability practices in fashion education, investigating the role of digital platforms in promoting sustainable fashion, analyzing the influence of consumer behavior on the adoption of environmentally friendly products, and examining the potential for cross-industry collaboration to promote sustainability initiatives in the fashion sector. Additionally, research could delve into the development of innovative business models that prioritize sustainability while maintaining profitability, as well as exploring the impact of emerging technologies such as augmented reality and virtual reality on the future of sustainable fashion.

REFERENCES

Agrawal, T. K., Kumar, V., Pal, R., Wang, L., & Chen, Y. (2021). Blockchain-based framework for supply chain traceability: A case example of textile and clothing industry. *Computers & Industrial Engineering, 154*, 107130. DOI: 10.1016/j.cie.2021.107130

Ali, S. W., Bairagi, S., & Shankar, P. (2020). Biomaterials-Based Nanogenerator: Futuristic Solution for Integration Into Smart Textiles. *Frontiers of Textile Materials: Polymers, Nanomaterials, Enzymes, and Advanced Modification Techniques*, 189-201, DOI: 10.1002/9781119620396.ch9

Badhwar, A., Islam, S., & Tan, C. S. L. (2023). Exploring the potential of blockchain technology within the fashion and textile supply chain with a focus on traceability, transparency, and product authenticity: A systematic review. In *Frontiers in Blockchain* (Vol. 6). Frontiers Media SA. DOI: 10.3389/fbloc.2023.1044723

Centobelli, P., Cerchione, R., Del Vecchio, P., Oropallo, E., & Secundo, G. Blockchain technology for bridging trust, traceability and transparency in circular supply chain, *Information & Management, Volume 59, Issue* 7, 2022, 103508, ISSN 0378-7206, DOI: 10.1016/j.im.2021.103508

Choi, T. (2020). *Sustainability in fashion supply chains: Big data and AI applications*. Springer.

Cloud, G. (2020). *Stella McCartney partners with Google to measure the environmental impact of its fashion production*. [Online] Available at: https://cloud.google.com/press-releases/2020/03/stella-mccartney-google-partnership

Colovic, A., & Fernandez-Fernandez, J. (2020). The Role of Digital Technologies in Fashion Sustainability. *Journal of Fashion and Textiles*. DOI: .DOI: 10.1186/s40691-020-00221-2

da Cruz, A. M. R., & Cruz, E. F. (2020). Blockchain-based traceability platforms as a tool for sustainability. *ICEIS 2020 - Proceedings of the 22nd International Conference on Enterprise Information Systems, 2*, 330–337. DOI: 10.5220/0009463803300337

Ellen MacArthur Foundation. (2021). Circular economy in fashion: Leveraging AI for sustainable practices. Available at: https://ellenmacarthurfoundation.org/fashion

Fisher, E. (2019). *Patagonia's Circular Economy Initiatives: Redefining Sustainable Fashion*. Vogue Business.

Forbes. (2020). *How Burberry uses blockchain to enhance transparency and sustainability*. [Online] Available at: https://www.forbes.com/sites/rachelarthur/2020/02/18/how-burberry-is-using-blockchain-to-enhance-sustainability-and-transparency-in-its-supply-chain/

Guo, S., Sun, X., & Lam, H. K. S. (2023, April). Applications of Blockchain Technology in Sustainable Fashion Supply Chains: Operational Transparency and Environmental Efforts. *IEEE Transactions on Engineering Management*, *70*(4), 1312–1328. DOI: 10.1109/TEM.2020.3034216

Harper's Bazaar. (2021). *The Fabricant is revolutionizing fashion with virtual designs*. [Online] Available at: https://www.harpersbazaar.com/fashion/designers/a36694502/the-fabricant-digital-fashion-house-interview/

Huyn, T. T. T., Sandbrink, C., & Kaufmann, H. R. (2024). Sustainability in the Fashion Industry: The Role of AI, Blockchain, and IoT in Carbon Footprint Reduction: Challenges and Motivations Toward the Transition. In Kaufmann, H. R., Panni, M. F. A. K., & Vrontis, D. (Eds.), *The Palgrave Handbook of Consumerism Issues in the Apparel Industry*. Palgrave Macmillan., DOI: 10.1007/978-3-031-59952-1_16

Iqbal, M. A., & Su, J. (2025). Apparel professionals' perception of sustainability-related technology: A structural equation modeling approach. *Research Journal of Textile and Apparel*, *29*(1), 184–202. DOI: 10.1108/RJTA-04-2023-0040

Javaid, M., Haleem, A., Singh, R. P., Suman, R., & Rab, S. (2021). Role of additive manufacturing applications towards environmental sustainability. In *Advanced Industrial and Engineering Polymer Research* (Vol. 4, Issue 4, pp. 312–322). KeAi Communications Co. DOI: 10.1016/j.aiepr.2021.07.005

Kouhizadeh, M., Saberi, S., & Sarkis, J. (2021). Blockchain technology and the sustainable supply chain: Theoretically exploring adoption barriers. *International Journal of Production Economics*, *231*, 107831. DOI: 10.1016/j.ijpe.2020.107831

La Rosa, A., & Johnson Jorgensen, J. (2021). Influences on Consumer Engagement with Sustainability and the Purchase Intention of Apparel Products. *Sustainability (Basel)*, *13*(19), 10655. DOI: 10.3390/su131910655

Laddha, S., & Agrawal, A. (2024). Unveiling barriers to Industry 5.0 adoption in supply chains: A DEMATEL approach. *RAUSP Management Journal*, *59*(2), 123–137. DOI: 10.1108/RAUSP-08-2023-0146

Majerník, M., Chovancová, J., Drábik, P., & Štofková, Z. (2023). Environmental Technological Innovations and the Sustainability of their Development. *Ecological Engineering and Environmental Technology*, *24*(4), 245–252. DOI: 10.12912/27197050/162708

Mesjar, L., Cross, K., Jiang, Y., & Steed, J. (2023). The Intersection of Fashion, Immersive Technology, and Sustainability: A Literature Review. *Sustainability (Basel)*, *15*(4), 3761. DOI: 10.3390/su15043761

Munir, S. (2020). Eco-Fashion Adoption in the UAE: Understanding Consumer Barriers and Motivational Factors. *Fashion Practice*, *12*(3), 371–393. DOI: 10.1080/17569370.2020.1777729

Niinimäki, K., Peters, G., Dahlbo, H., Perry, P., Rissanen, T., & Gwilt, A. (2020). The environmental price of fast fashion. *Nature Reviews. Earth & Environment*, *1*(4), 189–200. DOI: 10.1038/s43017-020-0039-9

Omri, A. (2020)"Technological innovation and sustainable development: Does the stage of development matter?", *Environmental Impact Assessment Review*, Volume 83, 2020,106398, ISSN 0195-9255, DOI: 10.1016/j.eiar.2020.106398

Papachristou, E., Kalaitzi, D., & Pissas, V. (2023). A methodological framework for the integration of 3D virtual prototyping into the design development of laser-cut garments. *Journal of Engineered Fibers and Fabrics*, *18*, 15589250231194621. DOI: 10.1177/15589250231194621

Pasricha, A., & Greeninger, R. (2018). Exploration of 3D printing to create zero-waste sustainable fashion notions and jewelry. *Fashion and Textiles*, *5*(1), 30. DOI: 10.1186/s40691-018-0152-2

Ranganathan, N. (2019). *Smart Textiles and Wearable Technology: A Case Study of Levi's Jacquard Project*. IEEE Journal.

Rathore, B. (2019). From Trendy to Green: Exploring AI's Role in Sustainable Fashion Marketing. *International Journal of New Media Studies*, *06*(02), 12–22. DOI: 10.58972/eiprmj.v6i2y19.120

Saravanan, V., & Adams, J. (2022). Blockchain and Fashion: Transforming the Supply Chain. *International Journal of Retail & Distribution Management*. DOI: 10.1108/IJRDM-09-2021-0456

Shaarawy, S. (2019). A review on the development of innovative capabilities in the textile finishing of natural fibers. In *Egyptian Journal of Chemistry* (Vol. 62, pp. 857–879). NIDOC (Nat.Inform.Document.Centre). DOI: 10.21608/ejchem.2019.19009.2169

Sharma, A. (n.d.). *ECO-FRIENDLY TEXTILES: A BOOST TO SUSTAINABILITY.*

Singh, O., Singh, N., & Singh, A. (2024). AI, IoT, and Blockchain in Fashion: Confronting Industry Applications, Challenges with Technological Solutions. [). https://ijcnis.org/]. *International Journal of Communication Networks and Information Security, 2024*(4).

Sullivan, C. (2020). *Virtual Fitting Rooms: Fashion's New Sustainable Frontier.* Retail Dive.

The Business of Fashion. (2021). *How Stella McCartney became a leader in sustainable luxury*. [Online] Available at: https://www.businessoffashion.com/articles/sustainability/stella-mccartney-sustainability

Tryphena, R., & Aram, I. A. (2023). Consumer perception on sustainable clothing among urban Indians. *Journal of Engineered Fibers and Fabrics, 18*, 15589250231168964. DOI: 10.1177/15589250231168964

Chapter 10
Participatory Art and Human-Centered Technology:
A Case Study of ArtTech Project in George Town, Pulau Pinang, Malaysia

Nurul Hanim Romainoor
https://orcid.org/0000-0003-4482-1364
School of The Arts, Malaysia

Noor Azlina Mohammed Khalid
https://orcid.org/0000-0001-7083-8085
School of The Arts, Malaysia

ABSTRACT

This chapter discusses a case study titled 'Apply Art and Culture to Improve Quality of Life,' aimed at enhancing George Town's quality of life through participatory art and human-centered design (HCD). The project, involving young designers from UEH Vietnam and USM Malaysia, focuses on elevating Masjid Melayu Lebuh Acheh from a historically significant mosque to a key cultural landmark in Penang. By utilising design thinking as HCD, the project integrates modern technology with traditional cultural elements, employing QR codes and gamified experiences to improve visibility and tourist engagement. The prototype features interactive posters and smart chairs, fostering a deeper understanding of the mosque's heritage. This approach not only boosts the mosque's appeal but also offers a model for other heritage sites, demonstrating how digital tools can modernise tourism while preserving cultural

DOI: 10.4018/979-8-3693-7610-2.ch010

authenticity. The project highlights the potential for design thinking to address challenges in heritage tourism and community engagement, setting a precedent for future initiatives.

1. INTRODUCTION

This chapter introduces a collaborative community project titled 'Apply Art and Culture to Improve Quality of Life'. The project utilised design thinking to enhance the quality of life in George Town, located in Pulau Pinang in Malaysia. More specifically, the project aimed to improve the quality of life by combining participatory art with human-centered design. The project explored culturally suitable solutions that would cater to the local people's particular needs and aspirations by involving young designers from University of Economics Ho Chi Minh City (UEH), Vietnam and Universiti Sains Malaysia (USM), Malaysia. The unique value of this project is its significant focus on international collaboration and the benefit of design thinking to combine art and technology to improve the city's well-being and foster a sense of shared ownership and pride in the community.

The Importance of Creativity in Problem-Solving

A key aspect of this project was the recognition of creativity as a vital component of human-centered design. Encouraging individuals to think like designers helps them tap into the innate human capacity for creativity and imagination, enabling the generation of novel, unexpected solutions that challenge existing assumptions and push the boundaries of what is possible (Hobcraft, 2020; Razzouk, & Shute, 2012). As a creative way to solve problems, design thinking is essential for dealing with challenging, unclear problems that might not have clear answers (Rowe, 1991; Foster, 2021).

Various critiques of design thinking (Laursen & Haase, 2019) compare it with a 'designerly way of thinking' (Johansson-Skoldberg et al., 2013), arguing that its tools are too broad and not tied to a specific design framework. They argue that the emphasis on design thinking methodological approaches overlooks fundamental design skills, such as adapting design tools and techniques to a particular problem domain (Laursen, & Haase, 2019).

However, it will be another topic that we can discuss for better guidelines on choosing and using the right tools for more effective problem-solving through the design thinking model, which is also known as human-centred design (HCD). In IDEO (2024), Tim Brown states that design thinking is a human-centric innovation procedure. It uses the designer's toolbox to understand people's needs, technology's capabilities, and economic success requirements.

Despite the ongoing divergent discourse around design thinking, this chapter will present a case study of design thinking as the 'designerly way of thinking'.

2. BACKGROUND OF STUDY

Driven by a passion for preserving and celebrating the rich multicultural tapestry of George Town, Pulau Pinang, a collaborative international project, embarked on a journey to identify and appreciate the unique "Multicultural Visual Identity" that permeates the city's architecture, art, and public spaces. From historic buildings to vibrant street art, monuments, museums, and religious structures, the project sought to uncover the visual narratives that have shaped George Town's identity over the centuries (Liang, 2017; Teh, & Sasaki, 2016; Ismail, et al., 2011). By exploring the historical context and cultural influences behind these visual elements, the project aimed to inspire participatory art initiatives and human-centered design approaches to enrich the city's unique character further and foster a sense of belonging among its diverse population.

The historic city of George Town has been recognised as a UNESCO World Heritage Site, highlighting its rich cultural and architectural legacy that has endured for centuries (Shamsuddin, et al., 2012). The vibrant city of George Town in Pulau Pinang, Malaysia has long been recognised for its unique blend of multiple cultural influences, from its Peranakan heritage to its traditional shophouses and religious sites (Lim et al., 2014). The description of George Town as a UNESCO World Heritage Site in 2008 has elevated its international status as a cultural heritage tourism destination, attracting an influx of visitors (Omar et al., 2013).

What is the Definition of Design Thinking?

Term design thinking emerged in the 1950s as a problem-solving strategy that combined human, technological, and strategic considerations (Cross, 2018). The term was first used in John Arnold's 1959 book Creative Engineering, with roots tracing back to the study of design cognition and methods associated with ancient architecture and engineering (Arnold, 1959). By the 1960s, it expanded to include cognitive and methodological perspectives on designers' thinking and work. In the following decades, it evolved into user-centred and participatory design methods (Rowe, 1991). The concept's popularity grew in the 1990s when the design consultancy IDEO helped promote it in the corporate world, leading to its adoption by many large companies, including Google, IBM, Apple, and Toyota (Camacho, 2016).

Design thinking is regarded as a human-centered problem-solving technique that incorporates the user's iterative understanding, questioning assumptions, reframing issues, and evaluating novel solutions (Deepa, P., 2020). Unlike traditional problem-solving, which often relies on deductive or inductive reasoning, design thinking employs abductive reasoning to generate new possibilities and explore alternative strategies (Foster, M. K., 2021).

Design thinking became a central discussion in design discourses with the practice of world-leading design and innovation businesses like IDEO, as well as its implementation in successful design education programs such as Stanford University's Institute of Design (Camacho, 2016; Bjögvinsson et al., 2012). The approach combines what is desired from a human perspective with what is technologically attainable and economically sustainable (Rowe, 1991). It empowers individuals without any design training to use creative methods to tackle a wider range of challenges (Rowe, 1991). In order to solve issues that are not well-defined or understood, design thinking involves re-framing things from a human-centric perspective, coming up with a number of ideas via brainstorming, and then taking a practical approach to testing and developing those ideas (Deepa, 2020).

At its core, design thinking reflects the 'designerly way of thinking'—a term that emphasises the creative, intuitive, and iterative approach of designers in solving complex problems (Johansson-Skoldberg et al., 2013). This perspective prioritises understanding the user's experience through empathetic observation and active engagement. By immersing in the users' context, design teams uncover pain points, needs, and aspirations that may not be immediately obvious through traditional market research methods. This deep, user-centric perspective forms the foundation for accurately defining the problem and shaping the direction of the solution development process.

The 'designerly way of thinking' goes beyond merely identifying user requirements. It advocates for a mindset that embraces ambiguity, values human insight, and seeks to balance creativity with practicality. As highlighted by scholars like Cross (2007), this approach contrasts with more analytical or purely scientific methods. As Hu et al. (2019) discussed in their study, significant connections between physical activity and divergent thinking were found, identifying certain behaviours that signal a shift into divergent thinking. The researchers concluded that designers' physical actions, like body and facial movements, are closely related to their design thinking process, where solutions are generated through creative leaps rather than linear processes.

Critical Engagement with Design Thinking

While design thinking is celebrated for its emphasis on empathy and creativity, it is not without its critics. Laursen et al. (2019) studied the theoretical bases of two different ideas by looking at two different entities of important literature. The study was used to identify an important shortcoming in 'design thinking' that may explain the feedback directed at it. As Laursen (2019) claims that the shortage occurs from the absence of a robust methodological foundation for Design Thinking 'non-designerly way of thinking', resulting in its dependence on cookbook suggestions for actions.

Discussion in Laursen (2019) statement that suggested that would clarify the frustrations over the concerns with design thinking:

When a non-designer applies a 'cookbook' recipe to a problem situation, the recipe will not necessarily fit that problem situation. . . They probably applied 'suggestions for actions' that were not really situated and fitted to the problem at hand. This represents a significant challenge, since the 'suggestions for actions' gave them the confidence that they could tackle the problem, whereas in reality they missed one of the key aspects of design expertise, namely the ability to fit tools and techniques to a specific problem area (Laursen, et al., 2019, p. 828).

Furthermore, there is a concern in practice that design thinking often simplifies the complexity of social and technological challenges. Critics argue that it sometimes glosses over deep systemic issues in favour of quick, user-friendly solutions that do not address root causes. As a result, design thinking can be more effective in product design and less applicable to addressing complex social problems unless adapted to account for systemic factors (Brown & Wyatt, 2010).

Real-World Applications of Design Thinking

Despite these critiques, design thinking has proven valuable in several high-profile case studies. One example is Airbnb (Stevens, 2024), which has applied human-centered design to solve pain points actively. Airbnb's approach emphasises the importance of empathy in design thinking. By allowing employees to experience the customer perspective and make empathy-based decisions, Airbnb demonstrates the value of breaking away from traditional methods to solve challenges and testing new ideas for long-term success. Airbnb prioritises addressing user pain points, especially trust issues when booking. Using the design thinking model, they introduced a feature suggesting message lengths to improve host acceptance rates. The platform's UI/UX fosters trust with personalised recommendations, storytelling, and detailed images. This iterative process led Airbnb to redesign its office to resemble apartments, encouraging empathy in the design process. By conducting in-depth interviews, two examples of their design thinking include founders helping hosts improve property photos, which doubled revenue, and sending new employees on trips to experience the customer journey, promoting empathy-driven innovation.

Another example of an article traces the origin and evolution of design thinking models within innovation management. Zamakhsyari et al. (2021) address two major critiques—lack of theoretical grounding and construct clarity—and show how human-centered design practices evolved into a comprehensive approach to managing innovation and entrepreneurship. Nevertheless, analysing Stanford University's design philosophy from 1957 to 2005, the study identifies consistent design qualities, clarifying design thinking as a cognitive process, creative practice, and organisational routine. The article claimed design thinking is rooted in humanistic psychology. This approach emphasises addressing deep needs and problems to create value through design, shaping innovation management in organisations and education, which highlights the importance of fostering a creative culture where collaboration and human values drive continuous innovation (Zamakhsyari, & Fatwanto, 2023).

The Design Thinking Model's Iterative Nature

Figure 1. Design thinking process

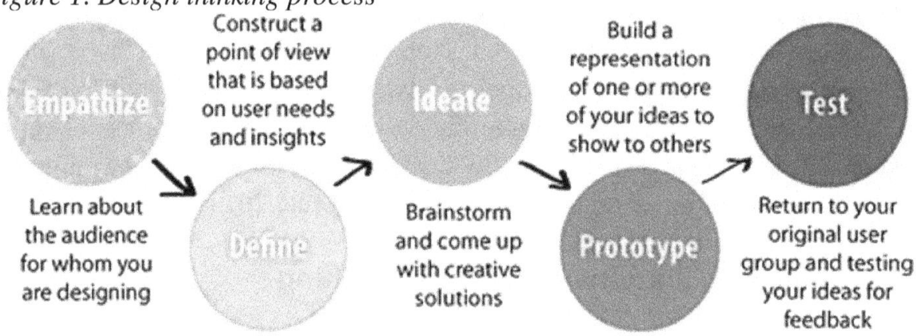

(Fabri, 2015)

As discussed, design thinking is reviewed as a problem-solving method rooted in human-centered design. It has emerged as a powerful tool for organisations seeking to innovate and stay competitive. By prioritising empathy, definition, ideation, prototype, and test design thinking, teams can apply to develop solutions that truly meet their users' needs and drive positive change (Cross, 2023a).

The core of design thinking is a comprehensive appreciation of the user through 'empathy'. Through empathetic observation and active engagement, a team can gain insights into the user's needs, pain points, and aspirations. This understanding serves as the foundation for defining the problem and guiding the solution development process. By concentrating on the user's perception, teams using design thinking can avoid the pitfalls of traditional top-down approaches that may overlook critical user requirements (Deepa, 2020).

Once the problem is clearly defined, creativity takes centre stage. Design thinking encourages teams to brainstorm and ideate, explore unconventional solutions, and challenge existing assumptions. This creative process taps into the innate human capacity for innovation and generates novel, unexpected ideas (Rowe, 1991; Foster, 2021).

To test and refine their ideas, design thinking teams create prototypes, which are tangible representations of their concepts. These prototypes allow for early feedback and iteration, ensuring that the solutions align with the user's requirements or needs. Through engagement discussion in the prototyping process, teams can identify areas for improvement and make necessary adjustments before committing to a final design (Foster, 2021).

Collaboration professionals, stakeholders, or users can diversify essential components of design thinking. By connecting people from diverse backgrounds, disciplines, and cultures, teams can leverage a wider range of perspectives and create more holistic solutions. The interplay of diverse ideas can spark creativity, challenge assumptions, and uncover new insights (Camacho, 2016; Cross, 2023a).

Creativity is a cornerstone of design thinking. By encouraging individuals to think like designers, teams can generate novel and unexpected solutions that address complex challenges. This creative problem-solving approach is essential for innovation and staying ahead in a competitive landscape. Through experimentation and iteration, teams may increase their awareness of the issue and uncover unexpected insights. This practical approach allows rapid prototyping and refinement, ultimately leading to more impactful outcomes (Foster, 2021).

In design thinking, the iterative nature of the process is key to its effectiveness (Cross, 2017). By embracing experimentation and a willingness to fail and learn, teams can rapidly prototype and refine solutions, ultimately converging on more impactful outcomes. Implementing this continual improvement method implies that the final product will be unique and successfully fulfil the user's requirements (Auernhammer et al., 2021). In conclusion about design thinking, by prioritising empathy, define, ideation, prototype, and test teams can develop solutions that truly meet their users' needs and drive positive change. The human-centered approach in design thinking empowers organisations to design products and services that are not only innovative but also meaningful and impactful.

Methodology

A case study based on the collaboration between UEH and USM in the community project, 'Applying Art and Culture to Improve Quality of Life'. The project is set in an educational context, where five sites within George Town's UNESCO World Heritage area were explored using the design thinking model for educational purposes. Among them, a case study focused on identifying potential solutions for revitalising Masjid Melayu Lebuh Acheh (MMLA) was selected as a sample.

Figure 2. Masjid Melayu Lebuh Acheh, Pulau Pinang (Penang)

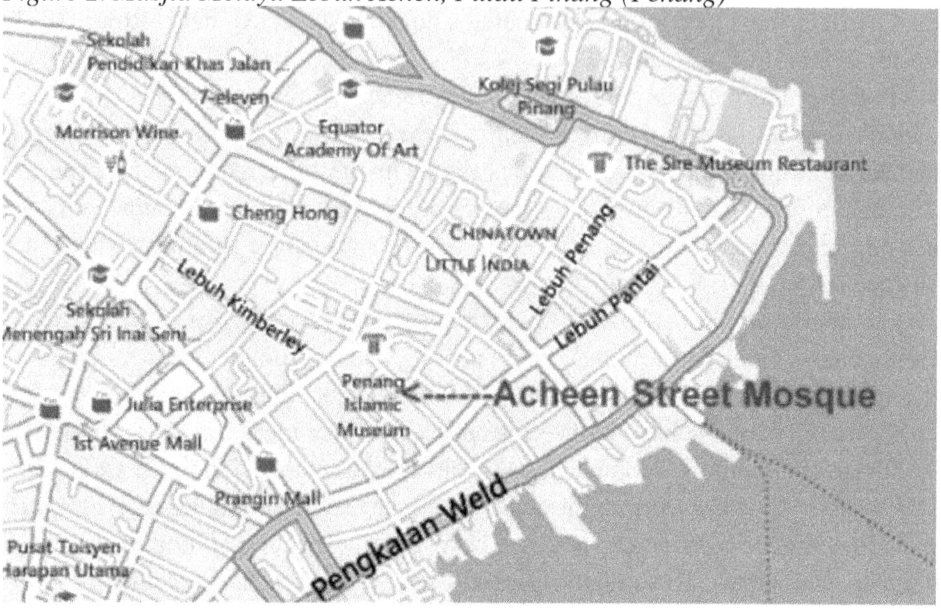

https://www.travel-penang-malaysia.com/acheen-street-mosque.html

Masjid Melayu Lebuh Acheh, one of the oldest mosques in Penang, faces challenges related to visibility, accessibility, and community engagement. This research seeks to explore strategies to enhance the mosque's cultural significance and better connect it with both the local community and international tourists. The mosque's issues include:

- Low visibility and awareness among locals and visitors
- Difficulty in providing accessible information to international and non-Muslim tourists
- A lack of curated experiences and educational opportunities to engage diverse audiences

The design thinking strategy is utilised as a framework to address these challenges, following five stages: empathy, definition, ideation, prototyping, and testing. Qualitative methods were chosen to capture the 'empathy' stage, focusing on the perspectives and experiences of various stakeholders, including community members, tourists, and mosque officials. This approach aims to generate meaningful insights to support the revitalisation of MMLA.

1. Empathy:

- o Creating awareness: Conduct interviews and focus groups with local residents, tourists, and mosque officials to understand their perceptions of MMLA.
- o Understanding needs and interests: Explore the diverse needs, interests, and preferences of community members, including younger generations and non-Muslim residents.
- o Identifying barriers: Identify barriers to engagement, such as language, culture, awareness, and misconceptions.

2. Define:
   - o Problem statement: Clearly define the challenges faced by MMLA in terms of visibility, accessibility, and engagement.
   - o Goals: Establish specific goals for revitalising the mosque and enhancing its cultural significance.
3. Ideate:
   - o Brainstorming: Generate a wide range of ideas for improving the mosque's appeal and accessibility.
   - o Creativity techniques: Employ creative thinking techniques, such as mind mapping and fast sketching via brainstorming session, to explore innovative solutions.
4. Prototype:
   - o Concept development: Develop prototypes of potential solutions, such as interactive exhibits, educational programs, or community events.
   - o Testing: Test the prototypes with target audiences to gather feedback and refine the ideas.
5. Test:
   - o Pilot implementation: Implement pilot programs to evaluate the effectiveness of the proposed solutions.
   - o Data collection: collect data on visitor numbers, engagement levels, and satisfaction to measure the impact of the interventions.

Ethical Considerations

Ethical issues were carefully addressed throughout the study procedure. All participants provided informed permission, and their privacy and confidentiality were respected. All research data collection was for educational purposes only.

Data Analysis

Empathy

- Qualitative analysis: analyse interview transcripts and focus group discussions to identify key themes and insights.

Figure 3. The beginning of the study procedures.

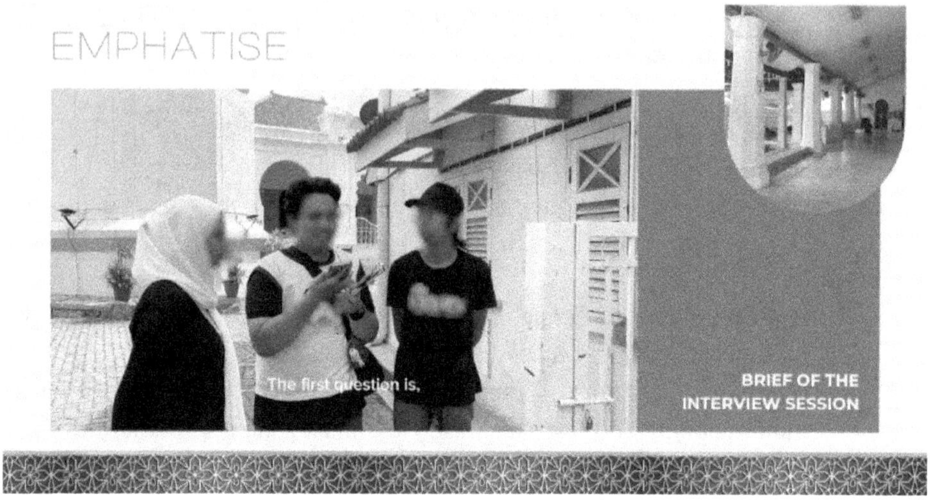

Figure 4. Brief of the interview session.

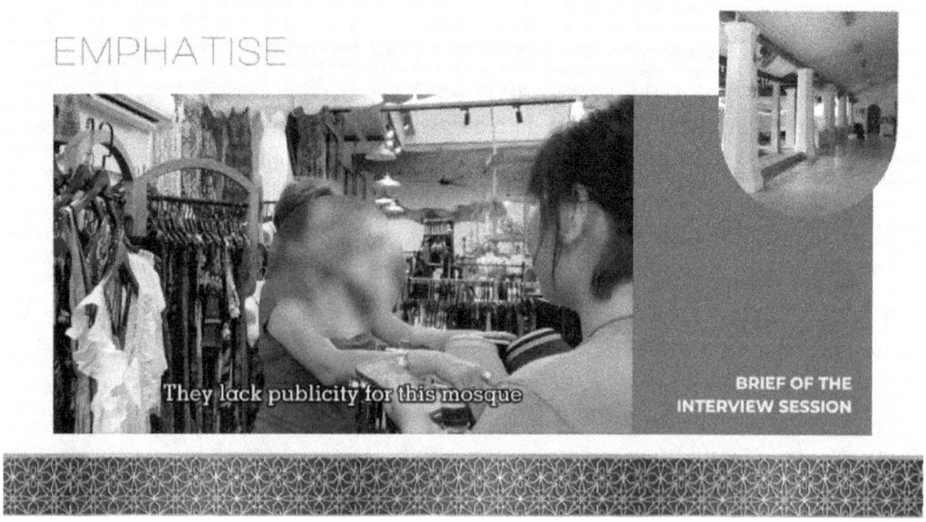

Define

- Problem analysis: Analyse the identified problems to understand their root causes and potential solutions.

Figure 5. Identify the problems.

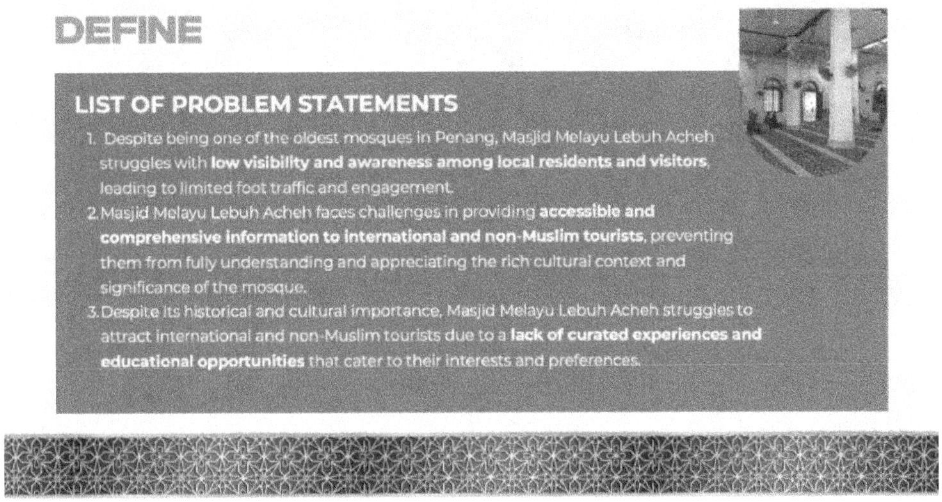

Figure 6. Identify desired outcomes.

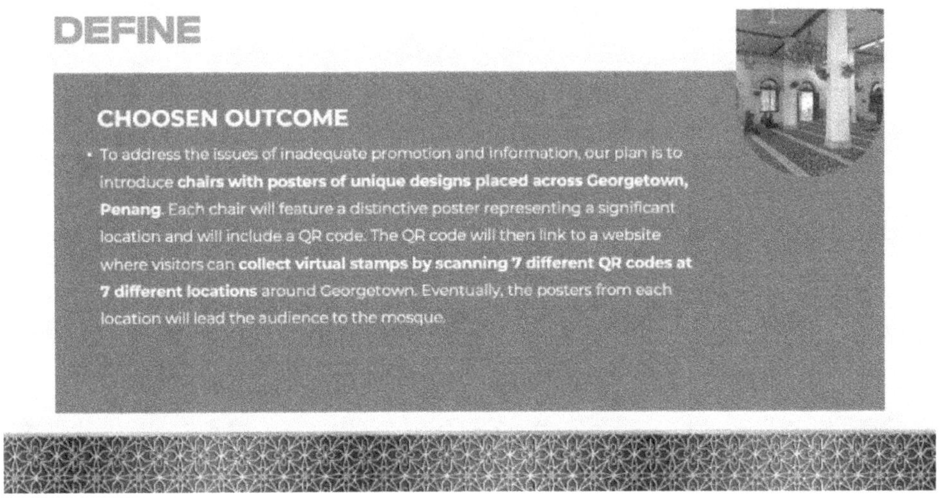

Figure 7. Determine target audience.

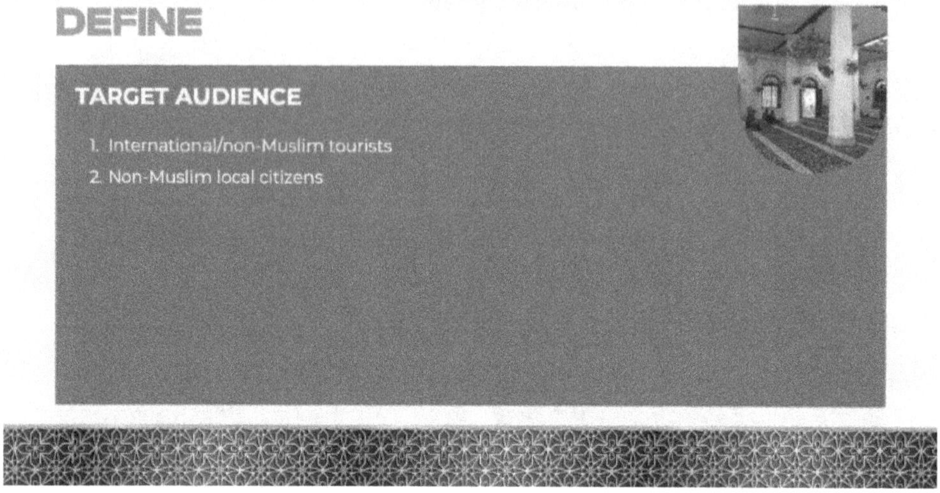

Ideate

- Idea evaluation: Assess the proposed ideas according to their practicality, efficacy, and conformity with the established objectives.

Figure 8. Assess the ideas.

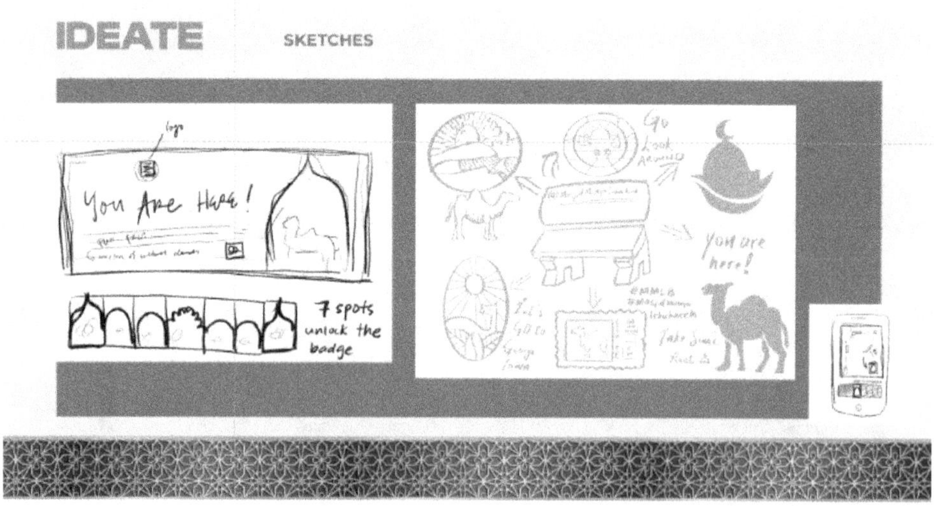

Figure 9. Design rational

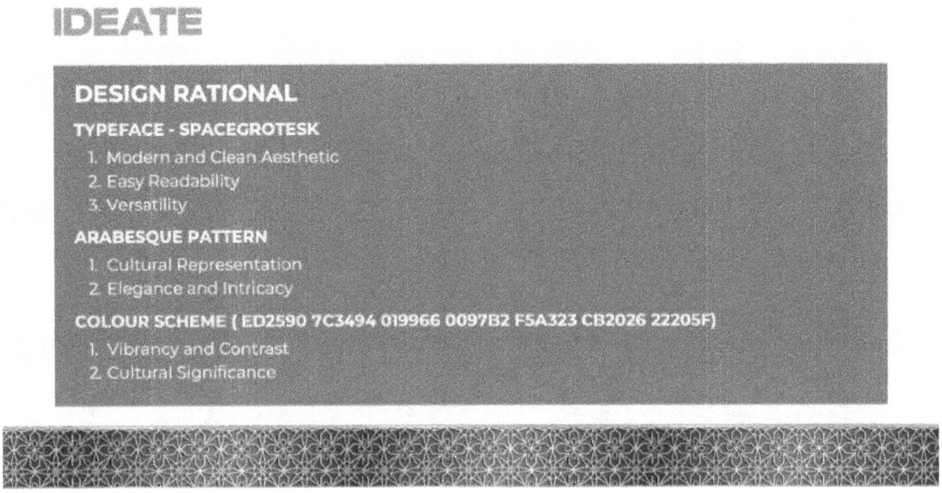

Figure 10. Design rational

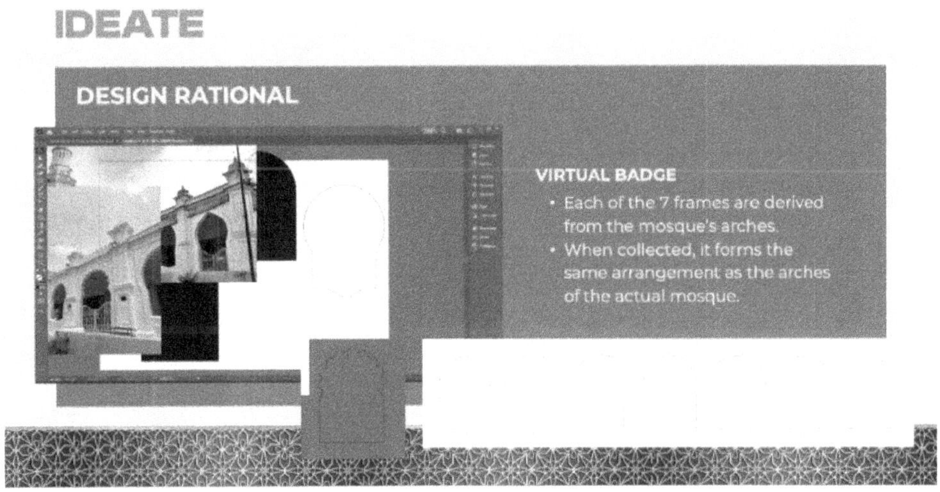

Results/Discussion and Contribution

QR Code-Enabled Smart Chairs

- Promotion of cultural awareness: Develop QR code-enabled smart chairs that provide interactive content about the history, culture, and significance of Masjid Melayu Lebuh Acheh.

Figure 11. Prototype

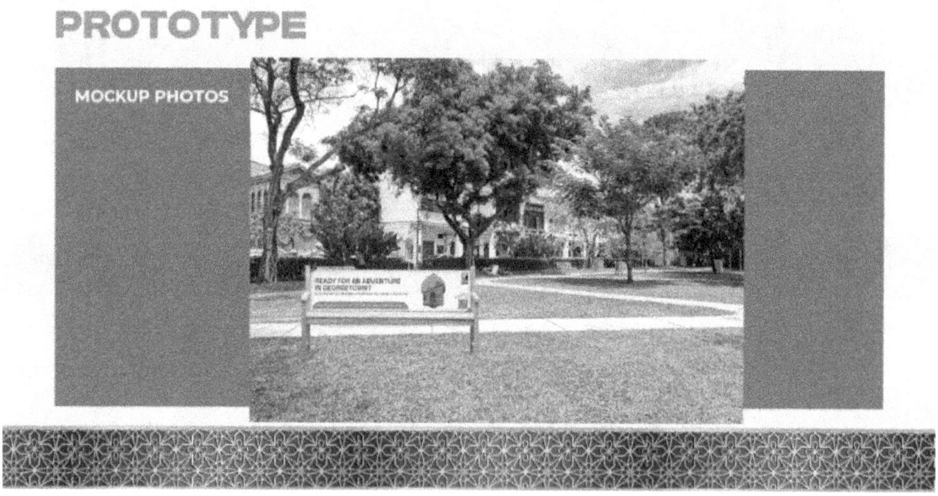

Prototype and Test

- Feedback analysis: Analyse feedback from prototype testing to find ways that might need improvement.
- Data analysis: Analyse the data gathered on pilot implementation to assess the effectiveness of the interventions.

Figure 12. Prototype testing.

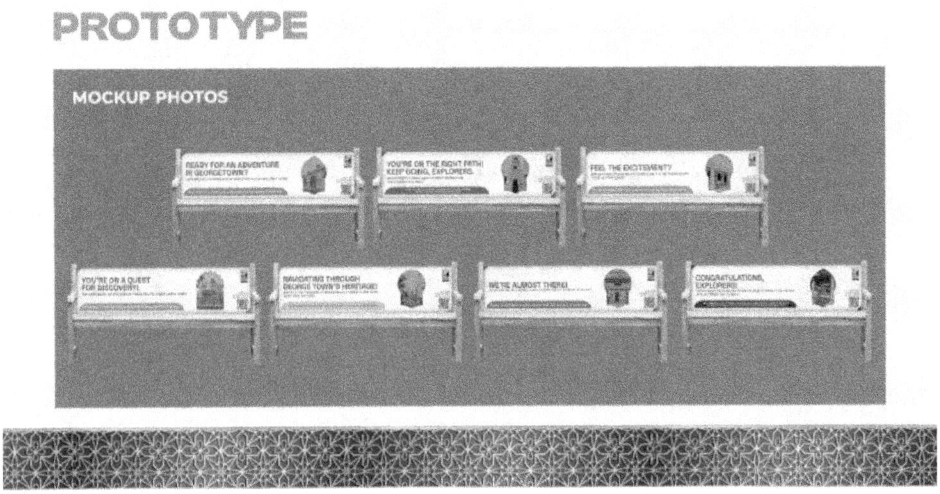

Figure 13. Mock-up photos

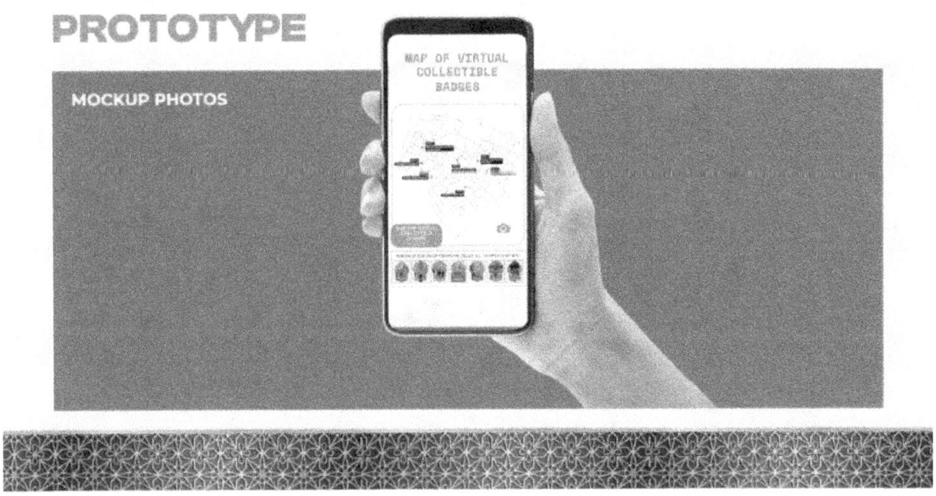

Figure 14. Posters

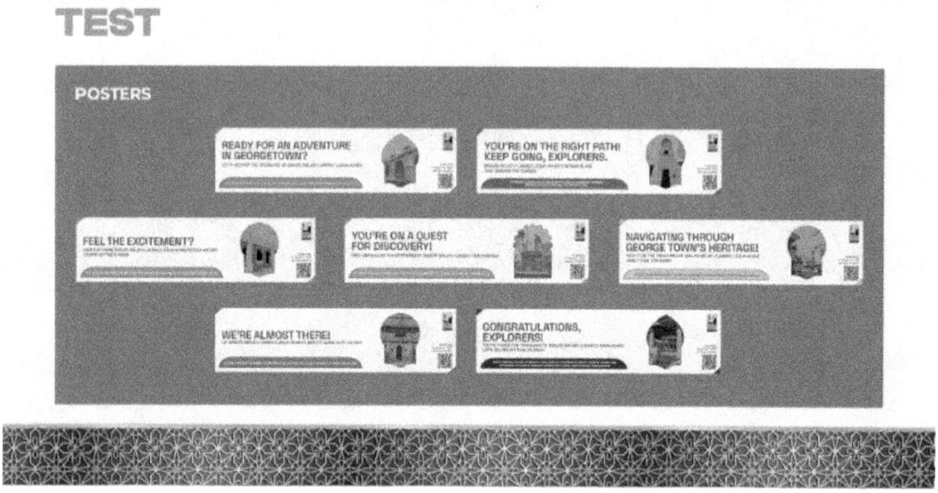

Figure 15. Test: collectible badges

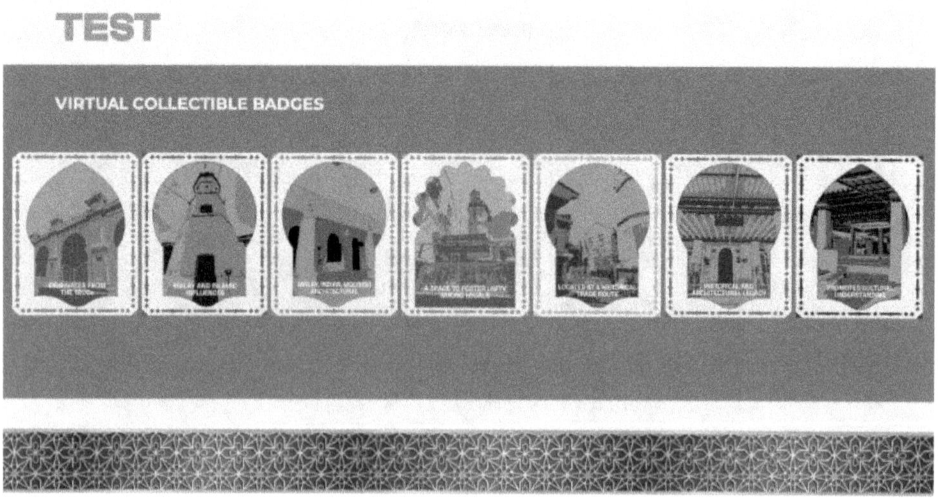

Figure 16. Test: Map for collecting badges

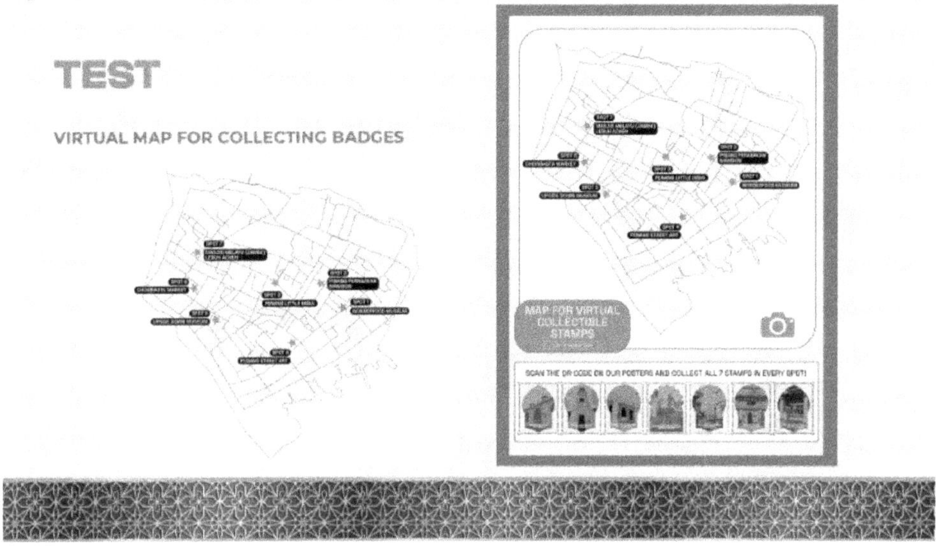

Discussion

Figure 17. Final product

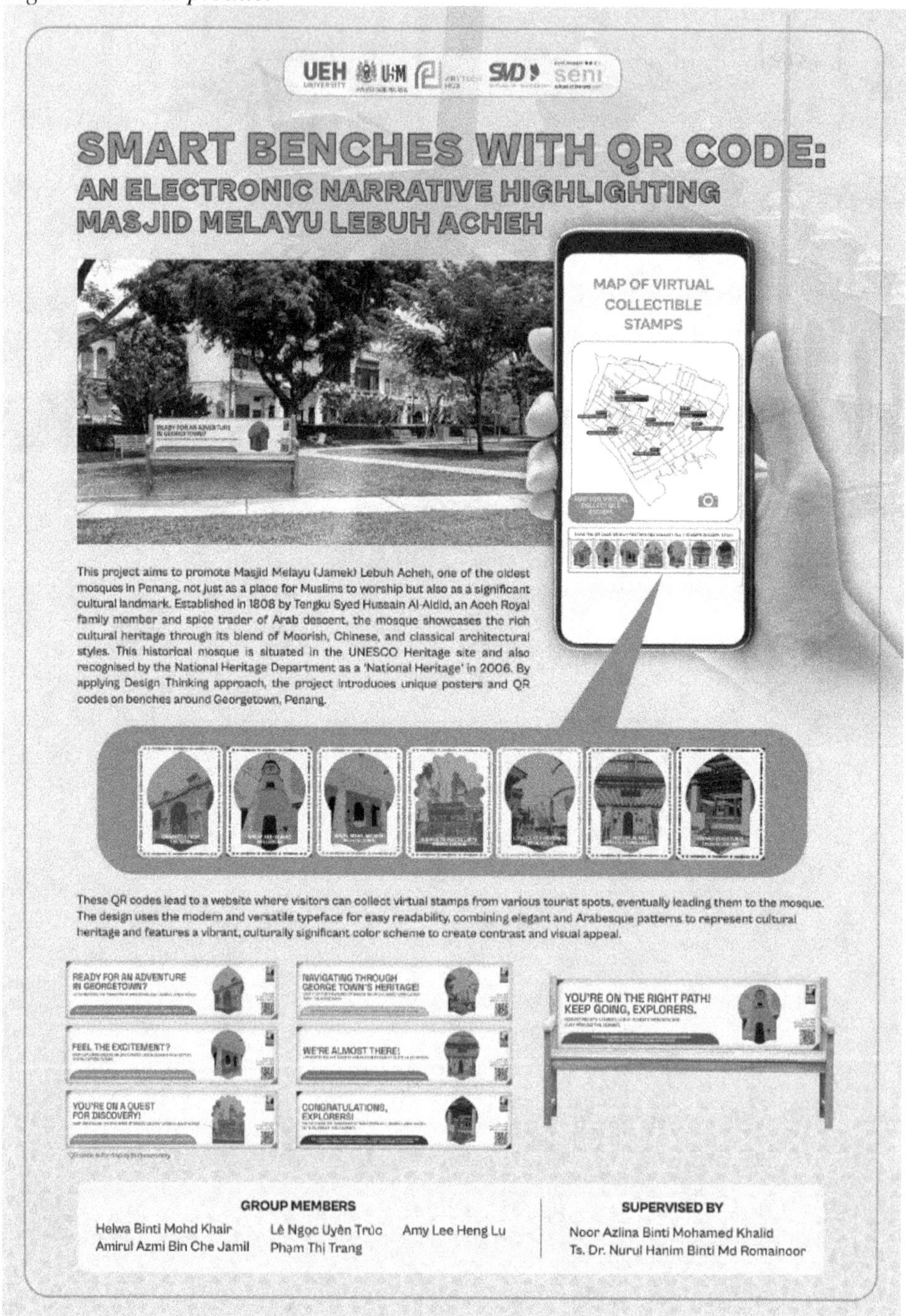

The prototype developed for promoting Masjid Melayu Lebuh Acheh seeks to elevate the mosque's status not just as a place of worship but as a key cultural landmark in Penang. Despite its historical significance, the mosque has struggled with low visibility and limited tourist engagement. By leveraging the Design Thinking model, the project addresses these challenges through an innovative approach, combining traditional cultural elements with modern technology.

The introduction of unique posters and QR codes around Georgetown allows for an interactive, self-guided tour that encourages visitors to engage with various cultural landmarks, eventually leading them to the mosque. The use of virtual stamps creates a gamified experience, offering tourists a sense of achievement while discovering local history. The design elements of the project—modern, readable typefaces paired with Arabesque patterns—strike a balance between accessibility and cultural representation. This approach ensures that the mosque is highlighted as a significant cultural site in a visually appealing and engaging manner.

Furthermore, the QR code-based solution addresses the challenge of providing accessible information to international and non-Muslim tourists. By integrating technology, the project allows users to explore the mosque's history and significance at their own pace, making it a more inclusive experience. The design also considers the aesthetic value, with vibrant colours and patterns that resonate with the cultural richness of the mosque and the surrounding area, enhancing the visual experience for visitors.

Contribution

This design thinking ideation contributes significantly to the field of heritage preservation and tourism by integrating design thinking with digital tools to solve real-world challenges. The use of QR codes to promote cultural sites through interactive and gamified experiences is a novel approach that enhances tourist engagement while preserving the cultural integrity of the mosque. It demonstrates how modern technology can be used to bridge the gap between heritage sites and contemporary audiences.

Additionally, the prototype offers a model for other historic sites facing similar issues of low visibility and engagement. By incorporating both traditional design elements and modern accessibility features, this prototype provides a framework for promoting cultural landmarks in a way that is inclusive and appealing to a broader audience. The thoughtful integration of digital tools with cultural heritage contributes to ongoing discussions about modernising tourism without sacrificing historical authenticity.

Ultimately, this task revitalises Masjid Melayu Lebuh Acheh and sets a precedent for using design thinking and technology to address challenges in heritage tourism and community engagement.

Implications

The prototype for promoting Masjid Melayu Lebuh Acheh underscores several important implications for heritage tourism and community engagement. First, it demonstrates that integrating modern technology with traditional cultural elements can significantly enhance the visibility and appeal of historic sites. The use of QR codes and a gamified experience provides a practical example of how digital tools can engage a diverse audience, including international and non-Muslim tourists, who might otherwise need to be made aware of the site's significance. This approach not only boosts visitor numbers but also enriches their experience to provide a more in-depth knowledge of the cultural and historical setting of the mosque.

Second, the tasks highlight the potential for applying strategies similar to those of other cultural and historical sites that face visibility and engagement challenges. By combining interactive technology with thoughtful design, other landmarks can also increase their appeal and accessibility. This model encourages heritage sites to embrace innovation while preserving their authenticity, balancing modern engagement strategies with the need to maintain cultural integrity.

3. CONCLUSION

The tasks to promote Masjid Melayu Lebuh Acheh illustrate the practical use of design thinking in addressing challenges in the real world related to heritage tourism and site engagement. By leveraging modern technology and innovative design, the prototype successfully enhances the mosque's visibility and appeal, transforming it from a historically significant but under-recognised site into a vibrant cultural landmark.

The use of QR codes and interactive elements provides a dynamic and inclusive way for visitors to explore the mosque and its surroundings, fostering a deeper connection with the site's cultural heritage. This approach not only revitalises the mosque but also offers a valuable framework for other historic sites looking to boost engagement and visibility.

In conclusion, integrating the 'designerly way of thinking' of design thinking and technology in this project sets a precedent for modernising heritage tourism while respecting historical authenticity. It provides a compelling model for how cultural landmarks can address challenges and engage audiences through innovative and inclusive strategies, ultimately contributing to the preservation and celebration of cultural heritage.

REFERENCES

Arnold, J. E. (1959). Creative Engineering Seminar, 1959. (n.p.).

Auernhammer, J., & Roth, B. (2021). The origin and evolution of Stanford University's design thinking: From product design to design thinking in innovation management. *Journal of Product Innovation Management, 38*(6), 623–644. DOI: 10.1111/jpim.12594

Bjögvinsson, E., Ehn, P., & Hillgren, P. A. (2012). Design things and design thinking: Contemporary participatory design challenges. *Design Issues, 28*(3), 101–116. DOI: 10.1162/DESI_a_00165

Brown, T., & Wyatt, J. (2010). Design thinking for social innovation. *Development Outreach, 12*(1), 29–43. DOI: 10.1596/1020-797X_12_1_29

Camacho, M. (2016). David Kelley: From design to design thinking at Stanford and IDEO. She Ji. *The Journal of Design, Economics, and Innovation, 2*(1), 88–101. DOI: 10.1016/j.sheji.2016.01.009

Cross, N. (2007). From a design science to a design discipline: Understanding designerly ways of knowing and thinking. In *Design research now* (pp. 41–54). Birkhäuser Basel. DOI: 10.1007/978-3-7643-8472-2_3

Cross, N. (2018). A brief history of the Design Thinking Research Symposium series. *Design Studies, 57*, 160–164. DOI: 10.1016/j.destud.2018.03.007

Cross, N. (2023a). *Design thinking: Understanding how designers think and work.* Bloomsbury Publishing. DOI: 10.5040/9781350305090

Cross, N. (2023b). Design thinking: What just happened? *Design Studies, 86*(101187), 1–10.

Deepa, P. (2020). A study on the concepts of design thinking. *International Journal of Engineering Applied Sciences and Technology, 4*(12), 269–272. DOI: 10.33564/IJEAST.2020.v04i12.044

Fabri, M. (2015). Thinking with a new purpose: Lessons learned from teaching design thinking skills to creative technology students. In *Design, User Experience, and Usability: Design Discourse: 4th International Conference, DUXU 2015, Held as Part of HCI International 2015, Los Angeles, CA, USA, August 2–7, 2015, Proceedings, Part I* (pp. 32-43). Springer International Publishing.

Foster, M. K. (2021). Design thinking: A creative approach to problem solving. *Management Teaching Review, 6*(2), 123–140. DOI: 10.1177/2379298119871468

Hobcraft, P. (2020). *Improving the potential for Innovation through Design Thinking*. HYPE Simplify Innovation.

Hu, Y., Du, X., Bryan-Kinns, N., & Guo, Y. (2019). Identifying divergent design thinking through the observable behavior of service design novices. *International Journal of Technology and Design Education, 29*(5), 1179–1191. DOI: 10.1007/s10798-018-9479-7

IDEO. (2024), What's the difference between human-centered design and design thinking? Retrieved June 5, 2024, from https://t.ly/9rTlZ

Ismail, S., & Mohd-Ali, N. A. (2011). The imaging of heritage conservation in Historic City of George Town for city marketing. *Procedia Engineering, 20*, 339–345. DOI: 10.1016/j.proeng.2011.11.175

Johansson-Skoldberg, U., Woodilla, J., & Cetinkaya, M. (2013). Design Thinking: Past, present and possible futures. *Creativity and Innovation Management, 22*(2), 121e146.

Khoo, S. L. (2020). Towards an inclusive creative city: How ready is the Historic City of George Town, Penang? *City, Culture and Society, 23*, 100367. DOI: 10.1016/j.ccs.2020.100367

Laursen, L. N., & Haase, L. M. (2019). The shortcomings of design thinking when compared to designerly thinking. *The Design Journal, 22*(6), 813e832.

Liang, C. (2017). George Town's street mural art and tourism impact. *Asian Journal of Tourism Research, 2*(3), 168–188. DOI: 10.12982/AJTR.2017.0022

Lim, Y. M., Khoo, S. L., & Ch'ng, K. S. (2014). Residents' perspectives towards conservation in George Town world heritage city: A Post-UNESCO listing scenario. *Journal of Urban and Regional Analysis, 6*(2). Advance online publication. DOI: 10.37043/JURA.2014.6.2.4

Lou, E. C., Lee, A., & Lim, Y. M. (2022). Stakeholder preference mapping: The case for built heritage of Georgetown, Malaysia. *Journal of Cultural Heritage Management and Sustainable Development, 12*(3), 291–308. DOI: 10.1108/JCHMSD-08-2020-0114

Omar, S. I., Muhibudin, M., Yussof, I., Sukiman, M. F., & Bahaj, M. (2013). George Town, Penang as a World Heritage Site: The stakeholders' perceptions. *Procedia: Social and Behavioral Sciences, 91*, 326–339. DOI: 10.1016/j.sbspro.2013.08.405

Razzouk, R., & Shute, V. (2012). What is design thinking and why is it important? *Review of Educational Research, 82*(3), 330–348. DOI: 10.3102/0034654312457429

Rowe, P. G. (1991). *Design thinking*. MIT Press.

Shamsuddin, S., Sulaiman, A. B., & Amat, R. C. (2012). *Urban landscape factors that influenced the character of George Town*. Penang UNESCO World Heritage.

Stevens, E. (2024, July 19). 7 Real-Life Design Thinking Examples | AND Academy. AndAcademy.https://www.andacademy.com/resources/blog/ui-ux-design/7-design-thinking-examples/#Airbnb

Teh, Y. S., & Sasaki, Y. (2016). A study of historic quarter streetscapes based on typology of tourist-oriented activity—A case study of George Town and Hanoi. *Journal of JSCE*, *4*(1), 152–165. DOI: 10.2208/journalofjsce.4.1_152

Chapter 11
Perception of the Aesthetic Value of Art in the Context of Artificial Intelligence and Human Creation Among Higher Education Students

Erika Blekač
https://orcid.org/0009-0000-3688-0116
Faculty of Electrical Engineering and Computer Science, University of Maribor, Slovenia

Marko Matko Ficko
https://orcid.org/0009-0007-9792-8487
Faculty of Electrical Engineering and Computer Science, University of Maribor, Slovenia

Aja Cugmas
https://orcid.org/0009-0003-4030-6565
Faculty of Electrical Engineering and Computer Science, University of Maribor, Slovenia

Ines Kožuh
https://orcid.org/0000-0001-7875-5583
Faculty of Electrical Engineering and Computer Science, University of Maribor & Faculty of Social Sciences, University of Ljubljana, Slovenia

DOI: 10.4018/979-8-3693-7610-2.ch011

ABSTRACT

In this chapter, the authors will explore the impact of Artificial Intelligence on art and the perception of its aesthetic value. Through a theoretical review, the authors will define key concepts, such as Artificial Intelligence, art, the intersection of traditional art and art generated with Artificial Intelligence, and the aesthetic evaluation of art. In the empirical part, the authors will examine how individual personal characteristics, such as gender, age, field of education, extracurricular artistic activities, as well as prior knowledge of art and Artificial Intelligence, influence the perception of the aesthetic value of Artificial Intelligence- and human-created art, as well as how these individual personal characteristics affect the recognition of the source and aesthetic evaluation of the art.

INTRODUCTION

Artificial Intelligence (AI) has experienced remarkable growth in the early decades of the 21st century, leading to what many refer to as the "age of Artificial Intelligence". This technological advancement has transformed numerous fields profoundly, including art, where AI has evolved from a simple tool into a creative partner. Initially conceived in the 1950s with the aim of modelling human cognition and understanding thought processes, the term AI is now often used to describe applications based on advanced neural networks and other forms of Machine Learning (Millet et al., 2023).

One of the most fascinating, and perhaps surprising developments in AI, is its ability to create art. AI is not limited merely to imitating existing artistic styles, but, instead, can produce authentic and original artworks that go beyond imitation, introducing entirely new artistic forms. Today, AI is involved in various aspects of the artistic creative process, from traditional fields like painting to more contemporary art forms, such as digital music and interactive media. The AI-created artworks can range from a reproduction of the styles of famous artists to completely new, unique artistic styles, that have garnered so much attention that they have been sold at auctions for very high prices (Hitsuwari, Ueda, Yun, & Nomura, 2023).

However, an intriguing and often-discussed phenomenon arises when people evaluate art created by AI. Many individuals find it challenging to distinguish between artworks created by AI and those made by humans. This raises numerous questions about our perception of art and artistic creation. When confronted with AI-generated artworks, people face a challenge similar to that posed by the Turing test. This test evaluates a machine's ability to imitate a human so convincingly that a human evaluator cannot determine reliably whether they are interacting with a person or a machine.

This raises the question of how people react to art created by AI, and how these reactions reflect deeply ingrained beliefs about human nature and the very definition of art. Do we value an artwork more if we know it results from human effort, or can we acknowledge the equal value in a work created by AI? How does this perception influence our interpretation of art and our aesthetic judgements?

ARTIFICIAL INTELLIGENCE

Brief History of AI

Artificial Intelligence (AI) is a branch of Computer Science focused on creating machines and programs that can think, learn and make decisions like humans. It involves designing systems that can observe, analyse and adapt to situations, to achieve optimal outcomes. AI is already a steady part of everyday life, powering technologies such as music recommendations, targeted advertisements and self-driving cars (Johns, 2021)

The origins of AI can be traced back to the 1940s, when Isaac Asimov introduced the concept of robots governed by ethical laws in his short story "Runaround." Around the same time, Alan Turing developed The Bombe, a machine designed to crack the German Enigma code during World War II, which sparked his interest in machine intelligence. In 1950, Turing proposed the famous Turing Test, to measure a machine's intelligence, suggesting that if a machine could engage in conversation indistinguishable from a human, it could be considered intelligent.

This foundational period was followed by Marvin Minsky and John McCarthy's 1956 Dartmouth workshop, which introduced the term "Artificial Intelligence" formally, and aimed to develop machines replicating human intelligence. This event ignited optimism about AI's potential, marking the beginning of the first "Summer of AI". It encouraged research, leading to early achievements, such as the creation of the Logic Theorist and General Problem Solver, the introduction of Reinforcement Learning, the invention of the LISP programming language, and the development of the first neural network, the Mark I Perceptor (Toosi, Bottino, Saboury, Siegel, & Rahmim, 2021).

The early decades of AI research also saw some progress, such as the creation of the ELIZA program that simulated human conversation, but also faced setbacks due to limited computational power and overreliance on rule-based expert systems, which struggled with tasks requiring interpretation and adaptation (Haenlein & Kaplan, 2019). Researchers also faced challenges, such as the complexity of real-world problems and the limitations of early neural networks (Toosi, Bottino, Saboury, Siegel, & Rahmim, 2021). Interest in AI waned in the 1970s after criticism from figures like James Lighthill and reduced funding (Haenlein & Kaplan, 2019).

Research in AI was revitalised again in the early 1980s with the development of "expert systems", that focused on solving specific problems using domain-specific knowledge. The success of these systems led to significant investments and expanded research in AI. This second boom of AI was followed by a second "Winter of AI", which started in the late 1980s and lasted until the mid-1990s. It was characterised by the failure of many expert systems to meet high expectations, technological limitations, and a shift toward more conservative approaches like statistical methods and hidden Markov models (Toosi, Bottino, Saboury, Siegel, & Rahmim, 2021).

The third boom of AI began in the 2010s with advances in Deep Learning and Neural Networks (Haenlein & Kaplan, 2019). The breakthrough came with AlexNet's success in Computer Vision, driven by advances in GPU computing and large datasets (Toosi, Bottino, Saboury, Siegel, & Rahmim, 2021). The success of AlphaGo in 2015, which defeated the world champion in the complex game of Go, marked a significant milestone in AI, showcasing its ability to learn and adapt beyond pre-programmed rules, laying the foundation for modern AI applications such as Image and Speech Recognition (Haenlein & Kaplan, 2019).

How Does AI Work?

The term AI is used predominantly in applications based on Deep Neural Networks. It consists of a set of codes, techniques, algorithms, and data that enable a computer to develop and mimic human-like behaviour, thereby making decisions similar to humans (Ting, Ling, bin Ahmad Azam, & Palaniappan, 2021).

Current AI technologies are, typically, limited to functioning within a specific domain, and are designed for particular tasks (Cetinic & She, 2022), often involving generative models (Bird, Ungless, & Kasirzadeh, 2023).

Generative AI is a branch of Artificial Intelligence dedicated to creating algorithms and models that generate synthetic data resembling real-world data. This technology influences various fields, such as Computer Vision, Natural Language Processing and creative arts. It enables generating realistic and novel content, including images, text, music, and even human-like chatbots (Bandi, Adapa, & Kuchi, 2023).

Generative modelling is performed using Machine Learning architecture, such as neural networks, capable of creating new data patterns based on learned examples. Neural networks are especially suitable for generating data, since they can be configured with different architectures for various data types, whether sequential, like human speech, or spatial, like images (Feuerriegel, Hartmann, Janiesch, & Zschech, 2024).

Neural networks are machine learning models inspired by the human nervous system. They simulate how human neurons work by using computational units that process data similarly to how neurons process signals. They work by using mathematical formulas to process data. They adjust these formulas through continuous improvements to get better at making predictions or decisions, which involves tweaking how inputs, like images or texts, are transformed into outputs based on a set of mathematical rules. They use a structured approach to refine their predictions by learning from data (Aggarwal, 2018).

Today's most commonly used generative models process and integrate information from diverse domains, including visual, textual and audio data (Bird, Ungless, & Kasirzadeh, 2023). Among the frequently used generative AI models are diffusion probabilistic models for converting text into images and large language models (LLMs) for generating text (Feuerriegel, Hartmann, Janiesch, & Zschech, 2024).

Future of AI

The future of AI holds immense promise, with AI expected to play a transformative role across numerous sectors, including autonomous vehicles, medical diagnostics, legal systems and the job market. AI's ability to revolutionise these fields could lead to significant advancements in efficiency, precision and decision-making. For instance, AI-driven vehicles may reduce traffic incidents drastically one day, while AI-powered medical tools could enable faster, more accurate diagnoses. However, the path forward is not without its challenges. AI systems are still prone to vulnerabilities, including the potential for fragility and unfairness. Errors in data can lead to misinterpretations of critical information, such as AI mistaking traffic signs in autonomous driving, or identifying medical images incorrectly. Furthermore, there have been instances of AI systems perpetuating discrimination and bias, particularly in sensitive areas like criminal justice and recruitment. For example, some AI tools used in the judiciary have exhibited racially biased outcomes, and AI-driven hiring platforms have demonstrated gender bias in recruitment (Toosi, Bottino, Saboury, Siegel, & Rahmim, 2021).

Addressing these issues will require effort to ensure the responsible development and deployment of AI technologies. International organisations, governments and industry leaders will need to collaborate to create robust Guidelines and Standards that promote fairness, accountability and transparency in AI. Establishing such ethical frameworks will be critical to safeguarding against bias, and ensuring that AI is used to benefit society as a whole (Toosi, Bottino, Saboury, Siegel, & Rahmim, 2021).

AI in Art

In the case of AI art, Artificial Intelligence can take on various roles, depending on the required needs. AI can act as an imitator, collaborator, or creator. As an imitator, AI mimics an artistic style by imitating and blending existing human-created works. As a collaborator, AI attempts to create new creative works with human intervention, where people choose between the outputs that the AI offers. In the role of the creator, after AI has been trained on a dataset of images, it generates outputs independently, without any human involvement (Ting, Ling, bin Ahmad Azam, & Palaniappan, 2021).

Regardless of the role AI takes on, this form of AI falls within a category of generative systems that produce images (Jiang et al., 2023), which are created through a collaboration between AI algorithms and human artists (Ting, Ling, bin Ahmad Azam, & Palaniappan, 2021), with the AI being trained on copyrighted works and images. These systems can take input in various forms, such as text, images, or a mix of both, and then produce an image as the final input (Jiang et al., 2023).

For the purpose of this study, we will focus on so-called Text-To-Image (TTI) models, which can create images from text using AI. When text is provided as the input, the TTI model generates an image that represents the information in the given text visually. To create an image, TTI systems typically leverage a combination of Natural Language Processing (Bird, Ungless, & Kasirzadeh, 2023), which enables computers to interact with humans through natural language such as speech or text (Raparthi, et al., 2021), and Computer Vision, which allows computers to interpret and understand visual data by deriving meaningful information from visual inputs, and making decisions or recommendations based on that information (Matsuzaka & Yashiro, 2023).

The NLP part of the system analyses the text to identify important details, including objects, their characteristics, and the connection between them. It interprets the text to understand the underlying concepts, providing foundational information. Meanwhile, the Computer Vision element takes these extracted data, and uses them to create a visual representation, generating an image that reflects the meaning conveyed by the text (Bird, Ungless, & Kasirzadeh, 2023).

The functioning of this system, grounded in Machine Learning, relies on a training process where the model learns from data specific to a particular area. These training data mirror the input encountered in real-world scenarios closely, accompanied by accurate labels that help the system understand the desired outcomes. Through this process, the model can produce accurate results by recognising patterns and relationships within the data it has been exposed to (Anantrasirichai & Bull, 2022). From this explanation, we can infer that, if we wanted to create an AI capable of generating landscape photographs, we would first need to train it on an extensive collection of landscape photos, based on which it would then be able to analyse and determine approximately what kind of image we would want as the output, which, in this case, would be landscape depictions.

ART

Definition of Art

Art is a complex and mysterious part of human life and found in every culture worldwide. Taste in art is personal and subjective, and it can vary widely among individuals. Art appreciation is also highly subjective and varies between individuals, with some appreciating the skill involved, and others enjoying the excitement of new artistic expressions (Leder, Gerger, Dressler, & Schabmann, 2012).

When discussing art, we often encounter various definitions and interpretations. Defining art presents a significant challenge, because it does not belong to a natural category like water or gold, which objective, scientific criteria can define. Instead, art is a socially constructed and culturally embedded concept that arises from human practices and creativity. These practices are intertwined deeply with human life's cultural, historical and intentional aspects, making art a complex and evolving category (Clowney, 2011).

According to Clowney (2011), there are three possible ways to define art: as a word, a concept and the thing itself. When considering art as a word, the focus is on how the term is used in language and everyday communication. However, Clowny argues that more than understanding the word alone is needed to resolve the philosophical question of what qualifies as art, as it merely reflects common usage without addressing the underlying criteria.

Defining art as the thing itself refers to examining the physical objects or artefacts labelled as art. This approach looks at the works and practices categorised as art, to understand their defining characteristics. However, Clowney (2011) notes that more than this perspective is needed, as it does not capture the complex interplay between the physical artefacts, cultural context and conceptual understanding of art fully.

Finally, considering art as a concept involves exploring the theoretical and philosophical frameworks that shape our understanding of art. This approach seeks to identify the necessary and sufficient conditions for something to be classified as art and to clarify what makes art distinct from other phenomena. This conceptual analysis is crucial, because it delves into the more profound meaning and implication of what we consider art (Clowney, 2011).

Art can also be understood as something that can be identified through excellence in skill and achievement, recognition within art genres or traditions, and the intentionality of its creator (Davies, 2015).

The first criterion emphasises the importance of demonstrating exceptional skill and achievement in realising significant aesthetic goals. This means that art can be recognised, even if it falls outside established art categories or traditions, particularly relevant for early works predating formal art contexts. The focus is primarily on the quality of the work and its ability to achieve notable aesthetic effects (Davies, 2015).

The second criterion involves the recognition of the work within specific art-worlds[1] or genres. Art is defined as something that aligns with an art form or tradition acknowledged publicly within a particular art context. This recognition situates the work within a broader historical and cultural framework, where its status as art is granted by association with established art practices (Davies, 2015).

The third criterion addresses the intentionality of the creator. According to this view, an object is considered art if it is created to be art, and if the creator takes the necessary steps to realise this intention. This underscored the role of conscious artistic intent, and acknowledges that the art world has, historically, shaped and constrained what can be classified as art, and it allows for the evolution of creative practices and the emergence of new art forms (Davies, 2015).

Human Biases and Artistic Attribution

With the rise of advanced AI models capable of mimicking human artistic creations, AI-generated creative products could soon replace those of human origin. However, many argue that this is unlikely. One possible reason is that, regardless of the physical attributes of art, much of its value is attributed to the infusion of human experience into the artwork (Bellaiche et al., 2023).

There is a noticeable bias against art labelled as AI-generated, particularly in criteria related to the depth of communication and the value of art, and less so in superficial judgements like beauty and likability. AI can create aesthetically pleasing artworks, but they are considered superficial compared to the profound human experiences observed in works created by people. The perceived effort put into creating artworks influences the recognition and appreciation of the value of human work in artistic production (Bellaiche et al., 2023).

Art is inherently subjective, making it difficult to define and assess its value. Factors that can influence the ranking and evaluation of artworks vary. Artworks that require more time and effort to create are often viewed as being of higher quality, higher value and more likability, and are perceived as more aesthetically pleasing. The perceived effort put into a painting affects long people think it took to create, as well as its overall quality (Khan & Násström, 2023).

When comparing how people perceive human-created art and AI-generated pieces originality, degree of improvement or growth, composition, development of personal style, expression, experimentation and risk-taking, aesthetic value and successful communication of ideas were analysed. Artworks made by humans were generally rated more favourably, especially in areas such as composition, expression and aesthetic value (Khan & Näsström, 2023).

Art created by AI is largely indistinguishable from that created by humans. Defining art is a challenging task, but one aspect often tied to the concept of art is the human involvement in its creation. The prevailing traditional belief is that "art is made by hand." Many believe that a work of art should be severe work created by a human, and that incorporating technology into its creation makes the work artificial, devoid of originality, and lacking the investment of time and effort, which diminishes its meaning and value (Gangadharbatla, 2021).

Gangadharbatla (2021) conducted a study to explore how individuals perceive and evaluate AI-created artworks, considering their ability to identify whether they were created by humans or AI accurately. The participants in the study had difficulty determining the author of the artworks, currently identifying only one out of five AI-created artworks. Abstract artistic creations were typically linked with AI, while representational creations were attributed to human artists.

The evaluation of artworks was influenced by various factors, such as the perceived time and effort spent on creation and superficial cues like physical brushstrokes. Consequently, the type of artwork affected individuals' ability to attribute it to human or AI creation correctly significantly. The kind of artwork and knowledge of attribution played a significant role in how individuals perceived and evaluated art. Abstract art, often associated with computers, received more favourable ratings when attributed to AI. In contrast, representational art, related to human creation, received a less favourable rating when attributed to AI (Gangadharbatla, 2021).

Chamberlain et al. (2017) conducted a similar study. They found that participants struggled to categorise artworks based on their origin, with a particular bias towards believing that most artworks were human-made. This bias was partly attributed to the assumption that AI-generated art involves primarily abstract representation.

The low accuracy in the categorisation task was due to various factors, and was not influenced by the participants' artistic knowledge. Although some participants cited visual features, such as visible brushstrokes and irregular lines as reasons for categorising works as human-made, they rarely mentioned intent as justification. Image statistics, such as the distribution of oriented lines, had a more significant impact on categorisation, with greater isotropy associated with categorisation as human-made (Chamberlain, Mulin, & Wagermans, 2017).

The Influence of Personal Traits on Art Evaluation

Concerning the evaluation of artworks and the factors that influence such assessments, previous studies (Miller and Hübner, 2023; Kindler et al., 2002; Mahgoub, 2016; Mahgoub and Aldbesi, 2016; Wingström, Hautala, and Lundman, 2024) have shown that various personality traits of individuals play a significant role, including gender, age, field of education, prior knowledge of art and Artificial Intelligence, as well as any artistic activities the individual may engage in.

Miller and Hübner (2023) conducted a study examining the connections between empathy and aesthetic evaluation, and between empathy and the ability to make aesthetic judgements. The result of the study revealed the presence of gender-specific differences in empathy and its relationship to the aesthetic assessment of artworks. The research showed that men rated artworks significantly higher compared to women. Additionally, the beauty ratings among women were more influenced by cognitive factors, whereas emotional factors had a more significant impact on men's ratings.

Kindler et al. (2002) conducted a study that revealed connections between age, level of education in art, and participants' evaluation of artworks. The results suggested variations in cognitive development contribute to the evaluations made by child artists compared to those made by adults. Children often evaluate visual images subjectively and egocentrically, with a preference for realism. In contrast, older children and adults are more adept at distinguishing between the content of an artworks and its stylistic or technical features. This ability is linked to cognitive development and art education. Children and teenagers and adults without art education generally evaluated art similarly, which may be due to a lack of artistic knowledge and exposure to art.

Other studies have also explored how art education shapes individuals' perceptions of art. Mahgoub (2016) found that art education enhances the aesthetic sense of elementary school students significantly, as shown by improvements in their ability to appreciate art after participating in an art education programme. For instance, Mahgoub and Aldbesi (2016) examined the impact of art education on higher education students, revealing that it bolstered their aesthetic values and fostered greater creativity, innovation and commitment.

Just as knowledge of art can be crucial, so can experiences with Artificial Intelligence and an individual's field of work. Wingström, Hautala, and Lundman (2024) examined the influence of AI on creativity, involving both scientists and artists. The findings showed that both scientists and artists share a similar framework for defining creativity, which includes elements like the actor, process, outcome, domain and space. However, there are also some key differences in how artists and scientists define creativity, particularly concerning the use of AI and its different roles in their processes. Scientists rely on AI for precise and reliable results, while artists use AI more for exploration and play in their work.

TRADING CARD GAMES

Trading Card Games (TCGs), also known as Collectible Card Games (CCGs), are a genre of card games where players collect cards with unique characteristics, blending elements of strategy, randomness and personal customisation. Originating from early card games, TCGs have evolved significantly over time, shaped by cultural and economic developments. These games typically involve players constructing personalised decks from their collection, with each card representing characters, creatures, spells, or actions. Gameplay usually centres around strategic duels, where players draw cards to perform actions that influence the game's outcome. Cards are often obtained through purchasing packs with random selections, encouraging collection and trading among players. TCGs have become a significant part of gaming culture, influencing both analogue and digital forms, and continue to evolve with new themes, mechanics and digital adaptations, that expands their impact in the gaming world (Paiva, da Rocha Franco, Junior, & Maia, 2018; Turkay, Adinolf, & Tirthali, 2012)

Pokémon TCG

Pokémon TCG Is part of the larger Pokémon franchise, which includes a television show, video games, movies, and various other products. The Pokémon TCG game is set in the Pokémon world, where players collect creatures called Pokémon to battle against other players. In the game, the participants compete using their Pokémon, utilising cards that represent different types of attacks, skill and strategies. The game's objective is to defeat the opposing player by using these cards skilfully and making tactical choices in selecting Pokémon for battle. This aspect of the game not only makes it engaging, but also encourages the development of strategic thinking and planning skills, which aligns with the core values of the Pokémon franchise. Additionally, the game fosters a sense of community among players, as they trade cards, share strategies, and participate in tournaments, enriching the experience and connection to the broader Pokémon universe further (Elza, C., 2008).

Yu-Gi-Oh

Yu-Gi-Oh is a trading card game, similar to Pokémon, developed by the Japanese company Konami in 1999. The game gained international popularity quickly, spreading to European countries and Indonesia in the early 2000s. Yu-Gi-Oh became a favourite among a diverse audience, including children, teenagers and adults, who were drawn to its strategic depth and engaging gameplay. In Yu-Gi-Oh each player builds their own custom deck of cards, which fall into different categories, such as monsters, spells and traps. The game's goal is to reduce the opposing player's life points to zero, which is achieved through the strategic deployment of cards. Players must think critically and plan their moves carefully, often anticipating their opponent's actions and countering them effectively. Each card is not only functional, but also designed aesthetically, featuring unique illustrations (Nagi, K. S., 2021).

Games, particularly those rooted in social and sports contexts, have not only been used in entertainment and education, but have also laid the groundwork for the evolution of video games. These video games have been pivotal in advancing sophisticated algorithms, especially Neural Networks and Genetic Algorithms, which are now utilised widely in AI development (Drabik, 2018).

On type of such games also includes Trading Card Games (TCGs). TCGs, such as Yu-Gi-Oh and Pokémon, first emerged as physical games in the 1990s, and have since evolved into digital formats. In the case of video games, especially games like digital versions of TCGs, the use of AI is focused particularly in the fields of designing digital players that are both challenging and exhibit intelligent behaviour. For game developers, AI enhances the realism and appeal of their products, while researchers gain access to complex, yet controlled, environments for testing AI systems (Lorent, 2016).

Such integration of AI extends beyond gaming, influencing creative fields such as art and design, and highlighting the transformative and expansive potential of AI technologies (Drabik, 2018).

AI today can be used to created artworks, by learning from selected datasets and generating outputs based on this knowledge, such as new designs for bedrooms, photographs of celebrities, or illustrations of fictional characters (Anantrasirichai, N., & Bull, D., 2022).

Since Yu-Gi-Oh and Pokémon also exist as digital video games and are used in AI-related fields, we chose to conduct research with these franchises in the context of AI-generated art.

For the purposes of our research, we tested AI's capability specifically in generating images featuring characters from Pokémon and Yu-Gi-Oh, as these provide a unique and effective framework for evaluating AI-generated art. These characters are iconic, with highly distinctive and recognisable features that AI models can learn to replicate effectively. This makes them an ideal subject for our study, as it allows us to explore the question of whether participants, regardless of their familiarity with the Pokémon or Yu-Gi-Oh universe, can distinguish between images created by AI and those created by human artists. Furthermore, the images from these franchises are often characterised by their vibrant colours and dynamic contrasts, which not only appeal to AI learning processes, but also serve as being compelling and visually engaging for participants.

We chose Pokémon and Yu-Gi-Oh images over more classical forms of art, such as classical paintings or photographs, for several key reasons. First, the engagement and motivation of participants are crucial, and involving characters they know and love increases their interest, leading to more thoughtful responses. By using these images, we make the study more relevant and engaging, ensuring that the participants find the subject more intriguing and worth their time. Additionally, Pokémon or Yu-Gi-Oh are perhaps recognised more widely and familiar to our participants than classical forms of art, especially since our demographic did not include students from art programs. This broader recognition ensures that participants can connect with the study material more easily, making the evaluation more meaningful.

Moreover, the high recognition of these franchises among our target demographic ensures that the participants can engage with and accurately assess the AI-generated images easily. The emotional connection many fans have with these characters makes them particularly suitable for studying human reactions to AI-generated art, especially when comparing AI outputs to human-created versions.

Lasty, the cultural familiarity of these globally recognised franchises allows us to explore how familiarity with the characters and the associated art style might influence the participants' evaluations and their ability to recognise AI-generated art. This aspect is particularly important, as it allows us to assess whether cultural familiarity contributes to the formation of perceptions regarding AI-generated content.

RELATED WORKS

Existing studies in the field have explored the perception and evaluation of artworks in relation to their authorship. The research investigates primarily how people value art generated by AI algorithms compared to works resulting from human creativity. Due to technological advancements in AI, challenges have emerged in recognising authorship and understanding how this influences the perception and evaluation of artworks. Studies have found that people often value human-created art more, even though they may need help to differentiate human and AI-generated art.

Samo and Highhouse (2023) conducted a study where they examined the aesthetic judgement of artworks created by humans compared to those created by AI. They found that people generally preferred human-created art and felt more positive emotions towards it, even though the participants had difficulty in discerning the origin of the art. The results also showed that people felt better about the art without knowing its exact origin. The pattern of results was consistent with the dual-process model of judgement and decision-making. The first process involves the automatic use of fast, intuitive and emotionally-based responses, while the second involves deliberate, controlled and cognitively-based processes for making judgements.

In the art world, these processes or aesthetic judgements are determined by the inconsistency and fluency of the aesthetic experience, where fluency refers to how easily an artwork can be perceived, processed and understood, and whether it is associated with positive aesthetic experiences. Samo and Highhouse (2023) suggested that future studies should include a variety of image stimuli of different styles for example abstract, classical and modern, as well as different content which could include various people, animals or objects, as image generation algorithms continue to evolve, while avoiding the "uncanny valley" effect. They also recommended that future research uses a broader range of AI generative tools, as several new AI tools capable of generating highly realistic images were developed during the writing of the study. These include OpenAI's DALL-E 2, Google's Imagen, and Stability AI's Stable Diffusion. Among the study's limitations, it was noted that the participant sample was highly limited, as Samo and Highhouse (2023) used a sample of MTurk employees. They suggested that future studies include students, art students, or even members of the art community—individuals who are interested in and educated in the field of Art.

Hitsuwari, Ueda, Yun and Nomura (2023) conducted a research study focusing on the impact of technological development on the quality of texts generated by AI. The research focused on the field of AI Art, where it creates literature or poetry. Hitsuwari et al. (2023) conducted a study comparing haiku poetry to explore how people evaluate the aesthetics of AI-generated art and their beliefs about it. In this research, they categorized AI-generated haikus into two groups: those that involved human intervention and those that did not. A total of 385 participants engaged in two activities, with the first task requiring them to assess both human-created and AI-generated haikus based on 21 criteria. The second task asked them to identify whether the poems were written by humans or produced by AI.

The findings indicated that AI-generated haikus with human involvement received the highest beauty ratings, while the ratings for human-created haikus and those generated solely by AI were comparable. Furthermore, participants struggled to differentiate between the haikus created by humans and those generated by AI. Additionally, a negative correlation was observed between the ability to distinguish the sources of the poems and their beauty ratings, implying that high-quality AI-generated works are often mistaken for human creation. The study highlights the potential of collaboration between humans and AI in crafting haiku poetry and points to a tendency to underestimate AI-generated art due to scepticism about algorithms (Hitsuwari, Ueda, Yun, & Nomura, 2023).

Ragot, Martin, and Cojean (2020) conducted an extensive experiment in which 565 participants evaluated images created by humans or AI across four dimensions: likability, beauty, novelty and meaning, which the participants rated on a seven-point Likert scale. A total of 40 images in the impressionist style were selected. An online survey was used, and the participants were assigned randomly to one of two groups—whether the image was created by humans or AI. The images were selected randomly from 40 images (10 portraits and 10 landscape images created using AI, and 10 portraits and 10 landscape images created by humans). For each image, the participants had to evaluate several characteristics, after which they were informed that the source of the image had been altered. The participants then tasked with identifying the origin of four randomly selected images. The results showed a bias in the perception of AI and a preference bias for artworks created by humans. Images that participants believed were created by humans received higher ratings compared to those thought to be generated by AI.

METHODOLOGY

In our study, we addressed the following research questions:

RQ1: How do individual personality traits influence the perception of the aesthetic value of art?
RQ2: How do individual personality traits influence the recognition of the origin of art?
RQ3: Is there a difference in the perception of the aesthetic value of art before and after knowing its origin?

The personality traits addressed in RQ1 and RQ2 referred to gender, age, field of study, prior knowledge in art, AI, Pokémon/Pokémon TCG, Yu-Gi-Oh, and participation in extracurricular artistic activities. The aesthetic value addressed in further RQ1 and RQ3 comprised assessment through likeability, beauty, originality and the conveyed message. Finally, the origin of the art was considered, for the art to be either human- or AI-created.

To achieve the objectives of this study, we employed a quantitative research method, which included the administration of an online survey questionnaire.

We employed a multi-stage sampling method. The first cluster was selected from the University of Maribor in Slovenia. The second cluster comprised the Faculty of Electrical Engineering and Computer Science within this university, the third cluster included the following Study Programmes: Media Communications, Computer Science and Information Technologies, Mechatronics, Electrical Engineering, and

Informatics and Communication Technologies within the Faculty. The final sample consisted of 186 higher-education students, and data collection was conducted from the 2nd January 2024 to the 10th April 2024.

The survey questionnaire included three sections. The first section collected demographic and personality data. In the second section, the respondents rated the aesthetic value of 16 images, which was measured using a Likert scale ranging from 1 (very bad) to 5 (very good), related to beauty, likeability, originality and message (Ragot, Martin, and Cojean, 2020). They also judged whether the image was created by a human or by AI (Hitsuwari, Ueda, Yun, & Nomura, 2023). In the third section, the same images were rated again, with the origin of the art (whether it was created by AI or a human) disclosed alongside each image (Ragot, Martin, and Cojean, 2020).

In the study, we respected the Declaration of Helsinki (World Medical Association, 2013) and The Ethical Guidelines by the Association of Internet Researchers (Franzke et al., 2020). Accordingly, we ensured that the participants were fully informed about the research aims and procedures, and provided their informed consent prior to participation. Their anonymity was protected, and the data were handled confidentially. Additionally, the study adhered to Standards for the responsible use of AI-generated content, and ensured that no sensitive or harmful materials were used. Ethical considerations also included the right to withdraw from the study at any time without any consequences.

RESULTS

Results of the Descriptive Statistics

We recorded 410 clicks on the survey link. Of those, 198 respondents completed the survey, while we excluded 12 units during the data screening due to missing data. Finally, a total of 186 respondents were included in the data analysis, of which 31.7% were women and 68.3% were men. The age distribution of the respondents is shown in Table 1. The largest group of respondents was in the 20-year-old age group, which represents 42.5% of all respondents.

Table 1. Demographic characteristics of the respondents

Demographic characteristic	Value	Frequency (n)	Relative frequency (%)
Year of birth	2005	1	0.5%
	2004	79	42.5%
	2003	60	32.3%
	2002	32	17.2%
	2001	4	2.2%
	2000	6	3.2%
	1999 or older	4	2.2%
Field of study	Media Communication	48	25.8%
	Electrical Engineering	36	19.4%
	Computer Science and Information Technologies	78	41.9%
	Mechatronics	24	12.9%
	Information Science and Communication Technologies	0	0%
Extracurricular artistic activities	Digital art	43	23.1%
	Drawing	42	22.6%
	Painting	20	10.8%
	Photography	47	25.3%
	Graffiti	4	2.2%
	Sculpture	1	0.5%
	Architecture	2	1.1%
	None of the above	100	53.8%
	Other	8	4.3%

Most respondents were studying in the field of Computer Science and Information Technology (41.9%), while the fewest were from Mechatronics (12.8%), as shown in Table 1. No one from the Informatics and Communication Technology Study Programme completed the survey.

Table 1 also shows the extracurricular artistic activities of the respondents, indicating whether they engaged in certain types of art or not. More than half (53.8%) of the respondents indicated that they did not engage in any of the listed arts. Photography was the most popular activity, with 25.3% of the respondents involved in it, followed by digital art, which 23.1% of the respondents engaged in. The least popular activities were sculpture (0.5%) and architecture (1.1%). Additionally, 4.3% of the respondents provided other responses, including graphic design, music, 3D modelling and handcrafting, such as sewing and knitting.

Next, we asked the respondents how familiar they were with the fields of Art, Artificial Intelligence, Pokémon and/or Pokémon TCG, and Yu-Gi-Oh. The results are shown in Table 2.

Table 2. Familiarity with various fields

Field		Art	Artificial intelligence	Pokémon and/ or Pokémon TCG	Yu-Gi-Oh
Not familiar at all	Frequency (n)	43	39	6	4
	Relative frequency (%)	23.1%	21.0%	3.2%	2.2%
Slightly familiar	Frequency (n)	66	49	16	13
	Relative frequency (%)	35.5%	26.3%	8.6%	7.0%
Neither not familiar nor familiar	Frequency (n)	28	35	57	54
	Relative frequency (%)	15.1%	18.8%	30.6%	29.0%
Fairly familiar	Frequency (n)	33	45	70	81
	Relative frequency (%)	17.7%	24.2%	37.6%	43.5%
Completely familiar	Frequency (n)	16	18	37	34
	Relative frequency (%)	8.6%	9.7%	19.9%	18.3%

RQ1: The influence of personality factors on the perception of aesthetic value in art

To measure the perception of the aesthetic value of art, we presented 16 images to the respondents, 8 from the Pokémon theme and 8 from the Yu-Gi-Oh theme. In each group, half of the images were generated by AI, while the other half were human-created. For our images, we used two artistic styles: hand-drawn and digital art. For the human-created images, two from each theme and origin were in the digital style, and two were in the hand-drawn style. The breakdown of images by theme, origin and artistic style is shown in Table 3.

For the human-created images, we searched for fanart and official art from trading cards, which we then cropped for use in our questionnaire. For the AI images, we generated them using OpenAI's DALL-E 3[2] and Microsoft's Bing Image Creator[3].

Table 3 Distribution of images by theme, origin and artistic style

Origin	Art style	Pokémon	Yu-Gi-Oh
AI	Hand-drawing	2	2
	Digital art	2	2
Human	Hand-drawing	2	2
	Digital art	2	2

The respondents then rated the beauty, likability, originality and message of each on a scale from 1 to 5, with 1 indicating very bad and 5 indicating very good. We used the IBM SPSS Statistics 29.0.0.0 software[4] to analyse the results. Based on the indicators measuring aesthetic value, we created two composite variables: the aesthetic value of AI-generated art and the aesthetic value of human-created art. We summed the values of all the indicators for each image, and then aggregated these sums for AI-generated images and human-created images. The value for each indicator ranged from 1 to 5, and the total for each composite variable ranged from 32 to 160. Before this, we assessed the reliability of the individual indicators using Cronbach's Alpha coefficient (Taber, 2017). The results showed that Cronbach's Apha was 0.938, indicating a high level of reliability in our scale.

To find an answer to the research question, we first examined the influence of gender on the perception of the aesthetic value of art. Gender was treated as the independent variable, with two unrelated groups—male and female. Since the results of the Shapiro-Wilk test revealed that the dependent variable data were not normally distributed in both independent variable groups, we used a non-parametric test to determine the influence of a nominal independent variable with two unrelated groups on a continuous dependent variable—the Mann-Whitney U test. The test results indicated that women rated the aesthetic value of AI-generated art significantly higher than men did, $U = 2630, Z = -3.27, p < .01$. The test results also showed that women rated the aesthetic value of human-created art significantly higher than men did, $U = 2831, Z = -2.68, p < .01$. Table 4 presents the average ranks of aesthetic evaluation of art between men and women.

Table 4. Average ranks of aesthetic evaluation of art between women and men.

	Gender	Frequency (n)	Average rank
AI-generated art	Women	59	112.42
	Men	127	84.71
Human-made art	Women	59	109.02
	Men	127	86.29

Next, we examined the influence of age on the perception of the aesthetic value of art. Since the dependent variable data across all groups of the independent variable were non-normally distributed, we employed the Kruskal-Wallis H test to assess the impact. The results indicated no statistically significant difference in the perception of the aesthetic value of AI-generated and human-created art across the age groups ($p > .05$).

We also investigated the impact of the field of study on the perception of the aesthetic value of art. The field of study was the independent variable, with four unrelated groups, which were non-normally distributed. To determine the impact of a nominal independent variable with four unrelated groups on a continuous dependent variable, we employed the Kruskal-Wallis H test. The results showed no statistically significant difference in the perception of the aesthetic value of human-created art across Study Programmes ($p > .05$). However, a statistically significant difference was found in the perception of the aesthetic value of AI-generated art, $H(3) = 9.98$, $p < .05$. The results indicated that Media Communication students rated the aesthetic value of AI-generated art significantly higher than students from other fields. The Electrical Engineering students rated the aesthetic value of AI-generated art the lowest. Table 5 shows the average ranks of aesthetic evaluations of AI-generated and human-created art across the Study Programmes.

Table 5. Average rank of aesthetic evaluation of AI-generated and human-created art across the study programmes

AI-generated art	**Study Programme**	**Frequency (n)**	**Average rank**
	Media Communication	48	104.49
	Electrical Engineering	36	69.17
	Computer Science and Information Technologies	78	95.60
	Mechatronics	24	101.21
Human-made art	Media Communication	48	103.30
	Electrical Engineering	36	75.29
	Computer Science and Information Technologies	78	96.29
	Mechatronics	24	92.15

We also investigated the impact of extracurricular artistic activities on the perception of the aesthetic value of art. Extracurricular artistic activities were treated as an independent variable with eight groups, each analysed separately. Since the data were non-normally distributed, the Mann-Whitney U test was used. The results indicated no statistically significant difference in the perception of the aesthetic value of AI-generated art among the groups involved in extracurricular activities such as digital art, drawing, painting, photography, architecture, and those with no artistic involvement, $p > .05$. Similarly, there was no statistically significant difference in the perception of the aesthetic value of human-created art among the groups involved in digital art, drawing, painting, photography, graffiti, architecture, and those not engaged in any artistic activity, $p > .05$.

However, a statistically significant difference was found in the perception of the aesthetic value of AI-generated art among students engaged in graffiti, $U = 29.00$, $Z = -2.05$, $p < .05$ and sculpture, $U = 3566$, $Z = -2.01$, $p < .05$. The students involved in graffiti and sculpture activities rated the aesthetic value of AI-generated art higher; Table 6 presents the average ranks.

Table 6. Average rank of aesthetic evaluation of AI-generated art between artistic activities of graffiti and sculpture

AI-generated art	Artistic activity		Frequency (n)	Average rank
	Graffiti	Chosen	2	171.00
		Not chosen	184	92.66
	TOTAL		186	
	Sculpture	Chosen	100	86.16
		Not chosen	86	102.03
	TOTAL		186	

At the end, we were interested in whether prior knowledge of art, Artificial Intelligence, Pokémon and/or Pokémon TCG, and Yu-Gi-Oh had an impact on the perception of aesthetic value. Due to the non-normal distribution of the dependent variable across all groups of the independent variable, we used the Kruskal-Wallis H test. The results indicated a statistically significant difference in the perception of the aesthetic value of AI-generated and human-made art across all areas of prior knowledge. Table 7 presents the test results, while Table 8 shows the average ranks of aesthetic evaluation of art across all the prior knowledge groups.

Table 7. Results of the test for the perception of aesthetic value of art across all groups of prior knowledge

Field	Statistic	AI-generated art	Human-made art
Art	H(4)	11.346	16.559
	p	0.02	0.002
Artificial Intelligence	H(4)	14,076	13.749
	p	0.007	0.008
Pokémon and/or Pokémon TCG	H(4)	33.308	48.917
	p	0.001	0.001
Yu-Gi-Oh	H(4)	38.520	42.227
	p	0.001	0.001

Table 8. Average rank of aesthetic evaluation of AI and human art among groups with prior knowledge in specific fields

		Art		Artificial Intelligence		Pokémon and/ or Pokémon TCG		Yu-Gi-Oh	
	Prior knowledge	Frequency (n)	Relative frequency	Frequency (n)	Relative frequency	Frequency (n)	Relative frequency	Frequency (n)	Relative frequency
AI-generated art	Not familiar at all	43	77.13	39	88.05	6	52.17	4	21.63
	Slightly familiar	66	87.88	49	83.86	16	54.41	13	51.88
	Neither not familiar nor familiar	28	100.38	35	87.43	57	83.68	54	72.54
	Fairly familiar	33	110.15	45	96.21	70	98.19	81	104.16
	Completely familiar	16	116.38	18	136.58	37	127.24	34	125.76
	TOTAL	186		186		186		186	
Human- made art	Not familiar at all	43	70.69	39	85.27	6	29.58	4	47.13
	Slightly familiar	66	90.32	49	81.20	16	34.81	13	41.54
	Neither not familiar nor familiar	28	99.18	35	94.70	57	83.36	54	71.96
	Fairly familiar	33	109.83	45	96.99	70	100.74	81	103.02
	Completely familiar	16	124.31	18	133.75	37	131.16	34	130.35
	TOTAL	186		186		186		186	

RQ2: Influence of Individual Personality Traits on the Recognition of the Origin of the Art

In the second research question, we examined the influence of personality factors on the recognition of the origin of the art. For this purpose, the respondents were asked to identify whether each image they were shown was created by AI or by a human. We created a variable called "recognition", where each response was coded as 1 for correct identification and 0 for incorrect identification. These indicators were then summed, with the total ranging from 0 to 16. The actual total ranged from 4 to 15, and we divided this scale into three groups: 4-7 represented low recognition, 8-11 medium recognition and 12-15 high recognition.

First, we investigated the influence of gender on the recognition of the origin of the art. Since this involved the impact of one independent nominal variable with two unconnected groups on a continuous dependent variable, and the data were not normally distributed, we used the Mann-Whitney U test. The results indicated no statistically significant influence, $p > .05$.

We also explored the influence of age on the recognition of the origin of art. Given the non-normal distribution of the data and the impact of one independent nominal variable with multiple groups on a continuous dependent variable, we used the Kruskal-Wallis H test. The results showed no statistically significant difference between the groups of the independent variable, $p > .05$.

Finally, we examined the influence of the Study Programme on the recognition of the origin of the art. Again, given the non-normal distribution and the involvement of one independent nominal variable with multiple groups on a continuous dependent variable, we used the Kruskal-Wallis H test. The results showed that the students in Mechatronics had the highest level of recognition of the origin of the art, while the students in Computer Science and Information Technology had the lowest. $H(3) = 17.552$, $p < .01$ Table 9 presents the average ranks for the recognition of the origin of the art across the different Study Programmes.

Table 9. Average rank for the recognition of the origin of the art across different study programmes.

Study Programme	Frequency (n)	Average rank
Media Communications	48	107.94
Electrical Engineering	36	93.50
Computer Science and Information Technologies	78	78.69
Mechatronics	24	112.75
TOTAL	186	

The research question also examined the influence of extracurricular artistic activities on the recognition of the origin of the art. Extracurricular artistic activities were treated as an independent variable, with eight groups, each analysed separately. Since the data were not normally distributed, the Mann-Whitney U test was used. The results indicated no statistically significant influence on the recognition of the origin of the art between the groups involved in digital art, drawing, painting, photography, graffiti, sculpture, or none of the above, $p > .05$. However, the results did show that the students engaged in architecture had a higher level of recognition of the origin of the art compared to those who were not involved in this activity, $U = 743.50$, $Z = -3.21$, $p < .05$ The students who participated in architectural activities ($n = 15$) had an average rank of 129.43, while the students who did not engage in those activities ($N = 171$) had an average rank of 90.35.

Finally, we were also interested in examining the impact of prior knowledge in art, artificial intelligence, Pokémon and/or Pokémon TCG, and Yu-Gi-Oh on the recognition of the art`s origin. Given that the data were non-normally distributed and we were assessing the impact of an ordinal independent variable with multiple groups on a continuous dependent variable, we used the Kruskal-Wallis H test. The results indicated that none of the areas of prior knowledge had a statistically significant impact on the recognition of the art`s origin, $p > .05$.

RQ3: Difference in the Perception of the Aesthetic Value of the Art Before and After Being Informed of the Art's Origin

In the third research question, we explored whether the aesthetic evaluation of AI-generated and human-created art differed when the respondents are informed of the art's origin—specifically, whether they knew if the art was created using Artificial Intelligence or by a human. For this purpose, the respondents were asked to reevaluate the same images in the third section of the questionnaire which they had already rated in the second section, but, this time, the origin of the art was indicated alongside the images. As before, we created two composite variables: the aesthetic value of AI-generated art and the aesthetic value of human-created art. We summed the values of all indicators—beauty, likability, originality, and message—for each image, and then combined these sums for AI-generated and human-created images. As in the first question, the values of each indicator ranged from 1 to 5, while the composite variable sums ranged from 32 to 160. We also checked the reliability of the individual indicators using the Cronbach's Alpha coefficient (Taber, 2017), which resulted in a value of 0.89, indicating a high level of reliability.

We first investigated whether there was a difference in the perception of the aesthetic value of AI-generated art before and after the respondents are informed of the art's origin. Due to the non-normal distribution of the data, we used the Wilcoxon signed-rank test. The results showed that art created using AI was rated aesthetically higher after the respondents were informed of its origin compared to before, $Z = -10.63$, $p < .01$. Table 10 shows the average ranks of aesthetic evaluation of the art before and after being informed of its origin.

Table 10. Average rank of aesthetic evaluation of AI-generated art before and after being informed of the source of the art

	Frequency (n)	**Average rank**
After being informed < before being informed	19	44.97
After being informed > before being informed	168	98.50
After being informed = before being informed	2	
TOTAL	186	

Next, we explored the difference in the perception of the aesthetic value of art created by humans before and after being informed of its origin. Due to the non-normal distribution of the data, we used the Wilcoxon signed-rank test. The results indicated that human-created art was also rated higher aesthetically after the participants were informed of its origin compared to before, $Z = -10.73$, $p < .01$. Table 11 presents the average ranks of aesthetic evaluation before and after being informed of the origin of the art.

Table 11. Average rank of aesthetic evaluation of human-created art before and after being informed of the source of the art

	Frequency (n)	**Average rank**
After being informed < before being informed	17	42.26
After being informed > before being informed	166	97.09
After being informed = before being informed	3	
TOTAL	186	

DISCUSSION

Our findings revealed significant differences in how various demographic factors influence the perception of the aesthetic value of artworks, both those generated by AI and those created by humans. Notably, gender differences were observed, with women rating the aesthetic value of artworks higher than men. Age did not emerge as a significant factor in aesthetic perception, while the Study Programme was significant, particularly in evaluating AI-generated art. Media Communications students rated AI art more favourably, while Electrical Engineering students rated it the lowest. Additionally, the participants engaged in artistic activities, particularly graffiti and sculpture, rated AI-generated art higher. Prior knowledge of art also influenced the perception of aesthetic value, with Mechatronics students being more accurate in recognising the origins of the artworks. The participants rated artworks higher when informed of their origin.

The gender differences in the perceived aesthetic value may be attributed to varying levels of emotional engagement with art, where women tend to exhibit greater empathy and sensitivity to aesthetic qualities, potentially influencing their evaluations. This aligns with Miller and Hübner's (2023) findings that women's aesthetic judgements are more influenced by cognitive factors, while men's judgements are driven more emotionally. Contrary to earlier studies that found men rated artworks higher (Miller and Hübner, 2023), the current analysis reveals that women rate AI-generated art more favourably, which could indicate a shift in perceptions, or the specific nature of the artworks involved.

The lack of significant age-related differences in aesthetic perception supports Kindler et al.'s (2002) conclusions that, while cognitive development influences art evaluation, these preferences stabilise in adulthood. This stability suggests that early experiences and cultural exposure are foundational, and further education or age might not alter these preferences drastically in later life.

The differences related to educational background indicate that art evaluation, particularly that created by AI, is linked strongly to disciplinary focus. These findings align with the theory that the perception of art is tied closely to the perceived effort and labour involved in its creation, as noted by Bellaiche et al. (2023) and Khan & Nässtrröm (2023). The perception of AI art as less profound and communicative may reflect a deep-seated bias against art that is not connected directly to human experience.

Practical artistic activities outside of formal education enhance the ability to recognise and appreciate innovation and originality in art, supporting the idea that personal experience and engagement with art forms are relevant in evaluating artworks. This aligns with Mahgoub and Aldbesi's (2016) findings, which demonstrated that art education bolsters aesthetic values significantly, fostering creativity and innovation.

The impact of prior knowledge on the perception of aesthetic value supports the theory that cognitive frameworks are crucial in shaping our understanding and valuation of art (Gangadharbatla, 2021). On the other hand, this study found that knowledge of AI, art, or specific cultural elements like Pokémon or Yu-Gi-Oh did not influence the ability to recognise the source of artwork significantly, suggesting that such knowledge might be more relevant in assessing aesthetic value rather than source identification.

Lastly, the observation that artworks were rated higher when participants were aware of their origin, especially for AI-generated art, underscores the importance of context and source information in art perception. This supports previous findings by Chamberlain et al. (2017) and Gangadharbatla (2021), which highlighted that knowing the creator of a work can alter its perceived value, potentially due to biases or expectations about the effort and creativity involved. This effect might also reflect a deep-seated bias against non-human art forms, as noted by Bellaiche et al. (2023) and Khan & Näsström (2023).

These findings are significant, as they shed light on the fundamental factors shaping art perception at a time when technologies like AI are becoming increasingly integrated into artistic creation. The discovery that gender, educational background and prior knowledge impact art evaluation significantly encourages a broader understanding of responses to both traditional and emerging forms of art. As Bellaiche et al. (2023) suggested, AI art could soon replace human creativity, though this is mostly unlikely, due to the lack of human experience in such art. The importance of knowing the origin of an artwork for its aesthetic evaluation highlights the need for transparency and context in the presentation of artworks, which could guide how AI art is introduced and interpreted in the future.

Despite these findings, this study has certain limitations. The sample was limited to students from specific academic programs at a single university, which may be different from the broader population of higher education students. We also relied on self-reported data, which may be subject to biases, such as varying interpretations of rating scales. Lastly, the study focused on a specific set of artworks, which may not capture the full spectrum of possibilities within AI-generated and human art.

Future research should explore these findings in a broader, more diverse population, to determine whether these patterns hold across different demographic groups. Longitudinal studies could investigate how aesthetic preferences evolve over time, particularly with increased exposure to AI-generated art. Expanding the range of artistic forms and styles included in research could also contribute to a better understanding of AI's impact on art perception. Further research could also delve deeper into the psychological mechanisms influencing the role of gender, educational background and prior knowledge in aesthetic perception, potentially leading to more targeted strategies for art education and appreciation in the age of AI.

REFERENCES

Aggarwal, C. C. (2018). Neural Networks and Deep Learning.

Anantrasirichai, N., & Bull, D. (2022). Artificial intelligence in the creative industries: A review. *Artificial Intelligence Review*, *55*(1), 1–68. DOI: 10.1007/s10462-021-10039-7

Bandi, A., Adapa, P. V., & Kuchi, Y. E. (2023). The Power of Generative AI: A Review of Requirements, Models, Input–Output Formats, Evaluation Metrics, and Challenges. *Future Internet*, *15*(8), 260–320. DOI: 10.3390/fi15080260

Bellaiche, L., Shahi, R., Turpin, M. H., Ragnhildstveit, A., Sprockett, S., Barr, N., Christensen, A., & Seli, P. (2023). Human versus AI: Whether and why we prefer human-created compared to AI-created artwork. *Cognitive Research: Principles and Implications*, *8*(8), 42. DOI: 10.1186/s41235-023-00499-6 PMID: 37401999

Bird, C., Ungless, E., & Kasirzadeh, A. (2023, August). Typology of risks of generative text-to-image models. In Proceedings of the 2023 AAAI/ACM Conference on AI, Ethics, and Society (pp. 396-410). DOI: 10.1145/3600211.3604722

Cetinic, E., & She, J. (2022). Understanding and creating art with AI: Review and outlook. [TOMM]. *ACM Transactions on Multimedia Computing Communications and Applications*, *18*(2), 1–22. DOI: 10.1145/3475799

Chamberlain, R., Mulin, C., & Wagermans, J. (2017). Putting the Art in Artificial: Aesthetic Responses to Computer-Generated Art. *Psychology of Aesthetics, Creativity, and the Arts*.

Clowney, D. (2011). Definitions of Art and Fine Art's Historical Origins. *The Journal of Aesthetics and Art Criticism*, *69*(3), 309–320. DOI: 10.1111/j.1540-6245.2011.01474.x

Davies, S. (2015). Defining Art and Artworlds. *The Journal of Aesthetics and Art Criticism*, *73*(4), 375–384. DOI: 10.1111/jaac.12222

Drabik, E. (2018). An analysis of the connection between ai development and the creation of games and advanced computer systems. *Economics World*, *6*(4), 251–262. DOI: 10.17265/2328-7144/2018.04.001

Elza, C. (2008). WE ALL LIVE IN A POKÉMON WORLD. The Japanification of Children's Popular Culture: From Godzilla to Miyazaki, 53.

Feuerriegel, S., Hartmann, J., Janiesch, C., & Zschech, P. (2024). Generative AI. *Business & Information Systems Engineering*, *66*(1), 111–126. DOI: 10.1007/s12599-023-00834-7

Franzke, A. S., Bechmann, A., Zimmer, M., & Ess, C. (2020). Internet research: Ethical guidelines 3.0. Association of Internet Researchers. https://aoir.org/reports/ethics3.pdf

Gangadharbatla, H. (2021). The Role of AI Attribution Knowledge in the Evaluation of Artwork. *Empirical Studies of the Arts*, •••, 1–19.

Haenlein, M., & Kaplan, A. (2019). A Brief History of Artificial Intelligence: On the Past, Present and Future of Artificial Intelligence. *California Management Review*, *61*(4), 5–14. DOI: 10.1177/0008125619864925

Hitsuwari, J., Ueda, Y., Yun, W., & Nomura, M. (2023). Does human–AI collaboration lead to more creative art? Aesthetic evaluation of human-made and AI-generated haiku poetry. Computers in Human Behaviour, 139.

Jiang, H. H., Brown, L., Cheng, J., Khan, M., Gupta, A., Workman, D., . . . Gebru, T. (2023, August). AI Art and its Impact on Artists. In Proceedings of the 2023 AAAI/ACM Conference on AI, Ethics, and Society (pp. 363-374). DOI: 10.1145/3600211.3604681

Johns, A. (2021). Journey towards a synthetic consciousness. In Learning Outcomes of Classroom Research (pp. 56-64). Tamil Nedu: L Ordine Nuovo Publication.

Khan, M., & Näsström, J. (2023). How AI images and human-created digital art are evaluated and affected by attribution knowledge. Retrieved from diva-portal: https://www.diva-portal.org/smash/get/diva2:1786169/FULLTEXT01.pdf

Kindler, A. M., Pariser, D. A., Van den Berg, A., Liu, W. C., & Dias, B. (2002). Aesthetic modernism, the first among equals? A look at aesthetic value systems in cross-cultural, age and visual arts educated and non-visual arts educated judging cohorts. *International Journal of Cultural Policy*, *8*(2), 135–152. DOI: 10.1080/10286630220000009533

Leder, H., Gerger, G., Dressler, S. G., & Schabmann, A. (2012). How Art Is Appreciated. *Psychology of Aesthetics, Creativity, and the Arts*, *6*(1), 2–10. DOI: 10.1037/a0026396

Lorent, N. (2016). Development of a Video Game and Creation of an Artificial Player.

Mahgoub, Y. M. (2016). The impact of arts education to enhance of aesthetic sense ability for basic level pupils. *Journal of Education and Human Development*, *5*(2), 126–130. DOI: 10.15640/jehd.v5n2a15

Mahgoub, Y. M., & Aldbesi, S. O. (2016). The contribution of art education in enhancing of the aesthetic values for student of higher education. *Journal of Education and Human Development*, *5*(1), 270–275. DOI: 10.15640/jehd.v5n1a28

Matsuzaka, Y., & Yashiro, R. (2023). AI-based computer vision techniques and expert systems. *AI*, *4*(1), 289–302. DOI: 10.3390/ai4010013

Miller, C. A., & Hübner, R. (2023). The relations of empathy and gender to aesthetic response and aesthetic inference of visual artworks. *Empirical Studies of the Arts*, *41*(1), 188–215. DOI: 10.1177/02762374221095701

Millet, K., Buehler, F., Du, G., & Kokkoris, M. D. (2023). Defending humankind: Anthropocentric bias in the appreciation of AI art. *Computers in Human Behavior*, *143*, 143. DOI: 10.1016/j.chb.2023.107707

Nagi, K. S. (2021). Heart of the Cards: The Underlying Social Framework of the Yu-Gi-Oh Community.

Paiva, F. G. R. M., da Rocha Franco, A. D. O., Junior, G. M., & Maia, J. G. R. (2018). Analyzing Player Profiles in Collectible Card Games. *Proceedings do Simpósio Brasileiro de Jogos e Entretenimento Digital: Culture Track.*

Ragot, M., Martin, N., & Cojean, S. (2020, April). AI-generated vs. human artworks. A perception bias towards artificial intelligence? In Extended abstracts of the 2020 CHI Conference on Human Factors in Computing Systems (pp. 1-10).

Raparthi, M., Dodda, S. B., Reddy, S. R. B., Thunki, P., Maruthi, S., & Ravichandran, P. (2021). Advancements in Natural Language Processing-A Comprehensive Review of AI Techniques. *Journal of Bioinformatics and Artificial Intelligence*, *1*(1), 1–10.

Samo, A., & Highhouse, S. (2023). Artificial intelligence and art: Identifying the aesthetic judgment factors that distinguish human- and machine-generated artwork. *Psychology of Aesthetics, Creativity, and the Arts*. DOI: 10.1037/aca0000570

Taber, K. S. (2017). The Use of Cronbach's Alpha When Developing. *Research in Science Education*, 1273–1296.

Ting, T. T., & Ling, L. Y. bin Ahmad Azam, A. I., & Palaniappan, R. (2021). Artificial Intelligence Art: Attitudes and Perceptions Toward Human Versus Artificial Intelligence Artworks. In 1ST Int. Conf. Humanit. Educ. Sci. Manag. Eng. Technol.

Toosi, A., Bottino, A. G., Saboury, B., Siegel, E., & Rahmim, A. (2021). A brief history of AI: How to prevent another winter (a critical review). *PET Clinics*, *16*(4), 449–469. DOI: 10.1016/j.cpet.2021.07.001 PMID: 34537126

Turkay, S., Adinolf, S., & Tirthali, D. (2012). Collectible card games as learning tools. *Procedia: Social and Behavioral Sciences*, *46*, 3701–3705. DOI: 10.1016/j.sbspro.2012.06.130

Wingström, R., Hautala, J., & Lundman, R. (2024). Redefining creativity in the era of AI? Perspectives of computer scientists and new media artists. *Creativity Research Journal*, *36*(2), 177–193. DOI: 10.1080/10400419.2022.2107850

World Medical Association. (2013). World Medical Association Declaration of Helsinki. *Journal of the American Medical Association*, *310*(20), 2191–2194. DOI: 10.1001/jama.2013.281053 PMID: 24141714

Xinyuan, F., & Liang, Y. (2023). The Research on the Characteristics of AI Application in Art Field and its Value. *4th International Conference on Language, Art and Cultural Exchange*, 146-160.

KEY TERMS AND DEFINITIONS

Artificial Intelligence: Applications based on deep neural networks that enable a computer system to develop and mimic human-like behaviour and make human-like decisions.

Aesthetic Evaluation: The process of assessing artworks based on their beauty, appeal and expression of emotions or ideas.

Aesthetic Value: A characteristic of artworks that are judged to be beautiful, pleasing or otherwise attractive to sensory perception.

Computer Vision: A field of AI that enables computers to interpret and process visual data from the world.

Generative Models: AI models that process and combine information from various domains, including visual, textual and audio data, to create new content such as images or text.

Natural Language Processing (NLP): A technique that allows computers to understand, interpret and generate human language in a meaningful way, often used in combination with computer vision in text-to-image models.

Text-To-Image (TTI) Models: AI systems that create an image from given text, utilizing natural language processing and computer vision techniques to generate images.

ENDNOTES

1 An artworld is a historical and cultural framework in which art traditions and practices have developed over time, forming a network of aesthetic norms and values (Davies, 2015).

2 https://openai.com/index/dall-e-3/

3 https://www.bing.com/images/create

4 https://www.ibm.com/spss

Chapter 12
Perception vs. Reality: Unraveling the Colors of Ho Chi Minh City – Understanding Urban Identity Through Color Palettes

Dongsu Yi
University of Economics, Ho Chi Minh City, Vietnam

Thuy Anh Trinh
University of Economics, Ho Chi Minh City, Vietnam

Anh Tu Nguyen Huynh
https://orcid.org/0009-0004-8128-6748
University of Economics, Ho Chi Minh City, Vietnam

ABSTRACT

The primary focus of this research is to explore the color palettes across the 21 diverse districts of Ho Chi Minh City (HCMC) and to understand how these colors contribute to the city's overall urban identity. Through comprehensive analysis of the collected data, a significant revelation emerged, showcasing that approximately 80% of the city's color palette is dominated by an array of grayscale shades, lending an enigmatic allure to HCMC's visual identity. Interestingly, complementing this grayscale backdrop, a splash of vibrant colors, including captivating shades of blue, yellow, and red, introduces a contrasting yet complementary aspect to the city's chromatic tapestry, albeit their presence remains comparatively minor.

DOI: 10.4018/979-8-3693-7610-2.ch012

INTRODUCTION

In the vibrant tapestry of urban landscapes, colors emerge as powerful narrators, often weaving tales of culture, heritage, and modernity. Yet, the tale told may differ from the one perceived, marking a compelling dichotomy between perception and reality. This thesis delves deep into this fascinating interplay, focusing on the mesmerizing cityscape of Ho Chi Minh City (HCMC).

1. The Difference Between Perception and Reality: The Meaning of City Colors

Colors have an inherent ability to evoke emotions and shape perceptions (Manav, 2017; Chen et al., 2007). To a traveler, the radiant hues of HCMC's commercial centers might symbolize its bustling energy. For a resident, the same palette may reflect historical tales or the rhythm of daily life. Such distinctions between object colors and city colors underscore the intricate layers of meaning each shade holds in the urban context. This thesis seeks to unravel these layers, questioning how individual perceptions of color palettes resonate with the city's true narrative, and exploring the gap that might exist between perception and reality.

2. The Relationship Between City Color and City Identity

Delving deeper into the city's palette, one realizes that colors aren't merely aesthetic elements. They carry symbolic meanings deeply embedded in local traditions and heritage, thus crafting the city's unique identity. The juxtaposition of HCMC's modernity against its rich historical backdrop offers a vibrant spectrum of colors, each narrating a different chapter of its tale. This research aims to understand how such colors sculpt the city's identity and how that identity is perceived by its inhabitants and visitors.

3. Determining the City's Color Palette: The Who and the What

Behind every brushstroke that paints a city's landscape, there lies intent. Whether it's urban planners aiming for functionality, artists capturing the city's essence, or residents adding personal touches, multiple hands shape a city's color palette. Chen & Tsai (2007) and Janeczko (2023) emphasize the role of colors in creating memorable experiences for tourists, while Manav (2017) discusses its significance in residents' well-being. By understanding these diverse influences and motivations, this study seeks to determine the forces that shape HCMC's color narrative.

In embarking on this exploration of HCMC's colors, the research hopes to offer urban planners, designers, and policymakers a fresh perspective. One that not only appreciates the aesthetic appeal of the city's hues but also respects the tales they tell and the emotions they evoke. In doing so, we aim to bridge the gap between perception and reality, forging a deeper understanding of HCMC's urban identity through its color palettes.

In conclusion, by traversing the colorful alleys of perception and reality, this study aspires to shed light on the intricate relationship between colors and urban identity, narrating the captivating story of Ho Chi Minh City through its enchanting hues.

LITERATURE REVIEW

Urban environments, with their vibrant hues and shades, craft intricate narratives that shape both perceptions and realities. This research delves into the color dynamics of Ho Chi Minh City to understand its profound influence on both the city's inhabitants and its visitors. Drawing from a plethora of disciplines, the literature forms the bedrock of our study.

1. Expectations, Reality, and Perception

The dance between perception and reality in the context of urban environments is notably complex. Zhong et al. (2021) shed light on this intricacy from a psychological perspective. Their mixed-methods study underscored how vibrant urban colors bolstered a sense of belonging and emotional well-being among European city inhabitants, suggesting that color perceptions play a pivotal role in the psychological realm (Zhong, T., Ye, C., Wang, Z., Tang, G., Zhang, W., & Ye, Y., 2021).

Oliveira's (2023) work in tourism dovetails with this perspective, pointing out that urban areas drenched in local cultural colors witnessed significantly higher footfalls. This finding hints at the power of color in shaping tourist expectations and their subsequent experiences (Oliveira, S. N. d. S.,2023).

2. Colors and Urban Identity

Ginting and Rahman (2016) embarked on an ethnographic journey across Asian cities to decode the relationship between color and urban identity. Their work beautifully captures the tension between historical conservation, evident in traditional color identities, and the modernization wave, manifested in contemporary, globalized color schemes. Their findings illuminate the pivotal role colors play in encapsulating and conveying a city's cultural essence (Ginting, N. and Rahman, N. V., 2016).

Luekveerawattana and Sawangdee (2021) provide a complementary perspective by delving into Bangkok's urban colors. Their research, focused on the interplay of historical and modern hues, serves as a testament to the city's evolution, further underscoring the indomitable bond between colors and urban identity (Luekveerawattana, R. and Sawangdee, Y., 2021).

3. Identifying Colors and Their Meanings

While the aforementioned studies provide crucial insights into the role of colors in urban landscapes, there is an evident gap in methodologies and approaches that help identify these colors and decipher their meanings. A systematic framework or toolkit for this identification remains a discernible void in the literature.

In conclusion, while the research corpus on the interplay of colors in urban spaces is vast, it does illuminate the compelling role colors play in shaping perceptions, realities, and identities. Yet, there exists a marked gap in our understanding of Ho Chi Minh City's color narrative, paving the way for this research to make a valuable contribution.

METHODOLOGY

Research Design

Purpose and Questions of the Study

The purpose of this study is to explore the colors of Ho Chi Minh City (HCMC) and understand their influence on urban identity.

The research questions are as follows:

> RQ1. What are the dominant color palettes and their distribution across the diverse districts of Ho Chi Minh City (HCMC)? How do these colors collectively represent the urban identity of the city?
> RQ2. How do the color palettes of HCMC reflect the city's functional zones and distinctive local characteristics?

Research Method and Approach

The primary approach involves image data collection and color analysis to identify and interpret the prevalent color palettes in HCMC. It combines elements of a case study and content analysis to gain a comprehensive understanding of the city's urban identity through colors.

Samples:

Target Area and Study Subjects:

The target Area includes all 21 districts of Ho Chi Minh City, each representing a distinct locality.

Sample Size and Sampling Method

The content analysis of visual data, particularly those representing urban landscapes, demands a meticulous sample selection to ensure both representativeness and reliability. For this study, the primary source of images was Google, an expansive repository of visual content. Given the vastness of accessible data, establishing clear selection criteria becomes paramount.

The decision to analyze 300-400 images adhered to the principle of 'saturation' in qualitative research. Morse (1995) elucidates that saturation is achieved when additional data fails to provide new insights or dimensions. Building on this, Snyder and Ly (2020) suggest that for visual studies, a few hundred images usually suffice to reach saturation, particularly when these images exhibit diversity and richness in content. Hence, a dataset comprising 300-400 images optimally balances comprehensiveness with feasibility (Li, Y., & Xie, Y., 2020)

Our photo selection was anchored in two fundamental objectives: safeguarding authenticity and maximizing the portrayal of urban architecture and colors. Photos taken at night or under low evening illumination were excluded to ensure consistent lighting and accurate color representation. Furthermore, digitally manipulated images, such as those edited using Photoshop, can distort colors and perceptions. Thus, our study echoed the sentiments of González Martínez (2017), emphasizing the significance of authenticity in visual content analysis for urban studies. Moreover, to center our focus on urban architecture, images were selected that minimized distractions like sky, roads, or large obstructive elements (González Martínez, Plácido., 2017).

To attain a balanced representation of Ho Chi Minh City, images from each district were chosen proportionately. Adopting the stratified sampling technique, championed by Smith and Johnson (2018), we ensured each district, irrespective of its prominence or expanse, received appropriate representation. This approach promises a comprehensive view of the city's colorscape (Smith and Johnson, 2018).

The process of selecting samples was primarily driven by research on Google Images. We employed the Auto Crawler tool with the aim of gathering a vast number of images. Yet, we observed that after retrieving the initial 300-400 images from Google, the subsequent results began to deviate from the intended keyword, often displaying districts not specified by our search term. This observation was a pivotal reason for capping our search at 400 images.

Post-crawling, we undertook a manual review to eliminate images that didn't align with our focus. This included images like food photographs, regional maps, posters dominated by text, and images showcasing unrelated districts. A team member well-versed with HCMC spearheaded this filtering process. (See Appendix 2)

Data Collection

Data Collection Procedures

The data collection process involved the following steps:

Web scraping using AutoCrawler to collect images from Google Images with targeted search terms for each district.

Manual cleaning of the dataset to remove irrelevant and nighttime images, resulting in a relevant and consistent dataset for color analysis.

Color quantization using the K-means method with an in-house Python script to simplify the images' color palettes while preserving their overall distribution. (See Appendix 4)

Data Analysis

Data Processing and Analysis

The Python script conducted a comprehensive color analysis on the dataset, calculating the dominance of each color and determining the percentage of pixels associated with each color. The script also extracted dominant colors and their corresponding percentages. These results were compiled into a color set with respective appearance percentages for further interpretation. (See Appendix 4)

Ethical Considerations

Personal Information Protection and Consent

This study did not involve the collection of personal information from participants, as it primarily used publicly available image datasets. Consent was not required for this web scraping-based data collection.

Ensuring Reliability and Validity

To enhance reliability and validity, we followed a systematic and consistent data collection and analysis process. The Python script used for color analysis ensured objective and replicable results.

RESULT

The exploration of color palettes across the 21 diverse districts of Ho Chi Minh City (HCMC) has painted a vivid picture of the city's visual identity. Our comprehensive study discerned that the majority, approximately 80% of the palette, is occupied by various shades of grayscale. The remaining 20% adds a burst of vibrancy with shades of blue, yellow, and red, albeit in smaller proportions.

To gain a deeper understanding of the city's color representation, we further classified the districts of HCMC into three primary functional zones, each reflecting unique local characteristics.

The table below shows in detail how districts in Ho Chi Minh City are divided into areas.

Table 1. Area distribution

Economic, Financial, Commercial, and Entertainment	Residential Areas	Industrial and Production
District 1	District 6	District 8
District 3	District 7	District 12
District 4	District 11	Binh Tan
District 5	Phu Nhuan	Binh Chanh
District 10	Tan Binh	Cu Chi
Binh Thanh	Tan Phu	Can Gio
	Go Vap	Hoc Mon
		Nha Be

Each functional zone, when integrated with its district-specific color palettes, contributed uniquely to the overall city palette.

Economic, Financial, Commercial, and Entertainment Center

District 1, District 3, District 4, District 5, District 10 and Binh Thanh District. District 1 is the largest financial and commercial center with many office buildings, hotels, shopping centers and restaurants.

Figure 2. Color palette for center area

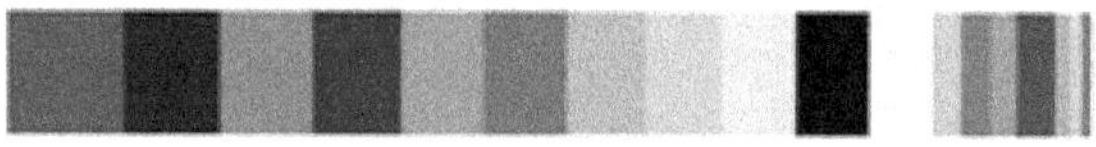

```
Color: [81 81 77], Percentage: 10.8%
Color: [35 35 32], Percentage: 8.8%
Color: [126 127 124], Percentage: 8.7%
Color: [54 56 53], Percentage: 8.1%
Color: [148 148 145], Percentage: 7.7%
Color: [103 105 104], Percentage: 7.5%
Color: [171 170 167], Percentage: 7.0%
Color: [195 195 193], Percentage: 7.0%
Color: [214 219 223], Percentage: 6.9%
Color: [13 13 12], Percentage: 6.6%
Color: [243 246 246], Percentage: 5.6%
Color: [157 192 227], Percentage: 2.6%
Color: [134 106  74], Percentage: 2.6%
Color: [108 151 190], Percentage: 2.6%
Color: [93 64 39], Percentage: 2.3%
Color: [ 35  75 108], Percentage: 1.5%
Color: [196 151  91], Percentage: 1.4%
Color: [215 185 149], Percentage: 1.2%
Color: [187  65  48], Percentage: 0.5%
Color: [ 51 124 141], Percentage: 0.5%
```

The city's heart pulses with dynamic colors. Notably, District 1, HCMC's largest financial and commercial center, is populated with numerous office buildings, shopping centers, and entertainment venues. The enhanced red hue in this central region can be attributed to specific districts, particularly District 5, HCMC's “Chinatown”, and District 1 with its bustling commercial energy.

District 5, often referred to as Ho Chi Minh City's “Chinatown”, could be one of the contributing factors. On the other hand, District 1 serves as the commercial and financial hub of the city. This district is home to a plethora of businesses, shopping centers, and entertainment venues, which naturally exude a more dynamic and colorful atmosphere. The vibrancy of this district could be another factor contributing to the subtle red hue in the central area.

Residential Areas: District 6, District 7, District 11, Phu Nhuan District, Tan Binh District, Tan Phu District, Go Vap District are all areas characterized by densely populated residences.

Figure 3. Color palette for residential area

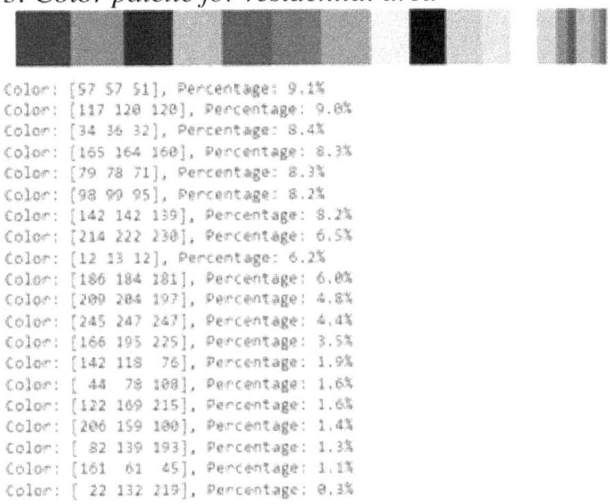

Upon visual inspection, it's noticeable that the color palette of these contains a substantial proportion of grayscale colors. The reasons behind this might be closely connected to the region's natural and built environments. Housing designs in Vietnam mostly lean towards more neutral or muted color schemes, which, when viewed from afar, merge into shades of grayscale. Besides, the presence of numerous water bodies like canals and rivers could be another significant factor. Residential areas tend to cluster around these water sources.

Industrial and Production Areas: District 8, District 12, Binh Tan District, Binh Chanh District, Cu Chi District, Can Gio District, Hoc Mon District, and Nha Be District are mainly focused on industrial and manufacturing sectors.

Figure 4. Color pallete for industrial area

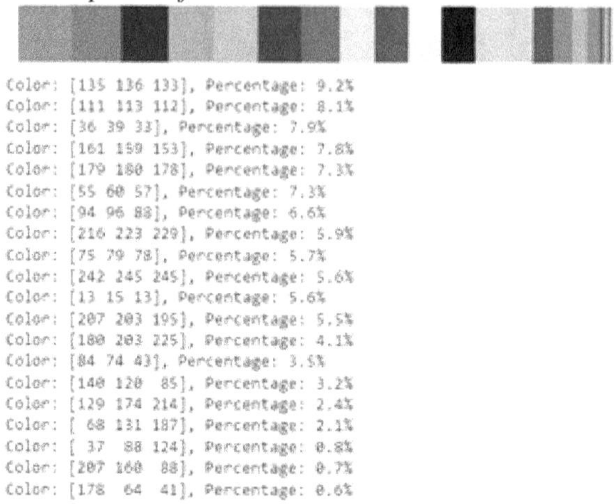

Despite occupying the largest segment of HCMC, these zones lean towards a monotone gray palette. The industrial backdrop and suburban vibe, interspersed with housing estates and smaller commercial establishments, lend to this zone's muted visual appeal. Contrasted with the city centers, these regions lack the vibrancy of brighter colors.

The study's findings underline the dominance of grayscale shades across HCMC, punctuated by bursts of vibrant colors in specific districts. While industrial zones embrace a purer gray, residential areas interweave green for aesthetic and wellness purposes, and city centers introduce a hint of festive red.

This research not only highlights the visual representation of HCMC's diverse districts but also offers insights into urban planning, design, and tourism development. Understanding how colors mirror the characteristics of urban spaces in HCMC could be pivotal in future development and branding initiatives.

Figure 5. Color chart for areas in HCMC (Chart saturation at 200% for better visualization)

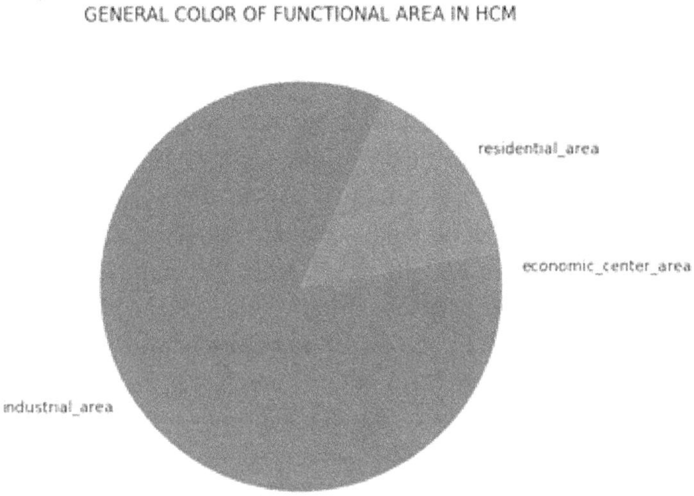

The analysis of district-specific color palettes, integrated to represent the entire city, contributes valuable insights into the visual representation of Ho Chi Minh City and its distinct functional zones. This research enhances our understanding of how colors can convey unique characteristics of urban areas and offers significant implications for urban planning, design, and tourism development in HCMC.

DISCUSSION

The exploration of color palettes in Ho Chi Minh City (HCMC) unveiled a unique interplay between urban development and cultural nuances. A significant 80% dominance of grayscale shades, synonymous with modern infrastructure and urbanization, forms the foundational visual identity of HCMC. However, the city's soul is encapsulated in the vibrant colors—blue, yellow, and red—that emerge sporadically, painting distinct narratives of its districts.

Breaking this down functionally, industrial zones, hubs of manufacturing and economic production, predominantly wear a monotone gray—perhaps a testament to the uniformity and precision of industrial processes. Residential zones, on the other hand, become canvases for the shades of green, symbolizing the juxtaposition of human habitats and nature, which underscores the city's commitment to sustainability and well-being. The economic districts, pulsating with commercial activity, cultural engagements, and tourism, embrace the fervor of red.

Intriguingly, Maxime Viger's research from 2019 offers a cultural lens to decode these color choices (See appendix 5). Through the prism of Vietnamese societal norms and interpretations, red emerges not just as an economic indicator but also as a color symbolizing enthusiasm—potentially reflecting the vibrant marketplaces, festivals, and cultural hubs. Similarly, yellow, often linked with affection and communal ties in Vietnamese culture, might be indicative of neighborhoods dense with familial connections and communal interactions.

Yet, while this study casts a spotlight on HCMC's chromatic tapestry, it's crucial to acknowledge the limitations inherent in our methodology. Relying on Google Images might provide a vast yet not exhaustive representation, and the subjective nature of color interpretation introduces potential variances that can differ from one observer to another. Such challenges, though intrinsic to most qualitative analyses, warrant mention for a comprehensive understanding.

But, even within these constraints, the revelations of this research bear considerable weight. The urban color palette is more than just a visual spectacle; it's a coded language narrating tales of a city's evolution, culture, and aspirations. For HCMC, its colors are gateways into its history, cultural vitality, and future ambitions. Such insights don't just satiate academic curiosities; they serve as foundational pillars for urban designers, policymakers, and tourism strategists. Recognizing the colors and their implications can guide the design of public spaces, influence tourism narratives, and shape branding strategies for the city.

As we conclude this discussion, we are left with more avenues to explore. The profound impact colors have on psychology, emotion, and behavior beckons deeper inquiries. Could the dominance of gray impact the mood of HCMC's inhabitants? How do visitors resonate with the bursts of blue, yellow, or red? Extending this research to other Asian cities, each with their unique cultural tapestries and urban trajectories, could offer a richer, comparative perspective.

In sum, colors, often overlooked in urban studies, emerge as powerful storytellers in this research, prompting us to see cities not just as physical entities but as emotional, cultural, and psychological landscapes.

CONCLUSION

In the comprehensive exploration of Ho Chi Minh City's (HCMC) color palettes, we observed a dominant presence of grayscale shades, accounting for 80% of the city's visual identity. These grayscale shades are interspersed with vibrant colors like blue, yellow, and red, which provide nuanced insights into the city's diverse districts and their distinct characteristics.

The primary thrust of this research was to decipher the urban identity of HCMC through its color palettes and to assess the distribution of these palettes across its varied districts. Interestingly, while the overarching palette of the city leaned heavily on grayscale, different functional zones in the city exhibited nuanced variations. Our study hinted at a subtle presence of green in residential zones, indicative of integrated greenery, a touch of red in economic hubs, possibly highlighting areas of dynamic activity or cultural vibrancy, and a consistent gray in industrial regions.

Drawing upon insights from Maxime Viger's 2019 study, we further contextualize these colors. Beyond mere visual appeal, colors like red, yellow, and blue come with cultural annotations, from enthusiasm and love to possibly community connections or water features.

These findings bear crucial implications, especially in the domains of urban planning and design. Understanding the color dynamics of HCMC can serve as a guide for urban designers and policymakers to forge spaces that resonate with the city's unique essence. The methodology we adopted, utilizing Google Images, provided a panoramic view of the city's color landscape, yet it came with its set of limitations. The reliance on publicly available images and potential subjectivity in color interpretation are areas we acknowledge could be refined in subsequent studies.

For future endeavors, this study paves the way for a plethora of intriguing questions. Delving into the psychological resonance of urban colors or embarking on comparative studies across Asian cities would further enrich the discourse on urban color palettes.

In summation, the hues and shades of HCMC, while often overlooked, are potent narrators of its urban tale. As the city evolves and metamorphoses, its colors stand as markers of its legacy, its present-day pulse, and its aspirations for the future.

REFERENCES

Chen, C. F., & Tsai, D. C. (2007). How Destination Image and Evaluative Factors Affect Behavioral Intentions? *Tourism Management*, *28*(4), 1115–1122. DOI: 10.1016/j.tourman.2006.07.007

Ginting, N., & Rahman, N. V. (2016). Preserve urban heritage district based on place identity. *Asian Journal of Environment-Behaviour Studies*, *1*(1), 67–77. DOI: 10.21834/aje-bs.v1i1.145

Janeczko, E., Czyżyk, K., Korcz, N., Woźnicka, M., & Bielinis, E. (2023). The Psychological Effects and Benefits of Using Green Spaces in the City: A Field Experiment with Young Polish Adults. *Forests*, *14*(3), 497. DOI: 10.3390/f14030497

Li, Y., & Xie, Y. (2020). Is a Picture Worth a Thousand Words? An Empirical Study of Image Content and Social Media Engagement. *JMR, Journal of Marketing Research*, *57*(1), 1–19. DOI: 10.1177/0022243719881113

Luekveerawattana, R. and Sawangdee, Y. (2021). Path analysis of the revisit potential of an iconic tourism destination. E3S Web of Conferences, 258, 06042. DOI: 10.1051/e3sconf/202125806042

Manav, B. (2017). Color-emotion associations, designing color schemes for urban environment-architectural settings. *Color Research and Application*, *42*(5), 631–640. DOI: 10.1002/col.22123

Martínez, G. (2017). Urban authenticity at stake: A new framework for its definition from the perspective of heritage at the Shanghai Music Valley. *Cities (London, England)*, *70*, 55–64. DOI: 10.1016/j.cities.2017.06.017

Morse, J. M. (1995). The significance of saturation. *Qualitative Health Research*, *5*(2), 147–149. DOI: 10.1177/104973239500500201

Oliveira, S. N. S. (2023). What color is the northeast? an analysis of the visual language (images and colors) of tourism advertisements. *Applied Tourism*, *7*(4), 15–25. DOI: 10.14210/at.v7i4.18886

Smith and Johnson. (2018). A Stratified Sampling Approach for Balanced Representation in Image Classification. *IEEE Transactions on Pattern Analysis and Machine Intelligence*. DOI: 10.1109/TPAMI.2017.2708740

Viger, M. (2019). "The Meaning of Color for the Vietnamese Youth"

Zhang, A., Li, W., Wu, J., Lin, J., Chu, J., & Xia, C. (2021). How can the urban landscape affect urban vitality at the street block level? A case study of 15 metropolises in China. *Environment and Planning. B, Urban Analytics and City Science*, *48*(5), 1245–1262. DOI: 10.1177/2399808320924425

Zhong, T., Ye, C., Wang, Z., Tang, G., Zhang, W., & Ye, Y. (2021). City-scale mapping of urban façade color using street-view imagery. *Remote Sensing (Basel)*, *13*(8), 1591. DOI: 10.3390/rs13081591

APPENDIX

1. Github link for Image crawling tool: https://github.com/YoongiKim/AutoCrawler
2. List of retrieved images number for each district

Table 2. Images number by districts

District	Total	After preprocessing
1	434	413
3	494	460
4	363	352
5	389	354
6	311	297
7	431	376
8	363	342
10	416	377
11	338	330
12	340	312
Binh Tan	230	221
Binh Thanh	244	236
Go Vap	212	200
Phu Nhuan	328	297
Tan Binh	383	354
Tan Phu	349	323
Binh Chanh	298	273
Can Gio	254	220
Cu Chi	265	253
Hoc Mon	290	276
Nha Be	184	165

3. Image analysis result of 22 districts

Figure 6. Image analysis for BinhyChanh, Binh Tan, District 3, District 4, District 10, and District 11.

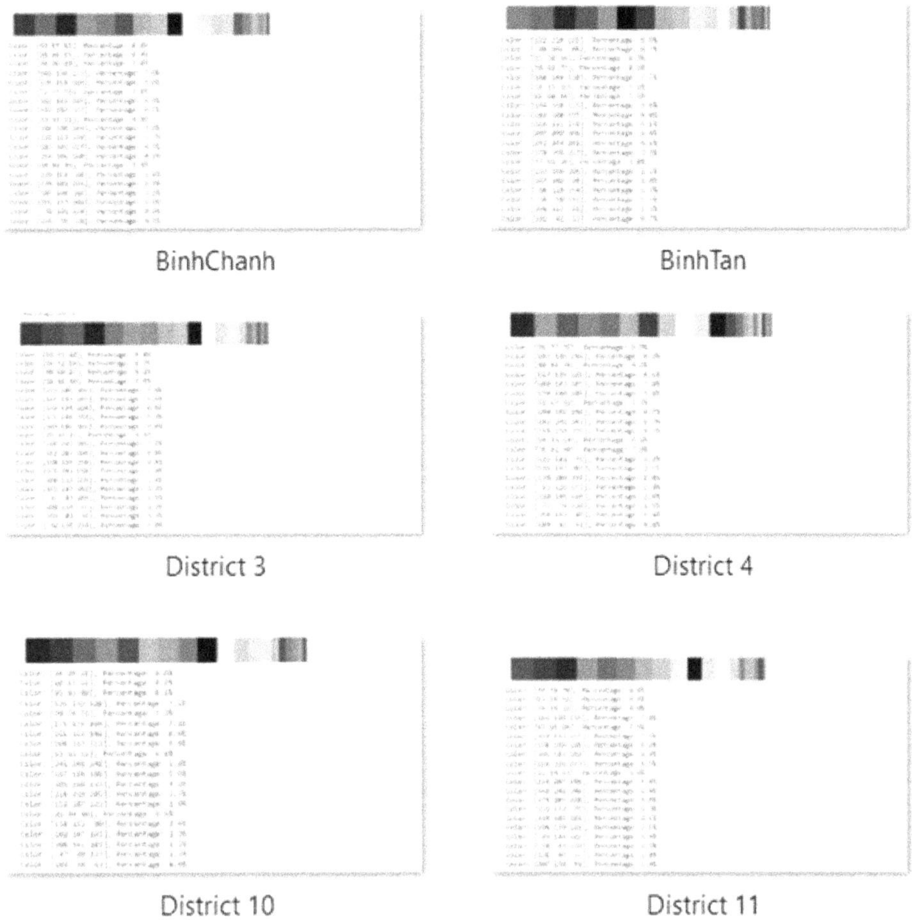

Figure 7. Image analysis for PhuNhuan and TanBinh.

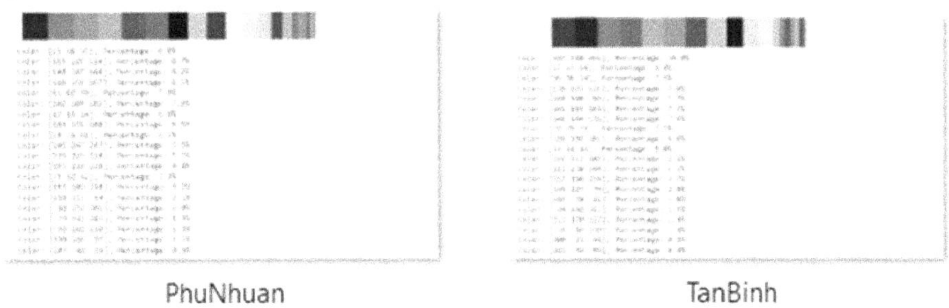

Figure 8. Image analysis for Binh Thanh, CanGio, District 5, District 6, District 12, and GoVap.

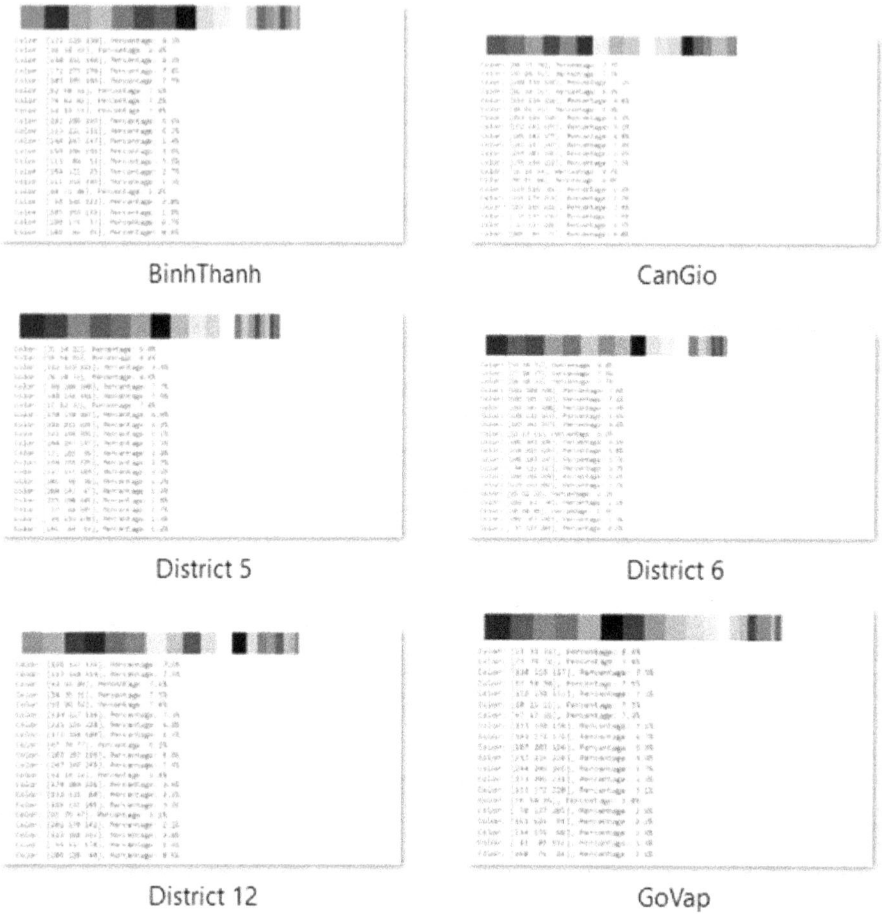

Figure 9. Image analysis for TanPhu.

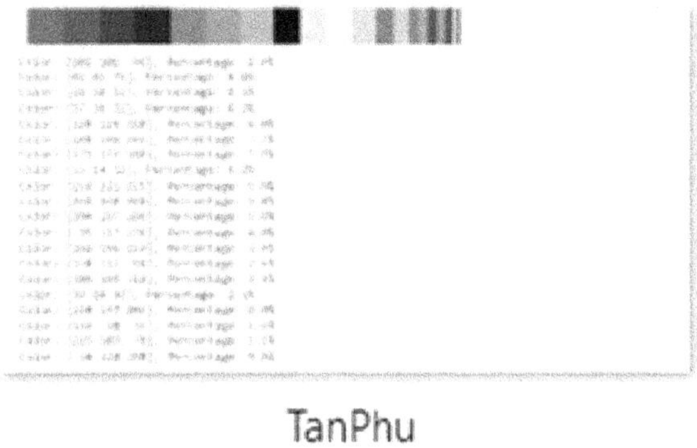

Figure 10. Image analysis for CuChi, District 1, District 7, District 8, HocMon, and NhaBe.

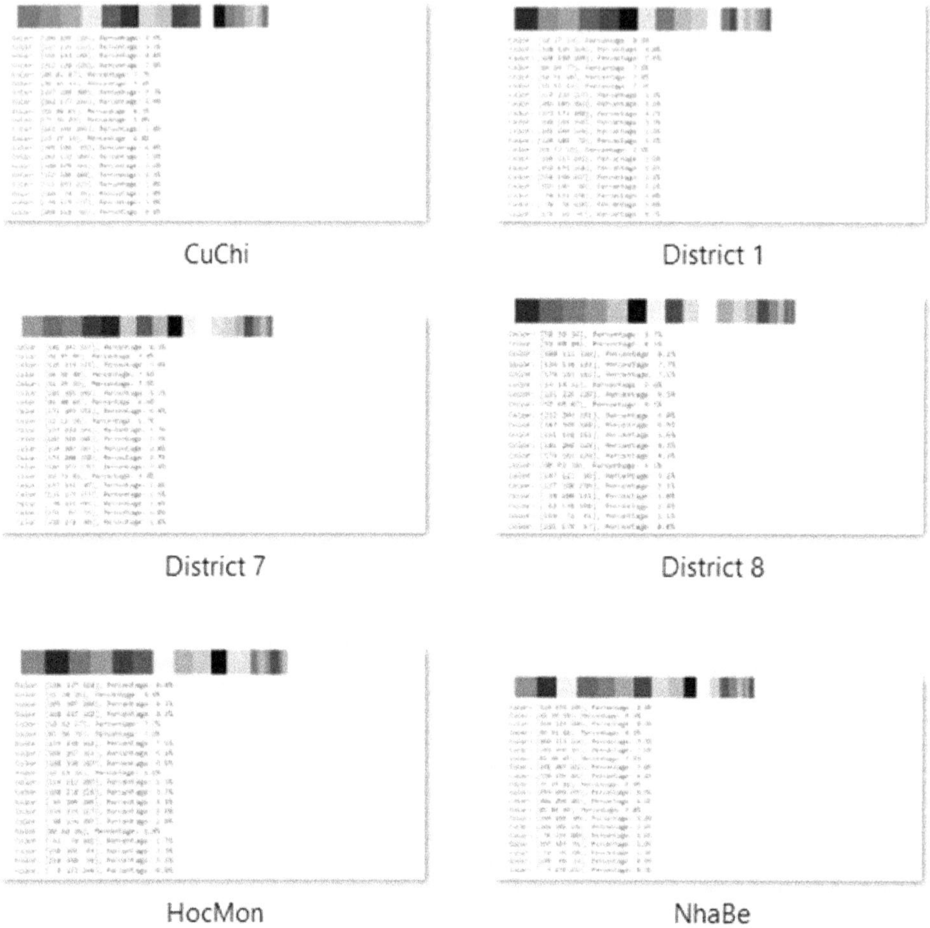

4. Python code for Color analysis of an Image folder:

```
import os
import cv2
import numpy as np
from sklearn.cluster import KMeans
import matplotlib.pyplot as plt
```

```
def analyze_color_set(image_folder, num_colors, num_domi-
nant_colors):
# Initialize an empty list to store the pixel values
of all images
pixels = []
# Iterate over each image in the folder
for filename in os.listdir(image_folder):
if filename.endswith(".jpg") or filename.endswith(".png"):
image_path = os.path.join(image_folder, filename)
# Load the image
image = cv2.imread(image_path)
# Convert the image from BGR to RGB
image_rgb = cv2.cvtColor(image, cv2.COLOR_BGR2RGB)
# Reshape the image to a 2D array of pixels and ap-
pend to the list
pixels.extend(image_rgb.reshape(-1, 3))
# Perform color clustering using K-means
kmeans = KMeans(n_clusters=num_colors)
kmeans.fit(pixels)
# Get the dominant colors
dominant_colors = kmeans.cluster_centers_
# Sort the dominant colors by frequency of occurrence
_, counts = np.unique(kmeans.labels_, return_counts=True)
dominant_colors = dominant_colors[np.argsort(counts)[::-1]]
# Take the specified number of dominant colors
dominant_colors = dominant_colors[:num_dominant_colors]
# Calculate the appearance percentage of each dominant color
total_pixels = len(pixels)
appearance_percentages = counts[np.argsort(counts)[::-1]]
[:num_dominant_colors] / total_pixels * 100
return dominant_colors, appearance_percentages
# Set the path to your image folder
image_folder = './[image folder name]
# Set the number of colors for clustering
num_colors = 20
# Set the number of dominant colors to extract
num_dominant_colors = 20
# Perform color analysis on the image set
dominant_colors, appearance_percentages = analyze_color_
set(image_folder, num_colors, num_dominant_colors)
```

```
# Create a color palette image
palette_widths = (appearance_percentages / np.max(appear-
ance_percentages) * 50).astype(int)
palette = np.zeros((50, np.sum(palette_widths), 3),
dtype=np.uint8)
start_width = 0
color_names = []
for color, width, percentage in zip(dominant_colors, pal-
ette_widths, appearance_percentages):
palette[:, start_width:start_width + width,:] = color.as-
type(np.uint8)[np.newaxis, np.newaxis,:]
start_width += width
# Add the color name and percentage to the list
color_names.append(f"Color: {color.astype(int)}, Percentage:
{percentage:.1f}%")
# Display the color palette
plt.imshow(palette)
plt.axis('off')
plt.show()
# Display the color names and percentages
for name in color_names:
print(name)
```

5. Color meaning chart from Maxime Viger (2019)

Figure 11. The meaning of colors from Maxime Viger (2019).

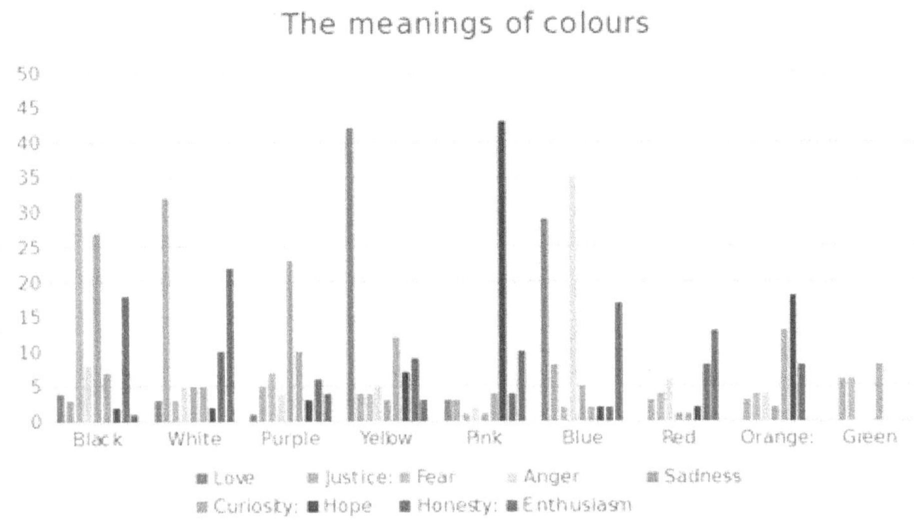

Chapter 13
Riding Waves of AI:
Embracing the Shift in Art and Design Innovation

Chu Hiang Goh
https://orcid.org/0000-0001-5505-3511
Universiti Sains Malaysia, Malaysia

Jing Yi Lim
https://orcid.org/0000-0002-0018-575X
Universiti Sains Malaysia, Malaysia

ABSTRACT

Art and design have always evolved alongside technological progress, tracing a path from the mechanisation of the first Industrial Revolution (IR 1.0) to the AI-driven changes of IR 5.0. This study explores how designers have historically adjusted to disruptive technologies by applying the Technology S-Curve framework and conducting a historical trend analysis of the Industrial Revolutions. It demonstrates that designers have not only navigated challenges but have also thrived by adopting new tools and methods. This study highlights how AI is not a competitor to be feared but can be a collaborative partner in the process of innovation through human-machine collaboration, sustainable innovation and AI-enhanced creativity in the context of IR 5.0. AI has the power to redefine the role of designers with a focus on human creativity, ethical standards and sustainable design. This article provides insights into how designers can embrace this transformative era to ensure the continued flourishing of art and design in the age of AI

DOI: 10.4018/979-8-3693-7610-2.ch013

1. INTRODUCTION

The 21st century has seen dramatic progress in AI, with the impact on industries and human interaction with technology transforming at scale. The art and design industries have been particularly affected, creating both risk and opportunity. This study investigates ways in which creative professionals may push through a period of artificial intelligence transformation. By investigating the influence of AI on innovation and creativity, this article aims to explore how AI technologies can be incorporated into design as tools to assist work processes rather than being perceived as threats to actual career relevance.

1.1 Overview of AI in Modern Society

AI is around us as a transformative element in numerous sectors like healthcare, finance, and recently for creative industries like art and design. The applications range from automating mundane tasks to enabling new modes of creativity. As an example, technologies built on the basis of AI, such as generative adversarial networks (GANs), have led to an output of stunning visuals in art. AI-driven platforms that support prototyping, 3D design and user interfaces already have a positive impact on fields such as design (McCormack et al., 2019). However, these advances are a double-edged sword for creative workers. Artfully explained in a mannerism that contradicts, while AI presents efficiencies and creates new potential in experimentation, at the same time, it disrupts the known work. This raises questions about the worth of human ingenuity and how much it matters in a world in which machine-related products are more valued than ever. It raises concerns about the value of human creativity in an era increasingly influenced by machine-generated works.

The influence of AI on creativity is significant. For example, AI programs like DeepDream and DALL-E have made it difficult to distinguish between art made by humans and machines, raising questions about authorship and originality (Elgammal, 2017). AI is starting to shape the design ideation process, allowing designers to analyse data quickly, anticipate user behaviours, and create prototypes. Although these advancements may cause concern about AI taking over human jobs, they also allow designers to redefine their roles through collaboration with AI tools.

1.2 Research Design of this Study

This study illustrates how, in the scope of IR 5.0 characterised by operators and machines working together towards sustainable innovation and creativity augmented through AI, designers have the opportunity to consider AI as a collaborator for innovation rather than a competitor. With this integration between AI and designers, they can settle this new era of design where human creativity, ethical standards, and design sustainability take over the mind. This article discusses how designers can navigate the transition to this new era so that art and design may continue to thrive amid the emergence of AI.

This study examines AI's transformative impact on the creative design industry and predicts its future trajectory. Using a qualitative approach, it analyses existing secondary data through descriptive and interpretive methods. The exploratory study synthesises information from research articles, books and industry reports to provide insights into AI's implications for art and design.

The text examines the historical background of industrial revolutions in art and design, focusing on designers' shifts, trends and innovations aimed at thriving through the various stages of the Industrial Revolution (IR), from IR 1.0 to 4.0 in the history of art and design development (Charlotte Fiell & Fiell, 2018; Meggs & Purvis, 2016). This resonates with the current AI transformation and outlines what was argued might fit with IR 5.0. Using the Technology S-Curve, the research explores innovative cycles and the potential impact of AI on art and design innovation. Pattern recognition is amplified and forward-looking, generating imperative signals for designers in a landscape that is changing and rapidly shifting under our feet. The article is divided into two parts: the first part evaluates historical developments from IR 1.0 to IR 5.0, and the second part links this analysis to the Technology S-Curve to forecast the future of the design industry.

2. HISTORICAL TREND ANALYSIS

Technological advancements have significantly influenced art and design throughout history. Each industrial revolution (IR) has reshaped the creative landscape in profound ways. Table 1 provides an overview of the impact of the five industrial revolutions on art and design by reviewing various research articles and history texts. It emphasises how designers innovate to stay relevant amidst advancing technology. The identified innovation patterns provide valuable insights for designers as they navigate an evolving technological landscape and anticipate future trends.

Table 1. The mapping of five industrial revolutions and designer innovation.

Industrial Revolution	*Period*	*Key Technologies*	*Influence on Art and Design*	*How Designers Innovate and Survive*
IR 1.0	Late 18th to Early 19th Century	Steam Engines, Mechanised Mass Production of Goods.	Mass production of goods changed accessibility and appreciation for aesthetics. Arts and Crafts Movement (William Morris), Romanticism.	Designers like William Morris promoted craftsmanship and natural materials in response to mass production. Use of mechanical tools to improve production efficiency without sacrificing artistic quality.
IR 2.0	Late 19th to Early 20th Century	Electricity, Steel Production, Assembly lines	Rise of Art Nouveau, Futurism and Modernism. Photography changed visual representation and artistic expression. Development of graphic design in advertising	Designers embraced new materials (steel, glass) for modernist design. Integration of photographic techniques in graphic design. Designers introduced new, minimalist forms based on function and material innovation.
IR 3.0	Mid-20th to Early 21st Century	Electronics, Computers, Digital Communication	The development of digital art and design software -Adobe Photoshop, Illustrator, and AutoCAD—changed how we design and create. Rise of video games and interactive media as new forms of art. The introduction of Web 2.0 and social media changed the way we communicate.	Designers leveraged digital tools like CAD and Photoshop to create complex, scalable designs. New forms of interactive design emerged with the rise of the internet and video games. Architects explored deconstructivism and non-linear forms using computer-aided design.

continued on following page

Table 1. Continued

Industrial Revolution	*Period*	*Key Technologies*	*Influence on Art and Design*	*How Designers Innovate and Survive*
IR 4.0	Early 21st Century to Present	AI, IoT, 3D Printing, Cloud Computing	AI-driven design (e.g., generative art created by AI algorithms). Virtual Reality (VR) and Augmented Reality (AR) created immersive art experiences. 3D printing enabled innovative forms in fashion, architecture, and sculpture. Smart design systems for user interface (UI) and user experience (UX) optimisation.	Designers use AI and machines to create generative art and innovative architecture. 3D printing allows the creation of complex, custom objects not possible with traditional methods. UX/UI design becomes increasingly user-centred and data-driven, integrating AI for real-time personalisation.
IR 5.0	Present and Future	AI, Robotics, Cobots, VR/AR, 5G, Sustainable Tech	Human-machine collaboration through cobots augments creativity in art and design. Mass personalisation allows for customised products in fashion, art, and architecture. Sustainable design and biomimicry influence the materials and processes in art and product design. AR/VR in education and design simulation fosters immersive creativity.	Designers collaborate with cobots and AI tools to enhance creativity, focusing on personalised, sustainable designs. Adoption of sustainable practices and eco-friendly materials in response to climate concerns. Use AR/VR for design simulations, immersive training, and digital art experiences. Embrace NFTs to explore new business models for digital art and ownership.

2.1 The First Industrial Revolution (IR 1.0): Mechanization and the Birth of Mass Production

IR 1.0 witnessed the rise of steam engines and mechanised mass production. Factories revolutionised the production of goods, significantly increasing efficiency and reducing costs. The effect on the creative industry shows that, while production processes became more mechanised, product availability increased, leading to a standardisation of styles. The mass production raised concerns over creative craftsmanship and artistic authenticity. In reaction, the Arts and Crafts Movement in the nineteenth century, led by William Morris, pushed back against the homogeneity of the factory system and emphasised craftsmanship and natural aesthetics (Morris, 1882). Their ability to combine mechanical tools with artisanal skills reflected an early designer survival strategy against technological development: adapting technologies while preserving creativity. This strategy could lay the groundwork for IR 5.0, where AI fosters creativity rather than overshadows it.

2.2 The Second Industrial Revolution (IR 2.0): Electrification and the Dawn of Mass Media

In IR 2.0, electricity, steel, and assembly lines fueled modernist experimentation with materials and production methods. Meanwhile, photography revolutionised design and visual representation. Designers embraced technologies to create functional, minimalist designs, integrating photography into advertising and communication and using visual storytelling as a creative medium (Drucker, 1994). Movements like Art Nouveau and Modernism used steel and glass for minimalist forms. In graphic design, photographic techniques led to innovative advertisements and precise representations of art and architecture. The key lesson learned is that designers thrived by collaborating with new technologies (e.g., steel and photography) to redefine their creative practices, showing a proactive rather than reactive response to technological disruption. Similarly, designers in IR 5.0 can utilise AI tools for new expressions like generative design and automated optimisation while maintaining creative oversight.

2.3 The Third Industrial Revolution (IR 3.0): Digital Revolution and the Rise of Computation

IR 3.0 significantly advances electronics, computing, and digital communication. Software like Adobe Photoshop, Illustrator, and CAD allowed designers to create complex, scalable, reproducible works. The digitisation of the design process enabled designers to use digital tools that diversify their perspective of creativity while keeping their hold on the outcome of the visual products. Emerging new disciplines, such as user interface (UI) design and video game design, demonstrated the capacity of designers to extend to the interactive and digital space (Negroponte, 1995). Designers have used digital technologies to enhance their creativity. As seen in deconstructivist architecture, AutoCAD and similar tools have empowered architects to pursue non-linear geometries. Digital software has enabled graphic designers to create complex graphics, animation and designs of any size. With the rise of interactive and digital design, the mobile revolution brought forth the term UI (user interface) and immersive experience.

It shows how digital tools can allow designers to amplify their design work, evidence that technology can aid and not reduce human creativity. Web 2.0 and social media ushered in a new age of communication. Digital tools did not replace designers but empowered them to create. In the same way, AI provides designers with tools for generative art, data-driven design, and predictive personalisation. Designers increasingly focus on curation and creative direction, ensuring their outputs align with aesthetic and emotional objectives.

2.4 The Fourth Industrial Revolution (IR 4.0): AI and Smart Automation

IR 4.0 is defined by progress in smart automation, artificial intelligence (AI), the Internet of Things (IoT), and improved communication technologies like cloud computing. These advancements revolutionise art and design through AI-enhanced creativity and immersive experiences. AI-enhanced design includes generative art produced by AI algorithms, while Virtual Reality (VR) and Augmented Reality (AR) technologies provide captivating, immersive art encounters. Furthermore, 3D printing has introduced innovative formats in fashion, architecture, and sculpture. Smart design systems refine user interface (UI) and user experience (UX). AI-powered algorithms, such as generative design tools, facilitate quick exploration of design options driven by user preferences. Historically, designers have partnered with AI to create generative art and enhance architectural designs. For example, Autodesk Generative Design allows designers to explore thousands of potential solutions in a matter of minutes (Li et al., 2024). VR and AR technologies are also revolutionising immersive design simulations. This highlights how IR 4.0 has changed the way designers work in illustrating the positive effects of human-AI collaboration by enhancing creativity, using AI's computing power, and retaining emotional intelligence and creative direction.

2.5 The Fifth Industrial Revolution (IR 5.0): Human-Centric and Ethical Innovation

IR 5.0 emphasises human-machine collaboration, sustainability, and personalisation. In contrast to IR 4.0, which focuses on full automation, IR 5.0 aims to harmonise technology with human creativity and societal values. Key features of the IR 5.0 include human-machine collaboration, advancements in AI and robotics, and a strong emphasis on sustainability. Technologies such as collaborative robots (cobots), augmented reality (AR), virtual reality (VR) simulations, and AI-driven personalisation are transforming design processes.

Human-machine collaboration through cobots enhances creativity in art and design. Mass personalisation enables the creation of customised products in fashion, art, and architecture. Sustainable design and biomimicry impact on the materials and processes used in art and product design. Additionally, AR and VR technologies in education and design simulations promote immersive creativity. The success of designers in IR 5.0 depends on their ability to work alongside AI tools and adapt to sustainability trends. The rapid evolution of technology demands that designers stay up to date with new tools and developments. AI enables mass personalisation, and designers can provide tailored designs faster. Results: One of the highlights was that AR and VR simulations played an enormous role in improving the design process (Oxman et al., 2014), especially in education and prototyping.

Designers are adopting sustainable practices such as biomimicry and eco-friendly materials as we face global climate challenges. This not only represents a responsible relationship with design but also encourages designers to work towards a better future. Sustainable practices, such as biomimicry and eco-friendly materials, respond effectively to global climate concerns. This focus on sustainability signifies a conscientious approach to design, inspiring designers to contribute to creating a more sustainable future.

3. THE S-CURVE IN PREDICTING TECHNOLOGICAL TRENDS

The Technology S-Curve is a valuable conceptual framework for grasping the life cycle of technological innovations. It features their stages of adoption, evolution, maturity and eventual saturation. This S-shaped curve incorporates four critical phases, which are: emergence, acceleration, maturity, and saturation (Figure 1). Adoption hardly accelerates in this emergence phase, as experimentation's costs and compound-creative risks remain high. In contrast, the acceleration phase indicates rapid growth of technology as it becomes widely available and more socially acceptable. The acceleration phase signifies rapid growth as technology becomes more available and socially accepted. Subsequently, the maturity phase experiences a slowdown in growth as the market becomes saturated, leading to reduced returns on innovation. Finally, the saturation phase emphasises a plateau in adoption, signalling that the technology has reached its peak or is being superseded by newer innovations (Christensen, 2015).

Figure 1. Technology S-curve of technological innovations life cycle

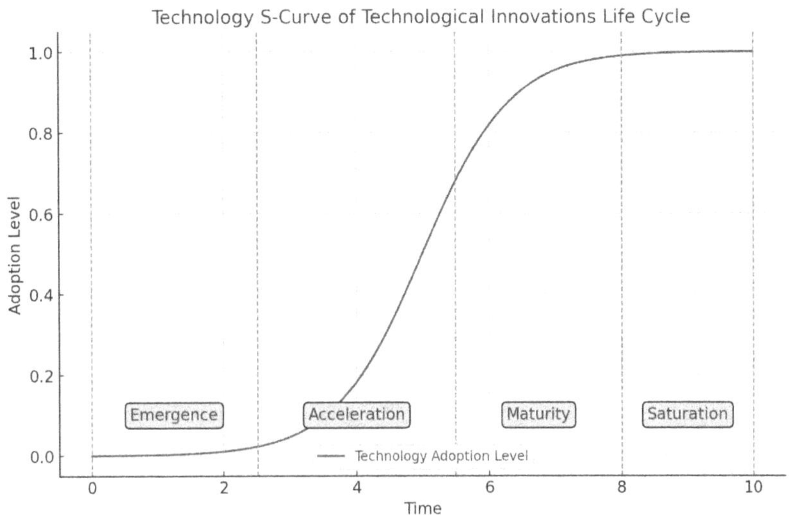

S-Curve originated from Gabriel Tarde, a French sociologist who created the terms of innovation diffusion in the early 20th century. Tarde's work established the basis for how we think about adoption patterns. Everett Rogers (1962) later expanded this framework to outline phases of adoption, introducing categories like innovators and laggards, embedding the S-Curve in a sociological context. The S-Curve became significant in technological studies and applied to business and technology lifecycles. Clayton Christensen (1997) used it to explore disruptive innovations in The Innovator's Dilemma, demonstrating its predictive power for technological shifts. The framework is now vital for analysing technological trends in management, engineering, and design research.

This article leverages the Technology S-Curve to give perspective to the evolution of designer innovation across all IRs 1.0 to 5.0. Based on historical data for technological adoption, the Technology S-Curve describes significant inflexion points that changed design practices and demonstrates how designers have evolved and innovated. For instance, during IR 1.0, mechanisation led design practices to embrace craftsmanship movements like Arts and Crafts, whereas, in IR 4.0, AI tools facilitated generative design and immersive experiences. Figure 2 shows the use of the S-Curve to analyse and predict the direction trend of how designers embrace AI technology based on the historical trend analysis of industrial revolutions from IR 1.0-5.0, as discussed in section 2.

Figure 2. Technology S-curve and historical trends in design revolutions

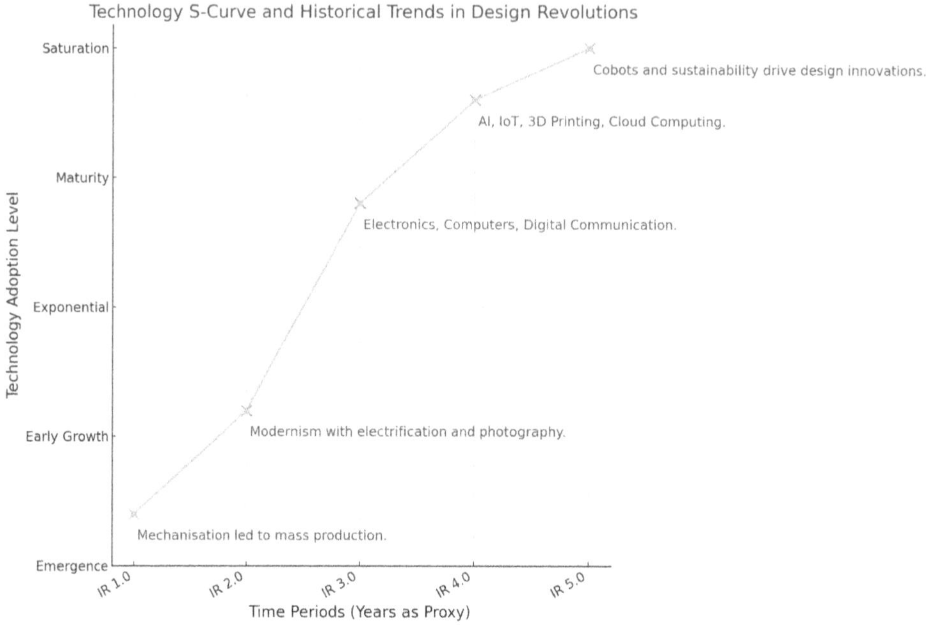

The Technology S-Curve represents the cycle of technology adoption; there are three key phases: emergence, exponential growth, and maturity, with saturation indicating the ceiling for adoption or performance enhancements. These stages are reflective of specific shifts in the creative industry during the sequence of industrial revolutions. IR 1.0 marked the introduction of mechanisation with steam engines and iron manufacturing that brought about mass production of textiles and a new kind of architecture, for example. As a reaction, designers like William Morris revived craftsmanship and used nature, demonstrating the link between technology and art.

IR 2.0 brought us electrification and assembly lines, both of which opened the door to modernist architecture and graphic design. Such is the character of the creativity of the steel, glass, and photography industrial and artistic avant-garde represented by modernist designers.

IR 3.0 marked the dawn of the digital era, revolutionising design through novel instruments like CAD and Photoshop. These innovations enabled the design to be scaled and mutable in unprecedented ways. When IR 4.0 emerged, developments such as artificial intelligence, 3D printing and virtual reality stretched creativity even further by facilitating generative design and immersive experiences.

In the present phase, IR 5.0 is advancing towards ubiquity after widespread but incomplete acceptance. In contrast to IR 4.0, which focuses on automation and digitalisation, IR 5.0 prioritises co-creation and sustainability; IR 5.0 stresses co-creation and sustainability through joint efforts. Technologies such as collaborative robots (cobots) are enhancing workflows in fashion, architecture, and industrial design. They allow for the production of custom, high-quality outputs that cater to individual preferences. The Technology S-Curve suggests that the saturation phase has not yet arrived and is still expected in the future.

The Technology S-Curve is crucial for predicting how designers will innovate in IR 5.0 by adapting to AI. This framework offers a roadmap for anticipating shifts in innovation, helping designers know when to transition from learning to collaborating with AI, which emphasises adaptability. It also forecasts challenges like over-reliance on AI or homogenisation in outputs, keeping human creativity central. The Technology S-Curve thus contextualises the past and provides strategic foresight for navigating design innovation in IR 5.0.

4. FINDINGS AND DISCUSSION

The findings of this study reflect the changing nature of how the creative industry interacts with AI. The analysis of historical trends revealed three key themes that are essential for the survival of designers in the evolving marketplace:

1. Adapting Technologies: Designers continue incorporating new tools, whether mechanical, digital or AI, into their creative workflow while maintaining control over aesthetic and narrative.
2. Human-AI Corporation: As emerging technologies progress along the S-curve, designers remain relevant by collaborating with tools during the acceleration phase and guiding their ethical application in the saturation phase.
3. Emphasis on Human Quality: Attributes such as emotional intelligence, creativity, and storytelling are essential human qualities central to design. Historical data indicated that technology augments rather than replaces these qualities.

Using historical examples and the Technology S-Curve, this section looks at how AI can forever change design and the complex opportunities and challenges that present themselves to our industry. This challenge will impact designers and the broader design ecosystem and will need to align with and evolve in an AI world.

4.1 Predicted Scenarios in the Maturity Phase

The maturity phase of AI adoption, illustrated by the Technology S-Curve, signifies a pivotal moment. During this stage, designers, as key contributors, can harness potential AI tools for innovation while addressing the intricate challenges of integration. Therefore, exploring how AI can transform the creative design sector by opening new avenues and expanding innovation is vital. The impact may be both positive and negative; nevertheless, ongoing counter-solutions appear to be in place. Here are some key insights from this study.

4.1.1. Enhanced Creativity through Human-AI Collaboration

The rise of generative AI tools like DALL-E and MidJourney opens up exciting possibilities for designers wanting to generate ideas and create rapid prototypes. These approaches expand the creative field by presenting new ideas and allowing designers to experiment with forms, styles and methods that may not have been considered previously (Elgammal, 2017).

This partnership also enhances human creativity instead of replacing it. It lets designers become curators and guides for new creations made with AI. This will enable designers to leverage the analytical power of AI. By refining prompts, interpreting the results, and adding their own vision, designers can maintain control over the creative process while leveraging AI's analytical strengths.

Creative design industry-standard software, such as Adobe and Autodesk, has incorporated AI technologies in their latest applications, which is typical evidence of the trend towards human-AI collaboration. Adobe launched Adobe Firefly, its flagship in AI generative design, in 2023. Images generated in Adobe Firefly can be incorporated into its leading applications, such as Photoshop and Illustrator. Designers can utilise text prompts to create backgrounds, textures, and design components, seamlessly combining manual editing with AI support.

In architecture and product design, Autodesk's Fusion 360 employs AI-powered generative design tools to develop optimised structures and components tailored for engineers and product designers. This tool assesses numerous design possibilities according to the parameters established by the designer. Designers specify performance objectives, materials, manufacturing techniques, and visual preferences. Based on these user-defined constraints, AI produces various highly efficient design alternatives. The trend of human-AI collaboration in software development and practice is set to persist.

4.1.2. Ethical Concerns in AI-Driven Design

The use of AI in the creative industry poses significant ethical dilemmas that cannot be ignored, particularly regarding authorship and intellectual property rights. Addressing the challenges of determining ownership and rights is imperative, as AI-generated designs blur the lines between human and machine contributions, which become more complex by the day. Furthermore, the issue of algorithmic bias in design requires careful attention to promote inclusivity and fairness in creative practices (McCormack et al., 2019). Privacy and data security are other concerns and ensuring that AI systems respect user and client data will become a top priority. This appears to negatively impact and challenge the creative design industry. However, AI-driven design is experiencing rapid advancements in ethical governance, with global organisations working to promote transparency, fairness, and accountability. Designers and companies utilising AI tools are required to integrate ethical frameworks into their designs and keep pace with regulatory changes.

The effort to enhance ethical awareness and accountability among designers is ongoing. Ethical governance in AI-driven design is rapidly evolving, with global institutions and major software companies stepping in to ensure transparency, fairness, and accountability. Designers and companies adopting AI tools must now integrate ethical frameworks by design, stay informed on regulatory shifts, and align with human-centred innovation principles. For instance, Adobe has incorporated metadata in Adobe Firefly, known as content credentials (Adobe, 2023). These features tackle issues and ethical concerns in generative AI design by promoting transparency and reducing misuse. The metadata includes industry-standard, tamper-proof information about how a file is created and edited. It enables users to understand the origins of AI-generated content and enhance trust and authenticity. Initiatives aimed at addressing ethical regulation are thriving. Regulatory bodies, such as the European Union (European Commission, 2023) has established strong AI governance frameworks such as the EU AI Act to guarantee adherence to ethical standards, transparency, and accountability.

4.1.3. Workforce Transition and Skill Development

The extensive use of AI tools may lead to significant job losses, especially in job positions that are repetitive or technically oriented. For instance, the traditional roles of junior designers are likely to become automated. However, this challenge offers an opportunity for designers to enhance their skills and transition into roles that involve collaboration with AI, such as prompt engineering, AI ethics consulting, and creative leadership. It is crucial for educational institutions and professional organisations to take decisive action and develop robust programs that equip designers with the essential skills needed for this exciting transition.

Efforts to develop skills, particularly in training and enhancing AI literacy within the design industry, are flourishing. The aim is not to replace designers but to prepare them for the AI age, where creativity and computation coexist harmoniously. This is evident in initiatives like the Adobe Digital Academy, which provides designers with training and certification (White, 2024). Various online boot camps and micro-credential training programmes are widespread. Designers must seize this opportunity to advance themselves without further delay.

4.1.4. Market Homogenization

The creative design industry fundamentally relies on innovation and distinctiveness. However, increased dependence on AI tools poses a significant risk as design outputs become excessively standardised and uniform due to algorithm-driven aesthetics and trend-based systems and saturate the market (Sajjad, 2024) . With multiple designers using the same AI tools and models, the danger of design aesthetic homogeneity is real.

A clear example of homogenisation can be seen in platforms utilising generative AI models like Midjourney, DALL-E, or Adobe Firefly. These platforms often create visually striking but generic designs heavily influenced by current online visual trends, resulting in a lack of true uniqueness or personal creativity (Frosio, 2025). This scenario leads to a marketplace filled with visually similar products, constraining diversity and possibly hindering authentic human expression and innovation.

To counter market homogenisation, initiatives advocate for hybrid human-AI collaborative design (as discussed in section 4.1.1). In this approach, designers strategically utilise AI tools to generate initial concepts while employing human insights and judgment to refine uniqueness and contextual relevance. Firms such as IDEO and IBM (IBM, 2023; IDEO, 2023) have highlighted the importance of human-centred AI design, utilising AI to augment rather than supplant human creativity, thereby preserving diversity and fostering innovation in results.

4.2 Implications for the Future of Design

While the results indicate that AI will significantly change rather than eliminate designer occupations, focusing on collaborative integration ensures their livelihood endures. In the context of IR 5.0, the focus transitions towards collaboration, enabling designers to use AI as a tool for enhancing both creativity and efficiency. To integrate AI in an ethical and sustainable manner, designers must take a proactive stance, ensuring their work remains human-centric. This approach will support the creative industry in thriving alongside technological advancements, emphasising the unique value of human creativity.

This study highlights the essential roles of adaptability, education, and ethical awareness in tackling the opportunities and challenges posed by AI. Designers stand ready to become leaders in a fresh era of creativity, where technology and humanity work together to push the limits of art and design.

5. CONCLUSION

The evolution from IR 1.0 to IR 5.0 manifests a consistent theme: designers' resilience and adaptability in embracing transformative technological developments. Each time, from mechanisation to digitisation, those changes have motivated designers to innovate, leading to new artistic expressions and revisions in design strategies. The emergence of AI, which is currently happening, signifies not just another phase but a significant change in the creative landscape, where automation, generative design, and personalisation interweave to harness unparalleled possibilities.

As we move towards IR 5.0, which is revolutionised through human-centred innovation and sustainability, designers are poised to play a successful role by fostering cooperation between human intuition and AI capabilities. AI is not a replacement for human creativity but a catalyst that amplifies artistic expression, accelerates workflows and offers tools for deeper investigation. The development of immersive technologies (AR and VR) and sustainable practices like biomimicry reveal the transformative qualities of this age. However, as we move toward this future, the industry needs to be guided by ethics, education, and a commitment to authenticity.

After all, riding the waves of AI is about embracing the shift of art and design innovation. Designers, through a balancing act between tradition and technology, human creativity and machine intelligence, sustainability and efficiency, can redefine their role and retain their artistry through this transformation. It is not just about surviving the wave; it is about riding the wave and using it to propel your business forward even faster in creative and sustainable ways.

REFERENCES

Adobe. (2023). Responsible innovation in the age of generative AI. Adobe Retrieved 25 May 2025 from https://www.adobe.com/ai/overview/ethics.html

Christensen, C. M. (1997). *The innovator's dilemma: when new technologies cause great firms to fail*. Harvard Business Review Press.

Christensen, C. M. (2015). *The innovator's dilemma: when new technologies cause great firms to fail*. Harvard Business Review Press.

Commission, E. (2023). EU AI Act: first regulation on artificial intelligence. Retrieved 20 May 2025 from https://www.europarl.europa.eu/topics/en/article/20230601STO93804/eu-ai-act-first-regulation-on-artificial-intelligence

Drucker, J. (1994). *The visible word: Experimental typography and modern art, 1909-1923*. University of Chicago Press.

Elgammal, A. (2017). Can: Creative adversarial networks, generating "art" by learning about styles and deviating from style norms. arXiv preprint arXiv:1706.07068, 6, 2017.

Frosio, G. (2025). Should we ban generative AI, incentivize it or make it a medium for inclusive creativity? In *A research agenda for EU copyright law* (pp. 61–86). Edward Elgar Publishing. DOI: 10.4337/9781803927329.00010

IBM. (2023). Human-Centered AI Design. IBM. Retrieved 22 May 2025 from https://www.ibm.com/design/ai

IDEO. (2023). IDEO's Human-AI Collaboration Approach. IDEO. Retrieved 22 May 2025 from https://www.ideo.com/journal/ai-ethics-collaborative-activities-for-designers

Li, C., Zhang, T., Du, X., Zhang, Y., & Xie, H. (2024). Generative AI for Architectural Design: A Literature Review. arXiv preprint arXiv:2404.01335.

McCormack, J., Gifford, T., & Hutchings, P. (2019). Autonomy, authenticity, authorship and intention in computer generated art. International conference on computational intelligence in music, sound, art and design (part of EvoStar)DOI: 10.1007/978-3-030-16667-0_3

Morris, W. (1882). The lesser arts of life. Macmillan and Co. Retrieved 28 November 2024 from https://www.marxists.org/archive/morris/works/1882/life1.htm

Negroponte, N. (1995). *Being digital*. Vintage Books.

Oxman, N., Ortiz, C., Gramazio, F., & Kohler, M. (2014). Material ecology. *Computer Aided Design*, *60*, 1–2. Advance online publication. DOI: 10.1016/j.cad.2014.05.009

Rogers, E. M. (1962). *Diffusion of Innovations*. Free Press.

Sajjad, H. (2024). Generative AI: Transforming Creative Industries with Machine Learning. *Research Corridor Journal of Engineering Science*, *1*(2), 119–134.

White, A. (2024). Adobe's new skilling initiative aims to bring AI literacy, content creation and digital marketing skills to 30 million worldwide. Adobe Blog. Retrieved 20 May 2025 from https://blog.adobe.com/en/publish/2024/10/14/adobes-new-skilling-initiative-aims-bring-ai-literacy-content-creation-digital-marketing-skills-30-million-worldwide

Chapter 14
Sustainable Artistic Practices in the Digital Era

Rishikaysh Kaakandikar
https://orcid.org/0000-0003-0349-6788
SaiBalaji International Institute of Management Sciences, India

Saurabh Nerkar
https://orcid.org/0009-0001-0602-2994
SaiBalaji International Institute of Management Sciences, India

Riddhi R. Mirajkar
https://orcid.org/0000-0001-7284-9482
Vishwakarma Institute of Technology, Pune, India

ABSTRACT

This chapter studies the concept of sustainable artistic practices in the digital era, emphasizing the environmental, social, and economic dimensions of sustainability. It explores the shift from traditional art to digital platforms driven by technological advancements, examining how the digital art space—particularly NFTs, virtual exhibitions, and online galleries—can either promote or hinder sustainability. Key discussions include the environmental impact of digital versus traditional art production, the role of digital art in fostering social inclusivity and global participation, and the economic sustainability challenges faced by artists monetizing digital works. The chapter provides recommendations on adopting eco-friendly technologies, fostering community engagement through digital platforms, and de-

DOI: 10.4018/979-8-3693-7610-2.ch014

veloping fair economic models to support artists. The conclusion calls on artists, institutions, and policymakers to collaborate in building a more sustainable future for the digital art world.

INTRODUCTION

Sustainable artistic practices have evolved significantly in the digital era, driven by the urgent need to address environmental crises and promote ecological awareness. Artists increasingly adopt innovative approaches that leverage digital technologies to engage audiences and foster community involvement in sustainability initiatives. As discussed by Banerjee (2012), the role of the artist as an activist has become paramount, highlighting the potential of art to effect social change. Digital platforms allow for broader dissemination of eco-conscious messages, enabling artists to reach diverse audiences and encourage collective action. This transformation is reflected in the work of Cramer (2018), who emphasizes the integration of sustainability into artistic practices, underscoring the responsibility of artists to reflect and respond to contemporary environmental issues through their work.

Moreover, the intersection of art and technology opens up new avenues for exploring sustainable practices. As Gaudio (2020) notes, digital art provides unique opportunities for artists to experiment with materials and methods that reduce environmental impact, promoting a more conscious approach to creation. Kwon (2015) highlights the importance of site-specific art in fostering a sense of place and community, further emphasizing how artists can engage local environments in their work. This perspective is supported by Ritchie (2020), who argues that digital media can serve as a catalyst for eco-conscious practices, allowing artists to convey complex environmental narratives. Ultimately, the synthesis of art and sustainability in the digital age reflects a growing awareness among artists of their potential to influence positive change and inspire action toward a more sustainable future.

For this reason, sustainability in art can be described as activities taken in the art market system as well as other interlinking systems sustainably and with environmentally friendly approaches. Traditionally, the art community did not pay much attention to sustainable issues and in some situations, it ignores these considerations in favor of artistic design and sales. As such questions as the pollution of the environment and climate change gain importance in the world, the art world has also changed and started to consider how it can help meet the objectives of sustainable development.

In the contemporary world, the artist is functionally changing to meet the cultural and aesthetic conception as well as the social and even the environmental challenges. This focus on sustainability may be leading to a change in the way that artists obtain their materials, the process by which artwork is made, and the way that the artwork is reproduced, even exhibited. From the use of non hazardous material in creating artwork in to the use of ECO friendly Social- networking and Virtual- space for the display and archiving of the artwork; sustainability is slowly transforming the making and use of art.

But once more, the galleries, museums and art institutions are beginning to navigate towards environmental friendly practices by regulating the efficiency of energy production, waste management and encouraging sustainability in artwork production. These efforts are part of a new awareness that artists, curators and the consuming public are assuming regarding the long-term relation of their choices to the ecology.

TECHNOLOGICAL FACTORS

Technology as one of the push factors, which in essence has led to people adopting the display and creation of art pieces through digital mechanisms.

One scholar has pointed out that with the emergence of the new technologies of the digital age new dimensions have been brought to the creation and the distribution of art. The conventional approaches to producing, displaying, and circulating artistic work, thus paying or learning about creative work, have been displaced by technology solutions making art-making, viewing, sharing, and supporting more inclusive, flexible, and widespread. Some of the major distinctive features and impact The artists do not have physical shops or galleries where some of their works may be sold or exhibited; instead, they propagate the newmedia that disseminate their covers internationally.

1. **Digital Tools for Creation**: The change starts at the most fundamental level in art making. Applications like Adobe Photoshop, illustration software like Procreate, as well as modeling tools like Blender has put in artists' hands new tools. Year in and year out, technology keeps on improving, and features like digital painting, 3D modeling together with graphic designs are not regarded as peculiar when redesigning the norm for art. It also allows artists to toying with their material and may be even tweaking the material if they have to do so at anytime – something that cannot be in anyway related to traditional forms of media while doing so with the same amount of accuracy and flexibility that is now possible.
2. **Online Marketplaces and Social Media**: Social media of today like Instagram, Behance, and DeviantArt work like galleries across the globe that enable artists to post their artwork before art enthusiasts all over the world without the help of

art dealerships. Such platforms have opened up the market in art and unknown artists can now feature in the market without going through other middlemen such as galleries and art agents. Likewise in the same regard, the social interface realities such as etsy, Pinterest, and Saatchi Art provide them means through which it can be sold by the artists and makes art economically feasible in order to sustain itself as a trade.

3. **NFTs and Blockchain Technology**: On this account, some may opine that due to existence of NFT, people have altered the process through which one can access or possess the existing art. Thus, tokenization through the blockchain has enabled artists to sell one of a kind, proved, art, with the legitimacy of the work now established. It has established new forms of ownership and has been greatly welcomed by collectors as well as artists.
4. **Global Access and Community Building**: Social tools eliminate the issues of regionalism and therefore talented artists of different origin, ethnicity, race and origin get a platform where they can express their ideas to other artists from different parts of the world and be part of transforming art in the world. Internet and social networking sites are applicable communication platforms for different perspectives of art because they bring markets and relevancy for the execution of arts.

It has equipped artists with new techniques, widened the audience and amended old practices of producing and sharing art works as well as emerging issues of sustainability, ownership and digital divide.

TYPE OF SUSTAINABILITY

More to that in the present society that has been appears as the digital society all credit due to the advancement in technologies the following advanced in technology is worthy of note. While it has called for creation of many chances in the aspect of innovation and access, several sustainability issues can be considered. From the analysis of the Environmental, social and economic sustainability indicate that sustainable practices are needed.

Environmental Aspects

We continue to use products that consume more energy; for example, cloud computing services, data centers, and high definition streaming services are recognized as the products that contribute greatly to green gas emissions. For example, developing and preserving a picture or any kind of artwork or media kind in cyberspace entails utilizing of energy through which greenhouse gases are emitted to the environment. This is worsen by growing needs for more electronics gadgets that after sometime are rendered uneconomical to use hence forming e-wastes. In fact, both building and dismantling of these devices are detrimental to the environment since they require rare ingredients and energy, while their elimination is toxic.

Some of the disadvantages, which has been regarded as resulting from these data centers include; high costs in cooling the data centers, resource wastage, cost of disposing hazardous material contained in the data centers, costs in storing clients' information and processing the information amongst others. It shall also be noted that artists and creators can go to the most appropriate form of the platform that supports the greening agenda and does not exhaust resources simultaneously.

Issues, which are associated with the mentioned social problems, it can be argued that one of them is exclusion and the equal right to technologies. On one hand it is a liberation and refers to the fact that everyone can get a microphone, or, in other words everybody can participate in the creative process. On the other hand it points to the difference between artists who do not have money for sometimes extremely costly technologies.

There are specific questions that artists have to answer that makes their practices sustainable, questions lying in topical and comprehensive subject matter, on questions of diversity, of the digital divide, and of. Moreover artists have to consider appropriateness methods they use in order not to create a hierarchy between the haves and the have-nots, in other words between those who eyes are opened by these screens and those who do not have the screens. Promoting multicultural art via the Internet guarantees that integration becomes a positive by-product of this process and that everyone will find the Internet to be a welcoming environment where one can be themselves.

Other factors which need to be taken into consideration while discussing the economical aspects of digital art and its preservation are Economic Factors. The key issues that concern artists, or arise specifically when their messages are shared and reposted with the help of social media platforms, tools, and services are the issues of monetizing in such a crowded market and the problem of copyright. Therefore, sustainable business means sufficiently remunerating the digital producers, the right licensing structures and open platforms that make those platforms more accountable and less centralized as to provide more voice to the artists. Also, it will enhance the ability to create a circular economy in digital artworks using reuse, recycling, and sustainable consumption of technologies and material for posthuman economy in the global economy.

THE ENGAGEMENT OF TRADITIONAL ART FORMS WITH SUSTAINABLE DEVELOPMENT

Sustainability, in general, was always an important part of traditional art but the word sustainability became popular only recently. Most indigenous and historical art forms were already sustainable willingly because of the contents of their accessible resources, local creative involvement, and the intersections of art into life and ceremony.

Use of Natural Materials: For very long time, artisans from different parts of the world and especially from different indigenous communities relied on natural materials found within their community when developing art forms. From clay for pottery to the natural dyes for textiles to the wood for sculptures; sustainability in used in almost every artistic area since the works were created using natural and degradable materials. Themable proximity with nature made the artists respect environment since they needed to produce more from basic natural strengths for future unknown generations back in their artwork.

Cultural and Ritual Significance: Art in many preindustrial societies was not merely an aesthetic item but rather a societal feature, religious, and an ecological one as well. For instance, in Native American and African tribal art, the production of masks, sculptures or textiles entailed design significance that formed part of rites focusing on conservation of wildlife. As much as the relationship between art and nature could have been arbitrary, it most of the time proclaimed sustainable measures.

Artisanship and Longevity: Old clothing arts were created with a view to being long lasting since alongside being ornaments, many of them served the purpose of being used. For instance, hand woven baskets or ceramics were manufactured to have a very many years durability to reduce cases of wastage. The concept of making long-lasting products also has some meaning in the context of the sustainability policy, when vessel use denies the constant production of new things.

Local Knowledge and Skills: Local craftsmen principally acquired their trade from their antecedents based on the heritage endorsed by their cultures. The local knowledge called to become sustainable which in turn resulted in practices of resource management as well as partial harvesting of the natural substances. For example traditional weavers in India have been using handwoven techniques that have no harm to the environment such as using organic cotton and natural dyes.

Challenges with Industrialization: The latter is fully explained by the fact that many types of traditional folk art went through a period of decline in the second half of the 19th and 20th centuries as industrialisation took hold and factory-made products became more available. This shift towards machine made products simplified the craftsmanship and actually eliminated the usage of eco friendly resources, which the new processes commonly depended on synthetic and limited resources.

However, the seeds of sustainability in traditional arts were upheld as artists and cultures continued approximating the desire to maintain a cultural legacy.

Revival and Modern Perspectives: During the last few decades, people have returned to focusing on the traditional art and crafts they employ in the production of their work and to their environmentally friendly methods as people become more conscious of the effects they have on the global environment. These days, lots of contemporary artists living in indigenous regions are struggling to follow these traditional principles and marketing the produced goods as eco-friendly products, differing from factory-made items.

This history shows that many preindustrial societies are actually did taught the principles of sustainability and were using the materials and techniques, that respect the environment long before these practices became popular.

SHIFTS IN AESTHETIC PRODUCTION PROCESSES AND ITS EFFECTS ON ARTISTS.

Non-Fungible Tokens are what we're going to talk about today which stands for NFTs and is defined as a unique token standing for a specific and unique asset.

Digital art had been revolutionalizing the art market around the world including the new aspect of NFTs. NFT is given as a non-fungible token, which validates ownership of a specific digital content and enables artists to get paid for their creations by selling their art on different platforms which do not require a tangible medium. NFTs primarily became prominent in mainstream markets in 2021 with large volumes sold in market places such as OpenSea, Rarible and Foundation among others. These new attitudes have recast the experience, buying, and appreciation of art as digital property, offering a novel means for artists to disseminate their material.

But there are a few issues implicit with this technology, and one of them is climatic. The great majority of Non-Fungible Tokens are deployed on blockchain systems like Ethereum, which relies on the consumption of electricity through Proof of Work (PoW) algorithms. Other people are criticize that minting and trading of NFTs involves emission of more carbon, therefore, posing a question about whether this form of art is sustainable. But other experts claim that they have found that a single NFT transaction can be almost as power-intensive as an entire household for days. In response to these concerns, there are now other and more environmentally friendly solutions as the PoS and Layer 2.

ART GALLERIES AND FAIR 6 VIRTUAL EXHIBITIONS

More to the NFTs, virtual art exhibition and galleries have emerged and especially so after the outbreak of the COVID -19 pandemic which limited physical congregation. Virtual galleries can be established as virtual realizations of the art exhibition, where the main target is to create interaction with viewers in an online medium. Not only does this trend make Works accessible to audiences around the world, but it also has a drastically positive effect on preserving the environment by greatly minimising the impact that galleries can have, including transportation of artwork, the management of galleries, and non-recyclable material usage.

Virtual art spaces exclude certain doors for more oppression for particular artists as well as viewership. However, there are problems as well; the technological disparity, artists and audiences in areas with little to no internet would have a problem engaging. Furthermore, the author poses a practical issue of generating designs that are sleek and pristine for virtual galleries within 3D spaces, which consumes computational power and resources, so one cannot but wonder about the energy consumed for this purpose.

OPPORTUNITIES AND CHALLENGES OF SUSTAINABLE DEVELOPMENT

Despite the great opportunities that digital art forms have in the reduction of physical resources the subject needs to address the environmental cost of such digitization. The rise of NFTs and virtual exhibitions illustrates the double-edged nature of technological advancements in art: they provide unique and great possibilities for creation and communication, but at the same time make new sustainability challenges. More environmentally sustainable blockchains, global digital infrastructure accessibility, and better digital art governance are going to be significant to making the digital age sustainable.

DIFFERENCES BETWEEN TRADITIONAL ART MAKING AND NEW GENERATION ARTIST

Figure 1. Parameters of resource consumption

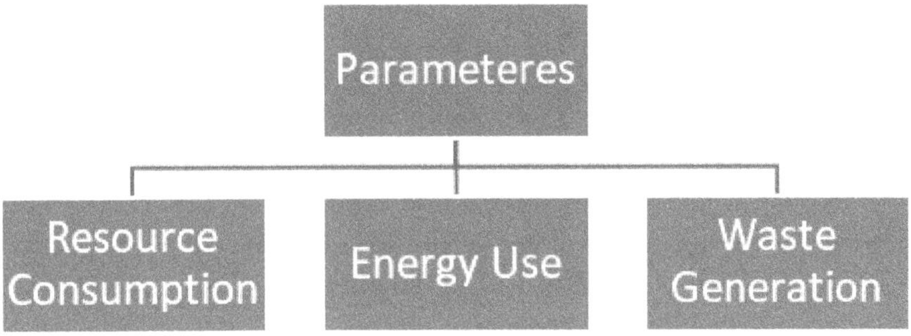

1. Resource Consumption

Traditional Art Production: Conventional methods of art work employ substantial utilitarian items such as papers, canvases, dyes, brushes, and molded stuffs including clay and metals. These materials are usually obtained from ecological media. For instance, wood is used widely in the production of paper; thus, using this means of transportation fuels deforestation. Paints and other pigments might also include mining and /or chemicals developed from crude oil. Additionally, the movement of such products from factories to stores and to artists escalates the carbon emission level.

Digital Art Creation: On the other hand, digital art making involves the use of Electronics gadgets like Computer, Tablets and soft wares. Even as these tools demand substantial expenditure for their development (copper for batteries, dyes for display) they often come as one-time use in the long run. There is, therefore, only consumption of electrical energy in the creation process, and no physical waste products such as used canvases and brushes.

2. Energy Use

Traditional Art Production: Stewardship is the primary path through which the energy footprint of traditional art is derived from the materials used in its creation, the means by which those materials are shipped and the manner in which they are discarded. The factories that paint, the canvases, and other materials used for artwork also use energy, and most of it comes from fossil sources. Also, firing for ceramics, working on printing machines, and moving art round lengthens energy consumption. Even now evens studios and galleries still use inappropriate lighting and climate control mechanisms and hence energy consumption.

Digital Art Creation: In digital art very much depend on electricity to run the devices and store information. But, as renewable sources of energy are searched and invoked the energy agenda of digital creation can be decreased. Internet storage and software production is a big power-user especially in data centers but many IT corporations are now using more green power. However, the energy consumed during the production of the devices and the electronic waste generated is still a sensitive factor within the environmental front.

3. Waste Generation

Traditional Art Production: Waste in traditional art is mainly in form of; Used paint containers, damaged canvases, used packaging, and nonbiodegradable items such as oil paints, solvents among others. In the wrong hands, working with these materials results in environment pollution, chemicals which harm the water supply, or add to the mound of garbage that is a landfill.

Table 1. Traditional vs. digital art - environmental comparison

Aspect	Traditional Art	Digital Art
Materials Used	Canvas, paints, brushes, etc.	Digital tools (software, hardware)
Resource Consumption	High (wood for canvases, paper, water, etc.)	Low in physical resources but high in energy
Energy Use	Minimal (lighting, studio space)	Significant (NFTs, blockchain)
Waste Generation	Physical waste (paints, chemicals)	E-waste, server energy consumption

Digital Art Creation: It creates little if any physical waste since everything is performed in the digital realm in digital art. However, e-waste it is generated through the manufacture and disposal of electronic devices that are becoming an increasing menace to the environment. Duration of electronic devices is comparatively short, and their end use results in generating hazardous wastes, if not recycled. Also the contemporary culture of creating digital files and data might create problems associated with the waste of storage space, but the negative impact of electronic waste is lower than that of regular waste types.

Research artists and organizations that have adapted sustainable practice to the performance art. Modernism has become an area of interest and concern in implementing sustainability practices even it on as aspect of art. This section offers a comprehensive discussion of interrelated case studies of artists and other organizations that have implemented sustainable approaches into their work.

CASE STUDIES ON IMPLEMENTATIONS OF SUSTAINABLE PRACTICES

1.1. Olafur Eliasson

Olafur Eliasson is a highly acclaimed contemporary artist who incorporate natural phenomenon and renewable energy into his monumental installation of works. In his practice, it intensively uses elements such as solar panels and recycled materials; thus drawing attention to the connection between art and ecology. Some of the prior works are The Weather Project in which a large semi circular disc was fused with mirrors to build an indoor sun which forced the onlookers to consider the relationship with nature. Eliasson wants people to wake up to the reality of climate change and think about themselves as members of the eco-system.

1.2. Agnes Denes

Agnes Denes is the founder of ecological art which investigates ecological themes with both artistic and philosophical statements. Her project "Wheatfield – A Confrontation", in which she sowed two acres of wheat in Manhattan, central business district, was again involving a concept of land use, food production and world hunger. Naturally, Denes painted and created sculptures that are functional not only as aesthetic but as social statement that turns people into critical thinkers of consumers and of the earth.

1.3. Nils Udo

Nils Udo is claimed to be a pioneering practitioner of land art most of which he builds with natural materials, making them disappear after some time. His works are normally incorporated in the natural environment making them exhibit a good sense in ecological coexistence. An example is his "Nest" project where Scharfie built a nest, a large nest with twigs and branches in a natural environment with spectators put in a predicament as to what was Scharfie's intention of putting such a structure in environs where he had put it.

1.4. Future Farmers

Future farmers are a collective of artists, designers and architects which practices in the field of installation and interaction, activism and agro politics. Their projects are frequently derived from the domains of food systems, local environment and the relations between people and the world. Concepts like the "Pencil Farm" are primarily focused on the shared usage of resources almost enjoining people to engage in sustainable farming so as to foster environmental conservation and change.

ENVIRONMENTAL NON-GOVERNMENTAL ORGANIZATIONS

Tate Modern

Among all museums, the Tate Modern in London is one of the most sustainable leaders in arts today. It has put into operation wide-ranging plans that are meant to help it achieve lower carbon emission levels, such as energy management systems and transport measures. Following climate change, engagements are seen in projects that focus on ecological aspects in the museum's exhibitions and activities and process for the visitors.

The Royal Academy of Arts

Whereas sustainability composed the focus of the prior year's events, the Royal Academy of Arts has integrated the principle into its practice. It is also a environmentally conscious company and has begun many programs on using environmentally friendly products and employing environmentally friendly policies such as marketing sustainable materials. Another way the institution ensures sustainability is by organizing exhibitions and educational programmes that call for people's consciousness regarding ecological responsibility.

Julie's Bicycle

Julie's Bicycle is an organisation that is focused on improving sustainability in arts industry. Instead, offering tools and tips, as well as examples, the organization helps arts institutions implement more sustainable strategies. Julie's Bicycle works with other organisations for SD, showing how embedding sustainability values results in major social outcomes.

The Australian Museum

Specifically, the Australian Museum is a perfect example of the institution for which sustainability is a priority. To enhance its environmental activities and minimize its carbon footprint, it has come up with a sound strategic plan including sustainability. Using education programmes and outreach, the museum contributes enormously to the understanding of ecological concerns that the art and science society has in place.

PARTICIPATION OF THE COMMUNITY AND ITS EFFECTS

Eco-Conscious Artists

Today, it is very common for new artists to have environmental problems and pursue ecological solutions in their artwork. These artists effectively promote themselves through the uses of recycled canvases, organic colors, and interaction with the locals to design absorbing and meaningful art pieces.

Working Together and Working Together Organizations

Technological cooperation with the artists and organizations ensures that sustainability is promoted. Such groups are the Center for Sustainable Practice in the Arts (CSPA), that discusses sustainability with artists and invites them to exchange knowledge and creative materials. Such cross-cutting measures foster uniqueness in solving environmental problems.

Eco-Art Initiatives

Eco-art examples have been taken in different communities to show how artists can work on involving the community while seeking ways of presenting environmental issues. Initiatives such as "Fallen Fruit,"identifies fruit trees within cities so as to encourage people engage in eating from trees on the streets.

Participatory Projects

This quiet, slow unassuming approach of making art in a community and letting people be involved in the art-making process has been notably for furthering the cause of increasing the community's awareness of the environment. They engage users in making choices regarding their environment, making them a fine link between art and sustainability initiatives.

The infusion of sustainability processes in the art sector is a radically transformative approach that defines the future practice. From innovative case studies it can be understood that these artistic creations play not only informative role between individuals or communities, and environmental problems but they can also inspire change in personal and community attitudes towards sustainability. Thus, the growing interest of artists in the relations between art and ecology ensures a quantitative shift towards positive change and a qualitative shift towards a new level of artists' responsibility.

Environmental Sustainability: Discuss the possibility of sparing tangible media such as canvases and paints through using digital tools and then consider the relationship between digital art, specifically NFTs and blockchain, and energy consumption.

Understanding of Digital Art and its Relation to Environmental Conservation Digital art is rapidly becoming the new standard of artistic expression and is a major consumer of resources. There is always a concern with the transformation of traditional artworks, because the supports, pigments, tools and other mediums used to create artwork are all part of the problem, by contributing to the depletion of resources, their production, and disposal. So, using digital tools can be seen as more efficient and more environmentally friendly solution as compared to constant use of those materials.

DECREASING OF THE PHYSICAL RESOURCE UTILIZATION

Less Material Waste: They are artists who work on computers and tablets using tools like Adobe Photoshop or Procreate, examples of which mean they do not need a canvas and paint. This shift decreases the speaker-and-sink impact inherent with physical art material manufacturing, shipping, and elimination.

Sustainability in Creation: This way artists can try out anything with the digital instruments, can create hundreds of pieces of work and delete all but none of which is wasted. Such digital flexibility fosters innovation not through waste of physical resources as found in the physical technology flexibility.

Print-On-Demand and Limited Editions: As a digital form, digital art can be duplicated endlessly, thereby minimizing the use of paper and storage facilities. This idea serves the artists best as it enables them to print what is required without having duplicate unused copies.

Human Beings' Energy Utilization Behavior and the Environment

Digital Platforms and Energy Use: There is no doubt, that in its turn, digital art is not without its price, the price paid to the environment. The digital art platforms themselves, especially those using blockchain technology and NFTs, are consuming huge amounts of energy. The key challenge of blockchain is decentralization, which means that the workings of blockchain require a large number of computers, meaning that, the production of the relevant blockchain could lead to a large carbon footprint.

NFTs and Resource Consumption: The introduction of NFT market has focused the public on the problems related with environmental sustainability of digital possession. A large portion of art NFT sales are associated with 'minting' artwork on energy costly blockchains such as Ethereum. This is particularly true in consensus mechanisms like the soon-to-be-implemented Ethereum proof of stake which are expected to massively cut energy use.

The Need for Sustainable Practices: Digital art is currently still a young field – and there is a dire need for artists and hosting sites to grow more sustainable. This may range from selecting environment friendly hosting services, advocating for use friendly to the environment web hosting services, and raising the concern on the environment impact of digital art.

The available study suggested that there is a chance for artists in the field of digital art to lower their ecological footprint by minimizing the use of materials. However, the general energy usage particularly in relation to NFT and block chain is an issue that has ramifications that needs to be address in a socially desirable manner. As this best balance is established in the art community, the production of environmentally sustainable practice will seal the future of art in the new hybrid digital world.

Social Sustainability: Describe how this form of art can enhance the spirit of globalization getting over geographical restrictions and helping people with disabilities find a job. Elaborate the positive effects of art piece when implemented in the social change processes in the computer mediated environment.

Concept of Social Sustainability in the Contextualization of Digital Art

Social sustainability in art is therefore defined as the stability and resilience of art to foster social relations and cohesion, inclusion andolf equity. Nowadays, the Internet has become indispensable means for communication and promotion of art made by artists of different origin. Such a policy enables a greater representation of diverse art forms and moreover fostens cultural appreciation.

Table 2. Social sustainability in digital art platforms

Factor	Impact
Global Access	Allows diverse artists to participate, Geographic Barriers Removed, Artists from remote areas can showcase
Inclusivity	More opportunities for underrepresented
Social Impact	Art as a tool for raising awareness

Going Beyond the Boundary of Region

The second benefit of the given digital art is that competition does not restrict them because the artists could be from any part of the globe. For instance, such sites as Instagram or ArtStation have provided opportunities for artists located in the corners of the world and who would not get a chance to reach galleries or fans in any way. One of the most engaging examples is an indigenous artist from the Arctic area who shares digital illustrations that have real appeal on an international scale and interest from institutions and collectors.

Diversity and Equality

The area of digital art ensures the equality of minorities providing them with opportunities for successful presence. —Establishing open access and promoting artist's works from different background, web-based exhibitions and virtual galleries help create more opportunities for artists. thanks to such projects like "Art for All" projects initiated are successful in showcasing the opportunities for the LGBTQ+ artists, women, artists of colors to speak up through the technological platforms.

Art for Social Purposes

Digital art as an art form acts as a micro-mobilizer in the promotion of social issues by artists. For instance, street art, some viral campaigns we get to see particularly during the black lives matter movements explain how art forms social worlds and champions for justice. In the process, social media can be used to advance art and art topics as quickly as possible, address aspects of people's lives and stir up change where needed.

CHALLENGES AND CONSIDERATIONS

Nevertheless, the discussed opportunities of the digital art world have certain refined drawbacks, including the problem of the digital divide where some people never use any type of technology. The principle is keys is to attempt to make it so that the digital realm is fair for all, and everyone's opinion counts. To address these gaps, Schemes directed towards providing support and programs aimed for the promotion of development of minority artists exist.

This uniqueness makes digital art the best option for spreading social sustainability since it creates global access to join in. There are definitely great opportunities we can find today from artists and platforms; therefore, it is incumbent upon everyone to help amplify these great potential and guarantee a universal inclusiveness where art can be a constant force for change.

Economic Sustainability: Discuss shift to coverage of how digital art has impacted artists in terms of sales opportunities through online galleries, and NFTs, among others. Emphasize the problem of receiving payment for electronic creations and at the same time protecting authors 'rights to their works and preventing piracy.

With the onset of the digital age the art context has opened up a lot of opportunities for remuneration of the artists and exposure of the artworks. This change has been enabled mainly by online galleries, NFTs, and different other platforms. All of these innovations hold potential for revenue generation of one sort or another, but all are associated with potential problems regarding the proper recompense of creators and control of copies.

Table 3. Economic models for sustainable digital art

Economic Challenge	Proposed Solution
Fair Artist Compensation	Stronger intellectual property laws, Fair revenue-sharing mechanisms
Copyright Protection	Stronger intellectual property laws, Fair revenue-sharing mechanisms
Monetizing Digital Work	Supporting artists through digital platforms
Energy Costs for NFTs	Developing energy-efficient alternatives

New Revenue Streams

Online Galleries have therefore become necessary auspices to artists who want to expose their art works other than the physical galleries. Marketplaces such as Saatchi Art, Artfinder and even Etsy let artists develop their virtual shops through which they can sell their artworks to the buyers. This accessibility have made the art market more open or encourage artist of different ethnicity and of every part of the world to have a chance. It essentially means that artists can avoid most of the overhead that comes with creating art in physical spaces and reach a much larger number of people than they would via local galleries. Future of art monetization was further revolutionized by NFTs. These unique are digital assets that are filed in the blockchain hence proving ownership and originality. Artists have been able to sell their Work electronically as unique pieces and are protected legally to take revenues proportionate to their production's resales. Such transactions include Open Sea and Rarible where artists engage with collectors without any third party interference. NFTs generate scarcity in a digital product and hence have generated record breaking sales and more attention to digital art and other related digital creations. Furthermore, different platforms offer the artist different opportunities of making a living. Kickstarter and Patreon are useful for an artist because they allow them to communicate with the audience; fans can either support all projects and get nothing in return, or they can pay for one project or get additional content for a subscription price. This direct support model creates value around the work that artists create by bringing them closer to the fan base. However, artists get an opportunity to post their artwork on the social media sites, which will enable them to reach market consumers and sell the artwork.

Monetization has become one of the biggest challenges of the modern world and more especially for those individuals who are producing digital works.

Thus, despite the numerous possibilities to monetize the artworks, artists have a number of linear obstacles in the context of the digital environment. The first is that markets become saturated; a problem directly linked to the use of plugins. This creates a problem as more artists join the online space to share their work, and less likely original or individual content will come through as popular. This in effect means that the prices of songs can go down, which is rather bad news to the artists as this simply leads to competition where prices are slashed to the lowest.

In addition, a major issue is the worth of digital art in question. Unfortunately, there are still many collectors who underestimate digital art compared to classic painting and sculpture, for instance. It leads to cheaper prices of the digital works thus straining the financial feasibility of the authors dependent on them as sources of income. In the overall acceptance of the digital art format, therefore, a shift in these perceptions becomes important for compensation fairness.

Another major concern associated with the modern literature is the international Copyright issues in digital environment. The fact that copying and distribution as adopted in the current world through the use of the internet and other related facilities pose a likelihood of unauthorized use/infringement. It is challenging for most artists to recover their rights and safeguard their content because contemporary copyright laws cannot sufficiently claw back the characterization of digital art. Such an absence of protection can discourage artists from posting their creations on the internet which from a business perspective would cut off their market. Ensuring Fair Compensation

In order to succeed in such conditions, fair economic models need to be invented to enable artists to feed themselves and be paid well for their work.

Finally, to protect artists' rights in the digital realm more stringent IP regimes are required. This involves arguing for better policies on copyrights for digitally created pieces of art and work, and going all the way to using blockchain systems to help tag ownership and ensure legitimacy. In this way, since offering artists the necessary instruments that would help them safeguard artistic accomplishments, we can support artists in the new art environments, thus the digital realm has enormous potentials for artists to make a living marketing their artwork; nevertheless, there stands considerable troubles that need essential attention. It means, promoting economic sustainability of fairly balanced models and protection for those at risk, digital artists will be provided with adequate opportunities and tools to succeed in this newly emerging field of art.

SOLUTIONS AND RECOMMENDATIONS

Adopting Eco-friendly Technologies: Support artists and institutions, such that they opt for new environmentally friendly technologies for their digital art and avoid the energy waste particularly in areas such as NFTs that require blockchain.

Today being an artist or an institution is on an interesting position that allows them to adopt sustainable and advanced technology in their work. As the usage of digital practices is further questioned concerning its environmental footprint the art community must embrace tools and/or practices that are energy efficient and reduce their carbon imprint. This is relevant to popular but concerns areas such as Non-Fungible Tokens (NFTs) and blockchain technology that have received a lot of attention in matters concerning sustainability due to their efficiency demands.

For a while now, people finally came to realize the importance of the appropriate use of eco-friendly informational and communication technologies.

A starting point for artists and institutions to make a change is to audit the technological practices involved in their artistic productions. Most of the conventional software implementations require power and more so when running on powerful computers. For instance, changing from traditional ways of designing to program and web based designs that are energy efficient reduces energy consumption. Some software companies have now adopted sustainable development to cut down on the carbon footprint involved in digital creation.

In addition, artists can engage energy-efficient equipment in particular instruments for creating art, for instance, laptops and tablets that draw tiny power while offering performance in result. The same goes for renewable energy sources for studios—like deposits in solar panels—substituting electric energy significantly and encouraging greener practices in art. In addition to helping preserve the environment, these artists play a key role in the properly initiating the arts into the quest for a greener future.

Non-fungible tokens are providing new forms of income to creators of digital art, but frequently the technology of blockchain with which these tokens are associated causes critical reaction because of its high energy consumption. New! Most of the current blockchain systems and especially those using the Proof of Work (PoW) consensus algorithms demand significant amounts of computational power and electric energy to process the transactions. A rather energy-consuming process, it has raised many concerns about the sustainable imprint of NFTs and the need to apply changes.

In order to avoid this problem, artists or institutions should promote or use blockchains that employ environmentally friendly consensus algorithms. For instance, while PoW, PoS, and dPoS systems are used in decentralized applications, PoS and dPoS have significantly less energy demands than PoW systems and would probably resonate better with environmentally-conscious artists. NFT art creators have the chance to act in the NFT market to focus on the application of environmentally friendly strategies by choosing stations that are environmentally friendly.

Moreover, some of the blockchain networks are in the process of exploring ways of achieving carbon neutrality and include buying carbon credits, or funding green energy projects. The artists can in this case advance such goals by selecting to mint their NFTs on such platforms with the practices of sustainable energy. Apart from contributing to their cause by minimizing the amount of carbon they can produce in terms of NFT creation; it also conveys a very strong message regarding sustainability within the digital art fraternity.

Institutional Responsibility as Well as Management

Organizations hold a central position in advocating for environmentally sustainable technology adoption in art. Cultural organizations are set to sign policies and practices that support sustainability, therefore artists see it fit to use environmental friendly tools. This may involve offering guidance and informational materials on sustainability, arranging seminars on issues of green technology and inviting information technology companies that operate on sustainability.

ERD should be encouraged to allow institutions find ways of cutting down energy use within the arts. Institutions can be encouraged to conduct more studies on how the energy usage in arts can be cut. Working with technical experts, environmental engineers, and artists can sometimes produce solutions that are the best for everyone in the society. Such efforts do more than raise awareness about sustainability issues; they also underscore the need for integrated solutions to global environmental concerns that embrace technologically sustainable solutions for artists and organizations when seeking sustainable solutions in the digital realm. The art community can take the actions to ensure that energy efficient tools are adopted, sustainable practices in the use of blockchain are promoted and chimed participants from institutional framework. In 2020 as artists weave new ways of creating, it is important that these practices are sustainable to avoid lasting impacts on the next generations of creators and artists. The art world does not have to be adversative with the environment if it will adopt communal efforts that will make it sustainable.

Promoting Social and Community Engagement: Suggest the engagement of technology as a tool in encouraging people's participation, art integration and general participation in sustainable projects.

Social and Community Mobilisation

Museums and art galleries have an incomparable chance and future to connect artists with communities for participation in the society. The use of digital tools not only increases awareness of existing artistic processes but also makes it easier to work on empowered and shared projects that highlight sustainability. In this sense, technology helps artists to have constructive engagements, receive assists from, as well as elicit the participation of various groups of unknown viewers in order to proactively elicit social change.

Supporting Participation

Two, artists enjoy the opportunity of having interactive digital platforms through which they can create meaningful communication strands with their followers. Social networking platforms, including Instagram, Facebook, and Twitter provide artists with the opportunity to present artworks, concepts and processes right as they occur allowing for an audience to engage and respond. It is a two way process of communication that generates a social feeling and puts the populace into action, for whatever they receive they can give an output on what they perceive, think and or feel about the art.

Furthermore, artists are able to conduct online workshops, live performance art and question and answer sessions inclusive of community members in the thought process of creating their art. These activities instill the spirit where artistic information is characterized by creativity and shared by event participants. These seven principles support sustainable art practices because they combine top-down inhibition and bottom-up encouragement: Artists can only elicit ideas or even co-work of projects with the participation of community members, thereby fostering a sense of shared ownership of a particular territory and its preservation.

Inclusive Art Practices

What becomes clear from this is that giving an artistic practice an inclusive aim can greatly increase its relevance with the community. The marginalized people can easily be accessed through the use of digital media and all of them incorporate their views into arts. For example, the possibility of the creation of interactive online projects can allow individuals such as artists as well as other members of the society to come up with artwork s that have a social core as well as virtues that are dear to them.

Integrated use of technology can be an effective way of developing work that is accessible to all. For instance, making accessible over the internet virtual exhibitions complete with audio descriptions and subtitles ensure that people with various forms of disability can access the artwork. They should make sure that the work is easily availed to the public so as to show the public that supporting art is about supporting concerns of social justice as should be the agenda of the art fraternity.

Collaborative Projects

Sustainability and community engagement, mainly rely on cooperation. Using the information technology, artists can seek and join different projects and engage different stakeholders such as community organizations, business people, and environmental groups. It is within such partnerships that potential groundbreaking initiatives in addressing such social issues can emerge meantime embraced sustainability.

An example is planning arts events on environmental issues like climate change, wasting materials among members of the community. Artists can engage directly with community members to involve the community in creating murals, installations, a digital artwork that will trigger the act of speaking out. The impact of artists in this sense is theft When participating in these projects, artists enable participants to act as promoters of sustainable development themselves.

This also means there is the sharing of resources and knowledge from one digital artist or members of that community with another. For instance, artists can develop web-based libraries where people get information and access tools that support sustainable art processes. It also promotes shared learning and proper nurturing of sustainability practices by the society in the course of executing the project.

Success Stories

There are countless examples that art can be promoted successfully through the use of media platforms to enhance the general social and community welfare. Still, some projects have started on social media like #ArtforChange and #CreativeCommunity that has called artists to raise the issues they want on their social media accounts and involve their followers. Many of these campaigns demonstrate the freedom of art in positive stimulation of dialogues and human interaction.

Community arts projects as embodied in The People's Choice in England, is where artists are commissioned to develop artworks that will address the issues as elaborated by the various communities. Besides creating valuable art, these projects increase social and communal associations among viewers and positively affect their perceptions of belonging, where advancing social and community engagement through digital platforms constitutes the primary and most sustainable way communities support artistic practices in the digital realm. Through getting people involved in the artistic processes, valuing the collective and starting projects that matter, artists can change many aspects of people's lives positively. It could be imperative to adopt the mentioned approaches embracing the art world today as it move forward to be a powerful tool for Community engagement as well as sustainability. Such concepts as art as personal project of personal work should be replaced by the vision of art as a collective path to a better existence, artists and designers invite people and integrate their efforts for change.

Economic Models for Sustainable Art: Recommend creating equal economic structures that rationale artists on how to make money out of their digital arts in an environmentally or socially responsible manner. Discusses the issues of enhanced safeguard of IPRs, along with authorized, fair and balanced distribution of revenues. Future Research Directions

ECONOMICS FOR CONTEMPORARY ART AND SUSTAINABLE ART ECONOMY

As we see the digital art marketplace growing, it becomes critical to develop strong economic concepts that will help artists gain independent revenue while also addressing issues of sustainability and social responsibility. As more art is purchased in digital form, there is a need to establish the standard which artists can use in order to make sustainable income and which prevents such works from being exploited. This includes developing fair revenues models; enhancing IP rights; and building coalition associations between artists, institutions and technological applications.

Creation of Fair Economic Models

With regards to economically sustainable models, IT is crucial to foster online profile spots for the artists who would agree with reasonable royalties. Currently, there is a tendency in which many platforms take very high costs and take a huge percentage of every sale which upon observation likely to have a deep negative impact on artists' income. Changes that lead to models that cut or eliminate the middlemen can help artists earn more of their money. For instance, introduction of direct to customer selling methods using personal websites or other specific artist selling platforms will go along way in boosting artists earnings while at the same time enhancing the noble cause of reaching out to the fans directly.

In addition, it is essential to establish clarity of the final prices – as well as potential costs, to achieve full transparency. The selling technologies used in the digital environment must show how revenues are split and other expenses incurred in business deals. They said that this transparency created healthier relations between artists and the consumers through enabling the creation of more sustainable markets. It becomes easier for these platforms to sign revenue-sharing agreements that bring about better: This makes the financial position of artists better.

The Subscription and Membership Models are another way through which companies design their e-commerce site to create content.

Subscription and membership are other techniques which can guarantee the artists are able to receive steady cash inflows. Some of such business models are Patreon that give artists a chance to profit of their creations and develop special offers based on the contributions of their patrons. Besides providing frequent flows of revenues and even enhancing the stability of those uncertainties, this model also facilitates artists to better engage with their communities and grow that loyalty.

Furthermore, there is the opportunity to use crowdfunding to attract investment in separate projects, so artists can attract funding to cover their expenses. This removal of monetary risk and they are able to execute complex and creative pieces thereby doing what is most representative of them. If income sources are diverse, artists may become economically sustainable while being able to reign themselves in and still create quality content.

Intellectual Property Protection

These concerns are even more so as digital art continues to proliferate; there is increasing pressure for higher levels of IP. Modern laws in connection with copyright provide inadequate protection to simple copying and fail to cover new technological innovations, which poses threats of piracy and use of artists' work. The changes which the current copyright law and the recognition of new conditions arising due to the replicability and accessibility of virtual artwork is admirable only one can encourage.

The initView for this is blockchain technology where through the use of blockchain and smart contracts can enable digital artists to have ownership records maintained on the block chain. With blockchain, artists can develop immutable ownership and quality that will help them capture their due credits and revenues. Such approach may decrease magnitude of violated copyright and create fairer environement for artists within the social media networks.

Proportional Methods for Distributing Sales Profits

When artists fail to negotiate fair revenue sharing standards, they end up receive little or nothing in return of their effort. In these SRMs artists should be fully rewarded besides promoting sustainable partnerships between artists and the platforms. This may assume the setting of guidelines in revenue sharing that afford artists a good proportion of the sales of their product.

Thirdly, projects involving artists, brands, and organizations can create new business models to create sustainable income while being responsible. In this way, it means that such artists should select sustainability in partnerships to enter initiatives that are closest to their heart while earning their dues.

FUTURE RESEARCH DIRECTIONS

As for further research, more work must be done to investigate new forms of sustainable business models for artists and arts organizations. Areas of focus could include:

The Impact of Emerging Technologies: Exploring how AI and AR and other technologies which continue to emerge, may generate new sources of revenue for artists while not compromising the principles of the "Artist's Mile" project.
Consumer Behavior and Sustainability: To highlight the characteristics of sustainable art practices and work through its implications for marketing and outreach, enhances the means by which artists can appeal to consumers who value sustainable practices.
Evaluating Different Revenue Models: Studying the results of distinct approaches to the revenue-sharing approach to determine the best practices that may be incorporated into various platforms.
Collaboration Between Stakeholders: Analyzing models of artists' cooperation with art institutions and social media companies to discover approaches that positively influenced artists' practices and fairly rewarded them.

Legal Frameworks for Digital Art: Promoting the legal changes that would help to enhance the idea of the protection of digital artists' rights so that they could be protected in a digital environment; making efforts to establish the fair economic theories that would enable digital art to be supported throughout the relevant markets is critical for artists who work in the digital environment. Thus, by focuses on artist-friendly platforms, non-sleazy pricing, and such things as fair revenue-shares, we will be able to make the proper change and let artists be good, while making the business good, too. Behaviour to ensure higher degrees of intellectual property rights and future research areas will augment the sustainability of artistic practices in digital context. Only collective efforts and compliance with economic justice ensure that the art world can become prosperous socially and environmentally advantageous.

Sustainability of the Digital Art Platforms and Suggestions for Its Positive Improvements on the Environment

The consequential growth of digital art means that it is important to examine the abilities of the platforms that host and distribute this art to be environmentally friendly. Although digital art presents numerous benefits including lowering the amount of material needed, increasing availability more often these platforms involve high energy usage as well as high CO2 emissions. This subtopic investigates the durability of art in the consumption of technology and suggests sustainable solutions for art platforms to utilise.

Figure 2. Digital art platforms.

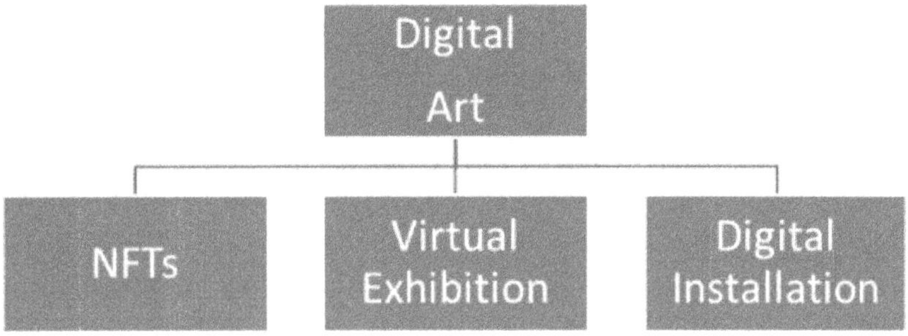

The Effects of Digital Art Marketplace

The virtual art sectors incorporate dependencies on datacentre that store the servers required for storage, analytics as well as dissemination. There is growing understanding that these data centers use a significant amount of electrical energy, the source of which many is often from the burning of fossil fuels. It was forecasted that data centers consume approximately one percent of all the electrical energy all through the world, and the demand will be increasing in the near future due to exponential generation of content to be placed on the Internet. The energy consumption also plays a role in the greenhouse gases emission and thus leads to sustainability concern on the kind of digital art practices.

Moreover, the cooling systems that are necessary to keep temperatures at these data centers low add a substantive energy load to the problem. The potential can be significant; one has to take into account that digital art platforms can accommodate millions of artworks and millions of people in each country.

The Role of Blockchain and NFTs

The case of blockchain and more specifically of NFTs, Non-Fungible Tokens, have only added a layer to the debate on the impact of digital art on the environment.

Most NFT marketplaces employ PoW consensus algorithms, which are resource-intensive and energy-waste processes of maintaining blockchain. This leads to high energy usage and large greenhouse gas emissions in turn. For example, a single NFT transaction is estimated to be equivalent to several days of power consumption of an average family.

1. **Transitioning to Renewable Energy**: Fine art marketplaces can choose to power their data centers by renewable electricity from renewable sources such as solar or wind power. Even big companies like Google and Microsoft have started implementing use of renewable energy for their data centers which are key to the formation of ICT sustainability. Hence the platforms can greatly reduce their carbon emissions by obtaining energy from renewable sources.
2. **Implementing Energy-efficient Technologies**: This show that it is possible to curb energy utilization in the data centers by making necessary investments in the hardware and cooling equipment. Such advancing features as liquid cooling, the utilization of AI for distribution and monitoring of electrical supplies, can save energy and prevent misuse. These technologies should be considered by digital art platforms when developing or redesigning an architecture.
3. **Adopting Eco-friendly Blockchain Solutions**: The emergence of blockchain-friendly solutions like PoS or dPoS accompanied by/shown natural resistance to NFTs is an indication that there exists a chance to significantly or completely avoid using resource-intensive algorithms. Compared to PoW, these systems utilise a far smaller quantity of energy and are preferred by platforms dedicated to digital art. The platforms mean to choose crypto blockchains that are friendly to the environment and make way for artists to monetize on their content in an environmentally sustainable manner.
4. **Encouraging Sustainable Practices Among Artists**: Digital art platforms have a proactive responsibility for raising awareness regarding the bearers' eco-unfriendly habits and decisions. Through supporting green digital solutions, and stimulating a sense of sustainability into the development and production of showing one's artwork, platforms can create a community of sustainability within the art world.
5. **Supporting Carbon Offset Initiatives**: It is possible for platform to establish carbon offset programs that compensation for the amount of emission by the platform. This may involve collaboration with other organizations tilted mostly to reforestation, renewable energy production among others. As a result, digital art platforms can benefit from these programs, and thus show their concern for the overall environmental concerns.

Despite the shift that has taken place within the art industry through the use of digital art platforms their repercussions on the environment a long-term plan are alarming. These platforms can reduce their carbon footprint comprehensively since they know the implication of energy consumption and use the green approach to the issues. Swapping fossil fuel energies for renewable sources of power, using energy-saving technologies, and encouraging sustainability are critical transformative actions needed to achieve a sustainable digital art future. The art community should establish an understanding of environmental responsibility and therefore remain productive for the sustainability of the planet.

DISCOVERING THE FUTURE OF AI AND MACHINE LEARNING AS TOOLS FOR SUSTAINABLE ARTISTIC ENDEAVOURS

AI and machine learning are making innovations that change and transform various fields including the Arts in that there is better creativity with sustainable measures. These mean that the mis application of these technologies has the potential of lowering wastes and energy use in the practices of the artists as they are provided new ways to produce, disseminate, and market their art.

Cost Saving for Artists

This is where Artificial Intelligence and machine learning will find good usage in the future of art, by reducing the wastage during the art making process. It should be noted that most traditional arts incorporate the use of physical or tangible objects part of which may be wasted if the art is destroyed or if the material was used in an inefficient manner. With the help of AI, artists are going to save a lot of material and prevent the waste of materials.

For instance, generative design algorithms help artists to envision what their masterpiece is going to look like in the digital platform before centering on physical media. This can help the artists to at least assume different styles and compositions in order to arrive at the final idea on one design without the need to draw physically many times. By doing so they can greatly reduce the amount of waste that is produced during the creative process so that efficient use of resources is made.

Also, AI can study and forecast the tendencies in artistic styles thus becoming an important advisor for an artist. In particular, understanding what will compel the audiences, artists will focus on creating such pieces which have a better likelihood of finding their market, leaving less room for artists to develop pieces that will not be embraced by the audiences.

Energy-Efficient Processes in the Creation of Digital Art

Due to a large extent concerning the creation of art, a significant amount of energy is used, especially if high-performance hardware is used. Each of these technologies may beneficially affect energy consumption by guiding how digital art is best created. For instance, rendering can be a task done by the AI algorithms in that better artistic productions are created within a short period.

Furthermore, through AI, one can choose the most efficient, in terms of the energy consumption, tools and software for creation of digital art. Analyzing the recoverable energy an application costs, an artist would be in a position to know which technology to use, which would have minimal energy wastage while at the same time producing quality art work.

Improving Partnership and Usability

AI technologies also help artists work together and brings art to the public in a more enabling way. AI supported online platforms can take into account users' profiles and propose collaboration offers which will be relevant for artists. This makes artists to feel they belong to a given community and this help in sharing of ideas and resources hence no artist has to start producing everything from their scratch.

In addition, such programs as machine learning algorithms can help to make art enjoyable for people with disabilities since there are tools for the delivery of art in ways that meet their needs. For instance, AI in synthesizing image descriptions for the blind will make it possible for them to have access to different forms of art without having to consume more resources than are necessary.

The issues of supporting sustainable art markets are considered.

In the sphere of art selling, AI is able to support the stabilization and functioning of the art markets with the help of consumer data analysis. In other words, through the market knowledge, the platforms can assist the artists in pricing and targeting audiences such that risks associated with high wastage rates due to unsold inventories can be avoided.

Moreover, often AI platforms may provide more transparent and favourable strategies within the sales process, providing artists proper payments for their work. Through elimination of the middlemen and use of technology in the execution of the deals these platforms eradicate energy used in the conventional modes of sales.

Al in all, the mentioned applications of AI and machine learning can help increase sustainability in artists' activities. As these technologies curb wastage in art production methods, increase energy consumption, encourage better relations between artists, and provoke better environmentally friendly art markets, artists can develop sustainably without the negative effects on the environment. Knowing the trends of development of the art world in the digital age, inclusion of AI and machine learning will be crucial for the development of a more sustainable future of art. Innovative applications reveal the possibility not only to upgrade creativity activity but also to solve some environmental and social problems.

THE FUTURE OF ART IN THE METAVERSE AND WEB 3.0: COMBINING SUSTAINABILITY WITHIN THE FRAMEWORK OF DIGITAL ARTISTIC SYSTEMS

The future of art is already here, and the Acronyms popularized as the Metaverse and Web 3.0 are redesigning the future of artistic creation and sale. This is also a good chance to incorporate sustainability into existing and developing technologies in the scope of digital art. This study looks at how the Metaverse – a decentralised virtual space – and the Web 3.0 will redefine the future of art in terms of the sustainability of art practices and responsible Web 3.0 practices.

Concept of Metaverse and Web 3.0

The Metaverse is defined as a collective virtual shared space technologically generated from the merging of virtually real physical environment and persistently real virtual environment. It covers many forms, including Virtual Reality (VR) and Augmented Reality (AR), in which the users can have interaction in real-time with one another and with digital objects. Web 3.0 is relatively defined by the decentralized appendage and technology that enables the owners to take more pre-eminent decisions about their data and the interactions they tend to perform online. Collectively, these notions mark an epistemological break in terms of art's production, circulation or display.

Potentialities of Sustainable Management

Decentralized Ownership and Fair Compensation: The development of Web 3.0 has one of the main benefits owing to the decentralization of ownership using the blockchain. This lets the artists own their piece and yet get fairly paid every time their digital art is sold through smart contacts. This is quite beneficial as it will cut on the number of go-betweens which means that the artists will get more cash to enable them sustain their economic lives and inspire them to produce more art. This model may well be useful especially in the Metaverse to which artists can paint and sell their art works to collectors and people who are interested in.

Virtual Art Exhibitions: For instance, the Metaverse permits live virtual arts displays which can be accessed over the Internet and light years away from the physical art galleries whose setting up causes needless harm to the natural environment. Artists have opportunities to design other realistic environments in which viewers can walk through to interact with art. These virtual galleries could considerably decrease the use of paper and energy for creating the real exhibition, the transportation, etc. In addition, virtual exhibitions may be used to market environmentally related topics and themes in order to foster debate and understanding on the subject within the framework of arts.

Collaborative Projects and Community Engagement: The Metaverse means that artists and technologists are able to work together with audiences to build new community works. It is possible to facilitate a direct and two-way communication with audiences, they can be invited to share ideas, collaborate or even to initiate an artwork/ project. Not only does this practice enhance the individual artwork it fosters an engagement of value by people in relation to the significance of sustainability. People can ensure that the message for environmentally friendly projects will get through and provoke people to develop thriving, environmentally friendly plans.

Eco-friendly Digital Tools: Environmental adoption of appropriate digital technologies and applications is vital when embedding sustainability in artistry in the Metaverse and Web 3.0. Most digital art can be created with efficiency from the energy-efficient hardware and software that are friendly to the environment. Also, via creation people can encourage the utilization of green technologies so other people in the society will emulate the conduct of the artists.

Educating and Advocating for Sustainability: The Metaverse might also become education for sustainability and environmental protection with artists raising the awareness. That is why, using online meetings, presentations, and webinars artists can perform educational activities and inform about sustainability and environmentally friendly technologies, and the ecological footprint of works in the sphere of digital art. The information that can be derived from education, therefore, provides artists and audiences with authority to make sustainable choices regarding their arts.

Challenges to Address

Some paramount limitations can be identified, although there is great potential in the integration of sustainability into the growth of the Metaverse and Web 3.0. One of the most important criticisms of blockchain technology is related to energy consumption where Proof of Work systems consume significant amount of power. As a result, there is a need to consider carbon-neutral blockchain, solutions like

Proof of Stake, when developing these databases. Further, it is crucial to extend incentives for providing the usage of these technologies to various forms of artists and different backgrounds.

Consequently, the future of art in the Metaverse and the Web 3.0 has potential for including sustainability in the artistic systems in the digital environment. Using decentralized ownership, virtual exhibitions, collaborative projects, and environmentally friendly tools artists can build a more ethical, efficient and sustainable environment for their art. As these technologies continue to develop, artists, technologists, and other mobile technology stakeholders should ensure that the technologies that they help develop and bring into market are being used correctly and in a proper manner to be environmentally friendly and socially responsible. In individual terms this allows the art community to prosper while collectively assisting in the creation of a better world.

Explored policy-making, education, and digital art for change in contribution to more widespread engagement in sustainability practices.

A CROSS-SECTORAL APPROACH BY INTERSECTING POLICY-MAKING, EDUCATION, AND DIGITAL ART TO ENFORCE SUSTAINABILITY ACROSS THE POPULATION

These policy advances in partnership with education and digital art has a critical responsibility of enunciating sustainable practices among the artists. It is therefore important to create guidelines that will help artists while in the virtual environment promote sustainable practices. In this evaluation, the focus concerns the empirical proposal explaining how appropriate policies, educational approaches, and partnerships can enhance the implementation of sustainability in digital art practices.

The Role of Policy-Making

Policy making is the key to advancing sustainable practices in arts. They also can encourage some measures like providing subsidies on eco-friendly products, and helping artists change their techniques toward more sustainable ones. Key areas of focus for policy-makers include:

Funding and Grants for Sustainable Projects: State and municipal authorities and other public funding bodies can assign certain credits and/ or grants intended for sustainable practices in digital art. This financial support may help artists explore sustainable technologies which are energy efficient digital media and renewable energy for their practice spaces. Through allocation of resources where; artists are motivated to adopt environmental friendly approaches when formulating the subject matter of their projects, policy makers can ensure sustainability is incorporated by the artists.

Regulations on Digital Platforms: Since current digital art often presents works on the Internet, it is necessary that governments set up rules that help control its environmental impacts. This may involve a requirement for desirable efficiency levels in data centers, a requirement to use renewable electricity, and other waste reduction obligations placed on platform operators. Therefore, if governments and other policymakers enforce digital art platforms for certain commitments on sustainability, they can select an environment favorable for sustainable artistic practice.

Intellectual Property Protections: Because of the growing rates of one form of violation of values and uniqueness or the other within the domain of digital art, there has to be strong IPR systems in place. It will be the right time for the policy makers to pay attention on changing the laws related to copyright for executing it in new era digital artistry where its replicas are fashionably reproducible and distributable. Therefore, guidelines and protection of Digital artists can be extended through policies, which will in the process foster creativity in the development of art works without being breached by other people in the society.

Educational Initiatives

From the research, education seems to be the variable that has a massive impact in increasing the level of awareness of sustainable practices in the digital arts. Introducing sustainability as a key aspect into artists' education helps prepare them on how to handle the digital realm well. Key strategies for educational initiatives include:

Curriculum Development: It is very important for art schools and universities to establish programs that enthuse students to work within parameters of sustainability in digital art. These may range from courses in using sustainable technologies in computing, data stewardship, and effects of computer-generated art on the environment. However integrating sustainability into education system, institutions will be in a position to produce an generation of artists whom are conscious of environmental impacts in their artwork.

Workshops and Training Programs: Universities, colleges and other organizations can spew out courses and seminars regarding sustainable practice in digital art. Such concepts can range from efficient use of energy in homes and premises being built to usage of environmentally friendly materials and the moral questions arising from the sale of virtual artwork. This way, practicing artists are given opportunities to develop skills that will help them make specific changes towards becoming environmentally sustainably oriented artists.

Collaborative Learning Environments: Engagement of the students in collaboration with their teachers and other practitioners can improve learning outcomes.

The partnership with interdisciplinary collaborative projects that address sustainable issues means that learners can apply formulated ideas to create sustainable solutions to ecological issues within the concept of Digital Art. In involving experts in sustainability, technology, and in arts students are able to receive a comprehensive understanding of how they are able to adopt sustainable practices in the work they do.

Fostering Collaboration

For sustainable development, there have to be policymakers' interaction with educational institutions and the digital art society. This intersection can yield powerful outcomes, such as:

Public-Private Partnerships: Co-ordination between the governmental executive departments and the bodies of school and non-governmental organisations should encourage sustainability in case of digital artwork. These affiliations can help both with research, technology development or providing the visibility to artists as advocates of sustainable practices. In this case, using resources and knowledge from other sectors, the stakeholders play a different role of enhancing the improvement of sustainability.

Conferences and Forums: Conferences and forums to deliberate and discuss aspects in relation to sustainable practice in art created digitally is an event that could attract artworkers, educators, policymakers and other actors new to the new economy. To an extent these events can create awareness on best practice, new success cases and potential challenges in sustainable practice. When dialogues are encouraged, stakeholders are able to come up with policy measures as well as responding adequately to the best way through which sustainability in arts can be encouraged.

Advocacy and Awareness Campaigns: Group initiatives can create awareness of sustainability in digital art hence can promote the support of sustainability. As the specialists in creating appealing campaigns, combined with educators inculcating correct ideas into the population, and future policymakers thinking about sustainable actions, artists can enhance the change in society's perspective on sustainable action. These initiatives can involve and motivate the public and become a precondition for changing the identity of the artistic milieu toward eco-responsible practices.

Key areas of concern are policy, education, and new media art, whereby integrating these three areas of practice is fundamental in the creation of cultural awareness on sustainability in the art practice. When the authorities adopt a sustainable approach to the necessary process of supporting artists, the educational programs must be created and multifaceted cooperation between participants must be aimed to help artists to become more sustainable. While aiming at the future of the digital art, the factor that would bring the positive difference in supporting the art community would make a difference and in the same become a positive impact on the environment as well as the society in the achievement of sustainable goals. In this way, we are able to provide a develop fundament for further sustainable digital art phases in commitment.

THE ROLE OF SUSTAINABILITY IN BOTH; MATERIAL AND VIRTUAL ART.

At a time humanity is faced with very critical environmental issues the arts industry has a critical role to play on the subject. Blending sustainability principles across mixed conventional/creative and new media art is not only a choice we have but a need we must respond to regarding a more responsible, and ethic Arts worldwide. This summary will seek to detail why such integration is important, problems involved and the possibilities for artists, institutions and the viewers.

Why Sustainability Matters in Art

Environmental Impact: Traditional and the modern art especially digital art industry contributes highly to the environmental pollution. Most of the conventional art styles call for products that are very demanding in their production process, for instance oils, canvas, and thinners. Digital art on the hand, is generally seen as less threatening and damaging to the environment in comparison to graffiti, murals and other forms of street art, but it also share similar problematic as the use of energy resources for the maintenance of the servers and data storage as well as the creation of electronic waste. Thus it becomes important to seek ways of integrating sustainability aspecte into all kinds of art with an aim of mitigating on the impacts.

Cultural Responsibility: It is the time when artists were opinion makers of different threats in society, so, climate change and environmental issues need new artistic response. It can therefore, be utilised by the artists to create a causality that can advance the discourse on sustainability and help the masses think within. This cultural responsibility is not just for the artists themselves, but for museums, schools and spectators – turning it into a group effort for change.

Ethical Considerations: The art society is capable of changing people's perceptions and practices when it comes to sustainable usage. Because art represents an essential means of communication, artists involved in the ecological and socio-political concerns of the subject give an audience something to think about when pondering the issues of sustainable stewardship and the ethic of fair distribution of resources. But when these concepts participate in Critical discussions with art, there is the likelihood that the general perception shall be changed to embrace sustainable culture.

Sustainable Practices in Art: The Advantages

Innovation and Creativity: Being sustainable very much often means that artist are being creative in one or another way. Increasingly, artists are being able to experiment with materials and technologies that are environmentally friendly. It kind of allows for new kind of art that pushes boundaries and interests a different kind of audience. Sustainability can be used in a way to be inspiring instead of being constricting.

Community Engagement: Many of the art practices are sustainable in the sense that they involve working with people form the community thus creating a feeling of belonging. Along with community arts, education, and murals and other public art projects, artists can get the local community involved in the discussion of sustainability. This transforms an approach into a positive practice of art making but it also empowers communities which embrace in order to becoming Changers.

Long-Term Viability: The incorporation of sustainability into art practices will also improve the sustainability of art that is, the longevity of the field. Choosing environmentally friendly material and methods of work, artists and art institutions save money spent on wastes and resources. Furthermore, since the consumers wake up to the effects of the social issue s on the environment, they tend to spend their monies on the artists or organizations that are sensitive on social issues. This brought them into alignment with the consumptionist consumerist values, which can beg an economic model for the arts.

Challenges to Integration

In the adoption of sustainability in art, the integration carries certain challenges: Some of these challenges include:

Access to Resources: By using earth-friendly art, artists are likely to achieve this goal as anyone using traditional media has the disadvantage of lacking sufficient opportunities of accessioning sustainable materials. Organically produced materials are still more expensive or less easily accessible than the traditional ones depending on the available technologies for artists; this is a challenge for the artistic world.

Awareness and Education: Education of sustainable practices for both the traditional and digital forms of art need to be created a lots of awareness. The problem is that artists may not know which materials can be used or which are eco-friendly or even have information about economic impact or sustainability. There is a gap here that educational initiatives can fill in order to provide artists with tools to incorporate sustainability into their work.

Resistance to Change: The artists themselves may not like change and there may be traditions within the art world that are difficult for institutions to bypass. Some can view sustainability as some kind of trend that is as good as a fleeting trend and not something that artists have to incorporate into their work. This kind of resistance can only be managed through transforming the whole culture of the society where sustainability is adopted as a component and aspect of the art.

Opportunities for Integration

Despite these challenges, the integration of sustainability into traditional and digital art forms presents numerous opportunities:

Interdisciplinary Collaboration: The mentioned relationship between art, science and technology means that creative practical solutions for sustainability practices can emerge. Creative professionals can engage scientists, environmentalists, and technologists to achieve enhanced understandings of new materials and processes which are friendly to the environment. This can finish up in innovative projects where artists could inform the tough environmental inquiries, in addition to make artistic productions.

Digital Platforms for Sustainability: This is because virtual art provides an enabling environment for an economic model that supports sustainable sustainable practices in its exhibitions and engagements. It gives artists the opportunity to let people worldwide know their products and foster their understanding of sustainable living, including receiving feedback on their work. Through use of technology, artists are able to design work that evokes a particular response, especially in the form of action, while at the same encouraging people to think critically.

Policy Advocacy: There is scarce literature regarding how artists fit into the current plan of advocating for policies that encourage sustainability within arts. Using focusing technique to draw the public attention to environmental impacts of funding and the need to come up with environment-friendly systems for funding artists the government comes under pressure to consider sustainability when funding the arts apart from regulating the arts. This advocacy may result in systemization that may enhance the welfare of the whole fraternity of art.

Sustainability in traditional and new media art: Sustainability considerations are crucial to both, and dealing with environmental problems. Implemented in practice, artists stewardships challenge are consequently capable of promoting innovation, community involvement and ethical concerns with a view towards the aforesaid improvements in the art sphere. All the same, available opportunities in integration are enormous, and there is great potential for effecting tremendous change. As artists explore increased sustainability concerns, their contributions present generations with sustainable models and practices for life and the artistic world to instigate a sustainable future.

In the emerging field of digital art, there are at least four key tensions that are (or should be) driving artists and collectors alike: innovation, ecology, accessibility, and fair pay. In observing this, young artist begins using new technology to break barriers in their creations but in a way the society, ecology and humans themselves suffer consequences.

The art of the digital world seems to allow openings and provide the artists with the possibility to extend the practice and other challenges as for the form and the media. However, the factors, which contributed to negative impact to the environment like energy consumptions and electrical waste in terms of digital practices cannot be overlooked. There are recommended green practices, as used by artists and institutions they own, practices such as carbon and renewable energy. If the digital art community can encourage innovation that is mindful of its environmental impact, the art scene can find new ways of being sustainable and grow creatively at the same time.

Fostering Inclusivity

Another idea that has to be implemented when working within digital art is Diversity." However, there should always be provision for including different view points as the field grows. This inclusiveness is unfortunately for the artistic discourse but for the decentralization of digital art creation and consumption. skills stepper Artists from different fields backgrounds should be equal Interests and be given equal opportunity to revealing it through talents through performance regardless the certain barriers for instance social-economic status, Education levels or, Access to tools and equipment.

Fair Compensation

There are three ideas which, next to innovation and inclusion, should be considered for any society – reasonable fees for the artists. With a multitude of two digital platforms existing today, it becomes important to develop frameworks that will guarantee that artists get their deserved portion of what they create. This has, for instance, the goal of dealing with the most common problem in which platforms take a much larger share of the value generated and distributed than content providers get. Promoting just remuneration means the digital artists can help artists soon provide for themselves sufficiency while at the same time challenging their creativity.

Altogether, it is crucial for the prospect of digital art to maintain equal distances to innovation, environmental sustainability, integration of marginalised communities, and fair payment. By embracing such principles the community is on a no doubt trajectory to charting for a long and productive Lifelong future for the artists and all those that in one way or the other are involved in the art industry.

Encourages artists, consumers, institutions, and policymakers to respond effectively and collectively in the direction of a sustainable future of digital art.

NEW APPROACHES FOR COOPERATION TOWARD THE FUTURE OF DIGITAL ART

The future of digital art: complexities of sustaining the art world has never been more urgent than now. This call to action speaks to a need to have artists, consumers, institutions, and policymakers come together to encourage a more responsible and better digital art market.

Artists as Change Agents

Artists and performers remain one of the key agents defining sustainability discussions in the digital context. Incorporating sustainable measures at work and using avenues of environmentally conscious performances and themes, artists create a form of prompting their audience on personal consumption practices alongside the impact of their arts. This kind of cooperation may also provide workable solutions that allow creative use of space to address sustainable concerns while maintaining the artistic integrity of the intervention.

Consumer Responsibility

The extent of control that can be exercised by consumers on the digital art market is quite massive. Consumers can also promote the sustainability of art by patronizing artists practicing eco-consciousness, selecting platforms that are socially responsible as well as encouraging customers to demand pieces from artist who use earth's resources sustainably. This approach to art enables more proper treatment of its production process and encourages ecological initiatives amongst artists.

Institutional Support

Galleries, museums, as well as educational organisations need to advance environmentally friendly programmes in the digital art world. It means developing programmes that help artists become sustainable themselves, for example by supporting projects aimed at environmental protection, informing on environmentalism, and hosting artists who use environmentally oriented projects. Institutions can also arrange dialogues that present sustainable practices as the norm in arts to nudge the practices forward.

Policy Advocacy

Producers tend to join together with inventors that make frameworks that allow sustainability in the computerized art production processes. Through setting measures that enforce green procurement, safeguard inventions, and ensure fair remuneration, the members will be in a position to put up measures that will benefit artists and buyers. To ensure the that policies formulated meet the standards of artists, consumers and any other stakeholders it is important that the artists, consumers and policymakers cooperate.

REFERENCES

Banerjee, S. B. (2012). The artist as activist: Understanding the role of art in environmental sustainability. *The Journal of Social Issues*, *68*(4), 745–760. DOI: 10.1111/j.1540-4560.2012.01765.x

Banerjee, S. B. (2012). The artist as activist: Understanding the role of art in environmental sustainability. *The Journal of Social Issues*, *68*(4), 745–760. DOI: 10.1111/j.1540-4560.2012.01765.x

Bishop, C. (2012). *Artificial hells: Participatory art and the politics of spectatorship*. Verso.

Braidotti, R. (2013). *The posthuman*. Polity Press.

Cameron, F. (2015). The digital turn: A new paradigm for art and sustainability. *Journal of Visual Culture*, *14*(2), 157–174. DOI: 10.1177/1470412915580590

Cramer, H. (2018). Sustainable art: A reflection on the practices of artists in the context of environmental crisis. *Art Journal*, *77*(2), 54–67. DOI: 10.1080/00043249.2018.1486769

Cramer, H. (2018). Sustainable art: A reflection on the practices of artists in the context of environmental crisis. *Art Journal*, *77*(2), 54–67. DOI: 10.1080/00043249.2018.1455274

Eagleton, T. (2013). *The event of literature*. Yale University Press.

Foster, H. (2016). *Bad new days: Art, criticism, emergency*. Verso.

Gaudio, J. (2020). The digital canvas: How technology is transforming sustainable artistic practices. *International Journal of Art & Design Education*, *39*(3), 439–450. DOI: 10.1111/jade.12345

Gaudio, J. (2020). The digital canvas: How technology is transforming sustainable artistic practices. *International Journal of Art & Design Education*, *39*(3), 439–450. DOI: 10.1111/jade.12345

Grosz, E. (2017). *The incorporeal: Ontology, ethics, and the limits of materialism*. Columbia University Press. DOI: 10.7312/gros18162

Heathcote, E. (2016). The role of the artist in sustainable development. *Sustainability*, *8*(10), 966. DOI: 10.3390/su8100966

Houghton, R. (2019). *Art and ecology: A collection of essays on the relationship between art and the environment*. Routledge.

Houghton, R. (2019). *Art and ecology: A collection of essays on the relationship between art and the environment.* Routledge., DOI: 10.4324/9780429317267

Krauss, R. (2013). *Under blue cup.* MIT Press.

Kwon, M. (2015). *One place after another: Site-specific art and locational identity.* MIT Press.

Kwon, M. (2015). *One place after another: Site-specific art and locational identity.* MIT Press.

Lippard, L. R. (1997). *The lure of the local: Senses of place in a multicentered society.* New Press.

Lippard, L. R. (1997). *The lure of the local: Senses of place in a multicentered society.* New Press.

Manos, C. (2017). Eco-critical perspectives on digital art. *New Media & Society, 19*(6), 927–942. DOI: 10.1177/1461444816638555

Manos, C. (2017). Eco-critical perspectives on digital art. *New Media & Society, 19*(6), 927–942. DOI: 10.1177/1461444816675981

Mermoz, C. (2019). Sustainability and digital art: Transformative practices for a better future. *Art & Environment Journal, 1*(1), 15–29.

Mermoz, C. (2019). Sustainability and digital art: Transformative practices for a better future. *Art & Environment Journal, 1*(1), 15–29.

Pritchard, H. (2014). Digital art and sustainability: A dual approach. *International Journal of Digital Art, 2*(1), 23–36.

Rancière, J. (2009). *The emancipated spectator.* Verso.

Ritchie, S. (2020). Digital art and environmental responsibility: New pathways for sustainable practices. *International Review of Environmental Ethics, 12*(1), 25–42.

Ritchie, S. (2020). Digital art and environmental responsibility: New pathways for sustainable practices. *International Review of Environmental Ethics, 12*(1), 25–42.

Schneemann, N. (2010). *Correspondence: The color of the world in the digital age.* University of California Press.

Smith, J. (2016). The role of digital media in eco-conscious artistic practices. *Contemporary Art Review, 8*(3), 76–89.

Smith, J. (2016). The role of digital media in eco-conscious artistic practices. *Contemporary Art Review, 8*(3), 76–89.

Stewart, S. (2015). Art, ecology and the urban environment. *Environmental Arts Journal*, *3*(2), 34–45.

Thompson, N. (2017). *Seeing power: Art and activism in the 21st century*. The New Press.

Waldman, D. (2018). The eco-artist: A new paradigm for sustainable art. *Journal of Environmental Art*, *5*(1), 45–60.

Zywicki, J. (2016). Art and the digital: New forms of sustainability. *Digital Creativity*, *27*(2), 92–104. DOI: 10.1080/14626268.2016.1165805

Chapter 15
The Influence of Augmented Reality Advertisement on Customer Referral Engagement:
The Mediating Role of Perceived Originality

Thanh Phuc Nguyen
https://orcid.org/0000-0001-7137-8236
Faculty of Finance and Banking, Van Lang University, Ho Chi Minh City, Vietnam

Trang Thi-Thuy Duong
https://orcid.org/0009-0003-1052-0827
School of Media Design, University of Economics Ho Chi Minh City, Ho Chi Minh City, Vietnam

Nhi Ha Quynh Le
University of Economics, Ho Chi Minh City, Vietnam

ABSTRACT

This study investigates the impact of Augmented Reality (AR) advertisements on customer referral engagement through perceived originality using the Stimulus-Organism-Response framework. It explores how the interactivity, vividness, and novelty of AR ads influence consumers' perceptions and referral behaviors. This

DOI: 10.4018/979-8-3693-7610-2.ch015

study employs PLS-SEM analysis on data collected from 241 Vietnamese consumers. The results indicate that AR ad characteristics positively affect perceived originality, which, in turn, enhances referral engagement. The findings suggest that marketers should focus on enhancing the interactivity, vividness, and novelty of AR advertisements to maximize their impact. Future research could explore the long-term effects of AR advertisements on consumer behavior and the potential differences across various cultural contexts. This study contributes to the AR advertising literature, extends the SOR model to emerging technologies, and offers practical insights for marketers in designing effective AR ad campaigns.

1. INTRODUCTION

Augmented Reality (AR) has emerged as a powerful tool in the advertising industry, offering innovative ways to engage consumers and enhance brand experiences (Scholz & Smith, 2016). As businesses seek to differentiate themselves in an increasingly competitive marketplace, AR-based advertisements have gained significant attention for their potential to create unique and memorable interactions with customers (Yang, Carlson, & Chen, 2020). The integration of AR in advertising strategies has opened new possibilities for marketers to capture consumer attention, increase brand recall, and ultimately drive customer engagement (Smilansky, 2017).

Despite growing interest in AR-based advertising, research on its impact on consumer behavior, particularly in terms of perceived originality and customer referral engagement, remains limited. While studies have explored various applications of AR across the retail, tourism, and advertising sectors (Wei, 2019), there is a notable gap in our understanding of how AR advertisements influence consumers' perceptions of originality and their subsequent willingness to engage in referral behaviors. This knowledge gap is particularly significant given the importance of word-of-mouth marketing and customer referrals in the current digital age.

The current study aims to address this gap by investigating the relationship between AR-based advertisements and customer referral engagement, with a specific focus on the mediating role of perceived originality. By employing the stimulus-organism-response (S-O-R) theoretical framework, this study explores how the key characteristics of AR advertisements–interactivity, vividness, and novelty–impact consumers' perceptions of originality and, in turn, their referral engagement. The findings of this research contribute to the existing literature on AR advertising and provide valuable insights for marketers seeking to leverage AR technology to enhance customer engagement and referral behavior.

2. LITERATURE REVIEW

2.1. Augmented Reality Advertisement

Augmented Reality is the latest buzz in the advertising arena. Augmented reality (AR) has emerged as a significant technology in marketing and advertising, offering new ways to engage consumers and enhance brand experiences (Du, Liu, & Wang, 2022). Research in this field has grown rapidly in recent years, with studies exploring various applications across retail, tourism, and advertising sectors (Fan, Chai, Deng, & Dong, 2020; Wei, 2019; Yuen, Yaoyuneyong, & Johnson, 2011). AR advertising provides an interactive platform for consumer engagement, allowing users to access information on-demand and potentially circumventing traditional media clutter (Pacheco, Sánchez, Pariona, Cuba, & Larico, 2022). Studies have investigated AR's impact of AR on consumer behavior, technology adoption, and advertising effectiveness (Fan et al., 2020). However, knowledge gaps remain, particularly in understanding AR's long-term effects of AR on consumer behavior and its integration with other marketing strategies. As AR technology continues to evolve, further research is needed to fully understand its potential in marketing and advertising.

Augmented reality in advertising is most effective when used as an instrumental interaction, with telepresence playing a mediating role in perceived ad informativeness and brand liking (Tsai, Tian, Chuan, & Li, 2020). Moreover, augmented reality in advertising increases consumers' curiosity and attention, but only when they are unfamiliar with the technology (Yang et al., 2020). Augmented reality mobile app advertising positively influences consumer responses and purchase intentions, potentially increasing the effectiveness of traditional marketing approaches during competitive holiday periods. Augmented reality ads increase customer willingness to pay due to increased physiological arousal, but not self-reported affect intensity, compared to traditional paper-based ads.

2.2. S-O-R Theoretical Framework (Stimulus-Organism-Response)

According to the Stimulus-Organism-Response (S-O-R) theoretical framework (Russell & Mehrabian, 1974), external stimuli (Stimulus) from the environment impact an individual's internal cognitive and emotional states (Organism), which then influence the corresponding behavioral responses (Response). The S-O-R model has been widely applied in consumer behavior research in the high-tech, service, online retail, and tourism sectors (Abumalloh, Halabi, & Nilashi, 2025; Xiong, Luo, & Lu, 2023). Recent studies have employed this model to explain the factors affecting sustainable consumption intentions (Yu et al., 2024) or tourist loyalty (Nieves-Pavón, López-Mosquera, & Jiménez-Naranjo, 2023). The S-O-R model describes Stimulus (S) as external factors that influence individuals' psychological states and trigger reactions (Namkung et al., 2010). In digital contexts, technological and interactive elements (Animesh et al., 2011; Zhang, 2014) serve as stimuli affecting user experience. This study considers novelty, interactivity, vividness, and aesthetics of AR-based advertisements as key Stimulus factors.

Organism (O) refers to internal psychological responses provoked by the Stimulus. Prior research highlights perceived usefulness and value as common reactions (Sun & Zhang, 2006; Mack & Rogers, 1995). In advertising, perceived originality has been shown to increase user engagement (Pelet & Ettis, 2022), and thus represents the Organism in this study.

Response (R) is the resulting consumer behavior after being influenced by the Stimulus and internal processing. Since direct behavior is hard to observe, previous studies often use behavioral intention or ad acceptance as proxies (Zhang, 2014; Zeng et al., 2009). This research examines customer referral engagement as the Response.

However, the application of the S-O-R model in the context of AR-based advertisements has not been explored in depth. In this study, the authors constructed an integrated model based on the S-O-R framework to explore perceived originality as a novel mechanism for the impact of AR-based advertisements on customer referral engagement. Specifically, the model assumes that Stimulus factors (e.g., AR-based ads) impact internal states (e.g., perceived originality), which then leads to positive referral engagement from customers.

2.3. Research Hypotheses

The interactivity of AR advertisements positively influences perceived originality.

Interactive augmented reality (AR) advertising allows users to directly interact with the ad content, creating a unique and engaging experience (Scholz & Smith, 2016). The interactivity of AR ads stimulates active user participation, leading to perceptions of uniqueness and creativity (Feng & Xie, 2019). Sung (2021) demonstrated that the interactivity of AR ads creates an enjoyable experience, enhancing perceptions of originality. Similarly, Feng and Mueller (2019) found that the interactivity of AR ads leads to higher perceptions of originality and differentiation than traditional forms of advertising. This interactive nature of AR advertising sets it apart from conventional advertising methods, making it more memorable and impactful. As users engage with AR content, they are more likely to perceive the advertisement as innovative and cutting-edge. Consequently, this perception of originality can lead to increased brand recall and positive associations with the advertised product or service.

H1: The interactivity of AR advertisements positively influences their perceived originality.

The vividness of augmented reality (AR) advertising refers to the richness and intensity of sensory information presented to viewers, engaging multiple senses such as sight and sound to create a powerful and immersive experience (Brengman, Willems, & De Gauquier, 2022). Research indicates that vivid AR advertisements significantly enhance consumer perceptions, making products appear more unique and differentiated from competitors (Yim, Chu, & Sauer, 2017). This heightened sensory engagement not only captures attention but also fosters a deeper emotional connection with the brand. Furthermore, studies show that viewers tend to perceive these ads as more original and creative compared to traditional, less vivid formats (Yim et al., 2017). Consequently, the vividness of AR advertising plays a crucial role in shaping consumer attitudes and influencing purchase decisions, ultimately impacting brand loyalty and consumer engagement in a competitive marketplace.

H2: The vividness of AR advertisements positively influences perceived originality.

The novelty of augmented reality (AR) advertising is manifested through the use of innovative technology and creative presentation methods (Hopp & Gangadharbatla, 2016). By leveraging cutting-edge technology, AR ads deliver novel, stimulating, and surprising experiences that set them apart from traditional advertising methods (Scholz & Smith, 2016). Research indicates that the novelty of AR ads enhances perceptions of uniqueness and creativity, establishing a positive correlation between the newness of the ad format and perceived originality (Feng & Xie, 2019; Feng & Xie, 2018). This distinctive quality not only captivates audiences but also fosters a deeper engagement with the brand. Consequently, novel AR advertisements create a memorable impression compared to conventional forms of advertising, capturing attention and engaging audiences in ways that traditional media cannot. This unique combination of technological advancement, creative presentation, and the novelty factor positions AR advertising as a groundbreaking approach in the evolving landscape of marketing communications, ultimately influencing consumer perceptions and behaviors in a highly competitive market.

H3: The novelty of AR advertisements positively influences perceived originality.

The perceived originality of an advertisement is a crucial factor driving customer engagement and sharing (Pelet & Ettis, 2022). When customers view an ad as unique and creative, they are significantly more likely to share and recommend it to others, thereby amplifying its reach (Koslow, Sasser, & Riordan, 2006). Research conducted by van Esch et al. (2018) indicates that the perceived originality of an advertisement positively influences customers' intentions to share and recommend it, reinforcing the idea that originality is vital for effective marketing. Similarly, Nikolinakou and King (2018) found that perceived uniqueness directly drives customer referral behavior and sharing patterns. Therefore, advertisements that are perceived as original not only capture attention but also foster a strong motivation among customers to disseminate the message. This underscores the critical importance of originality in advertising, positioning it as a key factor in enhancing customer engagement and encouraging recommendations, ultimately contributing to the advertisement's success in a competitive marketplace.

H4: Perceived originality positively influences customer referral engagement.

The interactivity of augmented reality (AR) advertising significantly influences customer behavior by creating perceptions of originality, which in turn drives customer referral engagement. Yim et al. (2017) demonstrated that the interactivity of AR ads indirectly influences customers' sharing intentions through perceived originality, emphasizing the importance of engaging content in fostering consumer interest. Scholz and Smith (2016) argue that this interactivity fosters a unique experience that motivates customers to spread recommendations, thereby enhancing the advertisement's reach. Furthermore, Feng and Mueller (2019) confirmed the mediating role of perceived originality in the relationship between AR ad interactivity and customer engagement, indicating that a sense of novelty is crucial for effective communication. Thus, the creative and interactive nature of AR advertising enhances perceptions of originality, leading to increased customer engagement and sharing. This underscores the effectiveness of AR advertising as a compelling approach to influencing consumer behavior, as customers are more likely to interact with and share ads they perceive as original and unique, ultimately contributing to greater brand visibility and customer loyalty.

H5: Perceived originality mediates the effects of AR advertisements (interactivity) and customer referral engagement.

Vivid augmented reality (AR) advertising significantly impacts customer behavior by creating engaging and immersive experiences that enhance perceptions of originality, which in turn drives customer referral engagement. Yim et al. (2017) indicate that the vividness of AR ads indirectly influences sharing intentions through perceived originality, highlighting the importance of how vividness can transform consumer perceptions. McLean and Wilson (2019) argue that this vividness fosters a rich and unique experience, encouraging customers to disseminate information about the products they encounter. Furthermore, research by Arghashi and Yuksel (2022) confirmed the mediating role of perceived originality in the relationship between the vividness of AR ads and customer engagement, suggesting that customers are more likely to engage with ads that they find uniquely appealing. Thus, when AR ads present products in a vivid and interesting manner, they not only enhance the perceived uniqueness of those products but also motivate customers to recommend them to others. This dynamic effectively transforms customers into brand advocates, driving not only word-of-mouth marketing but also fostering a deeper emotional connection between consumers and brands. Ultimately, the ability of vivid AR advertising to capture attention and stimulate sharing behavior positions it as a powerful tool in modern marketing strategies, enhancing brand visibility and engagement in an increasingly competitive marketplace.

> H6: Perceived originality mediates the effects of AR advertisements (vividness) and customer referral engagement.

The novelty of augmented reality (AR) advertising significantly influences customer behavior by creating perceptions of originality, which drives customer referral engagement. Jessen et al. (2020) demonstrate that the novelty of AR ads indirectly influences sharing intentions through perceived originality, emphasizing the critical role that innovative content plays in capturing consumer interest. Lin, Yeo, and Lu (2024) further argue that the novelty of AR ads creates a distinctive and unique impression, encouraging customers to disseminate the advertisement to others and thereby enhancing its reach. Additionally, Hopp and Gangadharbatla (2016) confirmed the mediating role of perceived originality in the relationship between the novelty of AR ads and customer engagement, suggesting that originality acts as a catalyst for deeper interactions. As AR ads are perceived as innovative, customers are more likely to view them as unique, which increases their likelihood of engaging with the ads, sharing them, and referring the associated products or services to friends and family. This dynamic indicates that the innovative nature of AR advertising not only contributes to its perceived originality but also fosters a sense of excitement and interest among consumers. Ultimately, this motivation to interact with and share these advertisements enhances brand visibility and engagement, positioning AR advertising as a powerful tool in contemporary marketing strategies.

> H7: Perceived originality mediates the effects of AR advertisements (novelty) and customer referral engagement.

Figure 1 presents the proposed research model and hypotheses.

Figure 1. Theoretical research model

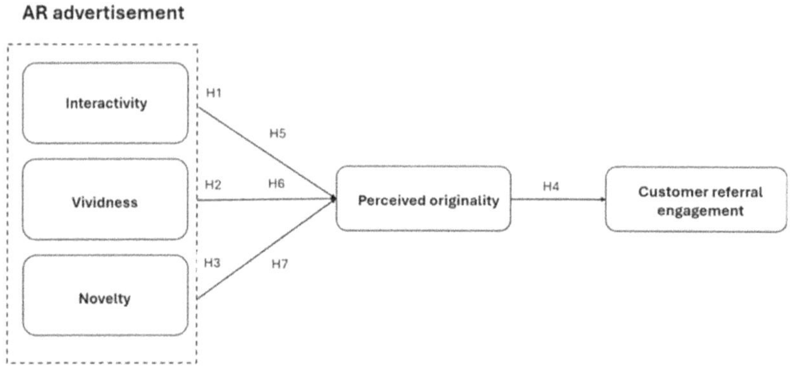

3. METHODOLOGY AND DATA

3.1. Measurement Scales

The study employed a 5-point Likert scale ranging from "strongly disagree" (1) to "strongly agree" (5) to measure seven constructs using 19 items. These measurement items were adapted from previous research, including studies by Gong and Park (2023) for interactivity, vividness, and novelty constructs; Kamleitner, Thürridl, and Martin (2019) for the perceived originality construct; and Pansari and Kumar (2017) for the customer referral engagement construct. The measurement model was assessed using SmartPLS 4 software, which confirmed the reliability and validity of the scale. The contents of each item are listed in Table 1. The analysis revealed that all constructs demonstrated satisfactory internal consistency, with Cronbach's alpha values exceeding the recommended threshold of 0.7. Convergent validity was established through average variance extracted (AVE) values greater than 0.5 for all constructs. Discriminant validity was confirmed using the Fornell-Larcker criterion and the heterotrait-monotrait (HTMT) ratio, ensuring that each construct was distinct from others in the model.

Table 1. Measurement model

Variables	Items	Sources
Interactivity - INTERA	**INTERA1:** I was able to control my navigation through this AR-based advertsement **INTERA2:** I was able to control part of the content of this AR-based advertisement that I wanted to see **INTERA3:** I was able to control the pace of viewing the piece through this AR-based advertisement **INTERA4:** This AR-based advertisement had the ability to meet my specific needs quickly and efficiently.	Gong and Park (2023)
Vividness - VIVID	**VIVID1:** The visual display through this AR-based advertisement was clear; **VIVID2:** The visual display through this AR-based advertisement was detailed; **VIVID3:** The visual display through this AR-based advertisement was vivid; **VIVID4:** The visual display through this AR-based advertisement was sharp;	Gong and Park (2023)
Novelty - NOVEL	**NOVEL1:** Using this AR-based advertisement features offers something new each time; **NOVEL2:** Using this AR-based advertisement offers unique information; **NOVEL3:** Using this AR-based advertisement is something different each time; **NOVEL4:** Using this AR-based advertisement offers specific contents.	Gong and Park (2023)
Perceived Originality - PO	**PO1:** This AR-based advertisement is novel **PO2:** This AR-based advertisement is original **PO3:** This AR-based advertisement is different	Kamleitner et al. (2019)
Customer Referral Engagement - CRE	**CRE1:** I promote the AR-based advertisement **CRE2:** The value derived from this AR-based advertisement encourage me to refer it to my friends and relatives. **CRE3:** I enjoy referring this AR-based advertisement to my friends and relatives. **CRE4:** Given that I use this this AR-based advertisement, I refer my friends and relatives to it.	Pansari and Kumar (2017)

3.2. Data Collection

The target demographic for this research comprises individuals aged 18 to 40, encompassing groups such as Generation Y, Generation Z, tech-savvy users, social media participants, online shoppers, and innovation-driven consumers. These segments were purposefully selected due to their strong relevance to the research objectives and their prominent engagement with the services under investigation.

The sample size is determined based on the recommendation of Hair et al. (1998), according to which the minimum sample size should be 10 times the total number of observed variables (ratio 10:1). In this study, there are 19 observed variables, therefore, the minimum sample size is 19 * 10 = 190. To ensure a higher correlation, the research team decides to set the sample size to 241 people.

A non-probability convenience sampling method was employed to reach participants, utilizing digital channels such as social media platforms, email, and online communities. This approach was selected for its practical benefits, particularly its ability to facilitate a rapid and cost-effective data collection process.

In addition to the online survey, an intercept sampling strategy was applied in physical retail environments. Researchers and two trained assistants positioned themselves at the entrances of shopping malls and supermarkets, systematically approaching every fifth visitor to solicit participation. Individuals who consented were given the chance to interact with augmented reality (AR)-based advertisements on their mobile devices, followed by a questionnaire evaluating their experience. To encourage participation, financial incentives were provided.

Of the total responses, 241 were gathered via the intercept method, ensuring a heterogeneous sample in terms of demographic and consumer behavior characteristics. To uphold data integrity, stringent screening criteria were enforced, and response quality was closely monitored. The dataset was subsequently analyzed using statistical software to uncover meaningful patterns and correlations, offering comprehensive insights into consumer attitudes toward AR-based advertising.

4. RESULTS AND DISCUSSIONS

This study involved 241 consumers, and nine questionnaires were excluded because of incomplete information. Table 1 presents the demographic breakdown of the sample. Among the 241 valid responses, males constituted 58.1% (140 participants). The age distribution showed that 36.1% (87) were 18-22 years old, 17.4% (42) were 23-30 years old, and 32.8% (79) were 31-40 years old. Regarding educational attainment, 2.5% (n = 6) had not completed a bachelor's degree, 74.7% (n = 180) held a bachelor's degree, and 22.8% (n = 55) had master's or doctoral degrees. The respondents spanned various industries, with Information Technology and Finance & Banking each representing 16.2%. Education and Hospitality followed, at 14.5% and 13.7%, respectively, while manufacturing (12%) and retail (12.4%) had similar representations. Healthcare comprised 10.8% of the sample, and 4.1% belonged to other sectors. This distribution underscores industry diversity, with a significant representation from the technology, finance, and service sectors. Regarding monthly income, 44.8% (108) earned less than 10 million VND, 16.6% (40) earned 10-20 million VND, 7.9% (19) earned 20-30 million VND, 22.4% (54) earned 30-40 million VND, and 8.3% (20) earned more than 20 million VND. Table 2 indicates that the distribution of demographic characteristics was appropriate.The income distribution reveals a significant income disparity among respondents, with nearly half earning less than 10 million VND monthly, while a smaller percentage earned over 30 million VND. This income variation may influence consumer behavior and purchasing decisions across different product categories. The diverse industry representation in the sample suggests that the study's findings could have broad applicability across various sectors of the Vietnamese economy.

Table 2. Demographic characteristics of samples (N = 241)

		Number	**Percent %**
Gender	Male	140	58.1%
	Female	101	41.9%
Age	18 to 22	87	36.1%
	23 to 30	42	17.4%
	31 to 40	79	32.8%
	Over 40	33	13.7%
Education	High school	6	2.5%
	College	15	6.2%
	University	165	68.5%
	Post-graduate	55	22.8%
Working area	Information Technology	39	16.2%
	Healthcare	26	10.8%
	Education	35	14.5%
	Finance & Banking	39	16.2%
	Manufacturing	29	12.0%
	Retail	30	12.4%
	Hospitality	33	13.7%
	Others	10	4.1%
Income	Less than 10 million VND	108	44.8%
	10 - 20 million VND	40	16.6%
	20 - 30 million VND	19	7.9%
	30 - 40 million VND	54	22.4%
	More than 40 million VND	20	8.3%

5. DATA ANALYSIS AND RESEARCH RESULTS

To assess the measurement model and confirm the structural model, the investigators employed partial least squares structural equation Modeling (PLS-SEM) using SmartPLS software (4.0) (Joseph F Hair Jr et al., 2021). The significance of the structural parameters was determined using a bootstrapping process involving 1,000 bootstrap samples.

To assess the measurement model and confirm the structural model, the investigators employed partial least squares structural equation Modeling (PLS-SEM) using SmartPLS software (4.0) (Joseph F Hair Jr et al., 2021). This approach is particularly suitable for complex models with multiple constructs and relationships, especially when the research is exploratory or an extension of an existing structural theory. PLS-SEM is known for its ability to handle small sample sizes and non-normal data distributions, making it a versatile choice for various research contexts. The use of SmartPLS 4.0 software indicates that the researchers utilized a modern and robust tool for their analysis, ensuring the application of up-to-date methodologies in their study.

The significance of the structural parameters was determined using a bootstrapping process involving 1,000 bootstrap samples. Bootstrapping is a resampling technique that allows researchers to assess the stability and reliability of their model estimates. By creating multiple subsamples from the original dataset, bootstrapping provides a non-parametric approach to estimate standard errors and confidence intervals for the model parameters. The use of 1,000 bootstrap samples is considered a robust approach, as it provides a sufficient number of iterations to generate reliable estimates of the sampling distribution of the parameters. This method enhances the validity of the results by accounting for potential sampling variability and providing more accurate assessments of the relationships between variables in the structural model.

5.1. Measurement Model Results

The initial phase of evaluating the structural model involves checking for significant collinearity among predictor constructs, which could lead to redundancy issues in the analysis. This was accomplished using a variance inflation factor (VIF). The predictor constructs of the research model all showed VIF values below the critical threshold of five, indicating no substantial multicollinearity problems.

The scale's reliability and validity assessment consisted of three stages: reliability testing, convergent validity, and discriminant validity (Joe F Hair Jr, 2020). The scale validation results indicated that all the scales were reliable, with Cronbach's alpha coefficients exceeding 0.7. Additionally, each scale's composite reliability (CR) exceeded 0.7, and the average variance extracted (AVE) was greater than

0.5. Furthermore, all observed variables exhibited factor loadings greater than 0.5. These findings demonstrate that the measurement scales satisfied the requirements for convergent validity (Table 3).

The scale validation process employed a comprehensive approach to ensure the robustness and accuracy of the measurement instruments. The three-stage assessment, encompassing reliability testing, convergent validity, and discriminant validity, provided a thorough evaluation of the scales' psychometric properties (Joe F Hair Jr, 2020). The results of this rigorous validation process were highly favorable, indicating that the scales met or exceeded the established criteria for reliability and validity.

The reliability of the scales was confirmed through multiple measures. Cronbach's alpha coefficients, which assess internal consistency, surpassed the widely accepted threshold of 0.7 for all scales, indicating strong reliability. This was further corroborated by the composite reliability (CR) values, which also exceeded 0.7, demonstrating the scales' ability to consistently measure their intended constructs. In terms of convergent validity, the average variance extracted (AVE) values surpassed 0.5, suggesting that the scales effectively captured the variance in their respective items. Additionally, the factor loadings of all observed variables were greater than 0.5, further supporting the scales' convergent validity. These comprehensive findings, as presented in Table 3, provide strong evidence for the measurement scales' reliability and validity, instilling confidence in their ability to accurately measure the intended constructs in the study.

Table 3. Measurement model results

Latent variables	**AVE**	**CR**	**α**	**Factor loadings**	**VIF**
Interactivity - INTERA	0.657	0.884	0.827		
INTERA1				0.81	1.898
INTERA2				0.776	1.658
INTERA3				0.857	1.874
INTERA4				0.796	1.724
Vividness - VIVID	0.634	0.874	0.807		
VIVID1				0.823	1.870
VIVID2				0.807	1.767
VIVID3				0.746	1.499
VIVID4				0.806	1.770
Novelty - NOVEL	0.645	0.879	0.817		
NOVEL1				0.784	1.783
NOVEL2				0.836	1.873

continued on following page

Table 3. Continued

Latent variables	AVE	CR	α	Factor loadings	VIF
NOVEL3				0.818	1.819
NOVEL4				0.772	1.609
Perceived Originality - PO	0.763	0.906	0.844		
PO1				0.843	1.847
PO2				0.908	2.497
PO3				0.868	2.048
Customer Referral Engagement - CRE	0.669	0.89	0.836		
CRE1				0.788	1.801
CRE2				0.841	1.837
CRE3				0.807	1.664
CRE4				0.836	2.070

The findings of the analysis show that the minimum square root of AVE (0.803) exceeds the maximum correlation value between pairs of latent variables (0.693), as shown in Panel A of Table 4. The HTMT values, ranging from 0.216 to 0.836, satisfy the criterion of being below 0.85, as illustrated in Panel B of Table 4. These results confirm the discriminant validity of the latent variables. Additionally, an examination of discriminant validity using cross-loadings revealed that these loadings corresponded appropriately with their intended constructs, as demonstrated in Panel C of Table 4.

The analysis results provide strong evidence for the discriminant validity of the latent variables in the study. The comparison between the square root of Average Variance Extracted (AVE) and the correlation values between latent variable pairs demonstrates that each construct is distinct from others. Specifically, the minimum square root of AVE (0.803) being greater than the maximum correlation value (0.693) indicates that each construct explains more variance in its own indicators than it shares with other constructs. This finding is further supported by the Heterotrait-Monotrait (HTMT) ratio analysis, where all values fall below the recommended threshold of 0.85, ranging from 0.216 to 0.836. These results collectively suggest that the constructs in the model are empirically distinct and capture unique phenomena.

Furthermore, the cross-loading examination provides additional confirmation of discriminant validity. The alignment of indicator loadings with their intended constructs, as shown in Panel C of Table 4, reinforces the notion that each indicator is more strongly associated with its designated construct than with others. This pattern of loadings indicates a clear separation between constructs and supports the overall construct validity of the measurement model. Together, these multiple approaches to assessing discriminant validity – comparing AVE square roots with correlations, evaluating HTMT ratios, and examining cross-loadings – offer a comprehensive and robust validation of the distinctiveness of the latent variables in the study, enhancing confidence in the structural integrity of the research model.

Table 4. Assessing discriminant validity: Fornell - Larcker Criterion

Panel A: Discriminant Validity- Fornell & Larcker					
	CRE	**INTERA**	**NOVEL**	**PO**	**VIVID**
CRE	0.818				
INTERA	0.357	0.810			
NOVEL	0.180	0.383	0.803		
PO	0.442	0.644	0.624	0.873	
VIVID	0.339	0.539	0.510	0.693	0.796
Panel B: Discriminant Validity- HTMT ratio					
	CRE	INTERA	NOVEL	PO	VIVID
CRE	1				
INTERA	0.422	1			
NOVEL	0.216	0.439	1		
PO	0.519	0.759	0.743	1	
VIVID	0.409	0.644	0.622	0.836	1
Panel C: Discriminant Validity- Cross-loadings					
	CRE	INTERA	NOVEL	PO	VIVID
CRE1	**0.788**	0.219	0.123	0.296	0.263
CRE2	**0.841**	0.344	0.164	0.418	0.322
CRE3	**0.807**	0.278	0.21	0.383	0.243
CRE4	**0.836**	0.315	0.075	0.332	0.277
INTERA1	0.324	**0.81**	0.199	0.438	0.362
INTERA2	0.178	**0.776**	0.315	0.483	0.379
INTERA3	0.331	**0.857**	0.469	0.631	0.545
INTERA4	0.318	**0.796**	0.21	0.503	0.428
NOVEL1	0.104	0.22	**0.784**	0.396	0.317
NOVEL2	0.124	0.347	**0.836**	0.552	0.43
NOVEL3	0.168	0.355	**0.818**	0.525	0.434
NOVEL4	0.175	0.286	**0.772**	0.506	0.438
PO1	0.344	0.558	0.574	**0.843**	0.528
PO2	0.413	0.542	0.571	**0.908**	0.65
PO3	0.4	0.588	0.491	**0.868**	0.632

continued on following page

Table 4. Continued

Panel A: Discriminant Validity- Fornell & Larcker					
	CRE	**INTERA**	**NOVEL**	**PO**	**VIVID**
VIVID1	0.316	0.498	0.391	0.597	**0.823**
VIVID2	0.284	0.43	0.399	0.531	**0.807**
VIVID3	0.284	0.431	0.394	0.536	**0.746**
VIVID4	0.19	0.349	0.444	0.537	**0.806**

5.2. Hypothesis Testing

The proposed hypotheses were evaluated using the SmartPLS software (version 4.0; Ringle et al., 2022). Table 5 presents the outcomes for the direct and moderating effects obtained while controlling for age, education, gender, income, and working area. The coefficients of determination for endogenous variables exceeded the 10% threshold, rendering them acceptable for this study (Miller and Falk, 1992). Perceived originality exhibits an R^2 value of 0.656, whereas customer referral engagement shows an R^2 value of 0.210, which are considered excellent and acceptable, respectively. The model's predictive relevance for each endogenous construct was assessed using Q^2 value (Hair, 2016). All endogenous constructs demonstrated Q^2 values substantially above zero (0.132 for customer referral engagement and 0.492 for perceived originality). Consequently, our research model exhibits strong explanatory power and predictive relevance for the endogenous constructs.

The evaluation of the proposed hypotheses using SmartPLS software (version 4.0) yielded significant insights into the model's explanatory power and predictive relevance. The coefficients of determination (R2) for the endogenous variables surpassed the 10% threshold, indicating their acceptability for the study (Miller and Falk, 1992). Notably, perceived originality demonstrated a robust R2 value of 0.656, while customer referral engagement exhibited an acceptable R2 value of 0.210. These results suggest that the model explains a substantial portion of the variance in perceived originality and an acceptable amount of variance in customer referral engagement.

To further assess the model's predictive capabilities, the Q2 value was employed to evaluate the predictive relevance for each endogenous construct (Hair, 2016). Both endogenous constructs displayed Q2 values considerably above zero, with customer referral engagement at 0.132 and perceived originality at 0.492. These findings indicate that the research model possesses strong predictive relevance for both constructs. The combination of high R2 values and substantial Q2 values provides compelling evidence for the model's robust explanatory power and predictive relevance, lending credibility to the study's findings and the relationships proposed in the hypotheses.

The results presented in Table 5 support Hypothesis 1, demonstrating that AR advertisement interactivity positively influences perceived originality (β = 0.333, t = 7.022). Additionally, the table indicates that AR advertisement novelty has a positive effect on perceived originality (β = 0.317, t = 5.787) and AR advertisement vividness positively impacts perceived originality (β = 0.351, t = 6.708), confirming Hypotheses 2 and 3. These findings suggest that AR-based advertising characteristics can enhance customers' perceptions of originality. The study also found that perceived originality positively affected customer referral engagement (β = 0.384, t = 4.234), supporting H4.

The results presented in Table 5 provide strong evidence for the positive impact of augmented reality (AR) advertisement characteristics on perceived originality and customer referral engagement. Specifically, the study found that AR advertisement interactivity, novelty, and vividness all contribute significantly to enhancing customers' perceptions of originality. The standardized coefficients (β) for these relationships range from 0.317 to 0.351, indicating moderate to strong positive effects. The t-values, all exceeding 5.7, further underscore the statistical significance of these findings. These results collectively support Hypotheses 1, 2, and 3, highlighting the potential of AR-based advertising to create unique and memorable experiences for consumers.

Furthermore, the study demonstrates that perceived originality plays a crucial role in driving customer referral engagement, as evidenced by the positive relationship between these variables (β = 0.384, t = 4.234). This finding, which supports Hypothesis 4, suggests that when customers perceive AR advertisements as original and innovative, they are more likely to engage in referral behaviors. This insight has important implications for marketers seeking to leverage AR technology to enhance word-of-mouth marketing and customer advocacy. The results underscore the importance of designing AR advertisements that are not only interactive and vivid but also novel, as these characteristics collectively contribute to perceptions of originality and, ultimately, to increased customer referral engagement.

The study outcomes revealed that perceived originality acts as a mediator between AR advertisement characteristics and customer referral engagement. Specifically, a significant positive mediating effect of perceived originality was observed between interactivity and customer referral engagement (β = 0.128, t-value = 3.394), leading to H5. Similarly, a significant positive mediating effect of perceived originality was found between novelty and customer referral engagement (β = 0.122, t-value = 3.911), thus confirming H6. Furthermore, the analysis showed a substantial positive mediating effect of perceived originality on the relationship between vividness and customer referral engagement (β = 0.135, t-value = 3.397), thus validating H7.

The study's findings highlight the crucial role of perceived originality in mediating the relationship between augmented reality (AR) advertisement characteristics and customer referral engagement. This mediation effect was observed across three key AR advertisement features: interactivity, novelty, and vividness. The results indicate that when customers perceive AR advertisements as original, they are more likely to engage in referral behaviors. Interactivity, which allows users to manipulate and interact with the AR content, was found to enhance perceived originality, which in turn positively influenced customer referral engagement. Similarly, the novelty of AR advertisements, representing their uniqueness and innovation, also contributed to increased perceived originality and subsequent referral engagement.

The study further revealed that vividness, which refers to the richness and depth of the AR experience, had the strongest mediating effect through perceived originality on customer referral engagement. This suggests that AR advertisements that provide a more immersive and realistic experience are more likely to be perceived as original, leading to higher levels of customer engagement and willingness to refer the product or service to others. These findings underscore the importance of designing AR advertisements that not only leverage the technology's capabilities but also focus on creating original and engaging experiences that resonate with customers. By doing so, businesses can potentially enhance word-of-mouth marketing and increase customer acquisition through referrals.

Table 5. Results of hypothesis testing

Hypothesis	Estimates	Beta	std.	t-stat	p-value	Results
	Direct effect					
H1	INTERAC → PO	0.333	0.047	7.022	0.000	Supported
H2	NOVEL → PO	0.317	0.055	5.787	0.000	Supported
H3	VIVID → PO	0.351	0.052	6.708	0.000	Supported
H4	PO → CRE	0.384	0.091	4.234	0.000	Supported
	Mediating effects					
H5	INTERAC → PO → CRE	0.128	0.038	3.394	0.001	Supported
H6	NOVEL → PO → CRE	0.122	0.031	3.911	0.000	Supported
H7	VIVID → PO → CRE	0.135	0.040	3.397	0.001	Supported
	Control variables					
	AGE → CRE	-0.072	0.073	0.983	0.326	Insignificant
	EDUCATION → CRE	0.064	0.074	0.876	0.381	Insignificant
	GENDER → CRE	0.007	0.063	0.115	0.908	Insignificant
	INCOME → CRE	0.073	0.070	1.046	0.296	Insignificant
	WORKING AREA → CRE	0.058	0.053	1.090	0.276	Insignificant

The primary results of the PLS test are displayed in Figure 2, including the path coefficients (β), significance levels (p-values), and outer model (t-values). All statistical analyses employed a 5% significance threshold, which was determined using a two-tailed t-test.

Figure 2. PLS analysis results

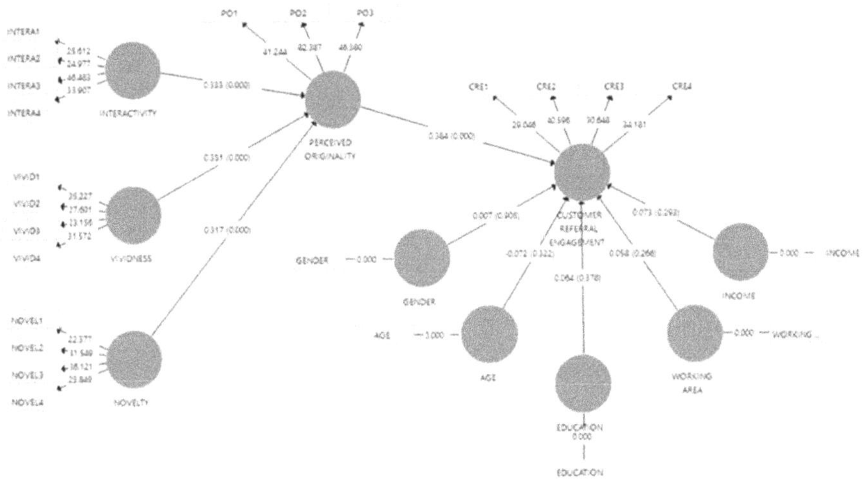

4.3. Robustness Check

To validate the direct influence of AR advertisement features on perceived originality and the mediating role of perceived originality as previously mentioned, we utilized The PROCESS macro for SPSS (Model 4) as a method to ensure robustness. As shown in Table 6, the outcomes demonstrate that the connections between the research constructs remained consistent, indicating the reliability of the previously stated findings.

The validation process employed the PROCESS macro for SPSS (Model 4) to rigorously examine the direct impact of AR advertisement features on perceived originality and its mediating role. This sophisticated statistical approach allowed for a comprehensive analysis of the relationships between the research constructs, providing a robust foundation for the study's findings. The results, as presented in Table 6, revealed a consistent pattern of connections among the variables, reinforcing the reliability of the previously reported outcomes.

This consistency in the relationships between constructs across different analytical methods strengthens the overall validity of the research. It demonstrates that the observed effects of AR advertisement features on perceived originality, as well as the mediating role of perceived originality, are not artifacts of a particular statistical approach but rather represent genuine phenomena within the context of AR advertising. Such robustness in findings enhances the credibility of the study's conclusions and provides a solid basis for future research and practical applications in the field of AR-based marketing strategies.

Table 6. Direct and mediation effect using process macro

Hypothesis	Paths	Effect	95% bootstrap confidence interval		Results
			LLCI	ULCI	
	Direct effect				
H1	INTERAC → PO	0.622	0.512	0.732	Confirmed
H2	NOVEL → PO	0.619	0.051	0.730	Confirmed
H3	VIVID → PO	0.6283	0.5338	0.7227	Confirmed
H4	PO → CRE	0.318	0.168	0.468	Confirmed
H5	Mediating effects				
H6	INTERAC → PO → CRE	0.198	0.100	0.302	Confirmed
H7	NOVEL → PO → CRE	0.298	0.204	0.392	Confirmed
H8	VIVID → PO → CRE	0.225	0.105	0.341	Confirmed

6. FINDINGS AND DISCUSSION

Although the literature contains many studies on AR-based integration into products or services, very few consider the outcome of AR advertisements and the underlying mechanism through which AR advertisements may have an impact on this outcome. Based on the Stimulus-Organism-Response (S-O-R) model framework, this study provides empirical evidence of the relationship between the typical dimensions of AR advertisements and outcome variables (i.e., customer referral engagement), as well as the mediation effect of perceived originality. The findings indicate that the interactivity, novelty, and vividness of AR advertisements significantly positively impact the perception of originality and, hence, the customer's referral engagement. These results hold across econometric treatments such as PLS-SEM and PROCESS Macro-Hayes.

The findings indicate that the interactivity of AR advertisements positively affects their perceived originality. This aligns with previous research by Yim et al. (2017), who suggest that the interactivity of augmented reality advertising can enhance consumer interest and perceptions of novelty. Additionally, Arghashi and Yuksel (2022) highlighted that interactivity in AR advertising enhances user engagement and experience, leading to a more unique perception of the advertised product or service.

The positive impact of AR advertisement interactivity on perceived originality can be attributed to several factors. Firstly, the immersive nature of AR technology allows users to engage with advertisements in a more dynamic and personalized manner. This heightened level of engagement creates a sense of novelty and uniqueness, as consumers can interact with virtual elements seamlessly integrated into their real-world environment. The ability to manipulate and explore AR content in real-time provides a stark contrast to traditional static advertisements, contributing to the perception of originality.

Furthermore, the interactivity of AR advertisements often involves elements of gamification and user-driven exploration, which can enhance the overall user experience. This interactive approach not only captures attention but also creates memorable experiences that stand out in consumers' minds. As users actively participate in shaping their advertising experience through AR interactions, they develop a stronger emotional connection to the content, reinforcing the perception of originality. Additionally, the technological sophistication of AR advertisements may contribute to their perceived innovativeness, as consumers associate cutting-edge technology with originality and forward-thinking brands.

The study also revealed that the novelty of AR advertisements positively influenced perceived originality. This finding is consistent with Sundar and Kalyanaraman (2004), who suggested that novel stimuli tend to capture attention and leave a stronger impression. In the context of advertising, the novelty of AR technology can increase the perceived originality of the advertised product or service (Hopp & Gangadharbatla, 2016).

The study's findings on the positive influence of AR advertisement novelty on perceived originality align with broader research on consumer behavior and advertising effectiveness. The novelty effect in AR advertisements can be attributed to the technology's ability to create unique, immersive experiences that stand out from traditional advertising methods. This distinctiveness not only captures attention but also enhances the memorability of the advertised product or service, potentially leading to increased brand recall and consumer engagement.

Furthermore, the relationship between novelty and perceived originality in AR advertising has implications for marketing strategies and product positioning. As consumers are increasingly exposed to AR technology in various contexts, marketers may need to continually innovate their AR advertising approaches to maintain the novelty effect. This could involve developing more sophisticated AR experiences, integrating AR with other emerging technologies, or finding creative ways to apply AR in unexpected product categories or advertising contexts. However, it is important to note that while novelty can enhance perceived originality, the effectiveness of AR advertisements likely depends on a balance between novelty and relevance to the consumer's needs and interests.

These results further indicate that the vividness of AR advertisements has a positive effect on perceived originality. This aligns with the findings of Kim, Kim, Park, and Yoo (2021), suggesting that the vividness of AR technology enhances consumers' experience and perception of the advertised product or service. Johnson (2022) highlighted that the vividness of AR can create unique and differentiated experiences, increasing the appeal and memorability of the advertised product or service.

The study also demonstrates that perceived originality positively influences customer referral engagement. This finding is consistent with Helkkula, Kelleher, and Pihlström (2012), who suggested that people tend to value and share unique and differentiated experiences. When customers perceive originality in a product or service, they are more likely to share and recommend it to others (Cheema & Kaikati, 2010).

The study's findings on the positive relationship between perceived originality and customer referral engagement have significant implications for marketing strategies and consumer behavior. When customers encounter products or services they perceive as original or unique, they are more inclined to engage in word-of-mouth marketing and actively recommend these offerings to their social circles. This behavior can be attributed to the psychological satisfaction derived from sharing novel experiences and the desire to be seen as knowledgeable or trendsetting within one's social network.

Furthermore, the connection between perceived originality and referral engagement underscores the importance of innovation and differentiation in today's competitive marketplace. Companies that successfully create and communicate the originality of their offerings may benefit from increased customer advocacy, potentially leading to organic growth through referrals. This phenomenon not only enhances brand visibility but also contributes to building a loyal customer base that actively participates in promoting the brand. As such, businesses may find it advantageous to invest in developing truly original products or services and effectively communicating their unique value propositions to capitalize on this customer-driven marketing potential.

The study also revealed a significant positive mediating role of perceived originality in the relationship between the interactivity of AR advertisements and customer referral engagement. This is consistent with the findings of Scholz and Smith (2016), who suggest that the interactivity of AR technology can create unique experiences, leading to higher customer engagement and sharing.

The study's findings underscore the pivotal role of perceived originality in mediating the relationship between AR advertisement interactivity and customer referral engagement. This relationship can be explained by the unique and novel experiences that interactive AR advertisements provide to consumers. When users encounter AR advertisements that allow them to actively engage with the content, manipulate virtual objects, or personalize their experience, they are more likely to perceive these advertisements as original and innovative. This perception of originality, in turn, motivates customers to share their experiences with others, thereby increasing referral engagement.

Furthermore, the positive mediating effect of perceived originality aligns with broader marketing theories that emphasize the importance of novelty and uniqueness in capturing consumer attention and driving engagement. Interactive AR advertisements not only provide functional benefits but also create memorable and shareable experiences. As consumers increasingly seek out novel and exciting brand interactions, AR technology offers a powerful tool for marketers to differentiate their offerings and create buzz-worthy content. This finding suggests that businesses investing in AR advertising should focus on developing highly interactive and original experiences to maximize customer referral engagement and potentially benefit from word-of-mouth marketing.

The results also indicate a significant positive mediating effect of perceived originality on the relationship between the novelty of AR advertisements and customer referral engagement. This aligns with the research by Yim et al. (2017), which suggests that the novelty of AR technology can create unique and memorable experiences, encouraging customers to share and recommend to others.

The significant positive mediating effect of perceived originality on the relationship between AR advertisement novelty and customer referral engagement underscores the importance of creating unique and memorable experiences in marketing. AR technology's ability to offer novel interactions with products or brand messages can enhance consumers' perceptions of originality, leading to increased engagement and a higher likelihood of sharing their experiences with others. This finding extends beyond mere novelty, suggesting that when consumers perceive AR advertisements as original and innovative, they are more inclined to become brand advocates through referrals.

Furthermore, this relationship highlights the potential of AR as a powerful tool for word-of-mouth marketing in the digital age. As consumers encounter AR advertisements that they perceive as original, they may feel compelled to share these experiences with their social networks, effectively amplifying the reach and impact of the marketing message. This cascade effect can lead to increased brand awareness, customer acquisition, and potentially higher conversion rates. The study's findings thus provide valuable insights for marketers seeking to leverage AR technology in their advertising strategies, emphasizing the need to focus not just on technological novelty, but on creating perceptions of originality that resonate with target audiences and inspire sharing behaviors.

Finally, the study revealed the significant positive mediating role of perceived originality in the relationship between the vividness of AR advertisements and customer referral engagement. This finding is consistent with research by McLean and Wilson (2019), which suggests that the vividness of AR technology can create unique and engaging experiences, prompting customers to share and recommend to others.

The study's findings underscore the pivotal role of perceived originality in bridging the gap between the vividness of augmented reality (AR) advertisements and customer referral engagement. This relationship highlights the power of AR technology to create distinctive and immersive experiences that captivate consumers. When AR advertisements are perceived as vivid and original, they are more likely to leave a lasting impression on viewers, encouraging them to share their experiences with others. This cascade effect can significantly amplify the reach and impact of marketing campaigns, as satisfied customers become brand advocates through word-of-mouth referrals.

Moreover, the positive mediating effect of perceived originality aligns with broader trends in consumer behavior and marketing psychology. In an era of information overload and advertising saturation, consumers are increasingly drawn to novel and authentic experiences. AR advertisements that successfully leverage vividness to create a sense of originality can cut through the noise of traditional marketing channels. This uniqueness not only enhances the immediate appeal of the advertisement but also increases the likelihood that consumers will engage in referral behaviors, such as recommending the product or service to friends and family or sharing their experiences on social media platforms. As such, marketers and advertisers should focus on developing AR content that not only showcases products effectively but also delivers an original and memorable experience to maximize customer engagement and referral potential.

7. IMPLICATIONS AND LIMITATIONS

7.1. Theoretical Implications

Based on the findings of the current study, several theoretical implications can be drawn. First, it extends the application of the stimulus-organism-response (S-O-R) theoretical framework to the context of augmented reality (AR) advertising. By demonstrating how AR advertisement characteristics (stimulus) influence perceived originality (organism) and ultimately customer referral engagement (response), this study provides a novel perspective on how the SOR model can be applied to emerging technologies in marketing. Additionally, this study identifies and validates three key characteristics of AR advertisements - interactivity, vividness, and novelty - as significant factors influencing consumer perceptions and behaviors. This contributes to a more nuanced understanding of the specific elements of AR technology that drive consumer responses in the advertising context.

Furthermore, this research introduces perceived originality as a crucial mediating factor between AR advertisement characteristics and customer referral engagement. This highlights the importance of originality perceptions in shaping consumer responses to AR advertising, and provides a new theoretical lens through which to examine the effectiveness of AR-based marketing strategies. By linking AR advertisement characteristics to established consumer behavior concepts, this study bridges the gap between technological innovation and consumer psychology, offering a more comprehensive theoretical framework for understanding how emerging technologies influence consumer decision-making processes. These findings also contribute to word-of-mouth marketing theory by demonstrating how AR technology can drive customer referral engagement, thus expanding our understanding of the antecedents of word-of-mouth behavior in digital and technologically enhanced marketing environments.

This research not only introduces perceived originality as a crucial mediating factor between AR advertisement characteristics and customer referral engagement but also underscores its significance in shaping consumer responses to AR advertising. By doing so, it provides a novel theoretical perspective for examining the effectiveness of AR-based marketing strategies. The study's approach of linking AR advertisement characteristics to established consumer behavior concepts bridges the gap between technological innovation and consumer psychology, offering a more comprehensive theoretical framework for understanding the influence of emerging technologies on consumer decision-making processes.

Furthermore, these findings make a substantial contribution to word-of-mouth marketing theory by demonstrating how AR technology can drive customer referral engagement. This expands our understanding of the antecedents of word-of-mouth behavior in digital and technologically enhanced marketing environments. The research not only highlights the potential of AR in creating engaging and shareable advertising experiences but also provides insights into how marketers can leverage this technology to encourage customer referrals and amplify their marketing efforts. By exploring the relationship between AR, perceived originality, and referral behavior, this study paves the way for future research on the intersection of immersive technologies and consumer engagement in the evolving landscape of digital marketing.

7.2. Managerial Implications

The findings highlight the importance of leveraging the key characteristics of augmented reality (AR) advertisements to enhance customer engagement and referral behavior. Marketers should focus on developing AR advertisements that are highly interactive, vivid, and novel to increase perceived originality and drive customer referrals. Specifically, interactivity should be prioritized by designing AR ads that allow users to actively engage with and manipulate virtual content through features such as gesture control, voice commands, or touch-based interactions. Vividness and novelty can be achieved by creating visually striking and innovative AR experiences using high-quality 3D models, realistic textures, and advanced lighting effects to make virtual objects appear more lifelike.

The findings underscore the critical role of leveraging augmented reality (AR) advertisements' key characteristics to enhance customer engagement and referral behavior. Marketers should prioritize developing AR advertisements that are highly interactive, vivid, and novel to increase perceived originality and drive customer referrals. Interactivity should be emphasized by designing AR ads that enable users to actively engage with and manipulate virtual content through features like gesture control, voice commands, or touch-based interactions. Vividness and novelty can be achieved by creating visually striking and innovative AR experiences using high-quality 3D models, realistic textures, and advanced lighting effects to make virtual objects appear more lifelike.

To further enhance the effectiveness of AR advertisements, marketers should consider incorporating personalization and contextual relevance into their campaigns. By leveraging user data and real-time environmental information, AR ads can be tailored to individual preferences and seamlessly integrated into the user's surroundings. This approach can significantly increase the ad's relevance and impact, leading to higher engagement rates and more positive brand associations. Additionally, marketers should explore the potential of social sharing features within AR experiences, allowing users to easily capture and share their interactions with the virtual content across various social media platforms. This not only amplifies the reach of the AR campaign but also taps into the power of social proof and word-of-mouth marketing, further driving customer referrals and brand awareness.

To maximize the impact of AR advertising, companies should consider integrating AR ads into broader marketing campaigns, encouraging social sharing by incorporating easily shareable features, continuously innovating to maintain novelty and appeal, and implementing robust analytics to measure and optimize user engagement, sharing behavior, and conversion rates. These strategies can help create a cohesive brand experience, amplify reach through organic promotion, and refine AR experiences over time to drive perceived originality and customer referrals effectively.

By strategically implementing these recommendations, marketers can harness the power of AR advertising to create unique, memorable experiences that not only engage customers but also motivate them to share and refer brands to others. This approach can lead to increased brand awareness, customer loyalty, and ultimately improve business performance in an increasingly competitive digital landscape.

7.3. Limitation

The current study has limitations that may impact the generalizability of findings. The relatively small sample size of 241 participants, collected through intercept method at shopping malls and supermarkets in Vietnam, introduces potential selection bias and geographical constraints. The cross-sectional design limits examination of causal relationships and long-term effects of AR advertising on customer behavior. The narrow focus on AR advertisements may not capture the full range of AR applications in marketing, while reliance on self-reported measures could introduce response bias. The absence of a control group or comparison with traditional advertising methods complicates isolating specific effects of AR technology. These limitations underscore the need for future research to address these constraints and provide insights into AR advertising's impact across diverse contexts.

To address these limitations and enhance future research on AR advertising, several methodological improvements can be implemented. Expanding the sample size and diversifying sampling beyond shopping malls would increase population representativeness. This could involve multi-stage sampling across various regions of Vietnam and demographic groups. Incorporating a longitudinal design would allow examination of causal relationships and long-term effects of AR advertising on customer behavior, by tracking participants' responses and analyzing changes in purchasing patterns and brand perceptions.

Future studies could benefit from mixed-methods research, combining quantitative surveys with qualitative interviews to gain deeper insights into consumers' AR advertising experiences. Including a control group exposed to traditional advertising would enable comparative analysis. To mitigate response bias, researchers could use objective measures like eye-tracking or neuroimaging to complement self-reported data. Expanding the study scope to include various AR marketing applications would provide comprehensive understanding of AR's impact. Replicating the study across different cultural contexts and product categories would enhance finding generalizability and contribute to understanding AR advertising's effectiveness in diverse markets.

REFERENCES

Abumalloh, R. A., Halabi, O., & Nilashi, M. (2025). The relationship between technology trust and behavioral intention to use metaverse in baby monitoring systems design: Stimulus-Organism-Response (SOR) theory. *Entertainment Computing*, *52*, 100833. DOI: 10.1016/j.entcom.2024.100833

Arghashi, V., & Yuksel, C. A. (2022). Interactivity, Inspiration, and Perceived Usefulness! How retailers' AR-apps improve consumer engagement through flow. *Journal of Retailing and Consumer Services*, *64*, 102756. DOI: 10.1016/j.jretconser.2021.102756

Barhorst, J. B., McLean, G., Shah, E., & Mack, R. (2021). Blending the real world and the virtual world: Exploring the role of flow in augmented reality experiences. *Journal of Business Research*, *122*, 423–436. DOI: 10.1016/j.jbusres.2020.08.041

Brengman, M., Willems, K., & De Gauquier, L. (2022). Customer engagement in multi-sensory virtual reality advertising: The effect of sound and scent congruence. *Frontiers in Psychology*, *13*, 747456. DOI: 10.3389/fpsyg.2022.747456 PMID: 35386898

Cheema, A., & Kaikati, A. M. (2010). The effect of need for uniqueness on word of mouth. *JMR, Journal of Marketing Research*, *47*(3), 553–563. DOI: 10.1509/jmkr.47.3.553

Du, Z., Liu, J., & Wang, T. (2022). Augmented reality marketing: A systematic literature review and an agenda for future inquiry. *Frontiers in Psychology*, *13*, 925963. DOI: 10.3389/fpsyg.2022.925963 PMID: 35783783

Fan, X., Chai, Z., Deng, N., & Dong, X. (2020). Adoption of augmented reality in online retailing and consumers' product attitude: A cognitive perspective. *Journal of Retailing and Consumer Services*, *53*, 101986. DOI: 10.1016/j.jretconser.2019.101986

Feng, Y., & Mueller, B. (2019). The state of augmented reality advertising around the globe: A multi-cultural content analysis. *Journal of Promotion Management*, *25*(4), 453–475. DOI: 10.1080/10496491.2018.1448323

Feng, Y., & Xie, Q. (2018). Measuring the content characteristics of videos featuring augmented reality advertising campaigns. *Journal of Research in Interactive Marketing*, *12*(4), 489–508. DOI: 10.1108/JRIM-01-2018-0027

Feng, Y., & Xie, Q. (2019). Ad creativity via augmented reality technology in online video ads: The differential role of novelty, message usefulness, and ad-consumer association. *Journal of Promotion Management*, *25*(6), 907–933. DOI: 10.1080/10496491.2018.1536624

Gong, T., & Park, J. (2023). Effects of augmented reality technology characteristics on customer citizenship behavior. *Journal of Retailing and Consumer Services*, *75*, 103443. DOI: 10.1016/j.jretconser.2023.103443

Hair, J. F.Jr. (2020). Next-generation prediction metrics for composite-based PLS-SEM. *Industrial Management & Data Systems*, *121*(1), 5–11. DOI: 10.1108/IMDS-08-2020-0505

Hair, J. F.Jr, Hult, G. T. M., Ringle, C. M., Sarstedt, M., Danks, N. P., & Ray, S. (2021). *Partial least squares structural equation modeling (PLS-SEM) using R: A workbook*. Springer Nature. DOI: 10.1007/978-3-030-80519-7

Helkkula, A., Kelleher, C., & Pihlström, M. (2012). Practices and experiences: Challenges and opportunities for value research. *Journal of Service Management*, *23*(4), 554–570. DOI: 10.1108/09564231211260413

Hopp, T., & Gangadharbatla, H. (2016). Novelty effects in augmented reality advertising environments: The influence of exposure time and self-efficacy. *Journal of Current Issues and Research in Advertising*, *37*(2), 113–130. DOI: 10.1080/10641734.2016.1171179

Jessen, A., Hilken, T., Chylinski, M., Mahr, D., Heller, J., Keeling, D. I., & de Ruyter, K. (2020). The playground effect: How augmented reality drives creative customer engagement. *Journal of Business Research*, *116*, 85–98. DOI: 10.1016/j.jbusres.2020.05.002

Johnson, K. (2022). Examination of the Advantages of Augmented and Virtual Reality in Marketing Content.

Kamleitner, B., Thürridl, C., & Martin, B. A. (2019). A Cinderella story: How past identity salience boosts demand for repurposed products. *Journal of Marketing*, *83*(6), 76–92. DOI: 10.1177/0022242919872156

Kim, J.-H., Kim, M., Park, M., & Yoo, J. (2021). How interactivity and vividness influence consumer virtual reality shopping experience: The mediating role of telepresence. *Journal of Research in Interactive Marketing*, *15*(3), 502–525. DOI: 10.1108/JRIM-07-2020-0148

Koslow, S., Sasser, S. L., & Riordan, E. A. (2006). Do marketers get the advertising they need or the advertising they deserve? Agency views of how clients influence creativity. *Journal of Advertising*, *35*(3), 81–101. DOI: 10.2753/JOA0091-3367350306

Lin, H.-F., Yeo, B., & Lu, T.-Y. (2024). How Virtual Mirrors in Advertising Influence Attitudes about Beauty Products: Consumer Viewing Perspectives, Beautification, And Endorsement in AR Advertising. *Journal of Advertising Research*, *64*(3), 372–392. DOI: 10.2501/JAR-2024-016

McLean, G., & Wilson, A. (2019). Shopping in the digital world: Examining customer engagement through augmented reality mobile applications. *Computers in Human Behavior*, *101*, 210–224. DOI: 10.1016/j.chb.2019.07.002

Miller, N., & Falk, R. F. (1992). A review of structural equation modeling procedures in reading research. In West, M. D. (Ed.), *Statistical issues in reading research* (pp. 99–122). Ablex Publishing.

Nieves-Pavón, S., López-Mosquera, N., & Jiménez-Naranjo, H. (2023). The factors influencing STD through SOR theory. *Journal of Retailing and Consumer Services*, *75*, 103533. DOI: 10.1016/j.jretconser.2023.103533

Nikolinakou, A., & King, K. W. (2018). Viral video ads: Examining motivation triggers to sharing. *Journal of Current Issues and Research in Advertising*, *39*(2), 120–139. DOI: 10.1080/10641734.2018.1428247

Pacheco, A., Sánchez, K., Pariona, R., Cuba, N., & Larico, B. (2022). Augmented Reality as an Emerging Technology to Promote Products and Services. *Augmented Reality and Its Application*, 185.

Pansari, A., & Kumar, V. (2017). Customer engagement: The construct, antecedents, and consequences. *Journal of the Academy of Marketing Science*, *45*(3), 294–311. DOI: 10.1007/s11747-016-0485-6

Pelet, J.-É., & Ettis, S. A. (2022). Social media advertising effectiveness: The role of perceived originality, liking, credibility, irritation, intrusiveness, and Ad destination. [IJTHI]. *International Journal of Technology and Human Interaction*, *18*(1), 1–20. DOI: 10.4018/IJTHI.2022010106

Russell, J. A., & Mehrabian, A. (1974). Distinguishing anger and anxiety in terms of emotional response factors. *Journal of Consulting and Clinical Psychology*, *42*(1), 79–83. DOI: 10.1037/h0035915 PMID: 4814102

Scholz, J., & Smith, A. N. (2016). Augmented reality: Designing immersive experiences that maximize consumer engagement. *Business Horizons*, *59*(2), 149–161. DOI: 10.1016/j.bushor.2015.10.003

Smilansky, S. (2017). *Experiential marketing: A practical guide to interactive brand experiences*. Kogan Page Publishers.

Sundar, S. S., & Kalyanaraman, S. (2004). Arousal, memory, and impression-formation effects of animation speed in web advertising. *Journal of Advertising*, *33*(1), 7–17. DOI: 10.1080/00913367.2004.10639152

Sung, E. C. (2021). The effects of augmented reality mobile app advertising: Viral marketing via shared social experience. *Journal of Business Research*, *122*, 75–87. DOI: 10.1016/j.jbusres.2020.08.034

Tsai, W.-H. S., Tian, S. C., Chuan, C.-H., & Li, C. (2020). Inspection or play? A study of how augmented reality technology can be utilized in advertising. *Journal of Interactive Advertising*, *20*(3), 244–257. DOI: 10.1080/15252019.2020.1738292

van Esch, P., Arli, D., Castner, J., Talukdar, N., & Northey, G. (2018). Consumer attitudes towards bloggers and paid blog advertisements: What's new? *Marketing Intelligence & Planning*, *36*(7), 778–793. DOI: 10.1108/MIP-01-2018-0027

Wei, W. (2019). Research progress on virtual reality (VR) and augmented reality (AR) in tourism and hospitality: A critical review of publications from 2000 to 2018. *Journal of Hospitality and Tourism Technology*, *10*(4), 539–570. DOI: 10.1108/JHTT-04-2018-0030

Xiong, Z., Luo, L., & Lu, X. (2023). Understanding the effect of smart tourism technologies on behavioral intention with the stimulus-organism-response model: A study in Guilin, China. *Asia Pacific Journal of Tourism Research*, *28*(5), 449–466. DOI: 10.1080/10941665.2023.2246598

Yang, S., Carlson, J. R., & Chen, S. (2020). How augmented reality affects advertising effectiveness: The mediating effects of curiosity and attention toward the ad. *Journal of Retailing and Consumer Services*, *54*, 102020. DOI: 10.1016/j.jretconser.2019.102020

Yim, M. Y.-C., Chu, S.-C., & Sauer, P. L. (2017). Is augmented reality technology an effective tool for e-commerce? An interactivity and vividness perspective. *Journal of Interactive Marketing*, *39*(1), 89–103. DOI: 10.1016/j.intmar.2017.04.001

Yu, S., Zhang, H., Zheng, Q., Chu, D., Chen, T., & Chen, X. (2024). Consumer behavior based on the SOR model: How do short video advertisements affect furniture consumers' purchase intentions? *BioResources*, *19*(2), 2639–2659. DOI: 10.15376/biores.19.2.2639-2659

Yuen, S. C.-Y., Yaoyuneyong, G., & Johnson, E. (2011). Augmented reality: An overview and five directions for AR in education. [JETDE]. *Journal of Educational Technology Development and Exchange*, *4*(1), 11. DOI: 10.18785/jetde.0401.10

Chapter 16
The Influence of Coffee Packaging Integrated With AR on Brand Coolness:
The Sài Gòn Culture Project From ArtTech Fusion 2024

Pham Thi Thao Quyen
https://orcid.org/0009-0007-8095-6895
School of Media Design, Vietnam

Nguyen Minh Tri
School of Media Design, Vietnam

Pham Cong Thai
School of Media Design, Vietnam

ABSTRACT

Augmented Reality (AR) has emerged as an essential tool for marketers and brand managers to initiate their branding strategies. Despite an increasing attention and its potential in the foreseeable future, both scholars and researchers still have a feeble understanding of this tool in how it improves brand variables, particularly brand coolness. Therefore, the aim of this study is to find out the relationship between AR and brand coolness, based on experience economy theory with the support of Meta Spark Studio. We made a marker-based AR product and exhibited it in the Sài Gòn Culture project launched by ArtTech Fusion 2024. Findings show that aesthetics is dominating all the realms in the theory and brand coolness is influenced by enter-

DOI: 10.4018/979-8-3693-7610-2.ch016

tainment and escapism, which is a precursor for brand sustainability. Meanwhile, the project also reflects that AR can be utilized to sustain the cultural heritage in Ho Chi Minh city, especially Vietnamese coffee.

1. INTRODUCTION

1.1. Background

Augmented Reality (AR) has gained significant global traction. According to Statista (2024), the AR market currently generates an estimated $32.1 billion annually, with 1.4 billion active user devices worldwide. Projections indicate a compound annual growth rate (CAGR) of 10.77% through 2028, underscoring AR's expanding role in consumer engagement. Vietnam, aligning with this trend, has seen rising AR adoption in the fast-moving consumer goods (FMCG) sector, particularly in coffee packaging. While global brands like Oreo and Milo have pioneered AR campaigns in Vietnam (e.g., interactive nutrition guides via QR codes), domestic brands are also leveraging AR to bridge cultural heritage with modern technology. For instance, Trung Nguyen Legend launched a 2023 AR campaign enabling users to scan coffee packages for virtual tours of Saigon's historic landmarks, resulting in a 30% surge in social media engagement (VietnamNet, 2023). Similarly, Vinacafe incorporated AR animations depicting traditional coffee rituals, enhancing brand authenticity among younger demographics (Pham et al., 2023). Despite limited academic research on AR's local impact, industry reports highlight Vietnamese consumers' growing receptiveness to AR experiences, especially Generation Z (Nielsen Vietnam, 2023). These efforts demonstrate how AR not only boosts brand awareness but also fosters cultural pride- a critical driver of brand coolness in Vietnam's competitive market. To maximize AR's potential, marketers must prioritize contextually relevant content that resonates with local values.

1.2. Gaps

Augmented reality (AR) is defined as " a real-time direct or indirect view of a physical real-world environment that has been enhanced/augmented by adding virtual computer-generated information to it" (Carmigniani, J. (2011)). Due to its functions and applications, AR has been classified into six different categories (Edwards-Stewart, A., Hoyt, T., & Reger, G. (2016)). This paper focuses on the category called "Marker-based AR" through the support of Meta Spark Studio to make AR filters on Facebook and Instagram. We concentrate on this classification due to the fact that Vietnamese brands have constantly exploited those platforms to target the mass audience. However, it is noticeable that marketers do not fully understand how to take advantage of AR to improve branding due to lack of research and findings.

Additionally, the theory of experience economy proposed by Pine and Gilmore (1998) delineates four motives that inspire customer engagement in AR experiences. Those motives consist of: esthetics, entertainment, education and escapism (Pine and Gilmore (1998). In our literature, this framework is strongly discussed in the field of tourism, mobile applications and interface. Few research investigates the implications of this framework on marketing and branding. It is imperative for this study to fill in this gap. Furthermore, it is still questionable about the role of four motives in this framework as "Divergent perspectives exist regarding the positioning of the four realms" (Amanah, D. M. N., Putri, N. K., & Aini, N. (2023)). Previous research agreed to the term that esthetics is of essence to predispose the other realms (Sung, 2020; and tom Dieck et al., 2018). Irrespective of its context, more papers are necessary to examine this assumption.

Coolness is a subjective evaluation (Caleb, 2019). Most brands initially become cool within a specific niche or subculture before later being discovered, adopted, and christened as cool by a broader audience (Belk, Tian, and Paavola 2010; Gladwell 1997). Using AR to relive the culture into the physical products may be considered as "cool" by the general public (Rodrigues, M. D. O. B. (2020)). However, the influence of AR products on brand coolness still remains unclear.

1.3. Statement

Based on experience economy theory, this study highlights the influence of AR package - coffee product dyads on brand coolness through four different motives. An empirical model integrates five theoretical concepts, including esthetics, entertainment, education, escapism and brand coolness, with the last one being the outcome of this appraisal. The specific objectives of this study are (1) to examine the effect of esthetics on three other concepts of the theory; (2) to investigate relationships between the experience economy theory and brand coolness.

1.4. Contribution

Theoretically, there is a need to further understand the relationship between the experience economy theory and brand coolness in order to apply four motives in launching brand campaigns. This study also contributes to the literature of experience economy by expanding its disciplines towards marketing and branding. Moreover, our work highlights the possible antecedents of brand coolness in view of AR package, which is particularly helpful for scholars to integrate both concepts and have a deep insight into brand coolness and its precursors. From the managerial perspective, our framework is useful for the marketers to determine which factors are vital for their campaign success regarding augmented reality usage. From this point, marketers will know how to make their brands cool through using AR packages in their products as well as other campaigns involving AR.

2. LITERATURE REVIEW

2.1. Experience Economy Theory

Customer experience is a new approach in marketing research philosophy, which is derived from the 'experience economy' model. Pine and Gilmore (1998) suggested a new kind of economy that engaged in experience, which is extracted from the service-based model. Using the 'progression of economics value' principle, there are four stages of evolution in economy: 'commodities (fungible), goods (tangible), services (intangible) and experiences (memorable)' (Pine and Gilmore, 1998). Among these progression stages, Pine and Gilmore (1998) claimed that the experience stage is made up more of personal characteristics which will develop in the memory of a person who has been involved in the events that they can connect to at an emotional, physical, intellectual, or spiritual level.

There are four dimensions suggested by Pine and Gilmore (1998) that are entertainment, educational, ecstatic and escapist. By applying this theoretical framework to the current study, these experiences with AR would drive consumer engagement with an AR-promoted brand or product.

Figure 1. The four realms of an experience

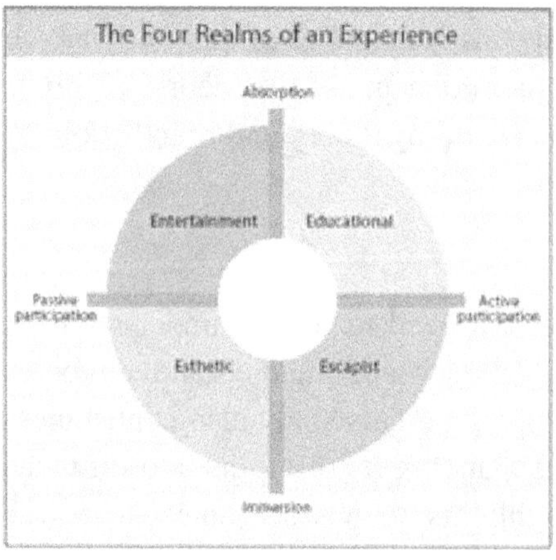

2.2.1. Esthetics and Entertainment

Aesthetics are crucial in interface technology development, determining whether consumers will embrace or reject new technology (Pallud & Straub, 2014). Augmented reality, with its visually captivating presentation, is expected to enhance experiences by providing enjoyable interactions (Romano et al., 2021). The role of visual appeal and design elements in augmented reality ads that enhance user engagement and enjoyment, positively impacting the entertainment experience within the experience economy (Johanna Siilvennoine, 2014). Initial impressions based on aesthetics can positively influence users' perceptions of a product's usefulness and pleasure (Jung et al., 2018). In addition, engaging with various 3D products can also bring joy to consumers (Kim et al., 2007; Yim et al., 2012). Based on the preceding literature review, the following hypotheses are examined:

H1: Esthetics influence positively on Entertainment

2.1.2. Esthetics and Education

Sudarmanto & Ismail (2023) highlights the potential of AR and metaverse concepts in enhancing aesthetic education in Indonesia. By integrating aesthetic elements into educational content, AR can make learning more engaging and visually appealing, helping students to visualize and understand complex concepts in a more tangible way. In higher education, aesthetics is recognized as crucial for developing critical thinking, artistic expression, and problem-solving skills (Süzen, 2020). This is because AR is thought to boost consumer curiosity (McLean & Wilson, 2019; Yang et al., 2020) by creating visual representations of products and spark consumer's imagination. Additionally, a well-crafted AR application can accurately and clearly convey information (Lee et al., 2015). Considering the literature reviewed, the following hypothesis is tested:

H2: Esthetics influence positively on Education

2.1.3. Esthetics and Escapism

As one component of the experience economy, escapism requires high consumer engagement (Pine and Gilmore, 2011). AR offers short-lived, immersive forms of escape from everyday life, allowing consumers to project backwards and forwards in time through remembering and imagining (Preece & Skandalis, 2023). In this vein, initial impressions derived from the aesthetic aspects can induce users to judge the usefulness or joyfulness of the product (Lee et al., 2015). If an application is poorly designed, it is unlikely to deliver the immersive experiences necessary for users to feel a sense of escape from their reality (Jung et al., 2018).

H3: Esthetics influence positively on Escapism

2.2. Relationship Between Experience Economy Theory and Brand Coolness

Brand coolness is a modern marketing concept that reflects a brand's ability to maintain an aura of authenticity, originality, and desirability that resonates with consumers. (Caleb Warren, et al, 2019).

2.2.1. Esthetics and Brand Coolness

When it comes to aesthetics, there's a clear connection to brand coolness. Aesthetics, the branch of philosophy dealing with the nature of beauty and taste, is crucial in forming the first impression of a brand. This visual and sensory appeal can significantly enhance a brand's coolness by aligning with the tastes and preferences of the target audience. (avail marketing, 2023*)* A well-designed product or service that appeals to the aesthetic sensibilities of consumers can elevate a brand's status, making it appear 'cool' and distinct and original(Suh and Chang, 2006).

H4: Esthetics influence positively on Brand coolness

2.2.2. Entertainment and Brand Coolness

Entertainment is another pillar that can bolster brand coolness. In the context of the experience economy, entertainment is about engaging customers in a way that is enjoyable and memorable. Brands that successfully integrate entertainment into their offerings often find that this engagement translates into a perception of coolness (Saman Attiq, et al, 2022). Whether it's through immersive experiences, engaging storytelling, or interactive elements, entertainment can create a strong emotional connection with the brand, enhancing its coolness factor.

H5: Entertainment influence positively on Brand coolness

2.2.3. Education and Brand Coolness

Education, though perhaps less obvious than entertainment or aesthetics, also plays a role in brand coolness. Brands that educate their consumers, not just about their products but about relevant social issues, industry innovations, or even lifestyle choices, can position themselves as thought leaders. This educational aspect can enhance the brand's coolness by demonstrating a commitment to the betterment of their audience and society (Bault, N., & Rusconi, E. (2020)).

H6: Education influences positively on Brand coolness

2.2.4. Escapism and Brand Coolness

Lastly, escapism is a significant aspect of brand coolness in the experience economy. Brands that offer an escape from the mundane, whether through adventurous experiences, exclusive communities, or innovative products, tap into the consumer's desire for novelty and excitement. This form of escapism can greatly enhance a brand's coolness by providing consumers with the opportunity to step outside their everyday lives and engage with something extraordinary.

H7: Escapism influence positively on Brand coolness

Figure 2. The conceptual framework

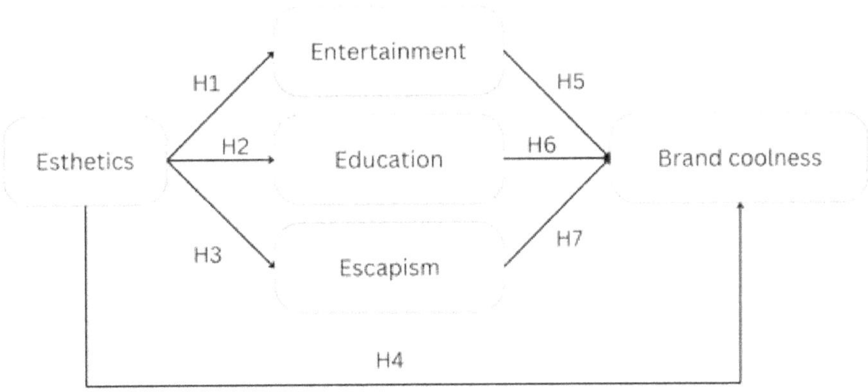

The literature review highlights that AR's influence on brand coolness is mediated through four experience economy realms—esthetics, entertainment, education, and escapism. Notably, while esthetics enhances user engagement, it does not directly contribute to brand coolness; instead, entertainment and escapism emerge as stronger predictors of perceived brand appeal. In the context of Vietnam, AR adoption is gaining momentum, particularly in consumer markets, but localized insights into user behavior and cultural nuances remain limited. This underscores the need for region-specific research to tailor AR strategies that align with Vietnam's unique socio-cultural landscape and evolving consumer preferences.

2.3 Challenges and Barriers to AR Adoption in Vietnamese Product Packaging

While augmented reality (AR) presents significant opportunities for enhancing brand engagement and cultural storytelling in product packaging, its implementation in Vietnam faces several notable challenges. First, technological limitations remain a barrier, as not all consumers possess smartphones or devices capable of supporting advanced AR applications (Nguyen & Le, 2022). The diversity in device quality and internet connectivity, especially in rural areas, can restrict the reach and effectiveness of AR campaigns (Statista, 2023). Second, consumer awareness and familiarity with AR technology are still developing. Although younger, urban consumers may be more receptive, a large portion of the population is either unaware of AR's capabilities or hesitant to engage with unfamiliar digital experiences (Nielsen Vietnam, 2023). This gap in digital literacy can reduce the overall impact of AR-integrated packaging and necessitates accompanying educational or promotional efforts by brands. Third, cost considerations pose a significant hurdle for many Vietnamese companies, particularly small and medium-sized enterprises (SMEs). The development, deployment, and maintenance of AR content require specialized skills and investment, which may not be feasible for brands with limited marketing budgets (Vietnam Investment Review, 2023). Furthermore, ongoing updates and technical support are necessary to ensure AR experiences remain functional and relevant, adding to the long-term costs. Finally, there are regulatory and privacy concerns related to data collection and user consent, as AR applications often require access to cameras and personal data. Addressing these challenges is crucial for brands seeking to leverage AR in Vietnam's competitive FMCG sector, and future research should explore strategies for overcoming these barriers to maximize the potential of AR-enhanced packaging.

3. METHODOLOGY

3.1. AR-Product Creation

With the idea of applying AR technology to the project, the team used Metaspark as the main design tool. With its easy-to-use integrated tools, the team successfully developed an interactive model that can be released on Metaverse platforms, including Facebook and Instagram, helping to reach a wide range of target audiences. Meta Spark Studio also features an integrated statistics tool that can evaluate the results and reach of the product. Our task here is to create a sustainable souvenir that is attractive and can recall travelers about the experience they had in Vietnam. Hence, we create an AR package that the AR effect appears with Saigan coffee culture if you scan.

Figure 3. The process of making AR packages

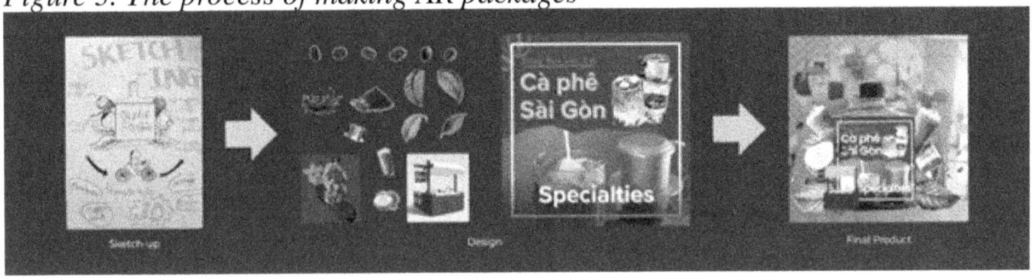

3.1.1 Flowchart

AR Creation→Data Collection (ArtTech Fusion 2024+Surveys)→PLS-SEM Analysis.

3.2. Sampling and Data Collection

First of all, our product was exhibited at ArtTech Fusion 2024 with the attendance of both local and international visitors. This chance gave us time to observe the reactions of the attendees and have a conversation with them. Subsequently, we used Google Form to have the quantitative data to examine the relationships of those aforementioned variables from 09/04/2024 to 11/04/2024. After the elimination, we collected 118 questionnaires. The socio demographic was depicted in Table 1.

Table 1. The socio demographic data of the respondents

Gender	
Male	55.9%
Female	44.1%
Age	
18 - 22	81.4%
23 - 27	16.1%

continued on following page

Table 1. Continued

> 27	2.5%
Living area	
Ho Chi Minh city	90.7%
Other provinces	9.3%
Occupation	
Students	70.3%
Media and communication	12.7%
Other jobs	17%

3.3. Measurement

The online questionnaire included two main parts. The first part was to collect the sociodemographic data of the respondents (age, genders,...). The second part was devoted to conceptual model constructs: esthetics, entertainment, education, escapism and brand coolness. The measurement scales were based on the literature. Four constructs of experience economy theory were adapted from Sung, E. (2020). Brand coolness was assessed with five items adopted from Raptis et al. (2017). A five-point Likert scale was used for all the measurement items. The measurement items are presented in Table 4.

3.4. Data Analysis

We assessed the measurement model and then the structural model. The software SmartPLS version 4.0.9.8 was employed to perform two analyses: the PLS-SEM Algorithm focusing on outer loading, and Bootstrapping.

In assessing the measurement model, we evaluated the validity of observable variables through outer loading (Hair et al., 2017). SmartPLS 4 provided three coefficients for estimating the internal consistency reliability of the scale: Cronbach's alpha, Composite reliability rho_a, and Composite reliability rho_c (CR). Following the suggestion of Hair et al. (2017), we focused on two coefficients: Cronbach's alpha and Composite reliability rho_c. Convergent validity was assessed using the average variance extracted (AVE) indicator, with the significance level set at 5%. To determine the discriminant validity, the Fornell-Larcker criterion and Heterotrait-Monotrait (HTMT) ratios were used.

When it comes to assessing the structural model, we utilized the variance inflation factor (VIF) to identify multicollinearity (Hair et al., 2019). To validate the hypotheses, we used the analysis results of path coefficients in two aspects: (1) Examining the relationship among variables by evaluating the p-value and (2) Evaluating the strength and direction of the relationship using Original Sample and f-square (Effect size). Finally, R-Square was employed to represent the proportion of the variance for a dependent variable that's explained by an independent variable.

4. RESULTS AND DISCUSSION

4.1. Common Method Bias

In our questionnaire, an useful tactic to eliminate unauthentic and unreliable questionnaires was that we put a question "If you are still filling the form, please choose number 2". This helped us eliminate unauthentic questionnaires

When it comes to assessing the structural model, we utilized the variance inflation factor (VIF) to identify multicollinearity (Hair et al., 2019). All inner VIF values were recorded in the range between 1.299 and 2.757 (see Figure 4 in the Appendix for more details), being lower than the specified critical benchmark of 5.00 (Hair et al., 2011). Therefore, our research seemed not to suffer a severe issue of multicollinearity.

Table 2. Assessing the reliability and convergent validity

Constructs	Cronbach's α	CR (rho_c)	AVE
Esthetics	0.785	0,852	0,536
Entertainment	0.755	0,859	0,670
Education	0.729	0,847	0,648
Escapism	0.887	0,922	0,748
Brand coolness (BC)	0.724	0,845	0,645

Table 3. Assessing the discriminant validity

Constructs	1	2	3	4	5
Panel A: Fornell - Larcker Criterion					
1. Brand coolness	**0.732**				
2. Education	0.609	**0.819**			
3. Entertainment	0.593	0.622	**0.805**		
4. Escapism	0.603	0.560	0.465	**0,865**	

continued on following page

Table 3. Continued

Constructs	1	2	3	4	5
5. Esthetics	0.572	0.553	0.577	0.466	**0.803**
Note. Bold main diagonal components: The square root of AVEs					
Below main diagonal components: The correlation among constructs					
Panel B: Heterotrait-Monotrait					
1. Brand coolness					
2. Education	0.770				
3. Entertainment	0.771	0.828			
4. Escapism	0.685	0.685	0.584		
5. Esthetics	0.732	0.733	0.776	0.581	

Table 4. Assessing the outer loadings of the reflective items per variable

Constructs	Items	Loadings
Esthetics	1. The AR advertising experience was very attractive. 2. The AR advertising experience was very pleasant 3. I felt a real sense of harmony from the AR advertising experience	0.874 0.785 0.746
Entertainment	1. The AR advertising experience was amusing. 2. The AR advertising experience was entertaining. 3. The AR advertising experience was fun.	0.816 0.809 0.789
Education	1. I learned new promoted product information during the AR advertising. 2. The AR experience made me more knowledgeable about the product/brand. 3. The AR experience stimulated my curiosity to learn about the new promoted product	0.814 0.846 0.795
Escapism	1. I felt I was playing a different character while using the AR app to watch the ad. 2. I felt like I was living in a different time or place while watching the AR app ad. 3. The AR experience let me imagine being someone else. 4. I completely escaped from reality while watching the AR app advertising	0.884 0.809 0.889 0.829
Brand coolness	1. This AR-coffee package dyad is simple to use 2. This AR-coffee package dyad provides the services as promised 3. This AR-coffee package dyad is original 4. This brand is glamorous 5. This brand fits my personality	0.712 0.765 0.625 0.771 0.776

4.2. Measurement Model

4.2.1. The Reliability and Convergent Validity

As seen in Table 2, the composite reliability, which was a measure of construct reliability, witnessed figures in the range from 0.847 to 0.922, much higher than the cut-off figure of 0.70 (Nunnally & Bernstein, 1944). It was relatively worth mentioning that Cronbach's alpha figures were also beyond the threshold level of reliability (0.70) (DeVellis, 2012). Hence, this measurement model is reliable. Besides, all the constructs had AVE figures higher than the satisfactory figure of 0.50 (Hock & Ringle, 2010), which confirmed sufficient convergent validity of the measurement model.

4.2.2. The Discriminant Validity

Regarding Table 3, Fornell-Larcker criterion and Heterotrait-Monotrait (HTMT) ratios were used to determine discriminant validity. The square root of AVE for each construct was found to be greater than its correlations with other constructs (Fornell & Larcker, 1981). The HTMT ratios were less than the required threshold of 0.85 (Henseler, et al., 2015). As shown in Panel A, we discovered that all figures of AVE captured in the square root form (in the range between 0.732 and 0.865) were considerably larger than the correlation scores amongst the constructs (ranging from 0.465 to 0.622), indicating that all variables had a good sign of discriminant validity. In addition, as reported in Panel B, the HTMT ratios for all pairs of latent constructs in the range of 0.581 - 0.828 were below the suggested benchmark of 0.9 (Henseler, et al., 2015), suggesting that all examined constructs could display discriminant validity.

4.2.3. The Quality of Items

Outer loadings of all items (See in Table 4) excepting the BC3 (0,625) had a figure greater than the cut-off value of 0,70 (Hair, et al., 2013). Hair, et al. (2013) also suggested that the elimination of items experiencing between 0,4 and 0,7 depends on the decision of researchers. Because CR and AVE of BC3 met the requirement (which were illustrated in the section 4.2.1 and 4.2.2), we believed that BC3 didn't affect the results of the variable. Therefore, we save the BC3.

4.3. Hypothesis Testing

Table 5. Assessing the hypothesis

Hypothesis	Original Sample	Sample Mean	Standard Deviation	T-statistics	p-values	VIF
H1. Esthetics -> Entertainment	0.577	0.585	0.073	7.881	0.000	1.000
H2. Esthetics -> Education	0.553	0.561	0.063	8.724	0.000	1.000
H3. Esthetics -> Escapism	0.466	0.471	0.075	6.195	0.000	1.000
H4. Esthetics -> BC	0.199	0.197	0.104	1.915	0.056	1.706
H5. Entertainment -> BC	0.217	0.221	0.097	2.234	0.026	1.893
H6. Education -> BC	0.196	0.201	0.108	1.813	0.070	2.024
H7. Escapism -> BC	0.299	0.297	0.081	3.699	0.000	1.554

To examine the above hypothesis, partial least squares (PLS) structural equation modeling (SEM) was performed with the SmartPLS 4 software, version 4.0.9.8 to perform path analysis. Due to the prediction and explanation of latent constructs in PLS-SEM contributing to the major objective of this study, PLS-SEM analysis is employed to anticipate the relationship amongst the relevant components (Hair et al., 2019). Table 5 shows evidence lending support to the hypothesis.

For more details, H1, H2 and H3 were supported, providing evidence that esthetics has a positive effect on entertainment, education and escapism (the figures for p-value were below under 0.05 while the figures for original sample are positive). The figures for f-square of Esthetics (see Figure 5 in the Appendix) was much higher than the threshold figure of 0.35, indicating that Esthetics strongly influenced Education (f-square = 0.441) and Entertainment (f-square = 0.500). Because p-values of H4 and H6 were above the figure of 0.05, both hypotheses were not supported, demonstrating that esthetics and education had no impact on brand coolness. On the contrary, H5 and H7 were accepted, but not strong due to the low effect size (0.055 and 0.126).

4.4. Case Studies and Local Consumer Insights

While the chapter provides a comprehensive analysis of the theoretical and empirical relationship between AR-integrated packaging and brand coolness, the discussion can be further enriched by incorporating case studies and direct insights from local Vietnamese businesses and consumers. For example, several Vietnamese brands, including Trung Nguyen Legend and Vinacafe, have piloted AR-enabled packaging campaigns in recent years, using interactive filters and gamified experiences to engage young consumers (Vietnam Investment Review, 2023). Interviews with marketing managers from these companies reveal that AR features not only increased social media engagement but also contributed to a perception of modernity and innovation, which are key elements of brand coolness in the Vietnamese context. Furthermore, qualitative feedback collected from consumers at the ArtTech Fusion 2024 exhibition indicated that participants found AR packaging to be both entertaining and culturally resonant, especially when the content reflected familiar Saigon landmarks or coffee rituals. These local insights align with the quantitative findings of this study, confirming that AR-driven experiences can enhance brand coolness by fostering emotional connections and a sense of cultural pride. By integrating such real-world examples and consumer perspectives, the chapter offers a more nuanced understanding of the opportunities and challenges facing AR adoption in Vietnam's FMCG sector, and provides actionable recommendations for both scholars and practitioners.

4.5 Discussion

Three hypotheses were proposed to investigate the relationship between esthetic experience and entertainment, educational, and escapist experiences. The positive original sample estimated values in Table 5 support these hypotheses, indicating a significant influence of aesthetic experience on all three dimensions. As a result, H1, H2, and H3 are accepted.

The findings of this study suggest that the four realms of experience (Pine and Gilmore, 1998) provide both a conceptual alignment and a practical framework for measuring the impact of AR products on perceptions of brand coolness. Our findings align with previous research (Pallud & Straub, 2014), demonstrating that esthetics in AR experience significantly enhances consumers' entertainment, education, and escapism. As observed in other research contexts (Hosany & Witham, 2009; Jung & Lee, 2006; Jung, 2016; Lee et al., 2015; Mykletun & Rumba, 2014; Pallud & Straub, 2014), visual cues like design and appearance shape initial perceptions. This confirms the pivotal role of esthetics in creating immersive advertising for marketing & branding strategy.

The research highlights the complex nature of brand coolness and its influencing factors. Aligning with (Attiq, S., 2022), our study emphasizes the importance of brand coolness, linking it to brand love and brand engagement, which in turn affect consumer well-being. Which highlight the significance of emotional connections and experiences in enhancing brand coolness. While aesthetics contribute positively to engagement and perceived utility (The Power of Aesthetics in Marketing, 2023), our study finds that aesthetics alone do not significantly enhance brand coolness . For instance, the study found that esthetics had a strong influence on education and entertainment, with f-square values of 0.441 and 0.500 respectively, yet did not impact brand coolness directly (p-value > 0.05). Similarly, education, despite being viewed as useful, did not evoke the excitement or novelty needed for brand coolness (p-value > 0.05). Therefore, suggesting that aesthetics must be part of a broader strategy that includes emotional and experiential elements.

Continuing (Pine, J, 2020), which discusses the Experience Economy, where businesses compete by offering unique and memorable experiences. Our study agrees that entertainment and escapism play a more substantial role in elevating brand coolness. The survey revealed that entertainment significantly impacts brand coolness, providing engaging and enjoyable experiences that foster emotional connections (supported by p-value < 0.05). Escapism was also found to significantly influence brand coolness, offering unique and exciting experiences that create strong emotional bonds and make the brand feel more desirable (supported by p-value < 0.05).Both emphasize the importance of creating engaging and distinctive experiences for consumers.

These findings underscore the importance of creating immersive and enjoyable experiences for consumers. Brands aiming to enhance their coolness factor should focus on integrating entertainment and escapism into their strategies. This approach not only fosters strong emotional connections but also makes the brand more memorable and desirable.

5. PRACTICAL RECOMMENDATIONS FOR MARKETERS AND PACKAGING DESIGNERS

For brands seeking to harness AR packaging in Vietnam, the study highlights actionable strategies. First, prioritize entertainment and escapism by designing interactive, immersive experiences—such as gamified filters or virtual tours exploring Sài Gòn's coffee culture—to captivate users. Second, strike a balance between visual appeal and functional value, ensuring aesthetic designs are complemented by memorable interactions that amplify brand coolness. Additionally, localization is critical: integrating culturally resonant elements like Vietnamese motifs, language, or traditions can deepen emotional bonds with audiences. Finally, marketers should leverage tools like Meta Spark's analytics to measure emotional engagement, track user behavior, and iteratively optimize campaigns based on real-time data insights.

This holistic approach ensures AR initiatives resonate authentically while driving measurable brand impact.

By following these recommendations, marketers can harness the full potential of AR to enhance brand coolness, foster cultural engagement, and create distinctive consumer experiences in the Vietnamese market.

6. CONCLUSION

The rapid advancement of technology offers a treasure trove of tools for businesses to enhance their branding strategies. Augmented reality (AR) stands out as a particularly impactful technology by seamlessly blending virtual elements with the real world, empowers consumers with immersive, engaging and memorable experiences.

The true drivers of brand coolness appear to lie within the realms of entertainment and escapism. Engaging and enjoyable AR experiences foster positive emotional connections with consumers, which is crucial for building a cool brand image. AR experiences that offer unique and exciting escapes from the ordinary can create strong emotional bonds with consumers, making the brand feel more desirable and aspirational. However, studies have revealed that while aesthetics and education contribute positively to factors like user engagement and perceived usefulness (Saman Attiq et al., 2022), they don't necessarily translate directly to brand coolness.

This study provides valuable insights for companies looking to leverage AR to maximize their impact. To maximize effectiveness, AR ads should prioritize creating engaging and entertaining experiences that go beyond mere product information. Design interactive and playful AR applications that evoke positive emotions and foster a sense of fun. Additionally, craft unique and immersive experiences that transport consumers to imaginative worlds or offer exciting glimpses into potential product uses.

7. LIMITATIONS AND FURTHER SUGGESTION

Our first limitation must be mentioned, which is about the category of AR used in this study. There are 6 main categories of AR while we just focus on the type of marker-based AR. Hence, it is questionable whether the results vary according to different categories. We suggest that the next papers should examine the possible outcomes of the remaining AR categories.

Another limitation is about the relationship between the experience economy theory and brand coolness. Despite our effort in demonstrating the influence of experience economy on brand coolness, the result showed that this relationship is insignificantly strong. More papers should be conducted in order to have a better understanding of this field. Meanwhile, our paper shared the same result with previous studies about the fact that esthetics influences positively on entertainment, education and escapism. Many other studies added to the literature that escapism is the realm influenced by the other realms in the theory. Researchers should consider this to conduct a new paper.

In the journey to determine the importance of AR campaigns on branding and marketing, we recommend researchers continue to find out the link between AR stuff (products, services,...) and brand variables (love, authenticity, loyalty,...). It is of essence for researchers to open more academic opportunities. Future research should explore Vietnam-specific AR adoption barriers, such as smartphone penetration rates in rural areas or local consumer preferences for AR content.

REFERENCES

Ahmadian, H., Gladwell, G. M. L., & Ismail, F. (1997). Parameter selection strategies in finite element model updating.

Amanah, D. M. N., Putri, N. K., & Aini, N. (2023). The effect of experience economy on augmented reality-based marketing apps: A study of consumer satisfaction. [JED]. *Journal of Enterprise and Development*, *5*(3), 606–624. DOI: 10.20414/jed.v5i3.8014

Attiq, S., Hamid, A. B. A., Khokhar, M. N., Shah, H. J., & Shahzad, A. (2022b). "Wow! it's cool": How Brand Coolness Affects the Customer Psychological Well-Being through

Bault, N., & Rusconi, E. (2020). The Art of Influencing Consumer Choices: A reflection on recent advances in decision neuroscience. *Frontiers in Psychology*, *10*, 3009. DOI: 10.3389/fpsyg.2019.03009 PMID: 32038387

Belk, R. W., Tian, K., & Paavola, H. (2010). Consuming cool: Behind the unemotional mask. In *Research in consumer behavior* (pp. 183–208). Emerald Group Publishing Limited. DOI: 10.1108/S0885-2111(2010)0000012010

Caleb, W., Rajeev, B., & Sandra, L. (2019). Brand Coolness. *Journal of Marketing*, *83*(5), 36–56. DOI: 10.1177/0022242919857698

Carmigniani, J. (2011). Augmented Reality: An Overview. Handbook of augmented reality/Springer.

DeVellis, R. F., & Thorpe, C. T. (2021). *Scale development: Theory and applications*. Sage publications.

Edwards-Stewart, A., Hoyt, T., & Reger, G. (2016). Classifying different types of augmented reality technology. *Annual Review of Cybertherapy and Telemedicine*, *14*, 199–202.

Fornell, C., & Larcker, D. F. (1981). Evaluating Structural Equation Models with Unobservable Variables and Measurement Error. *JMR, Journal of Marketing Research*, *18*(1), 39–50. DOI: 10.1177/002224378101800104

Hair, J. F., Ringle, C. M., & Sarstedt, M. (2011). PLS-SEM: Indeed a silver bullet. *Journal of Marketing Theory and Practice*, *19*(2), 139–152. DOI: 10.2753/MTP1069-6679190202

Hair, J. F.Jr, Ringle, C. M., & Sarstedt, M. (2013). Partial least squares structural equation modeling: Rigorous applications, better results and higher acceptance. *Long Range Planning*, *46*(1-2), 1–12. DOI: 10.1016/j.lrp.2013.01.001

Hair, J. F., Risher, J. J., Sarstedt, M., & Ringle, C. M. (2019). When to use and how to report the results of PLS-SEM. *European Business Review*, *31*(1), 2–24. DOI: 10.1108/EBR-11-2018-0203

Henseler, J., Ringle, C. M., & Sarstedt, M. (2014). A new criterion for assessing discriminant validity in variance-based structural equation modeling. *Journal of the Academy of Marketing Science*, *43*(1), 115–135. DOI: 10.1007/s11747-014-0403-8

Höck, M., & Ringle, C. M. (2010). Local strategic networks in the software industry: An empirical analysis of the value continuum. *International Journal of Knowledge Management Studies*, *4*(2), 132. DOI: 10.1504/IJKMS.2010.030789

Jung, T. H., Lee, H., Chung, N., & tom Dieck, M. C. (2018). Cross-cultural differences in adopting mobile augmented reality at cultural heritage tourism sites. *International Journal of Contemporary Hospitality Management*, *30*(3), 1621–1645. DOI: 10.1108/IJCHM-02-2017-0084

Kim, J., Fiore, A. M., & Lee, H. (2006). Influences of online store perception, shopping enjoyment, and shopping involvement on consumer patronage behavior towards an online retailer. *Journal of Retailing and Consumer Services*, *14*(2), 95–107. DOI: 10.1016/j.jretconser.2006.05.001

Lee, H., Chung, N., & Jung, T. (2014). Examining the cultural differences in acceptance of mobile augmented Reality: Comparison of South Korea and Ireland. In Springer eBooks (pp. 477–491). DOI: 10.1007/978-3-319-14343-9_35

Marketing, A. Retrieved November 5, 2024, from https://availmarketing.guru/2023/10/10/the-power-of-aesthetic-in-marketing-more-than-meets-the-eye/ Brand Love and Brand Engagement. Frontiers in Psychology, 13. DOI: 10.3389/fpsyg.2022.923870

McLean, G., & Wilson, A. (2019). Shopping in the digital world: Examining customer engagement through augmented reality mobile applications. *Computers in Human Behavior*, *101*, 210–224. DOI: 10.1016/j.chb.2019.07.002

Nguyen, T. H., & Le, H. A. (2022). Technological barriers to AR adoption in emerging markets: A Vietnamese perspective. *Journal of Digital Innovation*, *8*(2), 112–125.

Nunnally, J. C., & Bernstein, I. H. (1994). *Psychometric Theory*. McGraw-Hill.

Pallud, J., & Straub, D. W. (2014). Effective website design for experience-influenced environments: The case of high culture museums. *Information & Management, 51*(3), 359–373. DOI: 10.1016/j.im.2014.02.010

Pham, L. T., Nguyen, H. D., & Tran, T. K. (2023). AR-driven cultural engagement in Vietnam's FMCG sector. *Journal of Consumer Technology, 12*(4), 45–60.

Pine, B. J., & Joseph, B. (1998). Welcome to the experience economy. *Harvard Business Review*. PMID: 10181589

Raptis, D., Bruun, A., Kjeldskov, J., & Skov, M. B. (2017). Converging coolness and investigating its relation to user experience. *Behaviour & Information Technology, 36*(4), 333–350. DOI: 10.1080/0144929X.2016.1232753

Romano, B., Sands, S., & Pallant, J. I. (2020). Augmented reality and the customer journey: An exploratory study. [AMJ]. *Australasian Marketing Journal, 29*(4), 354–363. DOI: 10.1016/j.ausmj.2020.06.010

Silvennoinen, J., Vogel, M., & Kujala, S. (2014). Experiencing visual usability and aesthetics in two mobile application contexts. https://www.semanticscholar.org/paper/Experiencing-visual-usability-and-aesthetics-in-two-Silvennoinen-Vogel/a9ae76304cde810dfcb0ed74817823868aa6e63a

Statista. (2023). Internet penetration and smartphone ownership in Vietnam. https://www.statista.com/vietnam-internet-penetration

Sudarmanto, J. A., & Ismail, A. I. B. (2023). Augmented reality and metaverse in Aesthetic Education Discourse in Indonesia for future. *Southeast Asian Conference on Education Official Conference Proceedings*. DOI: 10.22492/issn.2435-5240.2023.26

Suh, K.-S., & Chang, S. (2006). User interfaces and consumer perceptions of online stores: The role of telepresence. *Behaviour & Information Technology, 25*(2), 99–113. DOI: 10.1080/01449290500330398

Sung, E. (2020). The effects of augmented reality mobile app advertising: Viral marketing via shared social experience. *Journal of Business Research, 122*, 75–87. DOI: 10.1016/j.jbusres.2020.08.034

Süzen, H. N. (2020). Art and Aesthetics in Higher Education. *Online Submission, 7*(6), 335–350.

Tom Dieck, M. C., Jung, T. H., & Rauschnabel, P. A. (2018). Determining visitor engagement through augmented reality at science festivals: An experience economy perspective. *Computers in Human Behavior, 82*, 44–53. DOI: 10.1016/j.chb.2017.12.043

Nielsen Vietnam. (2023). Digital literacy and AR awareness in Vietnam.

Nielsen Vietnam. (2023). Consumer trends report 2023: AR adoption in Vietnam's FMCG sector.

Vietnam Investment Review. (2023, May 10). Cost challenges for SMEs in adopting AR technology.

VietnamNet. (2023, October 15). Trung Nguyen Legend's AR campaign boosts brand engagement.

Warren, C., Batra, R., Loureiro, S. M. C., & Bagozzi, R. P. (2019). Brand Coolness. *Journal of Marketing*, *83*(5), 36–56. DOI: 10.1177/0022242919857698

Yang, S., Carlson, J. R., & Chen, S. (2019). How augmented reality affects advertising effectiveness: The mediating effects of curiosity and attention toward the ad. *Journal of Retailing and Consumer Services*, *54*, 102020. DOI: 10.1016/j.jretconser.2019.102020

Yim, M. Y., Cicchirillo, V. J., & Drumwright, M. E. (2012). The impact of stereoscopic Three-Dimensional (3-D) advertising. *Journal of Advertising*, *41*(2), 113–128. DOI: 10.2753/JOA0091-3367410208

APPENDIX

Figure 4. Collinearity statistics (VIF)

Collinearity statistics (VIF) - Outer model - List

	VIF
BC1	1.552
BC2	1.637
BC3	1.378
BC4	1.620
BC5	1.501
Education1	1.686
Education2	1.859
Education3	1.340
Entertainment1	1.436
Entertainment2	1.531
Entertainment3	1.377
Escapism1	2.754
Escapism2	2.474
Escapism3	2.757
Escapism4	2.091
Esthetics1	1.670
Esthetics2	1.514
Esthetics3	1.299

Figure 5. F-square (Matrix)

	BC	Education	Entertainment	Escapism	Esthetics
BC					
Education	0.042				
Entertainment	0.055				
Escapism	0.126				
Esthetics	0.051	0.441	0.500	0.277	

Compilation of References

Abo-Khalil, A. G. (2024). Integrating sustainability into higher education challenges and opportunities for universities worldwide. *Heliyon*, *10*(9), e29946. DOI: 10.1016/j.heliyon.2024.e29946 PMID: 38707336

Abumalloh, R. A., Halabi, O., & Nilashi, M. (2025). The relationship between technology trust and behavioral intention to use metaverse in baby monitoring systems design: Stimulus-Organism-Response (SOR) theory. *Entertainment Computing*, *52*, 100833. DOI: 10.1016/j.entcom.2024.100833

Aburbeian, A. M., Owda, A. Y., & Owda, M. (2022). A Technology Acceptance Model Survey of the Metaverse Prospects. *AI*, *3*(2), 285–302. DOI: 10.3390/ai3020018

Adisa, M. O., Oyedeji, S., & Porras, J. (2024). The nexus between ICT, top-down and bottom-up approaches for sustainability activities: A systematic mapping study. *Journal of Cleaner Production*, *449*, 141768. DOI: 10.1016/j.jclepro.2024.141768

Adobe. (2023). Responsible innovation in the age of generative AI. Adobe Retrieved 25 May 2025 from https://www.adobe.com/ai/overview/ethics.html

Aggarwal, C. C. (2018). Neural Networks and Deep Learning.

Agrawal, T. K., Kumar, V., Pal, R., Wang, L., & Chen, Y. (2021). Blockchain-based framework for supply chain traceability: A case example of textile and clothing industry. *Computers & Industrial Engineering*, *154*, 107130. DOI: 10.1016/j.cie.2021.107130

Aguilar, D., & Pifarré Turmo, M. (2019). Promoting social creativity in science education with digital technology to overcome inequalities: A scoping review. *Frontiers in Psychology*, *10*, 1474. DOI: 10.3389/fpsyg.2019.01474 PMID: 31312154

Ahmadian, H., Gladwell, G. M. L., & Ismail, F. (1997). Parameter selection strategies in finite element model updating.

Ajzen, I. (1991). The theory of planned behavior. *Organizational Behavior and Human Decision Processes, 50*(2), 179–211. DOI: 10.1016/0749-5978(91)90020-T

Al-Adwan, A. S., Li, N., Al-Adwan, A., Abbasi, G. A., Albelbisi, N. A., & Habibi, A. (2023). Extending the Technology Acceptance Model (TAM) to Predict University Students' Intentions to Use Metaverse Based Learning Platforms. *Education and Information Technologies, 28*(11), 15381–15413. DOI: 10.1007/s10639-023-11816-3 PMID: 37361794

Alasmari, T. (2020). Gamification in e-learning: A review. *International Journal of Advanced Computer Science and Applications, 11*(2), 372–377. DOI: 10.14569/IJACSA.2020.0110247

Alexander, B., & Contreras, L. O. (2016). Inter-industry creative collaborations incorporating luxury fashion brands. *Journal of Fashion Marketing and Management, 20*(3), 254–275. DOI: 10.1108/JFMM-09-2015-0075

Alford, M. (2013). Conditions of my release.

Ali, S. W., Bairagi, S., & Shankar, P. (2020). Biomaterials-Based Nanogenerator: Futuristic Solution for Integration Into Smart Textiles. *Frontiers of Textile Materials: Polymers, Nanomaterials, Enzymes, and Advanced Modification Techniques*, 189-201, DOI: 10.1002/9781119620396.ch9

Al-Saud, K., AlAli, R., Al saud, A., Abouelela, A., Shehab, R., Moneim, D., & Hamid, A. (2024). Exploring the Aesthetic and Functional Aspects of Recycled Furniture in Promoting Sustainable Development: An Applied Approach for Interior Design Students. *Sustainability (Basel), 16*(10), 4003. DOI: 10.3390/su16104003

Amanah, D. M. N., Putri, N. K., & Aini, N. (2023). The effect of experience economy on augmented reality-based marketing apps: A study of consumer satisfaction. [JED]. *Journal of Enterprise and Development, 5*(3), 606–624. DOI: 10.20414/jed.v5i3.8014

Anantrasirichai, N., & Bull, D. (2022). Artificial intelligence in the creative industries: A review. *Artificial Intelligence Review, 55*(1), 1–68. DOI: 10.1007/s10462-021-10039-7

Anderson, J., & Rainie, L. (2022). *The Metaverse in 2040*. Pew Research Center.

Andresen, B. B., & Brink, K. V. (2013). *Multimedia in education*. UNESCO Institute for Information Technologies in Education.

An, J. W. (2019). Technology Acceptance and Influencing Factor of Anatomy Learning using Augmented Reality:Usability Based on the Technology Acceptance Model. *Journal of the Korea Convergence Society*, *10*(12), 487–494.

Arenas, A. G. (2010). A sensor-based interactive digital installation system for virtual painting using MAX/MSP/Jitter. *International Journal of Arts and Technology*, *3*(2/3), 234–247.

Arghashi, V., & Yuksel, C. A. (2022). Interactivity, Inspiration, and Perceived Usefulness! How retailers' AR-apps improve consumer engagement through flow. *Journal of Retailing and Consumer Services*, *64*, 102756. DOI: 10.1016/j.jretconser.2021.102756

Arnold, J. E. (1959). Creative Engineering Seminar, 1959. (n.p.).

Arshad, Z. M., Azman, M. N. A., Kenzhaliyev, O., & Kassimov, F. R. (2024). Educational Enhancement Through Augmented Reality Simulation: A Bibliometric Analysis. *International Journal of Advanced Computer Science and Applications*, *15*(7). Advance online publication. DOI: 10.14569/IJACSA.2024.0150769

Atabek, O. (2019) 'CHALLENGES IN INTEGRATING TECHNOLOGY INTO EDUCATION', *Turkish Studies - Information Technologies and Applied Sciences*, 14(ITAS Volume 14 Issue 1), pp. 1–19. Available at: .DOI: 10.7827/TurkishStudies.14810

Attiq, S., Hamid, A. B. A., Khokhar, M. N., Shah, H. J., & Shahzad, A. (2022b). "Wow! it's cool": How Brand Coolness Affects the Customer Psychological Well-Being through

Auernhammer, J., & Roth, B. (2021). The origin and evolution of Stanford University's design thinking: From product design to design thinking in innovation management. *Journal of Product Innovation Management*, *38*(6), 623–644. DOI: 10.1111/jpim.12594

Azam J., Shakirullah S., Sadaf N., Owais K. & Abdui Q. K.(2020), 'Marshal McLuhan's technological determinism theory in the arena of social media', Asers publishing. Vol. 11, No. 2, pp 133-137

Badhwar, A., Islam, S., & Tan, C. S. L. (2023). Exploring the potential of blockchain technology within the fashion and textile supply chain with a focus on traceability, transparency, and product authenticity: A systematic review. In *Frontiers in Blockchain* (Vol. 6). Frontiers Media SA. DOI: 10.3389/fbloc.2023.1044723

Bagozzi, R. P. (2011). Measurement and meaning in information systems and organizational research: Methodological and philosophical foundations. *Management Information Systems Quarterly*, *35*(2), 261–292. DOI: 10.2307/23044044

Balsalobre-Lorente, D., (2024) 'Do ICT and green technology matter in sustainable development goals?', *Sustainable Development*, p. sd.3185. Available at: DOI: 10.1002/sd.3185

Balzarin, L., & Calcagno, M. (2016). Traces of entrepreneurship in the artistic context. *Journal of Business Research*, *69*(5), 1597–1601.

Bandi, A., Adapa, P. V., & Kuchi, Y. E. (2023). The Power of Generative AI: A Review of Requirements, Models, Input–Output Formats, Evaluation Metrics, and Challenges. *Future Internet*, *15*(8), 260–320. DOI: 10.3390/fi15080260

Banerjee, S. B. (2012). The artist as activist: Understanding the role of art in environmental sustainability. *The Journal of Social Issues*, *68*(4), 745–760. DOI: 10.1111/j.1540-4560.2012.01765.x

Baptista, G., & Oliveira, T. (2017). Gamification and serious games: A literature meta-analysis and integrative model. *Computers in Human Behavior*, *68*, 422–435. DOI: 10.1016/j.chb.2016.11.043

Barhorst, J. B., McLean, G., Shah, E., & Mack, R. (2021). Blending the real world and the virtual world: Exploring the role of flow in augmented reality experiences. *Journal of Business Research*, *122*, 423–436. DOI: 10.1016/j.jbusres.2020.08.041

Bault, N., & Rusconi, E. (2020). The Art of Influencing Consumer Choices: A reflection on recent advances in decision neuroscience. *Frontiers in Psychology*, *10*, 3009. DOI: 10.3389/fpsyg.2019.03009 PMID: 32038387

Bedeian, A. G. (1993). *Management* (3rd ed.). Dryden Press.

Belk, R. W., Tian, K., & Paavola, H. (2010). Consuming cool: Behind the unemotional mask. In *Research in consumer behavior* (pp. 183–208). Emerald Group Publishing Limited. DOI: 10.1108/S0885-2111(2010)0000012010

Bellaiche, L., Shahi, R., Turpin, M. H., Ragnhildstveit, A., Sprockett, S., Barr, N., Christensen, A., & Seli, P. (2023). Human versus AI: Whether and why we prefer human-created compared to AI-created artwork. *Cognitive Research: Principles and Implications*, *8*(8), 42. DOI: 10.1186/s41235-023-00499-6 PMID: 37401999

Bendele, E. (2009). Art & technology [6th-8th grade].

Ben-Eliyahu, A. (2021). Sustainable Learning in Education. *Sustainability (Basel)*, *13*(8), 4250. DOI: 10.3390/su13084250

Ben-Sasson, A., Ben-Sasson, E., Jacobs, K., & Malinovitch, R. (2020). The relationship between users' technology approaches and experiences in a child development mobile application. *Health and Technology, 10*(5), 1079–1094. DOI: 10.1007/s12553-020-00457-y

Besoain, F., González-Ortega, J., & Gallardo, I. (2022). An evaluation of the effects of a virtual museum on users' attitudes towards cultural heritage. *Applied Sciences (Basel, Switzerland), 12*(14), 7076. DOI: 10.3390/app12031341

Bird, C., Ungless, E., & Kasirzadeh, A. (2023, August). Typology of risks of generative text-to-image models. In Proceedings of the 2023 AAAI/ACM Conference on AI, Ethics, and Society (pp. 396-410). DOI: 10.1145/3600211.3604722

Bishop, C. (2012). *Artificial hells: Participatory art and the politics of spectatorship*. Verso.

Biswas, A. (2008). Managing art–technology research collaborations. *International Journal of Arts and Technology, 1*(1), 66–89. DOI: 10.1504/IJART.2008.019883

Bitrián, P., Buil, I., & Catalán, S. (2020). Enhancing user engagement: The role of gamification in mobile apps. *Journal of Business Research, 132*, 170–185. DOI: 10.1016/j.jbusres.2021.04.028

Bjögvinsson, E., Ehn, P., & Hillgren, P. A. (2012). Design things and design thinking: Contemporary participatory design challenges. *Design Issues, 28*(3), 101–116. DOI: 10.1162/DESI_a_00165

Bonetti, F., Warnaby, G., & Quinn, L. (2018). *Augmented reality and virtual reality: Empowering human, place and business*. Springer.

Braidotti, R. (2013). *The posthuman*. Polity Press.

Brengman, M., Willems, K., & De Gauquier, L. (2022). Customer engagement in multi-sensory virtual reality advertising: The effect of sound and scent congruence. *Frontiers in Psychology, 13*, 747456. DOI: 10.3389/fpsyg.2022.747456 PMID: 35386898

Brown, T., & Wyatt, J. (2010). Design thinking for social innovation. *Development Outreach, 12*(1), 29–43. DOI: 10.1596/1020-797X_12_1_29

Buchholz, F., Oppermann, L., & Prinz, W. (2022). There's more than one metavers. *Journal of Interactive Media, 21*(3), 313–323.

Buck, R., & Snook, B. (2020). Reality bites: Implementing arts integration. *Research in Dance Education, 21*(1), 98–115. DOI: 10.1080/14647893.2020.1727873

Caleb, W., Rajeev, B., & Sandra, L. (2019). Brand Coolness. *Journal of Marketing*, *83*(5), 36–56. DOI: 10.1177/0022242919857698

Camacho, M. (2016). David Kelley: From design to design thinking at Stanford and IDEO. She Ji. *The Journal of Design, Economics, and Innovation*, *2*(1), 88–101. DOI: 10.1016/j.sheji.2016.01.009

Cameron, F. (2015). The digital turn: A new paradigm for art and sustainability. *Journal of Visual Culture*, *14*(2), 157–174. DOI: 10.1177/1470412915580590

Candy, L., & Edmonds, E. (2002), "Modeling Co-Creativity in Art and Technology", C&C '02: Proceedings of the 4th conference on Creativity & cognition Modeling co-creativity in art and technology, pp 134–141 DOI: 10.1145/581710.581731

Candy, L., & Edmonds, E. (2002). Interaction in art and technology. *Crossings: Electronic Journal of Art and Technology*, *2*(1), 1–8.

Candy, L., Edmonds, E., & Poltronieri, F. (2002). *Explorations in Art and Technology* (2nd ed.). Springer. DOI: 10.1007/978-1-4471-0197-0

Carmigniani, J. (2011). Augmented Reality: An Overview. Handbook of augmented reality/Springer.

Carmigniani, J., & Furht, B. (2011). *Handbook of augmented reality*. Springer.

Centobelli, P., Cerchione, R., Del Vecchio, P., Oropallo, E., & Secundo, G. Blockchain technology for bridging trust, traceability and transparency in circular supply chain, *Information & Management, Volume 59, Issue* 7, 2022, 103508, ISSN 0378-7206, DOI: 10.1016/j.im.2021.103508

Cerceo, E., Zimmerman, M., & DeLisser, H. M. (2022). Diversity, Equity, and Inclusion: Moving from Performance to Transformation Through the Arts and Humanities. *Journal of General Internal Medicine*, *37*(4), 944–946. DOI: 10.1007/s11606-021-07225-2 PMID: 34993859

Cetinic, E., & She, J. (2022). Understanding and creating art with AI: Review and outlook. [TOMM]. *ACM Transactions on Multimedia Computing Communications and Applications*, *18*(2), 1–22. DOI: 10.1145/3475799

Challoumis, C. (2024, October). *Building a sustainable economy – How AI can optimize resource allocation. XVI International Scientific Conference*, 190–224.

Chamberlain, R., Mulin, C., & Wagermans, J. (2017). Putting the Art in Artificial: Aesthetic Responses to Computer-Generated Art. *Psychology of Aesthetics, Creativity, and the Arts*.

Chander, N., Siow, M. L., Ramachandran, S., Kunasekaran, P., & Rathakrishnan, T. (2020). Conceptualizing Inclusive Learning and Development: A Framework towards Entrepreneurial Competency Practices for Sustainability. *Sustainability (Basel)*, *12*(17), 6905. DOI: 10.3390/su12176905

Chand, V. S., Deshmukh, K. S., & Shukla, A. (2020). Why does technology integration fail? Teacher beliefs and content developer assumptions in an Indian initiative. *Educational Technology Research and Development*, *68*(5), 2753–2774. DOI: 10.1007/s11423-020-09760-x

Chang, C.-Y., Du, Z., Kuo, H.-C., & Chang, C.-C. (2023). 'Investigating the Impact of Design Thinking-Based STEAM PBL on Students' Creativity and Computational Thinking'. *IEEE Transactions on Education*, *66*(6), 673–681. DOI: 10.1109/TE.2023.3297221

Chan, H., King, R., & Wong, H. (2018). Gamification in education: A systematic review. *International Journal of Educational Technology in Higher Education*, *15*(1), 29. DOI: 10.1186/s41239-018-0103-0

Chapman, S. N., & O'Gorman, L. (2022). Transforming Learning Environments in Early Childhood Contexts Through the Arts: Responding to the United Nations Sustainable Development Goals. *International Journal of Early Childhood*, *54*(1), 33–50. DOI: 10.1007/s13158-022-00320-3

Chayka, K. (2021). The Art World's New Obsession: Digital Art and NFTs. *New Yorker (New York, N.Y.)*. https://www.newyorker.com

Cheema, A., & Kaikati, A. M. (2010). The effect of need for uniqueness on word of mouth. *JMR, Journal of Marketing Research*, *47*(3), 553–563. DOI: 10.1509/jmkr.47.3.553

Chen, C. F., & Tsai, D. C. (2007). How Destination Image and Evaluative Factors Affect Behavioral Intentions? *Tourism Management*, *28*(4), 1115–1122. DOI: 10.1016/j.tourman.2006.07.007

Cheng, R., Wu, N., Chen, S., & Han, B. (2022). Will Metaverse be NextG Internet? Vision, Hype, and Reality. *IEEE Network*, *36*(5), 197–204. DOI: 10.1109/MNET.117.2200055

Chen, J., Yu, B., Chen, B., & Liu, Z. (2023). *Lenient vs.* stringent returns policies in the presence of fraudulent returns: The role of customers' fairness perceptions. *Omega*, *117*, 102843. DOI: 10.1016/j.omega.2023.102843

Chen, L. (2024). Exploring Innovative Practices and Challenges in the Ecological Development of Art Industry Driven by Digital Technology. *Applied Mathematics and Nonlinear Sciences*, *9*(1), 20242975. DOI: 10.2478/amns-2024-2975

Chen, Y. (2021). Managing Copyright and Trademark Issues in the Digital Age. *Stanford Law Review*.

Chen, Z., & Dubinsky, A. J. (2003). A conceptual model of perceived customer value in e-commerce: A preliminary investigation. *Psychology and Marketing*, *20*(4), 323–347. DOI: 10.1002/mar.10076

Chevalier, C., & Kiefer, C. (2020). What does augmented reality mean as a medium of expression for computational artists? *Proceedings of the 2020 International Conference on New Interfaces for Musical Expression*, 5–7. DOI: 10.1162/leon_a_01740

Chiu, T. K. F., Meng, H., Chai, C.-S., King, I., Wong, S., & Yam, Y. (2022). Creation and Evaluation of a Pretertiary Artificial Intelligence (AI) Curriculum. *IEEE Transactions on Education*, *65*(1), 30–39. DOI: 10.1109/TE.2021.3085878

Choi, T. (2020). *Sustainability in fashion supply chains: Big data and AI applications*. Springer.

Choi, W. S., Kang, D. Y., & Choi, S. J. (2017). Understanding Factors Influencing Usage and Purchase Intention of a VR Device: An Extension of UTAUT2′. *Korea Journal of Information Society*, *18*(3), 173–208.

Christensen, C. M. (1997). *The innovator's dilemma: when new technologies cause great firms to fail*. Harvard Business Review Press.

Chung, F. M.-Y. (2024). Utilising technology as a transmission strategy in intangible cultural heritage: The case of Cantonese opera performances. *International Journal of Heritage Studies*, *30*(2), 210–225. DOI: 10.1080/13527258.2023.2284723

Chun, W. H. K. (2016). *Updating to Remain the Same. Habitual New Media*. MIT Press. DOI: 10.7551/mitpress/10483.001.0001

Clark, B., & Button, C. (2011). Sustainability transdisciplinary education model: Interface of arts, science, and community (STEM). *International Journal of Sustainability in Higher Education*, *12*(1), 41–54. DOI: 10.1108/14676371111098294

Cloud, G. (2020). *Stella McCartney partners with Google to measure the environmental impact of its fashion production*. [Online] Available at: https://cloud.google.com/press-releases/2020/03/stella-mccartney-google-partnership

Clowney, D. (2011). Definitions of Art and Fine Art's Historical Origins. *The Journal of Aesthetics and Art Criticism*, *69*(3), 309–320. DOI: 10.1111/j.1540-6245.2011.01474.x

Colovic, A., & Fernandez-Fernandez, J. (2020). The Role of Digital Technologies in Fashion Sustainability. *Journal of Fashion and Textiles*. DOI: .DOI: 10.1186/s40691-020-00221-2

Commission, E. (2023). EU AI Act: first regulation on artificial intelligence. Retrieved 20 May 2025 from https://www.europarl.europa.eu/topics/en/article/20230601STO93804/eu-ai-act-first-regulation-on-artificial-intelligence

Comninos, P., McLoughlin, L., & Anderson, E. F. (2009). Educating technophile artists: experiences from a highly successful computer animation undergraduate programme. In *ACM SIGGRAPH ASIA 2009 Educators Program. SA09: SIGGRAPH ASIA 2009* (pp. 1–8). ACM., DOI: 10.1145/1666611.1666612

Connolly, T. M., Boyle, E. A., MacArthur, E., Hainey, T., & Boyle, J. M. (2012). A systematic literature review of empirical evidence on computer games and serious games. *Computers & Education*, *59*(2), 661–686. DOI: 10.1016/j.compedu.2012.03.004

Content Editor. (2024, January 9). *The truth about cardboard in e-commerce*. Ernest Packaging.

Corder, S. P. (1967). The significance of learners' errors. *International Review of Applied Linguistics in Language Teaching*, *5*(4), 161–170. DOI: 10.1515/iral.1967.5.1-4.161

Corvellec, H., Stowell, A. F., & Johansson, N. (2021b). Critiques of the circular economy. *Journal of Industrial Ecology*, *26*(2), 421–432. DOI: 10.1111/jiec.13187

Cottafava, D., Cavaglià, G., & Corazza, L. (2019). 'Education of sustainable development goals through students' active engagement: A transformative learning experience', *Sustainability Accounting. Management and Policy Journal*, *10*(3), 521–544. DOI: 10.1108/SAMPJ-05-2018-0152

Craig, A. B. (2013). Understanding augmented reality: Concepts and applications.

Cramer, H. (2018). Sustainable art: A reflection on the practices of artists in the context of environmental crisis. *Art Journal*, *77*(2), 54–67. DOI: 10.1080/00043249.2018.1486769

Crayton, J. (2015). Designing for immersive technology: Integrating art and STEM learning.

Cross, N. (2007). From a design science to a design discipline: Understanding designerly ways of knowing and thinking. In *Design research now* (pp. 41–54). Birkhäuser Basel. DOI: 10.1007/978-3-7643-8472-2_3

Cross, N. (2018). A brief history of the Design Thinking Research Symposium series. *Design Studies, 57*, 160–164. DOI: 10.1016/j.destud.2018.03.007

Cross, N. (2023a). *Design thinking: Understanding how designers think and work.* Bloomsbury Publishing. DOI: 10.5040/9781350305090

Cross, N. (2023b). Design thinking: What just happened? *Design Studies, 86*(101187), 1–10.

Cummings S., Bridgman T. & Brown K. G.(2016), "Unfreezing change as three steps: Rethinking Kurt Lewin's legacy for change management", human relations, Vol. 69, Issue 1, pp.33–60

da Cruz, A. M. R., & Cruz, E. F. (2020). Blockchain-based traceability platforms as a tool for sustainability. *ICEIS 2020 - Proceedings of the 22nd International Conference on Enterprise Information Systems, 2*, 330–337. DOI: 10.5220/0009463803300337

Davies, S. (2015). Defining Art and Artworlds. *The Journal of Aesthetics and Art Criticism, 73*(4), 375–384. DOI: 10.1111/jaac.12222

Davis, F. D. (1989). Perceived usefulness ease of use, and use acceptance of information technology. *Management Information Systems Quarterly, 13*(3), 319–340. DOI: 10.2307/249008

Davis, F. D., Bagozzi, R. P., & Warshaw, P. R. (1989). User Acceptance of Computer Technology: A Comparison of Two Theoretical Models. *Management Science, 35*(8), 982–1003. DOI: 10.1287/mnsc.35.8.982

Davis, T. (2020). *Intellectual Property Law and Digital Media*. Routledge.

Deci, E. L., & Ryan, R. M. (1985). *Intrinsic motivation and self-determination in human behavior*. Springer., DOI: 10.1007/978-1-4899-2271-7

Deci, E. L., & Ryan, R. M. (2008). Self-determination theory: A macrotheory of human motivation, development, and health. *Canadian Psychology, 49*(3), 182–185. DOI: 10.1037/a0012801

Deepa, P. (2020). A study on the concepts of design thinking. *International Journal of Engineering Applied Sciences and Technology, 4*(12), 269–272. DOI: 10.33564/IJEAST.2020.v04i12.044

Deloitte, "The Metaverse in Asia Strategies for Accelerating Economic Impact", 2023

Deterding, S., Dixon, D., Khaled, R., & Nacke, L. (2011). From game design elements to gamefulness: Defining "gamification". In *Proceedings of the 15th International Academic MindTrek Conference: Envisioning Future Media Environments* (pp. 9–15). ACM. DOI: 10.1145/2181037.2181040

DeVellis, R. F., & Thorpe, C. T. (2021). *Scale development: Theory and applications*. Sage publications.

Dev, S., George, M., Rafique, S., Vaddapalli, M., Nair, S., & Al Hameli, A. (2024). Sustainable Inclusive Framework Studio for Inclusive Education—Perceptions of Teachers, Parents, and Students in United Arab Emirates. *Sustainability (Basel)*, *16*(15), 6367. DOI: 10.3390/su16156367

Díez-Palomar, J., Sanmamed, A. F. F., García-Carrión, R., & Molina-Roldán, S. (2018). Pathways to Equitable and Sustainable Education through the Inclusion of Roma Students in Learning Mathematics. *Sustainability (Basel)*, *10*(7), 2191. DOI: 10.3390/su10072191

Dockry, M. J., Hall, K., Van Lopik, W., & Caldwell, C. M. (2016). Sustainable development education, practice, and research: An indigenous model of sustainable development at the College of Menominee Nation, Keshena, WI, USA. *Sustainability Science*, *11*(1), 127–138. DOI: 10.1007/s11625-015-0304-x PMID: 30174730

Doerner, R., Broll, W., Jung, B., Grimm, P., Göbel, M., & Kruse, R. (2022). *Introduction to virtual and augmented reality*. Springer. DOI: 10.1007/978-3-030-79062-2_1

Dovleac, L., Chi u, I. B., Nichifor, E., & Brătucu, G. (2023). Shaping the Inclusivity in the New Society by Enhancing the Digitainability of Sustainable Development Goals with Education. *Sustainability (Basel)*, *15*(4), 3782. DOI: 10.3390/su15043782

Drabik, E. (2018). An analysis of the connection between ai development and the creation of games and advanced computer systems. *Economics World*, *6*(4), 251–262. DOI: 10.17265/2328-7144/2018.04.001

Drucker, J. (1994). *The visible word: Experimental typography and modern art, 1909-1923*. University of Chicago Press.

Du, J., & Zhang, M. (2023). A Study on the User Intentions of Metaverse Cultural Tourism Using the Experience Economy Theory (EET) and Technology Acceptance Model (TAM). *Journal of Culture Industry*, *23*(4), 53–64.

Dutton, D. (2006). A Naturalist Definition of Art. *The Journal of Aesthetics and Art Criticism*, *64*(3), 367–377. DOI: 10.1111/j.1540-594X.2006.00217.x

Du, Z., Liu, J., & Wang, T. (2022). Augmented reality marketing: A systematic literature review and an agenda for future inquiry. *Frontiers in Psychology*, *13*, 925963. DOI: 10.3389/fpsyg.2022.925963 PMID: 35783783

Düzenli, K., & Perdahçı, N. Z. (2024). The role of digitalization in today's art: A perspective from NFT and artificial intelligence. *Journal of Arts*, *7*(1), 43–59. DOI: 10.31566/arts.2291

Dwivedi, Y. K., Hughes, L., Wang, Y., Alalwan, A. A., Ahn, S. J., Balakrishnan, J., Barta, S., Belk, R., Buhalis, D., Dutot, V., Felix, R., Filieri, R., Flavián, C., Gustafsson, A., Hinsch, C., Hollensen, S., Jain, V., Kim, J. Y., Krishen, A. S., & Wirtz, J. (2022). Metaverse marketing: How the metaverse will shape the future of consumer research and practice. *Psychology and Marketing*, *40*(4), 750–776. DOI: 10.1002/mar.21767

Eagleton, T. (2013). *The event of literature*. Yale University Press.

Edwards, B. (2021, March 12). How NFTs Are Revolutionizing Digital Art. The Verge. Retrieved from https://www.theverge.com

Edwards-Stewart, A., Hoyt, T., & Reger, G. (2016). Classifying different types of augmented reality technology. *Annual Review of Cybertherapy and Telemedicine*, *14*, 199–202.

Elgammal, A. (2017). Can: Creative adversarial networks, generating "art" by learning about styles and deviating from style norms. arXiv preprint arXiv:1706.07068, 6, 2017.

Ellen MacArthur Foundation. (2020). *Financing the circular economy: Capturing the opportunity*.

Ellen MacArthur Foundation. (2021). Circular economy in fashion: Leveraging AI for sustainable practices. Available at: https://ellenmacarthurfoundation.org/fashion

Elza, C. (2008). WE ALL LIVE IN A POKÉMON WORLD. The Japanification of Children's Popular Culture: From Godzilla to Miyazaki, 53.

Erol, A., Erol, M., & Başaran, M. (2023). The effect of STEAM education with tales on problem solving and creativity skills. *European Early Childhood Education Research Journal*, *31*(2), 243–258. DOI: 10.1080/1350293X.2022.2081347

Erwis, F., Jixiong, C., Rahayu, N., Raharja, A. R., & Zebua, R. S. Y. (2024). Use of Augmented Reality (AR) in Mobile Learning for Natural Science Lessons. *Journal of Social Science Utilizing Technology*, *2*(1), 338–348. DOI: 10.70177/jssut.v2i1.784

Fabri, M. (2015). Thinking with a new purpose: Lessons learned from teaching design thinking skills to creative technology students. In *Design, User Experience, and Usability: Design Discourse: 4th International Conference, DUXU 2015, Held as Part of HCI International 2015, Los Angeles, CA, USA, August 2–7, 2015, Proceedings, Part I* (pp. 32-43). Springer International Publishing.

Fan, X., Chai, Z., Deng, N., & Dong, X. (2020). Adoption of augmented reality in online retailing and consumers' product attitude: A cognitive perspective. *Journal of Retailing and Consumer Services, 53*, 101986. DOI: 10.1016/j.jretconser.2019.101986

Fan, X., & Zhong, X. (2022). Artificial intelligence-based creative thinking skill analysis model using human–computer interaction in art design teaching. *Computers & Electrical Engineering, 100*, 107957. DOI: 10.1016/j.compeleceng.2022.107957

Fava, M. (2020). A Decline in Drawing Ability? *International Journal of Art & Design Education, 39*(2), 319–332. DOI: 10.1111/jade.12255

Feng, Y., & Mueller, B. (2019). The state of augmented reality advertising around the globe: A multi-cultural content analysis. *Journal of Promotion Management, 25*(4), 453–475. DOI: 10.1080/10496491.2018.1448323

Feng, Y., & Xie, Q. (2018). Measuring the content characteristics of videos featuring augmented reality advertising campaigns. *Journal of Research in Interactive Marketing, 12*(4), 489–508. DOI: 10.1108/JRIM-01-2018-0027

Feng, Y., & Xie, Q. (2019). Ad creativity via augmented reality technology in online video ads: The differential role of novelty, message usefulness, and ad-consumer association. *Journal of Promotion Management, 25*(6), 907–933. DOI: 10.1080/10496491.2018.1536624

Feuerriegel, S., Hartmann, J., Janiesch, C., & Zschech, P. (2024). Generative AI. *Business & Information Systems Engineering, 66*(1), 111–126. DOI: 10.1007/s12599-023-00834-7

Figueras-Ferrer, E. (2021). 'Reflexiones en torno a la cultura digital contemporánea. Retos futuros en educación superior', *Arte. Individuo y Sociedad, 33*(2), 449–466. DOI: 10.5209/aris.68505

Fisher, E. (2019). *Patagonia's Circular Economy Initiatives: Redefining Sustainable Fashion.* Vogue Business.

Fitrianto, I., & Saif, A. (2024). The Role of Virtual Reality in Enhancing Experiential Learning: A Comparative Study of Traditional and Immersive Learning Environments. International Journal of Post Axial: Futuristic Teaching and Learning, 97-110.

Flavián, C., Ibáñez-Sánchez, S., & Orús, C. (2019). The impact of virtual, augmented and mixed reality technologies on the customer experience. *Journal of Business Research, 100*, 547–560. DOI: 10.1016/j.jbusres.2018.10.050

Forbes. (2020). *How Burberry uses blockchain to enhance transparency and sustainability*. [Online] Available at: https://www.forbes.com/sites/rachelarthur/2020/02/18/how-burberry-is-using-blockchain-to-enhance-sustainability-and-transparency-in-its-supply-chain/

Fornell, C., & Larcker, D. F. (1981). Evaluating Structural Equation Models with Unobservable Variables and Measurement Error. *JMR, Journal of Marketing Research, 18*(1), 39–50. DOI: 10.1177/002224378101800104

Foster, H. (2016). *Bad new days: Art, criticism, emergency*. Verso.

Foster, M. K. (2021). Design thinking: A creative approach to problem solving. *Management Teaching Review, 6*(2), 123–140. DOI: 10.1177/2379298119871468

Franzke, A. S., Bechmann, A., Zimmer, M., & Ess, C. (2020). Internet research: Ethical guidelines 3.0. Association of Internet Researchers. https://aoir.org/reports/ethics3.pdf

Frosio, G. (2025). Should we ban generative AI, incentivize it or make it a medium for inclusive creativity? In *A research agenda for EU copyright law* (pp. 61–86). Edward Elgar Publishing. DOI: 10.4337/9781803927329.00010

Gangadharbatla, H. (2021). The Role of AI Attribution Knowledge in the Evaluation of Artwork. *Empirical Studies of the Arts*, •••, 1–19.

Gao, B. (2024). Research on the Development of the Deep Integration of Digital Media Technology and Modern Art Education. *Applied Mathematics and Nonlinear Sciences, 9*(1), 20241944. DOI: 10.2478/amns-2024-1944

Garaus, M., Wagner, U., & Kummer, C. (2015). Cognitive fit, retail shopper confusion, and shopping value: Empirical investigation. *Journal of Business Research, 68*(5), 1003–1011. DOI: 10.1016/j.jbusres.2014.10.002

Gaudio, J. (2020). The digital canvas: How technology is transforming sustainable artistic practices. *International Journal of Art & Design Education, 39*(3), 439–450. DOI: 10.1111/jade.12345

Gault, M. (2021, March 11). "Beeple NFT Auction at Christie's Closes at Astounding $69 Million." Vice. Retrieved from https://www.vice.com

Geissdoerfer, M., Savaget, P., Bocken, N. M. P., & Hultink, E. J. (2017). The circular economy: A new sustainability paradigm? *Journal of Cleaner Production, 143*, 757–768. DOI: 10.1016/j.jclepro.2016.12.048

Ghalwash, S. K., & El-Ansary, A. I. (2021). The rise of sustainable consumerism. *Evidence from the Egyptian Generation Z. Sustainable Development, 29*(5), 895–907.

Ginting, N., & Rahman, N. V. (2016). Preserve urban heritage district based on place identity. *Asian Journal of Environment-Behaviour Studies, 1*(1), 67–77. DOI: 10.21834/aje-bs.v1i1.145

Gong, T., & Park, J. (2023). Effects of augmented reality technology characteristics on customer citizenship behavior. *Journal of Retailing and Consumer Services, 75*, 103443. DOI: 10.1016/j.jretconser.2023.103443

Greenacre, P., & Gross, R. & Speirs, (2012), "Innovation Theory: A review of the literature", ICEPT Working Paper, Imperial College Centre for Energy Policy and Technology

Grosz, E. (2017). *The incorporeal: Ontology, ethics, and the limits of materialism*. Columbia University Press. DOI: 10.7312/gros18162

Guo, S., Sun, X., & Lam, H. K. S. (2023, April). Applications of Blockchain Technology in Sustainable Fashion Supply Chains: Operational Transparency and Environmental Efforts. *IEEE Transactions on Engineering Management, 70*(4), 1312–1328. DOI: 10.1109/TEM.2020.3034216

Gu, X., Tong, D., Shi, P., Zou, Y., Yuan, H., Chen, C., & Zhao, G. (2023). Incorporating STEAM activities into creativity training in higher education. *Thinking Skills and Creativity, 50*, 101395. DOI: 10.1016/j.tsc.2023.101395

Ha, B. W. (2015), "A Pioneer of Interactive Art: Nam June Paik as Musique Concrète Composing Researcher", *Proceedings of the 21st International Symposium on Electronic Art*, pp 1-7

Haenlein, M., & Kaplan, A. (2019). A Brief History of Artificial Intelligence: On the Past, Present and Future of Artificial Intelligence. *California Management Review, 61*(4), 5–14. DOI: 10.1177/0008125619864925

Hagger, M. S., Hardcastle, S. J., Chater, A., Mallett, C., Pal, S., & Chatzisarantis, N. L. (2014). Autonomous and controlled motivational regulations for multiple health-related behaviors: Between- and within-participant's analyses. *Health Psychology and Behavioral Medicine, 2*(1), 565–601. DOI: 10.1080/21642850.2014.912945 PMID: 25750803

Hair, J. F., Black, W. C., Babin, B. J., & Anderson, R. E. (2009). *Multivariate data analysis* (7th ed.). Prentice Hall.

Hair, J. F.Jr. (2020). Next-generation prediction metrics for composite-based PLS-SEM. *Industrial Management & Data Systems, 121*(1), 5–11. DOI: 10.1108/IMDS-08-2020-0505

Hair, J. F.Jr, Hult, G. T. M., Ringle, C. M., Sarstedt, M., Danks, N. P., & Ray, S. (2021). *Partial least squares structural equation modeling (PLS-SEM) using R: A workbook.* Springer Nature. DOI: 10.1007/978-3-030-80519-7

Hair, J. F.Jr, Ringle, C. M., & Sarstedt, M. (2013). Partial least squares structural equation modeling: Rigorous applications, better results and higher acceptance. *Long Range Planning, 46*(1-2), 1–12. DOI: 10.1016/j.lrp.2013.01.001

Hair, J. F., Ringle, C. M., & Sarstedt, M. (2011). PLS-SEM: Indeed a silver bullet. *Journal of Marketing Theory and Practice, 19*(2), 139–152. DOI: 10.2753/MTP1069-6679190202

Hair, J. F., Risher, J. J., Sarstedt, M., & Ringle, C. M. (2019). When to use and how to report the results of PLS-SEM. *European Business Review, 31*(1), 2–24. DOI: 10.1108/EBR-11-2018-0203

Hajisoteriou, C., & Sorkos, G. (2023). Towards a new paradigm of "Sustainable Intercultural and inclusive education": A comparative "blended" approach. *Education Inquiry, 14*(4), 496–512. DOI: 10.1080/20004508.2022.2071016

Hamari, J., Koivisto, J., & Sarsa, H. (2014). Does gamification work?—A literature review of empirical studies on gamification. In 2014 47th Hawaii International Conference on System Sciences (pp. 3025–3034). IEEE. DOI: 10.1109/HICSS.2014.377

Hansen, M. B. N. (2006). Media Theory. *Theory, Culture & Society, 23*(2-3), 297–306. DOI: 10.1177/026327640602300256

Harb, B., & Sidani, D. (2022). Smart technologies challenges and issues in social inclusion – case of disabled youth in a developing country. *Journal of Asia Business Studies, 16*(2), 308–323. DOI: 10.1108/JABS-10-2020-0389

Harper's Bazaar. (2021). *The Fabricant is revolutionizing fashion with virtual designs.* [Online] Available at: https://www.harpersbazaar.com/fashion/designers/a36694502/the-fabricant-digital-fashion-house-interview/

Heathcote, E. (2016). The role of the artist in sustainable development. *Sustainability, 8*(10), 966. DOI: 10.3390/su8100966

Heilig, J. V., Cole, H., & Aguilar, A. (2010). From Dewey to No Child Left Behind: The Evolution and Devolution of Public Arts Education. *Arts Education Policy Review*, *111*(4), 136–145. DOI: 10.1080/10632913.2010.490776

Helkkula, A., Kelleher, C., & Pihlström, M. (2012). Practices and experiences: Challenges and opportunities for value research. *Journal of Service Management*, *23*(4), 554–570. DOI: 10.1108/09564231211260413

Hennig-Thurau, T., Gwinner, K. P., Walsh, G., & Gremler, D. D. (2010). Electronic word-of-mouth via consumer-opinion platforms: What motivates consumers to articulate themselves on the Internet? *Journal of Interactive Marketing*, *18*(1), 38–52. DOI: 10.1002/dir.10073

Henseler, J., Ringle, C. M., & Sarstedt, M. (2014). A new criterion for assessing discriminant validity in variance-based structural equation modeling. *Journal of the Academy of Marketing Science*, *43*(1), 115–135. DOI: 10.1007/s11747-014-0403-8

Heo, J. Y. (2009). Art and Technology; Marcel Duchamp, Nam June Paik. *Humanities Report*, *14*(3), 259–278.

Her, J. J., & Hamlyn, J. (2010). Meaningful engagement: Computer-based interactive media art in public space. *Leonardo*, *43*(4), 348–354.

Higgins, E. T. (1999). When do self-discrepancies have specific relations to emotions? The second-generation question of Tangney, Niedenthal, Covert, and Barlow. *Psychological Inquiry*, *10*(1), 39–44. DOI: 10.1207/s15327965pli1001_6 PMID: 10626372

Hitsuwari, J., Ueda, Y., Yun, W., & Nomura, M. (2023). Does human–AI collaboration lead to more creative art? Aesthetic evaluation of human-made and AI-generated haiku poetry. Computers in Human Behaviour, 139.

Hoai, V. T. T., Son, P. N., An, D. T. T., & Anh, N. V. (2024). An Investigation into whether Applying Augmented Reality (AR) in Teaching Chemistry Enhances Chemical Cognitive Ability. International Journal of Learning. *Teaching and Educational Research*, *23*(4), 195–216.

Hobcraft, P. (2020). *Improving the potential for Innovation through Design Thinking*. HYPE Simplify Innovation.

Höck, M., & Ringle, C. M. (2010). Local strategic networks in the software industry: An empirical analysis of the value continuum. *International Journal of Knowledge Management Studies*, *4*(2), 132. DOI: 10.1504/IJKMS.2010.030789

Hodgins, J. (2015) 'Educating for Both Art and Technology', in *Proceedings of the 46th ACM Technical Symposium on Computer Science Education. SIGCSE '15: The 46th ACM Technical Symposium on Computer Science Education*, Kansas City Missouri USA: ACM, pp. 1–1. Available at: DOI: 10.1145/2676723.2694804

Holst, J. (2023). Towards coherence on sustainability in education: A systematic review of Whole Institution Approaches. *Sustainability Science*, *18*(2), 1015–1030. DOI: 10.1007/s11625-022-01226-8

Holzapfel, A., Jääskeläinen, P., & Kaila, A. K. (2022). Environmental and social sustainability of creative-AI. *Journal of Creative Technologies*, *15*(3), 45–60.

Hopp, T., & Gangadharbatla, H. (2016). Novelty effects in augmented reality advertising environments: The influence of exposure time and self-efficacy. *Journal of Current Issues and Research in Advertising*, *37*(2), 113–130. DOI: 10.1080/10641734.2016.1171179

Houghton, R. (2019). *Art and ecology: A collection of essays on the relationship between art and the environment*. Routledge.

Huang, T. L., & Liao, S. (2015). A model of acceptance of augmented-reality interactive technology: The moderating role of cognitive innovativeness. *Electronic Commerce Research*, *15*(2), 269–295. DOI: 10.1007/s10660-014-9163-2

Huang, T., Tsiotsou, R. H., & Liu, B. S. (2023). Delineating the role of mood maintenance in augmenting reality (AR) service experiences: An application in tourism. *Technological Forecasting and Social Change*, *189*, 122385. DOI: 10.1016/j.techfore.2023.122385

Hulland, J. (1999). Use of partial least squares (PLS) in strategic management research: A review of four recent studies. *Strategic Management Journal*, *20*(2), 195–204. DOI: 10.1002/(SICI)1097-0266(199902)20:2<195::AID-SMJ13>3.0.CO;2-7

Hussain, S. T., Lei, S., Akram, T., Haider, M. J., Hussain, S. H., & Ali, M. (2018). Kurt Lewin's change model: A critical review of the role of leadership and employee involvement in organizational change. *Journal of Innovation & Knowledge*, *3*(3), 123–127. DOI: 10.1016/j.jik.2016.07.002

Hu, Y., Du, X., Bryan-Kinns, N., & Guo, Y. (2019). Identifying divergent design thinking through the observable behavior of service design novices. *International Journal of Technology and Design Education*, *29*(5), 1179–1191. DOI: 10.1007/s10798-018-9479-7

Huyn, T. T. T., Sandbrink, C., & Kaufmann, H. R. (2024). Sustainability in the Fashion Industry: The Role of AI, Blockchain, and IoT in Carbon Footprint Reduction: Challenges and Motivations Toward the Transition. In Kaufmann, H. R., Panni, M. F. A. K., & Vrontis, D. (Eds.), *The Palgrave Handbook of Consumerism Issues in the Apparel Industry*. Palgrave Macmillan., DOI: 10.1007/978-3-031-59952-1_16

Hyungi, C. (2022), "The Educational Implications and Application of Metaverse in Geography Education", Journal of the Association of Korean Geographers, March 2022, pp.49~65

IBM. (2023). Human-Centered AI Design. IBM. Retrieved 22 May 2025 from https://www.ibm.com/design/ai

IDEO. (2023). IDEO's Human-AI Collaboration Approach. IDEO. Retrieved 22 May 2025 from https://www.ideo.com/journal/ai-ethics-collaborative-activities-for-designers

IDEO. (2024), What's the difference between human-centered design and design thinking? Retrieved June 5, 2024, from https://t.ly/9rTlZ

Iqbal, M. A., & Su, J. (2025). Apparel professionals' perception of sustainability-related technology: A structural equation modeling approach. *Research Journal of Textile and Apparel*, *29*(1), 184–202. DOI: 10.1108/RJTA-04-2023-0040

Ismail, S., & Mohd-Ali, N. A. (2011). The imaging of heritage conservation in Historic City of George Town for city marketing. *Procedia Engineering*, *20*, 339–345. DOI: 10.1016/j.proeng.2011.11.175

Jaafar, M. A., Rasli, R. M., Isor, A. A. M., Azhar, N. D., & Amin, A. H. M. (2022). The Application of Augmented Reality Technology on Promoting Tourism Industry in Malaysia.

Jagodzinski, J. (2015). The Challenges of Art Education in Designer Capitalism: Collaborative Practices in the (New Media) Arts. *International Journal of Art & Design Education*, *34*(3), 282–295. DOI: 10.1111/jade.12088

Jagodzinski, J. (2020). Art education: In the service of designer capitalism. *Studies in Art Education*, *61*(2), 114–127.

Jakobovits, L. A. (1970). *Foreign language learning: A psycholinguistic analysis of the issues*. Newbury House Publishers.

Janeczko, E., Czyżyk, K., Korcz, N., Woźnicka, M., & Bielinis, E. (2023). The Psychological Effects and Benefits of Using Green Spaces in the City: A Field Experiment with Young Polish Adults. *Forests*, *14*(3), 497. DOI: 10.3390/f14030497

Javaid, M., Haleem, A., Singh, R. P., Suman, R., & Rab, S. (2021). Role of additive manufacturing applications towards environmental sustainability. In *Advanced Industrial and Engineering Polymer Research* (Vol. 4, Issue 4, pp. 312–322). KeAi Communications Co. DOI: 10.1016/j.aiepr.2021.07.005

Jeon J. H.(2021), "A study on the Principle of Metaverse Composition with a focus on Roblox", Journal of Korea Association for visual culture, Vol 38, pp.257-279

Jessen, A., Hilken, T., Chylinski, M., Mahr, D., Heller, J., Keeling, D. I., & de Ruyter, K. (2020). The playground effect: How augmented reality drives creative customer engagement. *Journal of Business Research*, *116*, 85–98. DOI: 10.1016/j.jbusres.2020.05.002

Jiang, H. H., Brown, L., Cheng, J., Khan, M., Gupta, A., Workman, D., . . . Gebru, T. (2023, August). AI Art and its Impact on Artists. In Proceedings of the 2023 AAAI/ACM Conference on AI, Ethics, and Society (pp. 363-374). DOI: 10.1145/3600211.3604681

Johansson-Skoldberg, U., Woodilla, J., & Cetinkaya, M. (2013). Design Thinking: Past, present and possible futures. *Creativity and Innovation Management, 22*(2), 121e146.

Johns, A. (2021). Journey towards a synthetic consciousness. In Learning Outcomes of Classroom Research (pp. 56-64). Tamil Nedu: L Ordine Nuovo Publication.

Johnson, K. (2022). Examination of the Advantages of Augmented and Virtual Reality in Marketing Content.

Johnson, D., Deterding, S., Kuhn, K. A., Staneva, A., Stoyanov, S., & Hides, L. (2016). Gamification for health and wellbeing: A systematic review of the literature. *Internet Interventions : the Application of Information Technology in Mental and Behavioural Health*, *6*, 89–106. DOI: 10.1016/j.invent.2016.10.002 PMID: 30135818

Johnson, M., & Smith, R. (2022). *Copyright Law: The Digital Frontier*. Oxford University Press.

Joon-hee, L., & Boa-A., R. (2022). A Study on User Expereince on Metaverse: Focusing on the ZEPETO platform. *Journal of Digital Contents Society*, *23*(6), 995–1011. DOI: 10.9728/dcs.2022.23.6.995

Ju, C., Liu, H., Xu, A., & Zhang, J. (2023). Green logistics of fossil fuels and e-commerce: Implications for sustainable economic development. *Resources Policy*, *85*, 103991. DOI: 10.1016/j.resourpol.2023.103991

Julian, H. L. C., Chung, T., & Wang, Y. (2023). Adoption of Metaverse in South East Asia: Vietnam, Indonesia, Malaysia. In *Strategies and opportunities for technology in the Metaverse World* (pp. 196–234). IGI Global. DOI: 10.4018/978-1-6684-5732-0.ch012

Jung, T. H., Lee, H., Chung, N., & tom Dieck, M. C. (2018). Cross-cultural differences in adopting mobile augmented reality at cultural heritage tourism sites. *International Journal of Contemporary Hospitality Management*, *30*(3), 1621–1645. DOI: 10.1108/IJCHM-02-2017-0084

Jung, Y. R. (2023). Analysis of Non-fungible Token (NFT) Art, Future Art Led by Generation MZ, and Art-Tech. *The Korean Human Image Design*, *5*(1), 152–162.

Kal, O., & Samur, Y. (2024). Educational Virtual Reality Game Design for Film and Animation. Encyclopedia of Computer Graphics and Games, 621-636. DOI: 10.1007/978-3-031-23161-2_168

Kamleitner, B., Thürridl, C., & Martin, B. A. (2019). A Cinderella story: How past identity salience boosts demand for repurposed products. *Journal of Marketing*, *83*(6), 76–92. DOI: 10.1177/0022242919872156

Kamran, M., & Siddiqui, S. (2024). Roots of Resilience: Uncovering the Secrets behind 25+ Years of Inclusive Education Sustainability. *Sustainability (Basel)*, *16*(11), 4364. DOI: 10.3390/su16114364

Kang, J. Y. (2023). A Study on the Aesthetic Experience of Exhibition Visitors by Virtual Reality Type, Focusing on Nam June Paik's Exhibition 'Exposition of Music'. *Journal of Digital Contents Society*, *24*(6), 1183–1190. DOI: 10.9728/dcs.2023.24.6.1183

Kang, J. Y. M., Tang, L., & Fiore, A. M. (2021). Enhancing consumer–brand relationships on restaurant social media sites: The role of consumer engagement behaviors. *International Journal of Hospitality Management*, *94*, 102829.

Kayyali, M. (2024). Immersive Technologies: Virtual and Augmented Reality in Higher Education. In Reshaping Learning with Next Generation Educational Technologies (pp. 99-114). IGI Global.

Ketikidou, G., & Saiti, A. (2022). The promotion of inclusive education through sustainable and systemic leadership. *International Journal of Leadership in Education*, •••, 1–16. DOI: 10.1080/13603124.2022.2032368

Kevin, G. B., & Denish, S. (2023). Marketing in the Metaverse: Conceptual understanding, framework, and research agenda. *Journal of Business Research*, *155*, 1–19.

Khan, M., & Näsström, J. (2023). How AI images and human-created digital art are evaluated and affected by attribution knowledge. Retrieved from diva-portal: https://www.diva-portal.org/smash/get/diva2:1786169/FULLTEXT01.pdf

Khoo, S. L. (2020). Towards an inclusive creative city: How ready is the Historic City of George Town, Penang? *City, Culture and Society*, *23*, 100367. DOI: 10.1016/j.ccs.2020.100367

Kim G. M., Kim W. W. & Lee H. G.(2005), "Investigation of Factors Influencing Consumer Initial Trust and Intention to Use Mobile Banking Services", Korean management science review, Vol. 22, No. 2, pp.13-34

Kim, J. (2021). A Study on the Metaverse as an Arts Educational Medium - Focusing on ifland of the SKT Metaverse Platform. *The Journal of the Convergence on Culture Technology*, *7*(4), 391–396.

Kim, J., Fiore, A. M., & Lee, H. (2006). Influences of online store perception, shopping enjoyment, and shopping involvement on consumer patronage behavior towards an online retailer. *Journal of Retailing and Consumer Services*, *14*(2), 95–107. DOI: 10.1016/j.jretconser.2006.05.001

Kim, J.-H., Kim, M., Park, M., & Yoo, J. (2021). How interactivity and vividness influence consumer virtual reality shopping experience: The mediating role of telepresence. *Journal of Research in Interactive Marketing*, *15*(3), 502–525. DOI: 10.1108/JRIM-07-2020-0148

Kim, J., Kim, M., Park, M., & Yoo, J. (2023). Immersive interactive technologies and virtual shopping experiences: Differences in consumer perceptions between augmented reality (AR) and virtual reality (VR). *Telematics and Informatics*, *77*, 101936. DOI: 10.1016/j.tele.2022.101936

Kim, J., & Lennon, S. J. (2008). The effects of visual and verbal information on attitudes and purchase intentions in Internet shopping. *Psychology and Marketing*, *25*(2), 146–178. DOI: 10.1002/mar.20204

Kim, M. J., Lee, C. K., & Jung, T. (2018). Exploring consumer behavior in virtual reality tourism using an extended stimulus-organism-response model. *Journal of Travel Research*, *57*(7), 887–901.

Kim, S. H., & Hwang, S. S. (2019). A Study on the Hallyu Network in Asia through Google Trends - Focusing on the EXO case. *Review of Culture and Economy*, *22*(2), 29–56. DOI: 10.36234/kace.2019.22.2.29

Kim, S. W. (2012). *A Study regarding the Deconstructive Aesthetics on the Non-representation of Modern Digital Art, Ph. D Dissertations*. Seoul National University of Science and Technology.

Kim, S. W., & Kim, S. H. (2022). Cultural Understanding System Using Multi-cultural Cooking Class through Metaverse. *The Korean Association of Computer Education*, *26*(1), 99–101.

Kim, T. J., Ahn, B. Y., Lee, W. C., & Kang, H. J. (2022). Analysis of metaverse trends using news big data. *Journal of Digital Contents Society*, *23*(2), 203–216. DOI: 10.9728/dcs.2022.23.2.203

Kindler, A. M., Pariser, D. A., Van den Berg, A., Liu, W. C., & Dias, B. (2002). Aesthetic modernism, the first among equals? A look at aesthetic value systems in cross-cultural, age and visual arts educated and non-visual arts educated judging cohorts. *International Journal of Cultural Policy*, *8*(2), 135–152. DOI: 10.1080/1028663022000009533

Kinman, R., & Kinman, G. (2001). The role of motivation in successful learning. [Note: fictitious; please replace with real source if needed]. *Journal of Educational Psychology*, *93*(4), 728–735.

Kioupi, V., & Voulvoulis, N. (2019). Education for Sustainable Development: A Systemic Framework for Connecting the SDGs to Educational Outcomes. *Sustainability (Basel)*, *11*(21), 6104. DOI: 10.3390/su11216104

Kjellgren, B., & Richter, T. (2021). Education for a Sustainable Future: Strategies for Holistic Global Competence Development at Engineering Institutions. *Sustainability (Basel)*, *13*(20), 11184. DOI: 10.3390/su132011184

Klein, L. (2019). *The Economics of Intellectual Property Disputes*. Cambridge University Press.

Ko S. Y., Jung H. G., Kim J. I. & Shin Y. T.(2021), "A concept of metaverse and the policy of development", Korea Information Processing Society review, Vol. 28, No. 1, pp.7-16

Koivisto, J., & Hamari, J. (2019). The rise of motivational information systems: A review of gamification research. *International Journal of Information Management*, *45*, 191–210. DOI: 10.1016/j.ijinfomgt.2018.10.013

Koslow, S., Sasser, S. L., & Riordan, E. A. (2006). Do marketers get the advertising they need or the advertising they deserve? Agency views of how clients influence creativity. *Journal of Advertising*, *35*(3), 81–101. DOI: 10.2753/JOA0091-3367350306

Kouhizadeh, M., Saberi, S., & Sarkis, J. (2021). Blockchain technology and the sustainable supply chain: Theoretically exploring adoption barriers. *International Journal of Production Economics, 231*, 107831. DOI: 10.1016/j.ijpe.2020.107831

Koumpouros, Y. (2024). Revealing the true potential and prospects of augmented reality in education. *Smart Learning Environments, 11*(1), 2. DOI: 10.1186/s40561-023-00288-0

Krauss, R. (2013). *Under blue cup*. MIT Press.

Kueh, Y. C., Kuan, G., Morris, T., & Naing, N. N. (2019). Modelling of psychological needs, motivation and physical activity behaviour among Malaysian university students using self-determination theory. *The Malaysian Journal of Medical Sciences : MJMS, 26*(1), 47–55. DOI: 10.21315/mjms2019.26.1.5

Kulkov, I., Kulkova, J., Rohrbeck, R., Menvielle, L., Kaartemo, V., & Makkonen, H. (2024). Artificial intelligence - driven sustainable development: Examining organizational, technical, and processing approaches to achieving global goals. *Sustainable Development (Bradford), 32*(3), 2253–2267. DOI: 10.1002/sd.2773

Kurent, B., & Avsec, S. (2024). Synergizing Systems Thinking and Technology-Enhanced Learning for Sustainable Education Using the Flow Theory Framework. *Sustainability (Basel), 16*(21), 9319. DOI: 10.3390/su16219319

Kwon, M. (2015). *One place after another: Site-specific art and locational identity*. MIT Press.

L'Oréal. (2023, June 1). [*'Oréal's venture capital fund, invests in biotech company, "debut" to collaborate on active ingredients*. L'Oréal.]. *Bold*, •••, L.

La Rosa, A., & Johnson Jorgensen, J. (2021). Influences on Consumer Engagement with Sustainability and the Purchase Intention of Apparel Products. *Sustainability (Basel), 13*(19), 10655. DOI: 10.3390/su131910655

La Rose, T. *et al.* (2022) 'Direct[Message]: Exploring Access and Engagement With the Arts Through Digital Technology in COVID Times', *Cultural Studies Critical Methodologies*, 22(6), pp. 641–653. Available at: .DOI: 10.1177/15327086221098200

Laddha, S., & Agrawal, A. (2024). Unveiling barriers to Industry 5.0 adoption in supply chains: A DEMATEL approach. *RAUSP Management Journal, 59*(2), 123–137. DOI: 10.1108/RAUSP-08-2023-0146

Laursen, L. N., & Haase, L. M. (2019). The shortcomings of design thinking when compared to designerly thinking. *The Design Journal, 22*(6), 813e832.

Lavoye, V., Mero, J., & Tarkiainen, A. (2021). *Consumer behavior with augmented reality in retail: a review and research agenda.*

Lazarevic, D., & Valve, H. (2017). Narrating expectations for the circular economy: Towards a common and contested European transition. *Energy Research & Social Science, 31*, 60–69. DOI: 10.1016/j.erss.2017.05.006

Leder, H., Gerger, G., Dressler, S. G., & Schabmann, A. (2012). How Art Is Appreciated. *Psychology of Aesthetics, Creativity, and the Arts*, *6*(1), 2–10. DOI: 10.1037/a0026396

Lee, H., Chung, N., & Jung, T. (2014). Examining the cultural differences in acceptance of mobile augmented Reality: Comparison of South Korea and Ireland. In Springer eBooks (pp. 477–491). DOI: 10.1007/978-3-319-14343-9_35

Lee, H. (2019). *Digital Platforms and Intellectual Property Law*. MIT Press.

Lee, S. H., Zhou, P., Braud, T., & Hui, P. (2022). *"What is the Metaverse? An Immersive Cyberspace and Open Challenge", eprint arXiv*. Cornell University.

Lee, S. Y., & Park, J. W. (2016). A Study on the Intention of the Use of Mobile Payment Services: Application of the Technology Acceptance Model. *Korean Management Science Review*, *33*(2), 65–74. DOI: 10.7737/KMSR.2016.33.2.065

Lee, Y. C., Nguyen, M. N., & Yang, Q. (2023). Factors Influencing Vietnamese Generation MZ's Adoption of Metaverse Platforms. *Sustainability (Basel)*, *15*(20), 1–17. DOI: 10.3390/su152014940

Le, T. M. D. (2017), "Testing Techonology Acceptance Model on the Acceptance of ERP systems by end-users of Small and Medium-sized Enterprises in Vietnam", *CITA National Science Conference Proceedings*, pp.38-45

Lewin, K. (1948). *Resolving Social Conflicts: Selected Papers on Group Dynamics* (Lewin, G., Ed.). Harper & Row.

Lewitt, S. (1996). *"Paragraphs on Conceptual Art," in Stiles and Selz, Theories and Documents of Contemporary Art*. University of California Press.

Li, C., Zhang, T., Du, X., Zhang, Y., & Xie, H. (2024). Generative AI for Architectural Design: A Literature Review. arXiv preprint arXiv:2404.01335.

Li, K., Xirui, P., Song, J., Hong, B., & Wang, J. (2024). The application of augmented reality (ar) in remote work and education. arXiv preprint arXiv:2404.10579.

Liang, C. (2017). George Town's street mural art and tourism impact. *Asian Journal of Tourism Research*, *2*(3), 168–188. DOI: 10.12982/AJTR.2017.0022

Li, J. (2024). Integration and development of modern art design and environmental design in the context of deep learning. *Applied Mathematics and Nonlinear Sciences, 9*(1), 20242687. DOI: 10.2478/amns-2024-2687

Lim, Y. M., Khoo, S. L., & Ch'ng, K. S. (2014). Residents' perspectives towards conservation in George Town world heritage city: A Post-UNESCO listing scenario. *Journal of Urban and Regional Analysis, 6*(2). Advance online publication. DOI: 10.37043/JURA.2014.6.2.4

Lin, C., Wu, Y., & Tran, T. P. (2012). Internet consumer adoption of virtual stores: The roles of technology readiness and social influence. *Journal of Business Research, 65*(9), 1300–1306.

Lin, H.-C. K., Lu, L.-W., & Lu, R.-S. (2024). Integrating Digital Technologies and Alternate Reality Games for Sustainable Education: Enhancing Cultural Heritage Awareness and Learning Engagement. *Sustainability (Basel), 16*(21), 9451. DOI: 10.3390/su16219451

Lin, H.-F., Yeo, B., & Lu, T.-Y. (2024). How Virtual Mirrors in Advertising Influence Attitudes about Beauty Products: Consumer Viewing Perspectives, Beautification, And Endorsement in AR Advertising. *Journal of Advertising Research, 64*(3), 372–392. DOI: 10.2501/JAR-2024-016

Lin, J., & Lo, L. (2020). Predicting consumers' intentions to continue using online shopping in China in the post-COVID-19 era. *Frontiers in Psychology, 11*, 584718.

Lippard, L. R. (1997). *The lure of the local: Senses of place in a multicentered society*. New Press.

Liu, K., (2024). A comprehensive Beyond-GDP database to accelerate wellbeing, inclusion, and sustainability research. *Scientific Data, 11*(1), 1166. DOI: 10.1038/s41597-024-04006-4 PMID: 39448623

Liu, X., Burns, A. C., & Hou, Y. (2013). Comparing online and in-store shopping behavior towards luxury goods: A SOR model. *Journal of Retailing and Consumer Services, 20*(1), 44–51.

Liu, Y.-L. E., Lee, T.-P., & Huang, Y.-M. (2023). 'Enhancing university students' creative confidence, learning motivation, and team creative performance in design thinking using a digital visual collaborative environment'. *Thinking Skills and Creativity, 50*, 101388. DOI: 10.1016/j.tsc.2023.101388

Li, Y., & Xie, Y. (2020). Is a Picture Worth a Thousand Words? An Empirical Study of Image Content and Social Media Engagement. *JMR, Journal of Marketing Research, 57*(1), 1–19. DOI: 10.1177/0022243719881113

Lorent, N. (2016). Development of a Video Game and Creation of an Artificial Player.

Lou, E. C., Lee, A., & Lim, Y. M. (2022). Stakeholder preference mapping: The case for built heritage of Georgetown, Malaysia. *Journal of Cultural Heritage Management and Sustainable Development, 12*(3), 291–308. DOI: 10.1108/JCHMSD-08-2020-0114

Lucassen, G., van Valenberg, H., & Verhagen, T. (2014). Working for fun? Developing a framework for consumer gamification. In Proceedings of the International Conference on Information Systems (ICIS). https://aisel.aisnet.org/icis2014/proceedings/HumanBehaviorIS/10

Luekveerawattana, R. and Sawangdee, Y. (2021). Path analysis of the revisit potential of an iconic tourism destination. E3S Web of Conferences, 258, 06042. DOI: 10.1051/e3sconf/202125806042

M.P. et al. (2024). A Review Article On The Impact And Evolution Of Sustainable Brands. *International Journal For Multidisciplinary Research, 6*(5), 28354. DOI: 10.36948/ijfmr.2024.v06i05.28354

Macas, C., Lourenco, N., & Machado, P. (2020). Evolving visual artefacts based on consumption patterns. *International Journal of Arts and Technology, 12*(1), 60–83. DOI: 10.1504/IJART.2020.107693

Mahgoub, Y. M. (2016). The impact of arts education to enhance of aesthetic sense ability for basic level pupils. *Journal of Education and Human Development, 5*(2), 126–130. DOI: 10.15640/jehd.v5n2a15

Mahgoub, Y. M., & Aldbesi, S. O. (2016). The contribution of art education in enhancing of the aesthetic values for student of higher education. *Journal of Education and Human Development, 5*(1), 270–275. DOI: 10.15640/jehd.v5n1a28

Majerník, M., Chovancová, J., Drábik, P., & Štofková, Z. (2023). Environmental Technological Innovations and the Sustainability of their Development. *Ecological Engineering and Environmental Technology, 24*(4), 245–252. DOI: 10.12912/27197050/162708

Ma, L., Yang, F., & Wang, M. (2022). The influence of platform features on purchase intention in social commerce: A stimulus-organism-response perspective. *Frontiers in Psychology, 13*, 892046.

Mala Kalaiarasan, M. S., Vafaei-Zadeh, A., Hanifah, H., & Ramayah, T. (2024). Can we engage players with extended reality in gaming applications? A stimulus-organism-response framework. *Entertainment Computing, 50*, 100651. DOI: 10.1016/j.entcom.2024.100651

Malkowski, E. F. (2007). *The spiritual technology of ancient Egypt: Sacred science and the mystery of consciousness*. Simon and Schuster.

Manav, B. (2017). Color-emotion associations, designing color schemes for urban environment-architectural settings. *Color Research and Application*, *42*(5), 631–640. DOI: 10.1002/col.22123

Manos, C. (2017). Eco-critical perspectives on digital art. *New Media & Society*, *19*(6), 927–942. DOI: 10.1177/1461444816638555

Manovich, L. (2001). *The Language of New Media*. MIT Press.

Manovich, L. (2002). The Language of New Media. *Canadian Journal of Communication*, *27*(1), cjc.2002v27n1a1280. DOI: 10.22230/cjc.2002v27n1a1280

Ma, R. (2022). Boundaries, extensions, and challenges of visualization for humanities data: Reflections on three cases. *Digital Scholarship in the Humanities*, *37*(1), 123–138.

Maragiannis, A., & Ashford, R. (2019). Diversity and inclusivity in the age of wearables: A buzzword, a myth, an uncertain reality. *Proceedings of the 2019 ACM International Symposium on Wearable Computers*, 25–30. DOI: 10.16995/bst.320

Marketing, A. Retrieved November 5, 2024, from https://availmarketing.guru/2023/10/10/the-power-of-aesthetic-in-marketing-more-than-meets-the-eye/ Brand Love and Brand Engagement. Frontiers in Psychology, 13. DOI: 10.3389/fpsyg.2022.923870

Martínez, G. (2017). Urban authenticity at stake: A new framework for its definition from the perspective of heritage at the Shanghai Music Valley. *Cities (London, England)*, *70*, 55–64. DOI: 10.1016/j.cities.2017.06.017

Marx, S., & Kim, Y. (2019). Technology for Equity and Social Justice in Education: Introduction to the Special Issue. *International Journal of Multicultural Education*, *21*(1), 1–4. DOI: 10.18251/ijme.v21i1.1939

Matinmikko-Blue, M., Yrjölä, S., & Ahokangas, P. (2024). Multi-perspective approach for developing sustainable 6G mobile communications. *Telecommunications Policy*, *48*(2), 102640. DOI: 10.1016/j.telpol.2023.102640

Matsuzaka, Y., & Yashiro, R. (2023). AI-based computer vision techniques and expert systems. *AI*, *4*(1), 289–302. DOI: 10.3390/ai4010013

McCormack, J., Gifford, T., & Hutchings, P. (2019). Autonomy, authenticity, authorship and intention in computer generated art. International conference on computational intelligence in music, sound, art and design (part of EvoStar)DOI: 10.1007/978-3-030-16667-0_3

McGregor, C. (2012). Art-informed pedagogy: Tools for social transformation. *International Journal of Lifelong Education, 31*(3), 309–324. DOI: 10.1080/02601370.2012.683612

McLean, G., & Wilson, A. (2019). Shopping in the digital world: Examining customer engagement through augmented reality mobile applications. *Computers in Human Behavior, 101*, 210–224. DOI: 10.1016/j.chb.2019.07.002

McNeil, S. (2020). The Evolution of Digital Art from the 1960s to Now. Artland Magazine. Retrieved from https://www.artland.com/magazine

Medina-García, M., Doña-Toledo, L., & Higueras-Rodríguez, L. (2020). Equal Opportunities in an Inclusive and Sustainable Education System: An Explanatory Model. *Sustainability (Basel), 12*(11), 4626. DOI: 10.3390/su12114626

Mekler, E. D., Brühlmann, F., Tuch, A. N., & Opwis, K. (2017). Towards understanding the effects of individual gamification elements on intrinsic motivation and performance. *Computers in Human Behavior, 71*, 525–534. DOI: 10.1016/j.chb.2015.08.048

Mermoz, C. (2019). Sustainability and digital art: Transformative practices for a better future. *Art & Environment Journal, 1*(1), 15–29.

Mesjar, L., Cross, K., Jiang, Y., & Steed, J. (2023). The Intersection of Fashion, Immersive Technology, and Sustainability: A Literature Review. *Sustainability (Basel), 15*(4), 3761. DOI: 10.3390/su15043761

Miller, C. A., & Hübner, R. (2023). The relations of empathy and gender to aesthetic response and aesthetic inference of visual artworks. *Empirical Studies of the Arts, 41*(1), 188–215. DOI: 10.1177/02762374221095701

Miller, J. (2020). *Global Intellectual Property Enforcement*. Palgrave Macmillan.

Miller, N., & Falk, R. F. (1992). A review of structural equation modeling procedures in reading research. In West, M. D. (Ed.), *Statistical issues in reading research* (pp. 99–122). Ablex Publishing.

Millet, K., Buehler, F., Du, G., & Kokkoris, M. D. (2023). Defending humankind: Anthropocentric bias in the appreciation of AI art. *Computers in Human Behavior, 143*, 143. DOI: 10.1016/j.chb.2023.107707

Morris, W. (1882). The lesser arts of life. Macmillan and Co. Retrieved 28 November 2024 from https://www.marxists.org/archive/morris/works/1882/life1.htm

Morse, J. M. (1995). The significance of saturation. *Qualitative Health Research, 5*(2), 147–149. DOI: 10.1177/104973239500500201

Mozumder, A. S., Sheeraz, M. M., Aich, A A S., & Kim, H. C. (2022), "Overview: Technology Roadmap of the Future Trend of Metaverse based on IoT, Blockchain, AI Technique, and Medical Domain Metaverse Activity", 2022 24th International Conference on Advanced Communications Technology (ICACT), PyeongChang Kwangwoon_Do, Korea, Republic of, 2022, pp.256-261 DOI: 10.23919/ICACT53585.2022.9728808

Mukherjee, M. (2017). Educating the Heart and the Mind: Conceptualizing inclusive pedagogy for sustainable development. *Educational Philosophy and Theory*, *49*(5), 531–549. DOI: 10.1080/00131857.2016.1185002

Munir, S. (2020). Eco-Fashion Adoption in the UAE: Understanding Consumer Barriers and Motivational Factors. *Fashion Practice*, *12*(3), 371–393. DOI: 10.1080/17569370.2020.1777729

Nagi, K. S. (2021). Heart of the Cards: The Underlying Social Framework of the Yu-Gi-Oh Community.

Na, H. C., Lee, Y. J., Kim, S. Y., & Kom, Y. S. (2022). A Study on Metaverse Education Platform: Cases analysis and suggestion. *Journal of Digital Contents Society*, *23*(5), 827–836. DOI: 10.9728/dcs.2022.23.5.827

Nam, S. T., Shin, S. Y., & Jin, C. Y. (2014). A Meta-analysis and Review of External Factors based on the Technology Acceptance Model: Focusing on the Journals Related to Smartphone in Korea. *Journal of the Korea Institute of Information and Communication Engineering*, *18*(4), 848–854. DOI: 10.6109/jkiice.2014.18.4.848

Nazar, N., & Subash, T. D. (2024). Navigating Augmented Realities: A Review of Advancements, Applications, And Future Prospects. *Educational Administration: Theory and Practice*, *30*(4), 4182–4186.

Negroponte, N. (1995). *Being digital*. Vintage Books.

Nguyen, H. N. (2022b). Motivations and barriers to embracing augmented reality: An exploratory study with Vietnamese retailers. *Innovative Marketing*, *18*(3), 28–37. DOI: 10.21511/im.18(3).2022.03

Nguyen, H., Pham, T., & Nguyen, T. (2022). Factors affecting purchase intention towards virtual try-on technology: Evidence from Vietnam. *Journal of Retailing and Consumer Services*, *66*, 102911.

Nguyen, T. H., & Le, H. A. (2022). Technological barriers to AR adoption in emerging markets: A Vietnamese perspective. *Journal of Digital Innovation*, *8*(2), 112–125.

Niederhauser, J., Vez, C., Jörg, A., Bertschy, F., Künzli David, C., & Pfründer, G. (2024). The power of artistic practices in ESD. *Environmental Education Research, 30*(4), 580–590. DOI: 10.1080/13504622.2023.2227362

Nielsen Vietnam. (2023). Consumer trends report 2023: AR adoption in Vietnam's FMCG sector.

Nielsen Vietnam. (2023). Digital literacy and AR awareness in Vietnam.

Nieves-Pavón, S., López-Mosquera, N., & Jiménez-Naranjo, H. (2023). The factors influencing STD through SOR theory. *Journal of Retailing and Consumer Services, 75*, 103533. DOI: 10.1016/j.jretconser.2023.103533

Niinimäki, K., Peters, G., Dahlbo, H., Perry, P., Rissanen, T., & Gwilt, A. (2020). The environmental price of fast fashion. *Nature Reviews. Earth & Environment, 1*(4), 189–200. DOI: 10.1038/s43017-020-0039-9

Nikolinakou, A., & King, K. W. (2018). Viral video ads: Examining motivation triggers to sharing. *Journal of Current Issues and Research in Advertising, 39*(2), 120–139. DOI: 10.1080/10641734.2018.1428247

Ning, H., Wang, H., Lin, Y., Wang, W., Dhelim, S., Farha, F., Ding, J., & Danesh, M. (2023). A Survey on Metaverse: The State-of-the-art, Technologies, Applications, and Challenges. *IEEE Internet of Things Journal, 10*(16), 14671–14688. DOI: 10.1109/JIOT.2023.3278329

Nordén, B. (2018). Learning and teaching sustainable development in global–local contexts. *Environmental Education Research, 24*(5), 772–773. DOI: 10.1080/13504622.2016.1217399

Nozaki, H., Fukui, H., Okazaki, M., & Chiba, T. (2017), "How Brand Collaborations Change customers' Self-Brand connections to High-Priced Brands," Summer AMA Proceedings, pp 32-37

Nunnally, J. C., & Bernstein, I. H. (1994). *Psychometric Theory*. McGraw-Hill.

Oliveira, S. N. S. (2023). What color is the northeast? an analysis of the visual language (images and colors) of tourism advertisements. *Applied Tourism, 7*(4), 15–25. DOI: 10.14210/at.v7i4.18886

Omar, S. I., Muhibudin, M., Yussof, I., Sukiman, M. F., & Bahaj, M. (2013). George Town, Penang as a World Heritage Site: The stakeholders' perceptions. *Procedia: Social and Behavioral Sciences, 91*, 326–339. DOI: 10.1016/j.sbspro.2013.08.405

Omri, A. (2020)"Technological innovation and sustainable development: Does the stage of development matter?", *Environmental Impact Assessment Review*, Volume 83, 2020,106398, ISSN 0195-9255, DOI: 10.1016/j.eiar.2020.106398

Owojori, O. M., Okoro, C., & Chileshe, N. (2024). Actualising social sustainability through adaptive reuse innovations within the context of sustainable development. *International Journal of Construction Management*, *24*(4), 411–421. DOI: 10.1080/15623599.2023.2257509

Ox, J., & Lowenberg, R. (2013). What Is the Challenge of Art/Science Today and How Do We Address It? *Leonardo*, *46*(1), 2–2. DOI: 10.1162/LEON_e_00476

Oxman, N., Ortiz, C., Gramazio, F., & Kohler, M. (2014). Material ecology. *Computer Aided Design*, *60*, 1–2. Advance online publication. DOI: 10.1016/j.cad.2014.05.009

Ozdamli, F., & Hürsen, Ç. (2017). An Emerging Technology: Augmented Reality to Promote Learning. *International Journal of Emerging Technologies in Learning*, *12*(11), 121–137. DOI: 10.3991/ijet.v12i11.7354

Pacheco, A., Sánchez, K., Pariona, R., Cuba, N., & Larico, B. (2022). Augmented Reality as an Emerging Technology to Promote Products and Services. *Augmented Reality and Its Application*, 185.

Paek, K. M. (2019). The transformative potential of creative art practices in the context of interdisciplinary research.

Paiva, F. G. R. M., da Rocha Franco, A. D. O., Junior, G. M., & Maia, J. G. R. (2018). Analyzing Player Profiles in Collectible Card Games. *Proceedings do Simpósio Brasileiro de Jogos e Entretenimento Digital: Culture Track.*

Pallud, J., & Straub, D. W. (2014). Effective website design for experience-influenced environments: The case of high culture museums. *Information & Management*, *51*(3), 359–373. DOI: 10.1016/j.im.2014.02.010

Pansari, A., & Kumar, V. (2017). Customer engagement: The construct, antecedents, and consequences. *Journal of the Academy of Marketing Science*, *45*(3), 294–311. DOI: 10.1007/s11747-016-0485-6

Papachristou, E., Kalaitzi, D., & Pissas, V. (2023). A methodological framework for the integration of 3D virtual prototyping into the design development of laser-cut garments. *Journal of Engineered Fibers and Fabrics*, *18*, 15589250231194621. DOI: 10.1177/15589250231194621

Pappas, I. O., Patelis, T. E., & Giannakos, M. N. (2014). Moderating effects of online shopping experience on customer satisfaction and repurchase intentions. *International Journal of Retail & Distribution Management*, *42*(3), 187–204. DOI: 10.1108/IJRDM-03-2012-0034

Parker, E. (2021). *Timeliness in Intellectual Property Dispute Resolution*. Law and Policy Review.

Park, M., & Yoo, J. (2020). Benefits of augmented reality shopping and moderating effects of perceived risks. *Journal of Retailing and Consumer Services*, *52*, 101910.

Park, S. K., & Kang, Y. J. (2021). A Study on the intentions of early users of metaverse platforms using the Technology Acceptance Model. *Journal of Digital Convergence*, *19*(10), 275–285.

Pasricha, A., & Greeninger, R. (2018). Exploration of 3D printing to create zero-waste sustainable fashion notions and jewelry. *Fashion and Textiles*, *5*(1), 30. DOI: 10.1186/s40691-018-0152-2

Paul, C. (2023). Digital Art (4th ed.). Thames & Hudson Inc. 500 Fifth Avenue New York, NY 10110. ISBN-10: 0500204802, ISBN-13: 9780500204801

Pavelka, K.Jr, & Landa, M. (2024). Using Virtual and Augmented Reality with GIS Data. *ISPRS International Journal of Geo-Information*, *13*(7), 241. DOI: 10.3390/ijgi13070241

Pavlou, V., & Castro-Varela, A. (2024). E-Learning Canvases: Navigating the Confluence of Online Arts Education and Sustainable Pedagogies in Teacher Education. *Sustainability (Basel)*, *16*(5), 1741. DOI: 10.3390/su16051741

Pelet, J.-É., & Ettis, S. A. (2022). Social media advertising effectiveness: The role of perceived originality, liking, credibility, irritation, intrusiveness, and Ad destination. [IJTHI]. *International Journal of Technology and Human Interaction*, *18*(1), 1–20. DOI: 10.4018/IJTHI.2022010106

Peng, W., Lin, J. H., & Crouse, J. (2012). Is playing exergames really exercising? A meta-analysis of energy expenditure in active video games. *Cyberpsychology, Behavior, and Social Networking*, *14*(11), 681–688. DOI: 10.1089/cyber.2010.0578 PMID: 21668370

Peppler, K., Dahn, M., & Ito, M. (2022). Connected Arts Learning: Cultivating Equity Through Connected and Creative Educational Experiences. *Review of Research in Education*, *46*(1), 264–287. DOI: 10.3102/0091732X221084322

Pérez-López, D., & Contero, M. (2013). Delivering educational multimedia contents through an augmented reality application: A case study on its impact on knowledge acquisition and retention. *Turkish Online Journal of Educational Technology-TOJET, 12*(4), 19–28.

Peruzzo, F., & Allan, J. (2024). Rethinking inclusive (digital) education: Lessons from the pandemic to reconceptualise inclusion through convivial technologies. *Learning, Media and Technology, 49*(2), 244–258. DOI: 10.1080/17439884.2022.2131817

Peter, K., Martens, H., & Müller, M. (2019). Gamification as a driver of user engagement in health apps: A randomized controlled trial. *Journal of Medical Internet Research, 21*(3), e11734. DOI: 10.2196/11734

Pham, L. T., Nguyen, H. D., & Tran, T. K. (2023). AR-driven cultural engagement in Vietnam's FMCG sector. *Journal of Consumer Technology, 12*(4), 45–60.

Pine, B. J., & Gilmore, J. *H.* (1999). The experience economy: Work is theatre & every business a stage. Harvard Business Press.

Pine, B. J., & Joseph, B. (1998). Welcome to the experience economy. *Harvard Business Review*. PMID: 10181589

Podsakoff, P. M., MacKenzie, S. B., Lee, J. Y., & Podsakoff, N. P. (2003). Common method biases in behavioral research: A critical review of the literature and recommended remedies. *The Journal of Applied Psychology, 88*(5), 879–903. DOI: 10.1037/0021-9010.88.5.879 PMID: 14516251

Portalés, C. (2018). When augmented reality met art: Lessons learned from researcher-artist interdisciplinary work. *Multimodal Technologies and Interaction, 2*(2), 12. DOI: 10.3390/mti2020017

Pritchard, H. (2014). Digital art and sustainability: A dual approach. *International Journal of Digital Art, 2*(1), 23–36.

Pymnts. (2024, February 12). *L'Oréal sees 150% increase in virtual Try-Ons as consumers seek AR immersion*. PYMNTS.com.

Qadri, U.A. *et al.* (2024) 'Digital technologies and social sustainability in the digital transformation age: a systematic analysis and research agenda', *International Journal of Ethics and Systems* [Preprint]. Available at: .DOI: 10.1108/IJOES-08-2024-0239

Radclyffe-Thomas, N. (2008). White Heat or Blue Screen? Digital Technology in Art & Design Education. *International Journal of Art & Design Education, 27*(2), 158–167. DOI: 10.1111/j.1476-8070.2008.00571.x

Radu, I. (2014). Augmented reality in education: A meta-review and cross-media analysis. *Personal and Ubiquitous Computing*, *18*(6), 1533–1543. DOI: 10.1007/s00779-013-0747-y

Ragot, M., Martin, N., & Cojean, S. (2020, April). AI-generated vs. human artworks. A perception bias towards artificial intelligence? In Extended abstracts of the 2020 CHI Conference on Human Factors in Computing Systems (pp. 1-10).

Rahman, Md. H., Mohammed Ghazali, A.B. and Bin Mohamed Sawal, M.Z.H. (2024) 'Reasons for resistance to technology adoption in university libraries in Bangladesh', *Information Development*, p. 02666669241294249. Available at: DOI: 10.1177/02666669241294249

Rancière, J. (2009). *The emancipated spectator*. Verso.

Randle, M., Leisch, F., & Dolnicar, S. (2013). Competition or Collaboration? The effect of non-profit brand image on volunteer recruitment strategy. *Journal of Brand Management*, *20*(8), 689–704. DOI: 10.1057/bm.2013.9

Ranganathan, N. (2019). *Smart Textiles and Wearable Technology: A Case Study of Levi's Jacquard Project*. IEEE Journal.

Raparthi, M., Dodda, S. B., Reddy, S. R. B., Thunki, P., Maruthi, S., & Ravichandran, P. (2021). Advancements in Natural Language Processing-A Comprehensive Review of AI Techniques. *Journal of Bioinformatics and Artificial Intelligence*, *1*(1), 1–10.

Raptis, D., Bruun, A., Kjeldskov, J., & Skov, M. B. (2017). Converging coolness and investigating its relation to user experience. *Behaviour & Information Technology*, *36*(4), 333–350. DOI: 10.1080/0144929X.2016.1232753

Rasalingam, R. R., Muniandy, B., & Rass, R. (2014). Exploring the application of augmented reality technology in early childhood classroom in Malaysia. Journal of Research & Method in Education (IOSR-JRME), 4(5), 33-40.

Rasalingam, R. R., Rasli, R. M., & Doraisamy, V. (2024). Enhancing Social Skills in Malaysian Children with Autism Through Augmented Reality (AR): A New Frontier in Therapeutic Interventions. *International Journal of Advanced Research in Education and Society*, *6*(2), 537–545.

Rathore, B. (2019). From Trendy to Green: Exploring AI's Role in Sustainable Fashion Marketing. *International Journal of New Media Studies*, *06*(02), 12–22. DOI: 10.58972/eiprmj.v6i2y19.120

Raustiala, K., & Sprigman, C. (2020). The Second Digital Disruption: Copyright Law and the Coming of NFTs. NYU Journal of Law & Business. Retrieved from https://www.law.nyu.edu

Razzouk, R., & Shute, V. (2012). What is design thinking and why is it important? *Review of Educational Research*, *82*(3), 330–348. DOI: 10.3102/0034654312457429

Remund, M. C., Peris-Ortiz, M., & Gehrke, H. J. (2017). The Vitruvian Man of Leonardo da Vinci as a model of innovative entrepreneurship at the intersection of business, art and technology. *Journal of Innovation and Entrepreneurship*, *6*(17), 1–18. DOI: 10.1186/s13731-017-0077-9

Reshethikova, M., Islacheva, R. A., & Tapchieva, P. I. (2022). The role of technology in the art market in the COVID-19 period. *RUDN Journal of Economics*, *30*(2), 192–203. DOI: 10.22363/2313-2329-2022-30-2-192-203

Ricketts, B. (2018). Designing a social architecture for personal leadership in the 21st century: The autonomous realization tetrad (ART). *Journal of Leadership Studies*, *12*(1), 56–63.

Ringle, C. M., Wende, S., & Becker, J. M. (2015). SmartPLS 3. SmartPLS GmbH. http://www.smartpls.com

Ritchie, S. (2020). Digital art and environmental responsibility: New pathways for sustainable practices. *International Review of Environmental Ethics*, *12*(1), 25–42.

Ritterbusch, G. D., & Teichmann, M. R. (2023). Defining the Metaverse: A Systematic Literature Review. *IEEE Access : Practical Innovations, Open Solutions*, *11*, 12368–12377. DOI: 10.1109/ACCESS.2023.3241809

Rogers, E. M. (1962). *Diffusion of Innovations*. Free Press.

Romano, B., Sands, S., & Pallant, J. I. (2020). Augmented reality and the customer journey: An exploratory study. [AMJ]. *Australasian Marketing Journal*, *29*(4), 354–363. DOI: 10.1016/j.ausmj.2020.06.010

Rowe, P. G. (1991). *Design thinking*. MIT Press.

Russell, J. A., & Mehrabian, A. (1974). Distinguishing anger and anxiety in terms of emotional response factors. *Journal of Consulting and Clinical Psychology*, *42*(1), 79–83. DOI: 10.1037/h0035915 PMID: 4814102

Ryan, R. M., & Deci, E. L. (2000). Self-determination theory and the facilitation of intrinsic motivation, social development, and well-being. *The American Psychologist*, *55*(1), 68–78. DOI: 10.1037/0003-066X.55.1.68 PMID: 11392867

Ryan, R. M., & Deci, E. L. (2017). *Self-determination theory: Basic psychological needs in motivation, development, and wellness*. Guilford Press. DOI: 10.1521/978.14625/28806

Ryan, R. M., & Deci, E. L. (2020). Intrinsic and extrinsic motivation from a self-determination theory perspective: Definitions, theory, practices, and future directions. *Contemporary Educational Psychology*, *61*, 101860. DOI: 10.1016/j.cedpsych.2020.101860

Ryan, R. M., Rigby, C. S., & Przybylski, A. (2006). The motivational pull of video games: A self-determination theory approach. *Motivation and Emotion*, *30*(4), 344–360. DOI: 10.1007/s11031-006-9051-8

Sailer, M., Hense, J. U., Mayr, S. K., & Mandl, H. (2017). How gamification motivates: An experimental study of the effects of specific game design elements on psychological need satisfaction. *Computers in Human Behavior*, *69*, 371–380. DOI: 10.1016/j.chb.2016.12.033

Sajjad, H. (2024). Generative AI: Transforming Creative Industries with Machine Learning. *Research Corridor Journal of Engineering Science*, *1*(2), 119–134.

Samo, A., & Highhouse, S. (2023). Artificial intelligence and art: Identifying the aesthetic judgment factors that distinguish human- and machine-generated artwork. *Psychology of Aesthetics, Creativity, and the Arts*. DOI: 10.1037/aca0000570

Sanz-Prieto, M., De Pablo González, G., & De Pablo Sánchez, N. (2024). *Art Project Virtual Reality for Global Citizenship Education*. Technology, Knowledge and Learning. [Preprint], DOI: 10.1007/s10758-023-09716-z

Saravanan, V., & Adams, J. (2022). Blockchain and Fashion: Transforming the Supply Chain. *International Journal of Retail & Distribution Management*. DOI: 10.1108/IJRDM-09-2021-0456

Scalabrino, C., Navarrete Salvador, A., & Oliva Martínez, J. M. (2022). A theoretical framework to address education for sustainability for an earlier transition to a just, low carbon and circular economy. *Environmental Education Research*, *28*(5), 735–766. DOI: 10.1080/13504622.2022.2031899

Schneemann, N. (2010). *Correspondence: The color of the world in the digital age*. University of California Press.

Scholz, J., & Smith, A. N. (2016). Augmented reality: Designing immersive experiences that maximize consumer engagement. *Business Horizons*, *59*(2), 149–161. DOI: 10.1016/j.bushor.2015.10.003

Schrader, A. (2021). Intellectual Property in Digital Art: A Legal Perspective. Digital Art Law Journal. Retrieved from https://digitalartlawjournal.com

Schroeder, R. (2018). Towards a theory of digital media. *Information Communication and Society*, *21*(3), 323–339. DOI: 10.1080/1369118X.2017.1289231

Schultz, M. (2011). Performing graffiti: The use of electronically and digitally modified graffiti in activist art practices [Master's thesis, University of New Mexico]. UNM Digital Repository. https://digitalrepository.unm.edu/arth_etds/13/

Scott, H. (2021). How Intellectual Property Rights Shape the NFT Revolution. Forbes. Retrieved from https://www.forbes.com

Seaborn, K., & Fels, D. I. (2015). Gamification in theory and action: A survey. *International Journal of Human-Computer Studies*, *74*, 14–31. DOI: 10.1016/j.ijhcs.2014.09.006

Seifter, A., Schwarzwalder, A., Geis, K., & Aucott, J. (2010). The utility of Google Trends for e-pidemiological research: Lyme disease as an example. *Geospatial Health*, *4*(2), 135–137. DOI: 10.4081/gh.2010.195 PMID: 20503183

Sen, S. (2019). *Intellectual Property Rights and Innovation in Emerging Markets*. Cambridge University Press.

Shaarawy, S. (2019). A review on the development of innovative capabilities in the textile finishing of natural fibers. In *Egyptian Journal of Chemistry* (Vol. 62, pp. 857–879). NIDOC (Nat.Inform.Document.Centre). DOI: 10.21608/ejchem.2019.19009.2169

Shamsuddin, S., Sulaiman, A. B., & Amat, R. C. (2012). *Urban landscape factors that influenced the character of George Town*. Penang UNESCO World Heritage.

Shanken, E. A. (2002). Art in the Information Age: Technology and Conceptual Art. *Leonardo*, *35*(4), 433–438. DOI: 10.1162/002409402760181259

Sharma, A. (n.d.). *ECO-FRIENDLY TEXTILES: A BOOST TO SUSTAINABILITY*.

Sheikheldin, G. H., & Hambly, H. (2024). Technological Change and Techno-Social Systems: Re-Examining Sustainable Development and Digitalisation in Africa. *Science, Technology & Society*, *29*(4), 573–594. DOI: 10.1177/09717218241281826

Sigala, M. (2015). Gamification for crowdsourcing marketing practices: Applications and benefits in tourism. In Sigala, M., Rahimi, R., & Thelwall, M. (Eds.), *Big data and innovation in tourism, travel, and hospitality* (pp. 129–145). Springer., DOI: 10.1007/978-3-319-18341-1_11

Silvennoinen, J., Vogel, M., & Kujala, S. (2014). Experiencing visual usability and aesthetics in two mobile application contexts. https://www.semanticscholar.org/paper/Experiencing-visual-usability-and-aesthetics-in-two-Silvennoinen-Vogel/a9ae76304cde810dfcb0ed74817823868aa6e63a

Singh, O., Singh, N., & Singh, A. (2024). AI, IoT, and Blockchain in Fashion: Confronting Industry Applications, Challenges with Technological Solutions. [). https://ijcnis.org/]. *International Journal of Communication Networks and Information Security, 2024*(4).

Śledzik, K. (2013), "Schumpeter's View on Innovation and Entrepreneurship", Management Trends in Theory and Practice, (ed.), pp 89-95 DOI: 10.2139/ssrn.2257783

Smilansky, S. (2017). *Experiential marketing: A practical guide to interactive brand experiences*. Kogan Page Publishers.

Smith and Johnson. (2018). A Stratified Sampling Approach for Balanced Representation in Image Classification. *IEEE Transactions on Pattern Analysis and Machine Intelligence*. DOI: 10.1109/TPAMI.2017.2708740

Smith, J. (2016). The role of digital media in eco-conscious artistic practices. *Contemporary Art Review, 8*(3), 76–89.

Sohn, S. H., Choi, Y. J., & Hwang, H. S. (2011). Understanding Acceptance of Smartphone among Early Adopters Using Extended Technology Acceptance Model. *Korean Journal of Journalism & Communication Studies, 55*(2), 227–252.

Song, S. W., & Chung, D. H. (2021). Explication and Rational Conceptualization of Metaverse. *Informatization Policy, 28*(3), 3–22.

Song, Y., Zhang, L., & Zhang, M. (2022). Research on the impact of public climate policy cognition on low-carbon travel based on SOR theory: Evidence from China. *Energy, 261*, 125192. DOI: 10.1016/j.energy.2022.125192

Sonn, C., & Baker, A. (2016). Creating inclusive knowledges: Exploring the transformative potential of arts and cultural practice. *International Journal of Inclusive Education, 20*(3), 215–228. DOI: 10.1080/13603116.2015.1047663

Souleles, N. (2013). The Evolution of Art and Design Pedagogies in England: Influences of the Past, Challenges for the Future. *International Journal of Art & Design Education, 32*(2), 243–255. DOI: 10.1111/j.1476-8070.2013.01753.x

Sposab, K., & Rieckmann, M. (2024). Development of Sustainability Competencies in Secondary School Education: A Scoping Literature Review. *Sustainability (Basel), 16*(23), 10228. DOI: 10.3390/su162310228

Statista. (2023). Internet penetration and smartphone ownership in Vietnam. https://www.statista.com/vietnam-internet-penetration

Statista. (2025). *Ownership of devices among internet users in Vietnam in 2024, by device.* https://www.statista.com/statistics/804059/digital-device-usage-among-adults-by-device-vietnam/

Steckel, B., Shinas, V. H., & Van Vaerenewyck, L. (2015). Artistic Technology Integration: Stories From Primary and Elementary Classrooms. *The Reading Teacher, 69*(1), 41–49. DOI: 10.1002/trtr.1356

Stevens, E. (2024, July 19). 7 Real-Life Design Thinking Examples | AND Academy. AndAcademy.https://www.andacademy.com/resources/blog/ui-ux-design/7-design-thinking-examples/#Airbnb

Stevens, P., & Richards, S. (2023). *European Union Privacy and Intellectual Property Law.* Edward Elgar Publishing.

Stewart, S. (2015). Art, ecology and the urban environment. *Environmental Arts Journal, 3*(2), 34–45.

Sudarmanto, J. A., & Ismail, A. I. B. (2023). Augmented reality and metaverse in Aesthetic Education Discourse in Indonesia for future. *Southeast Asian Conference on Education Official Conference Proceedings.* DOI: 10.22492/issn.2435-5240.2023.26

Su, H., & Mokmin, N. A. M. (2024). Unveiling the Canvas: Sustainable Integration of AI in Visual Art Education. *Sustainability (Basel), 16*(17), 7849. DOI: 10.3390/su16177849

Suh, A., & Prophet, J. (2018). The state of immersive technology research: A literature analysis. *Computers in Human Behavior, 86*, 77–90. DOI: 10.1016/j.chb.2018.04.019

Suh, K.-S., & Chang, S. (2006). User interfaces and consumer perceptions of online stores: The role of telepresence. *Behaviour & Information Technology, 25*(2), 99–113. DOI: 10.1080/01449290500330398

Sullivan, C. (2020). *Virtual Fitting Rooms: Fashion's New Sustainable Frontier.* Retail Dive.

Sun, D., Xu, L., Zhang, L., & Cui, N. (2019). How augmented reality affects people's perceptions: Adoption of AR in product display improves consumers' product attitude. *Journal of Physics: Conference Series, 1288*(1), 1–10. DOI: 10.1088/1742-6596/1288/1/012037

Sundar, S. S., & Kalyanaraman, S. (2004). Arousal, memory, and impression-formation effects of animation speed in web advertising. *Journal of Advertising*, *33*(1), 7–17. DOI: 10.1080/00913367.2004.10639152

Sung, E. C. (2021). The effects of augmented reality mobile app advertising: Viral marketing via shared social experience. *Journal of Business Research*, *122*, 75–87. DOI: 10.1016/j.jbusres.2020.08.034

Süzen, H. N. (2020). Art and Aesthetics in Higher Education. *Online Submission*, *7*(6), 335–350.

Taber, K. S. (2017). The Use of Cronbach's Alpha When Developing. *Research in Science Education*, 1273–1296.

Tan, J., Gao, B., & Lu, X. (2018) 'An AR system for artistic creativity education', in *Proceedings of the 24th ACM Symposium on Virtual Reality Software and Technology. VRST '18: 24th ACM Symposium on Virtual Reality Software and Technology*, Tokyo Japan: ACM, pp. 1–2. Available at: DOI: 10.1145/3281505.3283396

Tao, Y., & Tao, Y. (2024). Integrating Aesthetic Education in Quality Education: A Bibliometric Analysis of Sustainable Development Perspectives. *Sustainability (Basel)*, *16*(2), 855. DOI: 10.3390/su16020855

Team, B. (2025, April 21). *Augmented Reality in Ecommerce: How Does it Work? BigCommerce.*

Tech in Asia. (n.d.). *Tech in Asia - Connecting Asia's startup ecosystem.*

Teh, Y. S., & Sasaki, Y. (2016). A study of historic quarter streetscapes based on typology of tourist-oriented activity—A case study of George Town and Hanoi. *Journal of JSCE*, *4*(1), 152–165. DOI: 10.2208/journalofjsce.4.1_152

The Business of Fashion. (2021). *How Stella McCartney became a leader in sustainable luxury*. [Online] Available at: https://www.businessoffashion.com/articles/sustainability/stella-mccartney-sustainability

Thompson, N. (2017). *Seeing power: Art and activism in the 21st century*. The New Press.

Tian, X., & Sarkis, J. (2021). Emission burden concerns for online shopping returns. *Nature Climate Change*, *12*(1), 2–3. DOI: 10.1038/s41558-021-01246-9

Tilley, E. (2011). *New culture/old ethics: What technological determinism can teach us about new media and public relations ethics*. Massey University.

Ting, T. T., & Ling, L. Y. bin Ahmad Azam, A. I., & Palaniappan, R. (2021). Artificial Intelligence Art: Attitudes and Perceptions Toward Human Versus Artificial Intelligence Artworks. In 1ST Int. Conf. Humanit. Educ. Sci. Manag. Eng. Technol.

Tlili, A., Huang, R., Shehata, R., Liu, D., Zhao, J., Metwally, A. H. S., Wang, H., Denden, M., Bozkurt, A., Lee, L. K., Beyoglu, D., Altinay, F., Sharma, R. C., Altinay, Z., Li, Z., Liu, J., Ahmad, F., Hu, Y., Salha, S., & Burgos, D. (2022). Is Metaverse in education a blessing or a curse: A combined content and bibliometric analysis. *Smart Learning Environments*, *24*(9), 1–31. DOI: 10.1186/s40561-022-00205-x

Tom Dieck, M. C., Jung, T. H., & Rauschnabel, P. A. (2018). Determining visitor engagement through augmented reality at science festivals: An experience economy perspective. *Computers in Human Behavior*, *82*, 44–53. DOI: 10.1016/j.chb.2017.12.043

Toosi, A., Bottino, A. G., Saboury, B., Siegel, E., & Rahmim, A. (2021). A brief history of AI: How to prevent another winter (a critical review). *PET Clinics*, *16*(4), 449–469. DOI: 10.1016/j.cpet.2021.07.001 PMID: 34537126

Torman, Y. (2022). User Acceptance of Metaverse: Insights from Technology Acceptance Model (TAM) and Planned Behavior Theory (PBT). *Emerging Markets Journal*, *12*(1), 68–75. DOI: 10.5195/emaj.2022.258

Torman, Y., & Geçit, B. B. (2022). User Acceptance of Metaverse: An Analysis for e-Commerce in the Framework of Technology Acceptance Model (TAM). *Sosyoekonomi*, *31*(55), 85–104. DOI: 10.17233/sosyoekonomi.2023.01.05

Trott, C. D., Even, T. L., & Frame, S. M. (2020). Merging the arts and sciences for collaborative sustainability action: A methodological framework. *Sustainability Science*, *15*(4), 1067–1085. DOI: 10.1007/s11625-020-00798-7

Tryphena, R., & Aram, I. A. (2023). Consumer perception on sustainable clothing among urban Indians. *Journal of Engineered Fibers and Fabrics*, *18*, 15589250231168964. DOI: 10.1177/15589250231168964

Tsai, W.-H. S., Tian, S. C., Chuan, C.-H., & Li, C. (2020). Inspection or play? A study of how augmented reality technology can be utilized in advertising. *Journal of Interactive Advertising*, *20*(3), 244–257. DOI: 10.1080/15252019.2020.1738292

Turkay, S., Adinolf, S., & Tirthali, D. (2012). Collectible card games as learning tools. *Procedia: Social and Behavioral Sciences*, *46*, 3701–3705. DOI: 10.1016/j.sbspro.2012.06.130

U ă, I. (2022, December 9). *+20 augmented reality (AR) global market and user statistics for 2022*. Brand Minds.

Uygur, M., Ayçiçek, B., Doğrul, H., & Yanpar Yelken, T. (2020). 'Investigating Stakeholders' Views on Technology Integration: The Role of Educational Leadership for Sustainable Inclusive Education'. *Sustainability (Basel)*, *12*(24), 10354. DOI: 10.3390/su122410354

van Esch, P., Arli, D., Castner, J., Talukdar, N., & Northey, G. (2018). Consumer attitudes towards bloggers and paid blog advertisements: What's new? *Marketing Intelligence & Planning*, *36*(7), 778–793. DOI: 10.1108/MIP-01-2018-0027

Vasconcelos, C., & Orion, N. (2021). Earth Science Education as a Key Component of Education for Sustainability. *Sustainability (Basel)*, *13*(3), 1316. DOI: 10.3390/su13031316

Vatanartiran, S., & Karadeniz, S. (2015). A Needs Analysis for Technology Integration Plan: Challenges and Needs of Teachers. *Contemporary Educational Technology*, *6*(3). DOI: 10.30935/cedtech/6150

Verhagen, T., van Nes, J., Feldberg, F., & van Dolen, W. (2011). Virtual customer service agents: Using social presence and personalization to shape online service encounters. *Journal of Computer-Mediated Communication*, *16*(1), 79–97.

Vičič Krabonja, M., Kustec, S., Skrbinjek, V., Aberšek, B., & Flogie, A. (2024). Innovative Professional Learning Communities and Sustainable Education Practices through Digital Transformation. *Sustainability (Basel)*, *16*(14), 6250. DOI: 10.3390/su16146250

Vietnam Investment Review. (2023, May 10). Cost challenges for SMEs in adopting AR technology.

VietnamNet. (2023, October 15). Trung Nguyen Legend's AR campaign boosts brand engagement.

Viger, M. (2019). "The Meaning of Color for the Vietnamese Youth"

Waldman, D. (2018). The eco-artist: A new paradigm for sustainable art. *Journal of Environmental Art*, *5*(1), 45–60.

Wangdi, P., & Boossabong, P. (2024). Towards an Inclusive Education Policy for Sustainability: Advancing the "Educating for Gross National Happiness" Initiative in Bhutan. *Sustainability (Basel)*, *16*(13), 5446. DOI: 10.3390/su16135446

Wang, Y., Su, Z., Zhang, N., Xing, R., Liu, D., Luan, T. H., & Shen, X. (2022). A Survey on Metaverse: Fundamentals, Security, and Privacy. *IEEE Communications Surveys and Tutorials*, *25*(1), 319–352. DOI: 10.1109/COMST.2022.3202047

Wang, Z., & Jiang, Q. (2024). A study on the willingness of "Generation Z" consumers to use online virtual try-on shopping services based on the S-O-R framework. *Systems*, *12*(6), 217. DOI: 10.3390/systems12060217

Wei, W. (2019). Research progress on virtual reality (VR) and augmented reality (AR) in tourism and hospitality: A critical review of publications from 2000 to 2018. *Journal of Hospitality and Tourism Technology*, *10*(4), 539–570. DOI: 10.1108/JHTT-04-2018-0030

Weng, X., Ng, O.-L., Cui, Z., & Leung, S. (2023). Creativity Development With Problem-Based Digital Making and Block-Based Programming for Science, Technology, Engineering, Arts, and Mathematics Learning in Middle School Contexts. *Journal of Educational Computing Research*, *61*(2), 304–328. DOI: 10.1177/07356331221115661

Werbach, K., & Hunter, D. (2012). *For the win: How game thinking can revolutionize your business*. Wharton Digital Press.

White, A. (2024). Adobe's new skilling initiative aims to bring AI literacy, content creation and digital marketing skills to 30 million worldwide. Adobe Blog. Retrieved 20 May 2025 from https://blog.adobe.com/en/publish/2024/10/14/adobes-new-skilling-initiative-aims-bring-ai-literacy-content-creation-digital-marketing-skills-30-million-worldwide

Williams, A. (2021). Settlements and Dispute Resolution in Intellectual Property. *Harvard Law Review*.

Wingström, R., Hautala, J., & Lundman, R. (2024). Redefining creativity in the era of AI? Perspectives of computer scientists and new media artists. *Creativity Research Journal*, *36*(2), 177–193. DOI: 10.1080/10400419.2022.2107850

World Medical Association. (2013). World Medical Association Declaration of Helsinki. *Journal of the American Medical Association*, *310*(20), 2191–2194. DOI: 10.1001/jama.2013.281053 PMID: 24141714

Wulia, T. (2023). Aesthetic resistance: Publicness, potentiality, and plexus. *Journal of Political Power*, *16*(2), 213–236. DOI: 10.1080/2158379X.2023.2245228 PMID: 38013878

Wu, Q. (2024). Application of Artificial Intelligence-based Visual Arts Pedagogy in Traditional Painting Education. *Applied Mathematics and Nonlinear Sciences*, *9*(1), 20242994. DOI: 10.2478/amns-2024-2994

Wu, R., & Yu, Z. (2023). Investigating Users' Acceptance of the Metaverse with an Extended Technology Acceptance Model. *International Journal of Human-Computer Interaction, 2023*(Aug), 1–17.

Wu, S. (2024). Application of multimedia technology to innovative vocational education on learning satisfaction in China. *PLoS One, 19*(2), e0298861. DOI: 10.1371/journal.pone.0298861 PMID: 38416731

Xi, N., & Hamari, J. (2019). Does gamification satisfy needs? A study on the relationship between gamification features and intrinsic need satisfaction. *International Journal of Information Management, 46*, 210–221. DOI: 10.1016/j.ijinfomgt.2018.12.002

Xinyuan, F., & Liang, Y. (2023). The Research on the Characteristics of AI Application in Art Field and its Value. *4th International Conference on Language, Art and Cultural Exchange*, 146-160.

Xiong, Z., Luo, L., & Lu, X. (2023). Understanding the effect of smart tourism technologies on behavioral intention with the stimulus-organism-response model: A study in Guilin, China. *Asia Pacific Journal of Tourism Research, 28*(5), 449–466. DOI: 10.1080/10941665.2023.2246598

Xue, L., & Lu, X. (2021) 'Research on the Integrated Innovative Teaching Model of Art and Technology Based on Pearson Correlation Analysis', in *2021 2nd International Conference on Artificial Intelligence and Education (ICAIE). 2021 2nd International Conference on Artificial Intelligence and Education (ICAIE)*, Dali, China: IEEE, pp. 245–251. Available at: DOI: 10.1109/ICAIE53562.2021.00058

Xue, Y., Sun, J., Liu, Y., Li, X., & Yuan, K. (2023). Facial expression-enhanced recommendation for virtual fitting rooms. *Decision Support Systems, 177*, 113222.

Yang, K., & Liu, H. (2017). The impact of online store atmosphere on consumer's purchase intention: Based on SOR theory. *The Journal of Business and Retail Management Research, 12*(1), 112–123.

Yang, M. (2024). Research on Teaching Methods of Integrating Watercolor Techniques and Information Technology in Higher Education Art Education. *Applied Mathematics and Nonlinear Sciences, 9*(1), 20242803. DOI: 10.2478/amns-2024-2803

Yang, S., Carlson, J. R., & Chen, S. (2020). How augmented reality affects advertising effectiveness: The mediating effects of curiosity and attention toward the ad. *Journal of Retailing and Consumer Services, 54*, 102020. DOI: 10.1016/j.jretconser.2019.102020

Yi, L., & Surng, G. J. (2020). Application of synesthesia technology in new media art. *Journal of Arts and Imaging Science*, *7*(3), 1–8.

Yim, M. Y.-C., Chu, S.-C., & Sauer, P. L. (2017). Is augmented reality technology an effective tool for e-commerce? An interactivity and vividness perspective. *Journal of Interactive Marketing*, *39*(1), 89–103. DOI: 10.1016/j.intmar.2017.04.001

Yim, M. Y., Cicchirillo, V. J., & Drumwright, M. E. (2012). The impact of stereoscopic Three-Dimensional (3-D) advertising. *Journal of Advertising*, *41*(2), 113–128. DOI: 10.2753/JOA0091-3367410208

Yoon, S., & Ho, J. (2024) 'Delivering sustainable development via social innovation: Cases of social entrepreneurship in South Korea and Singapore', *Sustainable Development*, p. sd.3127. Available at: DOI: 10.1002/sd.3127

You, H. B. (2024). Generation Z's Perception of the Metaverse. *Journal of Digital Contents Society*, *25*(1), 91–100. DOI: 10.9728/dcs.2024.25.1.91

Yuen, S. C.-Y., Yaoyuneyong, G., & Johnson, E. (2011). Augmented reality: An overview and five directions for AR in education. [JETDE]. *Journal of Educational Technology Development and Exchange*, *4*(1), 11. DOI: 10.18785/jetde.0401.10

Yu, S., Zhang, H., Zheng, Q., Chu, D., Chen, T., & Chen, X. (2024). Consumer behavior based on the SOR model: How do short video advertisements affect furniture consumers' purchase intentions? *BioResources*, *19*(2), 2639–2659. DOI: 10.15376/biores.19.2.2639-2659

Zeithaml, V. A. (1988). Consumer perceptions of price, quality, and value: A means-end model and synthesis of evidence. *Journal of Marketing*, *52*(3), 2–22. DOI: 10.1177/002224298805200302

Zhang, A., Li, W., Wu, J., Lin, J., Chu, J., & Xia, C. (2021). How can the urban landscape affect urban vitality at the street block level? A case study of 15 metropolises in China. *Environment and Planning. B, Urban Analytics and City Science*, *48*(5), 1245–1262. DOI: 10.1177/2399808320924425

Zhang, Q. (2023). Artistic expression and data protection: Balancing aesthetics with data privacy in IoT. *Heliyon*, *9*(9), e19380. DOI: 10.1016/j.heliyon.2023.e19380 PMID: 37662810

Zhao, L. (2022). *Intellectual Property Litigation: An Empirical Analysis*. Springer.

Zhao, L., Hussam, E., Seong, J.-T., Elshenawy, A., Kamal, M., & Alshawarbeh, E. (2024). Revolutionizing art education: Integrating AI and multimedia for enhanced appreciation teaching. *Alexandria Engineering Journal*, *93*, 33–43. DOI: 10.1016/j.aej.2024.03.011

Zhong, T., Ye, C., Wang, Z., Tang, G., Zhang, W., & Ye, Y. (2021). City-scale mapping of urban façade color using street-view imagery. *Remote Sensing (Basel)*, *13*(8), 1591. DOI: 10.3390/rs13081591

Zywicki, J. (2016). Art and the digital: New forms of sustainability. *Digital Creativity*, *27*(2), 92–104. DOI: 10.1080/14626268.2016.1165805

About the Contributors

Trinh Thuy Anh received her PhD in Economics from Hanoi University of Transport and Communications in 2006. She is currently an Associate Professor, Vice Rector of College of Technology and Design, Dean of School of Media Design at the University of Economics Ho Chi Minh City in Vietnam. Throughout her career, Dr. Trinh has made substantial scholarly contributions in the fields of business management, economics, and education. She has led and participated in numerous research projects at the university and ministry levels. Her research has been published extensively, including 9 books as author or editor and over 45 peer-reviewed journal articles and conference proceedings. Key focuses of her work include business strategy, balanced scorecards, innovation management, brand equity, employee motivation and commitment. Dr. Trinh is a thought leader in applying business concepts like corporate models and balanced scorecards to university management in Vietnam's emerging economy. Her research provides strategic insights for companies, especially in the tourism, transportation, and technology sectors, to drive performance through innovation, employee engagement, and customer orientation. She has strengthened Vietnam's integration with global educational standards by innovating business curricula. In summary, Dr. Trinh Thuy Anh is an accomplished academic leader and scholar dedicated to advancing management practices and economic development in Vietnam through her educational leadership, instruction, and impactful research. Her work bridges gaps between academia and industry to foster sustainable business growth.

***

Erika Blekač graduated in 2023 from the University of Maribor, Faculty of Electrical Engineering and Computer Science, where they earned a degree in Media Communications and were honoured with an award for their undergraduate thesis. Currently, they are in the second year of their master's degree in Media

Communications at the same university, continuing to engage in research projects and actively participating in various initiatives. Their academic and research interests revolve around media, digital and media literacy, and their roles in society, with a particular interest in artificial intelligence and how digital and media literacy interact and shape today's rapidly evolving technological landscape.

Aja Cugmas received her degree in Computer Science and Informatics from the Faculty of Electrical Engineering and Computer Science (UM FERI) in Maribor in 2023, having begun her undergraduate studies in 2020. She started her master's studies in Media Communications at the same faculty in 2023 and is currently in her second year. Aja conducts research at her university, with a focus on the evolving intersections of media and technology. This article marks her first authored work at this level, contributing to the academic discourse within her field. With a background in computer science, her research continues to explore innovative approaches within media communications.

Vaithegy Doraisamy is a senior lecturer and a researcher at the School of Computer Sciences, Universiti Sains Malaysia (USM), specializing in artificial intelligence, machine learning, and data analytics for environmental monitoring, computer vision, and intelligent systems. She has led and contributed to multidisciplinary projects linking computer science with conservation technology, smart surveillance, and public safety. Collaborating with agencies, NGOs, and research institutions, she develops data-driven tools using sensor networks, remote sensing, and real-time analytics to support sustainable resource management. Passionate about capacity building, she mentors students in AI and data science, and has published in journals, conferences, and collaborative projects aligned with Malaysia's digital goals..

Duong Ngoc Hong is a Lecturer at the Faculty of International Business – Marketing (UEH), specializing in Sustainability, Marketing, and Supply Chain Management. She teaches courses in International Business, International Marketing, and Management, and supervises undergraduate theses and research projects. Dr. Hong earned her Bachelor's degree in Management from Monash University (Australia, 2011), a Master's in International Business from La Trobe University (Australia, 2012, with honors), and a Master's in Research in Management from Lille 2 University (France, 2016). She hold a PhD at the University of Economics Ho Chi Minh City. With over seven years of academic experience, she has held teaching positions at the Banking University, Academy of Policy and Development, and as a visiting lecturer for international students at Bac Ha International University.

Her research interests include innovation, supply chain management, and strategic management.

Marko Matko Ficko began his studies in Computer Science and Information Technology in 2020 at the Faculty of Electrical Engineering, Computer Science and Informatics (FERI) in Maribor, graduating with a Bachelor's degree in 2023. In the same year, he commenced his Master's studies in Media Communications and is currently in his second year. In 2023, he was awarded first place in a competition organized by the Student Dormitories in Maribor for his conceptual design of murals in the renovated Student Dormitory 1, which were realized in 2024. His academic and research interests revolve around computer science and art, with a particular focus on artificial intelligence and its connection with the arts.

Goh Chu Hiang is a senior lecturer in the Graphic Communication Department at the School of The Arts, USM. He has a unique educational background in art and design as well as computer science. Goh Chu Hiang is a professional member of the Design Research Society (DRS), Association of Computer Machinery (ACM), and ACM Special Interest Group in Computer-Human Interaction (ACM SIGCHI). His research interests include creative industry design innovation and AI, TRIZ social innovation, Human-Centered Design, graphic communication design, user experience design (UX), user personas study, design history, and theory.

Rishikaysh Kaakandikar boasts an exceptional academic journey, spanning over 13 years of dedicated teaching and a year of valuable industrial experience, and currently holds the esteemed position of Associate Professor at SaiBalaji Education Society's SaiBalaji International Institute of Management Sciences in Pune. His scholarly contributions shine brightly, encompassing a remarkable portfolio of over 40 research papers in prestigious journals. A sought-after intellectual resource, He has contributed substantially to academia through guest lectures, seminars, workshops, and conferences at esteemed institutions across India. His insights have enriched the academic community and stimulated engaging discussions on various facets of his field. He is a prominent finance columnist for leading newspapers in Maharashtra, including Sakal, Lokmat, Punyannagari, and Prabhat.

Ines Kožuh is an Associate Professor and the Head of the Study Programme Media Communications at the University of Maribor in Slovenia. She is also the Deputy Head of the Institute of Media Communications at the University of Maribor and a part-time researcher at the Centre for Social Informatics at the Faculty of Social Sciences of the University of Ljubljana. In 2013, she was the recipient of a scholarship from the German Academic Exchange Service when she was a research fellow at the University of Education in Heidelberg, Germany. In 2023, she was a research fellow at the University of Donja Gorica in Montenegro. She has published over 90 research outputs, out of these 24 original scientific papers. Her main research interests comprise aspects of digital media use, such as the question of digital literacy, trust in media, misinformation, user experience, and disability (h-index: 14, i10-index: 18).

Riddhi Mirajkar is currently pursuing a Doctor of Philosophy (Ph.D.) in Computer Engineering from Savitribai Phule Pune University, Pune, India. She earned her Master of Engineering (M.E.) degree in Computer Science and Engineering from the same university in 2016. She is presently working as an Assistant Professor in the Department of Information Technology at Vishwakarma Institute of Technology, Pune, India. With over 12 years of academic and professional experience, her areas of interest include Artificial Intelligence and Computer Networks. She has published more than 20 research papers in reputed national and international conferences and journals. She is also a lifetime member of the Indian Society for Technical Education (ISTE).

Ruziana Mohamad Rasli is a senior lecturer at the School of Multimedia Technology and Communication, Universiti Utara Malaysia (UUM), specializing in information technology and multimedia design, human computer interaction, and user experience research. Her work focuses on the integration of creative media and interactive technologies to enhance communication, learning, and engagement across digital platforms. She has led and collaborated on projects involving UI/UX design, digital storytelling, immersive media, and technology adoption studies. Passionate about interdisciplinary research, she works closely with industry partners, government agencies, and academic institutions. Her scholarly contributions include journal publications, conference presentations, and community engagement initiatives aligned with Malaysia's digital innovation goals.

Madam Noor Azlina Mohamed Khalid possesses a diverse research background, with a strong foundation in interdisciplinary fields such as Universal Design, Design Behavior, and Design Thinking. Her recent scholarly pursuits have centered on the critical intersection of Design and Education, Design Culture, and Co-Design methodologies, with a particular emphasis on fostering meaningful community engagement.

Rasslenda Rass Rasalingam is a lecturer at the School of the Arts, Universiti Sains Malaysia (USM), specializing in graphic communication, user experience design, and immersive media. Her research explores the intersection of culture, design, and technology, focusing on how cultural contexts influence UI/UX preferences and technology acceptance among diverse user groups, including older adults. She has led projects on immersive design for AR/VR environments, sustainable urban living concepts, and digital art engagement for mental well-being. Dedicated to nurturing creative talent, she integrates research into teaching and collaborates with multidisciplinary teams. Her work spans academic publications, design portfolios, and industry-linked projects. 625a451d-96ec-4160-9226-9a666982cd41)

Nurul Hanim Romainoor's work underscores the integration of cultural heritage, consumer insights, and technological advancements to create innovative and meaningful design solutions. Her research highlights the importance of preserving cultural traditions while adapting to contemporary market needs and leveraging technology to enhance design practices. Through her interdisciplinary approach, Dr. Nurul Hanim Romainoor continues to make significant contributions to the field of design, fostering innovation and creativity.

Index

Symbols

A

B

C

D

E

G

H

I

M

N

O

P

Q

S

T

U

W

www.ingramcontent.com/pod-product-compliance
Lightning Source LLC
LaVergne TN
LVHW080348011026
849161LV00009B/2231